Lecture Notes in Artificial Intelligence 2671

Edited by J. G. Carbonell and J. Siekmann

Subseries of Lecture Notes in Computer Science

Springer
Berlin
Heidelberg
New York
Hong Kong
London
Milan
Paris
Tokyo

Yang Xiang Brahim Chaib-draa (Eds.)

Advances in Artificial Intelligence

16th Conference of the Canadian Society
for Computational Studies of Intelligence, AI 2003
Halifax, Canada, June 11-13, 2003
Proceedings

Springer

Series Editors

Jaime G. Carbonell, Carnegie Mellon University, Pittsburgh, PA, USA
Jörg Siekmann, University of Saarland, Saarbrücken, Germany

Volume Editors

Yang Xiang
University of Guelph
Department of Computing and Information Science
College of Physical and Engineering Science
Guelph, Ontario, Canada N1G 2W1
E-mail: yxiang@cis.uoguelph.ca

Brahim Chaib-draa
Université Laval
Dépt. Informatique-Génie Logiciel
Pavillon Pouliot, Ste-Foy, PQ, Canada, G1K 7P4
E-mail: Chaib@ift.ulaval.ca

Cataloging-in-Publication Data applied for

A catalog record for this book is available from the Library of Congress.

Bibliographic information published by Die Deutsche Bibliothek.
Die Deutsche Bibliothek lists this publication in the Deutsche Nationalbibliografie; detailed bibliographic data is available in the Internet at <http://dnb.ddb.de>.

CR Subject Classification (1998): I.2

ISSN 0302-9743
ISBN 3-540-40300-0 Springer-Verlag Berlin Heidelberg New York

Springer-Verlag Berlin Heidelberg New York,
a member of BertelsmannSpringer Science+Business Media GmbH

http://www.springer.de

Printed in Germany

Typesetting: Camera-ready by author, data conversion by DA-TeX Gerd Blumenstein
Printed on acid-free paper SPIN: 10927465 06/3142 5 4 3 2 1 0

Preface

The AI 2003 conference was the 16th in the series of artificial intelligence conferences sponsored by the Canadian Society for Computational Studies of Intelligence (CSCSI)/Société Canadienne pour l'Étude de l'Intelligence par Ordinateur (SCEIO). The conference showcases the excellent research work done by Canadians and their international colleagues. As in the case of many past Canadian AI conferences, AI 2003 was organized in conjunction with its sister Canadian conferences, Vision Interface (VI) and Graphics Interface (GI), enriching the experience for all participants. The conferences were held on the campus of Dalhousie University, at Canada's largest Atlantic port city, Halifax.

This year, we received a record number of paper submissions. A total of 116 abstracts were received, out of which 106 papers were submitted by the due date. As at past conferences, there was strong international participation. Among the submitted papers, about 41% were from non-Canadian researchers. From the 106 papers, we accepted 30 full papers and 24 short papers. Following the success in AI 2002, the Graduate Student Symposium was continued in AI 2003, with 11 extended abstracts accepted from 16 submissions. All these accepted papers are included in this volume. They cover a wide range of topics, including knowledge representation, search, constraint satisfaction, natural language, machine learning and data mining, reasoning under uncertainty, agent and multiagent systems, AI and Web applications, AI and bioinformatics, and AI and E-commerce.

We invited three distinguished researchers representing three very active subfields of AI: Victor Lesser (multiagent systems), Tom Mitchell (machine learning), and Pierre Baldi (AI and bioinformatics). The extended abstracts of their invited talks also appear in this volume.

Many contributed to the organization of AI 2003. Members of the Program Committee made helpful suggestions on the conference organization. They and the associated referees carefully and critically reviewed all submissions and ensured a high-quality technical program. The National Research Council of Canada and the Canadian Society for Computational Studies of Intelligence provided travel support for the Graduate Student Symposium. CSCSI's past president Bob Mercer and president Bruce Spencer gave us much guidance whenever needed. The conference chair Charles Ling and the local organizer Malcolm Heywood attended to many organizational details. We thank the invited speakers, all authors who submitted their work to AI 2003, and the conference participants. We thank the AI-GI-VI Steering Committee and the organizers of GI and VI for their cooperation. Our home institutions, the University of Guelph and Laval University, and the host institution of the conference, Dalhousie University, provided much assistance and support. Alfred Hofmann and Ursula Barth at Springer-Verlag assisted the publication of this volume. Graduate students Feng Zou, Junjiang Chen, Xiaoyun Chen and Xiangdong An assisted in developing and maintaining the program management website and in preparing the proceedings.

June 2003

Yang Xiang
Brahim Chaib-draa

Executive Committee

Conference Chair:	Charles Ling (U. Western Ontario)
Program Co-Chairs:	Yang Xiang (U. Guelph)
	Brahim Chaib-draa (Laval U.)
Local Organizer:	Malcolm Heywood (Dalhousie U.)

Program Committee

Aijun An (York U.)
Cory Butz (U. Regina)
Nick Cercone (Dalhousie U.)
David Chiu (U. Guelph)
Jim Delgrande (Simon Fraser U.)
Jorg Denzinger (U. Calgary)
Renee Elio (U. Alberta)
Richard Frost (U. Windsor)
Ali Ghorbani (U. New Brunswick)
Scott Goodwin (U. Windsor)
Jim Greer (U. Saskatchewan)
Gary Grewal (U. Guelph)
Howard Hamilton (U. Regina)
Bill Havens (Simon Fraser U.)
Michael Horsch (U. Saskatchewan)
Finn Jensen (Aalborg U.)
Stefan Kremer (U. Guelph)
James Little (U. British Columbia)
Stan Matwin (U. Ottawa)
Gord McCalla (U. Saskatchewan)
Bob Mercer (U. Western Ontario)
Evangelos Milios (Dalhousie U.)
Guy Mineau (U. Laval)
Eric Neufeld (U. Saskatchewan)
Petra Perner (IBaI Leipzig)
David Poole (U. British Columbia)
Fred Popowich (Simon Fraser U.)
Gregory Provan (Rockwell)
Dale Schuurmans (U. Waterloo)
Weiming Shen
(National Research Council Canada)
Danel Silver (Acadia U.)
Bruce Spencer
(National Research Council Canada
and U. New Brunswick)
Deb Stacey (U. Guelph)
Stan Szpakowicz (U. Ottawa)
Andre Trudel (Acadia U.)
Peter van Beek (U. Waterloo)
Julita Vassileva (U. Saskatchewan)
Michael Wong (U. Regina)
Jia You (U. Alberta)
Eric Yu (U. Toronto)
Kaizhong Zhang (U. Western Ontario)

Additional Reviewers

Mohamed Aoun-allah, Gilbert Babin, Behnam Bastani, Julia Birke, Pierre Boulanger, Caropreso, Ralph Deters, Dan Fass, Julian Fogel, Frédérick Garcia, Ali Ghodsi, Daniel Gross, Jimmy Huang, Andrija Ifkovic, Nadeem Jamali, Anthony Kusalik, Sonje Kristtorn, Lang, Lingras, Lin Liu, Yang Liu, Sehl Mellouli, Ronnie Mueller, Xiaolin Niu, Relu Patrascu, Elhadi Shakshuki, Pascal Soucy, Finnegan Southey, Sykes, Davide Turcato, Hussein Vastani, Qian Wan, Steven Wang, Yao Wang, Pinata Winoto, Sadok Ben Yahia, Harry Zhang

Sponsor

National Research Council of Canada
Canadian Society for Computational Studies of Intelligence

Table of Contents

Invited Talks

Full Papers

Knowledge Representation

Search

Constraint Satisfaction

Machine Learning and Data Mining

AI and Web Applications

Reasoning under Uncertainty

Agent and Multiagent Systems

AI and Bioinformatics

AI and E-commerce

Poster Papers

Knowledge Representation

Machine Learning and Data Mining

Natural Language

AI and Web Applications

Reasoning under Uncertainty

Agents and Multiagent Systems

AI and E-commerce

Graduate Student Symposium

Experiences Building a Distributed Sensor Network

Victor Lesser

Department of Computer Science, University of Massachusetts/Amherst
Amherst, MA 01003-9264 USA
Lesser@cs.umass.edu

1 Extended Abstract

A central challenge in building advanced sensor networks will be the development of distributed and robust control for such networks that scales to thousands of intelligent sensors [8]. Appropriately structuring where and when control and interpretation activities are done is key to the effective operation of the network. This structuring must be adaptive to changing network conditions such as new sensors being added, existing sensors malfunctioning, and communication and processor resource modifications. Together with this adaptive re-structuring of long-term roles and responsibilities, there is also a need for short-term adaptivity related to the dynamic allocation of sensors. This involves allocating the appropriate configuration of sensing/processing resources for effectively sensing the phenomena but also the resolution of conflicting resource assignments that may occur when there are multiple phenomena occurring in the environment that need to be tracked concurrently. More generally, this structuring can be thought of as organizational control. Organizational control is a multilevel control approach in which organizational goals, roles, and responsibilities are dynamically developed, distributed, and maintained to serve as guidelines for making detailed operational control decisions by the individual agents. The parameters guiding the creation and adaptation of the organization can have a dramatic impact on the performance of the sensor network. We have recently completed work on a small-scale sensor network (approximately 36 low-cost, adjustable radar nodes) for multi-vehicle tracking [5,7], that exemplifies in a simplified form many of the issues discussed above (see Fig. 1). This lecture will discuss how we approached the design of the sensor network and what technologies we needed to develop.

The sensor network hardware configuration consists of sensor platforms that have three scanning regions, each with a 120-degree arc encircling the sensor (see Fig. 1, top left). Only one of these regions can be used to perform measurements at a time. The communication medium uses a low-speed, unreliable, radio-frequency (RF) system over eight separate channels. Messages cannot be both transmitted and received simultaneously regardless of channel assignment, and no two agents can transmit on a single channel at the same time without causing interference. The sensor platforms are capable of locally hosting one or more processes, which share a common CPU (in this case a commodity PC and signal processing hardware). The goal of this application is to track one or more targets that are moving through the sensor environment (in this case model railroad trains traveling on railroad tracks whose pattern is unknown, see Fig. 1: top right). The radar sensor measurements consist of only amplitude and

Y. Xiang and B. Chaib-draa (Eds.): AI 2003, LNAI 2671, pp. 1-6, 2003.

frequency values, so no one sensor has the ability to precisely determine the location of a target by itself. The sensors must therefore be organized and coordinated in a manner that permits their measurements to be used for triangulation.

Fig. 1. Sensor Network. Top left: radar unit with three sensing heads. Top right: vehicle being tracked. Bottom: an example configuration with 35 sensors and 3 vehicles

The need to triangulate a target's position requires frequent, closely coordinated actions amongst the agents, ideally three or more sensors performing their measurements at the same time. In order to produce an accurate track, the sensors must therefore minimize the amount of time between measurements during triangulation, and maximize the number of triangulated positions. Ignoring resources, an optimal tracking solution would have all agents capable of tracking the target taking measurements at the same precise time as frequently as possible. Restrictive communication and computation, however, limits our ability to coordinate and implement such an aggressive strategy. Low communication bandwidth hinders complex coordination and negotiation, limited processor power prevents exhaustive planning and scheduling, and restricted sensor usage creates a trade-off between discovering new targets and tracking existing ones. These considerations led us to an overall design philosophy that includes the use of an agent organization and satisficing behavior in all aspects of problem solving.

Our approach is built upon a soft, real-time agent architecture called SRTA, which we constructed as part of this effort [6]. The SRTA architecture provides a robust planning, scheduling and execution subsystem capable of quantitatively reasoning over deadlines and resource constraints. This provides a useful layer of abstraction, enabling the agent's higher level reasoning components to operate at a more tractable level of granularity, without sacrificing fine-grained control and reactivity.

Built upon this agent architecture is a virtual agent organization based on partitioning the environment into geographically self-contained *sectors* each with its own local management. Each of these sectors has a *sector manager*, a role in the organization which has several responsibilities associated with information flow and activity within the sector. Among these responsibilities is the dissemination of a scan schedule to each of the sensors in its sector, specifying the rate and frequency that should be used to scan for new targets. This information is used by each sensor to create a description of the scanning task, which is in turn used by the SRTA architecture to schedule local activities. When a new target is detected, the sector manager selects a *track manager*, a different organization role responsible for tracking that target as it moves through the environment. This allocation process uses an abstract view of what activities are presently being conducted in the sector to make a choice that load balances processor and communication requirements. Track manager activities entail estimating future location and heading, gathering available sensor information, requesting and negotiating over the sensors, and fusing the data they produce. Upon receipt of such a commitment to perform tracking, a sensor takes on a *data collection* role. Like the scan schedule, these commitments are used to generate task descriptions used by SRTA to schedule local activities. If conflicting commitments are received by a sensor that imply that the agent has been asked to perform multiple concurrent data collection roles, SRTA will attempt to satisfy all requests as best possible. This provides a window of marginal quality in which a conflict can be detected and then potentially resolved through negotiation with the competing agent to find an equitable long-term solution. As data is gathered, is it fused and interpreted to estimate the target's location, which allows the process to continue. We call this a virtual agent organization since a particular sensor/processor node may be multiplexing among different roles, e.g. sector manager and data collection. The SRTA architecture does the detail scheduling of activities associated with different roles based on their priority and deadline. The planning and scheduling ability of the SRTA architecture also allows us to approach the dynamic allocation of sensors to tracking tasks at an abstract level. Commitments made at this abstract level are then mapped into detail allocations of sensor resources and data processing activities.

The organizational structuring we have discussed so far involves setting up long-term patterns of control and information processing. There is also a need for setting up more short-term and dynamic patterns involving the allocation of groups of sensors (sensor platforms and sensor heads) to the tracking of the movement of a specific vehicle. Since sensor heads have limited sensing range and orientation and the vehicle is moving, this allocation process must be repeated as the current group of sensors become inappropriate for tracking the vehicle. Further, the need for this allocation process may be occurring simultaneously in different parts of the sensor network when there are multiple vehicles moving in the environment. Finally, this allocation process is intimately tied with information fusing activities that are tracking the current locations of vehicles and predicting where they are likely to be going. The real-time ability to do this prediction accurately is key to having sensing resources appropriately allocated to sense the vehicle when it arrives in their sensing region. Resource contention is introduced when more than one target enters the viewable range of the same sensor platform.

This type of resource allocation can be too complex and time consuming to perform in a centralized manner when the environmental characteristics are both distributed and dynamic, because the costs associated with continuously centralizing the necessary information are impractical. Negotiation, a form of distributed search [12] has been viewed as a viable alternative to handling complex searches that include multi-linked interacting subproblems [1]. Researchers in this domain have focused primarily on resource allocation scenarios that are formulated as distributed constraint satisfaction problems [11,13]. In our approach, we extend this classic formulation in two ways. First, we introduce soft, real-time constraints on the protocol's behavior. These require the negotiation to adapt to the remaining available time, which is estimated dynamically as a result of emerging environmental conditions. Second, we reformulate the resource allocation task as an optimization problem, and as with the distributed Partial Constraint Satisfaction Problem (PCSP) [2,3,4], we use constraint relaxation techniques to find a conflict-free solution while maximizing the social utility of the tracking agents. Of course, when more than one tracking agent desires a particular resource these two goals may contradict each other.

Our approach, called SPAM (The Scalable Protocol for Anytime Multi-level negotiation [9,10]), is a real-time, distributed, mediation-based negotiation protocol that takes advantage of the cooperative nature of the agents in the environment to maximize social utility. By mediation based, we are referring to the ability of each of the agents to act in a mediator capacity when resource conflicts are recognized. As a mediator, an agent gains a localized, partial view of the global allocation problem and makes suggestions to the allocations for each of the agents involved in the mediation. This allows the mediator to identify over-constrained subproblems and make suggestions to eliminate such conditions. In addition, the mediator can perform a localized arc-consistency check, which potentially allows large parts of the search space to be eliminated. Together with the fact that regions of mediation overlap, the agents rapidly converge on solutions that are in most cases good enough and fast enough. Overall, the protocol has many characteristics in common with distributed breakout [14], particularly its distributed hill-climbing nature and the ability to exploit parallelism by having multiple negotiations occur simultaneously.

In summary, the use of a sophisticated agent architecture (that includes capabilities for planning and scheduling) and distributed resource allocation mechanisms for short-term agent control and resource allocation, together with an organization structure for long-term agent control, create a powerful paradigm for building the next generation of large scale and intelligent sensor networks. More generally, we see these techniques as applicable to the building of advanced multi-agent applications.

Acknowledgements

This represents the combined work of a number of researchers in the Multi-Agent Systems Laboratory at the University of Massachusetts. The main contributors were Bryan Horling, Roger Mailler, Jiaying Shen and Dr. Regis Vincent.

This effort was sponsored in part by the Defense Advanced Research Projects Agency (DARPA) and Air Force Research Laboratory Air Force Materiel Command, USAF, under agreements number F30602-99-2-0525 and DOD DABT63-99-1-0004. The U.S. Government is authorized to reproduce and distribute reprints for Governmental purposes notwithstanding any copyright annotation thereon. This material is also based upon work supported by the National Science Foundation under Grant No.

IIS-9812755. The views and conclusions contained herein are those of the authors and should not be interpreted as necessarily representing the official policies or endorsements, either expressed or implied, of the Defense Advanced Research Projects Agency (DARPA), Air Force Research Laboratory or the U.S. Government.

References

[1] S.E. Conry, K.Kuwabara, V.R. Lesser, and R.A. Meyer. Multistage negotiation for distributed constraint satisfaction. IEEE Transactions on Systems, Man, and Cybernetics, 21(6), Nov. 1991.

[2] E.C. Freuder and R.J. Wallace. Partial constraint satisfaction. Artificial Intelligence, 58(1-3):21-70, 1992.

[3] K. Hirayama and M. Yokoo. Distributed partial constraint satisfaction problem. In G. Smolka, editor, *Principles and Practice of Constraint Programming* (CP-97), volume 1330 of Lecture Notes in Computer Science, pages 222-236. Springer-Verlag, 1997.

[4] K. Hirayama and M. Yokoo. An approach to overconstrained distributed constraint satisfaction problems: Distributed hierarchical constraint satisfaction. In *International Conference on Multi-Agent Systems* (ICMAS), 2000.

[5] B. Horling, R. Vincent, R. Mailler, J. Shen, R. Becker, K. Rawlins, and V. Lesser. Distributed sensor network for real time tracking. In *Proceedings of the Fifth International Conference on Autonomous Agents*, pages 417-424, 2001.

[6] B. Horling, V. Lesser, R. Vincent, and T. Wagner. The soft real-time agent control architecture. University of Massachusetts/Amherst Computer Science Technical Report 2002-14, 2002.

[7] B. Horling, R. Mailler, J. Shen, R. Vincent, V. R. Lesser. Using Autonomy, Organizational Design and Negotiation in a Distributed Sensor Network. Accepted for publication in *Distributed Sensor Nets: A Multiagent Perspective*.

[8] V. Lesser, C. Ortiz, and M. Tambe. *Distributed Sensor Networks: A multiagent perspective*. Kluwer Publishers, 2003 (to appear).

[9] R. Mailler, R. Vincent, V. Lesser, J. Shen, and T. Middlekoop. Soft real-time, cooperative negotiation for distributed resource allocation. In *Proceedings of the 2001 AAAI Fall Symposium on Negotiation*, 2001.

[10] R. Mailler, V. Lesser, B. Horling. Cooperative Negotiation for Soft Real-Time Distributed Resource Allocation. Accepted for publication in *Proceedings of the Second International Joint Conference on Autonomous Agents and Multi-Agent Systems (AAMAS)*, Melbourne, Australia, 2003. Also available as University of Massachusetts/Amherst Computer Science Technical Report 2002-49.

[11] P. J. Modi, H. Jung, M. Tambe, W.-M. Shen, and S. Kulkarni. Dynamic distributed resource allocation: A distributed constraint satisfaction approach. In J.-J. Meyer and M. Tambe, editors, Pre-proceedings of the Eighth International Workshop on Agent Theories, Architectures, and Languages (ATAL-2001), pages 181-193, 2001.

[12] T. Moehlman, V. Lesser, and B. Buteau. Decentralized negotiation: An approach to the distributed planning problem. *Group Decision and Negotiation*, 1(2):161-192, 1992.

[13] M. Yokoo, E. H. Durfee, T. Ishida, and K. Kuwabara. The distributed constraint satisfaction problem: Formalization and algorithms. *Knowledge and Data Engineering*, 10(5): 673-685, 1998.

[14] M. Yokoo and K. Hirayama. Distributed breakout algorithm for solving distributed constraint satisfaction problems. In *International Conference on Multi-Agent Systems* (ICMAS), 1996.

Artificial Intelligence and Human Brain Imaging

Tom M. Mitchell

Center for Automated Learning and Discovery
Carnegie Mellon University, USA

Abstract. For many years AI researchers have sought to understand the nature of intelligence primarily by creating artificially intelligent computer systems. Studies of human intelligence have had less influence on AI, partly because of the great difficulty in directly observing human brain activity. In recent years, new methods for observing brain activity have become available, notably functional Magnetic Resonance Imaging (fMRI) which allows us to safely, non-invasively capture images of activity across the brain once per second, at millimeter spatial resolution. The advent of fMRI has already produced dramatic new insights into human brain activity, and how it varies with cognitive task. This breakthrough in instrumentation (and others as well) shifts the balance of utility between building artificial intelligent systems and studying natural intelligence. As a result, we should expect a growing synergy in the future between studies of artificial and natural intelligence.

One intriguing open question regarding fMRI is whether it is possible to decode instantaneous cognitive states of human subjects based on their observed fMRI activity. If this were feasible, it would open the possibility of directly observing the sequence of hidden cognitive states a person passes through while performing cognitive tasks such as language comprehension, problem solving, etc.

We present initial results showing that it is indeed possible to distinguish among a variety of cognitive states of human subjects based on their observed fMRI data. In particular, we have developed machine learning algorithms that can be trained to discriminate among a variety of cognitive states based on the observed fMRI data of the subject at a particular time or time interval. These machine learning algorithms, including Bayesian classifiers, support vector machines, logistic regression, and other methods, use the training data to discover the spatial-temporal patterns of fMRI activity associated with different cognitive states. They can then classify new fMRI observations to distinguish among these states.

This talk will describe results in which our machine learning methods were able to successfully discriminate between states such as "the subject is reading a sentence" versus "the subject is viewing a picture"; "the sentence is ambiguous" versus "the sentence is unambiguous"; and "the word is a noun" versus "the word is a verb." These classifiers are typically trained separately for each human subject, but in one case we were able to train a classifier that applies to new human subjects outside the training set. We will describe these results, the machine learning methods used to achieve them, and a number of directions for future research.

Y. Xiang and B. Chaib-draa (Eds.): AI 2003, LNAI 2671, p. 7, 2003.

Machine Learning Methods for Computational Proteomics and Beyond

Pierre Baldi

Institute for Genomics and Bioinformatics
University of California, Irvine, CA, USA

Abstract. Predicting protein structure is a fundamental problem in biology, especially in the genomic era where over one third of newly discovered genes have unknown structure and function. Because sequence and structure data (hence training sets) continue to grow exponentially, this area is ideally suited for machine learning approaches. Neural networks, in particular, have had remarkable success and have led, for instance, to the construction of the best secondary structure predictors. We will provide an overview of our own work and the state-of-the-art for several structure prediction problem including:

(1) prediction of protein secondary structures;
(2) prediction of relative solvent accessibility;
(3) prediction of contacts;
(4) prediction of three-dimensional protein structures;
(5) prediction of interchain beta-sheet quaternary structures; using machine learning methods.

The methods we have developed are based on the theory of graphical models but use deterministic recursive neural networks to speed up learning. We will discuss their applicability to other problems and the lessons learnt for the design of complex neural architectures.

Y. Xiang and B. Chaib-draa (Eds.): AI 2003, LNAI 2671, p. 8, 2003.

On the Structure Model Interpretation of Wright's NESS Test

Richard A. Baldwin and Eric Neufeld

Department of Computer Science, University of Saskatchewan
Saskatoon, Canada SK S7H 3A8
{rab831,eric}@cs.usask.ca
http://www.cs.usask.ca/index.html

Abstract. Within the law, the traditional test for attributing causal responsibility is the "but-for" test, which asks whether, 'but for' the defendant's wrongful act, the injury complained of would have occurred. This definition conforms to common intuitions regarding causation, but gives non-intuitive results in complex situations of overdetermination where two or more potential causes are present. To handle such situations, Wright defined the NESS Test, considered to be a significant refinement of Hart and Honore's classic approach to causality in the law. We show that though Wright's terminology lacks the mathematical rigor of Halpern and Pearl, the Halpern and Pearl definition essentially formalizes Wright's definition, provides an alternative theory of the test's validity, and fixes problems with the NESS test raised by Wright's critics. However, the Halpern and Pearl definition seems to yield puzzling results in some situations involving double omission, and we propose a solution.

1 Introduction

Ashley [1] writes that the legal domain is of interest to AI research because it is between those formal domains so amenable to knowledge representation and those commonsense domains whose representation remains so elusive. Here we discuss *actual causation* in the law from both perspectives. The generally accepted test for determination of actual causation in the law is the *but-for* test. If the specified injury would not have occurred 'but for' the defendant's wrongful conduct, then actual causation is established. The but-for test assumes that it is somehow possible to remove the defendant's wrongful conduct from the scenario describing the occurrence of the injury and determine whether the injury would have still occurred. The test is straightforward enough to assign its application to juries. However, the test is not comprehensive. It is known to fail when the scenario describing the injury includes other potential causes that would have caused the specified injury in the absence of the defendant's wrongful conduct. This is known as *overdetermined* causation.

Y. Xiang and B. Chaib-draa (Eds.): AI 2003, LNAI 2671, pp. 9-23, 2003.

Wright [10, pp. 1775-76] divides cases of overdetermined causation into preemptive and duplicative causation cases. In preemptive causation, the effect of other potential causes is preempted by the effect of the defendant's wrongful act. For example, the defendant stabs and kills the victim before a fatal dose of poison previously administered by a third party can take effect. In duplicative causation, the effect of the defendant's act combines with, or duplicates, the effect of other potential causes where the latter were alone sufficient to bring about the injury. For example, the defendant and another party start separate fires that combine to burn down the victim's house where each fire was independently sufficient to do so. Since in these cases it is not true that 'but for' the defendant's wrongful act the specified harm would not have occurred, according to the but-for test, in neither scenario is the defendant's conduct an actual cause of the injury. Such a result is contrary to intuitions about responsibility and, by implication, about causality.

To cope with overdetermination, Wright [10] proposes a comprehensive test for actual causation, the NESS (Necessary Element of a Sufficient Set) test: "a particular condition was a cause of (condition contributing to) a specific consequence if and only if it was a necessary element of a set of antecedent actual conditions that was sufficient for the occurrence of the consequence". He adopts the view that there is an intelligible, determinate concept of actual causation underlying and explaining common intuitions and judgments about causality and that this concept explains the "intuitively plausible factual causal determinations" of judges and juries when "not confined by incorrect tests or formulas." Wright [10, p. 1902] contends that, not only does the NESS test capture the common-sense concept underlying these common intuitions and judgements, the NESS test defines the concept of actual causation.

Pearl [9, pp. 313-15] claims that while the intuitions underlying the NESS test are correct the test itself is inadequate to capture these intuitions because it relies on the traditional logical language of necessity and sufficiency, which cannot capture causal concepts. Pearl [7,3,4,9] proposes a mathematical language of (graphical) causal models employing structural equations for formalizing counterfactual and causal concepts. Pearl [8; 9, Chap. 10] first applies this structural language to define actual causation using a complex construction called a causal beam. Halpern and Pearl [5] develop a "more transparent" definition, but still using structural models.

In the sequel, we investigate the relationship between the NESS definition and the Halpern-Pearl definition, in particular, whether the NESS test is an adequate informal, or semi-formal, application of the Halpern-Pearl definition and, correspondingly, whether the Halpern-Pearl definition formalizes the NESS test.

2 The NESS Test

In circumstances where only one actual or potential set of conditions is sufficient for the result, the NESS test reduces to the but-for test [10]. To illustrate that the NESS test matches common intuitions where the but-for test fails Wright considers three variations of a two-fire scenario: fires X and Y are independently sufficient to destroy house H if they reach it and they are the only potential causes of house H's destruction so that if neither reach the house it will not be destroyed. In the first situation, X

reaches and destroys H and Y would not have reached H even if X were absent. The **common** intuition here is that X was a cause of the destruction of H but not Y. In this case there is a single actually sufficient set of conditions and no other even potentially sufficient set of conditions. (This assumes that actually sufficient sets of conditions are minimal.) X was a necessary element (necessary for the sufficiency) of that single, actually sufficient set, a NESS condition. It was also a but-for condition.

In the second situation, X and Y reach H simultaneously and combine to destroy it. Here Wright claims that the common intuition is that both (individually) X and Y were causes of the destruction of the house. There are two overlapping sets of actually sufficient conditions. X is necessary for the sufficiency of the set including itself but not Y and Y is necessary for the sufficiency of the set including itself buy not X. Neither X nor Y is a but-for cause of the destruction of H but each is a duplicative NESS cause of the destruction.

In the final situation, X reaches and destroys H before Y can arrive and, if X had been absent, Y would have destroyed H. Here the common intuition is unquestionably that X caused the destruction of H and Y did not. Fire Y is not a NESS condition for the destruction of H since any actually sufficient set of conditions, given the assumptions of the scenario, must include X, and Y is not necessary for the sufficiency of any set of conditions that includes X. Fire X, on the other hand, is necessary for the sufficiency of the actually sufficient set of which it is a member. Because the set containing Y but not X would have been sufficient in the absence of X, X is not a but-for cause of the destruction of H. X was a preemptive NESS cause because it preempted the actual sufficiency of the potentially sufficient set including Y.

3 The Structure Equation Model

Following [5,9] a *signature* $\mathcal{S}$ is a 3-tuple $(\mathcal{U}, \mathcal{V}, \mathcal{R})$, where $\mathcal{U}$ is a finite set of exogenous variables, $\mathcal{V}$ is a set of endogenous variables, and $\mathcal{R}$ is a relation associating with each variable $Y \in \mathcal{U} \cup \mathcal{V}$ a nonempty set $\mathcal{R}(Y)$ of possible values for Y (the *range* of Y).

A *causal model* over a signature $\mathcal{S}$ is a 2-tuple $M = (\mathcal{S}, \mathcal{F})$, where $\mathcal{F}$ is a relation associating each $X \in \mathcal{V}$ with a function denoted F_X such that describes the outcome of X given the values of other variables in the model. This function is simplified by assuming that there is a total ordering $\prec$ of $\mathcal{V}$ such that if $X \prec Y$, then the value of F_X is independent of Y (i.e., $F_X(\ldots, y, \ldots) = F_X(\ldots, y', \ldots)$ for all $y, y' \in \mathcal{R}(Y)$). If PA_X is the minimal set of variables in $\mathcal{V}$ - X and U_X the minimal set of values in $\mathcal{U}$ that together suffice to represent F_X, then the causal model gives rise to a *causal diagram*, a directed acyclic graph (DAG) where each node corresponds to a variable in $\mathcal{V}$ and the directed edges point from members of PA_X and U_X to X. The set PA_X, connoting the *parents* of X, are the *direct causes* of X. Causal diagrams encode the information that a variable's value is independent of its other ancestor variables in the diagram given the values of its parents and, also, that the value of a variable can only affect the value of its descendents in the diagram. The edges in a causal diagram represent the non-parameterized (or arbitrary) form of the function for a variable, $X = F_X(U_X, PA_X)$.

An external *intervention* (or *surgery*) setting $X = x$ (representing contingencies outside of the model perturbing a causal mechanism), where $X \in \mathcal{V}$, is denoted $X \leftarrow x$ and amounts to pruning the equation for X from the model and substituting $X=x$ in the remaining equations. In the corresponding causal diagram, it amounts to removing the edges from $PA_X \cup U_X$ to X. An intervention that forces the values of a subset of $\mathcal{V}$ (sometimes written as a vector $\vec{X}$, and the setting of variables therein written as $\vec{X} \leftarrow \vec{x}$) prunes a subset of equations, one for each variable in the set and substitutes the corresponding forced values in the remaining equations.

For a given signature $\mathcal{S} = (\mathcal{U}, \mathcal{V}, \mathcal{R})$, a *primitive event* is a formula of the form $X = x$, where $X \in \mathcal{V}$ and $x \in \mathcal{R}(X)$. A *basic causal formula* is written $[Y_1 \leftarrow y_1, \ldots, Y_k \leftarrow y_k]\varphi$, where φ is a Boolean combination of primitive events, $Y_1, \ldots, Y_k$ are distinct variables in $\mathcal{V}$, and $y_i \in R(Y_i)$. Basic causal formulas are abbreviated as $[\vec{Y} \leftarrow \vec{y}]\varphi$ or just φ when $k = 0$. A *causal formula* is a Boolean combination of basic causal formulas.

A basic causal formula is true or false in a causal model given a context $\vec{u}$. (A context is a given setting of variables in $\vec{u}$.) Where ψ is a causal formula (or a Boolean combination of primitive events), $(M, \vec{u}) \models \psi$ means ψ is true in the causal model M in the context $\vec{u}$. $(M, \vec{u}) \models [\vec{Y} \leftarrow \vec{y}](X = x)$ means X has value x in the unique solution to the equations in the submodel $M_{\vec{Y} \leftarrow \vec{y}}$ in context $\vec{u}$. In other words, in the world in which $\mathcal{U} = \vec{u}$, the model predicts that if $\vec{Y}$ had been $\vec{y}$ then X would have been x; that is, in the counterfactual world $M_{\vec{Y} \leftarrow \vec{y}}$, resulting from the intervention $\vec{Y} \leftarrow \vec{y}$, X has the value x. Causes are conjunctions of primitive events of the form written $\vec{X} = \vec{x}$.

Definition (*Actual Cause*): $\vec{X} = \vec{x}$ is an *actual cause* of φ in a model M in the context $\vec{u}$ (i.e., in $(M, \vec{u})$) if the following conditions hold:

C1. $(M, \vec{u}) \models (\vec{X} = \vec{x}) \wedge \varphi$.

C2. There exists a partition $(\vec{Z}, \vec{W})$ of $\mathcal{V}$ with $\vec{X} \subseteq \vec{Z}$ and some setting $(\vec{x}', \vec{w}')$ of the variables in $(\vec{X}, \vec{W})$ such that, where $(M, \vec{u}) \models Z = z^*$ for each $Z \in \vec{Z}$ (i.e., the actual value of z in context $\vec{u}$

(a) $(M, \vec{u}) \models [\vec{X} \leftarrow \vec{x}', \vec{W} \leftarrow \vec{w}']\neg\varphi$, and

(b) $(M, \vec{u}) \models [\vec{X} \leftarrow \vec{x}, \vec{W} \leftarrow \vec{w}', \vec{Z}' \leftarrow \vec{z}^*]\varphi$ for every subset $\vec{Z}'$ of $\vec{Z}$.

C3. $\vec{X}$ is minimal; no subset of $\vec{X}$ satisfies conditions C1 and C2.

4 Examples of NESS and the Halpern-Pearl Definition

4.1 Preemptive Causation

To illustrate preemptive causation, Wright [10, p. 1795] considers two scenarios: in the first, *D* shoots and kills *P* before *P* can drink tea fatally poisoned by *C* and, in the second, *D* shoots and instantly kills *P* after *P* drinks tea fatally poisoned by *C* but before the poison can take effect. With respect to the first scenario, in Wright's [10, p. 1795] NESS analysis, *D*'s shot was necessary for the sufficiency of a set of actual antecedent conditions that did not include the poisoned tea. Conversely, *C*'s poisoning of the tea was not a necessary element of any sufficient set of actual antecedent conditions. A set that included the poisoned tea but not the shooting would be sufficient only if *P* actually drank the tea, but this was not an actual condition. The shooting preempted the potential causal effect of the poisoned tea.

In this scenario, the story of death by poisoning would have occurred (the intake of the poison through consumption of the tea will have occurred) but for *D* shooting *P*. This is reflected in the following causal model. (Henceforth we do not write the context and details of the structural equations.) The model has the following binary variables: *DS* (representing "*D* shoots"), *PT* ("*C* poisons the tea"), *CP* ("*P* consumes poison"), and *PD* ("*P* dies").

The structural equations are:

$$CP = \begin{cases} 0 & \text{if } PT = 0 \text{ or } DS = 1 \\ 1 & \text{if } PT = 1 \text{ and } DS = 0 \end{cases};$$

$$PD = \begin{cases} 0 & \text{if } DS = 0 \text{ and } CP = 0 \\ 1 & \text{if } DS = 1 \text{ or } CP = 1 \end{cases}.$$

The causal diagram corresponding to these equations is:

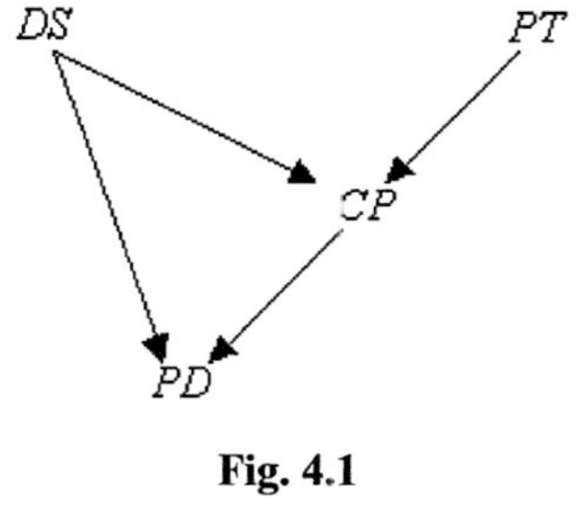

Fig. 4.1

To show that $DS = 1$ is an actual cause of $PD = 1$, for condition C2, let $\vec{Z} = \{DS, PD\}$ and $\vec{W} = \{CP, PCP\}$. Setting $DS = 0$ and $\vec{W} = \vec{w} = (0,0)$ satisfies conditions C2(a) and C2(b) because when $PCP = 0$, $PD = DS$. (When C1 and C2 are trivially satisfied, as they are here, this will be assumed and not referred to.) On the other hand, to show that $CP = 1$ is an actual cause of $DS = 1$, condition C2(a) requires that *DS* not be in the set $\vec{Z}$ or else $PD = 1$ and the condition fails. If *DS* is in

$\vec{W}$, to satisfy condition C2(a), DS must be set $DS = 0$. However, in that case, letting $\vec{Z}' = \{PCP\}$ in condition C2(b) results in $PD = 0$ and condition C2 fails again. In other words—the words of Wright's NESS analysis above—a set that "included the poisoned tea but not the shooting would be sufficient only if P actually drank the tea, but this was not an actual condition." Rather, the "shooting preempted the potential causal effect of the poisoned tea."

For the second example, Wright's [10, p. 1795] NESS analysis of why *D*'s shooting was a cause of *P*'s death is the same as that for the first example; as to whether *C*'s poisoning of the tea was a cause: "Even if *P* actually had drunk the poisoned tea, *C*'s poisoning of the tea still would not be a cause of *P*'s death if the poison did not work instantaneously but the shot did. The poisoned tea would be a cause of *P*'s death only if *P* drank the tea and was alive when the poison took effect. That is, a set of actual antecedent conditions sufficient to cause *P*'s death must include poisoning of the tea, *P*'s drinking the poisoned tea, and *P*'s being alive when the poison takes effect. Although the first two conditions actually existed, the third did not. *D*'s shooting *P* prevented it from occurring. Thus, there is no sufficient set of actual antecedent conditions that includes *C*'s poisoning of the tea as a necessary element. Consequently, *C*'s poisoning of the tea fails the NESS test. It did not contribute to *P*'s death."

In this scenario, the death itself, or the timing of the death, prevents the effect of the poisoning. This "late preemption" [5] or "temporal preemption" [9] problem is best modelled with time-indexed variables. The binary variables are:

P_i represents whether the tea was poisoned at time t_i;
CP_i represents whether the poisoned tea was consumed at time t_i;
PTE_i represents whether the poison took effect at time t_i;
S_i represents whether there was a shot taken at time t_i;
VSH_i represents whether the victim was shot at time t_i and
D_i represents whether the victim was dead at time t_i

The structural equations are:

$CP_i = P_i$;

$$PTE_i = 0 \text{ when } i = 1 \text{ and } PTE_i = \begin{cases} 0 & \text{if } CP_{i-1} = 0 \text{ or } D_{i-1} = 1 \\ 1 & \text{if } CP_{i-1} = 1 \text{ and } D_{i-1} = 0 \end{cases} \text{ when } i > 1;$$

$VSH_i = S_i$; and

$D_i = VSH_i$ when $I = 1$, and

$$D_i = \begin{cases} 0 & \text{if } D_{i-1} = 0 \text{ and } PTE_i = 0 \text{ and } VSE_i = 0 \\ 1 & \text{if } D_{i-1} = 1 \text{ or } PTE_i = 1 \text{ or } VSE_i = 1 \end{cases} \text{ when } i > 1.$$

These equations include implicit simplifying assumptions that time is discrete, poison takes effect in one time unit, a gunshot and impact are instantaneous; and death is immediate upon a gunshot impact or upon poison taking effect.

Figure 4.2 is the causal network corresponding to these equations. The context for this scenario requires that $P_1 = 0$, $P_2 = 1$, $S_1 = 0$, $S_2 = 1$, and $S_3 = 0$.

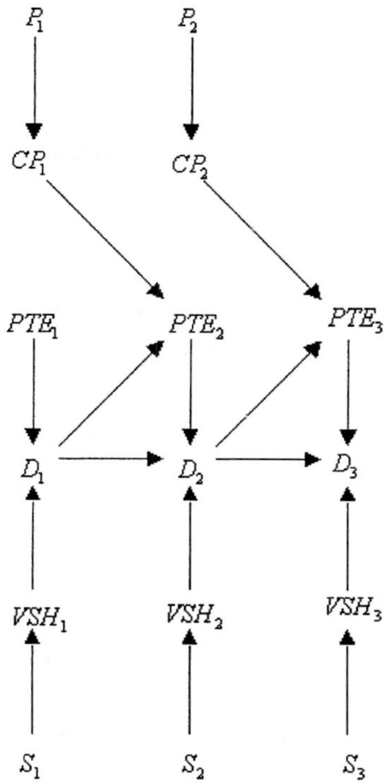

Fig. 4.2

To show that $S_2 = 1$ is an actual cause of $D_3 = 1$, let $\vec{Z} = \{S_2, VSH_2, D_2, D_3\}$. The only variable in $\vec{W}$ (the complement of $\vec{Z}$ in V) whose value must be changed to satisfy C2(a) is PTE_3, which must be set $PTE_3 = 0$. C2(b) is satisfied since, when S_2 is returned to its original value, all variables in $\vec{Z}$ (including D_3) return to their original values irrespective of the values of the variables in $\vec{W}$. To show $P_2 = 1$ is not an actual cause of $D_3 = 1$, notice that for D_3 to depend counterfactually upon P_2 that PTE_3 must be an element in any set $\vec{Z}$ required for condition C2. Since $(\vec{Z}, \vec{W})$ is a partition of V, D_2 must be an element in one of $\vec{Z}$ and $\vec{W}$. If D_2 is in $\vec{Z}$ then $D_3 = 0$ and condition C2(b) fails since changing the value of P_2 has no effect on the value of D_2. If D_2 is in $\vec{W}$ then to satisfy condition C2(a) D_2 must be set $D_2 = 0$. In that case, when $\vec{Z}' = \{PTE_3\}$ for condition C2(b) (that is, when PTE_3 is returned to its original value $PTE_3 = 0$), $D_3 = 0$ and the condition fails. Thus $P_2 = 1$ is not an actual cause of $D_3 = 1$.

In Wright's application of the NESS test to both scenarios, the competing causal stories are considered separately. Causal interactions between the conditions that comprise the actually and potentially sufficient sets are left implicit through consideration of a missing condition that must be instantiated for the potentially sufficient set to be actually sufficient. In the first scenario, it was the drinking of the poisoned tea; in the second, it was the victim being alive when the poison would take effect. That the condition is missing is due to the causal influence of conditions in the actually sufficient set on conditions in the potentially sufficient set. Again, because causal influences within the potentially and actually sufficient sets and the interaction between them are not explicitly represented in the application of the NESS test, Wright [10, p. 1795] places special emphasis on the causal effect (the injury) under consideration: "As the last example illustrates, a necessary condition for the sufficiency of any set of actual antecedent conditions is that the injury not have occurred already as a result of other actual conditions outside the set. The determination of whether this condition existed, as with all the other conditions, is an empirical judgment."

4.2 Duplicative Causation Scenarios

Among the duplicative causation cases, of particular interest are a group of pollution cases where defendants were found liable though none of their individual acts (their "contributions" to the pollution) was sufficient, or necessary given the contributions of the other defendants, to produce the plaintiff's injuries (some adverse effect on the use of his property).[1] Wright [10, p. 1793] applies the NESS test to two idealized examples. In the first, five units of pollution are necessary and sufficient for the injury and seven defendants discharge one unit each. In the second example, again five units of pollution are necessary and sufficient for the injury but there are two defendants one of whom discharges five units of pollution and the other two units.

In the first example, the NESS test requires only that a defendant's discharge be necessary for the sufficiency of *a* set of actual antecedent conditions [10, p. 1795]. In this sense, for each defendant's discharge there are 15 distinct actually sufficient sets of antecedent conditions, one for each possible choice of any four of the six remaining defendant's units of pollution.

The causal model for this example can be given by a single equation:

$$DP = \sum_{i=1}^{7} X_i \, .$$

where each X_i indicates whether defendant i contributed a unit of pollution, and DP, "destruction of property," represents whether the plaintiff was injured $(DP \geq 5)$—that is, whether his property was damaged—or not $(DP < 5)$.

Figure 4.3 shows the causal network for the scenario that describes the damage suffered as a direct result of the discharges.

[1] For example, Wright (2001, p 1100) cites the case of Warren v. Parkhurst, 92 N.Y.S. 725 (N.Y. Sup. Ct. 1904), *aff'd*, 93 N.Y.S. 1009 (A.D.1905), *aff'd*, 78 N.E. 579 (N.Y. 1906), where each of twenty-six defendants discharged "nominal" amounts of sewage into a creek which individually were not sufficient to destroy the use of downstream plaintiff's property but the stench of the combined discharges was sufficient.

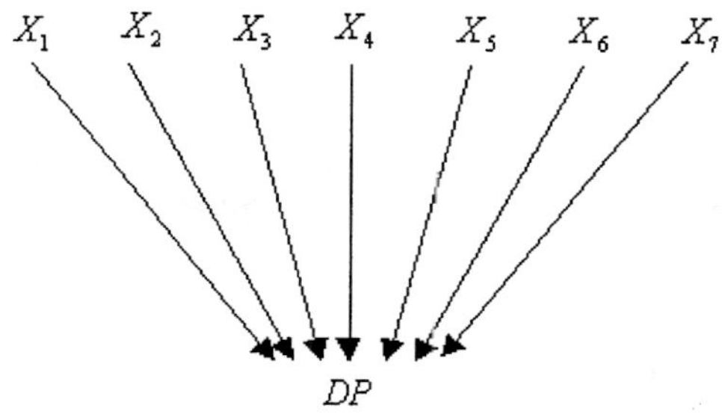

Fig. 4.3

To show each X_i is a cause of $DP \geq 5$, it is enough to show, without loss of generality, that $X_1 = 1$ is an actual cause of $DP \geq 5$. Let $\vec{Z} = \{X_1, X_2, X_3, X_4, X_5, DP\}$ and $\vec{W} = \{X_6, X_7\}$. Setting $X_1 = x_1' = 0$, the contingency in which $\vec{W} = \vec{w}' = (x_6, x_7) = (0,0)$ satisfies condition C2(a), since $X_1 = 0$ and $\vec{W} = \vec{w}'$ imply $DP \leq 5$. C2(b) is satisfied as well since, the values of $X_2, ..., X_5$ being unaffected by setting $\vec{W} = \vec{w}'$, with X_1 set to its original value ($X_1 = 1$) $DP = 5$.

Notice, however, that $\vec{Z}$ is not minimal—which is evident from the causal diagram (Figure 4.3) as every variable in a minimal set $\vec{Z}$ (an active causal process) must lie on a path from X_1 to *DP*. It is not hard to see that the partition $(\vec{Z}, \vec{W}) = (\{X_1, DP\}, \{X_2, ..., X_7\})$ satisfies condition C2, but so does any partition in which $\vec{W}$ is any two-member subset of $\{X_2, ..., X_7\}$: it is necessary to consider contingencies affecting the mechanisms (equations) for exactly two of the defendants' (other than X_1's) pollution discharges. Four of the discharges could have been treated as background conditions and their effect, modeled by an extraneous variable $U_{DP} = 4$, on *DP* so that the structural equation for *DP* becomes:

$$DP = F_{DP} = (U_{DP}, PA_{DP}) = 4 + \sum_{i=1}^{3} X_i \ .$$

Figure 4.4 is the new causal diagram.

Returning to the NESS analysis, a possible interpretation of removing (wiping out) two pollution discharges known to be present in the scenario in order to construct an actually sufficient set for which X_1 is a NESS condition is that it represents an intervention or contingency affecting the explicit model of the scenario as a set of relevant conditions describing the scenario in question. The working out of the consequences of these "interventions" is dependent on the underlying mental model of the flow of causal influences.

For the second pollution scenario, with two defendants one of whom discharges five units of pollution and the other two units, here is Wright's [10, p. 1793] NESS test analysis: "The two units still mix with the five units to produce the injurious seven units. More rigorously, the two units were necessary for the sufficiency of a set of actual antecedent conditions that included only three of the first defendant's five units, a set whose sufficiency was not affected by the existence of two additional duplicative units also provided by the first defendant."

A causal model for this scenario requires only two variables, X_1 and X_2, representing the two discharges. Figure 4.5 is the causal diagram corresponding to the single structural equation, $DP = X_1 + X_2$. To show $X_1 = 2$ is an actual cause of $DP \geq 5$ in the context in which $X_2 = 5$, let $\vec{Z} = \{X_1, DP\}$ and $\vec{W} = \{X_2\}$. Setting $X_1 = 1$ and $X_2 = 3$ satisfies C2(a) of the Halpern-Pearl definition, since $DP = 4$, and satisfies C2(b), since when X_1 is returned to its original value $(X_1 = 2)$ $DP = 5$.

Notice that this causal model does not correspond to the model implied by Wright's NESS actually sufficient set, $\{X_1, X_2, Y_1, ..., Y_5\}$, where the X_i represent the two units of pollution discharged by defendant *X* (individually), and the Y_i represent the 5 units of pollution discharged by defendant *Y* (individually). The corresponding structural causal model would have a single structural equation, $DP = X_1 + X_2 + \sum_{i=1}^{5} Y_i$, and the causal diagram shown in Figure 4.6.

Wright cannot have a single condition for each defendant's discharge of pollution because in that case it would not be possible to exclude two of defendant *Y*'s discharged pollution units from the actually sufficient set; that is, there would be no way to represent that contingency by removing conditions from the set.

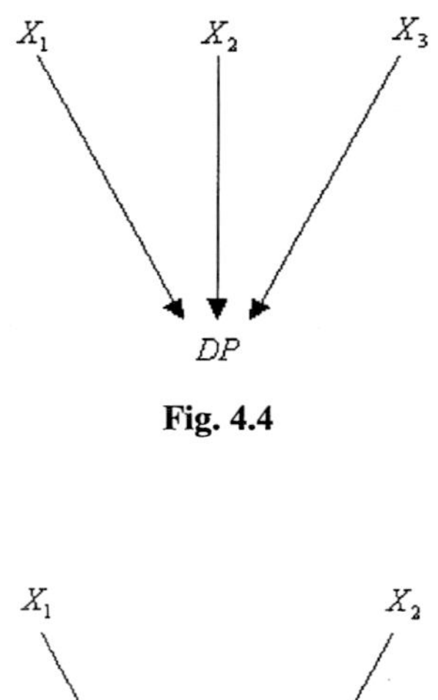

Fig. 4.4

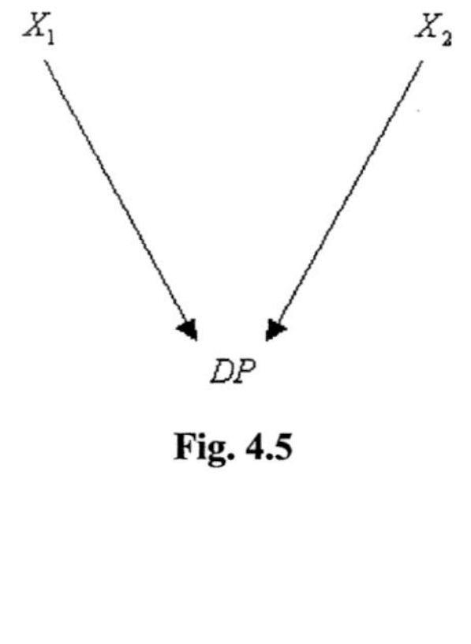

Fig. 4.5

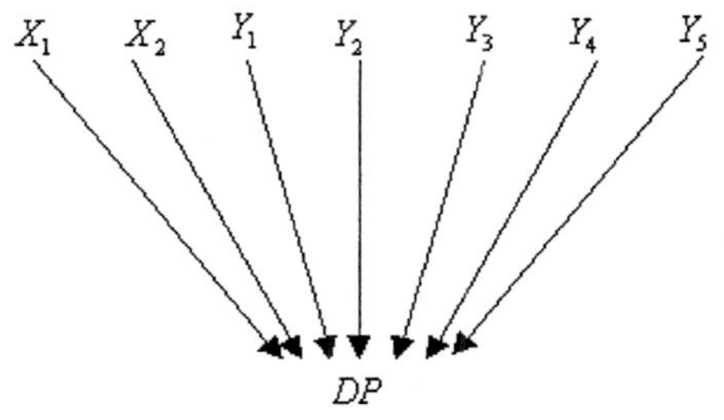

Fig. 4.6

4.3 Double Omission Cases

A class of cases that have proved problematic for the NESS test, the so-called double omission cases, suggest that modelling is an important aspect of a NESS enquiry in practice: "Some of the most difficult overdetermined-causation cases, at least conceptually, are those involving multiple omissions, which usually involve failures to attempt to use missing or defective safety devices or failures to attempt to read or heed missing or defective instructions or warnings." [12, pp. 1123-1124].

Wright [10, p. 1801; 12, p. 1124 ff.] considers in detail the case of *Saunders System Birmingham Co. v. Adams*[2] where a car rental company negligently failed to discover or repair bad brakes before renting a car out. The driver who rented the car then negligently failed to apply the brakes and struck a pedestrian. In general, courts have held that individuals who negligently fail to repair a device (or provide proper safeguards or warnings) are not responsible when (negligently) no attempt was made to use the device (or use the safeguards or observe the warnings). According to Wright [12, p. 1124], the court's decisions reflect a "tacit understanding of empirical causation in such situations": not providing or repairing a device (or not providing proper safeguards or warnings) can have no causal effect when no attempt was or would have been made to use the device (or use the safeguard or observe the warning)—unless no attempt was made because it was known that the device was inoperative (or the safeguards or warnings were inadequate).

Wright's [10, p. 1801] NESS analysis (where *D* represents the driver, *C* represents the car rental company, and *P* represents the pedestrian) is as follows: "It is clear that *D*'s negligence was a preemptive cause of *P*'s injury, and that *C*'s negligence did not contribute to the injury. *D*'s failure to try to use the brakes was necessary for the sufficiency of a set of actual antecedent conditions that did not include *C*'s failure to repair the brakes, and the sufficiency of this set was not affected by *C*'s failure to repair the brakes. A failure to try to use brakes will have a negative causal effect whether or not the brakes are defective. On the other hand, *C*'s failure to repair the brakes was not a necessary element of any set of antecedent actual conditions that was sufficient for the occurrence of the injury. Defective brakes will have an actual causal effect only if someone tries to use them, but that was not an actual condition here. The potential negative causal effect of *C*'s failure to repair the brakes was preempted by *D*'s failure to try to use them."

---

[2] Saunders Sys. Birmingham Co. v. Adams, 117 So. 72 (Ala. 1928).

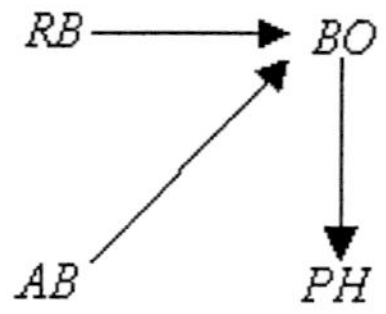

Fig. 4.7

The binary variables for this causal model are: *RB* for "repairs brakes", *AB* for "applies brakes", *BO* for "brakes operate", and *HP* for "pedestrian is hit".

Figure 4.7 gives the causal diagram for the model. The structural equations are:

$$BO = \begin{cases} 0 & \text{if } RB = 0 \text{ or } AB = 0 \\ 1 & \text{if } RB = 1 \text{ and } AB = 1 \end{cases}$$

$$PH = \begin{cases} 0 & \text{if } BO = 1 \\ 1 & \text{if } BO = 0 \end{cases}.$$

The context requires that $RB = 0$ and $AB=0$.

It is indeed the case that $AB=0$ is an actual cause of $PH=1$ (take $\vec{Z} = \{AB, BO, PH\}$ and $\vec{W} = \{RB\}$ for condition C2). But, as is evident from the symmetry in the model between variables *RB* and *AB*, substituting *RB* and *AB* in a proof that $AB = 0$ is an actual cause of $PH = 1$ will give a proof that $RB = 0$ is an actual cause as well. According to Wright (2001, p.1125): "At the time that I wrote this explanation, I was aware that it was too brief and cryptic, relied upon an insufficiently elaborated notion of causal sufficiency and 'negative causal effect,' and therefore could seemingly be reversed to support the opposite causal conclusions merely by switching the references to the two omissions. Nevertheless, I thought it roughly stated the correct analysis in very abbreviated form."

Wright [12, pp. 1125-1131] then expands on the earlier analysis, invoking notions of "negative causal effects" and "positive causal effects." Whatever the merits of that analysis, it does not appear necessary. As described in Section 4.2.1, to decide between two competing variables—here $RB = 0$ and $AB = 0$—as to which one is the actual cause in a given context for a model, it is necessary that the model include a variable whose value changes depending on which event is the actual cause. *BO* is the only variable on intersecting paths form *RB* and *AB* to *PH* and does not serve this function. A variable that would is "brakes fail". Define a new model that differs from the previous one by replacing *BO* with:

BF for "brakes fail" with values 0 (they do not) and 1 (they do).

The structural equations become:

$$BF = \begin{cases} 0 & \text{if } RB = 1 \text{ or } AB = 0 \\ 1 & \text{if } RB = 0 \text{ and } AB = 1 \end{cases}$$

$$PH = \begin{cases} 0 & \text{if } BF = 0 \text{ and } AB = 1 \\ 1 & \text{if } BF = 1 \text{ or } AB = 0 \end{cases}.$$

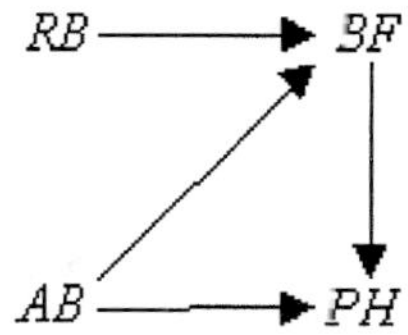

Fig. 4.8

Figure 4.8 is the causal diagram for the model.

It is easy to show that $AB = 0$ is an actual cause of $PH = 1$ (taking $(\vec{Z},\vec{W}) = (\{AB,PH\},\{RB,BF\})$ for condition C2 of the Halpern-Pearl definition). To show that $RB = 0$ is not an actual cause of $PH = 1$, note that AB must be in $\vec{W}$ for condition C2 since its value must be changed to make $PH = 0$ for C2(a). BF lies on the only path from RB to PH and must be in the set $\vec{Z}$. Setting $(RB, AB) = (1,1)$ makes $PH = 0$ $(\neg\varphi)$ satisfying condition C2(a). However, condition C2(b) fails when the subset $\{BF\}$ of $\vec{Z}$ is returned to its original value (that is, $PH = 0$ $(\neg\varphi)$ when $BF = 0$ and $AB = 1$). In the language of the NESS test, an actually sufficient set for which not repairing the brakes is a necessary condition includes the brakes being applied and the brakes failing. The difference between the two outcomes to the causal enquiry is a difference of modeling: in legal language, the difference in outcome depends on how the case is framed.

According to Wright's exception, the failure to fix the breaks would be a cause of the pedestrian being hit where no attempt was made to use the brakes because it was known that the brakes were inoperative. The assumption is that if the brakes had been repaired then they would have been used. In that case, the failure to repair the brakes has a causal influence on whether or not the brakes are applied. A model for this altered scenario differs from the previous model by modification of the equation for AP: $AP = RB$. (In the previous model, AP is a function of non-specified extraneous variables and no endogenous variables.) Figure 4.9 gives the new causal diagram.

To show that in this case $RB = 0$ is a cause of $PH = 1$, let $(\vec{Z},\vec{W}) = (\{RB,AB,PH\},\{BF\})$ and set $(RB,BF) = (1, 0)$ to satisfy condition C2(a) (i.e., leave BF at its original value). C2(b) is satisfied since when RB is returned to its original value, all variables are returned to their original values. Notice, however, than $AB = 0$ is still a cause of $PH = 1$ in this model in a context in which $RB = 0$ (take $(\vec{Z},\vec{W}) = (\{AB,BF,PH\},\{RB\})$ and set $(AB,RB) = (1, 1)$ for condition C2(a)).

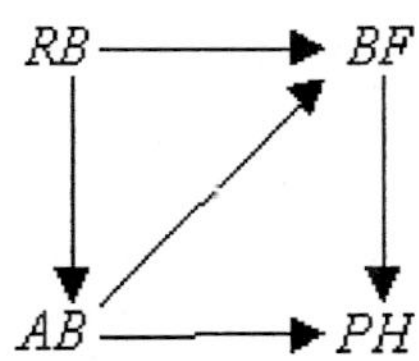

Fig. 4.9

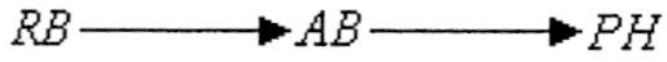

Fig. 4.10

Following Halpern and Pearl, the result that AB = 0 is a cause of PH = 1 in the model corresponding to Figure 4.9 might be explained as follows: the inclusion of BF in the model contemplates the contingency that the brakes may have operated even though they had not been repaired and therefore by failing to even try to apply the brakes the driver causally contributed to the pedestrian being hit. This suggests that if BF were left out then, in the resulting model (Figure 4.10), AB = 0 should not be a cause of PH = 1 in a context in which FB = 0. However, according to the Halpern-Pearl definition AB = 0 is a cause of PH = 1: taking $(\vec{Z},\vec{W}) = (\{AB,PH\},\{FB\})$ and setting (AB, FB) = (1, 1) satisfies condition C2(a); when AB is *forced* back to its original value (AB = 0) by the intervention $\vec{X} \leftarrow \vec{x}$ of condition C2(b), $PH = 1$ (i.e., φ) holds, satisfying C2(b). The intervention $\vec{X} \leftarrow \vec{x}$ is required in this case since the intervention $\vec{W} \leftarrow \vec{w}'$ of condition C2 (FB = 1) changes the value of $\vec{X}$ In other words, the proof that AB = 0 is a cause of PH = 1 in a context in which FB = 0 requires considering a contingency under which AB = 0 would not have occurred (would not be true).

It is not clear whether Halpern and Pearl intended that a proof that A caused B could depend on a contingency under which A would not have even occurred. The alternative would be to require that $\vec{X} = \vec{x}$ under the intervention $\vec{W} \leftarrow \vec{w}'$. This can be represented formally by amending condition C2(b) of the Halpern-Pearl definition (see Section 3.5) as follows:

C2′ There exists a partition $(\vec{Z},\vec{W})$ of $\mathcal{V}$ with $\vec{X} \subseteq \vec{Z}$ and some setting $(\vec{x}',\vec{w}')$ of the variables in $(\vec{X},\vec{W})$ such that, where $(M,\vec{u}) \models Z = z^*$ for each $Z \in \vec{Z}$,

(a) $(M,\vec{u}) \models [\vec{X} \leftarrow \vec{x}', \vec{W} \leftarrow \vec{w}']\neg\varphi$, and

(b) $(M,\vec{u}) \models [\vec{W} \leftarrow \vec{w}, \vec{Z} \leftarrow \vec{z}](\vec{X} = \vec{x} \wedge \varphi)$ for every subset $\vec{Z}'$ of $\vec{Z}$.

The consequences of this redefinition remain to be explored.

5 Conclusions and Future Work

Pearl [9] argues that Wright's NESS test, being based on traditional logic, is insufficient to capture the idea of actual cause because it lacks a causal notation. The preceding supports Pearl's argument, and, if viewed as providing formal rigour to Wright, suggests that at least one of Wright's revisitations of the NESS was not necessary. Nonetheless, the Halpern and Pearl definition appears to run into difficulties in certain cases involving double omission. We have presented a solution and continue to investigate this issue [2].

Acknowledgements

This research is supported by a grant from the Natural Science and Engineering Research Council of Canada.

References

[1] Ashley, Kevin D. (1990) Modeling legal arguments: reasoning with cases and hypotheticals. Cambridge : MIT Press, 329 pages.

[2] Baldwin, Richard A (to appear). A Structural Model Interpretation of Wright's NESS test. Department of Computer Science, University of Saskatchewan, MSc thesis.

[3] Galles, D., and Pearl, J. (1997). Axioms of causal relevance. *Artificial Intelligence*, 97 (1-2), 9-43.

[4] Galles, D., & Pearl, J. (1998). An axiomatic characterization of causal counterfactuals. *Foundations of Science*, 3 (1), 151-182.

[5] Halpern, J.Y., and Pearl, J. (2000). Causes and explanations: a structural-model approach. Retrieved from http://www.cs.cornell.edu/home/halpern/topics.html#rau September 3, 2001 (Part I, Causes, appears in *Proceedings of the Seventeenth Conference on Uncertainty in Artificial Intelligence*, San Francisco, CA: Morgan Kaufmann, 194-202, 2001.)

[6] Hart, H.L.A., and Honoré, A.M. (1985). *Causation in the law* (2nd ed.). Oxford University Press.

[7] Pearl, J. (1995). Causal diagrams for empirical research. *Biometrika*, 82 (4), 669–710.

[8] Pearl, J. (1998). On the definition of actual cause. Technical Report (no. R-259), Department of Computer Science, University of California, Los Angeles.

[9] Pearl, J. (2000). *Causality: Models, reasoning, and inference.* New York: Cambridge University Press.

[10] Wright, R.W. (1985). Causation in tort law. *California Law Review*, 73, pp. 1735-1828.

[11] Wright, R.W. (1988) Causation, responsibility, risk, probability, naked statistics, and proof: Pruning the bramble bush by clarifying the concepts. *Iowa Law Review*, 73, pp. 1001-1077.

[12] Wright, R.W. (2001). Once more into the bramble bush: Duty, causal contribution, and the extent of legal responsibility [Electronic version]. *Vanderbilt Law Review*, 54 (3), pp. 1071-1132.

Answer Formulation for Question-Answering

Leila Kosseim[1], Luc Plamondon[2], and Louis-Julien Guillemette[1]

[1] Concordia University
1455 de Maisonneuve Blvd. West, Montréal (Québec) Canada, H3G 1M8
{kosseim,l_guille}@cs.concordia.ca
[2] RALI, DIRO, Université de Montréal
CP 6128, Succ. Centre-Ville, Montréal (Québec) Canada, H3C 3J7
plamondl@iro.umontreal.ca

Abstract. In this paper, we describe our experimentations in evaluating answer formulation for question-answering (QA) systems. In the context of QA, answer formulation can serve two purposes: improving answer extraction or improving human-computer interaction (HCI). Each purpose has different precision/recall requirements. We present our experiments for both purposes and argue that formulations of better grammatical quality are beneficial for both answer extraction and HCI.

1 Introduction

Recent developments in open-domain question answering (QA) have made it possible for users to ask a fact-based question in natural language (eg. *Who was the Prime Minister of Canada in 1873?*) and receive a specific answer (eg. *Alexander Mackenzie*) rather than an entire document where they must further search for the specific answer themselves. In this respect, QA can be seen as the next generation of daily tools to search huge text collections such as the Internet.

To date, most work in QA has been involved in *answer extraction*; that is, locating the answer in a text collection. In contrast, the problem of *answer formulation* has not received much attention. Investigating answer formulation is important for two main purposes: human-computer interaction (HCI) and answer extraction. First, answer formulation can improve the interaction between QA systems and end-users. As QA systems tackle more difficult issues and are extended to dialog processing systems, a text snippet or a short answer will not be enough to communicate naturally with the user; a full natural sentence that is grammatical and responsive will be required. On the other hand, answer formulation can be used as a reverse engineering method to actually improve the extraction of the answer from a large document collection. For example, when looking for the answer to *Who was the Prime Minister of Canada in 1873?* and knowing that the answer could have the form `"In 1873, the Prime Minister of Canada was` <PERSON-NAME>`"` or `"In 1873,` <PERSON-NAME> `was the Prime Minister of Canada"`, the QA system can search for these formulations in the document collection and instantiate <PERSON-NAME> with the matching noun phrase.

Y. Xiang and B. Chaib-draa (Eds.): AI 2003, LNAI 2671, pp. 24–34, 2003.

Depending on the purpose of answer formulation, different goals will be enhanced at the expense of others. Answer formulations used to extract answers will need to have a high recall rate. The goal here is to produce a large number of possible formulations hoping that one of them will retrieve an answer. If the system produces formulations that are linguistically incorrect or awkward, the consequences are not great; the information retrieval component will simply not find any occurrence of the answer pattern. On the other hand, answer formulation performed to improve HCI will need to aim for high precision. The goal here is not to produce a great number of approximate formulations, but only a few (or only one) of good linguistic quality.

2 Previous Work in Answer Formulation

The field of QA has been chiefly driven by the DARPA initiative through the Text Retrieval Conferences (TREC) [12, 13, 14, 15]. This is why most work has been concentrated on issues related to question parsing (what are we looking for?), information retrieval (what document contains the answer?), and answer extraction (how can we pinpoint the specific answer?). Some research teams follow a more knowledge-rich approach ([6, 7]), while others use statistical approaches ([9]). However, regardless of how the steps are performed, the goal is always to extract an answer or a text snippet, rather than to compose an answer.

The need to investigate answer formulation has already been felt by the QA community [4]; however, to our knowledge, little research has yet addressed this issue. A first step toward answer formulation was done at the previous TREC-10 conference, where several teams saw the value of the Web as a tremendous source of additional texts to improve answer extraction (eg. [5, 3]) and as part of work in query expansion to improve information retrieval [1, 8]. In the work of [3, 2], the system searches the Web for a list of possible answer formulations generated by permutating the words of the questions. For example, given a question of the form:

$$\textit{Who is } w_1\ w_2\ w_3\ \ldots\ w_n\textit{?}$$

the system will generate:

$$\texttt{"}w_1\ \texttt{is}\ w_2\ w_3\ \ldots\ w_n\texttt{"}$$
$$\texttt{"}w_1\ w_2\ \texttt{is}\ w_3\ \ldots\ w_n\texttt{"}$$
$$\texttt{"}w_1\ w_2\ w_3\ \texttt{is}\ \ldots\ w_n\texttt{"}$$
$$\ldots$$

and will search the Web for such phrases. Given the question: `"Who is the world's richest man married to?"`, the following phrases will be searched for: `"the is world's richest man married to"`, `"the world's is richest man married to"`, `"the world's richest man is married to"`... Hopefully, at least one phrase (more likely, the last one in our example) will retrieve the expected answer. Although simple, this strategy is very efficient when combine with the Web. Using this method, [3] received the 9th best score out of 37 teams at the TREC-10 conference.

In the work of [1, 8], answer formulations are produced specifically to improve Web search engines. The formulations produced are precise, but they are used for query expansion to improve the retrieval of documents, not the retrieval of exact answers. While in [8] reformulation rules to transform a question like *What does NASDAQ stand for?* into `"NASDAQ stands for"` or `"NASDAQ means"` have been developed by hand, [1] uses n-grams with part-of-speech filtering to learn reformulation rules from a corpus of question-answers pairs.

To our knowledge, however, answer formulation has not been investigated in the context of human-computer interaction (HCI) to generate answer sentences rather than exact answers only. In the following, we will discuss our experiments in answer formulation for extraction and for HCI purposes, and argue that improving the linguistic quality of formulations is beneficial for both purposes.

3 Formulation Templates

Our first experiments with answer formulation were geared toward improving our results in answer extraction at the recent TREC-11 conference [15]. In this scenario, a high recall rate of the formulations was important in order to increase our chances of extracting the correct answer.

Because the TREC-11 questions are of general domain, we used the Web as an additional source of information for answering questions and we used answer formulation to drive the search. That is, we searched the Web for an exact phrase that could be the formulation of the answer to the question. For example, given the question *Who is the prime minister of Canada?*, our goal was to produce the formulation `"The prime minister of Canada is` <PERSON-NAME>`"`. Then, by searching the Web for this exact phrase and extracting the noun phrase following it, our hope was to find the exact answer. Syntactic and semantic checks were then performed to ensure that the following noun phrase is indeed a PERSON-NAME. This prevented us from finding answers such as `"The prime minister of Canada is (a native of Shawinigan/very controversial/...")`.

To formulate an answer pattern from a question, we turn the latter into its declarative form using a set of hand-made patterns. We used the 200 questions of TREC-8 and the 693 questions of TREC-9 as training set to develop the formulation patterns and used the 500 questions of TREC-10 and the 500 questions of TREC-11 for testing.

Before the formulation is done, the question's grammatical form is normalized in order to restrict the number of cases to handle. For example, any question starting with *What's ...* is changed to *What is ...*, *What was the name of ...* is changed to *Name ...* In total, 17 grammatical rules are used for normalization. The formulation proper is then performed using a set of formulation templates that test for the presence of specific keywords, grammatical tags and regular expressions. Figure 1 shows an example. The formulation template is composed of

Formulation Template	**Example**
`When did ANY-SEQUENCE-WORDS-1 VERB-simple ?`	*(# 22) When did the Jurassic Period end?*
`ANY-SEQUENCE-WORDS-1 VERB-past TIME`	`the Jurassic Period ended TIME`
`TIME ANY-SEQUENCE-WORDS-1 VERB-past`	`TIME the Jurassic Period ended`
`TIME, ANY-SEQUENCE-WORDS-1 VERB-past`	`TIME, the Jurassic Period ended`

Fig. 1. Example of a formulation template

2 sets of patterns: A question pattern that defines what the question must look like, and a set of answer patterns that defines a set of possible answer formulations. The patterns take into account specific keywords (eg. `When did`), strings of characters (`ANY-SEQUENCE-WORDS`) and part-of-speech tags (eg. `VERB-simple`). Answer patterns are specified using the same type of features plus a specification of the semantic class of the answer (eg. `TIME`). The semantic classes are used later, during answer extraction, to validate the nature of the candidate answers from the document. In the current implementation, about 10 semantic classes are used.

A particular phenomenon that could not be dealt with using simple pattern-matching is the case of verb tenses. Many questions in the TREC collections are in the past tense; but the past tense is exhibited only in the auxiliary verb, while the main verb stays in its citation form. When formulating a declarative sentence, the tense information must be transferred to the main verb. In order to do this transformation, yet keep formulation rapid and straightforward, we

Table 1. Answer templates for each type of question

Question Type	**Example**	**Nb of Templates**	**Average Nb of Answer Patterns**
when	*(# 398) When is Boxing Day?*	6	1.7
where	*(# 73) Where is the Taj Mahal?*	9	1.6
how many	*(# 214) How many hexagons are on a soccer ball?*	11	1.1
how much	*(# 203) How much folic acid should an expectant mother get daily?*	6	1.0
how (other)	*(# 177) How tall is Mt. Everest?*	11	1.4
what	*(# 257) What do penguins eat?*	21	1.0
which	*(# 108) Which company created the Internet browser Mosaic?*	2	1.0
who	*(# 55) Who started the Dominos Pizza chain?*	7	1.3
why	*(# 6) Why did David Koresh ask the FBI for a word processor?*	2	1.0
name	*(# 213) Name a flying mammal.*	2	1.0
Total		**77**	**1.2**

extracted all the verbs from WordNet and built a hash table mapping their simple tense to their past tense.

To increase our chances of finding the exact answer, the formulation module can also generate conjunctions of formulations. For example, the question *(# 970) What type of currency is used in Australia?* is reformulated as <CLAUSE> `"is used in Australia"` AND <CLAUSE> `"is a type of currency"` where <CLAUSE> can be any string.

In total, 77 formulation templates are used. The templates are tried sequentially and all question patterns that are satisfied are activated. Table 1 shows the distribution of the templates by question type. For example, 6 templates can be used to transform *when*-type questions, and, on average, 1.7 answer formulations are produced for questions of that type. The 77 templates cover 93% of the 200 TREC-8 questions and 89.5% of the 693 TREC-9 questions. By coverage, we mean that at least one formulation template is applicable. The templates generate 412 formulations for the 186 processed TREC-8 questions and 1226 formulations for the 620 processed TREC-9 questions. So, on average, 2 answer formulations were produced per question.

4 Evaluation

To evaluate the performance of the answer formulation module, we conducted three sets of experiments. The first was aimed at evaluating the answer formulation for answer extraction, the second experiment was meant to investigate HCI purposes, and the last was meant to evaluate how the grammatical quality of the formulation influences the score in answer extraction.

All experiments were performed on the TREC-10 and the TREC-11 question sets. The templates cover 448 of the 500 TREC-10 questions (89.6%) and 432 of the 500 TREC-11 questions (86.4%). This is shown in table 2. These numbers are consistent with the TREC-8 and TREC-9 questions used as training sets, and they are particularly high, especially considering that only 77 templates are used. In total, the templates generated 730 formulations for the 448 TREC-10 questions and 778 formulations for the TREC-11 questions. So, on average, 1.7 answer formulations were produced per question.

Table 2. Coverage of the formulation templates on different TREC question sets

Corpus	**Nb questions**	**Coverage**	**Nb of formulations**
TREC-8 (training)	200	93.0%	412
TREC-9 (training)	693	89.5%	1226
TREC-10 (testing)	500	89.6%	730
TREC-11 (testing)	500	86.9%	778

4.1 Evaluation for Answer Extraction

Evaluation for answer extraction was performed to specifically evaluate the improvement in answer extraction. To do so, we enhanced our QUANTUM QA system [10] with the answer formulation module and used *Yahoo!* to search for Web pages that contained the answer formulation. We then identified answer candidates by unification, and performed validity checks on candidates to ensure that the semantic class of the formulation was satisfied. Currently, semantic validation is rather simple and is based on the surface form of the candidates (eg. testing for length, capitalization, ...).

Only for 10% of the questions do we find one of the answer formulation in the TREC-10 document collection. However, when we search on the Web, we find at least one occurrence of a formulation for 43% of the questions. Of these, the answer identified by unification is correct 51% of the time. In clear, 10 % of the TREC-9 and TREC-10 questions are correctly answered only by searching for answer formulations on the Web and performing minimal semantic checking. For answer extraction, this simple technique of answer formulation seems interesting.

We further evaluated the answer formulation as part of the recent TREC-11 conference [15]. For 454 questions[1], without answer formulation, our system found 93 "good" answers[2] (20%). With answer formulation, our system found 110 "good" answers (24%). These results seem to show that using simple regular expressions based on keywords and part-of-speech tags in conjunction with a large document collection such as the Web can improve answer extraction. Table 3 shows the percentage of good answers by question type on the TREC-11 corpus. *When*, *where*, *how-much* and *who*-type questions seem to benefit the most from answer formulation. We suspect that this is because declarative sentences introducing this type of information are more stereotypical; thus a small number of reformulation patterns are sufficient to cover a larger number of answers.

4.2 Evaluation for HCI Purposes

To evaluate our answer formulation for HCI purposes, we generated answer formulations for the TREC-10 and TREC-11 questions. In total, 1510 answer formulations were generated for 1000 questions. We then asked 3 humans to judge these formulations on the basis of their grammaticality. The judgment could be one of the following:

Type U (ungrammatical) The formulation is not grammatically correct. For example, `"it from Denver to Aspen is"` <DISTANCE> `"away"`.

[1] 46 of the 500 TREC-11 questions were removed from the experiment because they had no answer in the TREC collection.

[2] By *good answer*, we mean an answer that is either correct, inexact with respect to its length or unsupported by its source document according to the NIST judgment. However, unlike for TREC, we consider in our evaluation all candidates tying for the best answer of a given question.

Table 3. NIST-like judgment of answers produced by QUANTUM with and without answer formulations, for the TREC-11 questions (no-answer questions excluded)

Question Type	% "good" answers without formulation	with formulation
when	14%	20%
where	29%	39%
how many	33%	33%
how much	10%	40%
how (other)	21%	18%
what	18%	22%
which	13%	13%
who	16%	31%
Total	**20%**	**24%**

Type A (awkward) The formulation is grammatically correct for answer extraction but not a natural and responsive answer to the original question. For example, *(# 907) Who was the first man to fly across the Pacific Ocean?* ⇒ `"the first man to fly across the Pacific Ocean,"` <PERSON-NAME>.

Type R (responsive) The formulation is grammatically correct and is natural and responsive to the original question. For example, *(# 914) Who was the first American to walk in space?* ⇒ `"the first American to walk in space was"` <PERSON-NAME>.

Inter-judge agreement was the following: 82% of the questions were judged similarly by all 3 judges; 18% of the questions were judged in two different categories by the 3 judges and 0% (1 out of 1508 answers) was judged differently by all judges.

Table 4 shows the results of the evaluation. On average, 56% of the formulations were considered correct for extraction as well as for HCI purposes; they were grammatical as well as natural and responsive to the question. 18% of the questions were considered awkward (appropriate for extraction, but not for HCI) and 19% were simply ungrammatical. Although the percentage of responsive formulations was higher than what we had originally expected, only one answer out of two being responsive is clearly unacceptable for human-computer interaction, where the end-users are humans, and more linguistically-motivated formulations are required.

4.3 Influence of the Type of Formulation for Answer Extraction

Finally, the last experiment that we performed was aimed at determining if the type of formulation (as determined for HCI purposes) has an influence on answer extraction. For example, do ungrammatical formulations really have no effect on answer extraction, or do they actually introduce noise and decrease the

Table 4. Human judgment of answer formulations for HCI

Question Type	% without a formulation	Judgment %U	%A	%R
when	10	22	15	63
where	5	14	34	47
how many	29	43	0	29
how much	72	6	0	29
how (other)	20	14	6	58
what	6	27	9	58
which	10	61	29	0
who	0.5	4	37	59
why	100	0	0	0
name	0	0	0	100
Total	**7**	**19**	**18**	**56**

performance of extraction? If this is the case, then producing only good-quality formulations will be worth the effort not only for HCI, but also for answer extraction. To verify this, we evaluated answer extraction with 3 different sets of formulations:

Type R: only formulations judged responsive by all 3 judges.
Type R+A: formulations judged responsive or judged awkward by all 3 judges (same judgment by all judges).
Type R+A+U: formulations judged responsive, awkward or ungrammatical by all 3 judges (same judgment by all judges).

Tables 5 and 6 show the result of this evaluation with the TREC-10 and TREC-11 corpora.

Table 5 shows that considering more formulation types covers more questions. However, table 6 shows that more formulation types does not result in better quality of the extracted answers. As expected, considering responsive and awkward formulations (types R+A) yields the best score for answer extraction in both the TREC-10 and the TREC-11 question sets (although the increase in score is slight and may not be statistically significant). It does, however, correlate with our expectations and our definitions of a *responsive* answer and an *awkward* answer. Awkward formulations may therefore be important for answer

Table 5. Coverage of the formulation templates according to their formulation type

Corpus	Coverage R	R+A	R+A+U
TREC-10	69.2%	73.8%	85.2%
TREC-11	58.4%	63.6%	79.2%

Table 6. Good answers found by QUANTUM, according to the responsiveness of the formulations

Corpus	% good answers		
	R	**R+A**	**R+A+U**
TREC-10	37.0%	38.3%	37.2%
TREC-11	16.5%	18.3%	17.4%
Total	**26.7%**	**28.3%**	**27.3%**

extraction. Considering ungrammatical answers (type U) has almost no effect on answer extraction and can actually introduce noise. In our experiment, ungrammatical formulations slightly decrease the score of answer extraction with both question sets (see table 6).

This last experiment shows that the linguistic quality of the formulations should be taken into account when used for QA. Although only responsive formulations should be generated for HCI purposes, responsive as well as awkward formulations should be used for answer extraction. Responsive formulations do, however, allow us to extract most of the answers. For both purposes, ungrammatical formulations should not be used as they are not acceptable for HCI, and have no effect positive on answer extraction.

5 Conclusion and Future Work

In this paper, we have shown that simple hand-made patterns for answer formulation can greatly benefit answer extraction. In addition, the formulations that are generated in this manner are of better linguistic quality than brute force word permutations, and this allows us to add a human-computer interaction dimension to QA. We have also shown that generating only formulations of good linguistic quality is beneficial for HCI purposes, without decreasing the performance of answer extraction when a large document collection such as the Web is used. However, with a smaller document collection (eg. the TREC corpus of ≈3GB), the effect of awkward (type A) reformulations might be larger.

Further work includes the generation of only grammatically correct and *natural* answer formulations. Most work on question reformulation, including the work presented here, has been done at the word level; whether using simple word permutations or including lexical variations such as synonyms. However, reformulations should take into account syntactic as well as semantic constraints. Identifying the syntactic structure of the question would allow us to reformulate more grammatically correct reformulations. Semantic constraints are also needed, for example, to identify the semantic type of prepositional phrases (eg. temporal, locative, ...) which cannot be placed in the same syntactic positions in the reformulations. Although our work only dealt with the production of single sentences, taking into account semantic information would lead us closer to work in natural language generation (in particular, micro-planning and surface realisation [11]) that try to produce *natural* texts from a semantic representation. In turn, this could be used as a starting point for the generation of answers that are not factual in nature, for example, to answer *why* or *how* questions which should be answered with a more complex answer (eg. an explanation or a procedure) where document planning is required. Currently, our work is based on the TREC question set, and thus only fact-based questions were considered. These questions can be answered with noun-phrases, which limits the scope of answer patterns.

Our work has investigated only the case of individual questions. However, in a dialog-based human-computer interaction with a QA system, users will need to be able to ask a series of related and follow-up questions. Such contextual questions have already been taken into account in the context of QA [14], but we have not yet included them in our experiments. Dealing with them will lead to interesting issues such as question interpretation and dialog modeling.

Acknowledgments

This project was financially supported by the Natural Sciences and Engineering Research Council of Canada (NSERC) and the Bell University Laboratories (BUL).

References

[1] E. Agichtein and L. Gravano. Snowball: Extracting relations from large plain-text collections. In *Proceedings of the 5th ACM International Conference on Digital Libraries*, 2000.

[2] E. Brill, S. Dumais, and M. Banko. An Analysis of the AskMSR Question-Answering System. In *Proceedings of the 2002 Conference on Empirical Methods in Natural Language Processing (EMNLP-2002)*, Philadelphia, 2002.

[3] E. Brill, J. Lin, M. Banko, S. Dumais, and A. Ng. Data-Intensive Question Answering. In *Proceedings of The Tenth Text Retrieval Conference (TREC-X)*, pages 393–400, Gaithersburg, Maryland, 2001.

[4] J. Burger, C. Cardie, V. Chaudhri, R. Gaizauskas, S. Harabagiu, D. Israel, C. Jacquemin, C-Y Lin, S. Maiorano, G. Miller, D. Moldovan, B. Ogden, J. Prager, E. Riloff, A. Singhal, R. Shrihari, T. Strzalkowski, E. Voorhees, and R. Weischedel. Issues, Tasks and Program Structures to Roadmap Research in Question & Answering (Q&A). Technical report, 2001. www-nlpir.nist.gov/projects/duc/roadmapping.html.

[5] C. L. A. Clarke, G. V. Cormack, T. R. Lynam, C. M. Li, and G. L. McLearn. Web Reinforced Question Answering (MultiText Experiments for TREC 2001). In *Proceedings of The Tenth Text Retrieval Conference (TREC-X)*, pages 673–679, Gaithersburg, Maryland, 2001.

[6] S. Harabagiu, D. Moldovan, M. Pasca, R. Mihalcea, M. Surdeanu, R. Bunescu, R. Girju, V. Rus, and P. Morarescu. The role of lexico-semantic feedbacks in open-domain textual question answering. In *Proceedings of the 39th Annual Meeting of the Association for Computational Linguistics (ACL-2001)*, pages 274–281, Toulouse, France, July 2001.

[7] E. Hovy, U. Hermjakob, and C.-Y. Lin. The Use of External Knowledge in Factoid QA. In *Proceedings of The Tenth Text REtrieval Conference (TREC-X)*, pages 166–174, Gaithersburg, Maryland, 2001.

[8] S. Lawrence and C. L. Giles. Context and page analysis for improved web search. *IEEE Internet Computing*, 2(4):38–46, 1998.

[9] T. Lynam, C. Clarke, and G. Cormack. Information extraction with term frequencies. In *Proceedings of HLT 2001 – First International Conference on Human Language Technology Research*, pages 169–172, San Diego, California, March 2001.

[10] L. Plamondon and L. Kosseim. Quantum: A function-based question answering system. In R. Cohen and B. Spencer, editors, *Proceedings of The Fifteenth Canadian Conference on Artificial Intelligence (AI'2002) - Lecture Notes in Artificial Intelligence no. 2338*, pages 281–292, Calgary, May 2002.

[11] E. Reiter and R. Dale. *Building Natural Language Generation Systems.* Cambridge University Press, 2000.

[12] E. M. Voorhees and D. K. Harman, editors. *Proceedings of The Eight Text REtrieval Conference (TREC-8)*, Gaithersburg, Maryland, November 1999. NIST. available at http://trec.nist.gov/pubs/trec8/t8_proceedings.html.

[13] E. M. Voorhees and D. K. Harman, editors. *Proceedings of The Ninth Text REtrieval Conference (TREC-9)*, Gaithersburg, Maryland, 2000. NIST. available at http://trec.nist.gov/pubs/trec9/t9_proceedings.html.

[14] E. M. Voorhees and D. K. Harman, editors. *Proceedings of The Tenth Text REtrieval Conference (TREC-X)*, Gaithersburg, Maryland, November 2001. NIST. available at http://trec.nist.gov/pubs/trec10/t10_proceedings.html.

[15] E. M. Voorhees and D. K. Harman, editors. *Proceedings of The Eleventh Text REtrieval Conference (TREC-11)*, Gaithersburg, Maryland, November 2002. NIST. to appear.

Pattern-Based AI Scripting Using *ScriptEase*

Matthew McNaughton, James Redford, Jonathan Schaeffer, and Duane Szafron

Department of Computing Science, University of Alberta
Edmonton, Alberta, Canada T6G 2E8
{mcnaught,redford,jonathan,duane}@cs.ualberta.ca

Abstract. Creating realistic artificially-intelligent characters is seen as one of the major challenges of the commercial games industry. Historically, character behavior has been specified using simple finite state machines and, more recently, by AI scripting languages. These languages are relatively "simple", in part because the language has to serve three user communities: game designers, game programmers, and consumers – each with different levels of programming experience. The scripting often becomes unwieldy, given that potentially hundreds (thousands) of characters need to be defined, the characters need non-trivial behaviors, and the characters have to interface with the plot constraints. In this paper, the ScriptEase model for AI scripting is presented. The model is pattern-template based, allowing designers to quickly build complex behaviors without doing explicit programming. This paper describes ScriptEase's behavior patterns and user interface. This is demonstrated by generating code for BioWare's *Neverwinter Nights* game. In addition to behaviors, the model is being extended to include encounter, dialog, and plot patterns.

1 Introduction

The commercial games industry is currently worth $15 billion. In the past, better computer graphics have been the major technological sales feature of games. With faster processors, larger memories, and better graphics cards, this has reached a saturation point. The perceived need for better graphics has been replaced by the demand for a more realistic gaming experience. All the major computer games companies are making big commitments to artificial intelligence (AI). This activity has been accelerated by the recent success of AI-based games like *The Sims* and *Black and White.*

Historically, the artificial intelligence research community has ignored the commercial games industry. However, the AI challenges that this industry faces are daunting. For a number of years, John Laird has been advocating commercial games as a fruitful venue for AI research (AI's "killer application") [10].

Computer games are the ideal application for developing characters that appear to have realistic, artificially-intelligent behavior. There is already a need for it, since human game players are dissatisfied with computer characters. The characters are shallow, too easy to predict, and, all too often, exhibit artificial stupidity. This has led to the success of on-line games where players compete

Y. Xiang and B. Chaib-draa (Eds.): AI 2003, LNAI 2671, pp. 35–49, 2003.

against other humans. The current state of the art in developing artificially intelligent characters can be described as rather primitive. The lack of sophistication is due to the lack of research effort [1] (Laird's group being a notable exception). This is changing, as more researchers recognize the value of the research problems facing the commercial games industry. Artificial intelligence allows us to create simulated environments where the human has the feeling that they are interacting in the real world. While an immediate application of this technology is games, the technology has wider applications (for example, training [8]).

As a first step, it is necessary only to create the illusion of intelligence. The state of the art has each character scripted, usually using a rule-based system or a finite state machine [11]. In both cases, behavior patterns are limited, repetitive, and non-adaptive. In contrast, human-level behavior should not be prescribed, should avoid repetition, and should adapt to changing conditions.

In designing a more ambitious, more robust system for defining behaviors, many issues must be considered:

- Knowledge management. There can be hundreds – even thousands – of characters in a game, each with a (possibly complex) combination of behaviors. All this information has to be organized to simplify maintenance issues.
- Knowledge acquisition. The system must simplify the task of defining characters and their behavior (especially important for game designers).
- Rapid prototyping. Game design is accomplished using an iterative approach. Typically one wants to quickly create the desired functionality, and then incrementally tune it to improve the quality of play.
- Simple model. The AI scripting facility will be used principally by three user communities: game designers (who, typically, have little programming experience), consumers (who want to create their own characters, but have variable programming experience), and game developers (usually programming experts). The programming model has to be simple enough to accommodate non-experts, but rich enough to allow developers to do anything that they want to do.
- Testing. Any definition of AI behavior must be easy to verify for correctness.
- Non-determinism. The system must support "intelligent" (pseudo-random) behavior selections to avoid predictability (while at the same time not hurting the testability of the system).
- Adaptive. The language must support learning – characters must adapt to their circumstances. Few commercial games do more than non-trivial types of learning.
- Rich set of behaviors. Realism demands that any AI behavior specification system must support a large and varied selection of behaviors.
- Complex behaviors. The system must support the creation of complex behaviors, either individual behaviors or a combination of simpler behaviors.
- Extensibility. The basic tool must support the addition of new behaviors and capabilities.

In effect AI scripting for a non-trivial game has all the problems of maintaining a large evolving software repository, while incurring the challenges of AI knowledge acquisition, maintenance, and usage.

Our experience with AI scripting languages comes from working with BioWare products *Baldur's Gate II* and *Neverwinter Nights.* These languages allow the game designer to define characters, and for users to create their own characters. The AI scripting has limited capabilities, and requires a lot of programming expertise to understand what is going on. As one adds more "intelligence" to the system, the scripts become unwieldy and hard to debug.

This paper introduces *ScriptEase*, a tool for defining complex behaviors. The objective is to address all of the above issues in a powerful yet easy-to-use tool. Behaviors are defined using *behavioral patterns* – taking an analogy from software engineering, these are the "design patterns" [7] of artificial intelligence behavior. This work builds on our experience with design patterns for parallel programming [5]. For example, one behavior pattern could be "to guard". The default would have a character stand guard over something and not allow any access to it without a fight. This behavior could be parameterized to, for example, allow the game designer to define how to guard (stand stationary; patrol around) or who to allow to have access to the object. To create a guard involves creating a character, assigning the guard behavior to it, and then customizing the behavior.

Our vision for a scripting language is to have it support a rich set of behavior patterns. And, as with our parallel programming tool CO_2P_3S[5], there is tool support for defining and refining these patterns. It is surprising to see that our research into parallel computing tools can be applied to something as seemingly remote as defining AI characters. The leap is not all that surprising given that the fundamental nature of both applications – defining and using patterns – is the same.

Note that there are multiple audiences for a scripting language, ranging from non-programmers to experts (this can be a serious issue in language design [4]). The former needs access to a simpler more intuitive interface to the language than the latter. Indeed, most users are not programmers, and exposing a textual programming language to them is undesirable. Hence, a visual representation – one that abstracts away textual programming – is important. Again, a CO^2P^3S-like approach seems to work here – parameterized behaviors can be defined graphically.

This paper describes the behavioral patterns in *ScriptEase*, and introduces the reader to our *behavior patterns.* Additional patterns, including those for encounters, dialogs and plot, are only briefly mentioned. We are fortunate to have access to industrial code to work with. *ScriptEase* is used to generate code for BioWare's multi-award-winning role-playing fantasy game *Neverwinter Nights.* Unfortunately, using a real application limits the expressiveness of behavior. The *Neverwinter Nights* scripting language does not support facilities for learning – something we want to see added to the language. Our hope is that our work will influence the future design of AI scripting languages.

Section 2 describes our patterns-based model. Section 3 illustrates our tool *ScriptEase* that implements the model. Section 4 discusses ongoing work, while Section 5 presents the conclusions.

2 Using Design Patterns to Design Computer Games

Consider the situation where a game designer of a fantasy role-playing game wants to include four icons (objects, or in this case, specifically shards), that when gathered together form a single larger icon called a moon-stone. Each shard is guarded, but the game designer wants the guarding done differently in each case:

1. Shard-1 is in a guarded chest. The guard should have a patrol route near the chest. However, if any "enemy" creature gets near the chest, the guard should warn the enemy and then run over to the chest and stand in front of it. If the enemy actually tries to open the chest then the guard should attack the enemy. If the "enemy" moves away from the chest without opening it, the guard should resume the patrol. Note that if a "friendly" creature approaches the chest, the guard will not react. In fact, if a friendly creature removes Shard-1 and takes it away, the guard will continue to guard the chest (not the shard).
2. Shard-2 is in a room with a single door. The guard attacks any enemy that gets close to the door. Again, the guard is guarding the door (not the shard) and the guard will continue to guard the door, even if the shard is removed from the room.
3. Shard-3 is in the possession of a creature. The guard will protect the creature (not the shard) from harm or from stealing. If an enemy comes near, the guard will shout and if the enemy tries to steal from the creature being guarded or attacks the creature, the guard will attack.
4. Shard-4 is protected by a guard who will attack any enemy who tries to possess it. Note that Shard-4 may be moved to any location by a friendly creature and the guard will follow along to attack any enemy that obtains it.

In addition, we want the guards in each of these scenarios to exhibit "natural" behaviors. For example, the designer wants the "chest" guard to have a fixed patrol path around the chest. However, this path should not be exactly identical each time around, since a real guard would have some variation. The second guard should be mostly stationary near the door. However, he should occasionally walk to one or more nearby objects. The third guard should stay close to the individual that is being guarded. The fourth guard should begin by staying near the icon. However, as time goes on without anything happening, this guard should become bored and move farther away. However, if any creature is spotted, the guard should immediately return to the shard and not wander far for a while (until the guard becomes bored again).

It would take considerable effort to program the behaviors of the four guards we have described in most computer game scripting languages. For example, we have manually programmed these four behaviors in the *Neverwinter Nights* scripting language and there are 500 lines of code (over 1,000 if you include white space and comments). However, these four behaviors have some similarities. They all have a common theme that something is being guarded. We should be able to abstract this commonality and use the abstraction to generate the game code for each of these four situations. This observation has already been made in other domains and has led to the construction of ***design patterns***. A design pattern is a mechanism for encapsulating the knowledge of experienced designers into a re-usable artifact. By definition, a design pattern is a descriptive device that fosters re-use during the design phase of an activity. Although design patterns have been used in architecture [2], they have also become an important tool in software development [7].

The most common form of a design pattern is a document, such as a chapter in a pattern catalog or a Web page. This form preserves the instructional nature of patterns, as a cache of known solutions to recurring design problems. Patterns in this form are easy to distribute and readily available to designers. Patterns provide a common design lexicon, and communicate not only the structure of the design but also the reasoning behind it. This common form of design pattern is called descriptive. In the context of role-playing fantasy games, humans use high-level patterns to describe characters and behaviors. For example, the notion of "wizard" or "shop-keeper" immediately infer attributes on the character they are ascribed to.

Until very recently, design patterns have only been applied during the design phase of software development. They have not been used to generate code. There are several reasons why design patterns are not used as generative constructs that support code re-use. The most fundamental reason is that design patterns describe a set of solutions to a family of related design problems and it is difficult to generate a single body of code that adequately solves each problem in the family. No adequate mechanism exists for a developer to understand the variations in code that spans the family of solutions and to adapt this code for an application. A second important reason is that it is difficult to construct and edit generative design patterns. This limits the number of design patterns that can be made generative and results in a poor selection of patterns for the end user. Faced with a small selection of rigid generative design patterns, end-users are reluctant to use such a limited approach for real software development.

We have created a new approach to generative design patterns that solves these difficult problems and have embodied our approach in tools called CO_2P_3S (Correct Object-Oriented Pattern-based Parallel Programming System) and $MetaCO_2P_3S$ (and their newer sequential counterparts). The first tool generates code for a wide variety of patterns that exist in the domain of general programming and the specialized domain of parallel programming. The second tool supports the design and implementation of new generative design patterns. Our approach solves the adaptation problem by parameterizing each design pattern with a fixed set of parameters. The programmer provides application domain-specific values for each of these parameters before generating code.

In the context of computer game design, the use of generative design patterns has six positive effects:

1. Pattern re-use. A pattern can be identified, designed and implemented once and then can be instantiated many different times across the same game and different games to amortize its development cost.
2. Pattern adaptation. A single pattern can provide a rich texture of different game experiences by varying its parameters.
3. Pattern abstraction. Game designers can discuss and design game components at a higher level of abstraction by discussing the design of new patterns and the adaptation of existing patterns to create new game situations.
4. Pattern code generation. Game designers can generate game code without knowing anything about programming.
5. Pattern prototyping. If a game designer has an idea for a novel new game construct, it can be evaluated more quickly. Instead of having a programmer code the new construct from scratch, an existing pattern can be adapted to generate code that implements a construct that is similar to the new idea, and this code can be modified by a programmer.
6. Pattern correctness. Once a pattern has been tested, the pattern instances that are generated from it will need less quality assurance time during game testing.

In the specialized domain of role-playing computer games, we have identified several kinds of generative design patterns that can be used by game designers with little or no programming experience: behavior, encounter, dialog, and plot patterns. In this paper, we will focus on behavior patterns, although we will also discuss encounter patterns.

Each specific pattern describes a set of roles. A role is a placeholder for a game object. For example, the guard behavior pattern defines two roles: the guard and the guarded. A pattern is instantiated by adapting it for a particular use in the game. For example, we will use four different instantiations of the Guard Pattern to generate the four different scenarios described earlier. To instantiate a pattern, each role is filled by an individual game object, who is said to play the role (in the movie sense, not the programming languages sense). For example, in the first scenario, a particular Orc (a monster) may be cast in the guard role and a particular chest may play the guarded role. In the third scenario, a particular fighter may play the guard and a particular wizard can be cast in the role of guarded.

Each game may have a different ontology for classifying the kinds of game objects it has. In this paper, we will use a simple ontology consisting of *actors* (animate game objects that can perform actions) and *props* (inanimate game objects that can be manipulated but cannot perform actions). Props can be further sub-classified as *containers* (that can hold other props) and *simple props* (that cannot hold other props). We use the term *object* to refer to a game object that might be an actor or a prop. Each role is typed. For example, in the Guard Pattern, the guard role must be played by an actor, but the guarded role may be played by any object.

One of the roles of each behavioral pattern is special and is called the principal role of the behavioral pattern. The other roles are called supporting roles. An actor (not a prop) must always play the principal role of a behavior pattern since it prescribes some actions that the actor will take. The actor that is cast in the principal role is called the principal of the behavioral pattern. In fact the goal of a behavior pattern is to prescribe all of the potential actions of the principal. We say that the principal is bound to a behavioral pattern since an actor can only be the principal of one behavioral pattern at any one time. The actions of a behavioral pattern's principal are completely determined by the behavioral pattern it is bound to. A principal stays bound to a behavioral pattern until it is unbound. This can be done if the principal is bound to a different behavioral pattern or is destroyed. Recently, complex schemes for allowing an actor to choose a principal role amongst several behavioral patterns have been proposed in the literature [6]. However, it is not clear that they will be easy to use in cases where the action taken by the character is significant to the plot of the game.

Although an actor may be cast in only one principal role at any given time, it may be cast in an arbitrary number of supporting roles simultaneously. For example, if the principal (guard role) of a Guard Pattern that is guarding something (chest, door, individual, shard, etc.) is itself being guarded by three other creatures, then the principal plays the guarded role in three other guard instantiations.

A pattern role is a special kind of pattern parameter. However, each pattern can have a set of other parameters as well as its roles. Every behavioral pattern has a situation list parameter that describes all of the possible basic situations that comprise the behavioral pattern. Each situation consists of a set of conditions and a set of actions. For example, in scenario 1, one situation is: if an enemy comes near the chest and the guard is currently patrolling, then warn the enemy and move near the chest. A second situation is: if an enemy opens the chest then attack the enemy.

In general, patterns can also have other parameters. Two other common parameter types are labels that refer to specific game objects and composite parameters that refer to other pattern instances. For example, the Guard Pattern has a list of patrols, where each patrol is an instance of another behavior pattern called a Patrol Pattern. At instantiation time, the game designer must assign a value to each pattern parameter. Of course, casting the roles of a pattern to specific objects is a special case of assigning pattern values to those parameters that are role parameters. In the next section, we provide an example of patterns, pattern parameters, and the instantiation of pattern parameters using the Shard-1 chest guard of this section as an example.

When patterns are used as parameters in other patterns there is sometimes a need to require roles from the two different patterns to be cast by the same object. For example, the guard in the Guard Pattern and the patroller in the Patrol Pattern that is attached to it, must be cast as the same actor. In the simplest case, the principal role of two patterns is shared and we say that we are attaching a pattern to another pattern. This is the only situation where an actor may play the principal role in more than one behavior. It is allowed since the attached behaviors are considered as components of the behavior they are attached to.

3 Designing Characters: A *ScriptEase* Walk through

Consider an example of the Guard Pattern, described as scenario 1 (Shard-1) from Section 2. As a default behavior, the guard patrols the room that the chest is in. When an enemy approaches the chest, the guard yells a warning, runs over to the chest, and stands in front of it. When the enemy moves away from the chest, the guard goes back to patrolling the room. If the enemy ignores the guard's warning and opens the chest, the guard attacks. Figure 1 describes all of the information needed to specify this instance of the Guard Pattern.

We have developed a tool called *ScriptEase* that allows this instance and many other variations of the Guard Pattern to be implemented quickly and easily. All user input is menu driven, with all options for behaviors and scenarios given in natural language. The user never does programming in the conventional senses and, indeed, never knows the existence of an underlying programming language. Figure 2 shows a screen shot of this tool.

Situations can be constructed by selecting conditions and actions from a list. The Situations panel on the left side of Figure 2 contains a list of all the situations that have been defined for this pattern instance. After a new situation has been created, it appears in this list and makes its condition and action lists available to be edited. Once a condition is added, it appears in a list inside the Conditions panel on the right side of Figure 2. Actions appear in the corresponding Actions panel. A condition or action can then be selected to make its parameters available for editing. In Figure 2, the first condition in the Conditions list is highlighted. Its parameters are shown inside of the Near Condition panel underneath the Situations panel.

Patrols are lower level patterns that can be attached to a Guard Pattern. All of the patrols that are attached to a Guard Pattern are listed in the Attached Patrols panel at the bottom of Figure 2. There are two types of Patrol Patterns used in this example. The "Room Patrol" from Figure 2 is an instance of a Way-point Patrol Pattern, which means the patrol is defined by a series of way-points that the guard walks along. The "Chest Post" is an instance of a Post Patrol Pattern, which means the guard just stands at a particular spot. Table 1 gives a description of these two instances. Any number of patrols can be attached to a guard, but only one is active at a time. There is a condition to test which patrol a guard is currently using, and an action to change a guards patrol.

Once all of the patrols and situations have been specified, code can be generated by clicking the "Generate" button at the very bottom of Figure 2. The user may further customize the situations using the *Situation Editor* tool of *ScriptEase*, shown in Figure 3. Finally, *ScriptEase* generates *Neverwinter Nights* scripting language code.

```
Pattern Type              : Guard Pattern
     Instance Name        : Chest Guard
     Guard Tag            : chest_guard
     Guarded Object Tag   : chest
     Friend Identifier    : guard1_friend

Attached Patrol Patterns:
     1. Instance Name     : Room Patrol
     2. Instance Name     : Chest Post

Situation List:
     Name                 : Spawn Situation
     Conditions           : The guard is created
     Actions              : Set the guard's patrol to "Room Patrol"

     Name                 : Warning Situation
     Conditions           : An creature is within 5 meters of the guarded
                            chest. The guard is currently using patrol
                            "Room Patrol".
     Actions              : The guard yells "Hey! Get away from there."
                            Set the guard's patrol to "Chest Post".

     Name                 : Continue Patrol Situation
     Conditions           : No enemy is within 5 meters of the guarded
                            chest. The guard is currently using patrol
                            "Chest Post".
     Actions              : Set the guard's patrol to "Room Patrol"

     Name                 : Attack Situation
     Conditions           : An enemy creature opens the guarded chest
     Actions              : The guard says "I warned you!".  The guard
                            attacks the enemy.
```

Fig. 1. The Chest Guard instance of the Guard Pattern

Table 1. Two patrol instances attached to the Guard Pattern

Pattern Type	Way-point Patrol Pattern	Pattern Type	Post Patrol Pattern
Instance Name	Room Patrol	Instance Name	Chest Post
Way-point Prefix	room 1	Post Tag	chest_post
Num of Way-points	8		
Initial Way-point	1		

Figure 4 shows a game scenario of a guard in action. Part of the *Neverwinter Nights* scripting code generated by *ScriptEase* for this scenario is shown in Figure 5. Notice that the code is self documenting, enabling the user to easily find

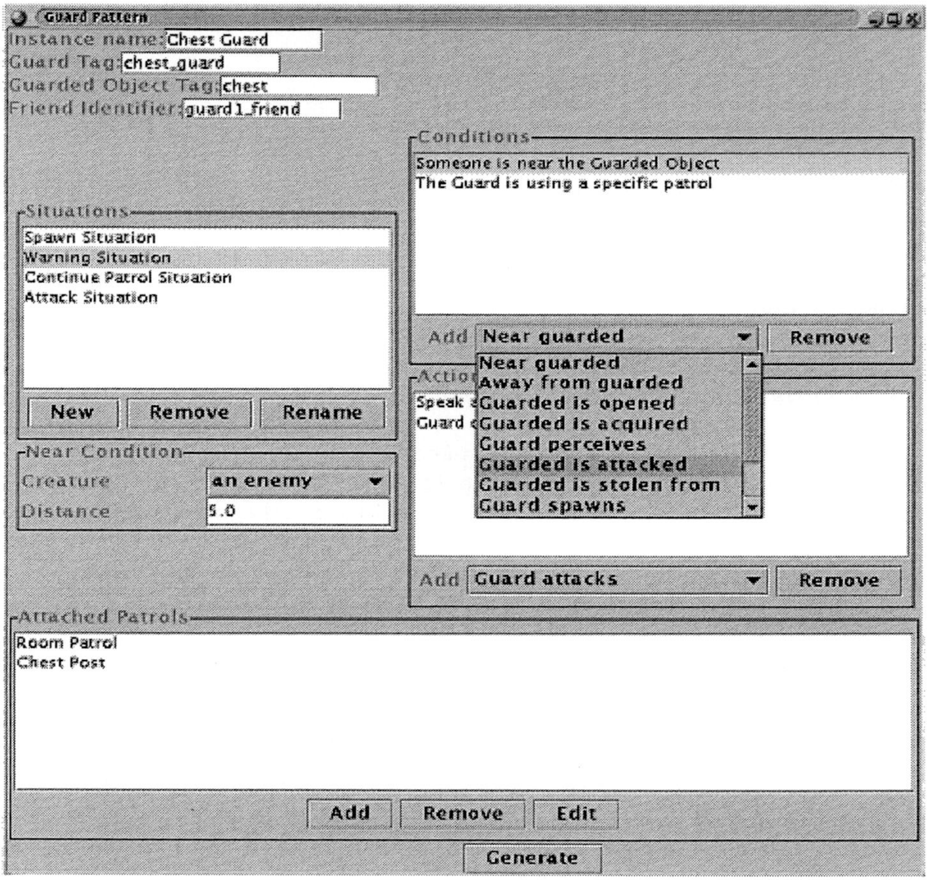

Fig. 2. Editing an instance of the Guard Pattern using *ScriptEase*

which portions of code correspond with the situations specified in *ScriptEase*. This is very useful if the user desires to fine tune the code on the lowest level.

We have also identified several *encounter* patterns. Instead of describing the behaviors of a principle actor, an encounter pattern defines a list of situations that describe some notable event in the game. For instance, in Baldur's Gate II, there is an interesting encounter in the Shade Lord's temple. There is a pedestal with an icon, called the Sun Stone, on it. There is also a ring of lights around the pedestal. When a particular type of monster, called a Shadow, enters the ring of lights, it is killed in a spectacular flash of light. If the Sun Stone is removed from the pedestal, the ring of lights disappears and the Shadows can then approach the pedestal without being killed. We have defined an encounter pattern called the Icon-Container Pattern. This pattern has 3 roles: an icon, a container, and an optional perimeter. The icon is a prop that can be placed

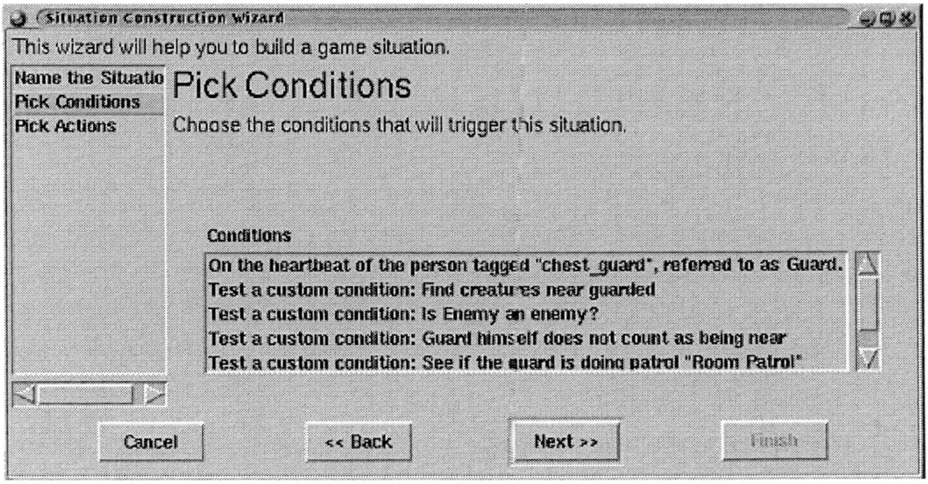

Fig. 3. Situation editing using *ScriptEase*

Fig. 4. *Neverwinter Nights* guarding scenario (using the Icon-Perimeter Pattern)

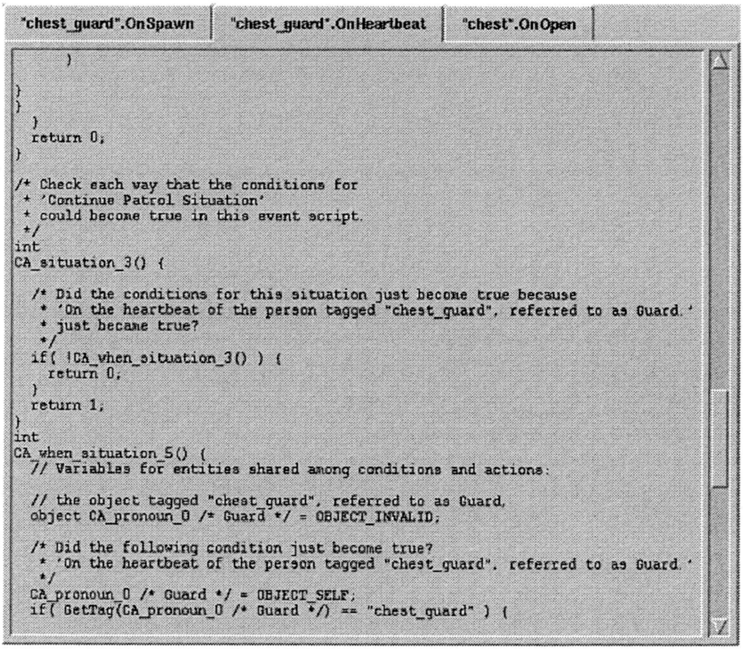

Fig. 5. *ScriptEase* code generation

into the container's inventory. The container is either an actor or a container prop. The perimeter is a polygonal area that an actor can enter and exit. This pattern involves four situations: adding the icon to the container, removing the icon from the container, an actor enters the perimeter while the icon is in the container, and an actor exits the perimeter while the icon is in the container. In each of these situations, the condition listed above is implicitly included in the condition list. The user can add more conditions to the list, and define actions to execute when the conditions are satisfied. Figure 6 shows these four situations instantiated for the Sun Stone Icon example.

We have identified multiple instances of this pattern in the Shade Lord temple alone, demonstrating that this pattern is useful in terms of abstraction, adaptation, and re-use. We have not yet created an interface specific to this particular pattern, however, all of the situations defined in Figure 6 have been implemented in the *ScriptEase* Situation Editor.

ScriptEase has been demonstrated to BioWare and we have received positive feedback. The tool is especially appreciated by the game designers, who prefer to work in terms of the story and characters, not at the level of programming. The tool is evolving, as we get more feedback from BioWare. Indeed, the project is expanding at a pace that is difficult to keep up with. The immediate goal is to give *ScriptEase* the functionality so that it can replicate all the capabilities in *Neverwinter Nights.* To do this requires adding a few more patterns (research)

```
Pattern Type               : Icon-Container
     Icon                  : Sun Stone
     Container             : Pedestal
     Perimeter             : Ring of Lights

Situation List:
     Implicit Condition : The Sun Stone is added to the Pedestal
     Other Conditions   : None
     Actions            : Activate the ring of lights

     Implicit Condition : The Sun Stone is removed the Pedestal
     Other Conditions   : None
     Actions            : Deactivate the ring of lights

     Implicit Condition : The Sun Stone is on the Pedestal and a~creature
                          enters the ring of lights.
     Other Conditions   : The entering creature is a~Shadow
     Actions            : Display an impressive visual effect.  Kill the
                          entering Shadow.

     Implicit Condition : The Sun Stone is on the Pedestal and a~creature
                          exits the ring of lights.
     Other Conditions   : None
     Actions            : None
```

Fig. 6. An instance of the Icon-Container Pattern

and a lot more scenarios (data input). The design of *ScriptEase* makes both issues easy to address.

4 Ongoing Work

Behavior patterns are only the beginning. The industry needs a tool that properly defines a complete game script, in much the same way that a script is used to outline a movie. A movie script must include information on each scene, including the physical arrangement of the scene, the characters that are present, how the characters interact, the dialogs, and the outcomes. A series of scenes has to be stitched together to give a coherent plot. Defining these components in isolation of each other (as is currently done in commercial games) is clearly wrong. Most (but not all) of these components touch on AI issues.

To cover the gamut of issues in game design, a ScriptEase-like tool needs other components, including dialog and plot. We believe that both of these can also be described by patterns. We have ideas for how to integrate these patterns into ScriptEase, and this is the subject of ongoing work.

The preceding description of ScriptEase described scripted behavior, where each character's behavior was predictable, modulo some random number generation. The reality is that creating realistic characters requires more sophisticated behavior. Machine learning is the answer. Unfortunately, compatibility with existing scripting languages (such as that in *Neverwinter Nights*) make this difficult. We expect our work to eventually lead us to the design of a new scripting language, one that supports core AI functionality (such as learning) as basic operators in the language.

Learning is a touchy issue in commercial games. Currently, machine learning plays a limited role in the commercial games industry. "[Learning] takes place as part of the game development cycle, never after the game ships" [9]. The reason for this is that the program developers have no control over how a learning game evolves; the results might be embarrassing. However, things are changing. The success of games like *The Sims* and *Black and White* have demonstrated the power (and commercial appeal) of games that learn.

The issue of testability of a learning algorithm before the product ships is of paramount importance to the games industry [3]. There are no guarantees with any learning algorithm, since the user (game player) can deliberately expose the learner to a contrived set of learning experiences. One way of addressing this is the ScriptEase approach of using patterns. Patterns can be tested individually and verified to be correct. Building on top of verified patterns allows one to create composite patterns that can have guarantees of correctness.

5 Conclusions

This paper discussed one aspect of ScriptEase – behavioral patterns. Our research and development efforts concentrated on this aspect of our vision for the simple reason that it has the highest potential for an impact in the short-term. Given the enormous effort that goes into defining behaviors in a complex game like *Neverwinter Nights*, any tool (such as ScriptEase) that can can reduce this effort translates into enormous costs savings and improved product reliability.

The commercial games industry is pushing AI technology into new and innovative directions. The demand for realism, high-performance, and real-time responses make the problems especially challenging. One could argue that this industry is one of the biggest receptors for AI technology, and yet it has historically been ignored by the AI community. There are wonderful opportunities here for ground-breaking innovative research.

Acknowledgments

Financial support was provided by the Institute for Robotics and Intelligent Systems (IRIS), the Natural Sciences and Engineering Research Council of Canada (NSERC), and Alberta's Informatics Circle of Research Excellence (iCORE). This research was inspired by our many friends at BioWare. We thank BioWare for their support and encouragement.

References

[1] E. Adams. In defense of academe. *Game Developer*, pages 55–56, November 2002.

[2] C. Alexander, S. Ishakawa, and M. Silverstein. *A Pattern Language.* Oxford University Press, New York, 1977.

[3] J. Barnes and J. Hutchens. Testing of undefined behavior as a result of learning. In S. Rabin, editor, *AI Game Programming Wisdom*, pages 615–623. Charles River, 2002.

[4] M. Brockington and M. Darrah. How not to implement a basic scripting language. In S. Rabin, editor, *AI Game Programming Wisdom*, pages 548–554. Charles River, 2002.

[5] S. Bromling, D. Szafron, J. Schaeffer, S. MacDonald, and J. Anvik. Generalising pattern-based parallel programming systems. *Parallel Computing*, 2002. To appear.

[6] R. Evans and T. Lamb. Social activities: Implementing wittgenstein, 2002. `http://www.gamasutra.com/features/20020424/evans_01.htm`.

[7] E. Gamma, R. Helm, R. Johnson, and J. Vlissides. *Design Patterns.* Addison Wesley, 1995.

[8] R. Hill, C. Han, and M. van Lent. Applying perceptually driven cognitive mapping to virtual urban environments. *AAAI National Conference*, pages 886–893, 2002.

[9] N. Kirby. GDC 2001 AI roundtable moderator's report, 2001. `http://www.gameai.com`

[10] J. Laird and M. van Lent. Human-level AI's killer application: Interactive computer games. *AAAI National Conference*, pages 1171–1178, 2000.

[11] P. Tozour. The evolution of game AI. In S. Rabin, editor, *AI Game Programming Wisdom*, pages 3–15. Charles River, 2002.

Enumerating the Preconditions of Agent Message Types

Francis Jeffry Pelletier and Renée Elio

Dept. Computing Science, Univ. Alberta
Edmonton, Alberta T6G 2H1
{jeffp,ree}@cs.ualberta.ca
http://www.cs.ualberta.ca/{~jeffp,~ree}

Abstract. Agent communication languages (ACLs) invoke speech act theory and define individual message types by reference to particular combinations of beliefs and desires of the speaker (feasibility preconditions). Even when the mental states are restricted to a small set of nested beliefs, it seems that there might be a very large number of different possible preconditions, and therefore a very large number of different message types. With some constraints on the mental attitude of the speaker, we enumerate the possible belief states that could serve as preconditions for individual message types, and we identify how these states correspond to different possible message types. We then compare these with FIPA's primitive message types. Our approach clarifies the nature of core message types in an ACL, and perhaps settles issues concerning just how many, and what types of, speech acts should be seen as primitive in such languages.

1 Introduction and Background

We are interested in the question of how many distinct communicative actions can be taken by an agent when communicating using an agent communication language (ACL). The sorts of actions under consideration are *speech acts*, and the general background for this, in the context of our investigation, is provided by FIPA's "Agent Communicative Act Library Specification" [7]. Communicative acts are a subset of the different possible actions that agents might perform. We restrict our attention to them because they seem to be a simple subset of the whole array of possible actions. We hope that the method suggested for communicative acts might carry over to other actions also.

1.1 Individuating Speech Acts

The notion of a speech act was introduced by Austin [1] and developed by both the philosophical community, especially by Searle [12, 13], and the linguistic community, as for example by Sadock [11] and the contributors to [6]. This general conception was adopted by the AI "agent paradigm" that started in the early 1990s with DARPA's

Y. Xiang and B. Chaib-draa (Eds.): AI 2003, LNAI 2671, pp. 50-65, 2003.

development of KQML [9], and has been carried over to FIPA's ACL. Key figures in this latter development have been Cohen & Levesque, Sadek, and Singh (e.g., [4], [10], [14]), see [8] for a survey. All of these later writers acknowledge their debt to Searle's [13] general account.

Austin's [1] initial descriptions of speech acts included such leading examples as *saying* "I hereby pronounce you man and wife" or "I order you to remain quiet," and thereby *making* the people become married, or *making* someone be under an obligation to be quiet. In these cases the speaker needs to hold a certain socially-defined position, the audience needs to be in a certain relationship to the speaker and (sometimes) to each other, and the specific form of words uttered has to be of a certain type, etc. If all these were the case, then the utterance would have a certain conventional effect—the people *would be* married, the subject *would have been* ordered, and so on. Searle [12] focused on cases like "I promise you that I will repay the loan," where the speaker has to have certain intentions and beliefs —such as believing that there is a loan, that the hearer wants the loan repaid, that the hearer will understand the utterance to place the speaker under an obligation, and so on. If all these were fulfilled, then the utterance of this sentence (or any other one that had the same speaker-intentions) would *be* a promise, that is, it would *be* the placing of the speaker under an obligation.

Austin thought that by varying the social relationships, the beliefs of the speaker or audience, or the specific forms of words used, he could account for all the different (conventionally recognized) speech acts there were. He had divided them into five major groupings, and found very many subtypes within each grouping. Famously, he estimated there to be "the third order of ten" different speech acts.

Since Austin and Searle, there has been much debate both in Linguistics and in Philosophy over the matter of how many speech acts there are. And this same issue has arisen, often implicitly, in the agent communication literature. We view ourselves as continuing this discussion, but employing a different methodology.

1.2 Individuating Speech Acts: The Role of Preconditions

It might seem that since there are an infinite number of different things that can be said, there must be an infinite number of different possible communicative acts. But the idea is to ask for the number of different *types* of things that can be said, and these are what are to be called "speech acts". Examples of speech acts are *informing, requesting, ordering,* and the like. If *p* and *q* are different, then there is a sense in which *inform-that-p* and *inform-that-q* are different; but there is also a sense where it is the same speech act that is directed at different "propositional contents." It is this latter sense, where these are the same speech act but with differing propositional contents, that we are interested in characterizing.

On the other hand, one can *inform-that-p, request-that-p, order-that-p,* and so on. These are each to be considered a different speech act, all directed to the same propositional content, *p*. It is also this sense, where these are different speech acts with the same propositional content, that we are interested in characterizing: How many different speech acts (i.e., different types of communicative acts) are possible for a given propositional content?

Austin used many different types of information when he came to "individuating" speech acts: they might differ in the circumstances and persons involved, differ in the sorts of conventions involved, differ in the mental state of the speaker, and finally they might differ in the resulting mental state of the hearer. Any of these might vary while the others stay constant, and the result could be a different speech act. In theory this would suggest there could be literally an infinite number of different possible speech acts, and it is just an accident of English and modern civilization that we only happen to have "the third power of ten" that are in actual use and codified in our language.

Searle on the other hand defined the various speech acts that happened to be already codified in the language as being "constituted" by two classes of conditions: preparatory conditions and sincerity conditions. The preparatory conditions described conditions of the world that need to happen in order for the speaker to correctly attempt that speech act, such as being in a "socially superior condition" in order to correctly attempt to give an order. The sincerity conditions distinguished "merely apparent" instances of a speech act from genuine ones, for example would distinguish a lie from a genuine case of informing.

The idea that speech acts were individuated by social convention (Austin) or were "constituted by" their preparatory and sincerity conditions (Searle) was not agreed to by all philosophers and linguists (e.g., not by the influential [2]). However, the current ACL design specifications (including FIPA's) do continue a general characterization of the difference between two distinct speech acts as a matter of the "preconditions" that are relevant to each. For instance, to (genuinely) request that another agent perform some action, the speaker (requestor) can't believe that the other agent would do the action anyway. An agent can't perform a (genuine) act of *confirming-p* if he doesn't believe p, and also if he doesn't believe that the hearer is uncertain about p. And so on. Thus, the difference between types of communicative acts becomes a matter of there being a difference in these "feasibility preconditions" (FPs), as they are called by FIPA.

Searle also held that a sincere and non-defective speech act would require that the hearer *in fact* fulfill some conditions. (For instance, in order for an utterance to be a promise, the hearer *in fact* had to desire the future action of the speaker). Although FIPA does not have promise speech acts, nor any commissive speech acts, if it were to add such an act, its version of a promise would have the FP that the speaker *believe* that the hearer desire the future action; but it would not require that the hearer *in fact* desire it. This is because the speaker is thought to engage in its communicative acts *only on account of its own, directly inspectable, mental attitudes.*

It might be thought, once again, that since there are an infinite number of mental attitudes that a speaker might have, there are an infinite number of FPs that could be involved even when we are restricting our attention to one propositional content, *p*. For example, it might be thought that "speaker believes that *p* but desires that *q*" could be a FP for *inform-that-p-while-desiring-that-q*. And if this is allowed, then it would be a different speech act than *inform-that-p-while-desiring-that-r*, and so on. In this paper we restrict our attention to the case where the FPs involved with a speech act only admit the same propositional content as the main speech act. Thus in the speech acts that have *p* as their propositional content, all the FPs will have speaker and hearer attitudes about *p*, and not about other propositions. In this we are following the majority of FIPA's speech act descriptions, although for some of their non-primitive speech acts they allow further modifications of the propositional content– such as complex actions that are "based on" *p*. Given that there are only a finite number of such further modifications, the considerations given below and our general method could be adapted to deal with them also; but for simplicity we will consider only the basic case where FPs are direct mental attitudes of the speaker and hearer about *p* and about each other's attitudes toward *p*.

1.3 Individuating Speech Acts: The Role of Effects

Speech acts can also be characterized by their intended effects, as can be seen from the statements made by Austin and Searle. Austin thought that speech acts required a communal convention that both the speaker and the hearer needed to be a conscious part of, and the hearer needed to have "uptake" of the speaker's desire to participate in the convention, in order that an utterance by the speaker should count as a speech act. Searle considered that a hearer would *in fact* have to believe that the speaker is under an obligation in order for a speech act to be a promise.

In FIPA's ACL specification, these are called "rational effects." The rational effect of an *inform-p* might be that the receiving agent now believes the propositional content of the inform. The rational effect of a promise might be that the hearer believe that the speaker is under an obligation. In FIPA's view, however, rational effects are not, strictly speaking, postconditions, because they are not guaranteed (messages may be lost; the mental state of the receiving agent is not in the control of the speaker, and in any case the hearer's mental response is generally unobservable to the sending agent). Thus speech acts are not even partially individuated by their rational effects. More generally, speech acts are a special case of an agent operating in a nondeterministic, partially observable environment over which it has only an indirect control, namely the mental state of another agent. And all an agent has to guide its actions are its own beliefs, desires, goals, and intentions concerning "external reality" (which includes other agents).

As a consequence, the rational effects of a speech act cannot be used to individuate one from another, since they are outside the speaker's control. To conclude: speech acts apparently cannot be individuated by their effects, but only by their preconditions.

1.4 Planning a Speech Act

The theory of an agent communicating crucially depends on being able to determine what FPs are currently satisfied. The general picture (due historically to [5], see [3] for discussion) is this. An agent desires to have the environment have a certain feature. (This desire is not necessarily a part of the communication process…it may have come about through other means such as being a feature of its design or being ordered by some outside agency. The feature might be as ephemeral as that another agent come to believe *p*.) The agent scans the various speech acts that are within its repertoire, finds one with the correct rational effect, then determines whether the FPs are satisfied. If they are, the agent performs that speech act. If not, then the agent might look to other speech acts to see if they have the desired rational effect, or it may set about the task to make the FPs become true. This picture of a dialog makes success be a matter of planning (in the classical AI sense); and as part of that plan it is required that a stash of speech acts with their associated FPs be accessible. For this reason it is necessary that we be able to give a clear accounting of what the range of possible FPs is.

2 The Semantics of FPs

Our strategy is going to be to investigate speech acts by inquiring into the class of possible FPs of speech acts. So we turn to a quick look at how FPs are given by FIPA.

2.1 The Semantic Language

The communicative acts offered by FIPA are assigned a semantics by means of statements in a Semantic Language (SL). Each speech act is associated with a formula of SL that describes the speech act; the speech act's FPs and rational effects are also given as formulas of SL. These SL statements are themselves interpreted in a possible worlds framework. The SL language is multi-modal, having belief, desire, uncertainty, and intend operators ($B_i\phi$ means that agent *i* believes that ϕ; $D_i\phi$ means that *i* desires ϕ; $U_i\phi$ means that *i* is uncertain about ϕ but thinks it more likely than $\neg\phi$, $I_i\phi$ means that *i* intends ϕ). The B operator, which is what we will mainly be concerned with in this paper, is described as a KD45 modal operator.[1] We shall not dwell in the details of such a logic (which is basically the S_5 logic, except that the T-axiom, $\Box\phi\Rightarrow\phi$, is replaced by the D-axiom, $\Box\phi\Rightarrow\neg\Box\neg\phi$). Instead we mention here some "Rules" about KD45 that we will use in what follows.

1. Self-contradictions inside the scope of one agent's B operator are contradictory: $B_i(\phi\&\neg\phi)$ is never true.
2. Beliefs of an agent cannot be contradictory: $B_i\phi$ and $B_i\neg\phi$ are never jointly satisfiable. (So in particular, $B_i\phi$ implies $\neg B_i\neg\phi$).
3. If an agent believes ϕ, then the agent believes the logical consequences of ϕ. (A special case is that an agent believes all tautologies).
4. Believing *p* is equivalent to believing that you believe it: $B_i\phi$ is equivalent to $B_iB_i\phi$.
5. Not believing *p* is equivalent to believing that you don't believe it: $\neg B_i\phi$ is equivalent to $B_i\neg B_i\phi$.
6. Although for a given proposition *p*, an agent might believe neither of *p* and $\neg p$, it is required that the agent *not believe* either *p* or $\neg p$: $[\neg B_i\neg p \vee \neg B_i p]$ is necessarily true.

---

[1] The D and I operators are described as KD logics. The U operator seems to be left formally undefined. It is not clear that it is even a normal K operator, since it is unclear that $U_i\phi$ and $U_i\psi$ would imply $U_i(\phi\&\psi)$; and this "aggregation" of a modal operator over & is true in all Kripke-normal modal logics. Consider: if ϕ is .7 likely and ψ is .6 likely and they're independent, isn't $(\phi\&\psi)$ .42 likely? (We won't pursue this issue in the present paper).

7. If all the propositional variables in ϕ are each in the scope of a B_i-operator (not necessarily the same one), then ϕ is equivalent to $B_i\phi$.

2.2 FIPA's Primitive Message Types

FIPA gives four primitive message types, which we state here, using a slightly different formalism than FIPA does by expanding their abbreviations.

1. <i, inform(h, ϕ)>
   FP: $B_i\phi$
   $\neg B_i[B_h\phi \vee B_h\neg\phi \vee U_h\phi \vee U_h \neg\phi]$
   RE: $B_h\phi$
2. <i, confirm(h, ϕ)>
   FP: $B_i\phi$
   $B_iU_h\phi$
   RE: $B_h\phi$
3. <i, disconfirm(h, ϕ)>
   FP: $B_i\neg\phi$
   $B_i[U_h\phi \vee B_h\phi]$
   RE: $B_h\neg\phi$
4. <i, request(h,α)>
   FP: $FP(\alpha)[i\backslash h]$
   B_i Agent(h, α)
   $\neg B_i\ I_h$ Done(α)
   RE: Done(α)

The request message type is more complicated than the others because it involves requesting the hearer to do an action α; and this involves issues concerning whether the requestor believes the hearer intends to do α anyway, and whether those parts of the FPs of α that are mental attitudes of *i* are satisfied, and so on. The more straightforward ones are the other three. An agent can *inform* a hearer of something if the agent believes it and believes the hearer does not believe it or its negation nor is uncertain of it or its negation. It can *confirm* something if it believes it and also believes the hearer is uncertain of it; it can *disconfirm* something if it disbelieves it but believes the hearer either believes it or is uncertain of it. We will contrast these primitive types with some further ones that we describe later.

3 Characterizing Feasibility Preconditions

We are interested in determining how many communicative acts there are by investigating the space of possible FPs for speech acts. Another way of putting our basic question is: How many different configurations of an agent's mental state might there be in a KD45 logic, concerning proposition *p* and a hearer, that in turn might be employed as feasibility preconditions for speech acts? Our aim is to specify a "grammar" that will exhaustively list the FPs that can be stated in the Semantic Language.

To make this question simpler, we will consider only what FIPA calls "primitive communicative acts." Non-primitive acts relevant to the propositional content *p* might turn out to "expand" on *p*, and therefore not be just concerning *p* simply. For instance, the non-primitive communicative act *query-if(i,j,ϕ)* means that agent *i* is requesting agent *j* to inform it of the truth of ϕ. This non-primitive speech act is defined in terms of *request* and *inform*; the FPs for this act mention more than just *i*, *j* and the content of ϕ.

So, we wish to consider how many primitive speech acts there can be that involve propositional content p, by considering how many different FPs there can be that mention only p as their propositional content and the beliefs of i and h, the speaker and hearer (respectively) of the speech act. The characterization of FPs in FIPA is not well-defined, but one can glean certain features from their examples. We will start with some of the simpler features and try to decide how many different FPs there can be using only these simple features. Then we will briefly talk about more complex ways of constructing FPs.

3.1 FP-Sets

First, we will define a *FP-set* to be a set of individual formulas, each one of which is a legitimate feasibility formula (which we call an FF). FIPA sometimes uses conjunction to conjoin these FFs and thereby make an FP just be one conjunctive formula; but sometimes it allows for there to be two or more different FFs and then the FP is that *group* of FFs…understood as their all being satisfied. We are approaching it in the latter way: we will give a number of simple formulas that are individual feasibility formulas, and will consider the FP-set to be a group of these FFs, and we will make sure that none of the individual formulas is itself a conjunction.

As we remarked before, FIPA allows not only the propositional content to play a role in individual FFs, but allows the speaker agent to have various mental attitudes towards this propositional content, such as believing it or being uncertain about it or desiring it, and the like. And it allows the speaking agent to have beliefs (etc.) about the beliefs (etc.) of the hearing agent. And so forth.

Although this sounds like it can lead to an infinite number of different FFs (agent i believes that agent j doesn't believe that agent i desires.....), in fact the examples suggest that FIPA keeps a tight limit on the amount of such iteration.[2] We will here give a very simple grammar designed only to accommodate the speaking agent (i), the hearing agent (h), the propositional content (p), and their beliefs (represented as B, with a subscript determining which agent has the belief). The FIPA examples allow negations and disjunctions, also. But again, they are limited and not allowed to generate an infinite number of FFs (at least, not in their examples). There is always uncertainty in trying to induce a general claim on the basis of limited examples, and our attempt to give regularity in the form of a grammar to FIPAs examples might result in something FIPA would reject. We would ask them to provide the specific grammar of allowable FFs so that we can more confidently apply our method.

We can begin by specifying a formal grammar of FFs for agents i and h, and propositional content p (letting α be a variable taking values of either i for speaker or h for

---

[2] The FIPA document [7] uses the sort of examples of FFs we are characterizing here, calling it "the operational semantics". But in footnotes it also gives a "theoretical semantics" for the FFs. The main difference, perhaps the only difference, is that the B operator is replaced by MB, standing for "mutual belief"—the infinitely iterated "i believes that h believes that i believes that…" Our grammar described below could also generate such statements by replacing the B operator with an MB operator, but we will instead follow the examples used in the operational semantics for simplicity of explanation.

hearer). In our initial analysis, we will be concerned only with a single modal operator, B. (That is, we will ignore for this document mental attitudes towards complex propositions, which themselves might be about mental attitudes, e.g., I believe you know that I desire that you know that I don't know p). The disjunctive possibilities we enumerate are in some of FIPA's examples.

BNF rule	Examples of generated formulas
1. <simple-statement> := p | ¬p	
2. <simple-attitude> := B_α<simple-statement> |	$B_\alpha p$, $B_\alpha \neg p$
¬B_α<simple-statement>	$\neg B_\alpha p$, $\neg B_\alpha \neg p$
3.<cmpd-attitude>:=[<simple-attitude>∨<simple-attitude>]	$[B_\alpha p \vee B_\alpha \neg p]$
4. <attitude> := B_i <simple-statement> |	$B_i p$, $\neg B_i p$…..
B_i<simple-attitude> |	$B_i B_\alpha \neg p$
¬B_i <simple-attitude> |	$\neg B_i \neg B_\alpha p$
B_i <cmpd-attitude> |	$B_i[B_\alpha p \vee B_\alpha \neg p]$
¬B_i <cmpd-attitude>	$\neg B_i[B_\alpha p \vee B_\alpha \neg p]$

The <attitude> strings allowed by this grammar each describe a mental activity of an agent, and any subset of these strings then constitutes a mental state of an agent, using only the Belief operator. Any such *string subset* is a candidate for use as a feasibility precondition of a speech act. Hence, an *FP-set* is a (non-empty) set of <attitude> FF's.

3.2 Some Semantic Restrictions on FP-Sets

There are various semantic constraints that exclude many of the sets that can be produced with this grammar. No such *set* is allowed to be contradictory for example, so no FP-set can contain both an <attitude> and its corresponding negation. (However, it might contain neither, as when the feasibility preconditions for some communicative act do not require that the speaker have any opinions about *p*–as for example the preconditions for *query-if* in FIPA's specifications).

Furthermore, being a KD45 operator imposes some other requirements on the FP-sets, such as that there can be no case of $B_i q$ and $B_i \neg q$ (for any *q*), as noted above in Rule 2. Rule 5 requires that $B_i q$ and $B_i B_i q$ are the same, and therefore (a) if one FF has the former as a subpart where another FF has the latter and that is their only difference, then they are the same FF, and so (b) if one FP has one of these formulas while the other FP has both formulas, and there is no other difference, then they are the same FP. Using the same Rule, since $B_i q$ and $B_i B_i q$ are the same, if an FP has $B_i q$ and also $\neg B_i B_i q$ [or the reverse negations], then this is an impossible FP. (The same holds for the beliefs of *j*).

More generally speaking, Rule 7 says that if the main operator of each of X and Y is B_i (for example, maybe X is the formula $B_i(B_j p \vee \neg p)$ and Y is the formula $B_i(q \vee \neg B_j p)$ – both X and Y have B_i as a main operator), then B_i(X v Y) is the same as (X v Y). In other words, the addition of a B_i to a formula that already has all sentence letters in the scope of a B_i does not yield a semantically different formula. (The same holds for the beliefs of *h*).

We modified the above grammar so that it incorporated some of the constraints mentioned above. The resulting grammar generated these sentences, plus their negations:

B_ip	$B_i\neg p$	B_iB_hp
$B_i\neg B_hp$	$B_iB_h\neg p$	$B_i\neg B_h\neg p$
$B_i[B_hp \vee B_hp]$	$B_i[\neg B_hp \vee B_hp]$	$B_i[B_h\neg p \vee B_hp]$
$B_i[\neg B_h\neg p \vee B_hp]$	$B_i[B_hp \vee \neg B_hp]$	$B_i[\neg B_hp \vee \neg B_hp]$
$B_i[B_h\neg p \vee \neg B_hp]$	$B_i[\neg B_h\neg p \vee \neg B_hp]$	$B_i[B_hp \vee B_h\neg p]$
$B_i[\neg B_hp \vee B_h\neg p]$	$B_i[B_h\neg p \vee B_h\neg p]$	$B_i[\neg B_h\neg p \vee B_h\neg p]$
$B_i[B_hp \vee \neg B_h\neg p]$	$B_i[\neg B_hp \vee \neg B_h\neg p]$	$B_i[B_h\neg p \vee \neg B_h\neg p]$
$B_i[\neg B_h\neg p \vee \neg B_h\neg p]$		

From these we remove "duplicates", that is, strings that merely have different syntactic orders of the components. This leaves us with the following 10, plus their negations (which we will discuss in Section 3.5); we divide them into three groupings:

Group 1	**Group 2**	**Group 3**
1. B_ip	7. $B_i[B_h\neg p \vee B_hp]$	8. $B_i[\neg B_h\neg p \vee B_hp]$
2. $B_i\neg p$		9. $B_i[B_h\neg p \vee \neg B_hp]$
3. B_iB_hp		10. $B_i[\neg B_h\neg p \vee \neg B_hp]$
4. $B_iB_h\neg p$		
5. $B_i\neg B_hp$		
6. $B_i\neg B_h\neg p$		

The embedded part of formula (7) expresses that the hearer has a definite belief about *p*, without stating what direction that belief takes. FIPA uses $Bif_h(p)$ as an abbreviation for this concept, and so formula (7) could also have been stated as $B_iBif_h(p)$. [Note also that $Bif_\alpha(p)$ is equivalent to $Bif_\alpha(\neg p)$.]

3.3 Further Semantic Restrictions on FP-Sets

It turns out that the members of Group 3 are not independently interesting. In KD45, formula 8 is equivalent to formula 6,[3] and formula 9 is equivalent to formula 4.[4] The embedded disjunction in formula 10 expresses a tautology, according to Rule 6. Therefore agent *i* must believe it, according to Rule 3, and thus 10 expresses no real requirement on FFs. We therefore have only the first seven formulas as FFs that can be used to form the feasibility preconditions for speech acts, at least when restricted as we have done to the propositional content of the speech act and the beliefs of the speaker. If it were true that any (non-empty) FP-set made up from these could deter-

[3] Since $\neg B_h\neg p$ implies $[\neg B_h\neg p \vee B_hp]$, it follows by Rule 3 that if *i* believes the former then *i* must believe the latter, so 6 implies 8. For the other direction, note that each disjunct of $[\neg B_h\neg p \vee B_hp]$ implies $\neg B_h\neg p$, the former because of identity, the latter because of Rule 2. Thus, if *i* believes the disjunction, then by Rule 3, *i* must believe $\neg B_h\neg p$.

[4] As with the previous case, 6 obviously implies 9, by Rule 3. For the other direction, each disjunct of $[B_h\neg p \vee \neg B_hp]$ implies $\neg B_hp$, and therefore since *i* believes the disjunction *i* must believe $\neg B_hp$ because of Rule 3.

mine a speech act, we would have $(2^7-1)=127$ different speech acts that could be defined from these formulas.

However, there are further relationships that hold in KD45 among the seven FFs. Obviously we cannot have both (1) and (2) in any FP-set, nor both (3) and (4), nor both (5) and (6). [Although for any of these pairs we might have neither in an FP-set.] It might also be noted that (3) implies (6),[5] and also that (3) implies (7).[6] (6) and (7) together imply (3).[7] This has various implications. Obvious ones are that any FP-set that has (3) must also include both (6) and (7), and any FP-set with both (6) and (7) must include also (3). At a somewhat deeper level of explanation, we might say that, since (3) is not really a separate FF from (6) and (7), we need to decide which is more fundamental: (3) itself, or the pair (6) and (7). To decide this, we need to determine whether there is an identifiable speech act that has (6) as a precondition but not (7)...or the reverse. If we decide this is not possible, then (6) and (7) should not count as separate FFs, but rather we should only use (3). If, on the other hand, we find there to be speech acts that have only one of them in their FP-set, then (3) should not count as a separate FF but instead we should allow (6) and (7) to occur separately sometimes, and sometimes together. And when they occur together that has the effect of adopting (3). We will not now dictate on this issue, but instead will present our analysis as two separate cases.

A similar situation holds among (4), (5), and a formula we have not yet considered,

7*. $B_i\neg[B_h\neg p \vee B_h p]$

This formula is not generated by our grammar for FFs, nor should it have been, because it is equivalent to (7*a), which in turn is equivalent to (7*b), in KD45

7*a. $B_i [\neg B_h\neg p \;\&\; \neg B_h p]$
7*b. $B_i\neg B_h\neg p \;\&\; B_i\neg B_h p$

which can be seen to be just the conjunction of formulas (5) and (6)...and our grammar only generates the individual conjuncts instead of the conjunctions. (The conjunction is represented by putting both conjuncts into the same FP-set).

Formula (4) implies (5) and (7*) for the same reasons that (3) implies (6) and (7). And similarly, (5) and (7*) imply (4). As was the case with (3) and (6)/(7), we note that (4) is not a separate FF from (5) and (7*), and so we need to decide whether to make (4) be a legitimate FF (and then (5) and (7*) wouldn't be), or whether to make (5) and (7*) be the primitive ones and (4) merely be implicit in the FP-sets that would have both. Recall that (7*) is really the conjunction of (5) and (6), and so the question becomes whether (5) and (6) can be pried apart from one another and appear in different speech acts.

Let us then give the two options: Option A treats (3) as the basic FF, thereby insisting that (6) and (7) cannot appear as basic FFs. Option B treats (6) and (7) as

---

5 By Rule 2, $B_h p$ implies $\neg B_h\neg p$, so since agent *i* believes $B_h p$, agent *i* must also believe $\neg B_h\neg p$, according to Rule 3. I.e., $B_i B_h p$ implies $B_i\neg B_h\neg p$.

6 Since $B_h p$ implies $[B_h\neg p \vee B_h p]$, $B_i B_h p$ must imply $B_i[B_h\neg p \vee B_h p]$ by Rule 3.

7 Since $\neg B_h\neg p$ and $[B_h\neg p \vee B_h p]$ together imply $B_h p$, and since *i* believes both of the former, *i* must also believe the latter, by Rule 3. I.e., (6) and (7) imply (3).

basic FFs, and (3) merely as a consequence that follows from other FFs in those FP-sets which happen to contain both (6) and (7). A similar state of affairs holds with the formulas (4) vs. (5) and (6). Note, however, that both (3) and (4) imply (6). This means that we need to treat the two states of affairs in the same way. That is, if we choose to treat (3) as a basic FF, we must do the same with (4); if we choose to treat (6) and (7) as basic, then we must also treat (5) and (6) as basic.

Employing our seven formulas, in the two Options, the basic FFs are:

Option A	**Option B**
1. B_ip	1. B_ip
2. $B_i\neg p$	2. $B_i\neg p$
3. B_iB_hp	5. $B_i\neg B_hp$
4. $B_iB_h\neg p$	6. $B_i\neg B_h\neg p$
	7. $B_i[B_h\neg p \vee B_hp]$

Any non-empty set of these is a FP-set. There are $(2^4-1)=15$ such sets in Option A, not all of which are legitimate (e.g., 1 and 2 can't appear in the same set). In Option B, there are $(2^5-1)=31$ FP-sets, not all of which are legitimate.

3.4 FP-Sets

Starting with Option A, we have already remarked that no FP-set can have both (1) and (2) in it, although it may have neither. No FP-set can have both (3) and (4) in it either, since agent *i* cannot believe that agent *h* believes both *p* and $\neg p$...at least not in a KD45 system of belief. (Each agent is consistent, and each agent believes that each agent is consistent). Again, though, an FP-set may contain neither. Each of (1) and (2) is independent of each of (3) and (4). There are nine sets that contain (a) at most one of (1) and (2), and (b) at most one of (3) and (4). One of these nine sets is empty, so there are eight legitimate FP-sets in Option A:

FP-1(A):	$\{ B_ip \}$	FP-5(A):	$\{ B_ip, B_iB_hp \}$
FP-2(A):	$\{ B_i\neg p \}$	FP-6(A):	$\{ B_ip, B_iB_h\neg p \}$
FP-3(A):	$\{ B_iB_hp \}$	FP-7(A):	$\{ B_i\neg p, B_iB_hp \}$
FP-4(A):	$\{ B_iB_h\neg p \}$	FP-8(A):	$\{ B_i\neg p, B_iB_h\neg p \}$

In Option B, once again FFs (1) and (2) can't both occur in the same FP-set (but perhaps neither does). But at least one of FF (5) and (6) must occur, according to Rule 6.[8] If both (5) and (6) are in an FP-set, then (7) cannot be in it.[9] We therefore generate the following 15 legitimate FP-sets in Option B.

FP-1(B):	$\{ B_i\neg B_hp \}$	FP-9(B):	$\{ B_i\neg B_h\neg p, B_i[B_h\neg p \vee B_hp]\}$
FP-2(B):	$\{ B_i\neg B_h\neg p \}$	FP-10(B):	$\{ B_ip, B_i\neg B_hp, B_i\neg B_h\neg p \}$
FP-3(B):	$\{ B_ip, B_i\neg B_hp \}$	FP-11(B):	$\{ B_ip, B_i\neg B_hp, B_i[B_h\neg p \vee B_hp]\}$
FP-4(B):	$\{ B_ip, B_i\neg B_h\neg p \}$	FP-12(B):	$\{ B_ip, B_i\neg B_h\neg p, B_i[B_h\neg p \vee B_hp]\}$

---

[8] By Rule 6, either $\neg B_hp$ or $\neg B_h\neg p$. It follows by Rule 3 that either $B_i\neg B_hp$ or $B_i\neg B_h\neg p$.

[9] As we remarked above, (5) and (6) imply (7*). But (7) and (7*) attribute contradictory beliefs to agent *i*, and so (5) and (6) together Rule out (7).

FP-5(B):	$\{ B_i\neg p, B_i\neg B_h p \}$	FP-13(B):	$\{ B_i\neg p, B_i\neg B_h p, B_i\neg B_h\neg p \}$
FP-6(B):	$\{B_i\neg p, B_i\neg B_h\neg p\}$	FP-14(B):	$\{ B_i\neg p, B_i\neg B_h p, B_i[B_h\neg p \vee B_h p]\}$
FP-7(B):	$\{B_i\neg B_h p, B_i\neg B_h\neg p\}$	FP-15(B):	$\{ B_i\neg p, B_i\neg B_h\neg p, B_i[B_h\neg p \vee B_h p]\}$
FP-8(B):	$\{ B_i\neg B_h p, B_i[B_h\neg p \vee B_h p]\}$		

3.5 Negative Feasibility Formulas

Although our grammar generated FFs that were negations of formulas expressing a belief of the speaker, we have not considered them so far. It might be thought that, since all feasibility conditions have to be truths about the mental states of the speaker, there could therefore be no FFs that did not have B_i as its main operator…a FF that started $\neg B_i$ would be illegitimate, since it says that *in fact* agent *i* does not believe such-and-so. Although this general reasoning is correct, in KD45 formulas of the form $\neg B_i\phi$ are equivalent to $B\neg B_i\phi$, as we saw in Rule 5, and therefore they are legitimate FFs.[10] However, the negated beliefs are logically quite difficult to deal with because there are two different reasons that $\neg B_i\phi$ could be true. It might be that $B_i\neg\phi$, and then from Rule 2 it follows that $\neg B_i\phi$; or it might be because the agent *i* has no beliefs about ϕ at all, neither $B_i\phi$ nor $B_i\neg\phi$, and from these facts it follows that $\neg B_i\phi$ by Rules 2 and 6. In other words, an agent does not believe ϕ if it believes $\neg\phi$ or if it has no beliefs about ϕ at all.

We will not embark on a full-scale investigation of the negative FFs that are allowed by our grammar, but we will just make some preliminary remarks. To start with, each of the 10 FFs that we presented in Section 3.2 has an FF just like it but with an initial $\neg$. Recall that we showed in that section that formula 8 was equivalent to formula 4, and 9 equivalent to 6. Their negations are also equivalent: $\neg$(8) is equivalent to $\neg$(4), and $\neg$(9) to $\neg$(6). We also showed there that the embedded formula of (10) was a tautology and so requiring that *i* believe it was not a real restriction. In the present case, the embedded formula of $\neg$(10) is a contradiction, so it is impossible for *i* to believe it, and so this is an impossible restriction. Thus, as in the positive case, we are left with the FFs $\neg$(1)–$\neg$(7).

But here the analysis diverges from the positive case. Since (3) implied (6) and (7), we now have that $\neg$(6) implies $\neg$(3), and $\neg$(7) implies $\neg$(3). But $\neg$(3) does not imply the conjunction of $\neg$(6) and $\neg$(7), but rather their disjunction, and so the analysis given for the positive case cannot be adapted to the negative one. Similarly $\neg$(5) implies $\neg$(4) and $\neg$(7*) implies $\neg$(4), but $\neg$(4) does not imply their conjunction.

A thorough analysis of the negative FFs is beyond the scope of this short paper, but it should be noted that there will now be many more FP-sets when we allow the negations to merge with the positives. (But a further thing to note is that no FP-set can have both the positive FF and the corresponding negative FF. Furthermore, there are a number of other illicit combinations, such as no FP-set can contain both (3) and $\neg$(6), or both (3) and $\neg$(7)…and so on.)

---

[10] The model that seems to be employed by implementations of these BDI theories is that an agent maintains a database of its beliefs, and scans through it on an as-needed basis to determine whether or not some belief is in it. If it fails to find the desired belief ϕ, it then adds $\neg B_i\phi$ to its belief-database, thus implementing Rule 5.

4 What Speech Acts Could There Be?

4.1 The Speech Acts Generated by Our Method

We look only at the positive FFs, and we start with Option A, to see what sort of speech act is correlated with each of the FP-sets. FP-sets 1(A) and 2(A) do not correspond to any speech act. This is because the mere belief of a proposition (or its negation) cannot by itself define a speech act in the absence of any other beliefs on the speaker's part. For, if it did, then corresponding to every belief one had there would be a speech act; and this subdivides the notion of speech act too finely. It would, for instance, not allow an agent to remain silent if it believes something (or else, it would define the silence as a type of speech act). FP-sets 3(A) and 4(A) also cannot generate a speech act, since they say only that the speaker believes that the hearer believes something. Without any further facts about the speaker's other beliefs this can't be enough to generate any particular speech act. If in addition to 3(A) the speaker did not believe *p* (for example) then these together might generate a type of disagreement, whereas if the speaker did believe *p* then together they might generate a confirmation of some type. But by itself 3(A) cannot determine any particular speech act.

The more interesting speech acts involve more FFs. FP-sets 5(A) and 8(A) are those cases where the speaker believes something and believes that the hearer believes it too. These both might be called "agree with", noting their difference from FIPA's 'confirm' that we gave in Section 2 (which required the speaker to believe that the hearer is uncertain about the proposition that the speaker believes).[11] The FP-sets 6(A) and 7(A) are those cases where the speaker believes that the hearer believes the opposite of what the speaker believes. These are the preconditions for the speech act of "disagree with", which is different from FIPA's 'disconfirm' that requires the speaker to believe that the hearer is uncertain about the negation of the proposition that the speaker believes.

Option B gives us a somewhat different set of speech acts. Similarly to Option A, FP-sets 1(B) and 2(B) do not give the speaking agent enough "mental life" to form a speech act. The mere fact that the agent does not believe that the hearer believes a proposition just cannot be enough content by itself to generate a speech act. FP-sets 3(B) and 6(B) have the hearer believe a proposition but not believe that the hearer does (recall that this "not believe" leaves open the possibility that the speaker thinks the hearer has no opinion about the proposition). This forms the preconditions necessary for what we might call "convince". FP-sets 4(B) and 5(B) are similar: the speaker believes a proposition but doesn't believe that the hearer believes the opposite. (Once again, it may be that the speaker thinks the hearer has no opinion on this opposite). Again, a possible name for the relevant speech act is "convince". But as in Option A, this is different from FIPA's 'disconfirm' and 'confirm'.

The remainder of the FP(B)-sets can be restated in terms of the Bif_h-operator. Recall that $Bif_h(p)=(B_h p \vee B_h \neg p)$, and hence that $\neg Bif_h(p)=(\neg B_h p \& B_h \neg p)$. Further note

---

[11] It is also different from FIPA's *agree*, which is a commitment on the part of the speaker agent to perform some future action. We discuss some implications of these differences in §4.2.

that $(Bif_h(p) \& \neg B_h p)$ implies $B_h \neg p$, while $(Bif_h(p) \& \neg B_h \neg p)$ implies $B_h p$. Using these facts we have

7(B):	$\{ B_i \neg Bif_h(p) \}$	10(B):	$\{ B_i p, B_i \neg Bif_h(p) \}$	13(B):	$\{ B_i \neg p, B_i \neg Bif_h(p) \}$
8(B):	$\{ B_i B_h \neg p \}$	11(B):	$\{ B_i p, B_i B_h \neg p \}$	14(B):	$\{ B_i \neg p, B_i B_h \neg p \}$
9(B):	$\{ B_i B_h p \}$	12(B):	$\{ B_i p, B_i B_h p \}$	15(B):	$\{ B_i \neg p, B_i B_h p \}$

It seems pretty clear that in FP-sets 7(B), 8(B), and 9(B) there can be no speech act that has just that precondition, for the speaker *i* is assumed to have no belief of its own, merely beliefs about the hearer. (Although perhaps they could be part of a complex speech act, such as a "request the hearer to inform the speaker", but such complex acts are a further step than is considered in this paper).

The more interesting cases occur when the speaker has some direct belief about the proposition *p* and also has a belief about the hearer's beliefs. FP-sets 10(B) and 13(B) make the speaker believe a proposition *p* but believe that the hearer has no direct beliefs about it. These are the preconditions for FIPA's "inform".

In FP-sets 12(B) and 14(B), the speaker believes some proposition and also believes the hearer shares this belief. This can be seen as forming the preconditions for the "agrees with" speech act we discussed in Option A. In FP-sets 11(B) and 15(B), the speaker believes the hearer has the opposite belief. And this would be the preconditions for the "disagree with" speech act. Again, though, it should be emphasized that these are different speech acts than FIPA's *confirm* and *disconfirm*.

So some of our FP sets are correlated with certain natural speech acts, namely

	FP-sets	**Corresponding Speech Act**
Option A:	FP-5(A) and FP-8(A):	agree with
	FP-6(A) and FP-7(A):	disagree with
Option B:	FP-3(B), FP-4(B), FP-5(B) and FP-6(B)	Convince
	FP-10(B) and FP-13(B)	Inform
	FP-12(B) and FP-14(B)	agree with
	FP-11(B) and FP-15(B)	disagree with

(Categorizing FP-5(A) and FP-8(A), for instance, as being in one group reflects the fact that the two FP-sets are identical except for their propositional content. FP-5(A) has *p* as its content while FP-8(A) has $\neg p$; and the same is true, mutatis mutandis, for all the other groups. We have already agreed that we were not going to individuate speech acts by their propositional content but only by the structure of their FP's; and this is why different FP-sets can correspond to the same speech act.)

4.2 The Speech Acts in FIPA

This method generates possible primitive speech acts that are not quite the same as FIPA's. For example, our *agree with* differs from FIPA's *confirm* and our *disagree with* differs from FIPA's *disconfirm*. And these differences are due to the same underlying feature: that FIPA has another modal operator that is not definable in our framework: $U_i\phi$, which means that *i* is uncertain about ϕ but thinks it more likely than $\neg\phi$. *Confirm(i,* ϕ*)* requires that *i* not only believe ϕ but also believe that the hearer is uncertain about ϕ (thinking it more likely than $\neg\phi$). *Disconfirm(i,* ϕ*)* requires that *i* disbelieve ϕ but think that the hearer either believes ϕ or is uncertain about ϕ. But our *agree-with(i, ϕ)* and *disagree-with(i, ϕ)* do not incorporate any notion of uncertainty.

It is important to note that our method could be used with an expanded language by adding the modal operator U_i to our SL and then adjusting our grammar so as to include this operator, possibly along with the others. And in doing this we would generate some FP-sets that give rise to FIPA's *confirm* and *disconfirm* speech acts. As well, we would no doubt generate many other types of speech acts that are not recognized by FIPA. But this would be a longer excursion than we can undertake in this paper.

We also did not allow the speaking agent to have a Bif_i attitude in general, but only in certain cases. Once again, we could alter the grammar so that the speaker itself could be the agent of a Bif. But this excursion is also to be saved for future work.

5 What Have We Shown?

We have given a kind of brute force method by which one can give a complete characterization of the communicative message types, or speech acts, in terms of their feasibility conditions. These feasibility conditions are themselves stated in a semantic language, and in our preliminary investigation we applied our method only to a very basic version of the semantic language – although we also indicated how it could be extended to more expressive languages. It remains to be seen whether the addition of further operators, e.g., U_i, or further types of legitimate FFs, will make this method become unwieldy. (If U_i is to be added to the language, as FIPA clearly wants, then some serious study of a semantics for U_i needs to be given before any analysis that involves our "modal reductions" can be undertaken, as we indicate in fn. 1. For, although we could easily add U_i to our grammars and mechanically produce a set of FFs with U_i, we would not be able to use our "semantic culling method" to reduce the sets.) With a very restricted grammar and assumptions about the content of an agent's mental state, we have shown that the space of possible combinations of beliefs is immense and that it is the KD45 semantics which reduces that dramatically. This is closely related to the conformance-verifiability problem [15].

Understanding the space of FPs is important, because FIPA assumes that an agent designer will use FIPA's core primitives, and that any newly-defined primitives will not semantically conflict with that core. We have shown that one of FIPA's four primitive acts is described by our method even in our impoverished semantic language. If the underlying semantic language were expanded so as to include some of FIPA's other operators (such as *U*), it seems clear that further omitted possible primitive speech acts would be uncovered. Our investigation has also described certain possible primitive communicative acts that are omitted from FIPA's list of primitive communicative acts: *agree-with*, *disagree-with*, and *convince*. We haven't argued that these message types should be added to the FIPA library, although we do not know of any reason why FIPA has omitted them. The issue of deciding on a core set of primitive message types has been a matter of debate ever since the notion of speech act was first introduced and subsequently adopted for agent communication. Our method gives a clear grip on how to investigate this topic.

References

[1] Austin, J.: How to do Things with Words. Harvard University Press (1962)

[2] Bach, K., Harnish, R.: Linguistic Communication and Speech Acts. MIT Press (1979)

[3] Breiter, P., Sadek, A Rational Agent as the Kernel of a Cooperative Spoken Dialogue System. In: Intelligent Agents III (LNAI Vol. 1193). Springer-Verlag (1997) 189-204

[4] Cohen, P., Levesque, H.: Communicative Actions for Artificial Agents. In: Proc. of the First International Conference on Multi-Agent Systems. AAAI Press (1995) 65-72

[5] Cohen, P., Perrault, R.: Elements of a Plan-Based Theory of Speech Acts. Cognitive Science 3 (1979) 177-212

[6] Cole, P., Morgan, J.: Syntax and Semantics, Vol. 3: Speech Acts. Academic Press (1975)

[7] FIPA: "Agent Communicative Act Library Specification" (2000 version) available at http://www.fipa.org/specs/fipa00037.

[8] Labrou, Y., Finin, T., Peng. Y.: Agent Communication Languages: The Current Landscape. IEEE Intelligent Systems, 14 (1999) 45-52

[9] Patil, R., Fikes, R, Patel-Schneider, P., McKay, D. Finin, T., Gruber, T., Neches, R.: The DARPA Knowledge Sharing Effort: Progress Report. In Rich, C., Swartout, W. Nebel, B. (eds.): Proc. Knowledge Representation and Reasoning (KR'92). Cambridge (1992) 777-788

[10] Sadek, M.: A Study in the Logic of Intention. In Rich, C., Swartout, W., Nebel, B. (eds.): Proc. Knowledge Representation and Reasoning (KR'92). Cambridge (1992) 462-473

[11] Sadock, J.: Toward a Linguistic Theory of Speech Acts. Academic Press (1975)

[12] Searle, J.: What is a Speech Act? In Black, M. (ed.): Philosophy in America. Cornell Univ. Press (1965) 221-239

[13] Searle, J.: Speech Acts. Cambridge University Press (1969)

[14] Singh, M.: A Semantics for Speech Acts. Annals of Math. and Art. Int. 8 (1993) 47-71

[15] Wooldridge, M.: Verifying that Agents Implement a Communication Language. In Proc. of 16th Conference on Artificial Intelligence (AAAI-99). AAAI Press (1999) 52-57

Monadic Memoization towards Correctness-Preserving Reduction of Search

Richard Frost

School of Computer Science, University of Windsor
Ontario, Canada
richard@uwindsor.ca

Abstract. Memoization is a well-known method which makes use of a table of previously-computed results in order to ensure that parts of a search (or computation) space are not revisited. A new technique is presented which enables the systematic and selective memoization of a wide range of algorithms. The technique overcomes disadvantages of previous approaches. In particular, the proposed technique can help programmers avoid mistakes that can result in sub-optimal use of memoization. In addition, the resulting memoized programs are amenable to analysis using equational reasoning. It is anticipated that further work will lead to proof of correctness of the proposed memoization technique.

1 Introduction

Search is ubiquitous in artificial intelligence. For many difficult problems, search time grows exponentially with respect to the problem size. In many cases, the time can be significantly reduced by making sure that parts of the search space are not revisited unnecessarily. In some cases a reduction in complexity is possible.

1.1 The Need for Selective Memoization

Some parts of a program can benefit from memoization whereas other parts will not. For example, the time complexity of the following naive Fibonacci program can be reduced from exponential to liner through memoization:

```
fib 0 = 1
fib 1 = 1
fib n = fib (n - 1) + fib (n - 2)
```

The reason for the improvement is that in the unmemoized form, the second call of `fib (n - 2)` repeats a computation carried out by the first call `fib (n - 1)`. Expansion of the computation tree will illustrate the extent of recomputation that can be prevented by memoization. On the other hand, consider a program that simply returns the first element of a list. This operation has constant complexity. Memoization would require that the list input be compared with lists

Y. Xiang and B. Chaib-draa (Eds.): AI 2003, LNAI 2671, pp. 66–80, 2003.

used as keys in the memo table. The complexity would now be O(length of the list).

A solution, therefore, is to provide the programmer with a function *memoize* which can be used to memoize selected parts of the program. The function *memoize* takes care of updating and using the memo tables when the memoized parts of the program are executed.

1.2 The Need for Pure Functionality?

One should only memoize parts of the program that are purely functional in the sense that the result should only depend on the input arguments, and there should be no side-effects, The reason for this is that memo-table lookup uses inputs as keys. If the result depends on other values that are accessible through non-functional calls, then the memo-table will return the wrong result. Also, if a component has side effects, such as having a subcomponent that updates a counter, then memoization will corrupt those side effects.

Therefore, a necessary, but not sufficient requirement for correct memoization, is that the components to be memoized must be purely functional. We use the term "correct" in the sense that a correct memoization process should not change the results returned by a program, or its termination properties. Many search algorithms are very complicated and programmers will be tempted to use non-functional features in their implementation. For example, the use of updateable global variables for various types of bookkeeping. It is difficult to determine which parts of a complicated program are purely functional, and can therefore be safely memoized. One solution to this is to use a pure-functional programming language such as Miranda (Turner 1985) or Haskell (Hudak et.al. 1992) to implement complicated search algorithms.

1.3 Memoization in a Pure-Functional Language

Use of a pure-functional programming language prevents certain types of inaccurrate use of memoization, and it also facilitates the construction of a memoization process that is amenable to analysis through equational reasoning, but it has a major disadvantage: memo tables cannot be implemented as updateable stores. Update is a side effect and is not allowed in a pure-functional language.

The solution is to provide the memo table as an extra argument to functions that are to be memoized. Memoized functions now begin by checking to see if the original input argument has an entry in the memo-table given as the additional input argument. If it has, then that result is returned with the original memo-table. If not, the body of the function is executed and the result is returned together with a new memo-table containing the additional entry. This is not as inefficient as it might first appear. Pure-functional programming languages use pointers to re-use parts of input arguments; this is safe owing to the fact that there is no update and therefore no possibility of corruption of a value that is pointed to.

1.4 The Need for a more Formal Technique

Two problems remain. Firstly, it is possible to make a mistake in threading the memo table through components resulting in sub-optimal use of memoization. For example, consider the following, which uses notation that is defined more fully in section 2.

```
(p $then q) inp = []      , if rp  = []
                = q rp    , otherwise
                  where  rp = p inp
```

This defines an infix higher-order operator `then` which takes two functions `p` and `q` as input and which returns a function `h` as result, such that when that function is applied to some input `inp` it begins by computing the value `rp` by applying `p` to `inp`. If `rp` is an empty list, then `h` returns an empty list as result. If `r` is not empty, then `h` returns the result obtained by applying `q` to `rp`.

The higher-order function `then` is similar to the operator of function composition, but differs in that the second function is not applied if the first function returns an empty list as result. This kind of operator can be used to prevent infinite looping that would otherwise occur when certain mutually-recursively defined functions are composed. Revising the definition of `then` in order to thread memo tables through `p` and `q` results in the following:

```
(p $mthen q) (inp, table) =  ([], table), if rp = []
                          =  q (rp, tp), otherwise
                             where
                             (rp, tp) = p (inp, table)
```

Even with this relatively simple definition, we have made a mistake. If the function `p` returns an empty list, possibly signifying that it failed in some sense when applied to the input, it may have done some work that has been recorded in the memo table `tp` returned as result. The definition above loses the results of this work. The correction is to replace `([], table)` with `([], tp)`. We show later that this error can result in exponential behavior for a top-down fully-backtracking language recognizer that would otherwise have cubic complexity after memoization.

A second problem is that the ad hoc memoization process can result in other errors which corrupt the result returned. The memoization process described so far requires that every function which is to be memoized, or which interacts with a function to be memoized, must be modified to accept the extra memo table input and return the table as part of its output.

To overcome these shortcomings, a more structured/formal technique for memoizing the search algorithm is required. We need to guarantee that the memo-tables are threaded through appropriate components of the search algorithm, and we need to prove that the memoization process preserves the correctness of the search algorithm.

1.5 Monadic Memoization

According to Wadler (1990), monads were introduced to computing science by Moggi (1989) who noticed that reasoning about programs that involve handling of state, exceptions, I/O, or non-determinism can be simplified, if these features are expressed using monads. Inspired by Moggi's ideas, Wadler proposed monads as a way of systematically adding such features to algorithms. The main idea behind monads is to distinguish between the type of values and the type of computations that deliver these values. This paper shows how monads can be used to systematically memoize search algorithms in a way that facilitates proof of correctness of the memoization process. A monad is a triple (`M, unit, bind`) where `M` is a type constructor, and *unit* **and** *bind* are two polymorphic functions. `M` can be thought of as a function on types, that maps the type of values into the type of computations producing these values. `unit` is a function that takes a value and returns a corresponding computation; the type of `unit` is `a -> Ma`. The function `bind` represents sequencing of two computations where the value returned by the first computation is made available to the second (and possibly subsequent) computation. The type of `bind` is

```
Ma -> (a -> Mb) -> Mb
```

In order to use monads to provide a structured method for adding new effects to a functional program, we begin by identifying all functions that will be involved in those effects. We then replace those functions, which can be of any type `a -> b`, by functions of type `a -> Mb`. In effect, we change the program so that selected function applications return a computation on a value rather than the value itself. This computation may be used to add features such as state to the program. In order to effect this change, we use the function `unit` to convert values into computations that return the value but do not contribute to the new effects, and the function `bind` is used to apply a function of type `a ->Mb` to a computation of type `Ma`. Having made these changes, the original program can be obtained by using the identity monad `idm`, as defined later. In order to memoize the program we simply replace the identity monad with the state monad `stm` and make a few local changes as required to the rest of the program.

1.6 Advantages of this Approach

The technique facilitates the systematic and controlled use of memoization in search algorithms, such that:

1. The approach is purely functional and equational reasoning can be used to analyze the program and to prove correctness of the memoization process. The use of monads further facilitates such proof.
2. As with many other proposed methods for memoization, the use of a "memoize" function allows the search engineer to selectively memoize parts of the search algorithm.
3. The approach helps to avoid mistakes in threading memo-tables through functions in the correct order and therefore facilitates optimal use of memoization.

1.7 Structure of the Rest of the Paper

We begin by briefly describing related work. We then introduce some notation. We follow this with a description of how monadic memoization can be used to improve the complexity of the naive Fibonacci program. At first, the reader may think that we are developing some heavy-duty techniques to achieve what can be achieved by a simple rewrite of the naive Fibonacci program. However, section 8 shows that **the same monad, and the same memoization function** can be used to systematically and easily improve the complexity of relatively complicated definitions of operators that can be used to quickly build top-down fully-backtracking language recognizers. Such recognizers are of interest in their own right as they are highly modular, simple to construct, and can accommodate ambiguous grammars. We then sketch out a proof of correctness of the memoization process. We conclude by discussing how the approach can be applied to other search problems.

2 Overview of Related Work

1. Memoization has a long history. Michie (1968) and Hughes (1985) are two of many publications on this subject.
2. Threading of memo tables though functional programs has been described by Field and Harrison (1988) and investigated in detail by Khoshnevisan (1990).
3. Wadler (1990) introduced the use of monads to add effects to pure functional programs. Subsequent publications (e.g. Wadler,1995) include discussion of the use of monads to structure functional recognizers and evaluators.
4. Koskimies (1990) convincingly explains how how top-down fully-backtracking language processors are considerably more modular than those constructed with alternative search strategies.
5. Norvig (1991) shows how memoization of top-down fully-backtracking language recognizers written in LISP results in processors that are as efficient and as general as Earley's algorithm, with the exception that they cannot accommodate. left-recursive productions. Norvig's recognizers have cubic complexity compared to exponential behavior of the unmemoized versions. Selective memoization is achieved through use of a memoization function defined in terms of an updateable memo-table. Owing to the fact that memoization involves updateable state Norvig's approach requires considerably more complex apparatus than equational reasoning to prove correctness of the memoization process.
6. The use of higher-order functions (combinators) to build functional language processors, which is described in detail in section 7, was originally proposed by Burge (1975) and further developed by Wadler (1985) and Fairburn (1986). It was first used to build evaluators for ambiguous natural-language by Frost and Launchbury (1989). It is now frequently used by the functional-programming community for language prototyping and natural-language processing. In the following, we describe the approach with respect

to language recognizers although the technique can be readily extended to parsers, syntax-directed evaluators and executable specifications of attribute grammars (Frost 1992 and 2002, Augusteijn 1993, and Leermakers 1993).

7. Leermakers (1993), Frost (1993), and Johnson (1995) have described different techniques by which the functional approach to building top-down backtracking language processors can be extended to accommodate left-recursive productions. It is interesting to note that Johnson's approach uses memoization, together with continuation-passing-style programming, to achieve efficiency and accommodate left-recursion.
8. Frost and Szydlowski (1995) show how purely-functional top-down backtracking language processors can be memoized, and proved that time complexity can be reduced from exponential to cubic.
9. The use of monads to systematically memoize purely-functional top-down recognizers was suggested to the author of this paper by an anonymous reviewer of the paper by Frost and Szydlowski. The reviewer identified the mistake in the threading of memo-tables through the **`$then`** operator as discussed earlier, and pointed out that this would result in exponential behaviour for certain inputs. A brief discussion of the potential use of monads in memoization of pure-functional recognizers was given at the end of their revised paper.
10. Panitz (1996) has developed a technique for proving termination for lazy functional languages by abstract reduction, and has used this technique to prove termination for a sub-set of recognizers that can be constructed using the combinators of Frost and Launchbury, a variation of which are used in section 7.

3 Notation

We use the notation of the programming language Miranda[1] (Turner 1985), rather than a functional pseudo-code, in order that readers can experiment with the definitions directly. The technique can be implemented in other languages.

- `f = e` defines `f` to be a constant-valued function equal to the expression `e`.
- `f a1 ... an = e` can be loosely read as defining `f` to be a function of `n` arguments whose value is the expression `e`. However, Miranda is a fully higher-order language — functions can be passed as parameters and returned as results. Every function of two or more arguments is actually a higher order function, and the correct reading of `f a1 ... an = e` is that it defines `f` to be a higher-order function, which when *partially-applied* to input `i` returns a function `f' a2 ... an = e'`, where `e'` is `e` with the substitution of `i` for `a1`.
- The notation for function application is simply juxtaposition, as in `f x`. Function application has higher precedence than any operator.

[1] Miranda is a trademark of Research Software Ltd.

- Function application is left associative. For example, `f x y` is parsed as `(f x) y`, meaning that the result of applying `f` to `x` is a function which is then applied to `y`. Round brackets are used to override the left-associative order of function application. For example, the evaluation of `f (x y)` requires `x` to be applied to `y`, and then `f` to be applied to the result.
- In a function definition, the applicable equation is chosen through pattern matching on the left-hand side in order from top to bottom, together with the use of guards following the keyword `if`.
- Round brackets with commas are used to create tuples, e.g. `(x, y)` is a binary tuple. Square brackets and commas are used to create lists, e.g. `[x, y, z]`. The empty list is denoted by `[]` and the notation `x : y` denotes the list obtained by adding the element `x` to the front of the list `y`. The notation `"x1 .. xn"` is shorthand for `['x1', .. ,'xn']`
- `t1 -> t2` is the type of functions with input type `t1` and output type `t2`. `f :: e` states that `f` is of type `e, and t1 == t2` declares t1 and t2 to be type synonyms.
- The notation `x => y` means that `y` is the result of evaluating `x`.

4 Rewriting the Fibonacci Program in Monadic Form – The Identity Monad

We begin by defining the identity monad `idm` (Wadler 1995), in which the computation simply returns its value, and `bind` is `postfix` function application. The star `*` means any type.

```
idm * == *

unit1 :: * -> idm *
unit1 x = x

bind1 :: idm * -> (* -> idm **) -> idm **
(p $bind1 k) = k p
```

We can use this monad to restructure the naive Fibonacci program given in section 1. This is the first step towards memoization:

```
fib1 0 = unit1 1
fib1 1 = unit1 1
fib1 n = fib1 (n - 1) $bind1 f
         where f a = fib1 (n - 2) $bind1 g
                     where g b = unit1 (a + b)
```

Such restructuring is relatively "clerical": Firstly, we apply `unit1` to all values which are returned by expressions that do not include calls to the `fib` function. Secondly, we analyze the expression `fib (n - 1) + fib(n - 2)` and work out an order of computation: begin with `fib (n - 1)` bind this result into the next computation `f` which involves `fib (n - 2)`, bind the result into the next part of the program `g` which returns a computation obtained by applying `unit1` to the result of the addition. The resulting program `fib1` acts like `fib` in all respects. Simple equational rewriting shows that `fib` and `fib1` are equal.

5 Adding a Counter to the Fibonacci Program – The State Monad

Before we memoize the `fib` function, we show how to add a counter to it using the state monad `stm` (Wadler 1995) defined as follows:

```
stm * == state -> (*, state)
state == num
unit2 :: * -> stm *
unit2 a = f where f t = (a, t)
bind2 :: stm * -> (* -> stm **) -> stm **
(m $bind2 k) = f
              where f x = (b, z)
                          where (b, z) = k a y
                                         where (a, y) = m x
```

In this case, the state is a numeric counter. The function `unit2` takes a value `v` and returns a computation of type `state -> (*, state)`, which takes a state as input and returns the value `v` paired with the state unchanged. For example when `unit2 5` is applied to state `6` (the counter), the result returned is `(5, 6)`.

The operator (infix function) `$bind2` is a little difficult to understand at first. Roughly, it takes a computation `m` which "involves" a value `v` of type `*` as one operand, and a function `k` of type `(* -> stm **)` as the other operand. It picks out the value `v`, applies `k` to it, and returns a computation that when applied to state returns a pair consisting of the result of the function application and the state unchanged. Basically, `$bind` creates a computation that threads the state through its components. To add a counter to the `fib` function, we simply replace the identity monad with the state monad, and make a small change so that the counter is incremented each time `cfib` is called:

```
fib 0 = unit2 1
fib 1 = unit2 1
fib n = cfib (n - 1) $bind2 f
        where f a =  cfib (n - 2) $bind2 g
                     where g b = unit2 (a + b)

cfib    =   count fib

count f n c =  (res, k + 1)
                where
                (res, k) = f n c
```

The function `cfib` computes the same value as before paired with the count. For example:

```
cfib 20 0 => (10946,21891)
```

6 Memoizing the Fibonacci Program

In order to memoize the `fib` function, we use the same state monad `stm`, change the type of the state from a numeric counter to a memo-table of type `[([char], [(num, num)])]`, and replace the count function with the function `memoize`. Note that the definition of `unit2` and `bind2` remain the same.

```
state == [([char],[(num, num)])]
fib 0 = unit2 1
fib 1 = unit2 1
fib n = mfib (n - 1) $bind2 f
        where f a =  mfib (n - 2) $bind2 g
                     where g b = unit2 (a + b)

mfib   =  memoize "fib" fib
```

The memoized function `mfib` has liner time and space complexity, compared to exponential behavior of the original `fib` program. To illustrate the flexibility of this approach. The definition above can be modified so that only the left-branching call of `fib` is memoized. Interestingly, the execution data for the resulting program `left_mfib` shown on the next page, suggests that such memoization results in polynomial complexity.

```
fib 20 => 10946                                        time  = 235015
fib 21 => 17711                                        time  = 380274
fib 22 => 28657                                        time  = 615308
fib 50 => ran out of heap space

mfib 20  [] => (10946, updated table)                  time  = 5494
mfib 21  [] => (17711, updated table)                  time  = 5775
mfib 22  [] => (28657, updated table)                  time  = 6056
mfib 200 [] => (453973694165307953197296969697410619233826,
                               updated table)          time  = 41046

left_mfib 20 []  => (33429, updated table)             time = 19171
left_mfib 50 []  => (20365011074, updated table)       time = 165170
left_mfib 100 [] => (573147844013817084101, table)     time = 1034095
left_mfib 200 [] => (453973694165307953197296969697410619233826,
                               updated table)          time  = 7133195
```

The memo table in this case is of type `[([char],[(num, num)])]`, i.e. a list of pairs. Each pair contains a string of characters identifying a function that has been memoized, followed by a list containing pairs of input/output values computed for that function. The reason for having multiple pairs in the table is that this allows a number of different functions in one program to be memoized and their results stored in a single table. We make use of this feature in later examples. The `memoize` function, defined below, creates a new function from the function to be memoized, such that the new function performs lookup and update operations on the memo table being threaded through the computation.

```
memoize name f inp table
   = (res, update newtable name inp res), if (table_res = [])
   = (table_res!0, table)                , otherwise
     where table_res       = lookup name inp table
           (res, newtable) = f inp table

lookup name inp table
  = [], if res_in_table = []
  = [res | (i, res) <- (res_in_table!0); i = inp], otherwise
    where
    res_in_table = [pairs | (n, pairs) <- table; n = name]

update [] name inp res  = [(name,[(inp, res)])]
update ((key, pairs):rest) name inp res
  = (key,(inp,res):pairs):rest, if key = name
  = (key,pairs): update rest name inp res, otherwise
```

Linear space complexity can be achieved by a simple modification to the memoize function to keep only the two most-recently computed values in the memo table.

7 A Modular Top-Down Fully-Backtracking Language Recognizer

One approach to implementing language processors in a modern functional programming language is to define a number of higher-order functions (combinators) which, when used as infix operators (denoted in this paper by the prefix `$`), enable processors to be built with structures that have a direct correspondence to the grammars defining the languages to be processed. For example, the function `s`, defined below is a recognizer for the language defined by the grammar `s ::= 'a' s s | empty`

```
s =  (a $then s $then s) $orelse empty
a =  term  'a'
```

The combinators that we use in this paper are from Frost and Launchbury (1989):

```
recognizer  == [char] -> [[char]]

term   :: char -> recognizer
term c   []    = []
term c (t:ts)  = [ts], if t  = c
               = []  , otherwise

orelse :: recognizer -> recognizer -> recognizer
(p $orelse q) inp =   unite (p inp) (q inp)

then   :: recognizer -> recognizer -> recognizer
(p $then q)  inp =  apply_to_all q (p inp)

apply_to_all q []      = []
apply_to_all q (r:rs) =  unite (q r) (apply_to_all q rs)

empty x = [x]

unite x y = mkset (x ++ y)
```

According to the approach, a recognizer is a function mapping an input string to a list of outputs. The input is a sequence of tokens to be analyzed. Each entry in the output list is a sequence of tokens yet to be processed. Using the notion of "failure as a list of successes" (Wadler 1985) an empty output list signifies that a recognizer has failed to recognize the input. Multiple entries in the output occur when the input is ambiguous. In the examples in this paper it is assumed that all tokens are single characters.

The simplest type of recognizer is one that recognizes a single token at the beginning of a sequence of tokens. Such recognizers may be constructed using the higher-order function `term` defined above. The following illustrates use of `term` in the construction of a recognizer for the character `'c'`. The empty list in the second example signifies that `c` failed to recognize a token `'c'` at the beginning of the input

```
c         =  term 'c'
c "cxyz" => ["xyz"]
c "xyz"  => []
```

Alternate recognizers may be built using the higher-order function `orelse` as defined above. When a recognizer `p $orelse q` is applied to an input `inp`, the value returned is computed by uniting the results returned by the separate application of `p` to `inp` and `q` to `inp`. The following illustrates use of `orelse` in the construction of a recognizer `c_or_d` and the subsequent application of this recognizer to three inputs.

```
c_or_d   = c $orelse d
c_or_d "cxyz" => ["xyz"]
c_or_d "abc"  => []
```

Sequencing of recognizers is obtained through use of the higher-order function **then** defined as above. When a recognizer `p $then q` is applied to an input `inp`, the result returned is a list obtained by applying `q` to each of the results in the list returned by `p`. The following illustrates use of **then** in the construction of a recognizer **c_then_d**, and the subsequent application of **c_then_d** to two inputs:

```
c_then_d = c $then d
c_then_d "cdxy" => ["xy"]
c_then_d "cxyz" => []
```

The "empty" recognizer always succeeds and returns a singelton list containing the input. The **unite** operation removes duplicates in the results returned by **orelse** and **then**. The example application given below illustrates use of the recognizer `s` from the previous page, and shows that the prefixes of the input ``aaa'' can be successfully recognized in different ways. The empty string in the output, denoted by `""`, corresponds to cases where the whole input ``aaa'' has been recognized as an `s`.

```
s   "aaa"  => ["","a","aa","aaa"]
```

Recognizers constructed in this way are easy to construct and are highly modular, but have exponential time complexity.

8 Use of the State Monad to Memoize Language Recognizers

The advantage of the proposed approach will now become apparent. In order to memoize recognizers that are constructed using the method described above, we simply rewrite the definitions of the combinators to use the state monad, change the state (memotable) to be of type `[([char],[([char], [[char]])])]` to be compatible with the input/output types of recognizers, and apply the **memoize** function from the Fibonacci example.

```
stm * == state -> (*, state)

state == [([char],[([char], [[char]])])]
term2 c   []     = unit2 []
term2 c (t:ts)   = unit2 [ts], if t  = c
                 = unit2 []  , otherwise
(p $orelse2 q) input
                = p input $bind2 f
                  where
                  f a =  q input $bind2 g
                         where
                         g b = unit2 (unite a b)
(p $then2 q)  input = p input }bind2 f
```

```
                              where
                              f a = apply_to_all2 q a
empty2 x = unit2 [x]
apply_to_all2 q []        = unit2 []
apply_to_all2 q (r:rs)    = q r $bind2 f
                                where
                                f a = apply_to_all2 q rs $bind2 h
                                      where
                                      h b = unit2 (unite a b)


ms = memoize "ms" (a2 $then2 ms then2 ms) $orelse2 empty2
a  =  term2  'a'
```

The memoized recognizer `ms` has worst-case cubic complexity (theoretically this is as good as is possible) compared to the exponential complexity of the original recognizer `s`:

```
s "aaaa" => ["","a","aa","aaa","aaaa"]          time =    5879
s "aaaaaaaaaa"
    => ["","a","aa","aaa","aaaa","aaaaa","aaaaaa","aaaaaaa",
          "aaaaaaaa","aaaaaaaaa","aaaaaaaaaa"] time = 1938151
s "aaaaaaaaaaaaaaaaaaaa"      => ran out of space

ms "aaaaaaaaaa" []            => as above       time =   43642
ms "aaaaaaaaaaaaaaaaaaaa" [] => correct result time =  388837
```

Notice that the structure of the definition of `ms` is the same as the original except for application of the memoize function. The monad and the memo-table function definitions are hidden from the programmer who is constructing the recognizer. Notice also that the programmer can choose which parts of the recognizer to memoize.

9 A Sketch of Proof of Preservation of Correctness

One of the advantages of the proposed approach is that the resulting memoized programs are completely functional and, therefore, equational reasoning can be used in their analysis. In particular, equational reasoning can be used to prove that the memoization process is correct in the sense that termination properties are preserved and that the memoized program returns the same results as the original:

1. Preservation of termination properties can be proven by:
    (a) Showing that the table size is bounded, that update and lookup terminate, and therefore that the `memoize` function terminates for finite input.

(b) Showing that rewriting the program in monadic form does not affect termination properties. For the recognition example, the technique of abstract reduction, which Panitz (1996) developed and has already used to prove termination of a sub-set of recognizers that can be built with the combinators given in the paper, can be used to show that the monadic form of the combinators have the same termination properties.

2. To prove that memoization does not change the results returned, we need to show that the values computed in the monadic form of the program are the same as those in the original, and that update and lookup do not corrupt those values. Although not trivial, it is anticipated that equational reasoning can be readily used to do this.

The resulting proofs apply to any program that is memoized using the technique described in this paper.

10 Concluding Comments

The approach described in this paper can be applied to other types of problem where memoization can be used to avoid reexamining already-visited parts of the search space. Such problems include scheduling, planning, sub-sequence analysis, pattern recognition, database query optimization, theorem proving, computational physics, conformational search in crystallography, and many others. Current work includes construction of the complete proof of preservation of correctness, and investigation of the use of the technique in other search problems.

References

[1] Augusteijn, L. (1993) *Functional Programming, Program Transformations and Compiler Construction.* Philips Research Laboratories. ISBN 90–74445–04–7.

[2] Burge, W. H. (1975) *Recursive Programming Techniques.* Addison-Wesley Publishing Company, Reading, Massachusetts.

[3] Fairburn, J. (1986) Making form follow function: An exercise in functional programming style. *University of Cambridge Computer Laboratory Technical Report* No 89.

[4] Field, A. J. and Harrison, P. G. (1988) *Functional Programming.* Addison-Wesley Publishing Company, Reading, Massachusetts.

[5] Frost, R. A. (2002) W/AGE The Windsor Attribute Grammar Programming Environment. *IEEE Symposia on Human Centric Computing Languages and Environments HCC'2002* 96–99.

[6] Frost, R. A. and Szydlowski, B. (1995) Memoizing purely-functional top-down backtracking language processors. *Science of Computer Programming" (27) 263 – 288.*

[7] Frost, R. A. (1993) 'Guarded attribute grammars'.*Software Practice and Experience.*23 (10) 1139–1156.

[8] Frost, R. A. (1992) Constructing programs as executable attribute grammars. *The Computer Journal* 35 (4) 376 – 389.

[9] Frost, R. A. and Launchbury, E. J. (1989) Constructing natural language interpreters in a lazy functional language'. *The Computer Journal – Special edition on Lazy Functional Programming,* **32** (2) 108 – 121.
[10] Hudak, P., Wadler, P., Arvind, Boutel, B., Fairbairn, J., Fasel, J., Hammond, K., Hughes, J., Johnsson, T., Kieburtz, D., Nikhil, R., Peyton Jones, S., Reeve, M., Wise, D. and Young, J. (1992) Report on the programming language Haskell, a non-strict, purely functional language, Version 1.2 *ACM SIGPLAN Notices* 27 (5).
[11] Hughes, R. J. M. (1985) Lazy memo functions. In proceedings. *Conference on Functional Programming and Computer Architecture* Nancy, France, September 1985. Springer-Verlag Lecture Note Series 201, editors G. Goos and J. Hartmanis, 129 - 146.
[12] Johnson, M. (1995) Squibs and Discussions: Memoization in top-down parsing. *Computational Linguistics* 21 (3) 405–417.
[13] Khoshnevisan, H. (1990) Efficient memo-table management strategies. *Acta Informatica* 28, 43–81.
[14] Koskimies, K. Lazy recursive descent parsing for modular language implementation. *Software Practice and Experience,* 20 (8) 749–772, 1990.
[15] Leermakers, R. (1993) *The Functional Treatment of Parsing.* Kluwer Academic Publishers, ISBN 0–7923–9376–7.
[16] Michie, D. (1968) 'Memo' functions and machine learning. *Nature* 218 19 - 22.
[17] Moggi, E. (1989) Computational lambda-calculus and monads. *IEEE Symposium on Logic in Computer Science,* Asilomar, California, June 1989, 14–23.
[18] Norvig, P. (1991) Techniques for automatic memoisation with applications to context-free parsing. *Computational Linguistics* 17 (1) 91 - 98.
[19] Panitz (1996) Termination proofs for a lazy functional language by abstract interpretation. `citeseer.nj.nec.com/panitz96termination.html`
[20] Turner, D. (1985) A lazy functional programming language with polymorphic types. *Proc. IFIP Int. Conf. on Functional Programmiong Languages and Computer Architecture.* Nancy, France. Springer Verlag Lecture Notes in Computer Science 201.
[21] Wadler, P. (1985) How to replace failure by a list of successes, in P. Jouannaud (ed.) *Functional Programming Languages and Computer Architectures* Lecture Notes in Computer Science 201, Springer-Verlag, Heidelberg, 113.
[22] Wadler, P. (1990) Comprehending monads. *ACM SIGPLAN/SIGACT/SIGART Symposium on Lisp and Functional Programming,* Nice, France, June 1990, 61–78.
[23] Wadler, P. (1995) Monads for functional programming, Proceedings of the Bastad Spring School on Advanced Functional Programming, ed J. Jeuring and E. Meijer. *Springer Verlag Lecture Notes in Computer Science* 925.

Searching Solutions in the Crypto-arithmetic Problems: An Adaptive Parallel Genetic Algorithm Approach

Man Hon Lo and Kwok Yip Szeto

Department of Physics
Hong Kong University of Science and Technology
Clear Water Bay, Hong Kong, SAR, China
phszeto@ust.hk

Abstract. The search for all solutions in the crypto-arithmetic problem is performed with two kinds of adaptive parallel genetic algorithm. Since the performance of genetic algorithms is critically determined by the architecture and parameters involved in the evolution process, an adaptive control is implemented on two parameters governing the relative percentages of preserved (survived) individuals and reproduced individuals (offspring). Adaptive parameter control in the first method involves the estimation of Shannon entropy associated with the fitness distribution of the population. In the second method, parameters are controlled by average values between the extreme and median fitness of individuals. Experiments designed to test two algorithms using crypto-arithmetic problems with ten and eleven alphabets are analyzed using the average first passage time to solutions. Results are compared with exhaustive search and show strong evidence that over 85% of the solutions in each problem can be found using our adaptive parallel genetic algorithms with a considerably faster speed. Furthermore, adaptive parallel genetic algorithm with the second method involving the median is consistently faster than the first method using entropy.

Keywords: Crypto-arithmetic problems, Parallel Search, Genetic Algorithm

1 Introduction

Crypto-arithmetic problem [1,2] is a difficult problem for searching. The landscape of its solutions is quite disjoint and the usual methods of search may find some solutions with relative ease, but will encounter increasing difficulties if all solutions are to be found. Therefore, it is an ideal case for testing the efficiency of various searching methods. Of particular interest here is the performance of different parallel algorithms, where the space of solutions is partitioned so that communication between groups with different searching techniques in different regions can be coordinated. Under this context, parallel genetic algorithm seems to be a good candidate not only

Y. Xiang and B. Chaib-draa (Eds.): AI 2003, LNAI 2671, pp. 81-95, 2003.

because of the intrinsic parallelism in genetic algorithm, but also because of the ease of testing various models of communications between different populations.

Genetic algorithms [3, 4] are adaptive search techniques, which differ from other stochastic optimization methods such as simulated annealing because a population of solutions is processed in parallel. Methods using statistical mechanics have been proposed to describe the evolution of the populations by deterministic equations of a small number of macroscopic quantities for the average effects of genetic operators [5]. This kind of approach complements a microscopic description of the dynamical systems in high-dimensional space [6] in that generic features can be extracted and the dimensionality of the problem is greatly reduced. Extension of this approach has been made on the investigation of the effect of correlation between generations on the dynamics [7]. There are other approaches to understand the dynamics of genetic algorithms by looking at the effective degrees of freedom of complex systems and the dependence of their evolution on scale under various coarse graining [8,9]. These recent approaches by physicists have added many new insights to this highly effective but rather ad-hoc method.

In GA, individuals with high fitness are always preserved, while the unfit ones are replaced by new individuals in the next generation. The merit of evolution is the preservation of the best group of potential solutions, which can take part in reproducing offspring with higher fitness. This often ensures a monotonic increase of the total fitness of populations, though sometimes leads to the problem of early convergence similar to the problem of trapping in the local optimum encountered in simulated annealing.

There are many applications of genetic algorithms because of its intrinsic parallelism and the success of the algorithms is more like an art because of the lack of guiding principles for the choice of parameters, genetic operators, and the method of representation. It is our attempt to use the method in stochastic dynamics and statistical physics to investigate the problem of early convergence and the optimization of first passage time to solution. An understanding of the relation between the diversity of the population and early convergence is very important. First of all, we can avoid trapping in local optima by maintaining certain level of diversity. Also, a proper control of the first passage time to solution can be used as a trade off in maximizing the mean rate of drift to the global optima. In this paper, we focus on parallel genetic algorithm as a method of search. In PGA, there is communication between several populations, so that individuals can be exchanged regularly during optimization to enhance the efficiency. Two key parameters of interest are the levels of communication between individual in a population and between neighboring populations [1,2]. Optimization by PGA in solving problems with a few variables and a unique solution is quite common, but its use in finding solutions of the crypto-arithmetic problem is so far not well tested. [2] In the past, we have used annealed genetic algorithms and parallel genetic algorithms to solve real life problems such as error message classification [10], financial time series forecasting [11-13]. Also, applications to resource allocation [14, 15] have been quite successful. One such approach will be to construct M parallel populations so that the effective size of GA is NM. This is effectively a coarse-grained parallel GA architecture and various population distributions and topologies have been suggested [16-22]. It is found that all the aforementioned cooperative methods show improvements in various degrees in the search of optimal solutions for constraint problems such as the crypto-arithmetic problem.

One of the common difficulties encountered in crypto-arithmetic problem is the application of the standard crossover and mutation operators, as there often appear many individuals representing illegal combinations. Moreover, the efficiency of any searching method in the crypto-arithmetic problem generally decreases when more and more solutions have been located. To address these typical difficulties in search, new method of crossover and mutation are used in PGA for the crypto-arithmetic problem. Moreover, we use the permutation operator to accelerate the searching process by periodically altering the searching space.

In order to install adaptive parameter control in the division of populations, we introduce a new method called the Median-Selection method, and compare it with both the entropy-estimating method [23,24] and exhaustive search. For the entropy-estimating method, Shannon's entropy is estimated by a periodic sampling on the fitness of individuals, which is used to determine the survival rate and reproduction rate of individuals in populations. In our Median-Selection method, the extreme values and the median of the distribution of fitness of the populations are used in scheduling the survival rate and reproduction rate of individuals in populations. Our experiments indicate that both adaptive methods improve the efficiency of PGA and are much better than exhaustive search, especially in the first 85% of the solutions. In section 2, we first define the crypto-arithmetic problem and the encoding scheme used. We then discuss the various genetic operators in section 3, followed by a discussion of the basic architecture of the parallel genetic algorithm in section 4. Two adaptive parameter-tuning methods are introduced in section 5 and 6. Finally, the performance evaluation, results and discussions are in section 7 and 8.

2 Crypto-arithmetic Function and Encoding Scheme

Crypto-arithmetic problem involves the assignment of integers to alphabets so that certain alphabetical equation is satisfied. This is therefore a searching problem, which difficulty is scalable. We will test two such problems with parallel genetic algorithms. The following two equations are used as examples,

$$NANCY + JASON = SZETO \tag{1}$$

$alphabets \in \{0,1,\ldots,9\}$. This problem involves ten alphabets. Therefore, the number of possible solutions is $10! \approx 3.63\times10^6$, though only 27 solutions are valid. The second equation is

$$TIME + SPACE = MONEY \tag{2}$$

$alphabets \in \{0,1,\ldots,10\}$. This problem involves eleven alphabets. There are $11! \approx 3.99\times10^7$ possible solutions, but only 120 are valid. In our convention, each word represents a number of base ten. For example,

$$TIME = T\cdot10^3 + I\cdot10^2 + M\cdot10^1 + E\cdot10^0$$

We find it convenient to use a *distance function* Ω to measure the distance to solutions of a chromosome. Fitness is then simply some constant minus Ω. Maximizing fitness corresponds to the minimization of distance. We define Ω as an absolute value of the difference between the two sides of the crypto-arithmetic equation. For example, (1) corresponds to the problem of:

$$\text{Minimize } \Omega = | NANCY + JASON - SZETO | \quad \textbf{(3)}$$

Equation (2) can be written in the same way. A high fitness of a chromosome will give a small distance value to solutions. With this data structure, chromosomes are encoded as a string of distinguishable numbers. As two or more alphabets representing a number is not allowed, classical methods for crossover and mutation will produce illegal individuals. This will require repair algorithms to ensure that they are legal. To avoid these hassles, we employ recombination crossover and concurrent transposition for mutation instead of the usual genetic operators.

3 Genetic Operators

3.1 Recombination Crossover

Recombination crossover is used to reproduce offspring by choosing two subsequences of genes from two individuals (or parents) separately, and swapping such subsequences without altering the order and position of other genes. A subsequence of genes is selected by two random cut points, which serve as boundaries for the swap. In order to reproduce legal individuals, such a swap requires a series of mappings of numbers. A number involved in the swap will be mapped to the other one with respect to their original position. For example:

Parent 1 = (1 2 3 4 5 6 7 8 9 0) ➔ Child 1 = (4 2 3 1 8 7 6 5 9 0)
Parent 2 = (4 5 2 1 8 7 6 9 3 0) ➔ Child 2 = (1 8 2 4 5 6 7 9 3 0)

with mapping: (1 ⇔ 4), (8 ⇔ 5), (7 ⇔ 6), and (6 ⇔ 7).

3.2 Mutation

Mutation operator is constructed by the method of simple inversion. It reproduces a child by randomly selecting two positions of genes on a parent and the subsequence between these points is reversed, i.e.

Parent 3 = (1 2 3 4 5 6 7 8 9 0) ➔ Child 3 = (1 2 6 5 4 3 7 8 9 0)

3.3 Permutation OperatorMutation

Continual exploration of different regions of the solution space is partially accomplished by the use of permutation operator. As crypto-arithmetic problem usually contains many solutions, there is always a danger for any search algorithm to get trapped in a particular region of the solution space. In order to escape from these traps, permutation operator can be used periodically in our parallel genetic algorithm, so as to accelerate the searching process and discover as many solutions as possible. The permutation operator builds a new population by making a shift of genes of all chromosomes in a population, without altering the relative orders of genes. Such a shift of genes is done by randomly dividing individuals into two subsequences of genes and swapping the positions of these two subsequences of genes, i.e.,

Population 1	➔	New Population 1
(1234567890)		(3456789012)
(1234567890)		(3456789012)
(1234567890)		(3456789012)
(2345678901)		(4567890123)
…………		…………

4 Basic Architecture

Only parallel genetic algorithms with invariable population scale (fixed number K of population and N individual) will be discussed in this paper. Given a randomly initialized population $P^k(0)$, $k = 1,2,\ldots K$, GA applies genetic operators on the k-th population to generate the next population $P^k(1)$, thereby yielding a series of generated populations $\boldsymbol{P^k} = \{P^k(0), P^k(1), \ldots, P^k(t), \ldots\}$ in general. In a PGA with our basic architecture, $P^k(t+1)$ is constructed by a preserved part $P_1^k(t)$, and reproduced parts $P_2^k(t)$ from crossover and $P_3^k(t)$ from mutation. Corresponding parameters R_S, R_C and R_M are introduced to the architecture to control the amount of each sub-population. In each generation, individuals are sorted according to their fitness (or distance value) and some fit ones are copied to form $P_1^k(t)$ in the k-th population. Then some individuals are selected out of the sorted ones with certain strategy and genetic operators are performed on them to generate $P_2^k(t)$ and $P_3^k(t)$. Finally, if the group of individuals in the preserved part remains unchanged for a certain number of generations, T, which means $P_1^k(t) = P_1^k(t+1) = \cdots = P_1^k(t+T)$, a permutation operator will be then be applied. If a solution is produced in the population, the position of that individual will be replaced by copying another one from another population, after the solution is recorded. The whole procedure is shown in Fig.1.

Parameters R_S, R_C and R_M are explained as follows.

R_S : *Preservation fraction.* It determines the number of individuals $N_1 = R_S N$ in $P^k(t+1)$ directly copied from $P^k(t)$. These copied individuals form the sub-population $P_1^k(t)$ and are the survivors.

R_C: *Reproduction fraction by crossover.* It determines the number of individuals $N_2 = R_C N$ in $P^k(t+1)$ generated by crossover. These individuals form the sub-population $P_2^k(t)$.

R_M: *Reproduction fraction by mutation.* It determines the number of individuals $N_3 = R_M N$ in $P^k(t+1)$ generated by mutation. These individuals form the sub-population $P_3^k(t)$.

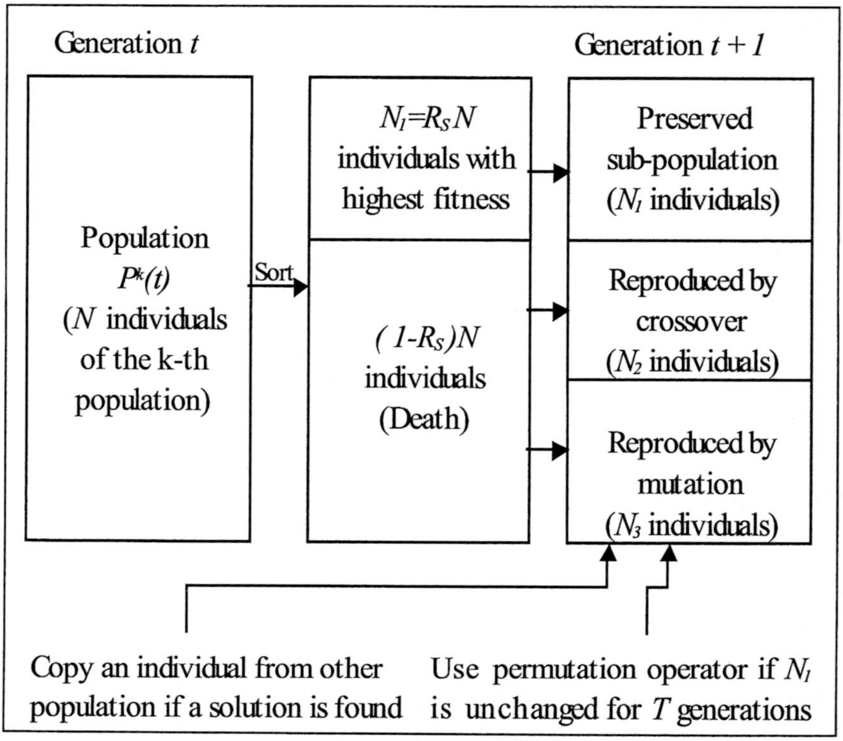

Fig. 1. The basic architecture

5 Entropy-Estimating Method

5.1 Estimation of Population Entropy

Shannon's entropy is introduced to measure the concept of population entropy [23]. Suppose that the solution space of a given problem can be divided into M different subspaces, denoted as $A_1, A_2, \ldots, A_M$. Then, we can check for a given individual from a given population to which solution space it belongs. Assume that the probability of that individual belonging to subspace A_i is p_i, $i = 1,2,\ldots,M$. With $p_i \geq 0$, and $\sum_{i=1}^{M} p_i = 1$, we define population entropy as follow,

***Definition* 1:** The *Population Entropy, S_p,* is the quantitative measure of the diversity of a population P. S_p can be calculated with the following equation.

$$S_p(p_1, p_2, \ldots, p_M) = -\sum_{i=1}^{M} p_i \ln p_i \tag{4}$$

The defining procedures of entropy estimation are:

Step 1: *Estimate the solution space S*. Let the minimum and maximum *distance value* of all populations $\{P^1(t), P^2(t), \ldots, P^K(t)\}$ be $\Omega_{\min}$ and $\Omega_{\max}$. Define $\hat{\xi}_{\min} = (1-\delta)\cdot\Omega_{\min}$, $\hat{\xi}_{\max} = (1+\delta)\cdot\Omega_{\max}$ and $\hat{\lambda} = \hat{\xi}_{\max} - \hat{\xi}_{\min}$, with δ is a small positive number (e.g. 0.05). The solution space S of that population is measured by the range $[\hat{\xi}_{\min}, \hat{\xi}_{\max}]$ with the length $\hat{\lambda}$.

Step 2: Estimate of the number M of subspaces in S. Let the scale of the total population be N_{total} and the first estimate of M be $M = N_{total}$. Divide the range of $[\hat{\xi}_{\min}, \hat{\xi}_{\max}]$ into $\hat{M}$ segments and label them as $i = 1,2,\ldots,M$. Therefore, the i-th segment is $[\hat{\xi}_{\min} + \hat{\lambda}\cdot(i-1)/\hat{M}, \hat{\xi}_{\max} + \hat{\lambda}\cdot i/\hat{M}]$, for $i = 1,2, \ldots, M-1$. Generally, the M-th one is $[\hat{\xi}_{\min} + \hat{\lambda}\cdot(\hat{M}-1)/\hat{M}, \hat{\xi}_{\max}]$. Count the number of individuals in each segment and denote this number by M_i, $i = 1,2,\ldots,\hat{M}$.

Step 3: Estimate of the probability distribution. Make use of $\hat{p}_i = M_i/\hat{M}$, $i = 1,2, \ldots, \hat{M}$ as the estimate for p_i, which is the probability that individual belong to the i-th segment.

Step 4: Estimate of the Population Entropy. Assuming the sampling size is large. We can use $\hat{S}_p(t) = -\sum_{i=1}^{M} \hat{p}_i \ln \hat{p}_i$ as the estimate of the population entropy in Equation (4).

5.2 The Adaptive Architecture of Entropy-Estimating Method

After installing the population entropy estimation on the basic architecture of our parallel genetic algorithm, we proceed to incorporate adaptive parameter control. The evolving procedure of such an adaptive algorithm is shown in Fig.2.

With such an adaptive architecture, the population entropy can be estimated regularly in a certain period of generations. $\alpha(t)$ and $\beta(t)$ are the controlling parameters that determined by the population entropy. Once these parameters are updated, they will be applied to generate new populations.

5.3 Parameter Adaptation

The controlling parameters $\alpha(t)$ and $\beta(t)$ are governed by the following equations:

$$\alpha(t) = A\cdot\exp(-B\cdot S(t)) \tag{5}$$

$$\beta(t) = C - D\cdot\exp(-B\cdot S(t)) \tag{6}$$

Here A, B, C and D are positive constants, and the exponential form is motivated by consideration the Boltzmann factor in statistical mechanics. We have $S_{min} = 0$ and $S_{max} = \ln N$. After simplification, these constants can be determined as below:

$$A = \alpha_{\max} \tag{7}$$

$$B = \frac{1}{\ln N} \cdot \ln\left(\frac{\alpha_{nax}}{\alpha_{\min}}\right) \tag{8}$$

$$C = \beta_{\min} + \alpha_{\max} \cdot \frac{\beta_{\max} - \beta_{\min}}{\alpha_{\max} - \alpha_{\min}} \tag{9}$$

$$D = \alpha_{\max} \cdot \frac{\beta_{\max} - \beta_{\min}}{\alpha_{\max} - \alpha_{\min}} \tag{10}$$

We choose $\alpha_{\min} = 0.1$, $\alpha_{\max} = 0.9$, $\beta_{\min} = 0.1$, $\beta_{\max} = 0.5$.

More information on this method can be found in [24]

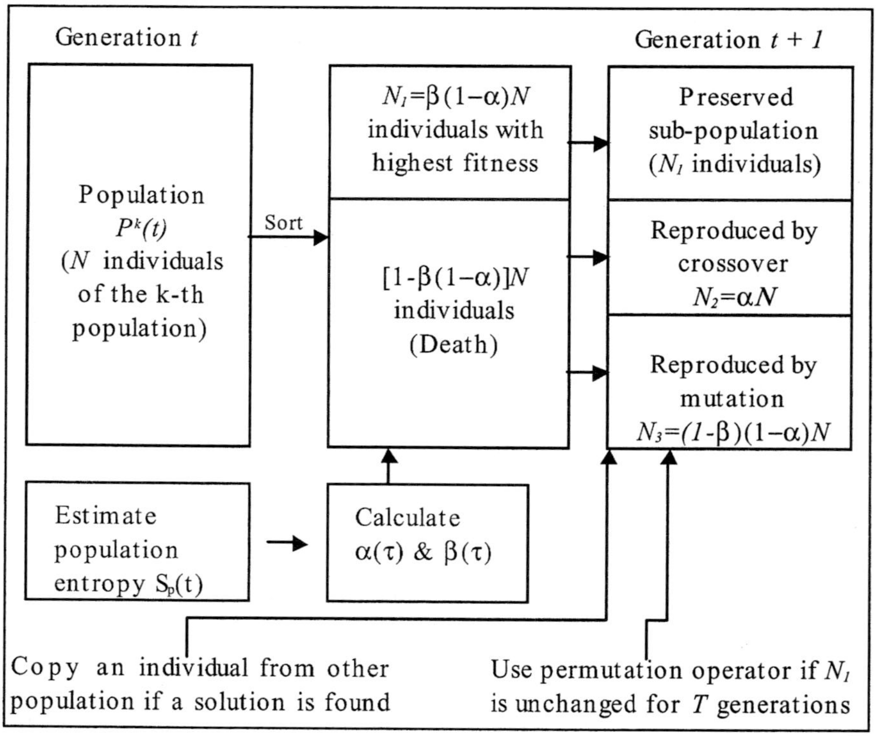

Fig. 2. The adaptive architecture of Entropy-estimating method

6 Median-Selection Method

6.1 Criteria in Selection Individuals

The importance of Darwinian evolution in the context of our optimization problem lies in the selection of survivors with high fitness. However, the fitness threshold for survival is quite arbitrary. To make a rather unbiased decision, we employ the *median* of the fitness distribution as the threshold. Statistically, an individual with fitness somewhere above the median is considered good and some of them are allowed to survive to the next generation. We thus introduce the following parameter,

$$\Psi = \Omega_{median} - \frac{1}{2}(\Omega_{median} - \Omega_{smallest}) \tag{11}$$

Individuals with distances to solution less than Ψ will survive. Furthermore, we only pick those individuals with distinguishable *distance* values smaller than Ψ as survivors, in order to increase the diversity of the survival group. Similarly, the allocation of the reproduction groups can be controlled as follows:

$$\Phi = \Omega_{median} + \frac{1}{2}\left(\Omega_{\text{largest}} - \Omega_{median}\right) \tag{12}$$

The number of individuals with distance values in the range $[\Psi,\Phi]$ will determine the mutation rate, while the ones greater than that of the Φ will determine the crossover rate.

6.2 The Adaptive Architecture of Median-Selection Method

By using the two parameters, the adaptive structure can be constructed as follow:

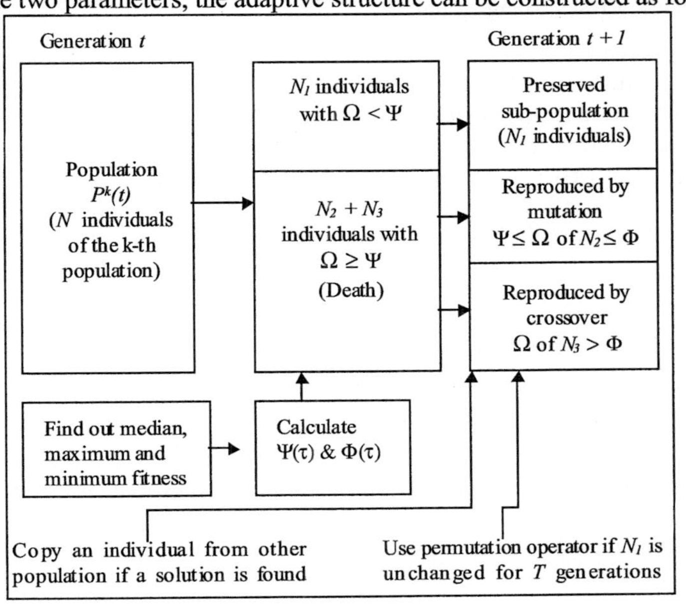

Fig. 3. The adaptive architecture of the Median-Selection method

Table 1. The setting of the PGAs

Number of populations K	10
Number of individuals N in each population	10
Total number of individuals ($K \times N$)	100
Permutation operator triggering period T	100 generations

Since searching process is computationally intensive, our Median-Selection method is specifically designed to minimize the computation involved in tuning the adaptive parameter in genetic algorithm. It is clear that this new method involves a lot less computation than the entropy estimating method.

7 Experimental and Results

We perform experiments to compare the performance of three methods of solution for the crypto-arithmetic problem. The first method is exhaustive search, which will ensure that we will find all the solutions. The second method is our adaptive PGA with entropy-estimating method (EPGA). The third method is called MPGA, which is the adaptive PGA with the Median-Selection method. The information of our parallel genetic algorithms is listed below:

7.1 Average First Passage Time

According to the descriptions of Eq.(1) and Eq.(2), there are many valid solutions that can fit the problems. In the searching process using parallel genetic algorithms, a particular solution may appear many times. In order not to duplicate the time record of a particular solution which has been found, we only record the CPU time that the particular solution first appears. This is called the first passage time. The searching process stops when all distinguishable solutions of the problems are found. Such experiments are done 100 times and we take an average of the first passage time to solutions.

7.2 Comparison with Parallel Genetic Algorithms and Exhaustive Search

We compare the performance of three different ways to solve the crypto-arithmetic problem. These include adaptive EPGA, MPGA and exhaustive search. The key element to measure the efficiency of such methods is the CPU time used to find solutions. All experiments are done on the same PC. The average time needed to find the last solution in EPGA is used as a normalization factor. The normalized average first passage times for PGAs are shown in Fig.4 and Fig.5.

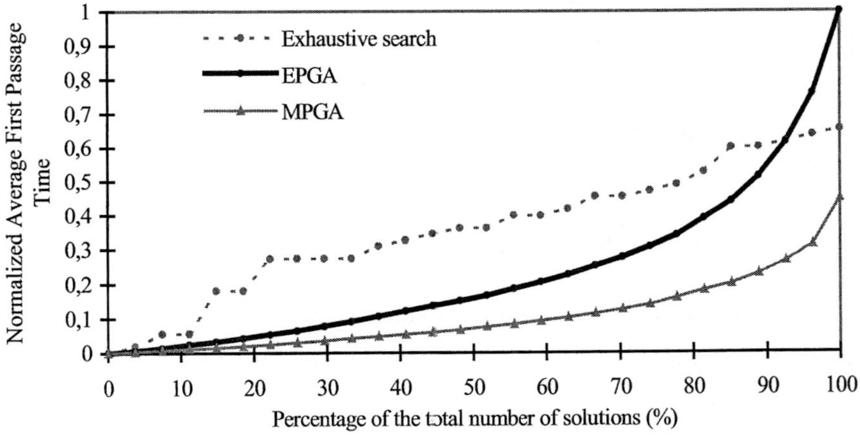

Fig. 4. Comparison of performance of Adaptive Parallel Genetic Algorithms and exhaustive search on crypto-arithmetic problem consisting of ten alphabets (Eq.1). EPGA and MPGA stands for entropy estimating PGA and Median-Selection PGA methods in controlling the adaptive parameters

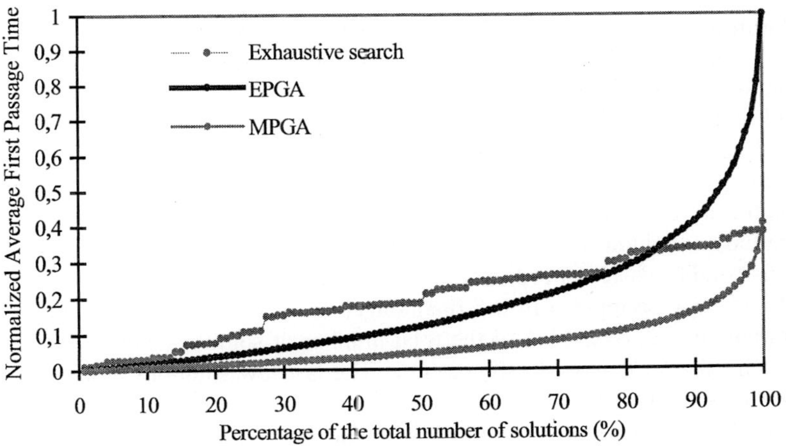

Fig. 5. Comparison of performance of Adaptive Parallel Genetic Algorithms and exhaustive search on crypto-arithmetic problem consisting of eleven alphabets (Eq.2). EPGA and MPGA stand for entropy estimating PGA and Median-Selection PGA methods in controlling the adaptive parameters

It can be seen that both curves of adaptive parallel genetic algorithm with entropy-estimating method (EPGA) and with Median-Selection method (MPGA) may have intersection with the curves of exhaustive search. Let the *percentage of the total number of solutions* be X, and let the *normalized average first passage time* be Y. Then these intersections can be summarized as follows.

Table 2. Summary of intersection points

Number of alphabets	Curve of intersection	X	Y	Total number of solutions
10	EPGA	92.6%	0.61	27
	MPGA	Nil	Nil	
11	EPGA	85%	0.33	120
	MPGA	100%	0.38	

7.3 Standard Deviation of the First Passage Time

The standard deviation of the distribution of first passage time to solution can be interpreted as the risk to find a solution within a given time. Using the standard deviation of the first passage time needed to find the *last* solution in EPGA as the normalization factor, we compare the risk for finding solutions with our two methods of PGA in Fig.6 and Fig.7.

8 Discussion

According to Fig.4 and Fig.5, parallel genetic algorithm with Median-Selection method (MPGA) generally out performs the entropy-estimating method (EPGA). This is due to the simplicity of parameters tuning in MPGA, so that all solutions can be found quickly. This result reveals that the choice of method in parameters control is quite important in searching solutions with genetic algorithm. We see that MPGA only involves computing the median and the extreme values of the fitness distribution, while the entropy estimation involves a lot more computation. We observe that during the initial and middle stages of the searching process, both PGAs locate solutions with a considerably faster speed than exhaustive search. However, this advantage of adaptive PGA disappears in the final stage, when most solutions have been found. From the table 2, over 85% of the total number of solutions can be found by PGAs with time shorter than exhaustive search. The last few solutions require considerable more times as the probability of finding a new solution to the problems during the searching process decreases rapidly with the number of known solution(s). PGAs inevitably consume some time in finding some known solutions again and again. This fact can also be supported by Fig.6 and Fig.7. Since the standard deviation of the first passage time is a measure of the risk of finding a solution, Fig.6 and Fig.7 reveal that the risk increases monotonically with the number of known solutions, and rises substantially at the final stage (90% to 100%).

Finally, the common problem of early convergence in optimization is handled well by MPGA. Usually, early convergence in genetic algorithm can be detected from the fitness distribution, which approaches a delta function. In MPGA, this is by design prevented, because we use the median in the selection mechanism for survivors, and also only distinguishable individuals are enlisted as survivors. Furthermore, MPGA has the advantage of the flexible choices in Ψ and Φ. These two time dependent adaptive parameters can be tuned, as we can choose different values in the denominator to replace our present choice of 2. This flexibility allows MPGA to cope with different searching problems.

We see that adaptive parallel genetic algorithm with the Median-Selection method of parameters tuning is quite good in solving search problem with rough solution space. The flexibility and simplicity of our method suggests its possible applications in many other kinds of search problems. K.Y. Szeto acknowledges the support of grant from RGC of Hong Kong, with grants HKUST 6144/00P and 6157/01P.

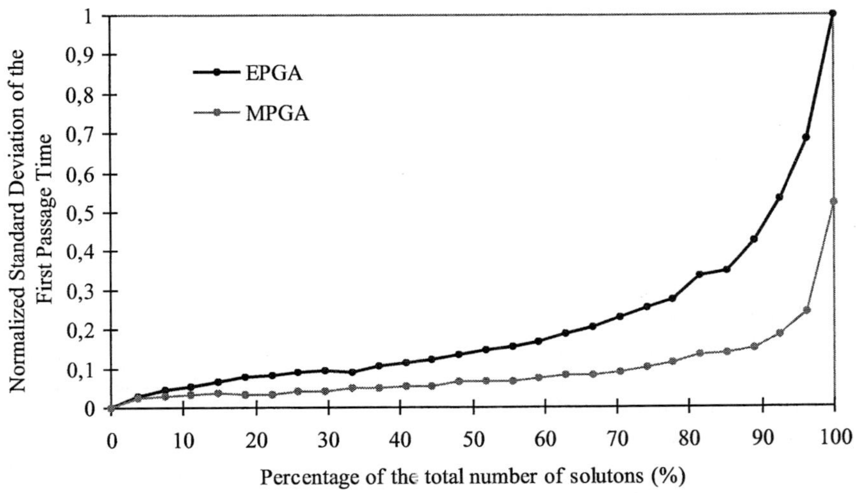

Fig. 6. Risk in finding solutions of Adaptive PGAs with entropy-estimating method and Median-Selection method on crypto-arithmetic problem consisting of ten alphabets (Eq.1)

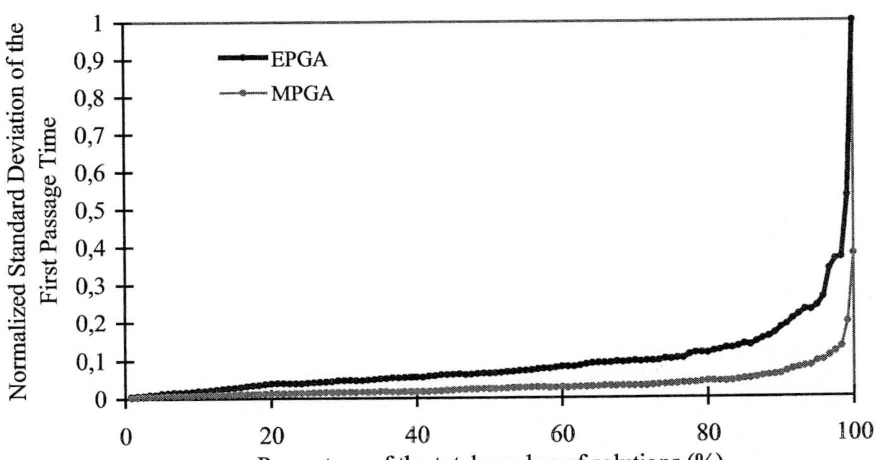

Fig. 7. Risk in finding solutions of Adaptive PGAs with entropy-estimating method and Median-Selection method on crypto-arithmetic problem consisting of eleven alphabets (Eq.2)

References

[1] K.Y. Szeto. K.H.Cheung and S.P. Li, Effects of dimensionality in parallel genetic algorithms. Proceeding of the World Multiconference on Systemics, Cybernetics, and Informatics, ISAS'98, Ed. N. Callaos, T. Yang, and J. Aguillar, Orlando, Vol.2, 322-326, 1998.

[2] S.P. Li, K.Y. Szeto, "Crytoarithmetic problem using parallel Genetic Algorithms," Mendl'99, Brno, Czech, 1999.

[3] I.H. Holland, Adaptation in Natural and Artificial Systems (1975) Ann Arbor, MI: University of Michigan Press.

[4] D.E.Goldberg, Genetic Algorithms in Search, Optimization, and Machine Learning, 1989, Addison- Wesley.

[5] M. Rattray and I.L. Shapiro, The dynamics of a genetic algorithm for a simple learning problem. I. Phys. A: Math. Gen. Vol.29, 7451-7473 (1996).

[6] M.D. Vose and G.E. Liepins. Complex systems. Vol.5. 31 (1991).

[7] S. Bornholdt, Genetic algorithm dynamics on a rugged landscape, Phys. Rev. E, Vol.57, 3853-3860 (1998).

[8] C.R. Stephens and H. Waelbroeck, Effective degrees of freedom in genetic algorithms, Phys. Rev. E, Vol.57,3251-3264(1998).

[9] A.B. Djurisic, J.M. Elazar, and A.D. Rakic, Genetic algorithms for continuous optimization problems-a concep of parameter-space size adjustment. J.Phys. A: Math.Gen. Vol.30, 7849-4861(1997).

[10] Lau, K.Y. Szeto, K.Y.M. Wong, and D.Y. Yeung; A Hybrid Expert System for Error Message Classification. (Proceedings of the International Workshop on Applications of Neural Networks to Telecommunications 2, Eds., J. Alspector. R. Goodman,and T.X. Brown, Lawrence Erlbaum Associates, 1995) p339-346.

[11] L.Y. Fong, K.Y. Szeto, "Rule extraction in short memory time series using genetic algorithms," *European Physics Journal B*, Vol.20, 569-572(2001)

[12] K. Y. Szeto and K.H. Cheung; Multiple Time Series Prediction using Genetic Algorithms Optimizer (Proceedings of the International Symposium on Intelligent Data Engineering and Learning) Hong Kong, IDEAL '98, Oct. 1998

[13] K. Y. Szeto, K.O. Chan, K.H. Cheung; Application of genetic algorithms in stock market prediction, Proceedings of the Fourth International Conference on Neural Networks in the Capital Markets: Progress in Neural Processing, Ed. A.S. Weigend, Y. Abu-Mostafa, and A.P.N. Refenes; World Scientific, NNCM-96, 1997. p95-103

[14] Tam, K. Y., Genetic Algorithm, Function Optimization, and Facility Layout Design, *European Journal of Operational Research,* Vol. 63, 1992, 322-346.

[15] Tam. K. Y. and S. K. Chan, "Solving Facility Layout Problems with Geometric Constraint using Parallel Genetic Algorithms: Experimentation and Findings..' *to appear in International of Production Research.*

[16] R. Tanese, Distributed genetic algorithms. Proceedings of Third International Conference on Genetic Algorithm, Lawrence Erlbaum Associates. Hillsdale, *N.J.,* 1989,434-439.

[17] H. Muehlenbein, M. Schomish and J. Born, The parallel genetic algorithm as function optimizer. Parallel Computing, 17(1991),619-632.

[18] J .H. Nang, A simple parallelizing scheme of genetic algorithm on distributed-memory multiprocessors. International Journal of High Speed Computing, 6, 3(1994). 451-474.

[19] R. Campanini, G. DiCaro, M. Villani, I. D'antone, and G. Giusti, Parallel architectures and intrinsically parallel algorithms: genetic algorithms. Inter. J. of Modern Physics CS, 1(1994)95-112.

[20] B.A. Shapiro and J. Navetta, A massively parallel genetic algorithm for RNA secondary structure prediction. The Journal of supercomputing. 8(1994),195-207.

[21] S.H. Clearwater, T. Hogg, B.A. Huberman. Cooperative Problem Solving, in Computation: the micro and the macro view; edited by B,A. Huberman, World Scientific, 1992. p.33-70.

[22] S.H.Clearwater, B.A. Huberman, and T.Hogg, Cooperative solution of constraint satisfaction problem. Science, V.254, 1991, p.l 181-1183.

[23] K.Y. Szeto, Seminar given in Kansei Advanced Research Center, CRL, Osaka, Japan 1999.

[24] Rui Jiang, K. Y. Szeto, Yupin Luo, Dongcheng Hu. An entropy-estimating approach to adaptive genetic algorithms. *IEEE Transactions on Evolutionary Computation*. Submitted. 2001.

Stochastic Local Search for Multiprocessor Scheduling for Minimum Total Tardiness

Michael Pavlin[1], Holger Hoos[1], and Thomas Stützle[2]

[1] Department of Computer Science, University of British Columbia
{mpavlin,hoos}@cs.ubc.ca
[2] Department of Computer Science, Darmstadt University of Technology
stuetzle@informatik.tu-darmstadt.de

Abstract. The multi-processor total tardiness problem (MPTTP) is an $\mathcal{NP}$-hard scheduling problem, in which the the goal is to minimise the tardness of a set of jobs that are processed on a number of processors. Exact algorithms like branch and bound have proven to be impractical for the MPTTP, leaving stochastic local search (SLS) algorithms as the main alternative to find high-quality schedules. Among the available SLS techniques, iterated local search (ILS) has been shown to be an effective algorithm for the single processor case. Therefore, here we extend this technique to the multi-processor case, but our computational results indicate that ILS performance is not fully satisfying. To enhance ILS performance, we consider the use of population-based ILS extensions. Our final experimental results show that the usage of a population of search trajectories yields a more robust algorithm capable of finding best known solutions to difficult instances more reliably and in less computation time than a single ILS trajectory.

1 Introduction

Given a set of tasks to complete and some set of processors which can complete them we find ourselves face to face with a scheduling problem. These problems arise in any number of situations ranging from fulfilling orders in a factory or scheduling processes on a multitasking computer to automated decision making in a robot. In this paper we consider the identical multi-processor scheduling problem, where the objective function is to minimise the total tardiness. Throughout this paper this problem is referred to as the MPTTP. The single processor variant, where only a single processor is available for processing the tasks, will be referred to as SPTTP.

The SPTTP was shown to be $\mathcal{NP}$-hard [10] and based on this result, MPTTP can be shown to be at least as hard via reduction [17]. This implies that it is unlikely that polynomial time algorithms exist to solve these problems [14]. The MPTTP is also very difficult to solve in practice, which is reflected by the fact that optimization algorithms for these problems rapidly become intractable as the problem size grows. Consequently, approximation algorithms of various forms have been developed. Construction heuristics and stochastic local search

Y. Xiang and B. Chaib-draa (Eds.): AI 2003, LNAI 2671, pp. 96–113, 2003.

(SLS) algorithms form the bulk of this work. We concentrate on a particular SLS algorithm, Iterated Local Search (ILS), which was shown to be the top performer on the SPTTP [7, 4]. However, on the MPTTP, the single search trajectory generated by ILS shows stagnation behaviour. To improve performance, we apply population-based extensions of ILS, where a population of search trajectories, each based on a single ILS trajectory, is evolved using operators gleaned from evolutionary computation and a memetic algorithm.

This paper is organised as follows. In Section 2 we introduce the problem formulation for the SPTTP and the MPTTP and give a brief review of algorithmic approaches to the MPTTP and related problems. Section 3 introduces ILS, the primary SLS technique considered in this paper, and Section 4 gives details on the single-trajectory ILS algorithms as well as the population-based extensions which were implemented. Section 5 presents the computational results for our new ILS algorithms and we conclude in Section 6.

2 The Multiprocessor Total Tardiness Problem

Problem Formulation. In the MPTTP we are given a set of jobs $\{job_0, job_1, \ldots, job_{(n-1)}\}$ that have to be processed on a set of m identical processors. Each job_i has associated an integer processing time p_i and an integer due date, d_i. A schedule consists of a list of jobs for each processor and a start time for each job such that the following conditions are satisfied:

- each job must be assigned to exactly one processor;
- jobs cannot be preempted;
- jobs cannot overlap on a single processor.

Given a schedule, the *tardiness* of job_i is $T_i := max\{0, C_i - d_i\}$, where C_i is the completion time of job_i and the total tardiness is given by $\sum T := \sum_{i=0}^{n-1} T_i$. The objective in the MPTTP is to find a schedule with minimal total tardinesss. Note that the SPTTP is a special case of the MPTTP with $m = 1$.

Total tardiness is a regular objective function, which means that it is monotonic with respect to all C_i. In the MPTTP, we only need to consider schedules without idle time on any single processor. Solving the MPTTP involves finding an assignment from jobs to processors and for each single processor finding a permutation of all the jobs assigned to it. One possible way to represent schedules is as an assignment of a permutation of the jobs to each processor (*permutation representation*). The order of the jobs assigned to a processor is determined by the order in which the jobs appear in the permutation.

An alternative to the above permutation representation is to translate a schedule into a single list of all jobs ordered by non-decreasing start times. From this list, a new schedule at least as good as the initial schedule can be created by greedily assigning jobs from the start of the list to processors. Together, the greedy algorithm and the list form a valid representation for minimizing tardiness which we will call the *priority-list representation.* This representation will be considered for both population and single trajectory algorithms.

Exact Algorithms. Several branch and bound algorithms for the SPTTP and MPTTP have been proposed and studied in the literature. Computational results show that even fairly large instances of the SPTTP with up to 500 jobs can be solved in reasonable computation time [5, 26]. This is possible by exploiting fundamental domination properties of the SPTTP reported by Emmons [11] and Lawler [17]. However, the good performance of exact algorithms for the SPTTP does not carry over to the MPTTP. The branch and bound algorithm by Azizoglu and Kirca becomes impractical for instances with more than 15 jobs on multiple processors [2]. This difference stems from the added difficulty of achieving an appropriate partitioning of jobs to processors. Because of the poor performance of exact algorithms, local search based algorithms have to be used for solving large MPTTP instances.

Note that the much worse performance of exact algorithms in the multi-processor version compared to the single-processor case appears to be rather typical and was observed also for exact algorithms attacking the related problem of minimising the number of tardy jobs [22].

Stochastic Local Search. Various inexact algorithmic strategies have been considered for the MPTTP. Approximation algorithms such as construction, list scheduling, and decomposition heuristics have been used to quickly find reasonable solutions [17]. In this paper we concentrate on Stochastic Local Search (SLS) approaches to this problem. SLS algorithms combine a local search algorithm with a probabilistic component. Well known SLS algorithms include tabu search, variable neighbourhood search, ant colony optimization (ACO) and evolutionary algorithms. All of these have been applied to MPTTP or, to closely related problems [22, 6, 9, 23, 12, 13, 4].

Currently, the best performing SLS algorithms for the single processor total tardiness and for the more difficult total weighted tardiness problem, where each job is given an additional weight, indicating its importance, are iterated local search algorithms [7, 4]. Therefore, we also considered this type of SLS algorithm first to attack the MPTTP; ILS is presented in more detail in the next subsection.

3 Iterated Local Search (ILS)

Iterated Local Search is a simple yet powerful SLS method, which is witnessed by excellent results computational results for a variety of combinatorial optimisation problems like the travelling salesman problem (TSP), the quadratic assignment problem (QAP) and several scheduling problems (see [18] for an overview). In a nutshell, ILS builds a biased random walk in the space of the local optima (with respect to some local search algorithm). This is done by iteratively perturbing a locally optimal solution, then applying a local search algorithm to obtain a new locally optimal solution, and finally using an acceptance criterion for deciding from which of these solutions to continue the search. To implement an ILS algorithm, the following four sub-procedures have to be defined: GenerateInitialSolution generates a starting point for the search, LocalSearch implements

```
procedure Iterated Local Search
    s0 = GenerateInitialSolution
    s* = LocalSearch(s0)
  repeat
      s' = Perturbation(s*)
      s*' = LocalSearch(s')
      s* = AcceptanceCriterion(s*, s*')
  until termination condition met
end
```

Fig. 1. Algorithmic outline of ILS

a (possibly complex) improvement procedure, Perturbation computes a perturbation of a given locally optimal solution, and AcceptanceCriterion chooses from which of two candidate solutions the search is continued. A general algorithmic outline of ILS is given in Figure 1.

An efficient ILS algorithm for the SPTTP was described by den Besten [9]; this ILS was extended to the single-machine total weighted tardiness problem (SMTWTP) [7], which is known to be significantly harder than the unweighted SPTTP [1]. Excellent results for the SMTWTP were also reported for the iterated Dynasearch algorithm of Congram, Potts and Van de Velde [4]. Den Besten's ILS for the SPTTP uses the interchange neighbourhood in the local search and also in the perturbation. This neighbourhood considers all moves which consist of selecting two jobs, job_i and job_j, $i \neq j$, and exchanging their positions. The local search is a best-improvement algorithm which terminates at the first local optimum encountered. The perturbation is implemented by applying a fixed number of random interchange moves to the candidate solution. New solutions are accepted if they are a strict improvement over the original solution and the algorithm terminates when a certain solution quality is reached or some maximum computation time expires. This algorithm performed well and found optimal solutions reliably.

Typically, ILS is a single-trajectory method. However, ILS can easily be extended into a population-based SLS method by independently applying a standard ILS algorithm to a population, that is, a set of candidate solutions, and allowing some limited interaction between the population elements. Such extensions have strong similarities to well-known population-based search metaphors such as evolutionary algorithms [3, 19] and, in particular, memetic algorithms [20, 21].

Population-based extensions of ILS were independently proposed in [15, 25] and applied to the TSP and the QAP. In particular, Stützle reported results for different levels of interaction among the individual ILS search threads: no-interaction, replace-worst and population-ILS. *No-interaction*, as the name implies, is simply a population of ILS trajectories run in isolation, when they have all completed the best solution is chosen. *Replace-worst* is similar but during the evaluation sometimes replaces the worst current solution by the best solution. *Population-ILS* generates a population of solutions and choses, based on a selection operator, one individual to pursue a number of ILS iterations. The new solution is inserted into the population and the process is iterated. Stützle had varying degrees of success with this approach. The performance of all three variants was found to be quite similar and appeared to depend strongly on the given problem instance. Similarly, Hong, Kahng, and Moon [15] presented computational results that did not indicate a significant improvement of the population-based ILS over a single-trajectory ILS for the TSP.

4 Our ILS Algorithms for the MPTTP

We implemented two single trajectory ILS algorithms and several population-based ILS algorithms plus a memetic algorithm for the MPTTP. These algorithms are based upon den Besten's ILS implementation for the SPTTP [9]. These two single trajectory algorithms, ILS3 and ILSRES, differ in how they perform the perturbation phase.

4.1 Single Trajectory ILS

Initialisation and Termination. In all the experiments reported here we considered random starting solutions. To do so, first a list is generated containing the jobs in random order. Then, the head of the list is recursively removed and assigned to the processor with the smallest total processing time. This randomised initialisation scheme is a reasonable choice for initialising a number of trajectories in a population based extension when the initial solution population should be scattered around the search space and was used for most experiments for both single and multiple trajectory algorithms.

Additionally, we considered ordering the list of jobs by non-increasing processing time (GPT) and by non-decreasing due date (EDD) and then assigning the jobs in the same way. Both GPT and EDD were used for testing selection strategies (below). GPT results in a poor initial schedule and EDD results in a very good initial schedule. The EDD construction heuristic was also used as an initialisation procedure in the protocol for finding optimal solution.

The algorithm terminates when a designated tardiness value is achieved or some maximum computation time limit is reached.

Local Search. The local search procedure is divided into two phases. The first phase applies a local search to the jobs assigned to each processor independently of the other processors and reorders the jobs to minimize the total tardiness on the individual processor (we call this local search procedure LocalSearchOnSingleProcessors). The second phase moves jobs between the different processors and, thus, modifies the assignment of jobs to processors (we call this local search procedure LocalSearchBetweenProcessors).

Both phases are iterative improvement algorithms which repeatedly interchange two jobs. The interchange neighbourhood was chosen based upon the

Table 1. Best and first improvement selection strategy time and solution qualities for finding local minimums over all 200 job single processor sample problems with three different initialisation schemes

Algorithm	Best Improvement		First Improvement	
init	Avg. time (s)	Avg. soln	Avg. time (s)	Avg. soln
EDD	1.47	140353	5.34	139793
GPT	1.86	140267	22.19	139807
Random	1.52	140493	10.01	139794

work of den Besten [9]. Both, best and first improvement selection strategies as well as several other variations were considered in some preliminary experiments. First improvement proved to find slightly better solution qualities than best improvement but it was much slower than the best-improvement algorithm, once the local search had been optimized (see Table 1 for sample results on single processor instances). Since local search has to be applied very frequently in ILS algorithms, we decided to use the best-imrpovement local search because of the much higher speed. The between processor search similarly performs interchange moves but considers only pairs of jobs which are on different processors.

Acceptance Criterion. In the single trajectory ILS algorithms a new solution is accepted only if the new solution has a smaller total tardiness value than that of the best solution currently known. We call this acceptance criterion Better and it is defined for minimization problems as:

$$\text{Better}(s^*, s^{*\prime}, \mathit{history}) = \begin{cases} s^{*\prime} & \text{if } f(s^{*\prime}) < f(s^*) \\ s^* & \text{otherwise} \end{cases} \tag{1}$$

where $f(\cdot)$ is the objective function value of a solution s. Note that this acceptance criterion implements an iterated descent in the search space of local optima.

Perturbation and Partitioning of Jobs. The two single trajectory ILS algorithms only differ in the kind of perturbation they apply. In ILS_i a number of insert moves is applied to the incumbent solution. This is done, because good perturbations should somehow be complementary to the type of moves done in the local search [18]. In particular, the perturbation allows to modify the number of jobs assigned to the processors, something which is not possible in the local search.

The perturbation first randomly selects a processor. A job is then randomly selected and removed from this processor. A second processor is then randomly chosen and the job inserted at a position on this processor which is also randomly selected.

```
procedure ILS_I
    s0 = GenerateInitialSolution
    s+ = LocalSearchOnSingleProcessors(s0)
    s* = LocalSearchBetweenProcessors(s+)
    repeat
        s' = PerturbationBetweenProcessors(s*)
        s+' = LocalSearchOnSingleProcessors(s')
        s*' = LocalSearchBetweenProcessors(s+')
        s* = Better(s*, s*')
    until termination condition met
end
```

Fig. 2. Algorithmic outline of ILS$_I$

The perturbation proceeds as follows: (i) First, a processor is randomly chosen from a uniform distribution. (ii) A job job_i is selected at random from a uniform distribution of the jobs on this processor and removed. (iii) job_i is then inserted at a position on a processor, both the position and the processor are also selected at random from uniform distributions. An outline of ILS$_I$ is shown in Figure 2.

In the problem formulation possible representations of schedules were discussed. Up to this point, we have considered only the permutation representation which was used throughout the previous algorithm. ILSRES tries to exploit the priority-list representation during the perturbation phase of each iteration. The ILSRES algorithm transforms the incumbent solution which is in permutation representation to the appropriate priority list before each perturbation. During the perturbation the priority list is modified by performing a predefined number of interchange moves. Following the perturbation a schedule is constructed by greedily assigning the jobs from the front of the list to the machine with the least load, as described in Section 4.1. At this point, the local search phase begins. Figure 3 gives the pseudo-code for this algorithm.

4.2 Population Based Algorithms for the MPTTP

Some preliminary results with the single-trajectory ILS algorithms showed that for the MPTTP stagnation behaviour becomes apparent, something that was not observed for the SPTTP. Therefore, we developped population-based extensions of the ILS algorithms to possibly avoid this behaviour. We adapted some earlier proposed population-based variants as well as new ones that include more advanced selection strategies. Finally, we considered also the extension to memetic algorithms [20, 21] by including a recombination operator that is applied with some probability to pairs of solutions; it returns a new solution that combines properties of both "parent" solutions.

We developed four algorithms for the study which range from the *No Interaction* scheme, mentioned in Section 3 to a memetic algorithm. All algorithms

```
procedure ILSRES
   s0 = GenerateInitialSolution
   s+ = LocalSearchOnSingleProcessors(s0)
   s* = LocalSearchBetweenProcessors(s+)
   repeat
      PL* = CreatePriorityList(s*)
      PL' = PerturbPriorityList(PL*)
      s' = MakeSchedule(PL')
      s+' = LocalSearchOnSingleProcessors(s')
      s*' = LocalSearchBetweenProcessors(s+')
      s* = Better(s*, s*')
   until termination condition met
end
```

Fig. 3. Algorithmic outline of ILSRES

```
procedure Population based ILS algorithm
   for each solution s[i]
      s[i] = GenerateRandomInitialSolution
   repeat
      if selection criteria reached
         then SelectionAlgorithm(s[])
      for each solution s[i]
         ILSRES Iteration(s[i])
   until termination condition met
end
```

Fig. 4. Algorithmic outline of population based algorithms

have the same general skeleton: they maintain a fixed size population of ILS trajectories. Each trajectory is composed of a single ILSRES trajectory with identical perturbation strength. During a run, each trajectory is initialised with a randomly generated solution. In the main loop, solutions are selected to apply one single iteration of the standard ILS algorithm. Finally, if appropriate, the algorithm performs any necessary interaction between trajectories and repeats.

The first two approaches are adaptation of the *No Interaction* (referred to as POPILS) and the *Replace-Worst* (referred to as POPREP) schemes [25], introduced already in Section 3. POPILS serves as a baseline control, whether the interaction among the ILS trajectories improves performance. In POPREP, the best schedule replaces every μ iterations the worst schedule. Stützle found that the parameter μ had a significant impact on the maintenance of variation during a search.

The following two algorithms, POPSEL and POPSTG, also use the the framework described in Figure 4 but employ a more advanced selection strategy which will be referred to as *genetic selection*. Genetic selection is imple-

Parents	α	=	1	2	3	4	5	6	7
	β	=	7	6	5	4	3	2	1
Modified parents	α'	=	1	b	b	b	5	6	7
	β'	=	b	b	b	4	3	2	b
Offspring, step 1	γ'	=	1				5	6	7
Offspring, step 2	γ	=	1	4	3	2	5	6	7

Fig. 5. Example of application of crossover operator to two schedules α and β resulting in a new schedule γ

mented according to an elitist roulette wheel strategy. In this scheme the selection probability is proportional to the fitness of a schedule; exceptions are that the best solution is always chosen and crossover does not make sense if two solutions are the same. The fitness of a schedule i is given by $fitness(schedule_i) = (T_{worst} - T_i) + \delta * (T_{worst} - T_{best})$, T_i is the tardiness of schedule i, T_{worst} and T_{best} are the best and the worst schedule in the population, and δ is a parameter.

The number of trajectories determined by crossover is determined by a parameter ψ which is the ratio k/n of crossover offspring to the total number of trajectories n, where k is an integer between 0 and $n-1$. One trajectory is reserved for the current best solution and the remaining trajectories are selected from all current solutions with probabilities determined by their relative fitness. POPSEL and POPSTG obey the population based ILS skeleton as described above. Both of these algorithms use the genetic selection algorithm but differ in when selection is applied, the selection criteria. POPSEL applies selection after a constant number of ILS iterations defined by a parameter μ. POPSTG tries to apply selection only when there is stagnation and there has been no improvement to the best trajectory for a constant number of ILS iterations defined by a parameter ν. Both of these algorithms generally employ crossover. POPSEL and POPSTG are "pure" population-based ILS algorithms only when $k = 0$.

The crossover operator operates on two parent schedules, α and β, represented by priority lists of jobs. The operator functions as follows (see also Figure 5 for an illustration): A random set of jobs in α are determined to be static and the nonstatic jobs in α are replaced by blanks (indicated by b in Figure 5) resulting in α'. The static jobs are then removed from β, resulting in β'. The offspring γ is build by first copying the static jobs of α into their positions and then filling the empty position with the jobs of β' maintaining their order in β'. The crossover operator has the properties that (i) all the jobs originating from α and β maintain their relative orderings and (ii) the jobs originating from α also maintain their positions in the priority list. Hence, we would expect that the start time of jobs in γ that were copied from α remain approximately similar to the ones they had in α. This operator is based upon the strategy of França [13] and the above two properties are present in their strategy as well. The two approaches differ in that França chooses an interval in α which remains static, while we choose the jobs randomly, and França's implementation is for a single processor scheduling problem, while ours is for the MPTTP.

5 Empirical Analysis

The algorithms described in the previous sections were evaluated empirically, it was necessary to perform empirical analysis. This required deriving appropriate sample problems and experimental protocol in order to accurately portray performance. We begin this section by describing the sample problems used followed by descriptions of the experiments and their results.

5.1 Benchmark Instances

We produced a set of forty 100 job and 200 job problem instances based on range of due date (RDD) and tardiness factor (TF) parameters using a widely applied algorithm [17, 16]. For each problem size, 20 instances were taken from a problem library maintained by Bahar Kara [16] with a single instance per RDD, TD pair taken from $RDD = \{0.2, 0.4, 0.6, 0.8, 1.0\}$ and $TF = \{0.2, 0.4, 0.6, 0.8\}$. The remaining 20 instances per problem size were generated by us using the same parameter values. We adapted these instances to the multi processor case by dividing their due dates by the number of processors and rounding to the nearest integer.

To evaluate the performance of our algorithms, we first tried to find very high quality solutions using the following protocol. A single trajectory ILS algorithms with perturbation set at 10% of the number of jobs was run ten times on each instance, five times with the earliest due date initialisation routine and five times with random initialisation. The termination condition requires that at least 1000 iterations have been completed. If this criteria has been satisfied, the termination condition will halt if the ILS did not find a better solution for $10n$ iterations. The best solution found was deemed to be the best-known solution and used as a goal for subsequent experiments.

This protocal reliably returned the known optimal solutions for the 100 and 200 job SPTTP instances of Bahar Kara; generally 90 to 100% of the runs returned the same potential optimal solution quality. This is a strong indication that the solutions found for the additional SPTTP instances using this protocol are likely optimal. However, this did not generally translate to the multiprocessor case where for the most difficult problems the runs resulted in different solutions; here we use the best solution returned by the 10 runs to evaluate the other algorithms.

5.2 Experimental Design

Most of the results reported in this paper are from runs on only a few instances, which were among the hardest ones. The instances were selected from the pool based on how quickly and easily known optimal solutions were found using the procedure described in the previous section. If the problem was solved in the first iteration, it was deemed trivial and not further studied. If the best solution was found in 80% or more of the runs, the problem was classified as easy. If on the other hand the best solution was found less than 20% of the time the problem was classified as difficult. The forty 200 job two processor instances divided into 57.5% difficult and 40% easy. We found that instances with RDD of 0.2 and 0.4 are rather easy and found consistent solutions 100% of the time in all but one case. On the instances with other RDD values, in almost all cases the best solution was only obtained in one trial, suggesting that there still may be some gap to the true optimum.

Three problems were arbitrarily selected from these sets; bk131 is an easy instance and both bk151 and 181 are difficult problems. mp101 was selected because its RDD parameter of 0.6 has been shown to be particularly difficult for the SPTTP [9].

All experiments were performed on the BETA laboratory compute cluster at the University of British Columbia. At the time of this work, the cluster consisted of 12 PCs running Redhat linux version 7.1 with 733MHz to 1GHz Pentium III processors and 1 to 4GB of RAM.

The cost model used throughout the experiments is based on the number of local search moves completed. The average CPU time per search step is dependent on the specific instance. However, on a given instance the CPU time per search step is consistent irrespective of algorithm or particular run. For problem bkara 151 on a 1GHz processor with 1GB RAM running a Linux executable written in C++ and compiled with g++ performs 839 search steps per second. This has been tested with both ILS3 and ILSRES and several predecessors. For bkara 131 the results are less consistent but is approximately 700 search steps per second.

5.3 Computational Experiments

Evaluation of ILS3 and ILSRES. An evaluation of perturbation parameters for MPTTP was performed with the ILS3 and ILSRES algorithms. The experiments were performed by running the ILS algorithms 25 times for each algorithm/ problem instance/perturbation level combination. The problem instances bkara 131 and bkara 151, adjusted to two processors, were considered. Perturbation levels of 2,4,6,8,10 were tested. This was repeated for ILSRES on problem 151 adjusted for 3 and 4 processors. All runs were limited to a maximum CPU time of 500 seconds. Analysis was performed by acquiring summary statistics for computational requirements and solution qualities as well as by analysing run-time distributions (RTDs).

The easy problem was solved to the best-known solution (which we conjecture to be optimal) within the given timeframe. This is not true for the difficult instance and here we can only consider results for solution qualities inferior to the best-known. Notably, in both instances and for both algorithms, the optimal perturbation appears at the low end of the spectrum, at level 2 in ILSRES and ILS3 (see Figure 6 for instance bkara 151 on two processors). As demonstrated

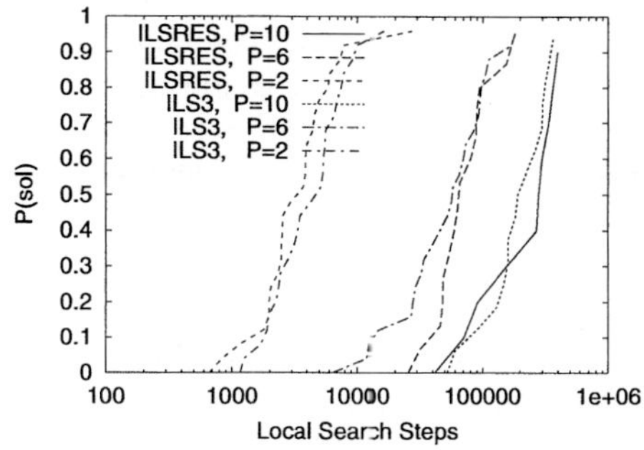

Fig. 6. Run time distribution for ILSRES and ILS3 run on 2 processor bkara 151

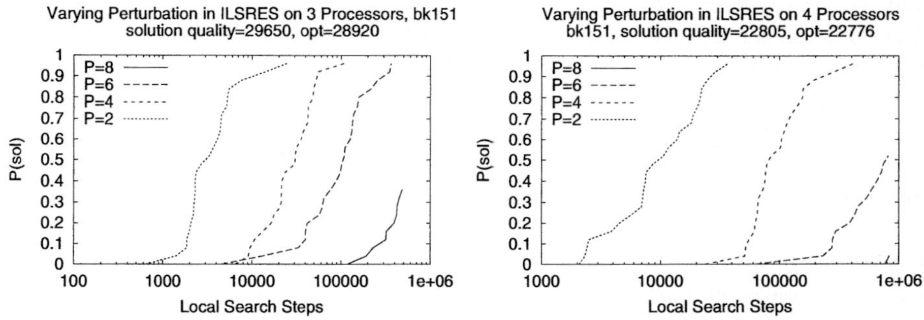

Fig. 7. Run time distribution for ILSRES run on 3 and 4 processor bkara 151

in Figure 6, these two algorithms perform almost identically on both of these instances. Figure 7 shows, that also for instances with three or four processors, the perturbation strength should be rather small.

Evaluation of Population Based Algorithms. All algorithms were evaluated with multiple parameter settings on problem instances bkara 131 and 151 on 2 processors, each run consisted of 25 repeats with a maximum processing time of 500 seconds. In addition ILSRES and POPILS with parameters optimized based on the bkara 151 experiments were run on bkara 181 and mp 101.

Throughout these experiments all population based algorithms' internal ILSRES trajectories used a perturbation strength of size 2 and constant population sizes equal to 20. POPREP was evaluated with μ equal to 1, 10 and 100. POPSEL was evaluated with μ equal to 5, 10 and 100 and the crossover frequency, ψ, held constant at 0.2. Similarly, POPSTG was considered with ν at 10, 100 and 500 with ψ contant at 0.2 and ν held constant at 10 with ψ at 0.2 and 0.4. All experiments were run with a population size of 20. The results of the application of these algorithms to bkara 151 are shown in Table 2 and Figure 9. Table 3 shows the application of the SLS algorithms to all four instances. Most significantly, on the difficult bkara 151 problem, the population based algorithms find the best-known solutions more often. Given the steep slope of the RTD in Figure 9, there is a strong indication that a small increase in alotted time will be sufficient to find this solution quality in all runs. In contrast, the slope of the single trajectory algorithms is very shallow and we can expect little benefit from increasing the allotted time. The stagnation of the single trajectory algorithms is supported by the fact that with a perturbation strength of 2 the single trajectory ILS algorithms usually have performed all their improvements before 250 seconds have elapsed. This is supported by the results in Table 3 which also indicate stagnation in the single trajectory algorithm on all difficult instances. Given these results it appears that the population based strategy is more promising than concentrating effort on a single trajectory.

On the easier bkara 131 instance most runs solved to the best known solution. Generally less than 5 iterations were required and there was no evidence of stagnation for the single trajectory algorithms. On this instance, very little difference could be observed between techniques. Problem 151 rarely completes in the 500 allotted seconds per run as shown in Table 2. In this time period, a population based algorithm performs up to 1000 iterations and characteristics of the algorithms become apparent. Both the runtime distributions in Figure 9 and Table 2 point to the benefits of a selection mechanism. The mean solution of POPILS is more than a standard deviation from the best POPSEL and POPSTG settings. In addition the number of optimal solutions found by strategies employing selection is consistently greater than 0, the number found by POPILS. The runtime distributions of Figure 17 also show that selection based strategies find the suboptimal solution 43350 much faster and more reliably.

Establishing the possible benefits of recombination is more difficult. We observe that in the run time distribution (RTD) of Figure 18, for a suboptimal solution, the run with no recombination appears to fare best. This is supported by the mean solution quality found which is least when ψ is 0. A very important measure however, which contradicts this point is the number of optimal solutions found which is greatest when recombination is at it's peak. These contradicting results are possibly due to the cap on runtime and the extra cost inferred when a recombination occurs. Recombination produces a new solution, which is likely to be farther from the optimal than either of it's parents. Observations on informal runs on problem bkara 151 indicate that when combining two schedules with quality in the neighbourhood of 43400, the child had solution quality of about 43600. The algorithms with recombination must absorb the added cost exploring this new solution before any benefits can be observed. It is likely that given more runtime the crossover will prove itself valuable at finding optimal solutions.

The results in Table 2 and Figure 9 enable us to gather an overall view of how the algorithms performed. Most significantly, the population based algorithms find more often the best-known solutions. Given the steep slope of the RTD in

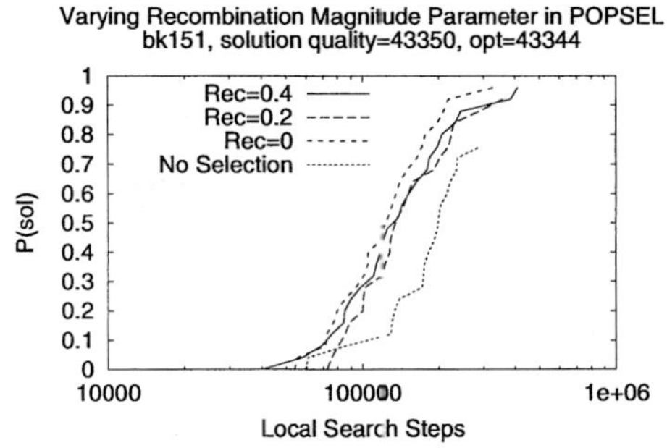

Fig. 8. Altering amount of recombination per selection operation

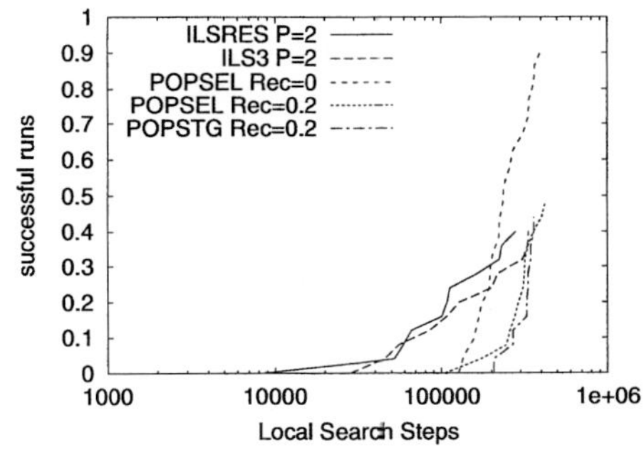

Fig. 9. RTD of Population based and Single Trajectory Algorithms on problem bkara 151

Figure 9, there is a strong indication that a small increase in alotted time will be sufficient to find this solution quality in all runs. In contrast, the slope of the single trajectory algorithms is very shallow and we can expect little benefit from increasing the allotted time. The stagnation of the single trajectory algorithms is supported by the fact that with a perturbation strength of 2 the single trajectory ILS algorithms usually have performed all their improvements before 250 seconds have elapsed. Given these results it appears that the population based strategy is more promising than concentrating effort on a single trajectory.

6 Conclusions and Future Work

In this paper we have considered the application of single trajectory ILS, population-based ILS algorithms, and memetic algorithms to the MPTTP, a very difficult scheduling problem arising in multi-processor environments. We have evaluated the algorithms on a large set of MPTTP benchmark instances, focussing in the presentation of the results on some of the hardest instances we

Table 2. Results for 25 application of each SLS algorithm to bkara 151 (best-known solution 43344)

	Time to find best		Solution Quality		
Algorithm	mean	SD	mean	SD	opt found(of 25)
ILS3 p=10	269.93	119.87	43368.52	5.15	0
p=6	274.94	143.49	43358.31	4.61	0
p=2	243.49	130.54	43347.68	3.06	2
ILSRES p=10	266.56	143.88	43371.56	5.96	0
p=6	288.66	113.36	43359.26	4.77	0
p=2	224.71	146.34	43347.28	2.03	1
POPILS s=20	368.81	74.47	43348.88	2.02	0
POPREP $\mu = 1$	376.04	113.31	43348.92	1.7	0
POPSEL μ=10 ψ=0	336.29	90.67	43345.76	1.33	3
μ=10 ψ=0.2	371.69	97.88	43346.52	1.82	4
μ=10 ψ=0.4	342.63	116.47	43346.16	1.86	7
μ=5 ψ=0.2	331.51	108.6	43346.36	2.03	4
μ=100 ψ=0.2	351.62	118.64	43347.28	1.33	0
POPSTG ν=10 ψ=0.2	391.62	62.82	43346.29	1.38	2 of 20
ν=10 ψ=0.4	341.11	102.26	43345.8	1.22	4
ν=100 ψ=0.2	345.59	96.25	43347.64	1.43	0
ν=500 ψ=0.2	358.77	102.79	43348.16	1.74	1

have encountered in our experiments. The main conclusion is that population-based ILS algorithms can offer significant advantages over single trajectory ILS implementations. Regarding the addition of recombination, we observed for single instances that the frequency of finding the best-known solutions for our instances increased slightly. However,the effect on the average solution quality was not very strong.

There are several ways to extend this research. One possibility is the use of local search algorithms based on variable neighbourhood descent (VND). For example, a VND local search was essential for the very good performance of ILS applied to the SPTWTP, the weighted version of the SPTTP [8]. However, it should be noted that we are already using a local search in two different neighbourhoods, but we could imagine other ways of combining the neighbourhood searches. Another possibility is to explore the usage of different acceptance criteria in the single trajectory ILS; this was shown to be essential for the performance of ILS applied to the TSP [24]; however, for the SPTWTP and the SPTTP the Better acceptance criterion we used was shown to perform best [8]. A further possible extension is to consider priority levels of the jobs by assigning them different weights. In the single processor case, this is known to strongly increase the difficulty of the tardness problem and the same is to be expected for the multi-processor case. Our algorithms have the advantage that they can be extended in a straightforward way also to this case, by simply changing the objective function.

Table 3. Results of application of SLS algorithms to other problem instances

		Time	Solution			
Instance	Algorithm	mean	best	median	worst	successes (%)
bk101	ILSRES	263.7479996	28127	28139.1	28195	10
TF=0.6,RDD=0.6	POPILS $\mu = 0$	430.9	28127	28128.5	28134	30
best=28127	POPILS $\mu = 0.4$	405.2	28127	28129.1	28135	30
bk131	ILSRES	0.8784	284	284	284	100
TF=0.8,RDD=0.4	POPILS $\mu = 0$	1.0348	284	284	284	100
best=284	POPILS $\mu = 0.4$	1.01	284	284	284	100
bk181	ILSRES	334.6	14159	14164.3	14177	0
TF=1.0,RDD=0.6	POPILS $\mu = 0$	452.8	14168	14176.4	14182	0
best=14160	POPILS $\mu = 0.4$	413.8	14163	14171.8	14180	0

The population based framework is generally applicable to all scheduling problems with regular objectives. In order to take advantage of the crossover operator which we have designed, more factors need to be taken into account. The problem must be able to be translated to and from a priority list such that the objective function is non-increasing. This puts conditions not only on the objective function but also on the machines and job constraints. The objective must be regular, machines must be identical and processing time of a job must be independent of the schedule.

[**Question — do the machines really have to be identical? It seems to me that if we reschedule jobs onto the faster machines first we should be OK.**]

Overall, ILS is applicable to small and easy MPTTP instances. As difficulty increases, stagnation becomes a dominating factor. Through the use of population based algorithms we have found an acceptable means to increase diversity and guide the search. In order to fully understand these algorithms however, we must study how they behave on a wider range of instances.

References

[1] E. J. Anderson, C. A. Glass, and C. N. Potts. Machine scheduling. In E. H. L. Aarts and J. K. Lenstra, editors, *Local Search in Combinatorial Optimization*, pages 361–414. John Wiley & Sons, Chichester, UK, 1997.

[2] Meral Azizoglu and Omer Kirca. Tardiness minimization on parallel machines. *International Journal of Production Economics*, 55(2):163–168, 1998.

[3] T. Bäck. *Evolutionary Algorithms in Theory and Practice.* Oxford University Press, New York, NY, 1996.

[4] R. K. Congram, C. N. Potts, and S. L. Van de Velde. An iterated dynasearch algorithm for the single–machine total weighted tardiness scheduling problem. *INFORMS Journal on Computing*, 14(1):52–67, 2002.

[5] F. Della Croce, R. Tadei, P. Baracco, and A. Grosso. A new decomposition approach for the single machine total tardiness scheduling problem. *Journal of the Operational Research Society*, 49:1101–1106, 1998.

[6] T. Davidovic, P. Hansen, and N. Mladenovic. Variable neighborhood search for multiprocessor scheduling with communication delays. 2001.

[7] M. den Besten, T. Stützle, and M. Dorigo. Configuration of iterated local search: An example application to the single machine total weighted tardiness problem. In *Applications of Evolutionary Computing*, volume 2037 of *Lecture Notes in Computer Science*, pages 441–451. Springer Verlag, Berlin, Germany, 2001.

[8] M. den Besten, T. Stützle, and M. Dorigo. Configuration of iterated local search: An example application to the single machine total weighted tardiness problem. In W. Egbert Boers et al., editor, *Applications of Evolutionary Computing*, volume 2037, pages 441–451, 2001.

[9] Matthijs Leendert den Besten. Ants for the single machine total weighted tardiness scheduling problem. Master's thesis, Universiteit van Amsterdam, April 2000.

[10] Jianzhong Du and Joseph Y. T. Leung. Minimizing total tardiness on one machine is NP-hard. *Mathematics of Operations Research*, 15(3):483–495, August 1990.

[11] H. Emmons. One-machine sequencing to minimize certain functions of job tardiness. *Operations Research*, 17:701–715, 1969.

[12] Paulo M. Frana, Michel Gendreau, Gilbert Laporte, and Felipe M. Muller. A tabu search heuristic for the multiprocessor scheduling problem with sequence dependent setup times. *International Journal of Production Economics*, 43(2-3):79–89, 1996.

[13] Paulo M. Frana, Alexandre Mendes, and Pablo Moscato. A memetic algorithm for the total tardiness total tardiness single machine scheduling problem. *European Journal of Operational Research*, 132:224–242, 2001.

[14] M. R. Garey and D. S. Johnson. *Computers and Intractability: A Guide to the Theory of $\mathcal{NP}$-Completeness.* Freeman, San Francisco, CA, USA, 1979.

[15] I. Hong, A. B. Kahng, and B. R. Moon. Improved large-step Markov chain variants for the symmetric TSP. *Journal of Heuristics*, 3(1):63–81, 1997.

[16] Bahar Kara. SMTTP problem library,
http://www.bilkent.edu.tr/ bkara/start.html, 2002.

[17] C. Koulamas. The total tardiness problem: Review and extensions. *Operations Research*, 42(6):1025–1041, November-December 1994.

[18] H. R. Lourenço, O. Martin, and T. Stützle. Iterated local search. In F. Glover and G. Kochenberger, editors, *Handbook of Metaheuristics*, volume 57 of *International Series in Operations Research & Management Science*, pages 321–353. Kluwer Academic Publishers, Norwell, MA, 2002.

[19] M. Mitchell. *An Introduction to Genetic Algorithms.* MIT Press, Cambridge, MA, 1996.

[20] P. Moscato. On evolution, search, optimization, genetic algorithms and martial arts: Towards memetic algorithms. Technical Report 790, Caltech Concurrent Comp. Program, 1989.

[21] P. Moscato. Memetic algorithms: A short introduction. In D. Corne, M. Dorigo, and F. Glover, editors, *New Ideas in Optimization*, pages 219–234. McGraw Hill, London, UK, 1999.

[22] Marc Sevaux and Philippe Thomin. Heuristics and metaheuristics for a parallel machine scheduling problem: a computational evaluation. Technical Report 01-1-SP, University of Valenciennes, March 2001.

[23] F. Sivrikaya-Serifoglu and G. Ulusoy. Parallel machine scheduling with earliness and tardiness penalties. *Computers and Operations Research*, 26(8):773–787, 1999.

[24] T. Stützle and H. H. Hoos. Analysing the run-time behaviour of iterated local search for the travelling salesman problem. In P. Hansen and C. Ribeiro, editors, *Essays and Surveys on Metaheuristics*, pages 589–611. 2001.
[25] Thomas Stützle. *Local Search Algorithms for Combinatorial Problems – Analysis, Improvements, and New Applications.* PhD thesis, Darmstadt University of Technology, 1998.
[26] B. Tansel, B. Y. Kara, and Sabuncuoglu. Single machine total tardiness scheduling problem. *IIE Transactions*, 33:661–674, 2001.

A Graph Based Backtracking Algorithm for Solving General CSPs

Wanlin Pang[1] and Scott D. Goodwin[2]

[1] QSS Group Inc., NASA Ames Research Center, Moffett Field, CA 94035
[2] School of Computer Science, University of Windsor
Windsor, Ontario, Canada N9B 3P4

Abstract. Many AI tasks can be formalized as constraint satisfaction problems (CSPs), which involve finding values for variables subject to constraints. While solving a CSP is an NP-complete task in general, tractable classes of CSPs have been identified based on the structure of the underlying constraint graphs. Much effort has been spent on exploiting structural properties of the constraint graph to improve the efficiency of finding a solution. These efforts contributed to development of a class of CSP solving algorithms called decomposition algorithms. The strength of CSP decomposition is that its worst-case complexity depends on the structural properties of the constraint graph and is usually better than the worst-case complexity of search methods. Its practical application is limited, however, since it cannot be applied if the CSP is not decomposable. In this paper, we propose a graph based backtracking algorithm called ω-CDBT, which shares merits and overcomes the weaknesses of both decomposition and search approaches.

1 Introduction

Many AI tasks can be formalized as constraint satisfaction problems (CSPs), which involve finding values for variables subject to constraints. While constraint satisfaction in its general form is known to be NP-complete, many CSPs are tractable and can be solved efficiently. Much work has been done to identify tractable classes of CSPs based on the structure of the underlying constraint graphs and many deep and insightful results have been obtained in this direction [12, 1, 15, 8, 6, 9, 28, 29, 3, 17, 18, 21, 10, 20, 24, 25]. A serious practical limitation of this research, however, has been its focus on backtrack-free conditions. Obviously, a CSP which has backtrack-free solutions is tractable, but a tractable CSP does not necessarily have backtrack-free solutions. In practice, many researchers have tried to improve the efficiency of finding a solution by exploiting the structural properties of the constraint graph. A class of structure-based CSP solving algorithms, called decomposition algorithms, has been developed [14, 16, 4, 7]. Decomposition algorithms attempt to find solutions by decomposing a CSP into several simply connected sub-CSPs based on the underlying constraint graph and then solving them separately. Once a CSP is decomposed into a set of sub-CSPs, all solutions for each sub-CSP are found.

Y. Xiang and B. Chaib-draa (Eds.): AI 2003, LNAI 2671, pp. 114–128, 2003.

Then a new CSP is formed where the original variable set in each sub-CSP is taken as a singleton variable. Usually the technique aims at decomposing a CSP into sub-CSPs such that the number of variables in the largest sub-CSP is minimal and the newly formed CSP has a tree-structured constraint graph. In this way, the time and space complexity of finding all solutions for each sub-CSP is bounded, and the newly formed CSP has backtrack-free solutions. The complexity of a decomposition algorithm is exponential in the size of the largest sub-CSP. The class of CSPs that can be decomposed into sub-CSPs such that their sizes are bounded by a fixed number k is tractable and can be solved by decomposition in polynomial time. This is the strength of CSP decomposition. A fatal weakness of CSP decomposition, however, is that the decomposition is not applicable to solving a CSP that is not decomposable, that is, its decomposition is itself. A secondary drawback of CSP decomposition is that, even if the CSP is decomposable, finding all solutions for all the sub-CSPs is unnecessary and inefficient.

In this paper, we propose a graph based backtracking algorithm, called ω-CDBT, which shares the strength of CSP decomposition and overcomes its weaknesses. As with CSP decomposition, ω-CDBT decomposes the underlying constraint hypergraph into an acyclic graph. Unlike CSP decomposition, however, ω-CDBT only tries to find one solution for a chosen sub-CSP, which is not separated from other sub-CSPs, and then tries to extend it to other sub-CSPs. The ω-CDBT algorithm uses a constraint representative graph called ω-graph [24, 22, 25]. The complexity of ω-CDBT is exponential in the degree of cyclicity of the ω-graph. Nevertheless, the significant contributions of this research on combining search with constraint structure are: 1) The class of CSPs with the property that the degree of cyclicity of the associated ω-graph is less than a fixed number k is tractable. As shown in [24, 22, 25], given a constraint hypergraph, the degree of cyclicity of an ω-graph is less than or equal that of the constraint hypergraph. Therefore, the class of CSPs that is ω-CDBT solvable in polynomial time includes the class of CSPs that is solvable in polynomial time by other decomposition algorithms such as hinge decomposition [16]. 2) For CSPs that do not have the above mentioned property, ω-CDBT still has a better worst-case complexity bound than other decomposition algorithms such as hinge decomposition [16], which in turn has a better worst-case complexity bound than search algorithms that do not exploit constraint structure. In both cases, ω-CDBT also has advantage over decomposition algorithms in that it finds only one solution for each sub-CSP which saves space and time. 3) In cases where CSPs are not decomposable, decomposition algorithms are not applicable whereas ω-CDBT degenerates to CDBT [23] which is still a practical CSP solving algorithm.

The paper is organized as follows. We first give definitions of constraint satisfaction problems and briefly overview constraint graphs and CSP decomposition. We then present the ω-CDBT algorithm, analyze its complexity, and compare it with decomposition algorithms.

2 Preliminaries

2.1 Constraint Satisfaction Problems

A *constraint satisfaction problem (CSP)* is a structure (X, D, V, S). Here, $X = \{X_1, X_2, \ldots, X_n\}$ is a set of variables that may take on values from a set of domains $D = \{D_1, D_2, \ldots, D_n\}$, and $V = \{V_1, V_2, \ldots, V_m\}$ is a family of ordered subsets of X called *constraint schemes*. Each $V_i = \{X_{i_1}, X_{i_2}, \ldots, X_{i_{ri}}\}$ is associated with a set of tuples $S_i \subseteq D_{i_1} \times D_{i_2} \times \ldots \times D_{i_{ri}}$ called *constraint instance*, and $S = \{S_1, S_2, \ldots, S_m\}$ is a family of such constraint instances. Together, an ordered pair (V_i, S_i) is a *constraint* or *relation* which permits the variables in V_i to take only value combinations in S_i.

Let (X, D, V, S) be a CSP, $V_K = \{X_{k_1}, X_{k_2}, \ldots, X_{k_l}\}$ a subset of X. A tuple $(x_{k_1}, x_{k_2}, \ldots, x_{k_l})$ in $D_{k_1} \times D_{k_2} \times \ldots \times D_{k_l}$ is called an *instantiation* of variables in V_K. An instantiation is said to be *consistent* if it satisfies all constraints restricted in V_K. A consistent instantiation of all variables in X is a *solution to the CSP* (X, D, V, S). The task of solving a CSP is to find one or more solutions.

A constraint (V_h, S_h) in a CSP (X, D, V, S) is *minimal* if every tuple in S_h can be extended to a solution. A CSP (X, D, V, S) is *minimal* if every constraint is minimal.

A *binary CSP* is a CSP with unary and binary constraints only, that is, every constraint scheme contains at most two variables. A CSP with constraints not limited to unary and binary is referred to as a *general CSP.*

We will also use some relational operators, specifically, *join* and *projection.* Let $C_i = (V_i, S_i)$ and $C_j = (V_j, S_j)$ be two constraints. The *join* of C_i and C_j is a constraint denoted by $C_i \bowtie C_j$. The *projection* of $C_i = (V_i, S_i)$ on $V_h \subseteq V_i$ is a constraint denoted by $\Pi_{V_h}(C_i)$. The *projection* of t_i on V_h, denoted by $t_i[V_h]$, is a tuple consisting of only the components of t_i that correspond to variables in V_h.

2.2 Graph Theory Background

In this section, we review some graph theoretic terms we will need later and we define constraint representative graphs, namely, the line graph, the join graph, and the ω-graph.

A *graph* G is a structure (V, E), where V is a set of *nodes* and E is a set of *edges*, with each edge joining one node to another.

A *subgraph of* G *induced by* $V' \subset V$ is a graph (V', E') where $E' \subset E$ contains all edges that have both their endpoints in V'. A *partial graph of* G *induced by* $E' \subset E$ is a graph (V, E').

A *path* or a *chain* is a sequence of edges $E_1, E_2, \ldots, E_q$ such that each E_i shares one of its endpoints with E_{i-1} and the other with E_{i+1}. A *cycle* is a chain such that no edge appears twice in the sequence, and the two endpoints of the chain are the same node. A graph is *connected* if it contains a chain for each pair of nodes. A *connected component* of a graph is a connected subgraph. A graph is *acyclic* if it contains no cycle. A connected acyclic graph is a *tree.*

Let $G = (V, E)$ be a connected graph. A node V_i is called a *cut node* (or *articulation node*) if the subgraph induced by $V - \{V_i\}$ is not connected. A *block* (or *nonseparable component*) of a graph is a connected component that contains no cut nodes of its own. An $O(|E|)$ algorithm exits for finding all the blocks and cut nodes [11].

Let $G = (V, E)$ be a connected graph. The *degree of cyclicity of G* is defined as the number of nodes in its largest block. A graph is *k-cyclic* if its degree of cyclicity is at most k.

A *hypergraph* is a graph with *hyper edges*; that is, an edge in a hypergraph may contain more than two nodes. The graph notations reviewed above can be extended to hypergraph, such as *sub-hypergraph*, *partial hypergraph*, *path*, *connected component*, *block*, and so on. These definitions can be found in [2].

A graph $G = (V, E)$ can be decomposed into a tree of blocks $T_B = (V_B, E_B)$: 1) choose a block $V_{B_i} \in V_B$, which contains at least one non-cut node, as the root node of T_B and mark it; 2) for each unmarked block X_{B_j} that has a node in common with block X_{B_i}, connect X_{B_j} as a child node of X_{B_i} with an edge (X_{B_i}, X_{B_j}) and mark it; 3) take each child node of X_{B_i} as the root node of a subtree, repeat 2) and 3); 4) stop when every block is marked.

For example, give a graph $G = (V, E)$ as shown in Figure 1 (A), we can have a block tree as in Figure 1 (B), where $B_1 = \{V_1, V_2, V_3, V_4\}$, $B_2 = \{V_2, V_5, V_6\}$, $B_3 = \{V_5, V_7, V_8\}$, $B_4 = \{V_6, V_9, V_{10}\}$, $B_5 = \{V_3, V_{11}, V_{12}\}$, $B_6 = \{V_3, V_{13}, V_{14}\}$, $B_7 = \{V_4, V_{15}, V_{16}\}$. The cut nodes in this graph are V_2, V_3, V_4, V_5, and V_6.

A block tree determines an order on the block set. For example, block set $B = \{B_1, B_2, B_3, B_4, B_5, B_6, B_7\}$ is in the depth-first order. For each block B_k $(2 \leq k)$ there is a cut node V_{a_k} of the graph that separates this block from its parent block, and there is a node V_{a_1} in B_1 which is not in any other blocks. These nodes are called *separating nodes*. For example, the separating nodes of the graph in Figure 1 (A) are V_1, V_2, V_3, V_4, V_5, and V_6

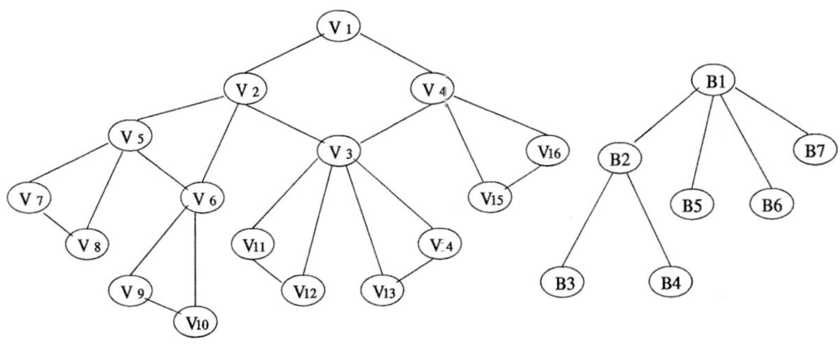

(A) A connected graph (B) A block tree

Fig. 1. A graph and its block tree

A binary CSP is associated with a simple constraint graph, which has been well studied and widely used for analyzing and solving binary CSPs [13, 7, 5]. A general CSP is associated with a constraint hypergraph, but the topological properties of the hypergraph have not been well studied in the area of constraint satisfaction problems. Instead, constraint representative graphs such as the *line graph*, the *join graph*, and the ω*-graph* have been studied and used to analyzing and solving general CSPs [20, 19, 16, 24, 25, 26, 27].

Given a CSP (X, D, V, S) and its hypergraph $H = (X, V)$, the *line-graph* [1] is a simple graph $l(H) = (V, L)$ in which nodes in V are hyperedges of the hypergraph and with two nodes joined with an edge in L if these two nodes share common variables. A *join graph* $j(H) = (V, J)$ is a partial linegraph in which some *redundant* edges are removed. An edge in a linegraph is redundant if the variables shared by its two end nodes are also shared by every nodes along an alternative path between the two end nodes. An ω-graph $\omega(H) = (W, F)$ is another constraint representative graph. The node set W of an ω-graph is a subset of nodes V in the line graph such that any node in $V - W$ is *covered* by two nodes in W; that is, if $V_k \in V - W$, then there exist V_i an V_j in V, such that $V_k \subset V_i \cup Vj$. There is an edge joining two nodes if either the two nodes share common variables or they cover a node that is not in W.

For example, given a hypergraph $H = (X, V)$ as in Figure 2 (A) with node set $X = \{X_1,X_2,X_3,X_4,X_5,X_6,X_7\}$ and edge set $V = \{V_1,V_2,V_3,V_4,V_5,V_6\}$, where $V_1 = \{X_1, X_2\}$, $V_2 = \{X_1, X_4, X_7\}$, $V_3 = \{V_2, V_3\}$, $V_4 = \{X_2, X_4, X_7\}$, $V_5 = \{X_3, X_5, X_7\}$, $V_6 = \{X_3, X_6\}$. Its line graph $l(H) = (V, L)$ is in Figure 2 (B). There is an edge, for example, between V_1 and V_2 because these two nodes share a common variable X_1. Edge (V_5, V_6) is redundant because the variable X_3 shared by V_5 and V_6 is also shared by every nodes on an alternative path between V_5 and V_6, that is, path (V_5, V_3, V_6). A join graph resulting from removing redundant edges is in Figure 2 (C), and an ω-graph is in (D) in which there is only 4 nodes, since node V_1 is covered by V_2 and V_4, and node V_3 by V_5 and V_6.

Since constraint representative graphs are simple graphs, all of those graph concepts mentioned previously are applicable. For example, an ω-graph (or a join graph) is *k-cyclic* if the number of nodes in its largest block is at most k. An ω-graph can be decomposed into a block tree.

Notice that the line graph or a join graph is also an ω-graph, but in general, an ω-graph is simpler than the line or join graph in terms of the number of nodes, the degree of cyclicity and the width. In particular, [22] gives an $O(|V|^3)$ algorithm for constructing an ω-graph for a hypergraph with the following property:

Proposition 1. *Given a hypergraph $H = (X, V)$, there exists an ω-graph whose degree of cyclicity is less than or equal the degree of cyclicity of any join graph.*

Note that the *degree of cyclicity of a hypergraph* is defined in [16] as the degree of cyclicity of its minimal join graph. The above proposition indicates that a hypergraph has an ω-graph whose degree of cyclicity is less than or equal that of the hypergraph.

[1] A line graph is also called an inter graph in [19] and a dual-graph in [7].

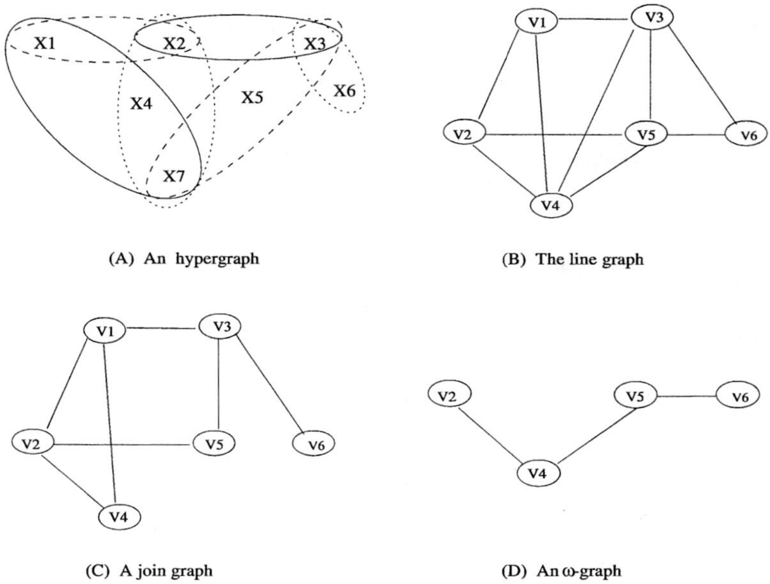

Fig. 2. A hypergraph and its representative graphs

2.3 CSP Decomposition

Decomposition algorithms attempt to find solutions more efficiently by decomposing a CSP into a set of sub-CSPs such that these sub-CSPs form a tree and the size of the largest sub-CSP is minimized. In general, a decomposition algorithm works as follows:

1. decompose the constraint hypergraph into a tree;
2. find all solutions to each sub-CSP associated with each node in the tree;
3. form a new CSP where the original variable set in each tree node is taken as a singleton variable;
4. find one solution to the new CSP.

Many decomposition algorithms have been developed [14, 16, 7, 4] and they usually differ in the first step. A comparison of most notable decomposition algorithms can be found in [14]. As pointed out in [14], each decomposition method defines a parameter as a measure of cyclicity of the underlying constraint hypergraph such that, for a fixed number k, all CSPs with the parameter bounded by k are solvable in polynomial time.

ω-graph fits well into this decomposition scheme in that we first construct an ω-graph from a given constraint hypergraph and then decompose the ω-graph into a tree. It is obvious that many graph decomposition methods can be used to decompose an ω-graph. For simplicity, however, we choose the block tree method to decompose ω-graphs in this paper.

The problem with the decomposition methods is that they cannot be applied if a given CSP does not possess some required properties (for example, non-decomposible). Moreover, even if the underlying constraint graph is decomposable, finding all solutions for every sub-CSP is inefficient and unnecessary. In the following, we propose a graph based backtracking algorithm called ω-CDBT that overcomes these weaknesses.

3 ω-Graph Based Backtracking

Let (X, D, V, S) be a CSP and $C = \{C_i = (V_i, S_i) | V_i \in V, S_i \in S\}$ a set of constraints. Let $\omega(H) = (W, F)$ be an ω-graph and $B = \{B_1, B_2, \ldots, B_l\}$ a set of blocks of $\omega(H)$ which is ordered in the depth-first manner according to the block tree, and each block $B_k = \{V_{k_1}, V_{k_2}, \ldots, V_{k_{|B_k|}}\}$ a set of nodes in which the first one is the separating node. Let $cks_a(V_i, V_j)$ denote the set of constraints on $V - W$ covered by V_i and V_j in W, that is, $cks_a(V_i, V_j) = \{V_k \in V - W | V_k \subset V_i \cup V_j\}$. The idea of the ω-CDBT algorithm is to search for a consistent assignment to variables involved in a block and then extend it to the child blocks. If at a block where no consistent assignment can be found, ω-CDBT backtracks to the parent block, reinstantiates variables in that block, and starts from there. Within a block, ω-CDBT uses a CDBT-like strategy [23] to find a consistent assignment to the variable subset in the block, which may involve backtracking within the block. The algorithm stops when a solution is found or when it proves that no solution exists.

3.1 Algorithm

The ω-CDBT performs backtrack at two nested levels which we call *outer-BT* and *inner-BT*. The inner-BT finds a consistent instantiation of variables involved in a block $B_k = \{V_{k_1}, V_{k_2}, \ldots, V_{k_{|B_k|}}\}$. The outer-BT calls inner-BT to find consistent instantiations for all blocks in the depth-first order. If a consistent instantiation of variables in the current block is found then outer-BT calls inner-BT again to find consistent instantiations of variables in its child blocks; otherwise, the outer-BT moves backward to the parent block and calls the inner-BT to find another consistent instantiation of variables in that block.

The function *DFS* corresponding to the outer-BT, the inner-BT, which is based on *CDBT* [23], consisting of two recursive functions *forward* and *goback*, and an auxiliary function *test* are given below. In these functions, some notations are explained as follows: tup_{B_k} is a consistent instantiation of variables in B_k; sol_{T_k} is a consistent instantiation of variables in the subtree rooted at B_k; $child_{B_k}$ is a set of child blocks of B_k; $changed_{B_k}$ is a flag indicating if the instantiation of variables in the separating node of B_k has changed; idx_{B_k} is the index of the separating node of B_k in the parent block; t_{B_k} is a current instantiation of variables in the separating node of B_k, initialized as a nil-tuple.

ω-*DFS*(B_k, V_I, tup_I)

1. **begin**
2. $tup_{B_k} \leftarrow \omega$-*forward*$(B_k, V_I, tup_I)$;

```
  if tup_{B_k} = ∅ then return ∅;
  for each B_j ∈ child_{B_k} do
    if changed_{B_j} then
      sol_{T_j} ← ω-DFS(B_j, V_{j_1}, t_{B_j});
      if sol_{T_j} = unsatisfiable then return unsatisfiable;
      if sol_{T_j} = ∅ then
        delete t_{B_j} from S_{j_1} and S*_{j_1};
        if S_{j_1} = ∅ then return unsatisfiable;
        V' ← ∪_{i=1}^{idx_{B_j}-1} V_{k_i}; tup' ← tup_{B_k}[V'];
        return (ω-DFS(B_k, V', tup'));
      changed_{B_j} ← false;
  end for
  return tup_{B_k} ⋈ (⋈_{B_j ∈ child_{B_k}} sol_{T_j});
end
```

forward(B_k, V_I, tup_I)

```
begin
  if V_I = ∪B_k then return tup_I;
  cks(V_{I+1}) ← ∪_{j=1}^{i} cks_a(V_{k_j}, V_{k_{i+1}});
  S*_{k_{i+1}} ← {tup | tup ∈ S_{k_{i+1}}, tup[V_I ∩ V_{k_{i+1}}] = tup_I[V_I ∩ V_{k_{i+1}}]};
  while S*_{k_{i+1}} ≠ ∅ do
    tup ← one tuple taken from S*_{k_{i+1}};
    tup_{I+1} ← tup_I ⋈ tup;
    if test(tup_{I+1}, cks(V_{I+1})) then
      for each B_j ∈ child_{B_k}
        if V_{k_{i+1}} ∈ B_j and tup ≠ t_{B_j} then t_{B_j} ← tup; changed_{B_j} ← true;
      return forward(B_k, V_{I+1}, tup_{I+1});
  end while
  return goback(B_k, V_I, tup_I);
end
```

goback(B_k, V_I, tup_I)

```
begin
  if V_I = V_{k_1} then return ∅;
  while S*_i ≠ ∅ do
    tup ← one tuple taken from S*_i;
    tup_I ← tup_{I-1} ⋈ tup;
    if test(tup_I, cks(V_I)) then
      for each B_j ∈ child_{B_k}
        if V_{k_{i+1}} ∈ B_j and tup ≠ t_{B_j} then t_{B_j} ← tup; changed_{B_j} ← true;
      return forward(B_k, V_I, tup_I);
  end while
  return goback(B_k, V_{I-1}, tup_{I-1});
end
```

test$(tup_I, cks))$

```
begin
  for each C_h = (V_h, S_h) in cks do
    if tup_I[V_h] ∉ S_h then return false;
  return true;
end
```

For a current block $B_k = \{V_{k_1}, V_{k_2}, \ldots, V_{k_{|B_k|}}\}$ and a partial instantiation tup_I of variables in $V_I = \cup_{j=1}^{i} V_{k_j}$, *DFS* tries to extend tup_I to a consistent instantiation sol_{T_k} of variables involved in the subtree rooted at B_k. Firstly, it tries to extend tup_I to a consistent instantiation tup_{B_k} of variables in V_{B_k}. This can be done by function *forward.* If *forward* succeeds, that is, if a consistent instantiation tup_{B_k} is found, then *DFS* moves forward to those of its child blocks that have not been instantiated at all or their instantiations have been changed due to backtracking to the parent block. *DFS* calls itself recursively for each of the subtrees, and then returns the joined tuple $tup_{B_k} \bowtie (\bowtie_{B_j \in child_{B_k}} sol_{T_j})$. If *forward* fails, that is, if it does not find a consistent instantiation tup_{B_k} of variables in V_{B_k} such that $tup_{B_k}[V_{k_1}] = tup_{k_1}$, then *DFS* reports that the tuple tup_{k_1} has no consistent extension to variables in V_{B_k}. Before the algorithm backtracks to the parent block, the tuple tup_{k_1} is deleted from S_{k_1}, since it will not be in any solution which will be explained in Section 3.3 and S_{k_1} is checked if it is empty. If it is empty then there is no solution to the problem, so *DFS* stops and reports *unsatisfiable.* If S_{k_1} is not empty then *DFS* moves up to the parent block and starts from there.

Within block B_k, suppose that we have already found a consistent instantiation tup_I of variables in $V_{k_1}, V_{k_2}, \ldots, V_{k_i}$ (their union is denoted by V_I), function *forward* extends this instantiation by appending to it an instantiation of variables in $V_{k_{i+1}}$ which is a node in the ω-graph. *forward* chooses a tuple tup from $S^*_{k_{i+1}}$ as an instantiation of variables in $V_{k_{i+1}}$ and joins tup and tup_I to form a new tuple tup_{I+1}, which is tested to see if it is consistent. Notice that the subset $S^*_{k_{i+1}}$ contains those tuples in $S_{k_{i+1}}$ that are compatible with tup_I. If tup_{I+1} is consistent, then *forward* is called recursively to extend tup_{I+1}; otherwise, another tuple from $S^*_{k_{i+1}}$ is tried. If no tuples are left in $S^*_{k_{i+1}}$, *goback* is called to re-instantiate variables in variable set V_{k_i}. Function *goback* tries to re-instantiate variables in V_{k_i} and to form another consistent instantiation of variables in $V_I = \cup_{j=1}^{i} V_{k_j}$. It first chooses another tuple from $S^*_{k_i}$ and forms a new tuple tup_I which is tested to see if it is consistent. If tup_I is consistent, then *forward* is called to extend tup_I; otherwise, another tuple from $S^*_{k_i}$ is tried. If $S^*_{k_i}$ is empty, then *goback* is called recursively to re-instantiate variables in variable set $V_{k_{i-1}}$. Note that *goback* does not re-instantiate variables in the separating node V_{k_1}. The tuple t_{B_k} for variables in V_{k_1} was chosen when the parent block was dealt with. If t_{B_k} cannot be extended to variables in B_k, *goback* returns $\emptyset$ and passes the control to *DFS* which deletes t_{B_k} from S_{k_1}. Backtracking across blocks occurs.

Function $test(tup_K, cks)$ returns $true$ if tuple tup_K satisfies all the constraints in cks, and *false* otherwise.

To find a solution to a given CSP $\mathbb{P} = (X, D, V, S)$, we need a main program such as the one given below to call *DFS* repeatedly until a solution is found or unsatisfiability is verified.

ω-*CDBT*($\mathbb{P}$, *sol*)

```
begin
  for each tup ∈ S_{1_1} do
    sol ← DFS(B_{k_1}, V_{k_1}, tup);
```

```
4.     if sol = unsatisfiable then return unsatisfiable;
5.     if sol ≠ ∅ then return sol;
6.   end for
7.   return unsatisfiable;
8. end
```

Algorithm *DFS* instantiates the variables in block B_j only if the values assigned to the variables in the separating node of B_j have been changed; that is, only if $changed_{B_j}$ is true (line 5 in the algorithm). At the first time of visiting B_j, $changed_{B_j}$ is true since the variables in the separating nodes have been instantiated when the algorithm visits B_k, the parent block of B_j. However, when the algorithm goes back to re-instantiates the variables in B_k, the variables in the separating node may not be affected, in which case the assignment to the variables in B_j will be retained. Needless to say, this saves time of repeatedly finding values for the variables in the subtree rooted at B_j. However, an immediate question to ask is whether this causes the algorithm to miss any solutions. The answer is *no* because even if the algorithm does re-instantiate variables in B_j, the instantiation will be the same if the values assigned to the variables in the separating node of B_j have not been changed.

3.2 Example

We consider a CSP $\mathbb{P} = (X, D, V, S)$ which has an ω-graph in Figure 1 (A) and we use this example to illustrate how the ω-graph based backtracking works.

We are given an ordered block set $B = \{B_1, B_2, B_3, B_4, B_5, B_6, B_7\}$, where each block is an ordered set of constraint schemes, that is: $B_1 = \{V_1, V_2, V_3, V_4\}$, $B_2 = \{V_2, V_5, V_6\}$, $B_3 = \{V_5, V_7, V_8\}$, $B_4 = \{V_6, V_9, V_{10}\}$, $B_5 = \{V_3, V_{11}, V_{12}\}$, $B_6 = \{V_3, V_{13}, V_{14}\}$, $B_7 = \{V_4, V_{15}, V_{16}\}$. Let V_{B_i} be the subset of variables involved in B_i.

We start from *ω-CDBT*($\mathbb{P}$, *sol*), choose a tuple $t_{B_1} \in S_1$ and call *DFS*(B_1, V_1, t_{B_1}). *DFS* first calls *forward*(B_1, V_1, t_{B_1}) to extend t_{B_1} to variables in V_{B_1}. If it fails, then it will choose another tuple from S_1 and start again. Suppose that it succeeds and it returns a tuple tup_{B_1} as a consistent instantiation of variables in V_{B_1}, then *DFS* will be called recursively for each child block B_2, B_5, B_6 and B_7. Recall that t_{B_i} is the instantiation of variables in the separating node. For the first child block B_2, *DFS*(B_2, V_2, t_{B_2}) is called to extend t_{B_2} to variables involved in the subtree rooted at B_2, which include the variables in V_5, V_6, V_7, V_8, V_9 and V_{10}. At first, *forward*(B_2, V_2, t_{B_2}) is called to extend t_{B_2} to variables in V_5 and V_6. Suppose that it succeeds and it returns a tuple tup_{B_2} as a consistent instantiation of variables in V_{B_2}, then *DFS* will be called for the child blocks of B_2. Again, suppose that they all succeeds, that is, tuples sol_{T_3} and sol_{T_4} are returned. So, *DFS*(B_2, V_2, tup_{V_2}) returns a tuple $sol_{T_2} = sol_{B_2} \bowtie sol_{T_2} \bowtie sol_{T_4}$ as a consistent instantiation of variables involved in the subtree rooted at B_2. For the second child block B_5, *DFS*(B_5, V_3, t_{B_5}) is called to extend t_{B_5} to variables involved in the subtree rooted at B_5. It calls *forward*(B_5, V_3, t_{B_5}) to extend t_{B_5} to variables in V_{B_5}. If it succeeds, then *DFS*(B_5, V_3, t_{B_5}) will return a tuple sol_{T_5}. However, suppose that *forward*(B_5, V_3, t_{B_5}) fails, which means that t_{B_5} cannot be extended to a consistent instantiation of variables in B_5, then *DFS*(B_5, V_3, t_{B_5}) returns sol_{T_5} which is a nil-tuple. Since sol_{T_5} is empty, tuple t_{B_5} is deleted from S_3, and S_3 is checked to determine if it is empty now. If it is, then there is no solution to the problem, *DFS*(B_1, V_1, t_{B_1}) will return *unsatisfiable* and *CDBT*($\mathbb{P}$, *sol*) will return *unsatisfiable*. We suppose that S_3 is not empty. Then *DFS*(B_1, V', tup') is called, where $V' = V_1 \cup V_2$ and $tup' = tup_{V_1} \bowtie tup_{V_2}$. This time, *forward*($B_1, V', tup'$) is called to extend tup' to a consistent instantiation of variables in V_{B_1}. If it finds one without re-instantiating variables in V_2 and V_1, then the instantiation of variables involved in the subtree rooted at B_2 is retained, and *DFS* is called for child nodes B_5, B_6, B_7. If variables in V_2 are re-instantiated, then the variables involved in the subtree rooted at B_2 may have to be re-instantiated. However, whether or not variables in V_{B_3} and V_{B_5} need to be re-instantiated depends on whether or not V_5 and V_6 are re-instantiated. If *forward*(B_1, V', tup') goes back to V_1, then *DFS*(B_1, V', tup') returns empty tuple, we will choose another tuple from S_1 and start from there.

3.3 Analysis

For analysis, we define *minimal constraint* and give a few technical lemmas, which have been proven in [22].

Let $\mathbb{P} = (X, D, V, S)$ be a CSP and $C = \{C_i = (V_i, S_i) | V_i \in V, S_i \in S\}$ a set of constraints. Let $H = (X, V)$ be the associated hypergraph, $\omega(H) = (W, F)$ an ω-graph, $B = \{B_1, B_2, \ldots, B_l\}$ a set of blocks ordered in the depth-first manner, and $A = \{V_{a_1}, V_{a_2}, \ldots, V_{a_l}\}$ a set of separating nodes. Let V_{B_i} denote the subset of variables involved in block B_i.

Definition 1. *Let (X, D, V, S) be a CSP, let V' be a subset of V and C' a subset of C restricted on V'. A* sub-CSP induced by V' *is a CSP (X', D', V', S') where $X' = \bigcup V'$, D' is a subset of the domains of variables in X', and S' is a set of constraint instances corresponding to V'. A constraint $C_i \in C'$ is said to be* minimal relative to (X', D', V', S') *if every tuple in S_i can be extended to a consistent instantiation of variables in X'. A constraint $C_i \in C$ is said to be* minimal *if it is minimal relative to (X, D, V, S). A CSP is said to be* minimal *if every constraint is minimal.*

Let $C_A = \{(V_{a_i}, S_{a_i}) | V_{a_i} \in A\}$ be a subset of constraints on A.

Lemma 1. *If every constraint in C_A is minimal, then every consistent instantiation of variables involved in each block can be extended to a solution.*

This lemma suggests that if every constraint on those articulation nodes is minimal, then the relation represented by the sub-CSP corresponding to each block is minimal. The following lemma indicates that minimizing the constraints on articulation nodes can be done by minimizing them relative to each block.

Lemma 2. *If every constraint (V_{a_i}, S_{a_i}) in C_A is minimal relative to the sub-CSP induced by the block to which V_{a_i} belongs, then they are also minimal.*

Lemma 3. *Let B_i be a block and V_{a_i} the separating node. If a tuple in S_{a_i} has no consistent extension to variables in V_{B_i}, then it cannot be extended to a solution.*

Based on this lemma, if a tuple in a constraint corresponding to an articulation node has no consistent extension to the variables involved in the block to which the articulation node belongs, it can be safely deleted. If every tuple in such a constraint is so, then there is no solution to the problem.

Lemma 4. *Let B_i be the parent block of B_j, and V_{a_j} the separating node in B_j. Let tup_{B_i} and tup_{B_j} be consistent instantiations of variable in V_{B_i} and V_{B_j} respectively. If $tup_{B_i}[V_{a_j}] = tup_{B_j}[V_{a_j}]$, then $tup_{B_i} \bowtie tup_{B_j}$ is a consistent instantiation of variables $V_{B_i} \cup V_{B_j}$.*

This lemma suggests that if we have a consistent instantiation tup_{B_i} of variables in a parent block B_i, extending tup_{B_i} to the variables in the child block B_j can be done by extending $tup_{B_i}[V_{a_j}]$ to the variables in B_j, so the consistent checking is restricted within the child block.

Theorem 1. *The ω-CDBT is correct.*

Proof. We prove that ω-CDBT is sound, complete, and it terminates. The CDBT algorithm has been proven to be correct in [23], the inner-BT consisting of *forward* and *goback* is correct with respect to each block.

Based on Lemma 4, when a consistent instantiation of variables in the parent blocks is extended to a child block, the new instantiation to variables including variables in the child block is consistent. In particular, when a consistent instantiation is successfully extended to variables in the last block, we have a whole assignment which is a solution. This proves the soundness.

The completeness follows from Lemma 3 and the fact that the inner-BT is complete.

The search space of *ω-CDBT* can be seen as a $|W|$-level tree, in which each level corresponds to a $V_i \in W$, and *ω-CDBT* visits every node in the search space at most once, it terminates. □

Suppose that the ω-graph is k-cyclic and has l blocks. Let $|s|$ be the size of the maximal constraint relations.

Lemma 5. *If every constraint in C_A is minimal, then any backtracking performed in* ω-CDBT *is restricted within each block, and the complexity of using* ω-CDBT *to solve a CSP with minimum constraints in C_A is $O(l|s|^k)$.*

Proof. Suppose that the algorithm has found a consistent instantiation of variables in V_{B_i} and it moves forward to a child block B_j. Finding a consistent instantiation of variables in V_{B_j} may require backtracking but it will not backtrack to the parent block B_i, since, according to Lemma 1, the existing consistent instantiation of variables in V_{B_i} can be extended to a solution.

The time complexity of finding a consistent instantiation of variables involved in a block is $O(|s|^k)$, and there are l blocks, so the time complexity of *ω-CDBT* is $O(l|s|^k)$. □

Theorem 2. *The time complexity of* ω-CDBT *is* $O(l|s|^k)$.

Proof. Based on the Lemma 2, minimizing constraints in C_A can be done by minimizing them relative to each block. The complexity of minimizing a constraint relative to a block is $O(|s|^k)$, so the complexity of minimizing constraints in C_A is $O(l|s|^k)$. In the worst case (that is equivalent to using ω-*CDBT* to find all solutions), every constraint in C_A will be minimized, which takes $O(l|s|^k)$ time, and then finding solutions with minimized constraint in C_A takes another $O(l|s|^k)$ time. Together, the time complexity of ω-*CDBT* is $O(l|s|^k)$. □

Since the complexity of solving the CSP by using ω-CDBT is exponential in k, a class of CSP where k is less than a fixed number is ω-CDBT solvable in polynomial time. Following directly from Proposition 1, this class of tractable CSPs includes the class of CSPs solvable by the hinge decomposition [16].

4 Comparison with Decomposition and other Search Methods

A general decomposition scheme is given in Section 2.3 and an ω-graph based decomposition algorithm can be easily constructed. To compare ω-CDBT with decomposition algorithms including ω-graph based decomposition, we argue that ω-CDBT shares the virtue of tree search algorithms in that it finds only one consistent assignment to variables in each block which corresponding to a sub-CSP in the decomposition scheme. Finding one solution is more cost-effective than finding all solutions.

Furthermore, the ω-CDBT algorithm has an additional two advantages over other search methods: 1) when a tuple t_{B_i} cannot be extended to a consistent instantiation of variables in V_{B_i}, it is deleted from the constraint on the separating node of B_i; then all the sub-regions of search space rooted at nodes containing t_{B_i} will be ruled out to avoid further exploration; 2) when the algorithm backtracks from a child block to the parent, the instantiation of the variables in the sibling blocks preceding this block may be retained, so that this sub-region of the search space does not need to be searched repetitively.

Another advantage of ω-CDBT is its ability to overcome the failure of decomposition methods when a given CSP is not decomposable. In this case, the decomposition method degenerates into whatever method is used to find all solutions which is expensive. ω-CDBT, on the other hand, degenerates to the original CDBT algorithm which is still a practical CSP solving algorithm.

5 Conclusion

Constraint satisfaction in its general form is known to be NP-complete, yet many CSPs are tractable and can be solved efficiently. Every CSP has an associated constraint graph. The key idea is that the efficiency of finding a solution can be improved by exploiting structural properties of the constraint graph. The contributions of this paper are both theoretical and practical. First, we have identified a new tractable class of CSPs that contains previously identified tractable classes. This extends the known set of CSPs that are solvable in polynomial time. Second, we have provided an algorithm that solves CSPs in this class in polynomial time, whereas other known algorithms cannot guarantee polynomial time solutions for this class. Third, even outside of this class, the provided algorithm has a better worst case complexity. This extends the limits of what is solvable in practice. Future empirical study is required to evaulate the actual improvement of the ω-CDBT algorithm against other decompostion and search algorithms.

References

[1] C. Beeri, R. Fagin, D. Maier, and M. Yannakakis. On the desirability of acyclic database schemes. *J. ACM*, 30(3):497–513, 1983.

[2] C. Berge. *Graphs and Hypergraphs.* North-Holland, New York, 1973.

[3] M. Cooper, D. A. Cohen, and P. G. Jeavons. Characterizing tractable constraints. *Artificial Intelligence*, 65:347–361, 1994.

[4] R. Dechter. Enhancement schemes for constraint processing: backjumping, learning, and cutset decomposition. *Artificial Intelligence*, 41:273–312, 1990.

[5] R. Dechter. Constraint networks. In S. C. Shapiro, editor, *Encyclopedia of Artificial Intelligence*, volume 1, pages 276–285. Wiley-Interscience, 2nd edition, 1992.

[6] R. Dechter. From local to global consistency. *Artificial Intelligence*, 55:87–102, 1992.

[7] R. Dechter and J. Pearl. Tree clustering for constraint networks. *Artificial Intelligence*, 38:353–366, 1989.

[8] R. Dechter and J. Pearl. Directed constraint networks: A relational framework for causal modeling. In *Proceedings of IJCAI-91*, pages 1164–1170, Sydney, Australia, 1991.

[9] R. Dechter and P. van Beek. Local and global relational consistency. In *Proceedings of the 1st International Conference on Principles and Practices of Constraint Programming*, pages 240–257, Cassis, France, September 1995.

[10] Y. Deville and P. Van Hentenryck. An efficient arc consistency algorithm for a class of CSPs. In *Proceedings of IJCAI-91*, pages 325–330, Sydney, Australia, 1991.

[11] S. Even. *Graph Algorithms.* Computer Science Press, Potomac, Maryland, 1979.

[12] E. Freuder. A sufficient condition for backtrack-free search. *J. of the ACM*, 29(1):25–32, 1982.

[13] E. Freuder. Backtrack-free and backtrack-bounded search. In L. Kanal and V. Kumar, editors, *Search in Artificial Intelligence*, pages 343–369. Springer-Verlag, New York, 1988.

[14] G. Gottlob. A comparison of structural CSP decomposition methods. *Artificial Intelligence*, 124:243–282, 2000.

[15] M. Gyssens. On the complexity of join dependencies. *ACM Transactions on Database Systems*, 11(1):81–108, 1986.

[16] M. Gyssens, P. Jeavons, and D. Cohen. Decomposing constraint satisfaction problems using database techniques. *Artificial Intelligence*, 66:57–89, 1994.

[17] P. Jeavons. Tractable constraints on ordered domains. *Artificial Intelligence*, 79:327–339, 1995.

[18] P. Jeavons, D. Cohen, and M. Gyssens. A test for tractability. In *Lecture Notes in Computer Science*, volume 1118, pages 267–281, Cambridge, MA, 1996. CP'96.

[19] P. Jegou. On some partial line graphs of a hypergraph and the associated matroid. *Discrete Mathematics*, 111:333–344, 1993.

[20] P. Jegou. On the consistency of general constraint satisfaction problems. In *Proceedings of AAAI-93*, pages 114–119, 1993.

[21] L. M. Kirousis. Fast parallel constraint satisfaction. *Artificial Intelligence*, 64:174–160, 1993.

[22] W. Pang. *Constraint Structure in Constraint Satisfaction Problems.* PhD thesis, University of Regina, Canada, 1998.

[23] W. Pang and S. D. Goodwin. Constraint-directed backtracking. In *The 10th Australian Joint Conference on AI*, pages 47–56, Perth, Western Australia, December 1997.

[24] W. Pang and S. D. Goodwin. A revised sufficient condition for backtrack-free search. In *Proceedings of 10th Florida AI Research Symposium*, pages 52–56, Daytona Beach, FL, May 1997.

[25] W. Pang and S. D. Goodwin. Characterizing tractable CSPs. In *The 12th Canadian Conference on AI*, pages 259–272, Vancouver, BC, Canada, June 1998.

[26] W. Pang and S. D. Goodwin. Consistency in general CSPs. In *The 6th Pacific Rim International Conference on AI*, pages 469–479, Melbourne, Australia, August 2000.

[27] W. Pang and S. D. Goodwin. Binary representation for general CSPs. In *Proceedings of 14th Florida AI Research Symposium (FLAIRS-2001)*, Key West, FL, May 2001.

[28] P. van Beek. On the minimality and decomposability of constraint networks. In *Proceedings of AAAI-92*, pages 447–452, 1992.

[29] P. van Beek and R. Dechter. On the minimality and global consistency of row-convex constraint networks. *Journal of the ACM*, 42:543–561, 1995.

Iterated Robust Tabu Search for MAX-SAT

Kevin Smyth[1], Holger H. Hoos[1,*], and Thomas Stützle[2]

[1] Department of Computer Science, University of British Columbia
Vancouver, B.C., V6T 1Z4, Canada
{hoos,ksmyth}@cs.ubc.ca
http://www.cs.ubc.ca/labs/beta

[2] Fachbereich Informatik, Technische Universität Darmstadt
Alexanderstr. 10, D-64289 Darmstadt, Germany
stuetzle@informatik.tu-darmstadt.de

Abstract. MAX-SAT, the optimisation variant of the satisfiability problem in propositional logic, is an important and widely studied combinatorial optimisation problem with applications in AI and other areas of computing science. In this paper, we present a new stochastic local search (SLS) algorithm for MAX-SAT that combines Iterated Local Search and Tabu Search, two well-known SLS methods that have been successfully applied to many other combinatorial optimisation problems. The performance of our new algorithm exceeds that of current state-of-the-art MAX-SAT algorithms on various widely studied classes of unweighted and weighted MAX-SAT instances, particularly for Random-3-SAT instances with high variance clause weight distributions. We also report promising results for various classes of structured MAX-SAT instances.

1 Introduction and Background

The satisfiability problem in propositional logic (SAT) is the task to decide whether a given propositional formula has a model. More formally, given a set of m clauses $\{C_1, \ldots, C_m\}$ involving n Boolean variables $x_1, \ldots, x_n$ the SAT problem is to decide whether an assignment of values to variables exists such that all clauses are simultaneously satisfied. This problem plays a prominent role in various areas of computer science, mathematical logic and artificial intelligence, but also in many applications [7, 13, 1].

MAX-SAT is the optimisation variant of SAT and can be seen as a generalisation of the SAT problem: Given a propositional formula in conjunctive normal form (CNF), the MAX-SAT problem then is to find a variable assignment that maximises the number of satisfied clauses. In *weighted MAX-SAT*, each clause C_i has an associated weight w_i and the goal becomes to maximise the total weight of the satisfied clauses. The decision variants of both SAT and MAX-SAT are $\mathcal{NP}$–complete [5]. Furthermore, it is known that optimal solutions to MAX-SAT are hard to approximate; for MAX-3-SAT (unweighted MAX-SAT with 3 literals per clause), *e.g.*, there exists no polynomial-time approximation algorithm

* To whom correspondence should be addressed.

Y. Xiang and B. Chaib-draa (Eds.): AI 2003, LNAI 2671, pp. 129–144, 2003.

with a (worst-case) approximation ratio lower than $8/7 \approx 1.1429$. It is worth noting that approximation algorithms for MAX-SAT can be empirically shown to achieve much better solution qualities for many types of MAX-SAT instances; however, their performance is usually substantially inferior to that of state-of-the-art stochastic local search (SLS) algorithms for MAX-SAT (see, *e.g.*, [8]).

Many SLS methods have been applied to MAX-SAT leading to a large number of algorithms for unweighted and weighted MAX-SAT. These include algorithms originally proposed for SAT, which can be applied to unweighted MAX-SAT in a straightforward way by keeping track of the best solution found so far in the search process. It is not clear that SLS algorithms that are known to perform well on SAT can be expected to show equally strong performance on unweighted MAX-SAT and some empirical evidence suggests that this is generally not the case. Therefore, many SLS algorithms were directly developed for unweighted and, in particular, weighted MAX-SAT or extended from existing SLS algorithms for SAT in various ways.

The currently best performing SLS algorithms for unweighted and weighted MAX-SAT fall into three categories: Tabu Search algorithms, Dynamic Local Search algorithms, and Iterated Local Search. Very good performance was reported for Reactive Tabu Search (H-RTS), a tabu search that dynamically adjusts the tabu tenure, on unweighted MAX-SAT instances [2]. High performing Dynamic Local Search algorithms include DLM by Wah and Shang [19], a later extension called DLM-99-SAT [21], and Guided Local Search (GLS) [15]. Computational results suggest that GLS is currently the top performing SLS algorithm for specific classes of weighted MAX-SAT instances, outperforming DLM and WalkSAT extensions to weighted MAX-SAT [11]. Also noteworthy is the recent Iterated Local Search by Yagiura and Ibaraki (ILS-YI) [23] that uses a local search algorithm based on 2- and 3-flip neighbourhoods. Particularly for MAX-SAT-encoded minimum-cost graph colouring and set covering instances, as well as for a big, MAX-SAT-encoded real-world time-tabling instance, the 2-flip variant of ILS-YI performs better than other versions of ILS-YI and a tabu search algorithm implemented by Yagiura and Ibaraki.

In this paper, we propose a new Iterated Local Search (ILS) algorithm and experimentally compare its performance to current state-of-the-art algorithms. The key idea behind ILS is to alternate between local searches and so-called perturbation phases which are designed to take the search away from the local optimum reached by the subsidiary local search procedure. Our new ILS algorithm, Iterated Robust Tabu Search (IRoTS), uses a Robust Tabu Search (RoTS) algorithm for both the subsidiary local search and perturbation phases. RoTS is a particular Tabu Search algorithm, originally applied to the Quadratic Assignment Problem [20], which we adapted to MAX-SAT.

Our empirical evaluation of IRoTS indicates that on a range of well-known benchmark instances for weighted and unweighted MAX-SAT this new algorithm performs significantly better than state-of-the-art MAX-SAT algorithms, such as GLS [15]. This is particularly the case for weighted MAX-SAT instances with highly variable clause weight distributions, as well as for highly overconstrained

procedure *Iterated Local Search*
  $s_0 = GenerateInitialSolution$
  $s^* = LocalSearch(s_0)$
  repeat
    $s' = Perturbation(s^*)$
    $s^{*\prime} = LocalSearch(s')$
    $s^* = AcceptanceCriterion(s^*, s^{*\prime})$
  until termination condition met
end procedure

Fig. 1. Algorithm outline of ILS

unweighted MAX-SAT instance; in both cases, IRoTS reaches quasi-optimal solutions[1] up to an order of magnitude faster than GLS. IRoTS also performs significantly better than many of the state-of-the-art algorithms on various classes of structured MAX-SAT instances, although on these instances it typically does not reach the performance of GLS.

A detailed analysis of the behaviour of IRoTS on individual problem instances shows that its performance over multiple runs as well as over multiple instances from the same test-set is typically less variable than that of GLS, which indicates that our Iterative Robust Tabu Search algorithm escapes more effectively from local optima than the Dynamic Local Search scheme underlying GLS.

The remainder of this paper is structured as follows. In the next section we introduce Robust Tabu Search for weighted MAX-SAT and our new Iterated Local Search algorithm, Iterated Robust Tabu Search. In Section 3, we describe the experimental protocol and benchmark instances used for our empirical analysis, whose results are presented and discussed in Sections 4 and 5. Finally, in Section 6 we draw some conclusions and briefly discuss several directions for future work.

2 ILS for MAX-SAT

In this section we describe our Iterated Local Search (ILS) implementation for MAX-SAT. ILS is a class of algorithms that essentially perform a biased random walk in the space of the local optima encountered by an underlying local search algorithm [14]. This walk is obtained by iteratively perturbing a locally optimal solution s^*, then applying local search to obtain a new locally optimal solution $s^{*\prime}$, and finally using an acceptance criterion to decide from which of the two solutions $s^*, s^{*\prime}$ to continue the search. An algorithm outline of ILS is given in Figure 1.

[1] Many of the test sets we experiment with in this study are intractable for complete solvers, so we are forced to empirically estimate the optimal solutions for some instances. Details of the protocol used for this estimation are given in Section 3.

Our ILS algorithm for weighted and unweighted MAX-SAT is strongly based on an adaptation of Robust Tabu Search (RoTS) [20] to MAX-SAT. RoTS is used in the local search phase and also in the perturbation phase. Since RoTS is actually itself a high-performing SLS algorithm for MAX-SAT, we first give some details on the RoTS algorithm, before describing how it is used in our ILS algorithm.

In each search step, the RoTS algorithm for MAX-SAT flips a non-tabu variables that achieves a maximal improvement in the total weight of the unsatisfied clauses (the size of this improvement is also called *score*) and declares it tabu for the next tl steps. The parameter tl is called the tabu tenure. An exception to this "tabu" rule is made if a more recently flipped variable achieves an improvement over the best solution seen so far (this mechanism is called aspiration). Furthermore, whenever a variable has not been flipped within a certain number of search steps (in our implementation: $10n$), it is forced to be flipped. This implements a form of long-term memory and helps prevent stagnation of the search process. Finally, instead of using a fixed tabu tenure, every n iterations the parameter tl is randomly chosen from an interval $[t_{min}, t_{max}]$ according to a uniform distribution. The tabu status of variables is determined by comparing the number of search steps that have been performed since the most recent flip of a given variable with the current tabu tenure; hence, changes in tl immediately affect the tabu status and tenure of all variables.

Our ILS algorithm, called IRoTS in the following, is initialised by setting each variable independently to true or false with equal probability (the same random initialisation is used by most other SLS algorithms for SAT and MAX-SAT). As previously stated, its subsidiary local search and perturbation procedures are both based on the RoTS algorithm described above. Each local search phase executes RoTS steps until no improvement in the incumbent solution has been achieved for *escape_threshold* iterations. This parameter is set by default to $n^2/4$, which was determined to give robust performance over a wide range of test sets. The default tabu tenure for the local search phase was set to $n/10 + 4$, which robustly achieves good performance on many of our test sets. The perturbation phase consists of a fixed number of RoTS search steps (default value: $9n/10$) with tabu tenure values that are substantially higher than the ones used in the local search phase (default tabu tenure for the perturbation is $n/2$). At the beginning of each local search and perturbation phase, all variables are declared non-tabu, irrespectively of their previous tabu status. If applying perturbation and subsequent local search to a candidate solution s results in a candidate solution s' that is better than the best candidate solution accepted since the search was initialised, the search is continued from s'. If s and s' have the same solution quality, one of them is chosen uniformly at random. In all other cases, the worse of the two candidate solutions s and s' is chosen with probability 0.1, and the better one otherwise.

The default parameter settings for IRoTS used in this study were determined in preliminary experiments, in which we also observed that IRoTS typically achieves significant performance improvements over RoTS. These default settings were used in all experiments reported here, with the exception of the experiments on the structured instances. Details on our experiments (including parameter settings) are given in Sections 4 and 5.

Throughout this paper, we compare IRoTS to two variants of Guided Local Search (GLS) as well as the ILS algorithm by Yagiura and Ibaraki (ILS-YI). GLS [15] iteratively modifies clause penalties to help the local search escape from local optima. GLS is based on HSAT [6] as the underlying local search method; in each search step, HSAT flips a variable with maximal score, breaking ties in favour of the variable which was flipped longest ago. When trapped in a local optimum, GLS modifies a penalty vector consisting of penalty values clp_i for each clause C_i in the given CNF formula. In GLS, clause weights in weighted MAX-SAT instances are only considered when computing the utility value of a clause, defined as $util(a, C_i) = w_i/(1 + clp_i)$ if clause i is unsatisfied under the current variable assignment a and zero otherwise. At each iteration of GLS, only the penalties of clauses with maximum utility are increased. The clause penalties are used when computing the variables' score when evaluating flips. In the GLS2 variant, all penalty values are regularly decayed, while in the basic GLS penalties never decrease. The reference implementations for GLS and GLS2 used for our experiments were kindly provided by Patrick Mills.

Yagiura and Ibaraki proposed and studied a simple ILS algorithm for MAX-SAT, ILS-YI, which initialises the search at a randomly chosen assignment, uses a subsidiary iterative first improvement search procedure, and a perturbation phase that consists of a fixed number of (undirected) random walk steps; the acceptance criterion always selects the better of the two given candidate solutions [22, 23]. The ILS-YI algorithm performs particularly well when using a 2- or 3-flip neighbourhood in the subsidiary local search procedure. The key to an efficient implementation of ILS-YI with this 2- and 3-flip local search procedure lies in an efficient caching scheme for evaluating moves in the respective larger neighbourhoods. An implementation of ILS-YI is publicly available at `http://www-or.amp.i.kyoto-u.ac.jp/members/yagiura/msat-codes/`.

3 Experiment Design

For the computational experiments conducted in this study, we compare the performance of the algorithms described in Section 2 on both random and structured instances. All experiments were run on a 1Ghz Pentium III with 1 GB RAM, 256KB L2 cache, running Linux RedHat 7.3 and using `gcc-3.2`. We first compared the performance of the algorithms on the `wjnh` and the `bor` test sets, which have been previously proposed and studied in the literature [18, 3, 12]. The `wjnh` test set consists of 44 randomly generated instances. The clause lengths vary in size, and the clause weights are randomly and uniformly chosen integers from the interval [1 . . . 1000]. Several of the instances are satisfiable — a clear distinction is made between the satisfiable and unsatisfiable instances when reporting results for this test set. The `bor` test set consists of both weighted and unweighted Random 2- and 3-SAT instances, resulting in four classes of instances

Table 1. Test-sets of unweighted MAX-SAT instances with varying clause to variable ratios (left), and weighted MAX-SAT instances with different variance σ^2 of clause weight distributions (right) used within this study

Name	n	m
`rnd50-250u`	50	250
`rnd100-500u`	100	500
`rnd100-700u`	100	700
`rnd100-850u`	100	850
`rnd100-1000u`	100	1000
`rnd200-1000u`	200	1000

Name	n	m	μ	σ
`rnd50-w50`	50	250	250	50
`rnd50-w250`	50	250	250	250
`rnd100-w100`	100	500	500	100
`rnd100-w500`	100	500	500	500
`rnd200-w200`	200	1000	1000	200
`rnd200-w1000`	200	1000	1000	1000

$\{weighted, unweighted\} \times \{2SAT, 3SAT\}$. Each of these classes is divided into three test sets consisting of 50, 100, and 150 variable instances for a total of 12 test sets. The number of instances in each test set is relatively small, ranging from 2 to 9, and each instance has a different clause to variable ratio (all instances are significantly overconstrained). The clause weights in the weighted test sets are randomly and uniformly chosen integers from the interval $[1 \ldots 10]$.

In order to be able to perform more systematic and detailed empirical evaluations, we generated twelve new test sets of benchmark instances with 100 instances each. Several of these test sets are unweighted, and sampled from the Uniform Random 3-SAT distribution [16] for various number of variables and clauses, corresponding to the over-constrained region of Uniform Random-3-SAT. The remaining test sets were obtained from this set by adding integer clause weights that were randomly generated according to discretised, truncated normal distributions. In all cases, the mean of the clause weight distribution was chosen as $\mu = 5n$, where n is the number of variables, and the distribution was symmetrically truncated such that all clause weights are restricted to lie in the interval $[1 \ldots 2\mu - 1]$. Symmetric truncation guarantees that the actual mean is close to μ. Within this class of distributions, standard deviations σ of n and $5n$ were used for generating our test-sets. The resulting test-sets are summarised in Table 1.

Additionally, we performed experiments on three test sets of structured MAX-SAT instances; these were obtained by encoding Minimum Cost Graph Colouring and Set Covering Problems, as well as and Level Graph Crossing Minimisation Problems into weighted MAX-SAT [23, 4]. We denote these test-sets as `YI-GCP`, `YI-SCP`, and `LGCMP`, respectively.

To evaluate the relative performance of IRoTS, ILS-YI, GLS, and GLS2, we measured the distribution of the CPU time (and number of search steps) required by each algorithm for reaching a certain (typically optimal) solution quality on each given instance. These run-time distributions (RTDs) [10] were measured by running each algorithm 100 times on each problem instance until the specified solution quality was reached or exceeded. We refer to the median

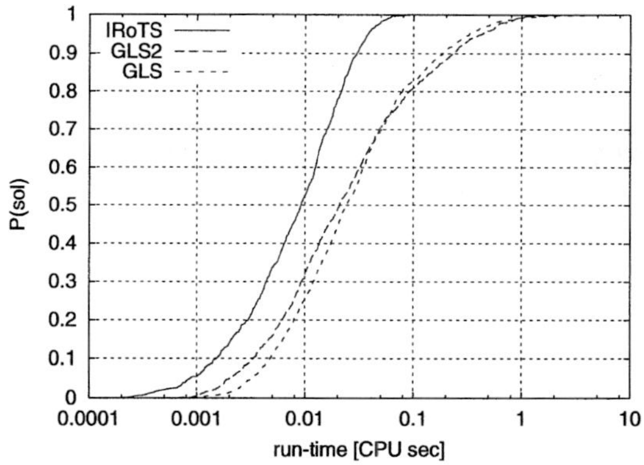

Fig. 2. RTDs for IRoTS, GLS, and GLS2 on the instance from the `rnd100-w100` test set with the median *sc* (in terms of run-time for GLS)

of the RTDs thus obtained as the *search cost* (*sc*) for the given algorithm and instance.

With the exception of the experiments on structured MAX-SAT instances, we generally measured RTDs for reaching provably optimal or best-known solution qualities. Where possible, we used Borcher and Furman's complete solvers **maxsat** and **wmaxsat** [3] to determine the optimal solution quality for each instance. (These are the best-performing complete MAX-SAT solvers we are aware of.) However, since the larger instances become intractable for these solvers, we estimated the quality of the optimal solutions by using an "iterative deepening" scheme for IRoTS. IRoTS is run for *base_cutoff* $= 10^6$ steps. Whenever an assignment is found that is better than any previously found assignment, the cutoff is set to the maximum of *base_cutoff* and ten times the number of search steps taken up to that point. This "iterative deepening" scheme is repeated 10 times per instance, and the best solution quality found over all 10 runs was reported as optimal. We verified the solution qualities reported as optimal following this protocol against the true optimal solution qualities for the test sets for which it was still possible to run the complete solver, and in all cases IRoTS had found the true optimal solution. We also verified the optimal solutions for a small, randomly selected set of larger instances (this required running the complete solver for multiple CPU days). In the remainder of this paper we treat the solutions returned by this protocol as optimal.

4 Results for Random Instances

In this section, we present our results for the randomly generated instances described in Section 3. Figures 2 and 3 show the run-time distributions of IRoTS, GLS, and GLS2 on the instances from the test set `rnd100-w100` with median and max *sc* respectively. It is clear from the fat right tails of the RTDs for

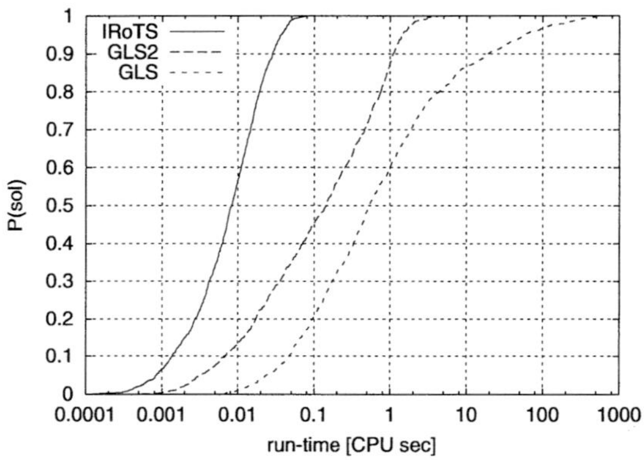

Fig. 3. RTDs for IRoTS, GLS, and GLS2 on the instance from the `rnd100-w100` test set with the highest *sc* (in terms of run-time for GLS)

GLS and GLS2 that both of these algorithms suffer from stagnation behaviour on these instances. This effect is most apparent in the hard instance (Figure 3), where we see a very pronounced right tail for GLS. The RTDs for IRoTS are approximately exponential.

This trend was present for all of the random test sets, and results in GLS2 performing better, in general, than GLS on all of the test sets; therefore we focus on GLS2 in our analysis. Another result of this stagnation behaviour is that the ratio of the mean to the median of the RTDs is much higher for GLS and GLS2 than for IRoTS, which is more "well-behaved". Because the median is a more stable summary statistic, we report statistics only of the median in all our results. When considering mean instead of median run-times, the ratios of the run-times of GLS and GLS2 to IRoTS are even higher than the ratios that we report.

The ILS-YI algorithm using the 1-flip neighbourhood (ILS-YI(1)) required multiple orders of magnitude more CPU time than IRoTS on all of the weighted and unweighted Random 3-SAT test sets, and was unable to solve some instances from the `wjnh` test set within 1 CPU hour. The ILS-YI algorithm using the 2-flip neighbourhood (ILS-YI(2)) performed significantly better than ILS-YI(1), though still required greater than an order of magnitude more CPU time than IRoTS in all cases, and performed particularly badly on the `wjnh` test set (there were instances from `wjnh` which required greater than 1 CPU hour for ILS-YI(2) to solve). Because of these poor results, for the sake of brevity we don't report further details for ILS-YI here.

Figure 4 shows a scatterplot of the median CPU time required for IRoTS and GLS2 for solving each of the `wjnh` instances. Some of the instances in this test set are actually satisfiable (in these cases, the clause weights are redundant, since an optimal solution will have a cost of zero), and have been marked in the plots. We see that the satisfiable instances tend to be easier for both IRoTS and GLS2. For 39 of the 44 instances in the test set, GLS requires fewer steps that

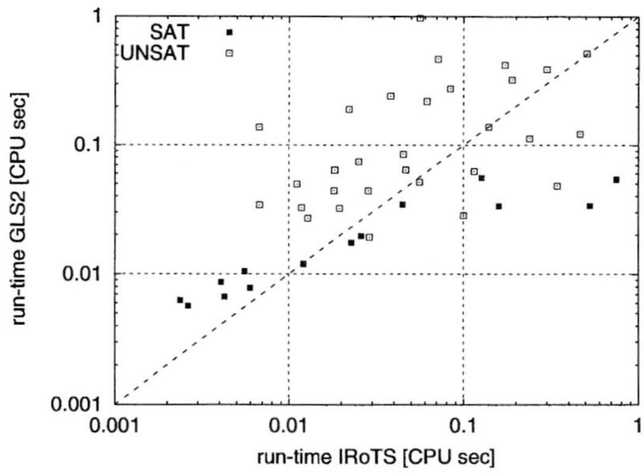

Fig. 4. Performance of IRoTS vs. GLS2 on the `wjnh` test set, measuring median CPU time for finding optimal solutions

IRoTS to find an optimal solution; the median *sc* for IRoTS is 14896, while the median *sc* for GLS2 is 2977 search steps. However, when we consider the median CPU time required to find an optimal solution we see that IRoTS requires less CPU time than GLS2 on 28 of the 44 instances, and the median CPU time for IRoTS to find a solution is 0.038 seconds, while the median CPU time for GLS2 is 0.050 seconds. In summary, IRoTS performs on par with GLS, the best known algorithm for the `wjnh` instances. Since GLS was shown to perform better than a variety of earlier proposed algorithms on this test set [18, 19, 21, 11], this fact also applies to IRoTS.

We ran all of the algorithms on the `bor` test set, and present a short summary of these results here. Overall, IRoTS was the best performing algorithm on these test sets. IRoTS typically required between 1.5 and 5 times less CPU time than GLS and GLS2 for finding optimal solutions. For example, on the 150 variable weighted 3-SAT test set, the mean run-time for IRoTS, GLS, and GLS2 are 0.0093, 0.024, and 0.018 CPU seconds, respectively. The instances tend to get easier (as the clause/variable ratio is increased) for IRoTS but harder for GLS and GLS2 (similar results are reported later in this section for the unweighted Random 3-SAT test sets). The ILS-YI algorithms both required over 5 times more CPU time to solve all of the test sets than all of the other algorithms, with the worst results for the larger test sets. RoTS performed as well as or better than GLS and GLS2, and worse than IRoTS in almost all cases.

Because there are so few instances in each of these test sets, the data presented above for the `bor` test set may not be representative of the typical behaviour of these algorithms on random test sets. To address this question, we now consider the performance of the algorithms on the weighted and unweighted Random 3-SAT test sets described in Section 3. Again, we report only results for IRoTS and GLS2, which were the two best performing algorithms on these test sets.

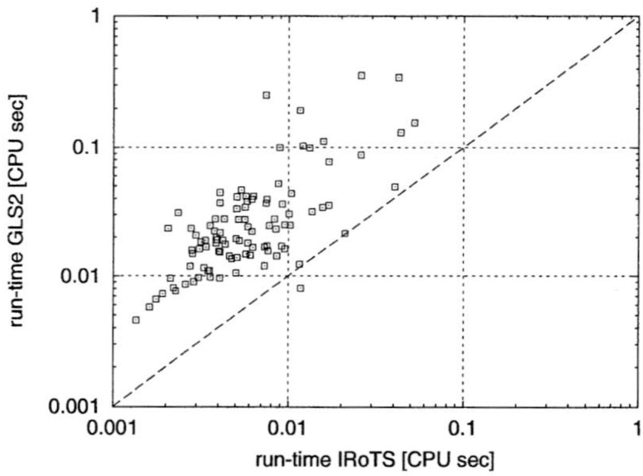

Fig. 5. Performance of IRoTS vs. GLS2 on the `rnd100-w100` test set, measuring median CPU time for finding optimal solutions

Figure 5 shows a scatter plot of the median CPU time required for IRoTS and GLS2 to optimally solve each instance in the `rnd100-w100` test set. We see that IRoTS requires less CPU time than GLS2 on all but one instance. We also notice that the CPU times are positively correlated, but that there is a significant amount of noise in the correlation especially for the harder instances. Interestingly, the amount of noise is proportional to σ^2 (the variance in the clause weights) — as the variance in the clause weight distribution increases, the correlation between the *sc* of IRoTS and GLS2 decreases.

Table 4 shows summary statistics of the distribution of search costs for IRoTS and GLS2 on the Random 3-SAT test sets. Clearly, IRoTS performs better than GLS2 on these test sets; IRoTS requires fewer flips for 4 out of the 9 test sets, and less CPU time than GLS2 in all cases. Table 4 shows the relative performance of IRoTS and GLS2 on the unweighted 100 variable Random 3-SAT test sets as the clauses/variables ratio increases. Note that the relative performance of IRoTS vs. GLS2 increases with the clauses/variables ratio. Furthermore, the instances become progressively easier for IRoTS as the level of constrainedness increases, while at the same time they become more and more difficult for GLS2. For the most overconstrained test sets, the median CPU time for finding optimal solutions is more than an order of magnitude less for IRoTS than for GLS2.

It may be noted that many of the Random-3-SAT instances are optimally solved within the first RoTS local search phase of the IRoTS algorithm (which is terminated after $n^2/4$ iterations without improvement), indicating that in these cases, RoTS alone is sufficient for finding optimal solutions. This is, however, not generally true for the hardest instances, where IRoTS shows substantially improved performance over RoTS; this performance advantage of IRoTS over RoTS is even more pronounced for the structured instances considered in the next section.

Table 2. Summary statistics of the search cost distribution for IRoTS and GLS2 on the Random 3-SAT test sets; q_x denotes the xth percentile; *f.b.* is the fraction of instances in the test set with $sc(\text{IRoTS}) < sc(\text{GLS2})$; *s.f.* is the "speedup-factor", *i.e.* the ratio $q_{50}(\text{GLS2}) / q_{50}(\text{IRoTS})$

	run-length [search steps]						run-time [CPU sec ×10^{-4}]					
	IRoTS		GLS2				IRoTS		GLS2			
Test Set	q_{50}	q_{90}/q_{10}	q_{50}	q_{90}/q_{10}	*f.b*	*s.f.*	q_{50}	q_{90}/q_{10}	q_{50}	q_{90}/q_{10}	*f.b.*	*s.f.*
rnd50-250u	**113**	7.9	142	9.6	0.7	1.3	**5**	3.5	18	4.7	1.0	3.6
rnd50-w50	**274**	8.0	448	8.7	0.19	1.7	**9**	3.8	41	6.2	1.0	4.5
rnd50-w250	**574**	10.1	754	19.6	0.37	1.3	**13**	6.1	68	15.6	0.99	5.2
rnd100-500u	639	10.3	**618**	8.1	0.39	0.97	**21**	5.6	88	4.6	1.0	4.2
rnd100-w100	2202	7.5	**2160**	10.6	0.54	0.98	**52**	6.0	207	9.1	0.99	4.0
rnd100-w500	6591	11.1	**6126**	39.5	0.5	0.93	**131**	10.6	570	36.7	0.88	4.4
rnd200-1000u	6630	13.3	**5665**	23.6	0.54	0.85	**240**	11.2	712	21.2	0.99	3.0
rnd200-w200	**45648**	18.7	69523	22.7	0.56	1.5	**1449**	18.2	8244	22.1	0.95	5.7
rnd200-w1000	318836	21.4	**217964**	24.4	0.26	0.68	**10166**	20.9	28277	27.5	0.71	2.8

Table 3. Summary statistics of the search cost distribution for IRoTS and GLS2 on 100 variable unweighted Random 3-SAT test sets with increasing clauses/variables ratio

	run-length [search steps]						run-time [CPU sec ×10^{-4}]					
	IRoTS		GLS2				IRoTS		GLS2			
Test Set	q_{50}	q_{90}/q_{10}	q_{50}	q_{90}/q_{10}	*f.b.*	*s.f.*	q_{50}	q_{90}/q_{10}	q_{50}	q_{90}/q_{10}	*f.b.*	*s.f.*
rnd100-500u	639	10.3	**618**	8.1	0.39	0.97	**21**	5.6	88	4.6	1.0	4.2
rnd100-700u	**514**	6.2	1016	9.5	0.95	2.0	**19**	3.5	139	6.8	1.0	7.3
rnd100-850u	**612**	5.9	1937	6.3	1.0	2.3	**24**	3.7	288	5.7	1.0	12.0
rnd100-1000u	**499**	6.3	2193	7.4	0.99	4.4	**22**	3.1	404	6.4	1.0	18.4

5 Results for Structured Instances

For the MAX-SAT encoded graph colouring, set covering, and crossing minimisation instances [4], IRoTS with the default parameters performs rather poorly. This is not surprising, since these instances are quite different from the previously considered random instances in terms of their syntactic properties (such as clause length and weight distributions). To obtain better performance, we changed the *escape_threshold* parameter to 100 steps, and used a different perturbation mechanism, in which instead of performing RoTS with a large tabu tenure, each variable is flipped independently at random with probability 0.05. The latter modification was motivated by the observation that using RoTS in the perturbation phase resulted in stagnation of the search process. We believe that the reason for this lies in the fact that RoTS is based on a greedy heuristic, and even though when using RoTS for perturbation the tabu tenure is set very high, the underlying greedy search mechanism seems to be unable to escape from the deep local optima that appear to be encountered when solving these instances.

Table 4. Summary statistics of search costs distribution on test sets of structured instances for each of the algorithms, measured in CPU seconds. Entries marked with a '–' indicate that the respective algorithm was unable to find the desired solution quality within 1 CPU hour

	YI-GCP		YI-SCP		LGCMP	
Algorithm	q_{50}	q_{90}/q_{10}	q_{50}	q_{90}/q_{10}	q_{50}	q_{90}/q_{10}
GLS	**0.36**	1.18	**0.35**	0.95	11.15	1.07
GLS2	2.12	1.18	1.27	0.92	11.56	1.07
IRoTS	4.46	1.75	3.39	1.05	**1.18**	0.92
ILS-YI(1)	–	–	–	–	2.79	0.93
ILS-YI(2)	0.78	1.19	–	–	16.38	1.10
RoTS	–	–	–	–	1.96	0.93

Due to the extremely large computation times required by some algorithms for finding optimal (or best known) solutions of the structured instances considered here, we performed our comparative analysis based on RTDs for suboptimal solution qualities. For each instance, we ran the worst-performing of IRoTS, GLS, and GLS2 10 times with a fixed cutoff of 10 seconds. Then we chose the 90th percentile of the solution quality distribution observed for that run-time as a target for all of the algorithms, and report statistics on the time required to find the respective (typically sub-optimal) solution quality.

The results from these experiments are shown in Table 5. The relative performance of IRoTS, GLS, and GLS2 is similar for the graph colouring and set covering instances, with GLS performing best by a large margin. IRoTS was able to solve all of the instances in these two test sets, but required approximately an order of magnitude more CPU time than GLS. The performance of GLS2 and IRoTS was more comparable, but GLS2 was still better by a factor of more than 2. Interestingly, the 2-flip ILS-YI algorithm performed very well on the graph colouring instances, but not on the set covering instances.

IRoTS shows more promise on the MAX-SAT encoded crossing minimisation instances, where it requires less than an order of magnitude less CPU time to find solutions of the given quality than GLS, GLS2, and the 2-flip ILS-YI algorithm. The 1-flip ILS-YI algorithm also performs well on these instances, though IRoTS is still a factor of 2 better than ILS-YI. Interestingly, this is the only test set where the 1-flip ILS-YI algorithm was among the best performing, indicating that Iterated Local Search in general may be well-suited to this type of MAX-SAT instances.

Additional experiments indicate that GLS and GLS2 perform better on the MAX-SAT encoded crossing minimisation instances when searching for higher quality solutions. Figure 6 shows the development of solution quality over time (SQT) for a 125 node crossing minimisation instance. We see that IRoTS finds much higher quality solutions than either GLS variant in short runs (this is reflected in the results reported in Table 5), but that both GLS variants find

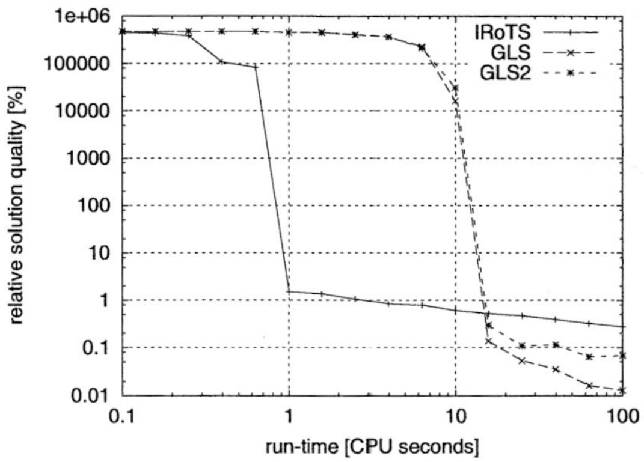

Fig. 6. SQT for a typical 125 node crossing minimisation instance. The y-axis shows the median relative solution quality found at each point in time, calculated as $sq(t)/sq^* - 1$, where $sq(t)$ is the median absolute solution quality reached at time t and sq^* is the best quality solution ever found by any of the algorithms studied in this paper

higher quality solutions if sufficiently long run-times are allowed. The results for random instances (where IRoTS outperforms GLS and GLS2) are qualitatively different, as Figure 7 shows. It is encouraging to note that IRoTS eventually finds solutions within 1% of the best known solution qualities, and that we see no evidence of stagnation for IRoTS in the SQTs.

The results of IRoTS on the structured instances also show a very strong improvement over RoTS at least for the graph colouring and set covering instances. This is further evidence that the underlying RoTS algorithm can be significantly improved by embedding it into the Iterated Local Search framework.

6 Conclusions and Future Work

In this work we introduced a new stochastic local search algorithm for MAX-SAT, Iterated Robust Tabu Search (IRoTS). This algorithm combines two SLS methods that have been used very successfully for solving a variety of other hard combinatorial optimisation problems, Iterated Local Search (ILS) and Robust Tabu Search (RoTS). Our empirical analysis of IRoTS on a range of MAX-SAT instances, including weighted and unweighted as well as randomly generated and structured instances, shows that in many cases IRoTS outperforms GLS, one of the best-performing MAX-SAT algorithms currently known, and ILS-YI, an earlier and simpler Iterated Local Search algorithm. However, we also observed cases in which the performance of IRoTS did not reach that of GLS, such as MAX-SAT-encoded Minimum Cost Graph Colouring and Set Covering problems.

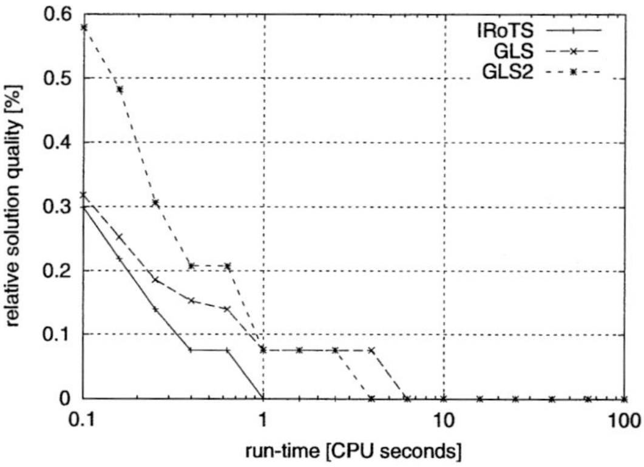

Fig. 7. SQT for an instances from the `rnd200-w1000` test-set with median *sc* for both IRoTS and GLS2. The y-axis shows the median relative solution quality found at each point in time, calculated as $sq(t)/sq^* - 1$, where $sq(t)$ is the median absolute solution quality reached at time t and sq^* is the best quality solution ever found by any of the algorithms studied in this paper

Like most other papers on MAX-SAT algorithms in the literature, we have focused mainly on randomly generated MAX-SAT instances and present only limited results on structured instances. We are currently extending this evaluation to additional sets of MAX-SAT-encoded instances from other domains with the goal of obtaining a better understanding of how the behaviour of state-of-the-art MAX-SAT algorithms differs between structured and random instances. Given an increased recent interest in using MAX-SAT algorithms for solving encoded instances of other combinatorial problems, such as MPE finding in Bayes Nets [17], the results from such a study should be highly relevant for the assessment and future development of MAX-SAT algorithms.

Our experimental results indicate that IRoTS performs particularly well on unweighted instances that are highly overconstrained, and therefore have optimal solutions with a large number of unsatisfied clauses, and on weighted instances with high variability clause weight distributions. In future work, we plan to further investigate how the performance of IRoTS and other MAX-SAT algorithms, in particular GLS, depend on features of the given problem instance. An important part of this is the analysis of the underlying search spaces.

We recently developed generalisations of Novelty$^+$, a state-of-the-art SLS algorithm for SAT [9], to weighted MAX-SAT. Preliminary experimental results indicate that in many cases, including the `wjnh` instances as well as some of the structured instance sets considered here, these algorithms outperform GLS and IRoTS. In many of the cases in which IRoTS is particularly successful, these Novelty$^+$ variants don't reach its performance. On the other hand, we have presented limited evidence in this paper that IRoTS does not achieve state-of-the-art performance on SAT instances. This suggests that inherently different

SLS strategies are required for efficiently solving SAT and at least certain types of MAX-SAT instances. This hypothesis will be further investigated in future research and might shed new light on the fundamental differences between solving decision and optimisation problems.

Overall, we see this present work as the first in a series of empirical studies that characterise and improve the state-of-the-art in solving MAX-SAT while providing deeper insights into the MAX-SAT problem and the behaviour of high-performance SLS algorithms for combinatorial optimisation problems. The fact that even at this early stage, we improved over state-of-the-art algorithms on a wide range of instances is very encouraging and, in our mind, illustrates the overall potential in this line of work.

Acknowledgments

This work has been supported by NSERC Individual Research Grant #238788 and by the "Metaheuristics Network", a Research Training Network funded by the Improving Human Potential programme of the CEC, grant HPRN-CT-1999-00106. The information provided is the sole responsibility of the authors and does not reflect the Community's opinion. The Community is not responsible for any use that might be made of data appearing in this publication. We thank Patrick Mills and Edward Tsang for providing us with their GLS implementation. Furthermore, we are indebted to Ewald Speckenmeyer and Mattias Gaertner for pointing out the Level Graph Crossing Minimisation Problem and for providing us with instances of this problem.

References

[1] P. Asirelli, M. de Santis, and A. Martelli. Integrity constraints in logic databases. *J. of Logic Programming*, 3:221–232, 1985.

[2] R. Battiti and M. Protasi. Reactive search, a history-based heuristic for MAX-SAT. *ACM Journal of Experimental Algorithmics*, 2, 1997.

[3] B. Borchers and J. Furman. A two-phase exact algorithm for MAX-SAT and weighted MAX-SAT problems. *Journal of Combinatorial Optimization*, 2(4):299–306, 1999.

[4] B. Randerath et al. A satisfiability formulation of problems on level graphs. Technical Report 40–2001, Rutgers Center for Operations Research, Rutgers University, Piscataway, NJ, USA, June 2001.

[5] M. R. Garey and D. S. Johnson. *Computers and Intractability: A Guide to the Theory of $\mathcal{NP}$-Completeness*. Freeman, San Francisco, CA, 1979.

[6] I. P. Gent and T. Walsh. Towards an understanding of hill–climbing procedures for SAT. In *Proceedings of AAAI'93*, pages 28–33. MIT Press, 1993.

[7] J. Gu and R. Puri. Asynchronous circuit synthesis with boolean satisfiability. *IEEE Transact. of Computer-Aided Design of Integrated Circuits and Systems*, 14(8):961–973, 1995.

[8] P. Hansen and B. Jaumard. Algorithms for the maximum satisfiability problem. *Computing*, 44:279–303, 1990.

[9] H. H. Hoos. On the run-time behaviour of stochastic local search algorithms for SAT. In *Proc. AAAI-99*, pages 661–666. MIT Press, 1999.

[10] H. H. Hoos and T. Stützle. Evaluating Las Vegas algorithms — pitfalls and remedies. In *Proceedings of the Fourteenth Conference on Uncertainty in Artificial Intelligence (UAI-98)*, pages 238–245. Morgan Kaufmann, San Francisco, 1998.

[11] Y. Jiang, H. Kautz, and B. Selman. Solving problems with hard and soft constraints using a stochastic algorithm for MAX-SAT. In *Proceedings of the 1st International Joint Workshop on Artificial Intelligence and Operations Research*, 1995.

[12] S. Joy, J. Mitchell, and B. Borchers. A branch and cut algorithm for MAX-SAT and weighted MAX-SAT. In D. Du, J. Gu, and P. M. Pardalos, editors, *Satisfiability problem: Theory and Applications*, volume 35 of *DIMACS Series on Discrete Mathematics and Theoretical Computer Science*, pages 519–536. American Mathematical Society, 1997.

[13] A.P. Kamath, N.K. Karmarkar, K.G. Ramakrishnan, and M.G.C. Resende. A continuous approach to inductive inference. *Mathematical Programming*, 57:215–238, 1992.

[14] H. R. Lourenço, O. Martin, and T. Stützle. Iterated local search. In F. Glover and G. Kochenberger, editors, *Handbook of Metaheuristics*, volume 57 of *International Series in Operations Research & Management Science*, pages 321–353. Kluwer Academic Publishers, Norwell, MA, 2002.

[15] P. Mills and E. Tsang. Guided local search for solving SAT and weighted MAX-SAT problems. In I. P. Gent, H. van Maaren, and T. Walsh, editors, *SAT2000 — Highlights of Satisfiability Research in the Year 2000*, pages 89–106. IOS Press, 2000.

[16] D. Mitchell, B. Selman, and H. Levesque. Hard and easy distributions of SAT problems. In *Proc. of AAAI'92*, pages 459–465. MIT Press, 1992.

[17] James Park. Using weighted MAX-SAT to approximate MPE. In *Proc. of AAAI-02*, pages 682–687. AAAI Press, 2002.

[18] M. G. C. Resende, L. S. Pitsoulis, and P. M. Pardalos. Approximate solution of weighted MAX-SAT problems using GRASP. In D. Du, J. Gu, and P. M. Pardalos, editors, *Satisfiability problem: Theory and Applications*, volume 35, pages 393–405. AMS, 1997.

[19] Y. Shang and B. W. Wah. Discrete lagrangian-based search for solving MAX-SAT problems. In *Proc. of IJCAI'97*, volume 1, pages 378–383. Morgan Kaufmann Publishers, San Francisco, CA, USA, 1997.

[20] É.D. Taillard. Robust taboo search for the quadratic assignment problem. *Parallel Computing*, 17:443–455, 1991.

[21] Z. Wu and B. W. Wah. Trap escaping strategies in discrete lagrangian methods for solving hard satisfiability and maximum satisfiability problems. In *Proc. of AAAI'99*, pages 673–678. MIT Press, 1999.

[22] M. Yagiura and T. Ibaraki. Efficient 2 and 3-flip neighborhoods seach algorithms for the MAX SAT. In W.-L. Hsu and M.-Y. Kao, editors, *Computing and Combinatorics*, volume 1449 of *Lecture Notes in Computer Science*, pages 105–116. Springer Verlag, Berlin, Germany, 1998.

[23] M. Yagiura and T. Ibaraki. Efficient 2 and 3-flip neighborhood search algorithms for the MAX SAT: Experimental evaluation. *Journal of Heuristics*, 7(5):423–442, 2001.

Scaling and Probabilistic Smoothing: Dynamic Local Search for Unweighted MAX-SAT

Dave A. D. Tompkins[1] and Holger H. Hoos[2,*]

[1] Department of Electrical Engineering
[2] Department of Computer Science
University of British Columbia
Vancouver, B.C., V6T 1Z4, Canada
davet@ece.ubc.ca,hoos@cs.ubc.ca
http://www.cs.ubc.ca/labs/beta

Abstract. In this paper, we study the behaviour of the Scaling and Probabilistic Smoothing (SAPS) dynamic local search algorithm on the unweighted MAX-SAT problem. MAX-SAT is a conceptually simple combinatorial problem of substantial theoretical and practical interest; many application-relevant problems, including scheduling problems or most probable explanation finding in Bayes nets, can be encoded and solved as MAX-SAT. This paper is a natural extension of our previous work, where we introduced SAPS, and demonstrated that it is amongst the state-of-the-art local search algorithms for solvable SAT problem instances. We present results showing that SAPS is also very effective at finding optimal solutions for unsatisfiable MAX-SAT instances, and in many cases performs better than state-of-the-art MAX-SAT algorithms, such as the Guided Local Search algorithm by Mills and Tsang [8]. With the exception of some configuration parameters, we found that SAPS did not require any changes to efficiently solve unweighted MAX-SAT instances. For solving weighted MAX-SAT instances, a modified SAPS algorithm will be necessary, and we provide some thoughts on this topic of future research.

1 Introduction and Background

The propositional satisfiability problem (SAT) is an important subject of study in many areas of computer science. Since SAT is $\mathcal{NP}$-complete, there is little hope to develop a complete algorithm that scales well on all types of problem instances; however, fast algorithms are needed to solve large problems from various domains. As with most other work on SAT algorithms, we consider only propositional formulae in conjunctive normal form (CNF), *i.e.*, formulae of the form $F = \bigwedge_i \bigvee_j l_{ij}$, where each l_{ij} is a propositional variable or its negation. The l_{ij} are called *literals*, while the disjunctions $\bigvee_j l_{ij}$ are called *clauses* of F.

* To whom correspondence should be addressed.

Y. Xiang and B. Chaib-draa (Eds.): AI 2003, LNAI 2671, pp. 145–159, 2003.

Unweighted MAX-SAT is the optimisation variant of SAT in which the goal is, given a CNF formula F, to find an assignment of truth values to the propositional variables in F that maximises the number of satisfied clauses. MAX-SAT is a conceptually simple $\mathcal{NP}$-hard combinatorial problem of substantial theoretical and practical interest; many application-relevant problems, including scheduling problems or Most Probable Explanation (MPE) finding in Bayes nets can be encoded and solved as MAX-SAT [10]. Although MAX-SAT is defined as a maximisation problem, it is usually more convenient to consider the corresponding minimisation problem, where the goal is to *minimise* the number of *unsatisfied* clauses. In *weighted MAX-SAT*, each clause c_i is associated with a weight w_i, and the goal is to minimise the total weight of the unsatisfied clauses. Obviously, unweighted MAX-SAT is equivalent to weighted MAX-SAT with each clause weight equal to one ($\forall i : w_i = 1$).

Some of the best known methods for solving SAT are Stochastic Local Search (SLS) algorithms; these are typically incomplete, *i.e.*, they cannot determine with certainty that a formula is unsatisfiable but they often find models of satisfiable formulae surprisingly effectively [6]. Although SLS algorithms for SAT differ in their details, the general search strategy is mostly the same. Starting from an initial, complete assignment of truth values to all variables in the given formula F, in each search step, the truth assignment of one variable is changed from true to false or vice versa; this type of search step is also called a *variable flip*. Variable flips are typically performed with the purpose of minimising an objective function that sums the number of unsatisfied clauses (in the case of weighted MAX-SAT, this would easily generalise into minimising the total weight of the unsatisfied clauses). Since the introduction of GSAT [15], a simple best-improvement search algorithm for SAT, much research has been conducted in this area. Major performance improvements were achieved by the usage of noise strategies [13], the development of the WalkSAT architecture [14], and further advancements such as the Novelty$^+$ variant of WalkSAT [5].

In parallel to the development of more refined versions of randomised iterative improvement strategies such as WalkSAT, another SLS method has become increasingly popular in SAT solving. This method is based on the idea of modifying the evaluation function in order to prevent the search from getting stuck in local minima or other attractive non-solution areas of the underlying search space. We call this approach *Dynamic Local Search (DLS)*. DLS strategies for SAT typically associate a clause penalty with each clause of the given formula, which is modified during the search process. These algorithms then try to minimise the total penalty rather than the number of the unsatisfied clauses. GSAT with clause penalties [13] was one of the first algorithms based on this idea, although it changes penalties only in connection with restarting the search process. Many variants of this scheme have been proposed: Frank [3] uses a DLS penalty scheme that is updated every time a variable is flipped. Morris' Breakout Method [9] simply adds one to the penalty of every unsatisfied clause whenever a local minimum is encountered. The Discrete Lagrangian Method (DLM) [18] is based on a tabu search procedure and uses a similar, but slightly more complicated penalty update scheme. Additionally, DLM periodically and deterministically invokes a smoothing mechanism that decreases all clause penalties by a constant amount. The Smoothed Descent and Flood (SDF) approach [11] introduced a more complex smoothing method, and the concept of multiplicative penalty updates, which evolved into the Exponentiated Sub-Gradient (ESG) method [12]. Our Scaling and Probabilistic Smoothing (SAPS) [7] method improved upon the ESG approach; SAPS will be described in detail in Section 2.

With the SAT problem, both complete solvers and SLS solvers have had a large amount of success. However, complete solvers often have difficulty with MAX-SAT problems, whereas SLS methods have been extremely effective. For MAX-SAT, much emphasis has been placed on developing polynomial-time algorithms that can achieve solutions within a bounded factor of the optimal solution, but in practice these algorithms are not as effective as SLS approaches. In principle, any SLS algorithm for SAT can be applied to the unweighted MAX-SAT problem with some simple modifications, but it is not clear that algorithms effective in the SAT domain are also effective in the MAX-SAT domain. Furthermore, in many cases the straightforward extensions of SLS algorithms for SAT to weighted MAX-SAT problems appear to perform rather poorly.

One of the first SLS techniques applied to MAX-SAT was the Steepest Ascent Mildest Descend (SAMD) algorithm [4], and numerous approaches have been used since. The Iterated Local Search (ILS) algorithm by Yagiura and Ibaraki [19] (ILS-YI) is an effective MAX-SAT solver, and is different from many approaches in that it implements a multi-flip neighbourhood. The Guided Local Search (GLS) approach of Mills and Tsang (GLSSAT2) [8] is currently considered one of the best-performing algorithms for MAX-SAT. In this paper, we apply SAPS, our recently developed, state-of-the-art DLS algorithm for SAT, to the unweighted MAX-SAT problem. Our empirical performance results show that for a wide range of problem instances, SAPS finds quasi-optimal (*i.e.*, provably optimal or best known) solutions significantly faster than the state-of-the-art GLSSAT2 algorithm. This suggests that extensions of SAPS to weighted MAX-SAT might also reach or exceed state-of-the-art performance.

The remainder of this paper is structured as follows. In Section 2 we review the SAPS algorithm and discuss some of its important characteristics. In Section 3, we report and discuss the results from our empirical study of SAPS on MAX-SAT. In Section 4 we discuss how SAPS can be extended from unweighted to weighted MAX-SAT. Finally, Section 5 contains conclusions and points out directions for future work.

2 Scaling and Probabilistic Smoothing

In this section, we describe the Scaling and Probabilistic Smoothing (SAPS) algorithm [7]. SAPS is a Dynamic Local Search (DLS) algorithm, developed as a variant of the ESG algorithm of Schuurmans *et al.* [12].

Like most DLS algorithms, SAPS associates a clause penalty clp_i with each clause i, which is dynamically changed throughout the search process.[1] The clause penalties help to direct the search, ideally away from local minima and toward a global optimum. There are two distinct stages involved in updating the clause penalties: a *scaling stage* and a *smoothing stage*. In the scaling stage, all currently unsatisfied clause penalties are multiplied by a scaling factor α. In the smoothing stage, all penalties are adjusted toward the clause penalty mean $\overline{clp}$ according to a smoothing factor ρ. In SAPS, outside of a local minimum the best flip candidate is always chosen, with ties broken randomly. Whenever a local minimum is encountered, a random walk step is taken with probability wp (by flipping a variable that has been selected uniformly at random from the set of all variables of F), otherwise scaling is performed, after which a smoothing stage is executed with probability P_{smooth}. While the SAPS algorithm described in [7] only performs probabilistic smoothing at local minima, recent experiments (not reported here) demonstrate that the smoothing stage can be performed outside of local minima (completely decoupled from the scaling stage) which provides for more robust values of P_{smooth}. Recent experiments (not reported here) also suggest that the random walk step is more effective when performed with probability wp outside of local minima. However, the performance enhancement is marginal, and for consistency we used the original SAPS algorithm for the experiments conducted in the context of this study.

In Figures 1 and 2 we provide the details of our SAPS algorithm. Figure 1 shows the algorithm outline of our penalty update procedure. Compared to ESG and other DLS algorithms with frequent smoothing, the time complexity incurred by the smoothing stage of SAPS is considerably reduced, since in each local optimum, smoothing is only performed with a probability P_{smooth}. Figure 2 shows the main SAPS algorithm and its underlying search procedure with penalties; overall, the main algorithm is conceptually very similar to ESG. The only modification to the SAPS algorithm for SAT required in the context of this work was the addition of a simple mechanism by which the best candidate solution found within a given run is stored and returned when the algorithm terminates.

The behaviour and performance of the SAPS algorithm depend on four parameters: α, ρ, P_{smooth}, and wp. For satisfiable instances, the performance of SAPS *w.r.t.* these parameters is very robust, and setting the values of (α,P_{smooth}, wp) to (1.3,0.05,0.01) will provide nearly optimal results for most instances. To adjust for differences in the smoothing parameter ρ, we developed a reactive variant of SAPS (RSAPS) that reactively changes the value of ρ when search stagnation is detected [7].

[1] To avoid potential confusion between the clause weights in Weighted MAX-SAT and the clause weights used by DLS algorithms, we strictly refer to the latter as *clause penalties*. This differs from the terminology we used in [7].

```
procedure UpdatePenalties(F, x, CLP, α, ρ, P_smooth)
   input:
      propositional formula F, variable assignment x, clause penalties CLP = (clp_i),
      scaling factor α, smoothing factor ρ, smoothing probability P_smooth
   output:
      clause penalties CLP
   C = {clauses of F}
   U_c = {c ∈ C | c is unsatisfied under x}
   for each i s.t. c_i ∈ U_c do
      clp_i := clp_i × α
   end
   with probability P_smooth do
      for each i s.t. c_i ∈ C do
         clp_i := clp_i × ρ + (1 − ρ) × avg(clp)
      end
   end
   return (CLP)
end
```

Fig. 1. The SAPS penalty update procedure; $\overline{clp}$ is the average over all clause penalties

3 Experimental Design and Results

To evaluate the performance of SAPS on the unweighted MAX-SAT problem, we conducted extensive experiments on several sets of well-known benchmark instances, in addition to some newly developed test sets of MAX-SAT instances that were designed to test the performance of MAX-SAT algorithms in more detail:

jnh The set of instances known as the DIMACS `jnh` set have been popular benchmark instances, and are available at SATLIB (`www.satlib.org`). These instances are generated with n variables such that each variable is added to each clause with probability $1/n$. The literals are negated with probability $1/2$ and all unit and empty clauses are removed. Instances generated in this manner are often referred to as Random P-SAT [16] or constant density model instances. Several of the `jnh` instances are satisfiable.

rnd$n$-mu We used several test sets of overconstrained (unsatisfiable) Uniform Random 3-SAT instances in our experiments. These instances are obtained by randomly and independently generating m clauses of length three as follows: The respective three literals are selected uniformly at random from the set of all possible literals over the given n variables; clauses that contain more than one literal with the same variable are discarded [16].

bor-ku These test sets consist of satisfiable and unsatisfiable MAX-2-SAT and MAX-3-SAT instances (both weighted and unweighted) and have been described and used in [1]. For each problem size and clause length, there are

```
procedure SAPS(F, α, ρ, wp, P_smooth)
   input:
      propositional formula F, scaling factor α,
      smoothing factor ρ, random walk probability wp,
      smoothing probability P_smooth
   output:
      variable assignment x
   x := Init(F)
   x̂ := x
   CLP := InitPenalties(F)
   while not terminate(F, x) do
      x' := PenalisedSearchStep(F, x, CLP)
      if x' = ∅ then
         with probability wp do
            x := RandomStep(F, x)
         otherwise
            CLP := UpdatePenalties(F, x, CLP, α, ρ, P_smooth)
         end
      else
         x := x'
      end
      if f(F, x) < f(F, x̂) then
         x̂ := x
      end
   end
   return (x̂)
end

procedure PenalisedSearchStep(F, x, CLP)
   input:
      propositional formula F, variable assignment x, clause penalties CLP
   output:
      variable assignment x̂ or ∅
   U_v = {variables of F that appear in clauses unsatisfied under x}
   X' := {x̂ | x̂ is x with variable v ∈ U_v flipped}
   best :=min{g(F, x̂, CLP) | x̂ ∈ X'}
   X := {x̂ ∈ X' | g(F, x̂, CLP) = best}
   if best ≥ 0 then
      x̂ := ∅
   else
      x̂ := draw(X)
   end
   return (x̂)
end
```

Fig. 2. The SAPS Algorithm for (unweighted) MAX-SAT. 'Init' generates a random variable assignment x, 'InitPenalties' initialises all clause penalties to 1. 'RandomStep(F,x)' returns an assignment obtained from x by flipping a variable that has been selected uniformly at random from the set of all variables of F; $f(F, \hat{x})$ and $g(F, \hat{x}, CLP)$ denote the number and the total penalty of the clauses in F that are unsatisfied under assignment $\hat{x}$, respectively. The function 'draw(X)' returns an element that is selected uniformly at random from set X

only 2–9 instances, and all instances are overconstrained. For our experiments, we only ran experiments on the unsatisfiable unweighted instances, which we grouped together in one MAX-2-SAT and one MAX-3-SAT test set.

rndu1000a These instances are unweighted variants of instances from a set originally used by Yagiura and Ibaraki [20].[2] They were generated in a fashion similar to the `jnh` instances and have 1000 variables and 7700 clauses each.

In total, we used 789 unique instances in our empirical evaluation of SAPS for unweighted MAX-SAT. All experiments were conducted on IBM servers with dual 2GHz Intel Xeon processors (hyperthreading disabled for accurate time results) with 512KB CPU cache and 4GB RAM, running Red Hat Linux 7.3. For each problem instance and algorithm, we measured empirical run-length and run-time distributions (RLDs and RTDs) [6] based on at least 100 successful runs, in each of which the algorithm was run until the respective quasi-optimal solution quality was reached. Run-times are reported in terms of the medians of the corresponding RLDs (measured in search steps) or RTDs (measured in CPU seconds). For the SAPS experiments, no instance-specific parameter tuning was conducted; the parameters (α,ρ,P_{smooth},wp) were set to (1.05,0.8,0.05,0.01) as generally good values, except for the heavily overconstrained instances, where we used $\alpha = 1.01$. For the GLSSAT2 software, the default settings were used (except for cutoff), and for the ILS-YI software, the neighbourhood size was set to 2.

In our empirical study, we generally measured the run-time and number of search steps for reaching provably optimal or best-known solution qualities. Where possible, Borcher and Furman's complete solver **`maxsat`** [1] was used to determine the optimal solution quality for each instance. (This is the best-performing complete MAX-SAT solver we are aware of.) For larger instances, which become quickly intractable for this solver, we used *quasi-optimal* solution qualities obtained from Iterated Robust Tabu Search, a state-of-the-art SLS algorithm for MAX-SAT, in conjunction with an "iterative deepening" scheme (for details, see [17], where exactly the same solution qualities are used). In all cases, the solution qualities thus obtained could not be improved upon with any method we are aware of (including SAPS), and in several cases their optimality was confirmed by the complete **`maxsat`** solver (which took several CPU days).

As we will demonstrate in Table 1, GLSSAT2 consistently outperforms ILS-YI, and so we compare the performance of SAPS primarily with that of GLSSAT2. Our first comparison between SAPS and GLSSAT2 is shown in Figure 3, where we compare the search step performance and time performance of the two algorithms on the `jnh` problem instances. Each data point in the figure represents a single problem instance, where points above and to the left of the diagonal represent instances where SAPS outperformed GLSSAT2. From Figure 3 (left) it is clear that GLSSAT2 generally requires fewer search steps than

[2] The respective weighted test set is available online at: **`http://www-or.amp.i.kyoto-u.ac.jp/members/yagiura/benchmarks.html`**.

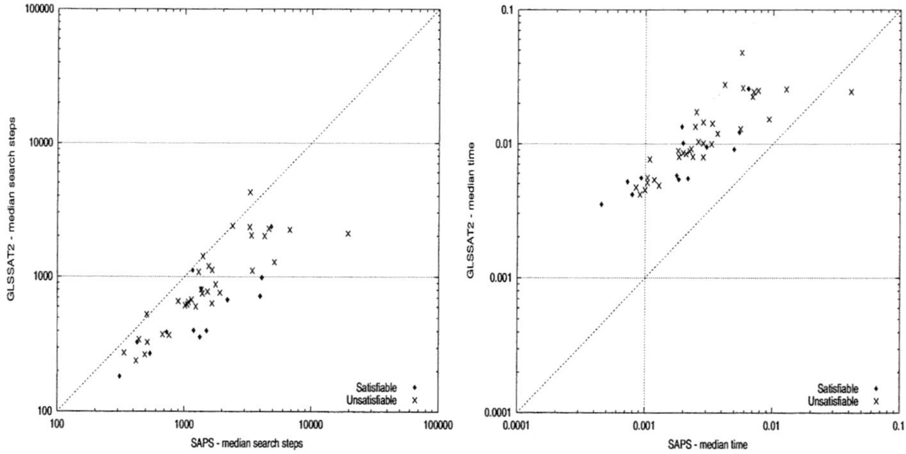

Fig. 3. Comparison between search step (left) and run-time (right) performance of SAPS and GLSSAT2 on the `jnh` test set. Every point correspond to the median performance over 100 runs of each algorithm on a single instance. Run-time is measured in CPU seconds

SAPS for finding quasi-optimal solutions. However, comparing the search step results to the time performance results in Figure 3 (right) clearly illustrates one of the key features of SAPS: fast search steps. When the comparison is made for time performance, SAPS outperforms GLSSAT2 by a median speedup factor *(s.f.)* of 3.9.

In Figure 4, we present similar results for the `rnd100-500u`, `rnd150-750u`, and `rnd200-1000u` test sets. All of these sets have the same clauses/variables ratio of 5, so we would expect to see similar differences in performance between the two algorithms. Considering that the solubility phase transition for Uniform Random-3-SAT occurs at a clauses/variables ratio near 4.3 [2], these instances are slightly overconstrained. The results in Figure 4 (left) and (right) closely resemble the results presented in Figure 3; for most instances, GLSSAT2 requires fewer search steps for finding quasi-optimal solutions, but when taking into account the CPU time per search step, SAPS typically performs better than GLSSAT2.

When analyzing the run-time performance of an SLS algorithm, it is important to study the distribution of the run-times on individual problem instances present the RLDs for the ILS-YI, GLSSAT2 and SAPS algorithms on a medium hardness instance from the set `rnd100-500u`. From this figure, it can be seen that GLSSAT2 consistently outperforms SAPS when measuring run-time in search steps, and SAPS outperforms ILS-YI; the RLDs for all three algorithms are closely approximated by exponential distributions, which is known to be typical for high-performance SLS algorithms for SAT when using optimal or close-to-optimal parameter settings [6]. This picture changes for the respective RTDs

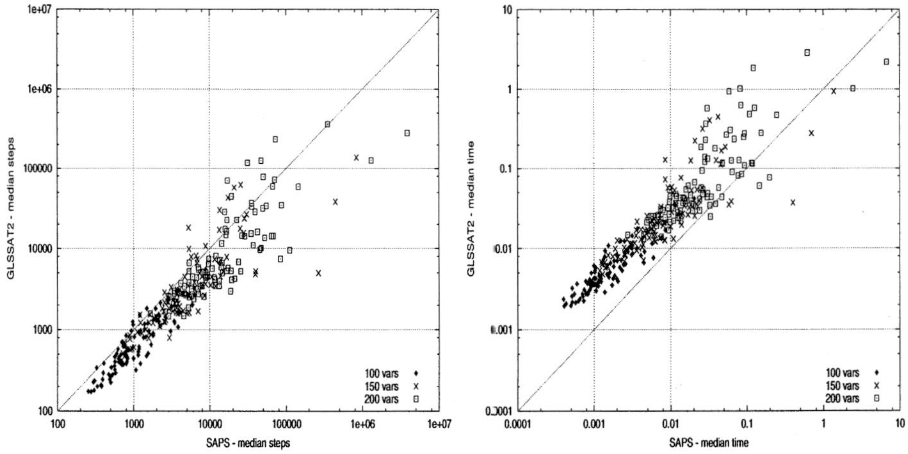

Fig. 4. Comparison between search step (left) and run-time (right) performance of SAPS and GLSSAT2 on the instances from the test sets **rnd100-500u**, **rnd150-750u**, and **rnd200-1000u**. All points correspond to the median performance for at least 100 runs of a single instance. Time is in CPU seconds

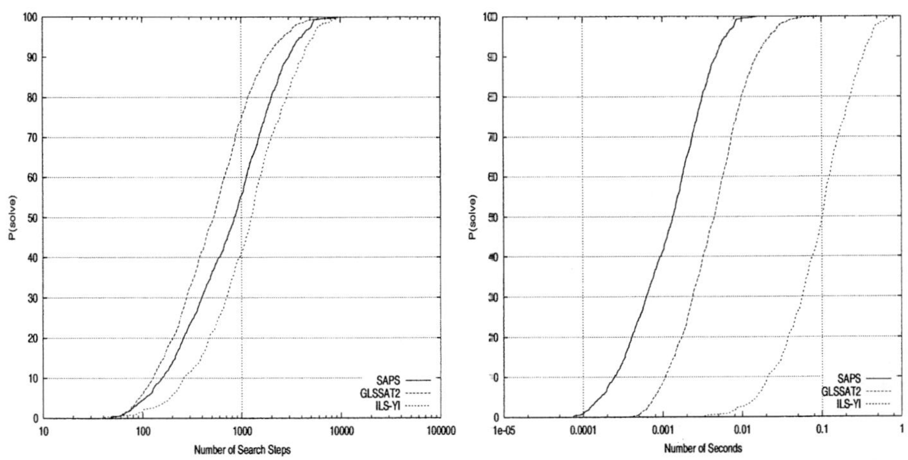

Fig. 5. RLD (left) and RTD (right) of SAPS, GLSSAT2 and ILS-YI on instance `uuf-100.500-017` (medium hardness) from test-set **rnd100-500u**. Runtime is measured in CPU seconds. Parameters for SAPS(α,ρ,P_{smooth},wp) are (1.05,0.8,0.05,0.01), GLSSAT2 is with default settings, and ILS-YI is with default settings, using the 2-flip neighbourhood

shown in Figure 5 (right); clearly, SAPS performs best when measuring CPU time, which again highlights the significant difference between search step performance and run-time performance.

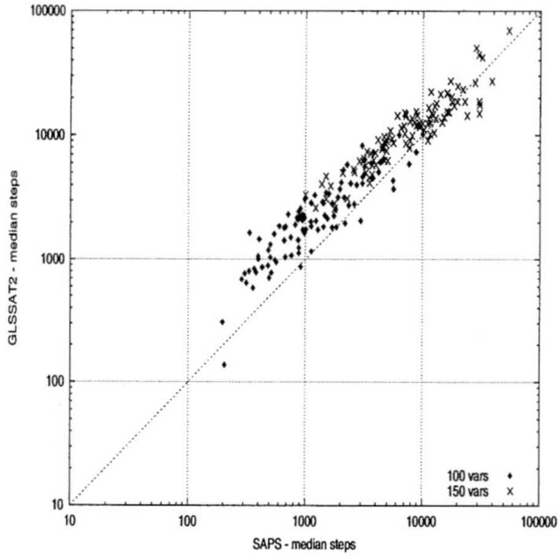

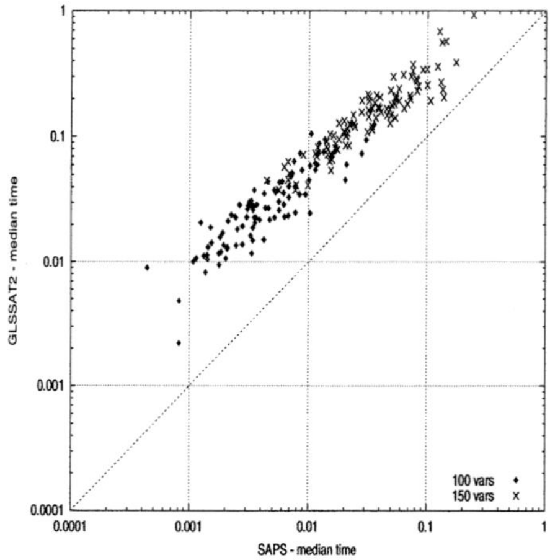

Fig. 6. Comparison between search step (left) and run-time (right) performance of SAPS and GLSSAT2 on the instances from test sets `rnd100-1000u` and `rnd150-1500u`. Every point corresponds to the median performance over 100 runs on a single instance. CPU time is measured in seconds

It is interesting to note that the optimal solutions of the instances in the slightly overconstrained test set `rnd100-500u` have between 1 and 5 unsatisfied clauses, with an average of 2.8 unsatisfied clauses per instance. This is in marked contrast to the sets of heavily overconstrained instances with a clauses/variables ratio of 10; *e.g.*, for the instances from test set `rnd100-1000u`, quasi-optimal solutions have between 24 and 36 unsatisfied clauses, with an average of 32.2 unsatisfied clauses per instance. While for all other instances used in this study, SAPS performed well using $\alpha = 1.05$, for these heavily overconstrained instances, a much smaller value of α is required for achieving good performance of SAPS (as previously stated, we use $\alpha = 1.01$). The significance of this difference in α will be addressed later in this Section. In Figure 6 we present a comparison of GLSSAT2 and SAPS performance on heavily overconstrained instances. From this figure, it is clear that SAPS outperforms GLSSAT2 for these test sets in terms of both search steps (left) and CPU time (right) required for finding quasi-optimal solutions.

In Table 1 we summarise the results from our experiments on all test sets used in this study. For each problem instance, at least 100 runs of each algorithm were performed, in each of which a quasi-optimal solution was found. From the RLDs and RLDs thus obtained, we determined the median number of search steps and median CPU time for finding a quasi-optimal solution of the respective instance; the values shown in the table are the medians of these search cost measures over the respective test-sets. To indicate the variability in instance hardness within each set, we also report the ratio of the 90% and 10% quantiles (q.90/q.10) of the instance search cost over the respective test set (measured in search steps). To help further illustrate the excellent time performance of SAPS, the speedup

Table 1. Performance comparison of ILS-YI, GLSSAT2, and SAPS over a range of unweighted MAX-SAT test sets. The precise meaning of the step and time performance is explained in the text, CPU times are measured in CPU milliseconds. The speedup factor *s.f.* shows the improvement in time performance of SAPS over GLSSAT2. The "fraction of best" measure *f.b.* indicates the fraction of instances within the respective test-sets for which SAPS performs better than GLSSAT2 in terms of CPU time. For SAPS, default parameters settings of $(\rho, P_{smooth}, wp) = (0.8, 0.05, 0.01)$ were used; GLSSAT2 annd ILS-YI were used with their respective default settings

Problem	ILS-YI			GLSSAT2			SAPS 1.0					
Set	steps	time	$\frac{q.90}{q.10}$	steps	time	$\frac{q.90}{q.10}$	α	steps	time	$\frac{q.90}{q.10}$	*f.b.*	*s.f.*
jnh	3,037	419.8	24.1	**751**	9.5	8.5	1.05	1,391	**2.4**	11.6	0.94	3.9
rnd100-500u	1,398	108.7	8.9	**563**	4.5	7.5	1.05	929	**1.2**	8.0	1.00	3.6
rnd125-625u	3,879	302.8	24.2	**1,329**	10.6	12.5	1.05	2,264	**3.3**	17.1	0.94	3.2
rnd150-750u	7,674	607.6	51.5	**2,552**	19.4	21.5	1.05	4,127	**6.4**	18.9	0.95	3.0
rnd175-875u	20,029	1,514.6	120.8	**4,119**	33.1	28.1	1.05	8,920	**15.2**	21.0	0.92	2.2
rnd200-1000u	31,968	2,440.8	29.7	**5,301**	44.2	23.5	1.05	13,343	**21.1**	18.3	0.91	2.1
rnd100-1000u	**884**	133.6	6.1	2,119	27.2	7.4	1.01	1,115	**3.9**	9.9	1.00	7.0
rnd150-1500u	**3,237**	499.7	15.5	11,035	148.1	4.8	1.01	7,723	**34.2**	10.0	1.00	4.3
bor-2u	76	5.6	18.1	88	1.1	14.1	1.05	73	**0.1**	71.2	0.80	7.7
bor-3u	740	65.3	32.0	425	4.7	30.9	1.05	487	**1.1**	39.3	1.00	4.5
rndu1000a	—	—	—	**20,812**	832.4	6.5	1.05	27,434	**67.4**	7.8	0.90	12.3

factor for the median instance is given, in addition to the fraction of instances for which the SAPS algorithm was best in terms of CPU time required for finding a quasi-optimal solution of a given instance.

For the heavily overconstrained instances, ILS-YI shows impressive search step performance, but as mentioned previously, when considering the time complexity of the search steps, this performance advantage is not amortised. GLSSAT2 does not perform well on the heavily overconstrained instances, but overall it shows a very impressive search step performance. However, the search steps in GLSSAT2 are expensive, and compared to the search steps of SAPS, they are slow.

Finally, we found that the `bor-`k`u` instances were very easy to solve for all of the algorithms tested here and that once again SAPS showed the best time performance. Furthermore, the most impressive median time speedup of SAPS over GLSSAT2 was found for the `rndu1000a` test set; for the same test set, even after 10 million search steps, less than 50% of the runs of the ILS-YI algorithm reached a quasi-optimal solution quality.

Overall, it is interesting to note that in order to achieve the reported excellent performance of SAPS, the only parameter that needed to be adjusted for the various test-sets was the scaling factor, α. When SAPS was tested on satisfiable instances, a parameter setting of $\alpha = 1.3$ was found to generally give good performance. On most satisfiable instances we tested, near-optimal performance of SAPS was obtained with that setting. However, initial experiments with SAPS on unweighted MAX-SAT with $\alpha = 1.3$ produced discouraging performance results; subsequently, we discovered that a lower value of α was required for unsatisfied, and particularly for heavily overconstrained instances.

Intuitively, this phenomenon can be explained as follows: The obvious difference between satisfiable and unsatisfiable instances is that in the latter case, any optimal solution leaves some clauses unsatisfied. It is reasonable to assume that for unsatisfiable instances, there are sub-optimal local minima in the objective function (number of unsatisfied clauses) that share unsatisfied clauses with the global optima. Clearly, when SAPS encounters such a local minimum, the penalties of these clauses will be increased along with those of all other unsatisfied clauses, which allows the search process to avoid stagnation in this area of the search space. This, however, may easily have the side effect of modifying the search space around the optimal solution(s) in a way that makes it harder for SAPS to efficiently reach an optimal solution. (Note that although it might be desirable to change the evaluation function in such a way that only the current local minimum is eliminated, changes of the clause penalties used by a DLS algorithm for SAT or MAX-SAT will usually affect large areas of the search space.)

For this reason, we would expect that aggressive scaling (*i.e.*, high α settings) becomes more detrimental to the efficiency of SAPS as the number of unsatisfied clauses, and hence the potential undesired side effects of scaling, increases. By using smaller α settings for more heavily overconstrained MAX-SAT instances, the impact of each single scaling stage, and hence presumably the magnitude of the unwanted side effects, is reduced, resulting in improved performance of SAPS, as observed in our empirical study.

On the other hand, when we examined the results (not shown) for different instances *within* the same test set, we found no correlation between the number of unsatisfied clauses in the respective optimal solution qualities and the optimal value of α. However, we did find strong evidence suggesting that within a test set, *harder* instances are solved faster when using a *smaller* value of α. As can be seen in Figure 6, the performance ratio between SAPS and GLSSAT2 appears to slightly decrease with instance hardness within the test set. We found that this effect can be avoided by decreasing the scaling factor α as the instance hardness increases. This could indicate that the hardness differences of MAX-SAT instance sampled from the same random distribution are partially due to the way in which global and local optima are coupled in terms of shared unsatisfied clauses.

Clearly, it would be highly desirable to shed further light on these issues by analysing the composition and distance of local minima in relation to the optimal solution, and by characterising the changes in the search landscape induced by the dynamic adjustment of the clause penalties in SAPS; both of these directions are currently being followed in our ongoing research. Furthermore, based on our observations and reasoning presented here, it would seem that in contrast to the reactive mechanism used in RSAPS [7] for automatically adjusting the smoothing parameter ρ, an adaption mechanism for the scaling factor α might be more beneficial to SAPS for MAX-SAT; devising and studying such mechanisms constitutes another direction for further research.

4 Initial Thoughts on SAPS for Weighted MAX-SAT

Applying the SAPS algorithm to unweighted MAX-SAT is a necessary stepping stone to developing an effective DLS algorithm for weighted MAX-SAT. When moving from unweighted to weighted MAX-SAT, DLS algorithms have to contend with an interesting issue: how should the fixed clause weights in a weighted MAX-SAT instance interact with the dynamically changing clause penalties? To date, three different DLS algorithms for MAX-SAT have used three very different approaches. In Shang and Wah's first DLM algorithm for weighted MAX-SAT [18], an evaluation function is used which sums the clause weights w_i and the clause penalties clp_i over all unsatisfied clauses. A variant of this algorithm known as DLM-99-SAT uses clause penalties only, but these are initialised to the clause weights, and during the search, the clause penalties are modified proportionately to the respective clause weights. Finally, the GLSSAT algorithm for weighted MAX-SAT defines a utility function as $clp_i/1 + w_i$ to determine which penalty weights are updated, but it does not use the clause weights directly to guide the search.

In addition to the three methods described above, a variety of other approaches can be used for incorporating clause weights and penalties into an extension of SAPS for weighted MAX-SAT. Limited preliminary results suggest that at least some of the resulting SAPS variants appear to perform at least as good as GLSSAT2 on standard benchmarks for weighted MAX-SAT, but a better understanding of the search dynamics and a more thorough empirical analysis is required to confirm these results.

5 Conclusions & Future Work

In this study, we applied the Scaling and Probabilistic Smoothing (SAPS) algorithm to the unweighted MAX-SAT problem; it extends our previous work, in which we developed the SAPS algorithm for the SAT problem, and established it as a state-of-the-art SLS algorithm for SAT. Here, we presented empirical evidence that SAPS performs similarly excellent on unweighted MAX-SAT, where it consistently outperforms GLSSAT2, one of the best performing MAX-SAT algorithms known to-date. For all of the problem test sets we examined, SAPS was at least 2 times faster than GLSSAT2 in finding optimal or best known solutions, and for some instances SAPS was over 10 times faster. We found that the performance of SAPS was relatively robust *w.r.t.* parameter settings; only for heavily overconstrained problem instances, a different setting of the scaling parameter was required to reach state-of-the-art performance. We provided some insight into this behaviour and some of the other phenomena we encountered.

This work provides a solid foundation for assessing and understanding the behaviour of SAPS on MAX-SAT, and provides a natural stepping stone for developing a SAPS variant for weighted MAX-SAT. Since SAPS is a Dynamic Local Search (DLS) algorithm, and uses dynamic clause penalties, there are many different ways of combining the clause penalties with the clause weights specified in a weighted MAX-SAT instance. Some of these variants are currently being implemented and empirically evaluated. When we proposed SAPS for SAT, we found it helpful to reactively tune the smoothing component of the algorithm, but from our work presented here, we found that unsatisfiable instances are more sensitive to the scaling component of the algorithm. Hence, we will turn our attention to developing a SAPS variant that dynamically adapts the scaling parameter during the search. Overall, based on the promising results reported here, we believe that SAPS has the potential to exceed the performance of the best-performing algorithms for MAX-SAT (weighted and unweighted) currently known.

Acknowledgements

This work has been supported by an NSERC Postgraduate Scholarship (PGS-B) to DT and by HH's NSERC Individual Research Grant #238788. We thank Patrick Mills and Edward Tsang for providing us with their GLS implementation.

References

[1] B. Borchers and J. Furman. A two-phase exact algorithm for MAX-SAT and weighted MAX-SAT problems. In *Journal of Combinatorial Optimization, Vol. 2*, pp. 299–306, 1999.

[2] P. Cheeseman, B. Kanefsky and W. M. Taylor. Where the Really Hard Problems Are. In *Proceedings of the Twelfth International Joint Conference on Artificial Intelligence, IJCAI-91*, pp.331–337, 1997.

[3] J. Frank. Learning Short-term Clause Weights for GSAT. In *Proc. IJCAI-97*, pp. 384–389, Morgan Kaufmann Publishers, 1997.

[4] P. Hansen and B. Jaumard. Algorithms for the maximum Satisfiability problem. In *Computing*, 44:279-303, 1990.

[5] H. H. Hoos. On the Run-time Behaviour of Stochastic Local Search Algorithms for SAT. In *Proc. AAAI-99*, pp. 661–666. AAAI Press, 1999.

[6] H. H. Hoos and T. Stützle. Local Search Algorithms for SAT: An Empirical Evaluation. In *J. of Automated Reasoning*, Vol. 24, No. 4, pp. 421–481, 2000.

[7] F. Hutter, D. A. D. Tompkins, and H. H. Hoos. Scaling and Probabilistic Smoothing: Efficient Dynamic Local Search for SAT. In *LNCS 2470:Proc. CP-02*, pp. 233–248, Springer Verlag, 2002.

[8] P. Mills and E. P. K. Tsang. Guided Local Search for solving SAT and weighted MAX-SAT problems. In *Journal of Automated Reasoning, Special Issue on Satisfiability Problems*, pp. 24:205–223, Kluwer, 2000

[9] P. Morris. The breakout method for escaping from local minima. In *Proc. AAAI-93*, pp. 40–45. AAAI Press, 1993.

[10] J. D. Park. Using Weighted MAX-SAT Engines to Solve MPE. In *Proc. AAAI-02*, pp. 682–687. AAAI Press, 2002.

[11] D. Schuurmans and F. Southey. Local search characteristics of incomplete SAT procedures. In *Proc. AAAI-2000*, pp. 297–302, AAAI Press, 2000.

[12] D. Schuurmans, F. Southey, and R. C. Holte. The exponentiated subgradient algorithm for heuristic boolean programming. In *Proc. IJCAI-01*, pp. 334-341, Morgan Kaufmann Publishers, 2001.

[13] B. Selman and H. A. Kautz. Domain-Independent Extensions to GSAT: Solving Large Structured Satisfiability Problems. In *Proc. IJCAI-93*, pp. 290–295, Morgan Kaufmann Publishers, 1993.
[14] B. Selman, H. A. Kautz, and B. Cohen. Noise Strategies for Improving Local Search. In *Proc. AAAI-94*, pp. 337–343, AAAI Press, 1994.
[15] B. Selman, H. Levesque, and D. Mitchell. A New Method for Solving Hard Satisfiability Problems. In *Proc. AAAI-92*, pp. 440–446, AAAI Press, 1992.
[16] B. Selman, D. G. Mitchell, and H. J. Levesque. Generating Hard Satisfiability Problems. In *Artificial Intelligence, Vol. 81*. pp. 17–29, 1996.
[17] K. Smyth, H. H. Hoos, and T. Stützle. Iterated Robust Tabu Search for MAX-SAT. In *Proc. of the 16th Canadian Conference on Artificial Intelligence (AI 2003)*, to appear, 2003.
[18] Z. Wu and B. W. Wah. An Efficient Global-Search Strategy in Discrete Lagrangian Methods for Solving Hard Satisfiability Problems. In *Proc. AAAI-00*, pp . 310–315, AAAI Press, 2000.
[19] M. Yagiura and T. Ibaraki. Analyses on the 2 and 3-Flip Neighborhoods for the MAX SAT. In *Journal of Combinatorial Optimization, Vol. 3, No. 1*, pp. 95-114, July 1999.
[20] M. Yagiura and T. Ibaraki. Efficient 2 and 3-Flip Neighborhood Search Algorithms for the MAX SAT: Experimental Evaluation. In *Journal of Heuristics, Vol. 7, No. 5*, pp. 423-442, 2001.

A Comparison of Consistency Propagation Algorithms in Constraint Optimization

Jingfang Zheng and Michael C. Horsch

Department of Computer Science
University of Saskatchewan
Saskatoon, SK, Canada
{jiz194,horsch}@cs.usask.ca

Abstract. This paper reviews the main approaches for extending arc consistency propagation in constraint optimization frameworks and discusses full and partial arc consistency propagation based on Larrosa's W-NC* and W-AC*2001 algorithms [Larrosa 2002]. We implement these full/partial propagation algorithms in branch and bound search and compare their performance on MaxCSP models. We empirically demonstrate that maintaining arc consistency is more efficient than other partial propagation. We also demonstrate that the end result of constraint propagation can be used as an effective heuristic for guiding search in constraint optimization problems.

1 Introduction

It is well known that arc consistency (AC) plays an important role in solving constraint satisfaction problems (CSP). Considerable research was invested in exploring the effectiveness of computing arc consistency, and in looking for effective partial consistency algorithms which might provide a better tradeoff between the costs of propagation and search [Nadel 1989, Bessiere and Regin, 1996].

Two general frameworks, SCSP and VCSP, have been proposed to generalize classical constraint satisfaction and constraint optimization [Bistarelli et al., 1995, Schiex et al. 1996]. Both of these frameworks generalize the idea of satisfiability to optimization of a global valuation, which can represent costs, preferences, fuzzy values, or other varieties of so-called "soft constraints."

Generalizations for arc consistency algorithms for soft constraints were initially proposed, with the restriction that the valuations must be combined with an idempotent operator [Bistarelli et al. 1996]. Idempotence is natural in many instances of the soft constraint framework, as well as for classical CSP problems (eg, the boolean operators AND and OR are idempotent), but for some other instances, such as the problem of maximizing the number of satisfied constraints (MaxCSP), idempotence is not natural (ie, integer addition is not idempotent). Recently, [Schiex, 2000] proposed a new extension of AC without this restriction and [Larrosa, 2002] improved this algorithm.

Y. Xiang and B. Chaib-draa (Eds.): AI 2003, LNAI 2671, pp. 160-174, 2003.

In this paper we present an exploration into the use of Larrosa's W-NC* and W-AC*2001 algorithms [Larrosa 2002] in conjunction with a simple branch and bound search. Drawing a parallel to the work of Nadel [1988], we introduce five variants of the basic Soft AC (SAC) propagation: SBC, SFC, SPL, SFL, and SRFL. Each of these represents a different tradeoff between propagation and search costs. We also define a value ordering heuristic function using the result information of SAC propagation. We investigate the performance of these variants in solving random MaxCSP problems. In addition, we compare these soft constraint propagation algorithms to related methods of [Verfaillie, Lemâıtre, & Schiex 1996].

Our experimental results suggest that computing full arc consistency in MaxCSP is more effective than partial consistency algorithms for the random MaxCSP problems we studied. We also present a surprising result, namely that the performance of one of the partial consistency algorithms, "soft forward lookahead" (SFL) is almost identical to full consistency in terms of search costs and propagation costs. Finally, we demonstrate that the value-ordering heuristic, which is computed as a side effect of the constraint propagation algorithms, reduces search costs significantly.

2 COP and Valued CSP Framework

The classical binary CSP is defined as a triple P = (X, D, C), where X is a set of variables, D is a set of finite domains associated to X, and C is a set of constraints that restrict the values the variables can simultaneously take. The task of solving CSP is to assign each variable a value that satisfies all the constraints.

With the definition of *soft constraint* that represents preference and uncertainty [Schiex, Fargier, & Verfaillie 1995], the CSP representation is extended to constraint optimization problems (COP). COPs take the violation of these constraints into account in a specific criterion that should be minimized (or maximized). Two frameworks were proposed in [Bistarelli et al., and Schiex et al. 1996], Semiring-based CSP (SCSP) and Valued CSP (VCSP), which cover classical CSP, fuzzy CSP, possibilistic CSP, additive CSP, probabilistic CSP, etc. We use VCSP as the framework to build our COP models.

A VCSP is a structure $<X, D, C, S, \varphi>$, where:

- X is a set of variables;
- D is the domains associated to each variable, for example D_i is the domain for variable i;
- C is a set of constraints. In the following sections we have C_{ij} for binary constriant between (i, j) and unary constraint C_i for variable i;
- S is a valuation structure $(E, \oplus, \bot, \mathrm{T}, >)$, where E is a set, > is a complete order on E, $\bot$ is the minimum element in E, T is the maximum element in E, and $\oplus$ is a binary closed operation on E, which satisfies the following properties: commutativity, associativity, monotonicity according to >, $\bot$ as identity and T as absorbing element;
- φ is a map from C to E.

E is a set of values given to constraints that defines the gradual notion of constraint violation and inconsistency. The mapping function φ assigns a valuation in E to each constraint in C. This valuation can be considered as the cost of the violation of constraint. When a constraint maps to the minimum element $\perp$, it is satisfied or consistent; when a constraint maps to the maximum element T, it represents constraint violation and complete inconsistency, and other elements between $\perp$ and T are the valuations for the partial constraint violations. Any pair of elements of E may be compared using >, and combined using the operation $\oplus$.

In the following sections, (i, a) represents the assignment of value a $(a \in D_i)$ to variable i $(i \in X)$; $A[0..k]$ represents the partial assignment of values to variables 0 through k; $\varphi(c)$ is the cost of the violation of constraint c $(c \in C)$; and $\varphi(A)$ is the cost of an assignment A. If we define the operation $\oplus$ as mathematical sum, the cost of an assignment A is the sum of the costs from the violations of the assigned constraints:

$$\varphi(A) = \bigoplus_{c \in C,\ A \text{ violates } c} \varphi(c) \tag{1}$$

Equation 1 is used for partial as well as complete assignments. In an *assigned constraint,* both variables have been assigned in a partial assignment.

3 Algorithms for Solving COPs

3.1 Branch and Bound Search

Branch and bound (BB) is a straightforward method of finding a global complete consistent assignment for COPs like backtracking for CSPs. In BB, a lower bound (*lb*) and an upper bound (*ub*) are defined as filters for the search. The *lb* is the possible cost of the current (partial) assignment, updated in each step of the BB search with the new violated costs. The parameter *ub* is the highest cost that an assignment is allowed to reach during search. Once a partial assignment has a *lb* higher than *ub*, the current branch of the search tree can be pruned.

Depending on the particulars of the algorithm, *lb* may be the cost of the assigned violated constraints; it may also include the cost of constraints that *will* be violated in any *future* assignment based on the current one. So the more quickly an algorithm can increase *lb* and decrease *ub*, the less work it will have to do during the search. However, increasing *lb* may require more effort at each search step. Obviously there is a tradeoff and we want to explore the value of it.

3.2 Calculating Lower Bounds

From the way that *lb* is calculated, by taking into account the violated constraints, LB methods can be looked on as the extension of consistency propagation in COP frameworks. [Verfaillie, Lemaıtre, & Schiex 1996] discusses two methods, called *Partial Assignment Valuation*, which are reviewed in this section.

Backward Checking (BC) is the natural extension of consistency checking in backtracking search (BT) for CSPs. It is the simplest way of bounding the valuation of a current assignment A, by only taking into account the constraints that are assigned in A. A partial assignment $A[0..k]$ $(0 \leq k \leq n-1)$ is *qualified* if its cost (LB_{bc}) of the assigned violated constraints is smaller than the current best upper bound ub. The bound $LB_1(A)$ is called the local valuation of A (Equation 2):

$$LB_1(A) = LB_{bc}(A) = \bigoplus_{\substack{c \in C \\ A \text{ violates } c}} \varphi(c) \tag{2}$$

Forward Checking (FC) attempts to increase lb more quickly by taking more constraints into account at each step. A partial assignment $A[0..k]$ is *qualified* if (1) its LB_{bc} cost is smaller than ub; (2) for any unassigned variable x $(k+1 \leq x \leq n-1)$, the minimum cost added by taking into account x should not lead the new lb to exceed ub. Thus we obtain the new bound $LB_2(A)$ as shown in Equation 3:

$$LB_2(A) = LB_{bc}(A) \oplus LB_{fc}(A)$$

$$LB_{fc}(A) = \bigoplus_{x \in X'} [\min_{val \in D_x} \Delta LB_{bc}(A, x, val)] \tag{3}$$

$$\Delta LB_{bc}(A, x, val) = \bigoplus_{\substack{c \in C \\ A \cup \{x[val]\} \text{ violates } c}} \varphi(c)$$

where X' is the set of unassigned variables and D_x is x's domain. $\Delta LB_{bc}(A, x, val)$ is the new local cost by bringing in variable x with value val.

The minimum cost from each unassigned variable can help not only increase the lb, but also prune future unqualified values. The future value val from variable x is not qualified if the local valuation LB_{bc} plus the minimum cost from all other future variables plus the cost val brings exceeds ub (See Formula 4).

$$\begin{aligned} & LB_{bc}(A) \oplus \Delta LB_{bc}(A, x, val) \\ & \quad \oplus [\bigoplus_{x' \in X' - \{x\}} [\min_{val' \in D_{x'}} \Delta LB_{bc}(A, x', val')]] \\ & \geq ub \end{aligned} \tag{4}$$

Since $LB_{fc}(A)$ is always non-negative, $LB_2(A)$ is no smaller than $LB_1(A)$, and takes into accounts the constraints between the assigned variables and the unassigned ones. Note that because there may be a lot of constraints between the unassigned variables $LB_2(A)$ leaves considerable room for improvement.

3.3 Node and Arc Consistency Propagation in COPs

Schiex [2000] proposed a new notion of AC for soft constraint frameworks, and Larrosa [2002] described an implementation of node and arc consistency propagation for Weighted CSP. This paper incorporates Larrosa's W-NC* and W-AC*2001 algorithms into BB search. First we review the definition of NC and AC in a VCSP framework <X, D, C, S, φ>:

Definition 1 [Schiex 2000] NC. *(i, a) is node consistent if* $C_i < T$. *Variable i is node consistent if all its domain values are node consistent. A VCSP is node consistent (NC) if all its domain values are node consistent.*

Here the maximum value T is used as a threshold to check node consistency. But to apply NC propagation in BB search, we have a lower threshold *ub*, which is decreasing in the process of search. Since the node value with higher node cost than *ub* is not eligible for the optimal assignment, using *ub* as a filter is more efficient than using T in BB search. We revise the definition, as follows:

Definition 2 NC_{ub}. *(i, a) is node consistent if* $C_i < ub$. *Variable i is node consistent if all its domain values are node consistent. A VCSP is node consistent* (NC_{ub}) *if all its domain values are node consistent.*

NC_{ub} can be achieved by pruning values whose cost C_i is not less than the current best *ub*. After pruning, each remaining value in each variable has its cost less than *ub*. But there is some common information that can be extracted from the costs. Larrosa [2002] defines a zero-arity constraint called C_ϕ, which is the combination of the minimum costs from each variable. Larrosa defines the operation subtraction □ , and two projection operations. First, the *projection of binary constraint* C_{ij} *over unary constraint* C_i transfers costs from C_{ij} to C_i by subtracting the minimum cost of any tuple in the constraint. Second, the *projection of unary constraint* C_i *to the zero-arity constraint* C_ϕ, which transfers the minimum cost from C_i to C_ϕ. With the extraction of the common information of C_ϕ, the original NC_{ub} problem can be made NC^*_{ub}. Note that C_ϕ is a lower bound on the cost of a full assignment from the current problem state.

Larrosa defines NC*, which extends Schiex's definition by using C_ϕ; our revised definition uses *ub* as the consistency criterion, as follows:

Definition 3 NC^*_{ub}. *Let P <X, D, C, S, φ> be a VCSP framework. (i, a) is node consistent if* $C_\phi \oplus C_i < ub$. *Variable i is node consistent if: 1) all its values are node consistent and 2) there exists a value* $a \in D_i$ *such that* $C_i(a) = \perp$. *Value a is a support for the variable node consistency. P is node consistent (*NC^*_{ub}*) if every variable is node consistent.*

Schiex defines arc consistency for soft constraint problems as follows.

Definition 4 [Schiex 2000] AC. *(i, a) is arc consistent with respect constraint* C_{ij} *if it is node consistent and there is a value* $b \in D_j$ *such that* $C_{ij}(a,b) = \perp$. *Value b is called a support of a. Variable i is arc consistent if all its values are arc consistent with respect every binary constraint affecting i. A VCSP is arc consistent (AC) if every variable is arc consistent.*

Enforcing NC^*_{ub} and AC in a COP framework is the procedure of the projection of binary constraints over unary constraints, then over zero-arity constraints. The algorithm has two basic operations, *FindSupports* and *PruneVar*, which do binary projection and the unary projection respectively [Larrosa, 2002]. In Figure 1, *FindSupports* and *PruneVar* are the same as those in [Larrosa 2002] except that C_ϕ is checked against *ub* every time C_ϕ is increased to make allow unqualified partial assignments to be pruned. The procedure *initSupport*, which is mentioned in [Larrosa 2002] with the addition of C_ϕ checking, is shown in Figure 2.

The procedures SNC (Figure 2) and SRFL (Figure 4) implement NC^*_{ub} and AC, respectively. Note that our procedures differ from W-NC* and W-AC*2001 in that we reduce the range of checked constraints. The original algorithms check the whole set of constraints, which is necessary to achieve AC, but not necessary if the algorithms are embedded in BB search and used in every step. In each step of propagation, full AC is achieved and the result is projected on C_ϕ and is brought to next step. We only need to deal with the changes that are brought by the new assignment from the new step. Since C_ϕ is the common information extracted after the propagation, it is the right *lb* value that we want to return from the LB method.

procedure FindSupports(i, j)
This procedure projects binary constraint C_{ij} over unary constraint C_i, then over zero-arity constraint $c0$ (See [Larrosa, 2002]). Add $c0$ checks after $c0$ increases and backtrack $c0$ exceeds ub.

  supported := **true**;
  for each $a \in D_i$ **if** $S(i, a, j) \notin D_j$ **do**
    $v := \text{argmin}_{b\in Dj}\{ C_{ij}(a,b) \}$; $\alpha := C_{ij}(a,v)$; $S(i, a, j) := v$;
    $C_i(a) := C_i(a) \oplus \alpha$;
    if ($a = S(i)$ **and** $\alpha \neq \perp$) **then** *supported* := **false**;
  if no*supported* **then**
    $v := \text{argmin}_{a\in Di}\{ C_i(a) \}$; $\alpha := C_i(v)$; $S(i) := v$;
    $c0 := c0 \oplus \alpha$;
    if ($c0 \geq ub$) **return and backtrack**;
    for each $a \in D_i$ **do** $C_i(a) := C_i(a) \ominus \alpha$;
endprocedure

function PruneVar(i): Boolean
This function prunes values from variable i whose node cost (unary cost plus zero-arity cost) is higher than ub (See [Larrosa, 2002]).

  change := **false**;
  for each $a \in D_i$ **if** $C_i(a) \oplus c0 \geq ub$ **do**
    $D_i := D_i \ominus \{a\}$; *change* := **true**;
  return (change);
endfunction

Fig. 1. FindSupports and PruneVar Methods

```
procedure initSupport(X, D, C)
This procedure initiate structure S(i) and S(i, a, j) before the arc consistency
propagation starts. S(i, a, j) is set to Nil and S(i) is set to an arbitrary supporting
value (See [Larrosa, 2002])
  for each i∈X do
    for each a∈D_i do
      for each j∈X do
        if (j≠i) then S(i, a, j) := Nil;
  for each i∈X do
    v := argmin_{a∈Di} {C_i(a)}; S(i) := v; α := C_i(v);
    if (α≠ ⊥) then
      c0 := c0 ⊕ α;
      if (c0 ≥ ub) then return and backtrack;
      for each a∈D_i do
        C_i(a) := C_i(a) θ α;
endprocedure

procedure SNC(firstV, currentV, D, C)
This procedure does node consistency propagation from variable firstV to
currentV.
  for each i∈[firstV..currentV] do
    v := argmin_{a∈Di} {C_i(a)}; α := C_i(v); c0 := c0 ⊕ α;
    if (c0 ≥ ub) then return and backtrack;
    for each a∈D_i do
      C_i(a) := C_i(a) θ α;
  for each i∈[firstV..currentV]
    for each a∈D_i do
      if (C_i(a) ⊕ c0 ≥ ub) then D_i := D_i - {a};
endprocedure
```

Fig. 2. initSupport and SNC Methods

3.4 Full and Partial Propagation

Similar to CSP solving, consistency propagation reduces backtracks but increases work in each step of search. To study the effectiveness of propagation, we define different degrees of propagation similar to those defined for CSP solving [Nadel, 1989].

Soft Backward Checking (SBC). SBC deals with the set of constraints C_{ij}, C_i, and C_ϕ that are assigned in the partial assignment $A[0..k]$. Since variable i has been assigned with value $A[i]$, there is only one available value in D_i which is $A[i]$. The projection of C_{ij} over C_i and finally over C_ϕ will transfer all of the cost from C_{ij} to the only C_i and then all to C_ϕ. SBC takes into account the same subset of constraints as BC (Section 3.2), thus C_ϕ obtained from SBC equals LB_1.

Soft Forward Checking (SFC). Unlike SBC, the SFC takes into account some of the unassigned variables and constraints. Given the current assignment $A[0..k]$, SFC deals with $C_{kj}\ (k < j \le n-1)$, $C_j\ (k \le j \le n-1)$ and projects them over C_ϕ. SFC considers more constraints than FC [Verfaillie, Lemaître, & Schiex 1996] mentioned in Section 3.2, thus C_ϕ obtained from SFC might be a little higher than LB_2.

Soft Partial Lookahead (SPL). SPL takes more constraints than SFC. Given the current assignment $A[0..k]$, it deals with constraints $C_{ji}\ (k \le j < i \le n-1)$, $C_i\ (k \le i \le n-1)$, and projects them over C_ϕ. SPL considers some of the constraints between unassigned variables while SFC does not; thus *lb* from SPL might be higher than that from SFC.

Soft Full Lookahead (SFL). SFL takes into account the whole set of constraints $C_{ji}\ (k \le j \ne i \le n-1)$ and $C_i\ (k \le i \le n-1)$; each constraint is considered only once.

procedure SBCprop(k)
This procedure does Backward Checking propagation and updates $c0$ for BB.
Queue Q keeps the variables that need finding supports.
  initSupport(X, D, C);
  if ($c0 \ge ub$) **then return and backtrack;**
  SNC(0, k);
  if ($c0 \ge ub$) **then return and backtrack;**
  for each $i \in [0..k\text{-}1]$ **do** FindSupports(k, i);
endprocedure

procedure SFCprop(k)
This procedure does Forward Checking propagation and updates $c0$ for BB.
Queue Q keeps the variables that needs finding supports.
  initSupport(X, D, C);
  if ($c0 \ge ub$) **then return and backtrack;**
  SNC(k, n-1);
  if ($c0 \ge ub$) **then return and backtrack;**
  for each C_{ki}, $i \in [k+1..n\text{-}1]$ **do** FindSupports(i, k);
  if ($c0 \ge ub$) **then return and backtrack;**
  for each $i \in [k+1..n\text{-}1]$ **do** PruneVar(i);
endprocedure

Fig. 3. SBC and SFC Propagation Methods

```
procedure SPLprop(k)
This procedure does Partial Forward Look ahead propagation and updates c0
for BB. Queue Q keeps the variables that needs finding supports.
  initSupport(X, D, C);
  if (c0 ≥ ub) then return and backtrack;
  SNC(k, n-1);
  if (c0 ≥ ub) then return and backtrack;
  for each j∈[k..n-1] do
    for each C_ij, i∈[j+1..n-1] do
      FindSupports(i, j);
    if (c0 ≥ ub) then return and backtrack;
    for each i∈[j+1..n-1] do PruneVar(i);
endprocedure

procedure SFLpropANDSRFLprop(k)
This procedure does Forward Look ahead propagation and Real Forward
Lookahead. Flag isSRFL is true when it does SRFLprop.
  initSupport(X, D, C);
  if (c0 ≥ ub) then return and backtrack;
  SNC(k, n-1);
  if (c0 ≥ ub) then return and backtrack;
  for each j∈[k..n-1] do
    for each C_ij, i∈[k..n-1] do
      if i≠j then FindSupports(i, j);
    if (c0 ≥ ub) then return and backtrack;
    for each i∈[k..n-1] do
      if PruneVar(i) then
        if isSRFL then Q := Q∪{i};
endprocedure
```

Fig. 4. SPL, SFL, and SRFL Propagation Methods

Soft Real Full Lookahead (SRFL). SRFL is an implementation of Larossa's W-AC*2001 [Larossa, 2002]. SRFL repeats SFL propagation by taking into account the variables whose domain values have been pruned, and its constraints again until nothing changes. Enforcing SRFL maintains node consistency and arc consistency in each step of search, thus it provides the highest *lb* than any of the others above.

As shown from SBC to SRFL, more and more propagation work is carried out in each step of BB search, as the result, higher and higher *lb* is produced, less and less backtrack occurs. The balance between search cost and propagation cost has become a problem for solving COPs as it does for CSPs. In the next section, we explore these five different combinations.

3.5 Heuristic Functions

The SAC propagation methods generate unary costs for each variable during projection. Recall that $C_i(a)$ is the unary cost of each value a in each variable i given the current assignment $A[0..k]$ (section 3.3). It is updated after propagation in each step of the search. It is straightforward to use this information as a dynamic value order for the heuristic. The idea behind the heuristic is that variables with relatively low $C_i(a)$ will have higher probability to be in the optimal solution. Therefore, we use the values in the order of increasing $C_i(a)$.

4 Experimental Results

We tested these algorithms using MaxCSP (or *partial CSP*) models, but the algorithms are not limited to only this framework. Let us recall the MaxCSP problem: the violations of each constraint are equal in cost (let us say 1). The goal is to find the solution that violates the least constraints, that is, the solution that has the smallest cost. We used the random flawless CSP generator described in [Gent. et. al. 1998]. The four parameters of this model are n (the number of the variables), m (the domain size, equal for all the variables), $p1$ (the density of the constraint graph), and $p2$ (the constraint tightness, equal for all the constraints). We converted the CSP problems into a Valued CSP problem where all failed tuples assigned with the cost 1.

In the following sections we perform comparisons among algorithms in different ways. We use several criteria to compare them:

- We count the number of nodes instantiated (#nodes). The number of instantiated nodes as a criteria has been used for comparing algorithms [Nadel 1989]. It can show how much of the search tree has been examined. It can also give the information about the number of backtracks.
- We count the number of times a binary constraint is projected onto a unary constraint (#bprojs). We count projections because we mentioned in Section 3.3 that the SAC propagation is actually the flow of cost from binary constraints to unary constraints and finally to zero-arity constraints. And the cost flowing is actually done by projection operations. This measure is similar to the count of constraint checks in classical CSPs.
- We also look at the run time (time). Java provides only wall clock time, so while this data is not highly significant, it provides some contextual information.

We chose several sets of problems to test the performance of SRFL, SFC, SPL and SFL (SBC was taking too much time and we knew already that it is bad, so we did not include it here). Our experiments are limited to small problems. This is a practical as well as theoretical issue. These experiments are a first step in our effort to apply soft constraint propagation to larger problems. Experiments on small problems are crucial to understanding the limitations of the algorithms applied to larger problems. For easy problems we generated 100 instances and for larger problems (Column 3, 4 and 5) we generate 30 instances for each of them. We show results from 5 sets in Table 1. We give the 4 parameters and the average solution costs for the problems in the first row. We provide the comparison result in 3 measures as #nodes, #bprojs and Time. For clarity of comparison, we also show the ratio value to SRFL in #nodes and #bprojs in parentheses after the data in each data cell.

In the last set <30, 15, 0.2, 0.2>, four algorithms have close performance (SFC is slightly better in projections). These problems are very easy and do not have many constraints; there are a lot of assignments with zero cost so all of the algorithms can easily find the first one with 0 cost. So there is not much difference among them.

As the of hardness of the problems increases, SRFL shows higher efficiency, just as MAC outperforms FC on large and hard CSP problems [Bessiere and Regin, 1996]. However, for CSP, FC and MAC are roughly equivalent for much wider range of problem classes, while SRFL outperforms other partial AC propagation algorithms much earlier, even when the four parameters are still small.

Figure 5 and Figure 6 show the comparison of these algorithms by the measure of #nodes and #bprojs. The graphs show the fraction of problems in a set that were solved for a given number of #nodes (#bprojs). SRFL is the most efficient algorithm in most of our experiments; SFL is the second best and is very close to SRFL. This result is consistent with Table 1.

We also tested the dynamic value ordering heuristic, using BB search algorithm and SRFL propagation in each step. Figure 7 shows these two algorithms on problem sets <10, 15, 0.5, p2> and <10, 15, p1, 0.5> . Note that the heuristic algorithm outperforms SRFL when p1, p2 are relatively small; when p1 or p2 is relatively high, the nodes number of heuristics quickly rises up close to SRFL.

Table 1. Performance of SRFL, SFC, SPL, and SFL on Flawless generated MaxCSP problems

		10,10,0.9,0.9 ave(cost)=18.03	10,15,0.7,0.7 ave(cost)=3.88	20,10,0.5,0.4 ave(cost) = 1.8	20,10,0.9,0.2 ave(cost) = 0	30,15,0.2,0.2 ave(cost) = 0
#nodes (ratio to SRFL)	SFC	18806 (3.36)	6106 (6.66)	404351 (9.71)	17358 (12.22)	207 (1)
	SPL	6488 (1.16)	1470 (1.60)	62317 (1.50)	2466 (1.74)	206 (1)
	SFL	5759 (1.03)	1119 (1.22)	46656 (1.12)	1637 (1.15)	206 (1)
	SRFL	5595	917	41640	1420	206
#bprojs (ratio to SRFL)	SFC	2451910 (1.06)	494685 (1.13)	10171557 (1.67)	184016 (2.26)	728 (0.98)
	SPL	2297038 (1)	446632 (1.02)	6624528 (1.09)	95251 (1.17)	734 (0.99)
	SFL	2304148 (1)	439244 (1)	6170519 (1.01)	84318 (1.03)	743 (1)
	SRFL	2304275	437499	6089149	81473	743
Time Ratio to SRFL	SFC	2.16	3.51	4.69	6.29	1
	SPL	1.15	1.50	1.41	1.51	1
	SFL	1.01	1.12	1.06	1.08	1
	SRFL	1	1	1	1	1

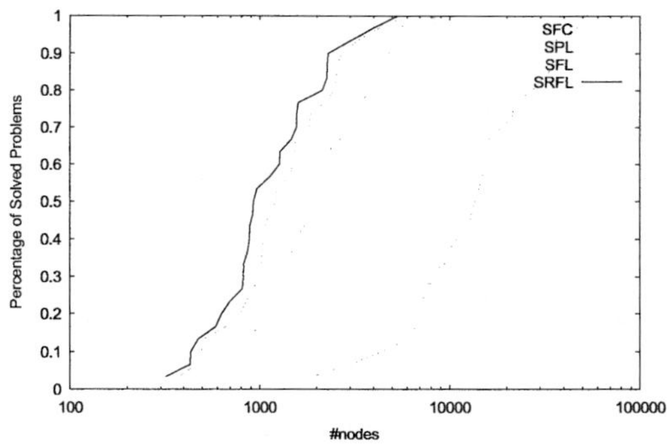

Fig. 5. Nodes Comparison among SFC, SPL, SFL and SRFL on <20, 10, 0.9, 0.2>

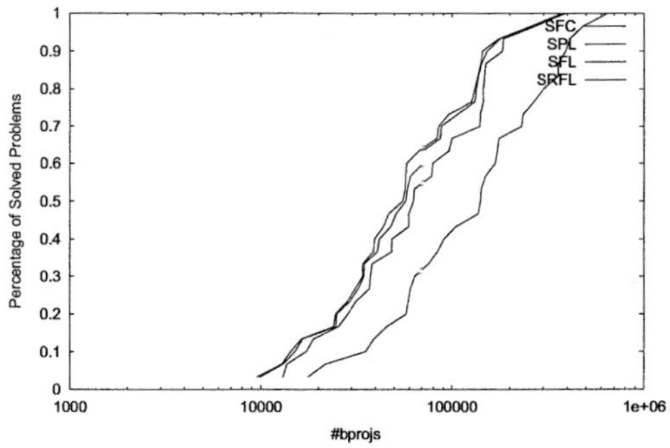

Fig. 6. Projections Comparison among SFC, SPL, SFL and SRFL on <20, 10, 0.9, 0.2>

We explored the reason from the aspect of satisfiability. Figure 8 gives the percentage of satisfiable problems in the example problems we used for Figure 7. We see from Figure 8 that in the area of <10, 15, 0.5, p2> (0.1≤p2≤0.5) and <10, 15, p1, 0.5> (0.1≤p1≤0.7), most problems are satisfiable. Corresponding from Figure 7, in these areas heuristic has obvious better performance than SRFL. Our implementation is configured to allow the search to end after finding a satisfiable assignment (since no better assignment will be found).

Figure 9 and Figure 10 explore 2 problem instances to confirm the argument. We randomly chose a satisfiable problem from <10, 15, 0.3, 0.5> and solved it. Figure 9 shows two graphs, one for SRFL, and one for SRFL with the heuristic. In each graph we show the progress each algorithm makes as #bprojs increases. The points represent the cost of a full or partial assignment at the time a backtrack occurs. The lines show the depth that the search reaches in the search tree. Notice that SRFL requires a number of backtracks (the depth decreases) before finding a solution of zero cost, whereas the heuristic does not. Both algorithms halt when a zero cost solution is found, because there is no need to continue the search for a better solution.

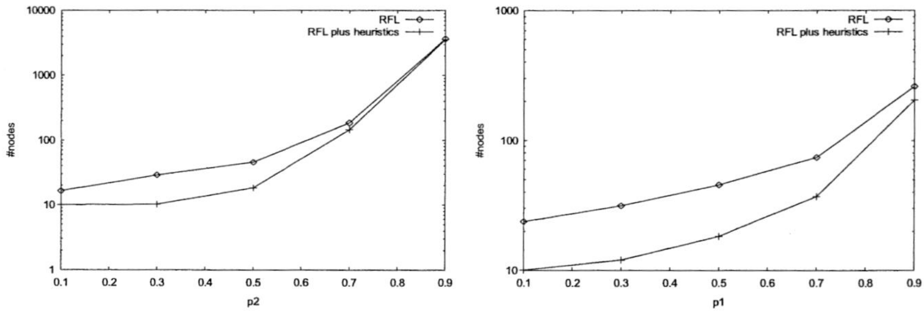

Fig. 7. Nodes Comparison between SRFL and Heuristics on <10,15,0.5,p2> and <10,15,p1,0.5>, 100 examples for each set of parameters

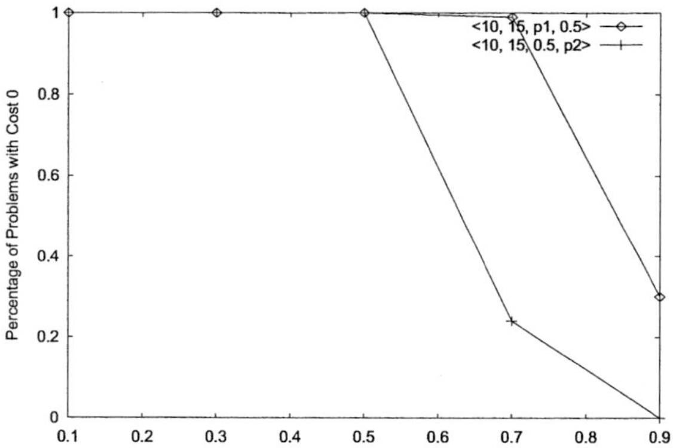

Fig. 8. Percentage of Strictly Satisfiable Problems of<10, 15,0.5,p2> and<10,15,p1,0.5>

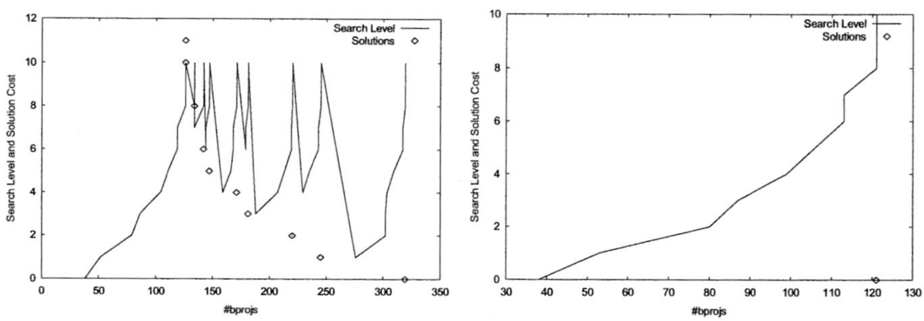

Fig. 9. Comparison between SRFL and Heuristic on satisfiable problem <10, 15, 0.3, 0.5>We randomly generated an over-constrained problem from <10, 15, 0.9, 0.9> and solved it. Figure 10 shows the progress of the solution by noting the cost of solutions found. Note that the SRFL and the heuristic algorithm find a solution with the same minimal cost; the heuristic algorithm finds it much earlier than SRFL. However, both algorithms have to do a lot of work to ensure that there is no better solution

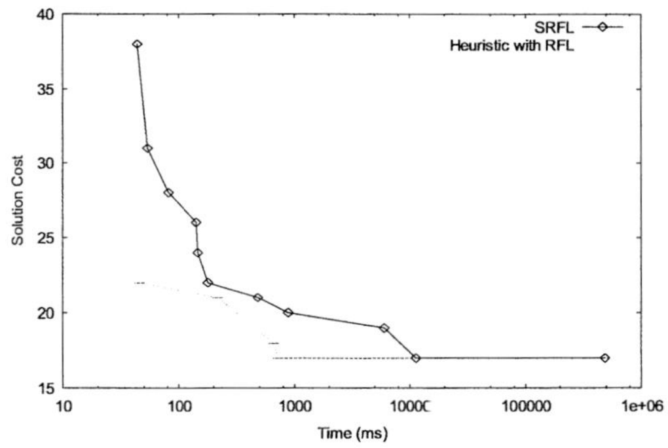

Fig. 10. Comparison of SRFL and Heuristic on an Unsatisfiable Problem <10, 15, 0.9, 0.9>

The COP instance in Figure 10 is an example of a hard problem in COP solving: the algorithm needs a lot of work to prove that the current solution is the best one. The proof takes the heuristic (resp., SRFL) 99.8% and (resp., 97.7%) of the total time for this example. Our data for this problem indicate that the average search level of the search tail is around 2.9 (maximum depth: 5, standard deviation: 0.43).

5 Conclusions and Future Work

In this paper, we implemented full and partial arc consistency propagations in a COP framework. The projection – pruning method can be combined with BB search using C_ϕ as the *lb* filter in BB search. We implemented five BB-SAC algorithms and applied them in solving COPs.

Our experiments found that maintaining soft arc consistency (SRFL) in each step was more effective than partial AC propagations. This is not too surprising, given the results of similar studies for related algorithms in the CSP domain [Bessier and Regin, 1996]. However, for COP, SRFL outperforms other partial consistency propagation methods even for relatively small problems. Since optimality must be proved, even a minor increase in pruning power will be multiplied many times over. We also observed that the partial propagation method SFL performed nearly as well as SRFL. This seems surprising, and we intend to investigate this further in future work.

We used $C_i(a)$ from SRFL propagation as dynamic value ordering heuristic. Our experiments show that it improves SRFL when the problem is satisfiable. Obviously, if a problem instance is known to be satisfiable, there are better methods for solving it than any BB-SAC method. When the problem is unsatisfiable, the heuristic method seems to require less work to find a reasonably good solution (sometimes optimal), but will spend almost the same effort as SRFL to achieve or prove optimality. A comparison of this heuristic to other heuristics for COP (e.g., [Larrossa and Mesguer, 1999; Kask, 2000; Horsch et al., 2002]) is needed.

For a significant improvement in effectiveness, the cost of proving optimality may seem a primary target for improvement. However, our experiments suggest that for harder COP problems, the insight provided by a heuristic, *e.g.*, $C_i(a)$, does not seem to help much; proving optimality is a problem requiring thoroughness rather than insight. As well, full SAC propagation (SRFL) is already limiting the search depth substantially; this does not seem to leave too much room for reducing the cost of the proof of optimality.

Because of the difficulty in proving the optimality [Givry et al. 1997], our experiments were limited to small problems. We are actively researching improvements to soft constraint propagation and search algorithms for larger problems. The tradeoff between the value of a "good" solution and the cost of the proof of optimality is also the subject of on-going work; we are interested in the problem of providing better control over choosing to continue search or to stop with the current best solution.

References

[1] Bessiere, C., and Regin, J.-C. MAC and combined heuristics: Two reasons to forsake FC (and CBJ?) on hard problems. CP-1996, *Lecture Notes in Computer Science* 1118:61–75, 1996.

[2] Bistarelli, S.; Montanari, U.; and Rossi, F. Semiring-based constraint satisfaction and optimization. *Journal of the ACM* 44(2):201–236, 1997.

[3] Gent, I., MacIntyre, E., Prosser, P., Smith, S., and Walsh, T. Random Constraint Satisfaction: Flaws and Structure. APES Research Report 98.23, 1998.

[4] Givry, S. de, and Verfaille, G. Optimum Anytime Bounding for Constraint Optimization Problems. In Proc. of the AAAI97 workshop on "Building Resource-Bounded Reasoning Systems", Providence, RI. 1997.

[5] Horsch, M., Havens, W. and Ghose, A. Generalized Arc Consistency with Applications to MaxCSP and SCSP Instances. In Proceedings of the Fifteenth Canadian Conference on Artificial Intelligence, 2002.

[6] K. Kask. New Search Heuristics for Max-CSP In Proceeding of CP'2000, pg. 262--277, 2000.

[7] Kumar, V., 1992. Algorithms for Constraint-Satisfaction Problems: A Survey. *AI Magazine* 13(1):32--44, 1992.

[8] Larrossa and P. Meseguer. Partition-based lower bound for max-csp. Proceedings CP, pages 303-315, 1999.

[9] Nadel, B. Constraint Satisfaction Algorithms. *Computational Intelligence* 5:188--224, 1989.

[10] Schiex, T., Fargier, H., and Verfaillie, G. Valued constraint satisfaction problems: hard and easy problems. In *IJCAI-95*, 631–637, 1995.

[11] Schiex, T. Arc consistency for soft constraints. In *CP-2000*, 411–424, 2000.

[12] Verfaillie, G.; Lemaıtre, M.; and Schiex, T. Russian doll search. In *AAAI-96*, 181–187, 1996.

[13] Wallace, R. Analysis of Heuristic Methods for Partial Constraint Satisfaction Problems. In CP-1996, pp482-496, 1996.

Discovering Temporal/Causal Rules: A Comparison of Methods

Kamran Karimi and Howard J. Hamilton

Department of Computer Science
University of Regina
Regina, Saskatchewan
Canada S4S 0A2
{karimi,hamilton}@cs.uregina.ca

Abstract. We describe TimeSleuth, a hybrid tool based on the C4.5 classification software, which is intended for the discovery of temporal/causal rules. Temporally ordered data are gathered from observable attributes of a system, and used to discover relations among the attributes. In general, such rules could be atemporal or temporal. We evaluate TimeSleuth using synthetic data sets with well-known causal relations as well as real weather data. We show that by performing appropriate preprocessing and postprocessing operations, TimeSleuth extends C4.5's domain of applicability to the unsupervised discovery of temporal relations among ordered data. We compare the results obtained from TimeSleuth to those of TETRAD and CaMML, and show that TimeSleuth performs better than the other systems.

1 Introduction

We consider the problem of discovering relations among a set of attributes that represent the state of a single system as time progresses. Given a sequence of temporally ordered records, with or without an explicit time attribute, the goal is to identify as many cases as possible where two or more attributes' values depend on each other. We may want to describe the system, predict future behavior, or control some of the attributes by changing the values of other attributes. For example, one observation may be that "$(y = 5)$ is always true when $(x = 2)$." From this statement, we could predict the value of y as 5 when we see that x is 2. This is an example of *co-occurrence* between two values. Alternatively, the same statement could be interpreted as the rule: **if** $\{(x = 2)\}$ **then** $(y = 5)$, and use forward chaining to predict that setting the value of x to 2 will result in y becoming 5. This rule is thus interpreted as a *causal relation*.

Mining information from temporal data is an active research subject with different approaches. A *time series* is a time-ordered sequence of observations taken over time [1,2]. In a *univariate time series*, each observation consists of a value for a single attribute, while in a *multivariate time series*, each observation consists of values for

Y. Xiang and B. Chaib-draa (Eds.): AI 2003, LNAI 2671, pp. 175-189, 2003.

several attributes. Most research on time series has assumed the presence of a distinguished attribute representing time and numeric values for all other attributes. Attempts have been made to fit constant or time-varying mathematical functions to time series data [1].

An *event sequence* is a series of temporally ordered events, with either an ordinal time attribute (which gives the order but not a real-valued time) or no time attribute. Each *event* specifies the values for a set of attributes. A recurring pattern in an event sequence is called a *frequent episode* [18]. Recent research has emphasized finding frequent episodes with varying number of events between the events that identify the event sequence. Algorithms such as Dynamic Time Warping and its variants measure the similarity of patterns that are stretched differently over time [15]. These methods have not been applied to searching for relations in causal data.

Two tools that were designed for performing unsupervised search for causal relations are CaMML [14, 23] and TETRAD [21]. They look for relationships among all attributes, resulting in a non-linear increase in running time as the number of attributes increase. Although these tools were not designed for the exact problem of finding atemporal and temporal rules from temporally ordered data from a single source, they can be applied to this problem and provide the most appropriate existing techniques for comparison purposes.

CaMML is a Minimum Message Length based causal discovery system that uses a Bayesian minimum encoding technique. Given a set of observed attributes, CaMML finds causal relationships between one or more causes and a single effect. As an example, in CaMML's notation $(A, B \rightarrow C)$ means that A and B are causes of C. The output of CaMML must be interpreted by a human expert.

TETRAD is a well-known causality discoverer that uses Bayesian networks [4] to find causal relations. It has its own notation for displaying the discovered causal rules. For example, $A \rightarrow B$ means that A causes B and $A \leftrightarrow B$ means that both A and B have a hidden common cause. Unfortunately TETRAD's results are not always precise. A •→ B means that either A causes B, or they both have a hidden common cause, A •–• B means that A causes B or B causes A, or they both have a hidden common cause (usually considered to mean the same thing as co-occurrence). This ambiguity opens the door to different interpretations of the results. In this paper we attempt to sidestep this ambiguity by using an artificial data set with known relations. TETRAD allows the user to provide it with information regarding the temporal order of the attributes. We exploited this feature in our experiments to give TETRAD all available information.

Interpreting co-occurrence relations as causal relations, as is done by software such as TETRAD, requires justification. The main trend in causality mining involves using the statistical concept of conditional independence as a measure of the control one attribute may have over another [19]. For example, given the three attributes x, y, and z, if x is independent from y given z, that is, $P(x, y \mid z) = P(x \mid z)$, then we can conclude that y is not a direct cause of x. In other words, z separates x and y from each other. This basic concept is used to build Bayesian Networks, which show the conditional dependence of attributes as arcs. These arcs are then *interpreted* as signifying causal relations.

The notion of conditional independence is void of time. The proponents of this popular method use temporal information, if it is available, to place constraints on the relationships among the attributes (if we know x always happens before y, then y cannot be a cause of x), but time is not essential to the working of their algorithms. Leaving out time when dealing with the notion of causality seemed counterintuitive to us. The result was an investigation into the use of a standard tool, C4.5 [19], to discover relations given temporally ordered input data. We chose C4.5 because it is available in source code form, and has been widely used.

In this paper, we describe TimeSleuth [12], an enhanced version of our RFCT software [9], for the problem of finding atemporal and temporal relations in causal data and compare it to two other causality miners. By performing appropriate preprocessing (rotation and flattening) and postprocessing (applying temporal constraints), TimeSleuth extends C4.5's domain of applicability to the unsupervised discovery of temporal relations among ordered nominal or numeric data. It searches for relations among attributes that characterize the behavior of a system. In general, such relations can be causal or acausal, but we consider data sets where causal relations exist, and evaluate the effectiveness of methods at finding these relations. We distinguish between *atemporal relations*, which involve values observed at the same time, and *temporal relations*, which involve values from different time steps. TimeSleuth further divides temporal relations into causal and acausal. TimeSleuth implements the TIMERS method (Temporal Investigation Method for Enregistered Record Sequences), which is formally introduced in [13]. The same reference describes how the method distinguishes between causal and acausal relations.

The remainder of this paper is organized as follows. Section 2 introduces the TimeSleuth method and software. Section 3 describes experiments with synthetic data from a simple problem domain that contains atemporal and temporal/causal relations. The simplicity of the domain allows us to judge the results with little ambiguity. Section 4 presents experiments on real-world data. Section 5 concludes the paper.

2 TimeSleuth

TimeSleuth is a tool for finding and analyzing atemporal and temporal predictive relations in data. It includes a variant of C4.5 to form decision rules. TimeSleuth provides a user interface and processes data before and after running C4.5. Many other rule discoverers could be used instead of C4.5. TimeSleuth assumes the existence of a temporal order among the input records, and based on that assumption, formulates predictive rules among the attributes. These rules are *temporally consistent*, i.e., condition attributes are referred to at or before the time of the decision attribute. TimeSleuth's mathematical model and method are explained in [11].

TimeSleuth requires a patched version of C4.5, which we call C4.5T (Temporal), which adds time indications to output rules. Patch files with all the necessary modifications are included with the TimeSleuth package. C4.5T's output can include both temporal decision trees and temporal rules [10]. The relations found by TimeSleuth may or may not be causal. For a discussion on causality, see [3, 5, 16, 22]. TimeSleuth finds relations that have a temporal relationship between a cause and an effect. It provides a metric to distinguish among causal and acausal relations.

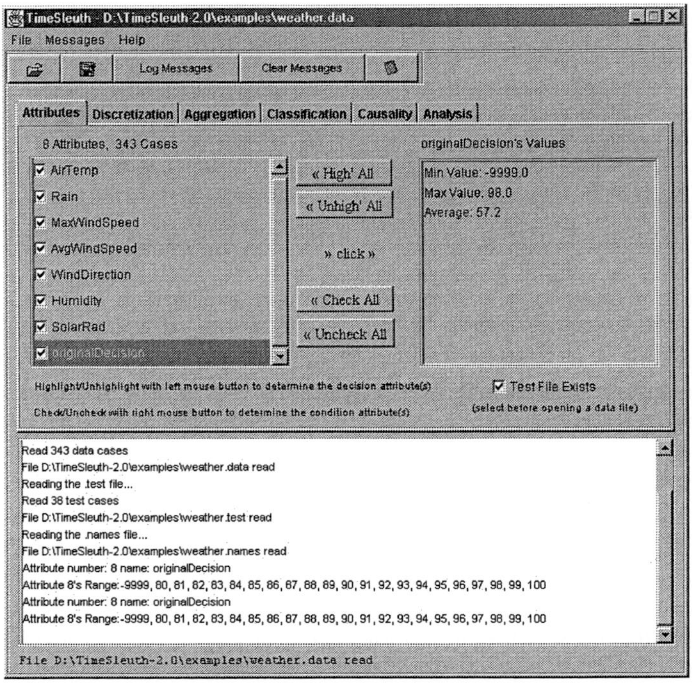

Fig. 1. Screen shot of TimeSleuth

TimeSleuth's graphical user interface is designed to encourage the user to experiment with the data and different scenarios. Unlike C4.5, which requires the user to select a single attribute as the decision attribute, TimeSleuth can iterate over many attributes and invoke C4.5T with a new decision attribute each time. It rotates the fields in the observation data, so that the value of the decision attribute appears last, as required by C4.5. The rules resulting from running C4.5T are sorted by it so that the attributes appear in correct temporal order, and are presented by TimeSleuth in tables that emphasize the temporal characteristics of the rules. The user can thus easily see any temporal relationship among the attributes, and how each attribute is used as time progresses. The user can also opt to have the rules output in the form of Prolog statements [7, 8], thus making the results readily executable. TimeSleuth is thus both a machine learning tool (which outputs machine-usable rules) and a data mining tool (which helps the user to discover temporal relations among data through experimentation). C4.5 assigns a confidence value to the rules it generates. The user can instruct TimeSleuth to prune the output rules so that only rules with a confidence value greater than a threshold are presented. Figure 1 shows TimeSleuth's user interface after loading a file that contains hourly weather observations. The decision attribute (here corresponding to Soil Temperature) is selected by being highlighted. The condition attributes to be used during rule generation have a check mark next to them. TimeSleuth can discretize real-valued attributes as needed.

TimeSleuth merges consecutive records into one record, which brings previous values together with later observations, helping in the discovery of relationships between temporally distant values. This process is called flattening [6, 13], and the number of records merged is determined by the window size (w). The assumption with bigger window values is that the events' effects have a longer delay. TimeSleuth's Analysis panel presents the output in different ways to help the user in discovering such properties. As an example, Figure 2 shows how often each attribute at each time step has been mentioned in the temporal rules. In this figure, TimeSleuth has generated rules with window values from 1 to 14, and the current window size is set to 5. The user can employ the slider to see the effects of selecting other window size values. In Figure 2 the decision attribute is soil temperature.

Finding the appropriate window size for mining data may be a challenge for the domain expert. For this reason, TimeSleuth can be run in batch mode, where different window sizes are tried automatically. The user can choose criteria, such as the error rate, to stop the search for an appropriate window size. When applied to sample weather data, this method found the best results with a window size of 3 (hours), as shown in Figure 4. These results are better than standard C4.5's results (w = 1), indicating an advantage of the temporal investigation of the data. TimeSleuth can also be used to distinguish between causal and acausal relations. It considers time to have two directions. The forward direction, which is the natural direction of time, is used to test the data for causality. Here the past observations are used to predict the value of the decision attribute. The backward direction of time is used to test the acausality of the data. In this case the future observations are used to predict the value of the decision attribute. In an acausal relation the value of the decision attribute is in a temporal "co-occurrence" relation with the condition attributes. The results determine the quality of the rules, and thus the verdict of the system. This verdict could be one of causal, acausal, or instantaneous (when window size 1 gives the best results). Causal and acausal relations are both considered temporal, and in the rest of this paper we will emphasize the temporal aspects of the rules discovered by TimeSleuth. See [13] for a treatment of the distinction between causality and acausality in TimeSleuth.

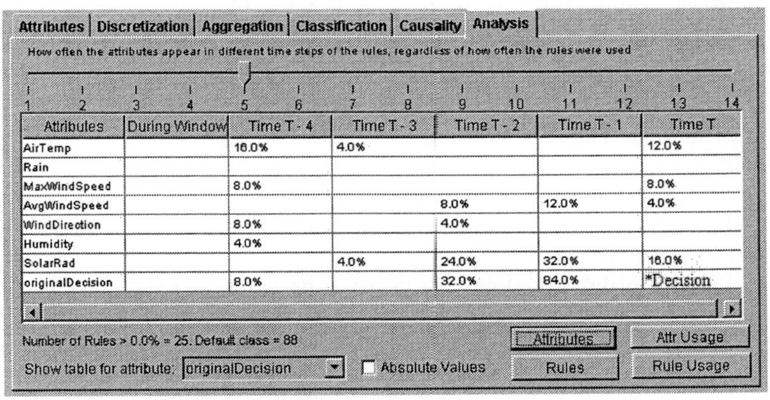

Fig. 2. Attribute usage in the weather data with window size of 5

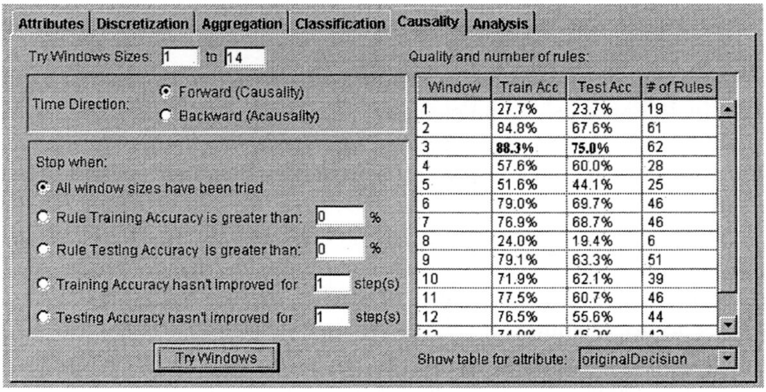

Fig. 3. The quality of the generated rules for different window sizes

Finally, TimeSleuth can use various aggregate values of the attributes in the rules. The sum, mean, median, mode, minimum (or logical-OR), and maximum (or logical-AND) of the values of an attribute at all time steps in the window can be computed and treated as new attributes. If a new attribute is identical to an existing attribute, it is discarded. If a new attribute is used as a condition in a rule, it will be described as "during time window" instead of "at time t." An example rule is: **if**{ *during time window*: *mean*(a) > 1 **and** *at time 1*: x = 1} **then** *at time 2*: x = 2.

3 Experiments on Synthetic Data

We used an Artificial Life [17] simulator called URAL [24] to generate data for the experiments described in this section. URAL is a discrete event simulator where known atemporal and temporal rules govern an artificial environment. Having complete knowledge about the URAL domain allows us to judge the quality of the discovered rules. Other kinds of data would have required interpretations as to the true nature of relations among the attributes, making the process of judging the output more complex and open to debate. The world in URAL is a rectangular, two-dimensional board with an agent living in it. Food exists at specific locations on the board. The agent can sense its position and also the presence of food at its current position. At each time-step, it randomly chooses one of the following actions: left (L), right (R), up (U), or down (D). Left and right correspond to moving along the x-axis and up and down to moving along the y-axis. The agent can sense which action it takes in each situation. If the agent attempts to move beyond the boundary of the board, the move is ignored and the location of the agent is left unchanged.

Data from URAL form an event sequence (i.e., records are in temporal order) with attributes $\{x, y, f, a\}$, where x and y give the agent's location coordinates, f indicates whether food was present at this location, and a tells which action was taken at the location. An example record is <2, 3, true, L>. The agent, moving around randomly, can visit the same location more than once.

A single record does not contain the effect of the move action. To bring the possible cause (action) and the possible effect (next position) together in the same record, flattening is required to merge consecutive records into one. A minimum window size of 2 is required to allow a method to find the correct temporal/causal rules for the URAL domain because the complete effect of a move is known in the following time step. An example flattened record with a window size of 2 is <2, 3, true, D, 2, 4, false, L>.

The purpose of the experiments in this section is to measure the effectiveness of TimeSleuth, TETRAD, and CaMML in discovering rules when provided with temporal data. First we apply the methods to unflattened data, which should allow them to discover atemporal rules. Then we apply the methods to data flattened with various window sizes, which should allow them to discover atemporal and temporal rules. The results show how flattening affects the output of the methods.

We applied the three methods to example data from the URAL domain. TETRAD restricts attributes to at most 8 values, so the size of the world was set to 8×8, with x and y ranging from 0 to 7. To ensure fairness to all methods, all results presented in this section are derived from a single run of 10,000 time steps in URAL where food existed at locations (0,6), (1,2), (3,5), (5,5), and (6,3). These results are representative of many experiments we have performed with varying number of time steps and a variety of locations for food. The confidence value of the correct rules generally increased with the number of records.

Table 1 shows the desired output of TimeSleuth, TETRAD, and CaMML in each tool's notation. The domain expert's beliefs about the relations actually present in the simulator are also given. Composite rules, such as "x_{w-2}, a_{w-2}, and a_{w-1} give x_w" are not included because of our preference for shorter rules. *FoodXY*() is an atemporal relation saying whether or not food is present at a given (x,y) location, while *MoveX*() and *MoveY*() are temporal relations describing the effects of moving along the x-axis and y-axis, respectively. For any window size $w \geq 2$, the result of a move depends only on the position and the move direction in the w-1 time step (time starts at 1 and ends at w in each flattened record). In Table 1, TETRAD's and CaMML's desired output is represented directly, but TimeSleuth's desired output is given in template form. The actual output has multiple rules, with one rule for each combination of the values for the attributes representing conditional attributes. Also, the actual output does not contain keywords such as *if*, *then*, or *and*, and has specific values instead of the α, β, γ and δ parameters. We expect the atemporal relations that hold for $w = 1$ to also hold for $w > 1$ because atemporal relations do not depend on time.

Window Size 1: To test their ability to find atemporal relations, we ran TETRAD, CaMML and TimeSleuth. The results for TETRAD, shown in Table 2, were generated by the "Build" command, assuming the existence of latent common causes, and using the exact algorithm. The best results were found at the significance levels from 0.001 to 0.01, where rules a, x •–• f and y •–• f are correct, because the action has no discernible cause and food is associated with both x and y. Other rules are incorrect in the context of a single record, because no other causal or atemporal rules exist among the attributes in a single record.

Table 1. The correct output for TimeSleuth, TETRAD, and CaMML

Window size	Domain Expert	TimeSleuth	TETRAD	CaMML
1	f = FoodXY(x, y)	**if** $\{(x = \alpha)$ **and** $(y = \beta)\}$ **then** $(f = \delta)$.	x •–• f, y •–• f	$(x, y \rightarrow f)$
	No relation for *a, x, y*	No rules	a, x, y	$(\rightarrow a), (\rightarrow x), (\rightarrow y)$
	f_w = FoodXY(x_w, y_w)	**if** $\{(x_w = \alpha)$ **and** $(y_w = \beta)\}$ **then** $(f_w = \delta)$.	x •–• f_w, y •–• f_w	$(x_w, y_w \rightarrow f_w)$
	x_w = MoveX(x_{w-1}, a_{w-1})	**if** $\{(x_{w-1} = \alpha)$ **and** $(a_{w-1} = \gamma)\}$ **then** $(x_w = \delta)$.	$x_{w-1} \rightarrow x_w$, $a_{w-1} \rightarrow x_w$	$(x_{w-1}, a_{w-1} \rightarrow x_w)$
	y_w = MoveY(y_{w-1}, a_{w-1})	**if** $\{(y_{w-1} = \beta)$ **and** $(a_{w-1} = \gamma)\}$ **then** $(y_w = \delta)$.	$y_{w-1} \rightarrow y_w$, $a_{w-1} \rightarrow y_w$	$(y_{w-1}, a_{w-1} \rightarrow y_w)$
$w \geq 2$	No cause for a_w	No rules	a_w	$(\rightarrow a_w)$

Table 2. Atemporal rules discovered by TETRAD ($w = 1$)

Significance Levels	Correct Rules	Incorrect rule
0.001, 0.005, 0.01	*f* •–• *x*, *y* •–• *f*, *a*	*x* •–• *y*
0.05, 0.1		y ↔ f, y ↔ x, x → f, a •→ x
0.2	*f* •–• *x*, *y* •–• *f*, *a*	*y* •–• *a*, *y* •–• *x*, *a* •–• *x*

Table 3. CaMML's results with unflattened records ($w = 1$)

Correct Rules	Incorrect rules
$(\rightarrow a), (\rightarrow x), (\rightarrow y), (x, y \rightarrow f)$	

For the same data, CaMML gave the results shown in Table 3. CaMML found all the correct atemporal rules. In fact, *x* and *y* do not cause *f* in URAL, but without any domain knowledge, it is reasonable to interpret this relationship as a causal one.

TimeSleuth gave the results shown in Table 4. The first two entries for predicting the value of *f* show that the C4.5rules component of TimeSleuth eliminated unneeded condition attributes when creating rules. In general, if the value of *x* is sufficient to predict the outcome regardless of the value *y*, the generated rule will not include *y* and vice versa. We accept all the rules generated for predicting *f* because together they correctly predict the presence or absence of food.

TimeSleuth's desired output for other attributes would be no rules, which can be achieved by not setting *x*, *y* or *a* as the decision attribute. For the sake of completeness we did try TimeSleuth with these attributes, with the results shown in Table 4. As a classifier, C4.5 creates rules regardless of whether or not they make semantic sense. However, the results were interesting. There is a strong co-occurrence between *f*, *x*, and *y*, and this is exploited by TimeSleuth for predicting the value of these attributes with high confidence levels. The value of *a*, however, is unrelated to any other observable attribute, and this is reflected in low confidence levels for the rules. From an atemporal, co-occurrence point of view, the results in Table 4 are satisfactory.

Table 4. TimeSleuth's results with unflattened records ($w = 1$)

Decision Attribute	Condition Attribute(s)	Number of Rules	Correctness	Min / Max Confidence	Training Accuracy
f	x	3	correct	99.9% / 99.9%	100%
	y	4	correct	99.9% /99.9%	
	x, y	20	correct	99% / 99.4%	
x	y, f	4	incorrect	52.9% / 99.4%	19.9%
y	x, f	5	incorrect	99% / 99.4%	21.2%
a	x, y	7	incorrect	30.3% / 33.9%	26.4%

Table 5. The rules discovered by TETRAD from the flattened records ($w = 2$)

Significance Level(s)	Correct Rules	Incorrect Rules
0.001	a_2	$y_1 \leftrightarrow f_1, y_1 \bullet\!\!\rightarrow y_2, y_1 \leftrightarrow f_2, f_1 \leftrightarrow x_1, f_1 \leftrightarrow y_2, f_1 \leftrightarrow x_2,$ $a_1 \leftrightarrow y_2, a_1 \leftrightarrow x_2, x_1 \leftrightarrow f_2, x_1 \bullet\!\!\rightarrow x_2, y_2 \leftrightarrow f_2, f_2 \leftrightarrow x_2,$
0.005, 0.01, 0.005	a_2	$y_1 \leftrightarrow f_1, y_1 \bullet\!\!\rightarrow y_2, y_1 \leftrightarrow f_2, f_1 \leftrightarrow x_1, f_1 \leftrightarrow y_2, f_1 \leftrightarrow x_2,$ $a_1 \leftrightarrow y_2, a_1 \leftrightarrow x_2, x_1\ y_2\#, x_1 \leftrightarrow f_2, x_1 \rightarrow x_2, y_2 \leftrightarrow f_2, x_2 \rightarrow f_2$
0.1	$x_1 \rightarrow x_2$,	$f_1 \bullet\!\!\rightarrow y_1, y_1 \leftrightarrow x_1, y_1 \leftrightarrow y_2, y_1 \leftrightarrow f_2, y_1 \leftrightarrow x_2,$ $f_1\ x_2\#, f_1 \leftrightarrow y_2, f_1 \leftrightarrow x_2, a_1 \leftrightarrow y_2, a_1 \bullet\!\!\rightarrow f_2,$ $a_1 \leftrightarrow x_2, x_1 \rightarrow y_2, x_1 \leftrightarrow f_2, x_1 \leftrightarrow a_2, y_2 \leftrightarrow f_2, f_2 \leftrightarrow x_2,$
0.2		$f_1 \bullet\!\!\rightarrow y_1, y_1 \leftrightarrow x_1, y_1 \leftrightarrow y_2, y_1 \leftrightarrow f_2, y_1 \leftrightarrow x_2, f_1 \leftrightarrow x_1,$ $f_1 \leftrightarrow y_2, f_1 \leftrightarrow x_2, a_1 \leftrightarrow y_2, a_1 \bullet\!\!\rightarrow f_2, a_1 \leftrightarrow x_2, x_1 \rightarrow y_2,$ $x_1 \leftrightarrow f_2, x_1 \leftrightarrow a_2, x_1 \leftrightarrow x_2, y_2 \leftrightarrow f_2, y_2 \leftrightarrow a_2, f_2 \leftrightarrow x_2,$

Table 6. CaMML's rules for the flattened records ($w = 2$)

Correct Rules	Incorrect rules
$(\rightarrow x_1), (\rightarrow y_1), (x_1, y_1 \rightarrow f_1), (x_2, y_2 \rightarrow f_2), (\rightarrow a_2)$	$(x_1, y_1, x_2, y_2 \rightarrow a_1), (\rightarrow x_2), (\rightarrow y_2)$

TimeSleuth can prune the rules based on the confidence level, and thus only the rules with a confidence level greater than a certain threshold will be displayed to the user.

Window Size 2: Flattening using a window size of $w = 2$, produced records with 8 attributes $\{x_1, y_1, f_1, a_1, x_2, y_2, f_2, a_2\}$. TETRAD, CaMML, and TimeSleuth were applied to determine whether they could discover the *FoodXY*() atemporal function and the *MoveX*() and *MoveY*() temporal functions.

TETRAD's output is summarized in Table 5. TETRAD has a mechanism to let the user specify the temporal order among the input attributes, and this information was provided in the input. Flattening the records to give TETRAD more relevant data resulted in many more rules being discovered, most of which are incorrect. TETRAD was thus unable to exploit the extra information provided to it. The rule "$f_1\ x_2\#$" means that TETRAD considered the input information concerning the relation between to f_1 and x_2 to be contradictory (some observations supporting f_1 to be the cause of x_2, and some vice versa).

The results of applying CaMML with a window size of 2 appear in Table 6. For CaMML, we were unable to discover any means of specifying a temporal order among the input attributes. It continued to discover the same relations as it had found with unflattened records, which is desirable, as the relations that existed in the previous case continue to exist in the flattened data. However, it failed to discover the relationship between the previous location and action, and the current location. It also discovered the rule ($x_1, y_1, x_2, y_2 \rightarrow a_1$), which is a valid relationship among these attributes. However, it is temporally invalid, as it refers to a time in the future to predict the past.

The results of applying TimeSleuth to the same data are given in Table 7. In our 8×8 board, 4 possible actions and 8 distinct values exist for each of x_1 and y_1. In this example, the agent has explored the entire world, and TimeSleuth created 32 (8×4) rules for predicting the next value of each of x_2 and y_2. It correctly pruned y_1 from the rules for x_2, because the rules for moving along the x-axis are independent of the value of y. Similarly, it pruned x_1 from the rules for y_2. The rules for predicting f_2 are the same as the rules given in Table 4 for predicting f in the atemporal case, because the rules for food are not dependent on time. TimeSleuth was also tried on the a_2

attribute, which is not caused by any of the observable attributes. We did not use x_1, y_1, f_1, and a_1 as decision attributes. Consistent with the results with unflattened data, the rules have low confidence levels and can be pruned out completely.

Window Sizes Larger Than 2: TimeSleuth obtained good results with larger window sizes. As previously demonstrated [6], C4.5 effectively handles the bigger input records that are created by larger window sizes by pruning irrelevant attributes. TETRAD yielded very unsatisfactory results, shown in Table 8, for $w = 3$ with a significance level of 0.01, and these results are typical of the results for significance levels from 0.001 to 0.2.

CaMML could not process the more complex data because the version we used could not handle the increased number of combinations. For $w > 3$, TETRAD's running time was too long (no results after days of computing). Table 9 shows the results obtained with window sizes from 3 to 10.

The overall results of our experiments are summarized in Table 10, where the number of correct and incorrect relations/rules discovered by each system, for a variety of window sizes, is given. For TETRAD, we use the 0.05 significance level and for TimeSleuth we assumed a threshold confidence of 80%.

Table 7. TimeSleuth's results for the flattened records ($w = 2$)

Decision Attribute	Condition Attribute(s)	Number of Rules	Correctness	Min/Max confidence	Training Accuracy
f_2	x_2	3	correct	99.9% / 99.9%	100%
	y_2	4		99.9% / 99.9%	
	x_2, y_2	20		99% / 99.4%	
x_2	x_1, a_1	32	correct	99.7% / 99.4%	100%
y_2	y_1, a_1	32	correct	99.5% / 99.6%	100%
a_2	x_1, a_1, y_2	16	incorrect	30.2% / 45.7%	29.8%
	$x_1, y_1, a_1,$	18			
	x_1, y_1, y_2	6			
	x_1, x_2, y_2	7			
	x_1, y_1, x_2	4			
	x_1, y_2	3			
	x_1, y_1	2			
	x_1, a_1	1			
	a_1, y_2	1			

Table 8. The rules discovered by TETRAD from flattened records ($w = 3$)

Significance Level	Correct Rules	Incorrect Rules
0.01	$a_3, y_2 \rightarrow y_3$	$y_1 \leftrightarrow f_1, y_1 \leftrightarrow y_2, y_1 \leftrightarrow f_2, y_1 \leftrightarrow y_3, y_1 \leftrightarrow f_3, y_1 \leftrightarrow x_3, f_1 \leftrightarrow x_1,$ $f_1 \leftrightarrow y_2, f_1 \leftrightarrow x_2, f_1 \leftrightarrow y_3, f_1 \leftrightarrow f_3, f_1 \leftrightarrow x_3, a_1 \leftrightarrow y_2, a_1 \leftrightarrow x_2,$ $a_1 \leftrightarrow y_3, a_1 \leftrightarrow x_3, x_1 \leftrightarrow y_2, x_1 \leftrightarrow f_2, x_1 \leftrightarrow x_2, x_1 \leftrightarrow f_3, x_1 \leftrightarrow x_3,$ $y_2 \leftrightarrow f_2, y_2 \leftrightarrow f_3, x_2 \rightarrow f_2, , f_2 \leftrightarrow y_3, , f_2 \leftrightarrow x_3, a_2 \leftrightarrow y_3, a_2 \leftrightarrow x_3, x_2 \rightarrow y_3,$ $x_2 \rightarrow f_3, x_2 \bullet\!\!\rightarrow x_3, y_3 \leftrightarrow f_3, f_3 \leftrightarrow x_3$

Table 9. Test results for larger window sizes

Window Size	Domain Expert	TimeSleuth	TETRAD	CaMML
$3 \leq w \leq 10$	FoodXY(x_w, y_w)	**if** $\{(x_w = \alpha)$ **and** $(y_w = \beta)\}$ **then** $(f_w = \delta)$.	Poor results with $w = 3$; running time too long for $w > 3$	Not tested because it cannot handle the input size
	MoveX(x_{w-1}, a_{w-1})	**if** $\{(x_{w-1} = \alpha)$ **and** $(a_{w-1} = \gamma)\}$ **then** $(x_w = \delta)$.		
	MoveY(y_{w-1}, a_{w-1})	**if** $\{(y_{w-1} = \beta)$ **and** $(a_{w-1} = \gamma)\}$ **then** $(x_w = \delta)$.		

Table 10. Summary of experimental results

Window Size	TETRAD		CaMML		TimeSleuth	
	Correct	Incorrect	Correct	Incorrect	Correct	Incorrect
W = 1	3	1	1	3	15	1
W = 2	3	15	1	7	79	0
W = 3	3	39	N/A		79	0
$4 \leq w \leq 10$	N/A		N/A		79	0

Table 11. Traing and testing accuracy for all attributes except rain (in percentages)

W	Soil Temp		Air Temp		Humidity		Wind Direc		AvgWindSp		MaxWindSp		Solar Rad	
	Tr	Ts	Tr	Ts	Tr	Ts	Tr	Ts	Tr	Ts	Tr	Ts	Ts	Tr
1	27.7	15.8	39.7	7.9	43.4	23.7	4.4	100	73.2	57.9	44.3	44.7	44.3	42.1
2	85.1	48.6	48.8	16.2	45.9	29.7	2	100	71.3	67.6	46.2	37.8	43.3	40.5
3	88.6	61.1	42.2	16.7	51	33.3	1.5	100	72.4	66.7	46.9	30.6	43.4	38.9
4	57.6	48.6	35.9	14.3	30	22.9	1.5	100	51.8	51.4	34.4	37.1	43.5	37.1
5	51.6	41.2	22.1	11.8	20.4	20.6	1.5	100	66.4	64.7	N/A	N/A	44.5	32.4
6	79	42.4	40.8	24.2	48.2	21.2	1.5	100	69.2	60.6	38.5	27.3	43.2	33.3
7	76.9	40.6	39.2	28.1	46.9	15.6	1.5	0	51.3	46.9	46.9	21.9	43	31.2
8	24.1	25.8	38.7	22.6	53	22.6	3.3	0	65.8	58.1	43.2	22.6	42.9	32.3
9	79.1	36.7	42.4	23.3	27.6	10	2.1	0	67.5	53.3	41.8	20	42.7	33.3
10	71.9	37.9	12.9	0	50.3	24.1	2.1	0	69.5	58.6	38.9	20.7	42.5	34.5

4 Experimental Results on Weather Data

We also tested TimeSleuth on a weather data set from the Louisiana AgriClimatic Information System [25], which contains observations of 8 environmental attributes gathered hourly from 22/7/2001 to 6/8/2001. The first 343 observations were used for training, and the last 38 hours' data were used for testing the rules. The result of trying TimeSleuth on all available attributes using window sizes from 1 to 10 hours appears in Table 11. "W" represents the window size, "Tr" the training accuracy, and "Ts" the testing (predictive) accuracy, all in percentages.

The training accuracy for Rain was 99.7% and the predictive accuracy was 100%. The reason for the high numbers is that there were few rainy days in the training data, and simply selecting the default value of "no rain" gave very good results. As evident in Table 11, Soil Temperature, Humidity, and Air Temperature have their highest accuracy for window sizes 3, 2, and 8, respectively. In these three cases, the results are better than for $w = 1$ (atemporal case). The user can interpret these results to mean that these attributes are temporally dependent on the previous values of the attributes, while the Wind Direction, Average Wind Speed, Max Wind Speed, and Solar Radiation attributes have little temporal dependence on previous observations.

These observations agree with common sense expectations. For example, we expect the soil temperature to be temporally related to the values of the available attributes at the current time and during the previous several hours. Other attributes such as wind direction and speed depend on factors that may not be available locally (difference of temperature between two regions). TimeSleuth's temporal rules for soil temperature will thus be more accurate than the atemporal rules that C4.5 could form from the unflattened data.

The available data allows a temporal investigation of the values of the Soil Temperature, Air Temperature, and Humidity attributes. The user can thus relate the current values to the previous values of the available attributes. For a window size of

3, a total of 62 rules were discovered. Table 12 summarizes the composition of the rules for predicting Soil Temperature. Each entry shows the percentage of rules in which a particular attribute at a particular time appears. Since the window size is 3, the current hour is time 3, the previous hour is time 2, and two hours ago is time 1. For example, the Air Temperature at time 2 appears in 14.5% of the rules for predicting the value of the Soil Temperature at time 3. The usage of attributes in rules with other window sizes is roughly consistent with Table 12, because most attributes that appear in rules are drawn from the current and previous two time steps. The general concentration of the attributes in the last 3 time steps can be seen also in Figure 2, which shows the attribute usage when the window size is 5.

We tried TETRAD with the same weather data (unflattened). The results appear in Appendix 1. Because weather is very complicated and one can argue that "to some degree" everything is related to everything else, we have refrained from categorizing the output as either correct or incorrect.

5 Concluding Remarks

We introduced a new unsupervised learning tool called TimeSleuth, which is based on C4.5 and relies on straightforward methods to extend its abilities. C4.5 is a supervised learning tool that requires the user to identify one attribute as the decision attribute. By applying C4.5 with each decision attribute in turn to flattened input, TimeSleuth was able to discover atemporal and temporal rules, which can be interpreted as causal rules.

TimeSleuth is specifically meant for cases where data is temporally ordered and generated by a single source. The results in this paper indicate that it is effective in finding atemporal and temporal/causal rules when presented with such data. On synthetic data with strong causal relationships among the attributes, TimeSleuth found all correct temporal rules. On the same data, TETRAD and CaMML discovered many incorrect rules and also stopped working when the input size increased. On real weather data, TimeSleuth's results agreed with common sense knowledge of weather. However, despite TimeSleuth's better performance in this paper, it is not meant to replace software such as TETRAD, as its domain of applicability is more restricted (temporally ordered output of a single source versus data generated by many sources, regardless of their temporal order). As well, we used a preliminary version of CaMML, and its authors may now have a better version. We will next apply TimeSleuth to many years worth of weather data.

Table 12. Attribute usage when predicting the value of Soil Temperature with a window size 3

Attribute	Time T-2	Time T-1	Time T
Air temperature	6.4%	14.5%	17.7%
Rain	0%	0%	0%
MaxWindSeed	1.6%	0%	9.6%
AvgWindSpeed	3.2%	4.8%	8.0%
WindDirection	8.0%	4.8%	6.4%
Humidity	3.2%	1.6%	3.2%
Solar Radiation	19.3%	9.6%	20.9%
Soil Temperature	19.3%	88.7%	N/A

TimeSleuth is written in Java and runs in any environment that supports the Java runtime environment and has a graphical user interface such as Microsoft Windows or X Window. The package includes full source code and online help, and is available from http://www.cs.uregina.ca/~karimi/downloads.html.

References

[1] Berndt, D. J. and Clifford, J., Finding Patterns in Time Series: A Dynamic Programming Approach, *Advances in Knowledge Discovery and Data Mining*. U.M. Fayyad, G. Piatetsky-Shapiro, P. Smyth, et al. (eds.), AAAI Press/ MIT Press, 1996, pp. 229-248

[2] Chatfield, C., *The Analysis of Time Series: An Introduction*, Chapman and Hall, 1989.

[3] Freedman, D. and Humphreys, P., *Are There Algorithms that Discover Causal Structure?*, Technical Report 514, Department of Statistics, University of California at Berkeley, 1998.

[4] Heckerman, D., *A Bayesian Approach to Learning Causal Networks*, Microsoft Technical Report MSR-TR-95-04, Microsoft Corporation, May 1995.

[5] Humphreys, P. and Freedman, D., The Grand Leap, *British Journal of the Philosophy of Science 47*, 1996, pp. 113-123

[6] Karimi, K. and Hamilton, H.J., Finding Temporal Relations: Causal Bayesian Networks vs. C4.5, *The Twelfth International Symposium on Methodologies for Intelligent Systems (ISMIS'2000)*, Charlotte, NC, USA, October 2000, pp. 266-273.

[7] Karimi, K. and Hamilton, H.J., Learning With C4.5 in a Situation Calculus Domain, *The Twentieth SGES International Conference on Knowledge Based Systems and Applied Artificial Intelligence (ES2000)*, Cambridge, UK, December 2000, pp. 73-85.

[8] Karimi, K. and Hamilton, H.J., Logical Decision Rules: Teaching C4.5 to Speak Prolog, *The Second International Conference on Intelligent Data Engineering and Automated Learning (IDEAL 2000)*, Hong Kong, December 2000, pp. 85-90.

[9] Karimi, K. and Hamilton, H.J., RFCT: An Association-Based Causality Miner, *The Fifteenth Canadian Conference on Artificial Intelligence (AI'2002)*, Calgary, Alberta, Canada, May 2002, pp. 334-338.

[10] Karimi, K. and Hamilton, H.J., Temporal Rules and Temporal Decision trees: A C4.5 Approach, *Technical Report CS-2001-02*, Department of Computer Science, University of Regina, Regina, Saskatchewan, Canada, December 2001.

[11] Karimi, K. and Hamilton, H.J., Discovering Temporal Rules from Temporally Ordered Data, *The Third International Conference on Intelligent Data Engineering and Automated Learning (IDEAL 2002)*, Manchester, UK, August 2002, pp. 334-338.

[12] Karimi, K., and Hamilton, H.J. TimeSleuth: A Tool for Discovering Causal and Temporal Rules, *The 14th IEEE International Conference on Tools with Artificial Intelligence (ICTAI 2002)*, Washington DC, November, 2002, pp. 375-380.

[13] Karimi, K., and Hamilton, H.J., Distinguishing Causal and Acausal Temporal Relations, *The Seventh Pacific-Asia Conference on Knowledge Discovery and Data Mining (PAKDD'2003)*, Seoul, South Korea, April/May 2003.
[14] Kennett, R.J., Korb, K.B., and Nicholson, A.E., Seabreeze Prediction Using Bayesian Networks: A Case Study, *Proc. Fifth Pacific-Asia Conference on Knowledge Discovery and Data Mining (PAKDD'01)*. Hong Kong, April 2001.
[15] Keogh, E. J. and Pazzani, M. J., Scaling up Dynamic Time Warping for Data Mining Applications, *The Sixth ACM SIGKDD International Conference on Knowledge Discovery and Data Mining (KDD 2000)*, August 2000.
[16] Korb, K. B. and Wallace, C. S., In Search of Philosopher's Stone: Remarks on Humphreys and Freedman's Critique of Causal Discovery, *British Journal of the Philosophy of Science 48*, 1997, pp. 543-553
[17] Levy, S., Artificial Life: A Quest for a New Creation, Pantheon Books, 1992.
[18] Mannila, H., Toivonen, H. and Verkamo, A. I., Discovering Frequent Episodes in Sequences, *Proceedings of the First International Conference on Knowledge Discovery and Data Mining*, 1995, pp. 210-215,
[19] Pearl, J., *Causality: Models, Reasoning, and Inference*, Cambridge University Press. 2000.
[20] Quinlan, J. R., *C4.5: Programs for Machine Learning*, Morgan Kaufmann, 1993.
[21] Scheines, R., Spirtes, P., Glymour, C. and Meek, C., *Tetrad II: Tools for Causal Modeling*, Lawrence Erlbaum Associates, Hillsdale, NJ, 1994.
[22] Spirtes, P. and Scheines, R., Reply to Freedman, In McKim, V. and Turner, S. (editors), *Causality in Crisis*, University of Notre Dame Press, 1997, pp. 163-176
[23] Wallace, C. S., and Korb, K. B., Learning Linear Causal Models by MML Sampling, *Causal Models and Intelligent Data Management*, Springer-Verlag, 1999.
[24] http://www.cs.uregina.ca/~karimi/downloads.html/URAL.java
[25] http://typhoon.bae.lsu.edu/datatabl/current/sugcurrh.html. Contents change.

Appendix 1

TETRAD's results with the weather data

Significance Level	Relations
0.001	airt •–• maxwnd, airt •–• humid, maxwnd •–• avgwnd, avgwnd •–• wnddir, solar •–• soilt, rain
0.005	Maxwnd •→ airt, Humid •→ airt, maxwnd •→ avgwnd, wnddir •→ avgwnd, solar •–• soilt, rain
0.01	Maxwnd •→ airt, humid •→ airt, maxwnd •→ avgwnd, wnddir •→ avgwnd, solar •–• soilt, rain
0.05	airt ↔ maxwnd, airt → avgwnd, humid •→ airt, maxwnd ↔ avgwnd, maxwnd → wnddir, avgwnd wnddir#, solar •–• soilt, rain
0.1	airt ↔ maxwnd, airt → avgwnd, humid •→ airt, maxwnd ↔ avgwnd, maxwnd → wnddir, avgwnd wnddir#, solar •–• soilt, rain
0.2	airt ↔ maxwnd, airt → avgwnd, humid •→ airt, rain •→ maxwnd, maxwnd → avgwnd, maxwnd → wnddir, avgwnd → wnddir, humid •–• soilt, solar •–• soilt

Airt = Air Temperature
Maxwnd = Max Wind Speed
Avgwnd = Average Wind Speed
Wnddir = Wind Direction
Solar = Solar Radiation
Soilt = Soil Temperature
Humid = Humidity
Rain = Rain

Selective Transfer of Task Knowledge Using Stochastic Noise

Daniel L. Silver and Peter McCracken

Intelligent Information Technology Research Laboratory
Jodrey School of Computer Science, Acadia University
Wolfville, Nova Scotia, Canada B4P 2R6
danny.silver@acadiau.ca

Abstract. The selective transfer of task knowledge within the context of artificial neural networks is studied using a modified version of ηMTL (multiple task learning) previously reported. sMTL is a knowledge based inductive learning system that uses prior task knowledge and stochastic noise to adjust its inductive bias when learning a new task. The MTL representation of previously learned and consolidated tasks is used as the starting point for learning a new primary task. Task rehearsal ensures the stability of related secondary task knowledge within the sMTL network and stochastic noise is used to create plasticity in the network so as to allow the new task to be learned. sMTL controls the level of noise to each secondary task based on a measure of secondary to primary task relatedness. Experiments demonstrate that from impoverished training sets, sMTL uses the prior representations to quickly develop predictive models that have (1) superior generalization ability compared with models produced by single task learning or standard MTL and (2) equivalent generalization ability compared with models produced by ηMTL.

1 Introduction

The majority of machine learning research has focused on the single task learning (STL) approach where an hypothesis for a single task is induced from a set of training examples with no regard to previous learning or to the retention of task knowledge for future learning. *Life-long learning* is a relatively new area of machine learning research concerned with the persistent and cumulative nature of learning [26]. Life-long learning considers situations in which a learner faces a series of different tasks and develops methods of retaining and using task knowledge to improve the effectiveness (more accurate hypotheses) and efficiency (shorter training times) of learning.

A challenge often faced by a life-long learning agent is a deficiency of training examples from which to develop accurate hypotheses. Machine learning theory tells us that this problem can be overcome with an appropriate *inductive bias* [13], one source being *prior knowledge* from related tasks [3]. Lacking a method of knowledge transfer [4, 26] that distinguishes knowledge from related and unrelated tasks, we have developed one and applied it to life-long learning problems, such as learning a more accurate medical diagnostic model from a small sample of patient data [21].

Y. Xiang and B. Chaib-draa (Eds.): AI 2003, LNAI 2671, pp. 190–205, 2003.

In [22] we define the difference between two forms of task knowledge transfer: *representational* and *functional*. Our previous research has focused on functional transfer that uses the parallel learning of related tasks to constrain the hypothesis space of back-propagation neural networks. In [22] we developed ηMTL, a modified version of the multiple task learning (MTL) method of parallel functional transfer, to provide a solution to the problem of selective transfer. Using a *measure of task relatedness*, an ηMTL network can favourably bias the induction of a hypothesis for a primary task. In [23] the *task rehearsal method* (TRM) was introduced as a method of retention and recall of learned task knowledge. Building on the theory of pseudo-rehearsal [18], previously learned but unconsolidated task representations are used to generate *virtual examples* as a source of functional knowledge. TRM uses either the standard MTL or the ηMTL learning algorithm to relearn or *rehearse* these secondary tasks in parallel with the learning of a new task. It is through the rehearsal of previously learned tasks that knowledge is transferred to the new task.

In this paper we turn our attention to the representational form of knowledge transfer in the hopes of overcoming a fundamental problem with functional transfer based on TRM and MTL: relearning secondary tasks within an MTL network starting from initial random weights is not efficient. This paper presents a theory of task knowledge transfer that is based on the existence of a large MTL network that contains all previously learned task knowledge in a consolidated form. This MTL representation is used as the starting point for learning a new task. Task rehearsal is used to ensure the stability of related secondary task knowledge within the MTL network and stochastic noise is used to create plasticity in the network so as to allow a new task to be learned. The transfer of knowledge under the method is therefore both representational and functional.

2 Background

2.1 Inductive Bias and Knowledge Transfer

The constraint on a learning system's hypothesis space, beyond the criterion of consistency with the training examples, is called *inductive bias* [13]. Inductive bias is essential for the development of an hypothesis with good generalization from a practical number of examples. Ideally, a life-long learning system can select its inductive bias to tailor the preference for hypotheses according to the task being learned [27]. One type of inductive bias is knowledge of the task domain. We define *knowledge-based inductive learning* as a learning method that uses knowledge of the task domain as a source of inductive bias. The method relies on the *transfer* of knowledge from one or more *secondary* tasks, stored in a domain knowledge database, to a new *primary* task. The problem of selecting an appropriate bias becomes one of selecting the appropriate task knowledge for transfer.

There are two forms of task knowledge transfer: *representational* and *functional*. Representational transfer involves the direct or indirect assignment of known task representation (weight values) to the model of a new task. In this way the learning system is initialized in favour of a particular region of hypothesis space within the modelling system. Since 1990 numerous authors have discussed methods of representational transfer [17, 19, 20, 24]. Representational transfer often results in substantially reduced training time with no loss in generalization performance.

In contrast to representational transfer, functional transfer does not involve the explicit assignment of prior task representation when learning a new task; rather, it employs the use of implicit *pressures* from training examples of related tasks [1, 25], the parallel learning of related tasks constrained to use a common internal representation [3, 4], or the use of historical training information (most commonly the learning rate or gradient of the error surface) to augment the standard weight update equations [12, 14, 26]. These pressures serve to reduce the effective hypothesis space in which the learning system performs its search. This form of transfer has its greatest value from the perspective of increased generalization performance.

2.2 Functional Transfer with MTL and ηMTL

An MTL network is a feed-forward multi-layer network with an output for each task that is to be learned [3, 4]. The standard back-propagation of error learning algorithm is used to train all tasks in parallel. Consequently, MTL training examples are composed of a set of input attributes as well as a target output for each task. The sharing of the *internal representation* (weights of connections) within the network is the method by which inductive bias occurs within an MTL network. This is a powerful method of knowledge transfer because it allows two or more tasks to share those portions of internal representation that are mutually beneficial.

To optimize the transfer of knowledge within an MTL network, the secondary tasks should be as closely related to the primary task as possible, otherwise negative inductive bias can result in a less accurate hypothesis. The ηMTL algorithm overcomes this problem with a separate learning rate, η_k, for each task output T_k [22]. η_k varies as a measure of relatedness between secondary task T_k and the primary task. In [21, 23] we define task relatedness and develop and test various mathematical measures of relatedness.

Selective functional transfer within an ηMTL network has been demonstrated to develop more accurate hypotheses [22]. However, the method suffers from lengthy training times due to the relearning of the secondary tasks from random initial weights. Assuming that a single MTL network exists that contains a consolidated representation of all previously learned tasks, then it would seem appropriate to consider the direct transfer of this representation when learning a new and potentially related task. The next section discusses some of the fundamental problems of representational transfer in neural networks and presents some of approaches that have been used.

2.3 Problems and Approaches to Representational Transfer in ANNS

Representational transfer involves the direct or indirect assignment of a known task representation (weight values) to a new task. The intention is to initialize the modelling system's parameters to a favourable region of hypothesis space that reduces learning time without loss of generalization accuracy.

In [16] two methods of representational transfer are defined; *literal* and *non-literal.* Literal transfer is the placement of neural network parameters (typically weight values) from a source network into a target network with no intermediate modification of those parameters. Approaches of this kind that have been studied by other researchers are *modular learning* [28], *compositional learning* [24] and *incremental learning* [5]. One might think that an ANN trained on one task would provide a good starting point for learning what would seem to be a closely related task. This is not necessarily the case (*e.g.* learning the logical *XOR* function starting from the logical *OR* representation). When a network is initialized to high magnitude weight values as a consequence of literal transfer the probability of finding local minima and prolonged training times increases [7]. This is because high magnitude weights places the output of the network nodes at the extremes of the sigmoid activation function.

A non-literal representational transfer of ANN knowledge is the placement of neural network parameters from a source network into a target network following some form of intermediate modification of those parameters. Two investigators who have looked at methods of modifying the weights of a source task to generate a good initial representation for a target task are Agarwal *et al.* [2] and Pratt [16]. Both take an approach based on the linear discriminate functions constructed by the hidden nodes of the network. Agarwal prescribes a method of retaining source network performance while perturbing the hidden node hyperplanes to accommodate the training data for the target task. Pratt describes the discriminability-based transfer (DBT) method that selects good initial weight values for transfer from a source network over poor values by examining the information theoretic value of the hidden node hyperplanes. Those weights associated with a hyperplane of high discrimination score are kept. Those weights associated with a hyperplane of low discrimination are randomized to small values. Two limitations of Pratt's approach are (1) due to the dynamics of gradient descent the initial combination of hidden node hyperplane positions may be more important than their individual discriminant abilities and (2) the method relies on the selection of a single related source task and does not consider combining knowledge from several related tasks.

In [15], the idea of using previously learned representations within an MTL network as a starting point for learning a new and potentially related task is explored. The intention is to improve both the generalization accuracy of the new task as well as the related secondary tasks. The method relies on the addition of an output node to the MTL network for the new task as well as one or more hidden nodes and modifications to the back-propagation learning algorithm. Experiments show that the method consistently develops models of higher generalization accuracy than STL but not as high as standard MTL (when all tasks are learned starting from initial random weights). The method suffers from the inability to mitigate the representational and functional bias of the unrelated secondary tasks.

2.4 Stochastic Noise and Hypothesis Development

It has been known for some time that stochastic noise can be beneficial to the development of mathematical models that use gradient descent on their error (or cost) function. Simulated annealing, the Boltzman Machine and related techniques employ noise as a means by which to escape local minima, which commonly frustrate the search for a good hypothesis. Given sufficient training and an appropriate schedule of noise, these algorithms can often converge to near optimal solutions.

A number of authors have shown that the back-propagation algorithm responds equally well to stochastic noise. In [8] Heskes studies the advantages of on-line learning over batch learning and shows that on-line learning produces superior models due to stochastic noise introduced to the weights by the random selection of training examples. In [10, 6] the addition of noise to weights during training is shown to result in models of equal or greater generalization accuracy when compared to models developed without noise. Closer to the spirit of this paper, [11, 9] establish that adding noise to the back-propagation training examples is a simple method of producing the same effect. The effect of noisy training data on learning speed and the ability to escape local minima is specifically examined in [29]. The article proves and empirically demonstrates that random noise injected into the target values of training examples "will yield in the mean the solution for the original optimization problem, i.e. without the noise added to the desired signal". In all of the above, the level of noise is depreciated to zero according to some schedule over the iterations of learning.

3 Selective Transfer Using Prior Representations and Stochastic Noise

This section describes a theory of task knowledge transfer that uses (1) the consolidated representation of previously learned tasks as a starting point for learning a new task within an MTL network, (2) task rehearsal to ensure the stability of related secondary task knowledge within the MTL network and (3) stochastic noise to create plasticity in the MTL network so as to allow the new task to develop. The theory builds on the task rehearsal method (TRM) of life-long learning previously reported in [23].

3.1 Combining Representation and Functional Transfer

The Need for Consolidated Domain Knowledge (CDK). TRM relies on a system of *domain knowledge* to store the representations for all previously learned tasks. In [23], domain knowledge is stored as a set of *unconsolidated* ANN representations; one independent representation for each previously learned task.

Such *unconsolidated domain knowledge* presents at least two problems. Independent representations of previously learned tasks makes it difficult to combine such representations as a starting point for learning a new and related task. Also, unconsolidated domain knowledge does not facilitate an *a priori* measure of relatedness between tasks in the domain. Shallow surface measures such as the correlation of the tasks' target values can be calculated prior to training. However, deeper structural measures based on the shared use of internal representations are not possible unless the domain tasks are consolidated within a single MTL network. Further information on surface and structural measures of task relatedness can be found in [21].

In the proposed version of TRM with *s*MTL, domain knowledge is stored as a single, consolidated MTL network. A forthcoming paper will report on the construction of such a consolidated domain knowledge (CDK) network.

Efficiency through Representational Transfer. The standard method of initializing a neural network prior to training is to use small random values for the connection weights. In line with Occam's Razor, such initial conditions provide a bias in favour of a simple linear discriminate function. This was the approach used in the original TRM that used the ηMTL network. In the proposed version of TRM, the weight values of the MTL network used to learn a new function are initialized to those of the CDK network described above. Only the weights of the output node for the primary task are initialized to small random values, because they have no corresponding weight values in the CDK. Provided that the CDK contains tasks that are related to the new primary task, the CDK representation will provide better than random initial weights from which to begin learning the primary task. Therefore, representational transfer should result in reduced training times for a new task and improve the efficiency of the inductive learning system.

Stability through Task Rehearsal and Functional Transfer. The rehearsal of *virtual examples* of secondary tasks in parallel with the learning of a new task is the key ingredient to success of the TRM system [23]. The virtual examples provide functional knowledge from previously learned tasks that constrain the development of the ηMTL network so as to create mutually beneficial internal representations for related tasks.

The proposed version of TRM continues to use the rehearsal of previously learned tasks but for a slightly different purpose – to ensure the stability of related task knowledge. In the new version of TRM, the MTL network will be initialized to the weights of the CDK and therefore the representation of each secondary task will exist within the network before training begins. Task rehearsal will, in the presence of noise, serve to maintain the knowledge of secondary tasks that are most related to the primary task.

sMTL: Plasticity from Stochastic Noise. In order to ensure that positive inductive bias occurs within an MTL network, the secondary tasks must be closely related to the primary task, in so much as they beneficially share internal representation. Unrelated tasks will create negative inductive bias that can result in ineffective models for the primary task. The original TRM approaches this problem by using a version of MTL called ηMTL that controls the learning rate, η, of each secondary task based on a measure of relatedness to the primary task. Related tasks are given learning rates close to that of the primary task while less related tasks are assigned lower learning rates. This approach has been demonstrated to be successful [21].

With the proposed TRM, representational transfer from domain knowledge poses a problem that ηMTL does not address. The initial representation from the CDK will contain high magnitude weight values which are indicative of a stable local minimum that is beneficial for the previously learned tasks. Such weight values can take the back-propagation algorithm many iterations to modify. Prolonged training is particularly likely in an MTL learning environment where the representations of secondary tasks (some of which are unrelated to the primary task) are continually reinforced by task rehearsal. In the worst case the standard back-propagation algorithm will be unable to escape the local minimum so as to develop an accurate hypothesis for the primary task.

The proposed modification to TRM is to replace ηMTL with a variant called *stochastic* MTL, or *s*MTL. *s*MTL is designed to create plasticity in the network and to minimize the effects of negative representational and functional bias from unrelated task knowledge transferred from the CDK. sMTL creates plasticity by injecting stochastic noise into the network during the training process. Like ηMTL, *s*MTL is a modification of the traditional back-propagation algorithm for feed-forward neural networks. Stochastic noise is added to training examples of unrelated tasks during the error-propagation phase. Noise is generated by randomly inverting, according to a given probability, the target class of each training example. The noise creates an unstable target for the unrelated tasks which impedes the back-propagation algorithm's ability to create accurate representations for them. Because the network representation used by the unrelated tasks is not continually reinforced with accurate training examples, it will become less stable, or more plastic. The training examples for the primary task and related secondary tasks will contain little or no noise and therefore the hypothesis for these tasks can take advantage of the representation abandoned by the unrelated tasks.

In *s*MTL, the probability for inverting a target class of a training example for a secondary task is determined by a base level of noise, a measure of relatedness of the secondary task to the primary task, and a schedule for applying the noise over the training process. The base level of noise, σ, is the initial probability of inverting the examples class during the first iteration through the training data. For each secondary task the base level of noise is adjusted according to a measure of relatedness, R_k, that ranges between 0 and 1. The intent is that stochastic noise is applied most to those secondary tasks that are least related to the primary task. The schedule for applying the noise is given by the formula $\sigma(I - i)/I$, where i is the current iteration number, and I is the total number of iterations during which noise should be applied. Thus, over the course of I iterations, the probability for any given training example class to be inverted decreases linearly, from a maximum of σ at the first iteration to 0 at the Ith iteration.

3.2 Benefits and Consequences of Using CDK and *s*MTL

The main advantage of consolidated domain knowledge is that it provides the means of transferring the representation of all previously learned tasks as a single structure. It is expected that this will dramatically increase the efficiency of developing a model for a new and related task. An additional benefit of using CDK is that a consolidated representation of tasks lends itself well to methods of measuring task relatedness based on the shared use of representation. Such measures of relatedness provide a deeper and more accurate assessment of relatedness than methods which consider only functional similarity.

An expected consequence of using CDK and representational transfer is that a CDK network must contain sufficient representation for all tasks, including the new primary task. If there is insufficient representation, the accuracy of the resulting model will be affected. Conversely, a large CDK network will require an equally large *s*MTL network even for the first few tasks that are learned. Using large *s*MTL networks will increase training times.

*s*MTL is expected to overcome any initial negative representational bias transferred from CDK through the selective use of stochastic noise. The noise should also mitigate negative functional transfer from the rehearsal of unrelated secondary tasks. In general, a source of noise will make it less likely for *s*MTL to become trapped in a local minimum. An expected consequence of using *s*MTL is that despite an ability to mitigate negative bias from representational transfer, some bias will remain. Therefore, it is expected that the *s*MTL models will be equal to but not better than ηMTL results (where training begins from random initial weights). It is also important to note that *s*MTL, like ηMTL, is intended to develop an accurate hypothesis for only the primary task.

4 Empirical Studies

To test our theory of selective transfer of knowledge using prior representation and stochastic noise we conducted a series of three experiments on a single domain. Our objective is to show that *s*MTL can selectively transfer representational and functional knowledge from CDK to a new task more efficiently and effectively than previous methods. The first experiment verifies that representational transfer without stochastic noise frustrates the ability to efficiently develop effective models. The second experiment determines which of the secondary tasks individually provides the best inductive bias under *s*MTL. The third experiment compares *s*MTL's ability to selectively transfer knowledge to standard MTL's and to ηMTL's.

4.1 Test Domain

The following experiments use a synthetic domain of tasks previously used to test TRM and ηMTL [23]. The seven tasks of the Band domain are characterized in Figure 1. Each is a band of positive examples (the shaded area) across a 2-dimensional input space. All tasks are non-linearly separable requiring two hidden nodes to form a proper internal representation. A visual inspection of

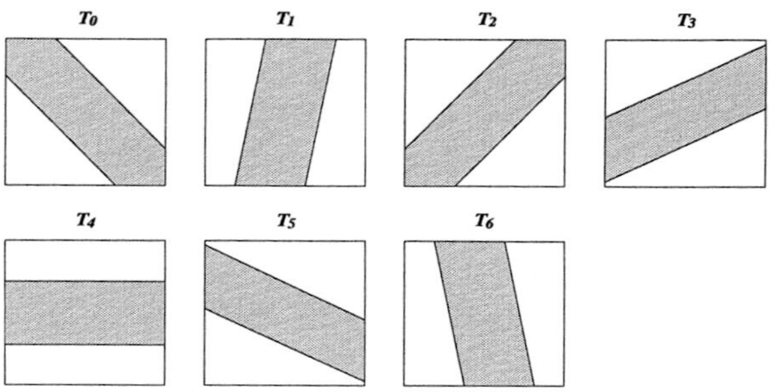

Fig. 1. The band domain. Each task is a 2-variable input space consisting of a band of positive examples bordered by negative examples

Figure 1 suggests that the primary task, T_0, varies in its relatedness to the secondary tasks T_1 through T_6 according to the similarity of the orientation of the band of positive examples. Previous experimentation using ηMTL has shown that T_4 and T_5 are the most related tasks to T_0.

A total of 50 training, 20 validation, and 200 test examples were randomly generated and their target values determined for each task. The sets of training and validation examples for each secondary task were shown to be sufficient to develop a model under the STL method such that the number of misclassifications on the corresponding test sets were always less than 30 (accuracy $>$ .85). The training set for the primary task was then impoverished by marking 40 of the examples as unknown[1] so that only 5 negative and 5 positive training examples remained. This impoverished training set was chosen to make the development of an accurate hypothesis very difficult for the learning methods. The test set was purposely made large so as to estimate the true error of the hypotheses as accurately as possible.

In order to create the CDK, all six secondary tasks were trained in a standard MTL network with sufficient training examples (200) and for a sufficient duration (100,000 iterations) to create accurate models for all tasks. Several CDKs were created from different sets of random initial weights, so that our results would not be biased by a single CDK.

4.2 General Method

The neural networks used in the following experiments have an input layer of 2 nodes, one hidden layer (common feature layer) of 28 nodes, and an output layer of 7 nodes, one for each task. The number of hidden nodes is more than is required for the standard MTL method, since at maximum two hidden nodes are needed to create the internal representation for each of the band tasks. In all experiments, the mean square error cost function is minimized by the back-propagation algorithm that uses a momentum term. The base learning rate, η, is 0.1 and the momentum term is 0.9. For all runs that do not use representational

[1] Target values marked as *unknown* make zero contribution to weight modifications.

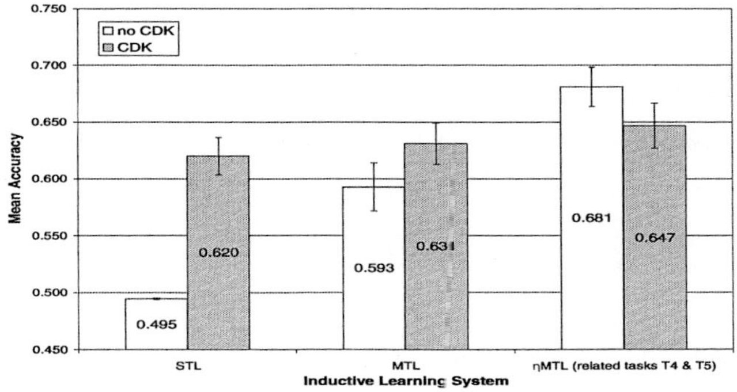

Fig. 2. Performance of T_0 hypotheses created by non-stochastic learning methods. Shown is the mean accuracy on a test set of 200 examples

transfer from CDK, random initial weight values are selected in the range -0.1 to 0.1. For all experiments involving *s*MTL, the base noise level is $\sigma = 0.5$.

The hypotheses are developed using the training and validation examples and then tested against the 200 test examples. Training continues up to a maximum of 10,000 iterations through the training data. Training is stopped at the point of minimum validation set error for the primary hypothesis. Each experiment reports the results of 30 repetitions using different random initial weight vectors.

Performance of the methods is compared in terms of the effectiveness of the primary task hypotheses and the efficiency in developing such hypotheses. Effectiveness is measured as the mean accuracy (proportion of correct classifications) of the primary hypotheses against a test set. Efficiency is measured as the mean number of iterations to develop the hypotheses.

4.3 Experiment 1: Representational Transfer without Stochastic Noise

Method. This experiment sets the baseline for inductive learning of the primary task T_0 under STL, MTL and ηMTL where the networks are initialized with small random weight values. The experiment also shows the effect of combining representational transfer with each of the learning methods; STL, MTL and ηMTL are trained after being initialized with the CDK representation.

Results and Discussion. The set of three results mark as "no CDK" in Figure 2 show the mean accuracy T_0 hypotheses developed from random initial weights. The consistently poor results of STL hypotheses indicates that knowledge transfer is necessary in this domain to create effective predictive models. The hypotheses developed by MTL are more effective than those of STL, showing the positive effect of functional transfer in learning a hypothesis. However, the high ratio of unrelated to related secondary tasks leads to some negative functional transfer, which interferes with development of optimal models. ηMTL provides a method of selectively transferring functional knowledge from the most related

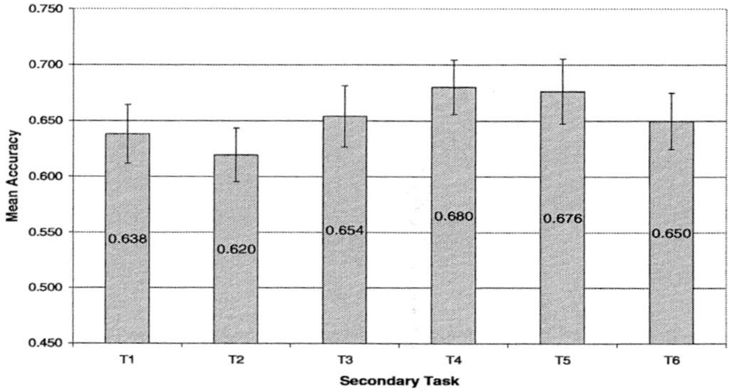

Fig. 3. Performance of T_0 hypotheses developed in parallel with each secondary task under *s*MTL. Shown is the mean accuracy on a test set of 200 examples

tasks to the primary task. The results show that when the learning rates of the unrelated tasks (T_1, T_2, T_3, T_6) are set to 0 then the most effective hypothesis are generated.

The set of three results marked as "CDK" in Figure 2 show the effect of representational transfer on the three inductive methods but without stochastic noise to create plasticity. The STL and MTL hypotheses benefit from the transfer, however the ηMTL hypotheses perform more poorly (with 95% confidence) than when started from random initial weights. This demonstrates that representational transfer requires a method to overcome the stability of the CDK representation and the negative inductive bias from the unrelated tasks.

4.4 Experiment 2: Inductive Bias Provided by Each Task

Method. We next examine the inductive bias provided to the primary task, T_0, by each of the secondary tasks as they are learned in an *s*MTL network that employs representational transfer and stochastic noise. The results of learning T_0 under 30 trials of *s*MTL are compared. For each trial k, the noise level of all secondary tasks except T_k were set to 0.5. This is equivalent to setting the measure of relatedness under ηMTL to $R_k = 1.0$ and $R_i = 0.0, i \neq k$. A constant noise level was maintained during learning (*e.g.* $I =$ infinity).

Results and Discussion. The results of training the pairs of tasks using *s*MTL are shown in Figure 3. The bar graphs represent the mean accuracy (and 95% confidence interval) on a 200 example test set.

When noise is injected into each of the secondary tasks except for one, the *s*MTL method isolates the inductive bias from that task. The results indicate that the inductive bias from T_4 and T_5 leads to development of the most effective hypotheses for T_0. This agrees with the task relatedness results for the domain reported in [21]. Therefore, in the remaining experiments we considered tasks T_4 and T_5 to be the related tasks and the other secondary tasks to be unrelated.

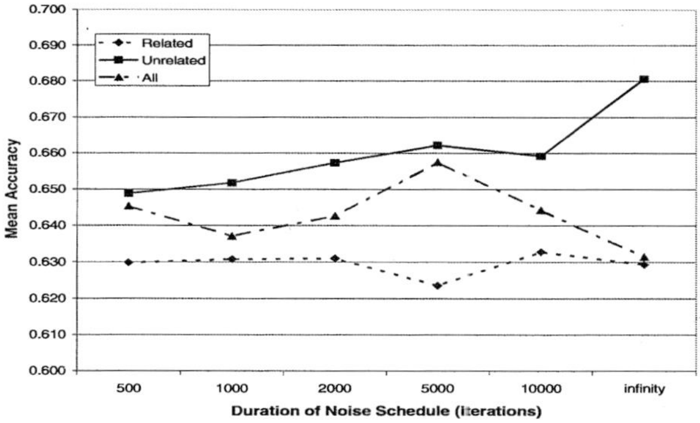

Fig. 4. Performance of T_0 hypotheses developed under *s*MTL and using different durations of noise injection

Note that a positive inductive bias from T_4 and T_5 under *s*MTL significantly improves upon the accuracy of the hypotheses generated by STL and MTL shown in Figure 2. The hypotheses perform as good as or better than the hypotheses developed by ηMTL.

4.5 Experiment 3: *s*MTL's Ability to Selectively Transfer Knowledge

Method. The final experiment tests the ability of the *s*MTL system to selectively transfer representational and functional knowledge from the most related tasks to the hypothesis of the primary task. The results of learning T_0 under three configurations of *s*MTL are compared. The first configuration has noise applied to all secondary tasks, the second has noise applied to just the related tasks T_4 and T_5 and the third configuration has noise applied to just the unrelated tasks T_1, T_2, T_3, and T_6. In addition, for each configuration five different noise schedules were tried, with I set to 500, 1000, 2000, 5000 iterations and *infinity*.

Results and Discussion. Figure 4 shows the mean accuracy of hypotheses developed using representational transfer from CDK, plus stochastic noise to create plasticity. The least accurate models are developed by *s*MTL when stochastic noise is applied only to the related tasks. The CDK representation of the unrelated tasks continues to be reenforced by task rehearsal and therefore the primary hypothesis receives only negative inductive bias. The most accurate models are developed by *s*MTL when stochastic noise is applied only to the unrelated tasks. In this case, representational and functional transfer from the related tasks of CDK have a positive influence on the development of the primary hypothesis. As the graph shows, longer schedules of noise injection result in more accurate hypotheses. The models are more effective than those produced by STL or MTL using representational transfer and are statistically equivalent to or better than

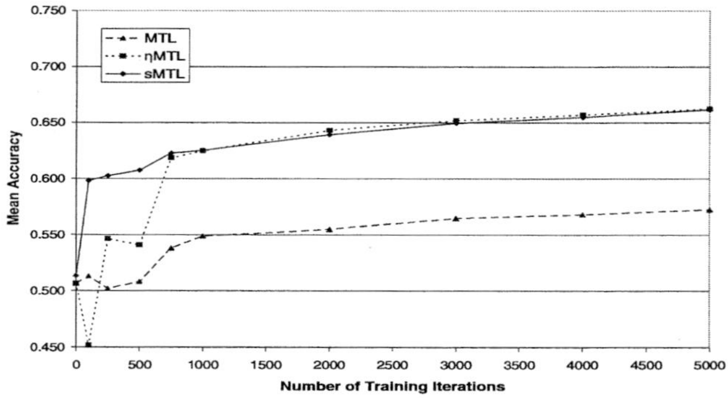

Fig. 5. Performance of T_0 hypotheses developed under MTL, ηMTL and sMTL for various durations of training

the models produced by ηMTL with no representational transfer (see Figure 2). These results demonstrate that, at least for the Band domain, noise can be used to create plasticity in an existing representation and to minimize the effects of negative inductive bias from unrelated tasks.

Another difference between the sMTL method and the older ηMTL method (without representational transfer from CDK) is the speed at which accurate hypotheses are developed. Figure 5 shows the mean accuracy of the two methods on the test set as a function of number of training iterations. The results indicated that early hypotheses (up to 1000 iterations) produced by sMTL are significantly more accurate than those of ηMTL. This efficiency comes from the use of related internal representation transferred from the CDK. Clearly, both methods are more effective and efficient than standard MTL.

5 Summary and Conclusion

This paper follows work reported in [21] on the selective transfer of task knowledge in the context of artificial neural networks. The theory of selective functional transfer through task rehearsal is extended to include representational transfer from a source of consolidated domain knowledge, CDK. sMTL, a modified version of the ηMTL system, is introduced. sMTL uses prior task knowledge and stochastic noise to adjust its inductive bias when learning a new task. The CDK representation of previously learned tasks is used to initialize the sMTL network for learning a new primary task. Task rehearsal ensures the stability of related secondary task knowledge within the sMTL network and stochastic noise is used to create plasticity in the network so as to allow the new task to be learned. sMTL controls the level of noise introduced to each secondary task based on a measure of secondary to primary task relatedness.

The results of repeated experiments on a synthetic domain of tasks demonstrates that representational transfer from CDK on its own is not enough to promote positive inductive bias for a primary task that suffers from impoverished training sets. Within 10,000 iterations, the hypothesis developed by STL, MTL and ηMTL networks initialized with CDK representation produce models with statistically lower generalization accuracy to an MTL network initialized with random weights.

Repeated experiments on the same domain and for the same primary task showed that stochastic noise added to the training examples of unrelated tasks is able to mitigate the negative inductive bias from representational and functional knowledge transferred from the CDK. This allows the representation of related tasks and their task rehearsal during learning to create a positive inductive bias for the primary task. The results are hypotheses that are statistically more effective than those of either STL or MTL and statistically equivalent in performance to hypotheses developed by the ηMTL method that trains from random initial weight values. Furthermore, the results verify that sMTL uses the prior representations from CDK to rapidly develop these accurate hypotheses. Figure 5 shows a significant increase in efficiency of sMTL over ηMTL during the early stages of learning.

In these initial experiments involving sMTL the relatedness between the primary task and each secondary task was determined via a brute force approach. In future work an *a priori* measure of task relatedness, similar to that presented in [22], will be implemented.

The scaling of this solution as a method of life-long learning comes under some scrutiny. The size of the sMTL network is dictated by the size of the CDK representation and with each new task that is learned the size of both would need to increase. This addition can be made as per [15] by adding hidden nodes to the sMTL network, however, the issue of scalability remains. For this reason we are of the opinion that short-term learning should involve selective functional transfer within small ηMTL networks where as long-term consolidation requires the use of both representational and functional transfer within larger sMTL networks.

This brings us to a further problem that is not addressed in this paper: the manner by which CDK is augmented with the new task knowledge after sMTL learning completes. As presented in this paper, sMTL is not capable of maintaining the accuracy of all secondary tasks (related and unrelated) while developing a hypothesis of the primary task. However, we are currently working on a method of domain knowledge consolidation that employs aspects of the sMTL method but minimizes the loss of any prior representational task knowledge.

References

[1] Yaser S. Abu-Mostafa. Hints. *Neural Computation*, 7:639–671, 1995.

[2] A. Agarwal, R. J. Mammone, and D. K. Naik. An on-line training algorithm to overcome catastrophic forgetting. *Intelligence Engineering Systems through Artificial Neural Networks*, 2:239–244, 1992.

[3] Jonathan Baxter. Learning internal representations. *Proceedings of the Eighth International Conference on Computational Learning Theory*, 1995.

[4] Richard A. Caruana. Multitask learning. *Machine Learning*, 28:41–75, 1997.

[5] S. E. Fahlman and C. Lebiere. The cascade-correlation learning architecture. *Advances in Neural Information Processing Systems 2*, 2:524–532, 1990. ed. D. S. Touretsky.
[6] S. J. Hanson. A stochastic version of the delta rule. *Physica D*, 42:265–272, 1990.
[7] J. Hertz, A. Krogh, and R. G. Palmer. *Introduction to the Theory of Neural Computation.* Adddison-Wesley Pub. Co., Redwood City, CA., 1991.
[8] Thomas Heskes and Bert Kappen. On-line learning processes in artificial neural networks. In J. Taylor, editor, *Mathematical Foundations of Neural Networks.* Elsevier, Amsterdam, Netherlands, 1993.
[9] L. Holmstrom and P. Koistinen. Using additive noise in back-propagation training. *IEEE Transactions on Neural Networks*, 3(1), 1992.
[10] Anders Krogh and John Hertz. Generalization in a linear perceptron in the presence of noise. *Journal of Physics*, A(25):1135–1147, 1992.
[11] K. Matsuoka. Noise injection into inputs in back-propagation learning. *IEEE Transactions on Systems, Man and Cybernetics*, 22(3):436–440, 1992.
[12] Tom Mitchell and Sebastian Thrun. Explanation based neural network learning for robot control. *Advances in Neural Information Processing Systems 5*, 5:287–294, 1993. ed. C. L. Giles and S. J. Hanson and J. D. Cowan.
[13] Tom M. Mitchell. *Machine Learning.* McGraw Hill, New York, NY, 1997.
[14] D. K. Naik and Richard J. Mammone. Learning by learning in neural networks. *Artificial Neural Networks for Speech and Vision; ed. Richard J. Mammone*, 1993.
[15] Joseph O'Sullivan. *Transfer of Learned Knowledge in Life-Long Learning Agents, A PhD Proposal.* School of Computer Science, Carnegie Mellon University, February 1997.
[16] Lorien Y. Pratt. Discriminability-based transfer between neural networks. *Advances in Neural Information Processing Systems 5*, 5:204–211, 1993. ed. C. L. Giles and S. J. Hanson and J. D. Cowan.
[17] Mark Ring. Learning sequential tasks by incrementally adding higher orders. *Advances in Neural Information Processing Systems 5*, 5:155–122, 1993. ed. C. L. Giles and S. J. Hanson and J. D. Cowan.
[18] Anthony V. Robins. Catastrophic forgetting, rehearsal, and pseudorehearsal. *Connection Science*, 7:123–146, 1995.
[19] Noel E. Sharkey and Amanda J. C. Sharkey. Adaptive generalization and the transfer of knowledge. *Working paper - Center for Connection Science*, 1992.
[20] Jude W. Shavlik and Geoffrey G. Towell. An appraoch to combining explanation-based and neural learning algorithms. *Readings in Machine Learning*, pages 828–839, 1990. ed. Jude W. Shavlik and Thomas G. Dietterich.
[21] Daniel L. Silver. *Selective Transfer of Neural Network Task Knowledge.* PhD Thesis, Dept. of Computer Science, University of Western Ontario, London, Canada, June 2000.
[22] Daniel L. Silver and Robert E. Mercer. The parallel transfer of task knowledge using dynamic learning rates based on a measure of relatedness. *Connection Science Special Issue: Transfer in Inductive Systems*, 8(2):277–294, 1996.
[23] Daniel L. Silver and Robert E. Mercer. The task rehearsal method of life-long learning: Overcoming impoverished data. *Advances in Artificial Intelligence, 15th Conference of the Canadian Society for Computational Studies of Intelligence (CAI2002)*, pages 2338:90–101, 2002.
[24] Satinder P. Singh. Transfer of learning by composing solutions for elemental sequential tasks. *Machine Learning*, 1992.
[25] Steven Suddarth and Y Kergoisien. Rule injection hints as a means of improving network performance and learning time. *Proceedings of the EURASIP workshop on Neural Networks*, 1990.

[26] Sebastian Thrun. Lifelong learning algorithms. *Learning to Learn*, pages 181–209, 1997.

[27] Paul E. Utgoff. *Machine Learning of Inductive Bias*. Kluwer Academc Publisher, Boston, MA, 1986.

[28] Alexander Waibel, Hidefumi Sawai, and Kiyoshiro Shikano. Modularity and scaling in large phonemic neural networks. *IEEE Transactions on Acoustics, Speech, and Signal Processing*, 37(12):1888–1898, December 1989.

[29] C. Wang and J. C. Principe. Training neural networks with additive noise in the desired signal. *IEEE-NN*, 10(6):1511, November 1999.

Efficient Mining of Indirect Associations Using HI-Mine

Qian Wan and Aijun An

Department of Computer Science, York University
Toronto, Ontario M3J 1P3 Canada
{qwan,aan}@cs.yorku.ca

Abstract. Discovering association rules is one of the important tasks in data mining. While most of the existing algorithms are developed for efficient mining of frequent patterns, it has been noted recently that some of the infrequent patterns, such as indirect associations, provide useful insight into the data. In this paper, we propose an efficient algorithm, called HI-mine, based on a new data structure, called HI-struct, for mining the complete set of indirect associations between items. Our experimental results show that HI-mine's performance is significantly better than that of the previously developed algorithm for mining indirect associations on both synthetic and real world data sets over practical ranges of support specifications.

1 Introduction

Since it was first introduced by Agrawal et al. [4] in 1993, association rule mining has been studied extensively by many researchers. As a result, many algorithms have been proposed to improve the running time for generating association rules and frequent itemsets. The latest includes FP-growth [6], which utilizes a prefix-tree structure for compactly representing and processing pattern information, and H-mine [8], which takes advantage of a novel hyper-linked data structure and dynamically adjusts links in the mining process.

While most of the existing algorithms are developed for efficient mining of frequent patterns, it has been noted recently that some of the infrequent patterns may provide useful insight into the data. In [13], a new class of patterns called indirect associations has been proposed and its utilities have been examined in various application domains. Consider a pair of items, x and y, that are rarely present together in the same transaction. If both items are highly dependent on the presence of another itemsets M, then the pair (x, y) is said to be indirectly associated via M. Fig. 1 illustrates a high-level view of an indirect association.

There are many advantages to mining indirect associations in large data sets. For example, an indirect association between a pair of words in text documents can be used to classify query results into categories [13]. For instance, the words *coal* and *data* can be indirectly associated via *mining*. If only the word *mining* is used in a query, documents in both mining domains are returned. Discovery of the indirect association between *coal* and *data* enables us to classify the retrieved documents into

Y. Xiang and B. Chaib-draa (Eds.): AI 2003, LNAI 2671, pp. 206-221, 2003.

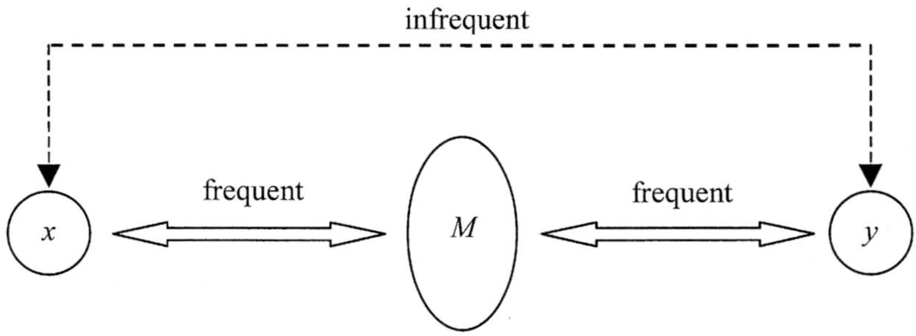

Fig. 1. Indirect association between x and y via mediator M

coal mining and *data mining*. There are also potential applications of indirect associations in many other real-world domains, such as competitive product analysis and stock market analysis [13].

For mining indirect associations between itempairs, an algorithm is presented in [11, 13]. There are two phases in the algorithm:

1. Extract all frequent itemsets using standard frequent itemset mining algorithms such as Apriori [3] or FP-growth [6];
2. Discover valid indirect associations by checking all the candidate associations generated from the frequent itemsets.

In this paper, we propose a new data structure, HI-struct, and a new mining algorithm, HI-mine, for mining indirect associations in large databases. We show that they can be used as a formal framework for discovering indirect associations directly, with no need to generate all frequent itemsets as the first step. Empirical evaluations comparing HI-mine to two versions of the algorithm described above show that HI-mine performs significantly better on both synthetic and real world data sets.

The remaining of the paper is organized as follows. Section 2 reviews related work and briefly exhibits the contribution of the paper. Next, we present the HI-struct data structure and the HI-mine algorithm in Section 3. Our empirical results are reported in Section 4. Finally, we conclude with a summary of our work and suggestions for future research in Section 5.

2 Related Work

Let $I = \{i_1, i_2, \ldots, i_m\}$ be a set of m literals, called items. Let the database $D = \{t_1, t_2, \ldots, t_n\}$ be a set of n transactions, each one consisting of a set of items from I and associated with a unique identifier called its TID. The *support* of an itemset A is the percentage of transactions in D containing A: $sup(A) = \|\{t \mid t \in D, A \subseteq t\}\| / \|\{ t \mid t \in D\}\|$, where $\|X\|$ is the cardinality of set X. An itemset is *frequent* if its support is more than a user-specified *minimum support* value.

2.1 Negative Association Rules

An *association rule* $A \Rightarrow B$ is a conditional implication among itemsets A and B, where $A \subset I$, $B \subset I$ and $A \cap B = \varnothing$. The *confidence* of an association rule r: $A \Rightarrow B$ is the conditional probability that a transaction contains B, given that it contains A. The support of rule r is defined as: $sup(r) = sup(A \cup B)$. The confidence of rule r can be expressed as $conf(r) = sup(A \cup B)/sup(A)$.

The importance of extending the current association rule framework to include negative association was first pointed out in [5]. In the case of *negative association rules* we are interested in finding itemsets that have a very low probability of occurring together. That is, a negative association between two itemsets A and B, denoted as $A \Rightarrow \overline{B}$ or $\overline{A} \Rightarrow B$, means that A and B appear very rarely in the same transaction. Mining *negative association rules* is impossible with a naïve approach because billions of negative associations may be found in a large dataset while almost all of them are extremely uninteresting. This problem was addressed in [14] by combining previously discovered positive associations with domain knowledge to constrain the search space such that fewer but more interesting negative rules are mined.

2.2 Indirect Association and INDIRECT Algorithm

Indirect association is closely related to negative association, they are both dealing with itemsets that do not have sufficiently high support. Indirect associations provide an effective way to detect interesting negative associations by discovering only "infrequent itempairs that are highly expected to be frequent" without using negative items or domain knowledge.

Definition 1 (Indirect Association)
An itempair $\{x, y\}$ is indirectly associated via a mediator M, if the following conditions hold:

1. $sup(\{x, y\}) < t_s$ (Itempair Support Condition)
2. There exists a non-empty set M such that:
   a) $sup(\{x\} \cup M) \geq t_f$, $sup(\{y\} \cup M) \geq t_f$ (Mediator Support Condition)
   b) $dep(\{x\}, M) \geq t_d$, and $dep(\{y\}, M) \geq t_d$, where $dep(P, Q)$ is a measure of the dependence between itemsets P and Q. (Mediator Dependence Condition)

The thresholds above are called *itempair support threshold* (t_s), *mediator support threshold* (t_f), and *mediator dependence threshold* (t_d), respectively. In practice, it is reasonably to set $t_f \geq t_s$.

In the database and probability theories, an indirect association is a well-know property of embedded multi-valued dependency (EMVD) and probability conditional independence, where it is sometimes called an "induced dependence". [16] includes a comprehensive discussion on an independence in a small context becoming a dependence in a larger context in both database and probability settings.

In this paper, we use the notation $<x, y \mid M>$ to represent the indirect association between x and y via M. And we use the IS measure [10] as the dependence measure for Condition 2(b). Given a pair of itemsets, say X and Y, its IS measure can be computed using the following equation:

```
1.  Extract frequent itemsets, L1, L2,...Ln, using frequent itemsets generation
    algorithm, where Li is the set of all frequent i-itemsets.
2.  P = ∅ (set of indirect associations)
3.  for k = 2 to n do
4.    Ck+1 = join(Lk, Lk)
5.    for each <x, y , M> ∈ Ck+1 do
6.      if (sup({x, y}) < ts and dep({x}, M) ≥ td and dep({y}, M) ≥ td)
7.        P = P ∪ {<x, y , M>}
8.      end
9.    end
10. end
```

Fig. 2. The INDIRECT algorithm

$$IS(X, Y) \equiv \frac{P(X, Y)}{\sqrt{P(X)P(Y)}} \tag{1}$$

where P denotes the probability that the given itemset appears in a transaction.

An algorithm for mining indirect associations between pairs of items is given in [11, 13], which is shown in Figure 2. There are two major phases in this algorithm: (1) extract all frequent itemsets using Apriori (step 1) and (2) discover all indirect associations by (a) candidate generation (step 4) and (b) candidate pruning (steps 5-8). In the candidate generation step, frequent itemset L_k is used to generate candidate indirect associations for pass $k+1$, i.e., C_{k+1}. Each candidate in C_{k+1} is a triplet, $<x, y, M>$, where x and y are the items that are indirectly associated via the mediator M. C_{k+1} is generated by joining the frequent itemsets in L_k. During the join, a pair of frequent k-itemsets, $\{x_1, x_2, \ldots, x_k\}$ and $\{y_1, y_2, \ldots, y_k\}$, are joinable if the two itemsets have exactly k-1 items in common and thus produce a candidate indirect association $<x, y, M>$, where x and y are the distinct items, one from each k-itemset, and M is the set of common items. For example, two frequent itemsets, $\{a, b, c, d\}$ and $\{a, b, d, e\}$, can be joined together to produce a candidate indirect association, $<c, e, \{a, b, d\}>$. Since the candidate associations are created by joining two frequent itemsets, they all satisfy the mediator support condition. Therefore, in the steps for candidate pruning, only itempair support condition and mediator dependence condition are checked.

There are two join steps in the INDIRECT algorithm. One is in the first phase for generating all the frequent itemsets with Apriori. In Apriori, the join operation is used to generate candidate frequent itemsets for pass $k+1$ based on the frequent itemsets in L_k. The other join operation is for generating candidate indirect associations, C_{k+1}, from L_k. Both candidate generation steps can be quite expensive, because each of them requires at most $O(\Sigma_k |L_k| \times |L_k|)$ join operations. The join operation for generating indirect association candidates is more expensive than that in Apriori because the items in an indirect itempair, x and y, do not have to be the last item in each frequent itemset, whereas Apriori only combines itemsets that have identical k-1 prefix items, assuming that all the items in an itemsets are sorted in lexicographic order. Moreover, no matter what implementation technique is applied, an Apriori-like algorithm may still suffer from nontrivial costs in situations with prolific frequent patterns, long patterns, or quite low minimum support thresholds.

Is there any other way that we may reduce these costs in indirect association mining? Can we avoid generating all the frequent itemsets and a huge set of candidates, and derive indirect association directly using some novel data structure or algorithm?

In the next section, we introduce our solution. The solution is based on the HI-struct data structure and the HI-mine algorithm, which were inspired by a novel hyper-linked data structure, H-struct, and an efficient algorithm, H-mine, presented in [8]. H-struct and H-mine are designed for the purpose of mining frequent patterns. We modify both of them for learning indirect association. With HI-struct and HI-mine, we do not need to find all the frequent itemsets before mining indirect associations nor we need to do any join operation for candidate generation. Instead we generate two new sets: *indirect itempair set* and *mediator support set* by recursively building the HI-struct data structures for the database. Then indirect associations are discovered from these two sets directly and efficiently.

3 Mining Indirect Association Using HI-Mine

In this section, we first define *indirect itempair set* (*IIS*) and *mediator support set* (*MSS*). We then illustrate the general idea of HI-mine (Hyper-structure Indirect-association Mining) using the two sets with an example.

Definition 2 (Indirect Itempair Set)
Let t_s be the itempair support threshold and L be the set of frequent itemsets of a database D with respect to t_s. We define the indirect itempair set *IIS* of *D* as:

$$IIS(D) = \{<x, y> \mid \{x\} \in L, \{y\} \in L, \text{ and } sup(\{x, y\}) < t_s\}$$

Definition 3 (Mediator Support Set)
Let L be the set of frequent itemsets of a database D. Let t_f be the mediator support threshold and t_d be the mediator dependence threshold. The mediator support set *MSS* of x ($\{x\} \in L$) is defined as:

$$MSS(x) = \{M \mid M \in L, sup(M \cup \{x\}) \geq t_f, \text{ and } dep(M, \{x\}) \geq t_d\}$$

It's trivial to prove that the following properties hold for each indirect association $<x, y \mid M>$ of database *D*:

1. $<x, y> \in IIS(D)$;
2. $M \in MSS(x)$ and $M \in MSS(y)$.

And on the other hand, given x, y and M that have the above properties, $<x, y \mid M>$ must be an indirect association of *D*.

3.1 HI-Struct: Design and Construction

The design and construction of HI-struct for efficient indirect association mining are illustrated in the following example. The original transaction database *TDB* is shown in Table 1. The HI-struct of *TDB* is a dynamic data structure that changes during the process of recursively generating the indirect itempair set and mediator support sets.

Table 1. The transaction database *TDB*

TID	List of item_IDs
T100	A, B, C, D
T200	A, B, E, F
T300	G, H
T400	B, C
T500	A, B, D, E, I
T600	B, C, D
T700	J, K
T800	L, M, N

The initial HI-struct is constructed in the following steps.

1. Scan the transaction database *TDB* once. Collect the set of frequent items *F* and their supports. Sort *F* in support descending order as *L*, the list of sorted frequent items. For the example database, *L* is {B, A, C, D, E}. Then a header table H is created, where each frequent item has an entry with three fields: an item-id, a support count, and a pointer to a queue.
2. For each transaction *Trans* in *TDB*, select and sort the frequent items in *Trans* according to the order of *L*. Let the sorted frequent item list in *Trans* be [*t*|*T*], where *t* is the first element and *T* is the remaining list. [*t*|*T*] is called the *frequent-item projection* of transaction *Trans*. Add [*t*|*T*] to a frequent-item projection array, and append [*t*|*T*]'s index of the array to *t*'s queue. Thus, all indexes of the frequent-item projections with the same first item (in the order of L) are linked together as a queue, and the entries in the header table *H* act as the heads of the queues.

The initial HI-struct of the example database is shown in Figure 3. Since all frequent item projections in our example database start with B, the queues for other items than B are empty at the moment[1]. After the initial HI-struct is constructed, the remaining mining process is performed on the HI-struct only, without referencing any information in the original database. Note that the frequent-item projection array contains only frequent items. Its size is usually much smaller than the original database. Therefore, the array may fit into main memory.

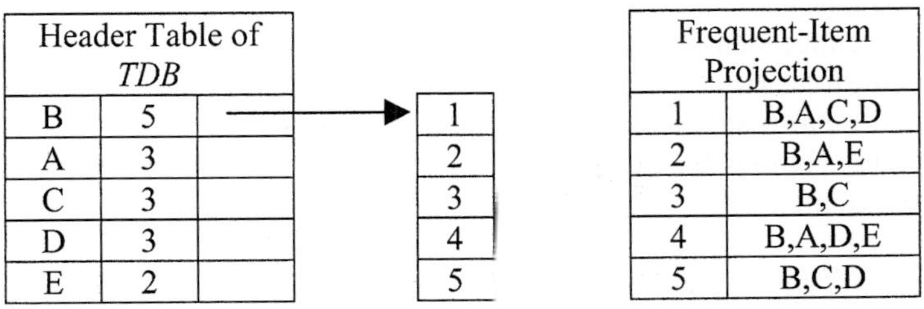

Fig. 3. The initial HI-struct of *TDB*

[1] The initial header table of a database may contain more than one queue. We use a simple example for the convenience of explanation.

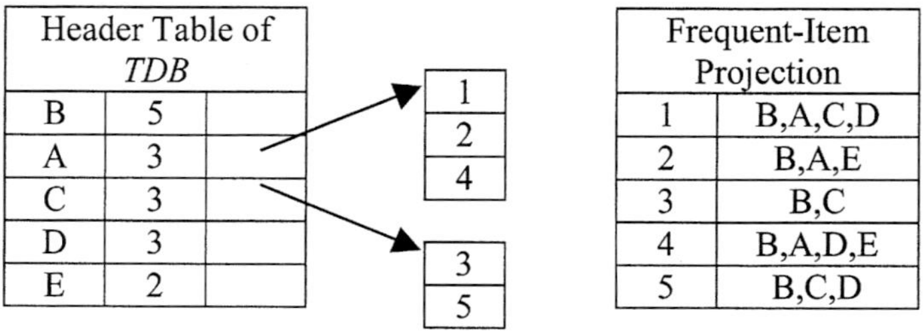

Fig. 4. HI-struct of *TDB* after mining B-projected database

The subsequent mining process involves building the *indirect itempair set* (*IIS*) of the database and the *mediator support set* (*MMS*) of each frequent item. We use a divide-and conquer strategy to build *IIS* and each *MMS* by partitioning each set into disjoined subsets and generating each subset in turn. Following the support descending order of frequent items: B, A, C, D, E, the complete *indirect itempair set* and *mediator support sets* of all the frequent items in our example database can be partitioned into 5 subsets as follows: (1) those containing item B; (2) those containing item A but no item B; (3) those containing item C, but no item B nor A; (4) those containing item D, but no item B nor A nor C; (5) those containing only item E. Clearly, all the frequent-item projections containing item B, referred to as the B-projected database, are already linked in the B-queue in the header table, which can be traversed efficiently. In the next section, we will show that, by mining the B-projected database recursively, HI-mine can find the *indirect itempair set* and *mediator support sets* (*MSS*) of all the frequent items in the first subset, i.e., all the *indirect itempairs* and *support mediators* containing item B. After that, each index in B-queue is added to the queue for the next item in the corresponding projection following B in the order of L to mine all the *indirect itempair set* and *mediator support sets* containing item A but not B. The HI-struct after this adjustment is shown in Figure 4. Note that B-queue is no longer needed and is thus removed. After the subsets containing A but not B are mined, other subsets of *indirect itempair set* and *mediator support sets* are mined similarly.

3.2 HI-Mine Algorithm

The HI-mine algorithm mines the complete set of indirect associations based on a dynamically-changed HI-struct. There are two phases in the algorithm. In the first phase, we construct HI-struct and generate the *indirect itempair set* of the database and *mediator support set* of each frequent item. In the second phase, we generate all the indirect associations based on the indirect itempair set and the mediator support sets. The algorithm is described as follows.

Algorithm: ***HI-mine***. (Mine indirect associations using an HI-struct)
Input: A transaction database (*D*); itempair support threshold (t_s); mediator support threshold (t_f); mediator dependence threshold (t_d);
Output: The complete set of indirect associations between itempairs.

Method:

```
build the initial HI-struct for D which includes a header table H and the frequent
item projection array.
for each item i in the header table of HI-struct
create header table H_i by scanning i-projected database in the same way as
building header table H except that item i is not considered (see Figures 5, 10 -
13)
    hi_mine(H_i)
    insert all the indexes in i-queue to the proper queues in H (see Figure 4)
end
if IIS(D) ≠ ∅ then
    for each itempair <x, y> in IIS(D)
        SM ← MSS(x) ∩ MSS(y)
        if SM ≠ ∅
            for each mediator M in SM
                output <x, y | M>
    end
else
    output "Indirect associations do not exit in this database"
end
```

procedure **hi_mine**(H_m)

(Recursively mine the header table of itemset m and update $IIS(D)$ and MSS(j), $j \notin$ m)

```
for each item j in the header table H_m
    if j's count > minimum mediator support count then
        if IS(j, m) > t_d then
            add m to MSS(j)
            create header table H_mj by scanning j-queue in H_m (i.e., mj-projected
        database) in the same way as building H except that item j and items in m
are
        not considered (see Figure 7)
        hi_mine(H_mj)
    else if the size of m is 1 and j's count < minimum itempair support count then
        add <m, j> to IIS(D)
    end
    insert all the indexes in j-queue to the proper queues in H_m (see Figure 6)
end
```

Figures 5 to 13 show the execution of the algorithm on the transaction database *TDB* given in Table 1. The itempair support threshold t_s and mediator support threshold t_f are set to be 25% (minimum support count and minimum mediator support count are both 2)[2], and the minimum dependence threshold t_d is 0.5.

First, to find all the *indirect itempairs* and *support mediators* containing item B, a B-header table H_B is created, as shown in Figure 5. In H_B, every frequent item, except

---

2 The two thresholds are of the same value here just for the convenience of explanation. They can be different.

for B itself, has an entry with the same fields as H, i.e., item-id, support count and a pointer to a queue. The support count in H_B records the support of the corresponding item in the B-queue. For example, since item A appears 3 times in the frequent-item projections of B-queue, the support count in the entry for A in H_B is 3.

By traversing the B-queue once, the set of locally frequent items, i.e., the items appearing at least 2 times, in the B-projected database is found, which is {A, C, D, E}. Since all the items in H_B are locally frequent, there is no indirect itempair contains item B, and *IIS(D)* is empty after this scan. Because the minimum mediator support count is 2, we compute the IS measure between B and each item in H_B:

$$IS(\{B\},\{A\}) = 3/\sqrt{3\times 5} = 0.77 \quad (2)$$

$$IS(\{B\},\{C\}) = 3/\sqrt{3\times 5} = 0.77 \quad (3)$$

$$IS(\{B\},\{D\}) = 3/\sqrt{3\times 5} = 0.77 \quad (4)$$

$$IS(\{B\},\{E\}) = 2/\sqrt{2\times 5} = 0.63 \quad (5)$$

They all pass the minimum dependence threshold 0.5. Therefore, {B} should be in the *MMS* of each of these items. The result is shown in Figure 5.

After {B} is inserted into *MSS*(A) in the above process, a header table H_{BA} is created by examining A-queue in H_B in the same manner as in generating H_B from the B-queue in *H*. The header table H_{BA} is shown in the most left part of Figure 6. Then, the algorithm recursively exams the BA-projected database to determine whether {B,A} belongs to the mediator support sets of items C, D and E. Since the local support count of C is less than 2, {B,A} is not added to *MSS*(C) and the search along path BAC completes. But the index in the C-queue of H_{BA} is inserted into the D-queue of H_{BA} because D follows C in the projection corresponding to the index, which is the first projection {B, A, C, D}. The resulting header table after this adjustment is shown in the middle of Figure 6. Since D is locally frequent and passes the dependence threshold, {B,A} is added to *MSS*(D). Then a header table H_{BAD} (not shown here) is created, which contains no local frequent items, and thus search along path BAD completes. Similarly, {B,A} is added to *MMS*(E), E-queue is adjusted, and the search along path BAE completes because header table H_{BAE} contains no frequent items. Thus, the process of mining the header table H_{BA} finishes.

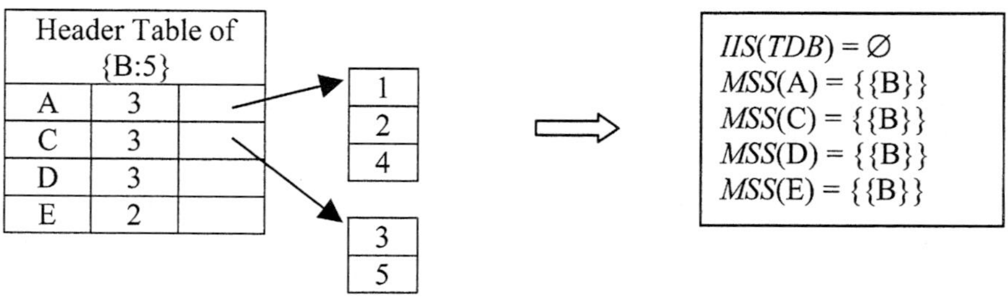

Fig. 5. Header table H_B and mining result

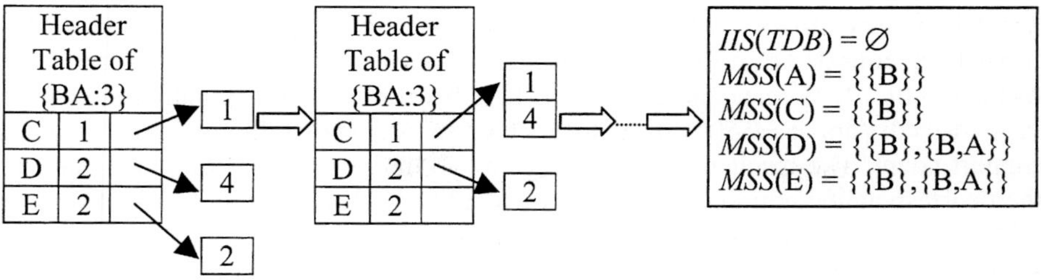

Fig. 6. Header table H_{BA} and mining result

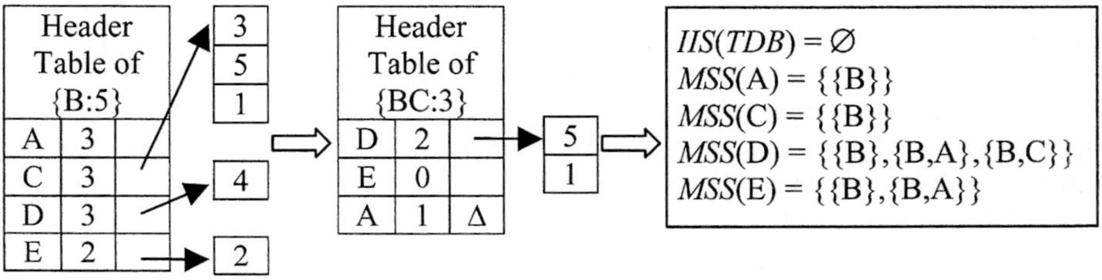

Fig. 7. Adjusted header table H_B, header table H_{BC} and mining result

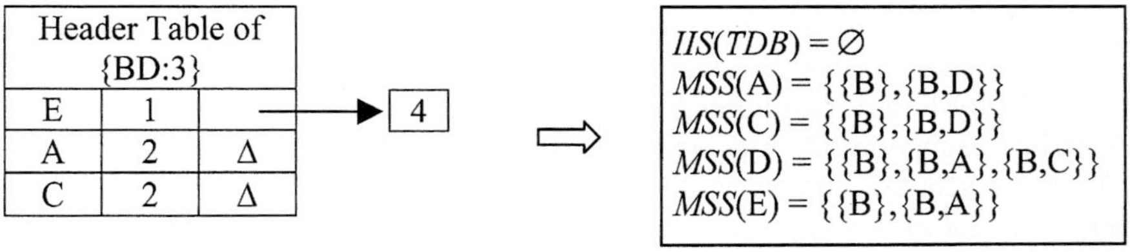

Fig. 8. Header table H_{BD} and mining result

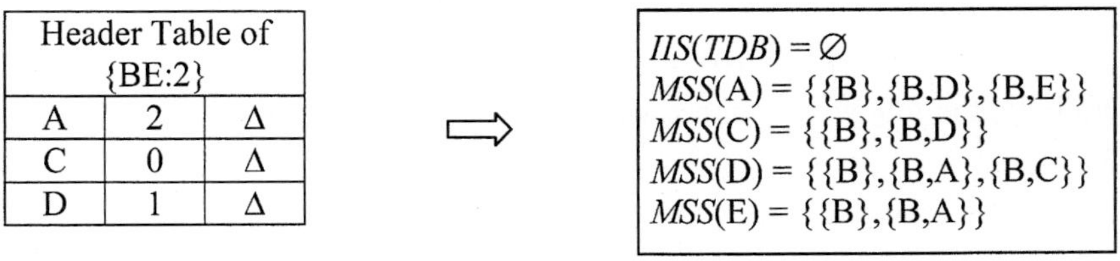

Fig. 9. Header table H_{BE} and mining result

After that, each index in the A-queue in table H_B is appended to the queue of the next frequent item in the corresponding projection according to the order of *L*. The adjusted header table H_B is shown in the most left part of Figure 7. After the above adjustment, the C-queue in H_B (also referred to as BC-queue) collects the complete set of frequent-item projections containing items B and C. Thus, by further creating a header table H_{BC} (shown in the middle of Figure 7), the *support mediators* containing item B and C but not A can be mined recursively. Please note that item A appears in H_{BC} because it does not belong to {B,C} and it appears in the frequent-item projections of BC-queue. However, its queue is always empty, that is, we will not append any index to its queue after D-queue or E-queue in H_{BC} has been mined since it has been considered in the mining of the BA-queue. Thus, the A-queue in H_{BC} is marked with "·". We need an entry for A here because we need to output the correct support mediators in *MSS*(A) if the local count of A is above the minimum mediator support count. The result is shown in Figure 7. The header table H_{BD} and H_{BE}, and their corresponding mining results are shown in Figure 8 and Figure 9 respectively.

After the *indirect itempairs* and *support mediators* containing item B are found, the B-queue is no longer needed in the remaining of mining. Since the A-queue in header table *H* includes all frequent-item projections containing item A except for those projections containing both B and A, which are in the B-queue, we need to insert all the projections in the B-queue to the proper queues in *H* to mine all the *indirect itempairs* and *support mediators* containing item A but not B, and other subsets of them. The header table *H* after this adjustment is shown in Figure 4.

By mining the A-projected database recursively, we can find the *indirect itempairs* and *support mediators* containing item A but no B. The header table H_A and the mining result are shown in Figure 10. Since C is locally infrequent with respect to A, pair <A,C> is added to the infrequent itempair set *IIS*(*TDB*). Notice that item B will not be considered in the rest mining processes since all the *indirect itempairs* and *support mediators* containing B are already found, and B is frequent with all the other frequent items.

Similarly, the mining process continues as shown in Figure 11 to 13. It is easy to see that the above mining process finds the complete *indirect itempair set* and *mediator support sets* because we partition the sets into disjoined subsets and mine each subset by further partitioning it recursively. The complete indirect itempair set and mediator support sets for our example database *TDB* are shown in Figure 13.

After the sets are computed, the second phase of the HI-mine algorithm is to compute the set of mediators for each indirect itempair in the indirect itempair set *IIS* (see steps 7-15 in the HI-mine algorithm). For example, the set of mediators for pair <A,C> in *IIS*(*TDB*) is computed by intersecting *MSS*(A) and *MSS*(C), which results in {{B},{D},{B,D}}. Therefore, three indirect associations are discovered for pair <A,C>:

<A, C | {B}>, <A, C | {D}>, <A, C | {B,D}>

Similarly, the following indirect associations are discovered for pairs <C, E> and <D, E>:

<C, E | {B}>
<D, E | {A}>, <D, E | {B}>, <D, E | {A,B}>

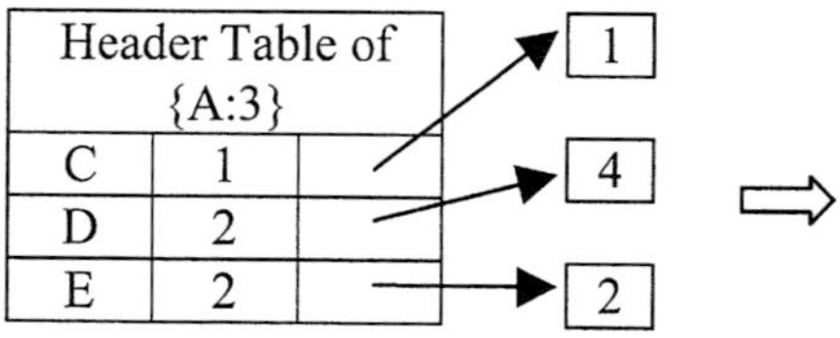

IIS(*TDB*) = {<A,C>}
MSS(A) = {{B},{B,D},{B,E}}
MSS(C) = {{B},{B,D}}
MSS(D) = {{B},{B,A},{B,C},{A}}
MSS(E) = {{B},{B,A},{A}}

Fig. 10. Header table H_A and mining result

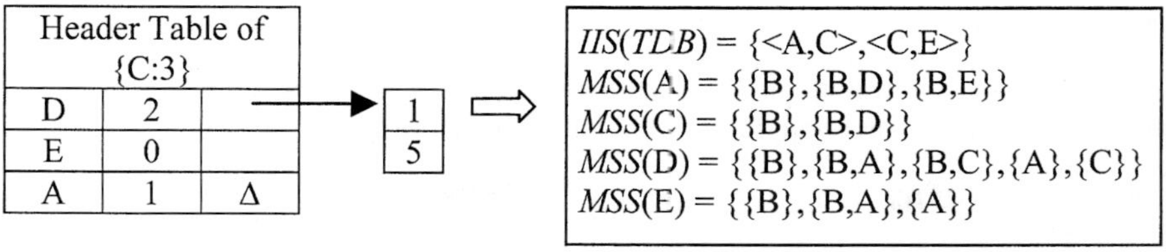

Fig. 11. Header table H_C and mining result

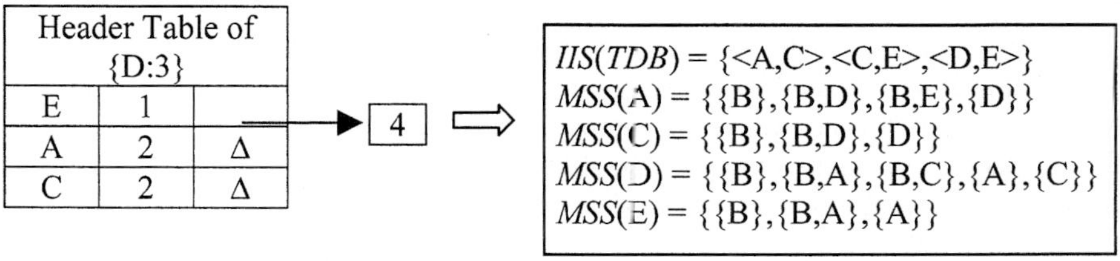

Fig. 12. Header table H_D and mining result

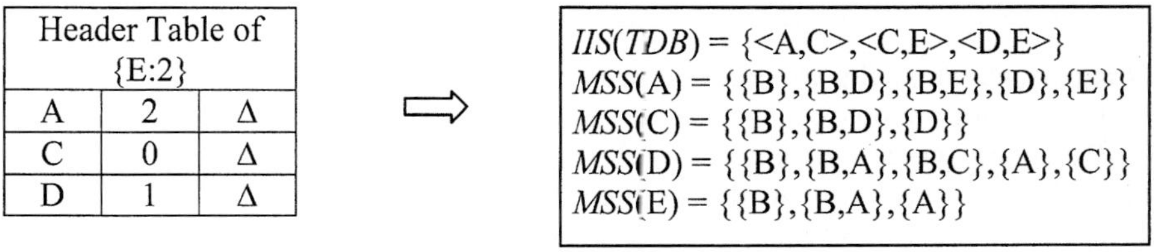

Fig. 13. Header table H_E and mining result

4 Experimental Evaluation and Performance Study

In this section, we report our experimental results on the performance of HI-mine in comparison with two versions of the INDIRECT algorithm, INDIRECT-A and INDIRECT-F, which extract frequent itemsets using Apriori and FP-growth in the first step, respectively.

All the experiments are performed on a 533-MHz Pentium PC machine with 128M main memory, running on Microsoft Window 2000 Professional. All the programs are written in Sun Java 1.3.1. We have tested the programs on various data sets. Due to space limitation, only the results on some typical data sets are reported here. Please note that *run time* used here means the total execution time, i.e., the period between input and output. Also, in all reports, the *run time* of HI-mine include the time of constructing HI-struct, and the *run time* of INDIRECT-F include the time of constructing FP-tree from the original database as well.

4.1 Test Data

The algorithms are tested on two types of datasets: synthetic data, which mimic market basket data, and anonymous web data, which belong to the domain of web log databases.

The synthetic datasets used in our experiments were generated using the program described in [3]. The first one is denoted as T10.I5.D20K. It contains 250 items and 20,000 transactions. In this data set, the average transaction size and average maximal potentially frequent itemset size are set to 10 and 5, respectively. The second data set, denoted as T10.I5.D50K, contains 250 items and 50,000 transactions.

The web dataset was obtained from http://kdd.ics.uci.edu/databases/msweb/msweb.html. It was created by sampling and processing the www.microsoft.com logs. The data records the use of www.microsoft.com by 38000 anonymous, randomly-selected users. For each user, the data lists all the areas of the web site that user visited in a one week timeframe. The data set contains 32711 instances (transactions) with 294 attributes (items); each attribute is an area of the www.microsoft.com web site.

4.2 Performance Comparison of HI-Mine and INDIRECT

Our experimental results are reported in Figures 14, 15 and 16. Each figure depicts a run time comparison of the three algorithms (HI-mine, INDIRECT-A and INDIRECT-F) on a synthetic or real data set over different mediator support thresholds. In our experiments, the itempair support threshold is set to be the same as the mediator support threshold and the dependence threshold is set to be 0.1. From the figures, we can observe that HI-mine is a clear winner on all the three datasets. At high support threshold values, HI-mine and INDIRECT-F have similar performance and they both outperform INDIRECT-A. However, as the support threshold goes lower, the gap between INDIRECT-F and HI-mine and the gap between HI-mine and INDIRECT-A become larger. It is interesting to observe that the lines for HI-mine in the figures are quite flat, which means that the run time of HI-mine does not increase much as the support threshold goes lower.

The reason that INDIRECT-F is better than INDIRECR-A is that FP-growth does not generate candidates when it generates frequent patterns and the generation of frequent patterns is based on a compressed tree structure (FP-tree), which is usually much smaller than the original database. However, INDIRECT-F generates candidates for indirect associations using a join operation. HI-mine does not perform any candidate generation. It discovers indirect associations directly based on the HI-struct data structure.

The reason that the run time of HI-mine does not change much with the support threshold is that, when the support threshold decreases, the number of frequent items increases, but the number of indirect associations may decrease because there are fewer indirect itempairs. On the other hand, the run time of INDIRECT depends primarily on the number of frequent itemsets generated by Apriori or FP-growth. Therefore, avoiding generating all the frequent itemsets in HI-mine makes it a big winner.

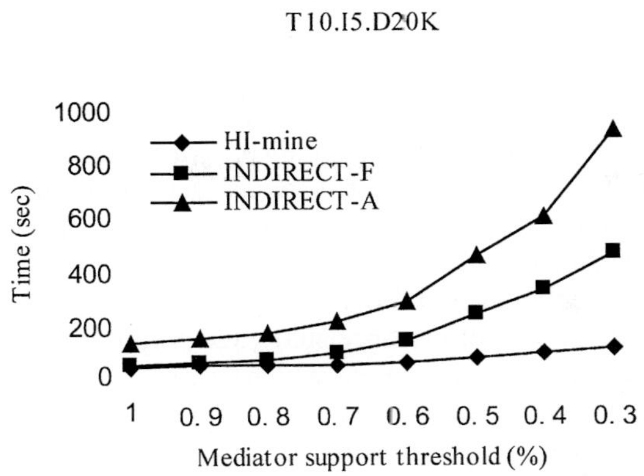

Fig. 14. Run time comparison on synthetic data set T10.I5.D20K

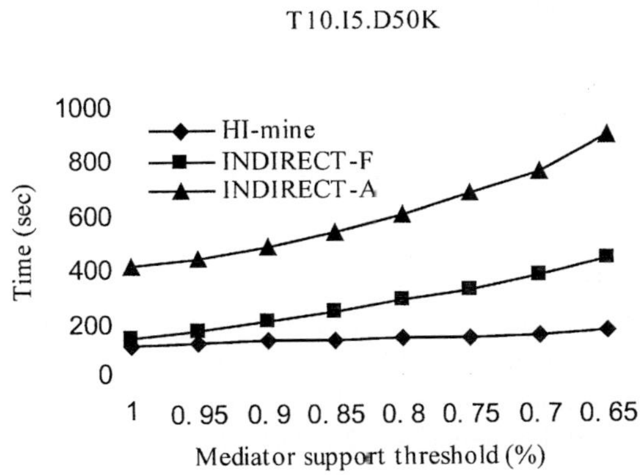

Fig. 15. Run time comparison on synthetic data set T10.I5.D50K

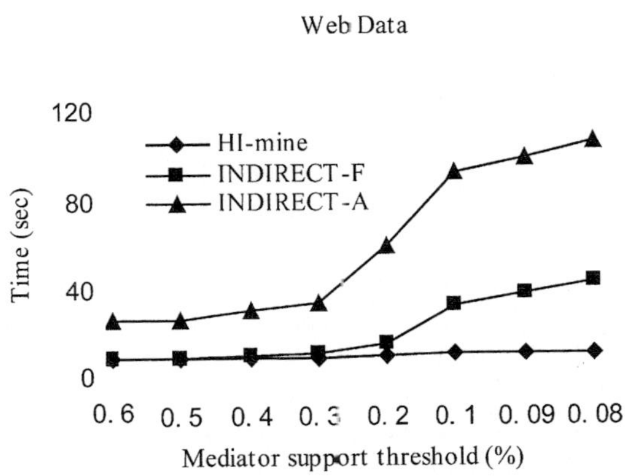

Fig. 16. Run time comparison on web log data

5 Conclusions

In this paper, we have proposed an efficient algorithm, HI-mine, which uses a new data structure, HI-struct, to discover all indirect associations between items. The salient features of HI-mine include that it avoids generating all the frequent items before generating indirect associations and that it generates indirect associations directly without candidate generation. We have compared this algorithm to the previously known algorithm, the INDIRECT algorithm, using both synthetic and real-world data. As shown in our performance study, the proposed algorithm significantly outperforms the INDIRECT algorithm, which uses a standard frequent itemset generation algorithm such as Apriori and FP-growth to extract the frequent itemsets before mining indirect associations.

In the future, we will work on scalability issues of HI-mine. The current version of HI-mine compresses the database into frequent-item projections. If the projected database fits into memory, there is no extra disk I/O in the subsequent mining process. Otherwise, multiple scans of (part of) the projected database (usually much smaller than the original database if the database is sparse) are needed in the process of learning the indirect itempair set and mediator support sets. We will work on the issue of how to further reduce disk I/Os when the database is huge, e.g., with millions of transactions.

Acknowledgments

This research is partially supported by a research grant from the Natural Sciences and Engineering Research Council (NSERC) of Canada. We would like to thank Mr. Miao Wen for his help in implementing the INDIRECT algorithm.

References

[1] R. Agarwal, C. Aggarwal, and V. V. V. Prasad. A tree projection algorithm for generation of frequent itemsets. *In J. of Parallel and Distributed Computing (Special Issue on High Performance Data Mining)*, 2000.

[2] C. Aggarwal and P. Yu. A new framework for itemset generation. *In Proc. of the Fourth Int'l Conference on Knowledge Discovery and Data Mining*, pages 129-133, New York, NY, 1996.

[3] R. Agrawal and R.Srikant. Fast Algorithms for mining association rules. *Proceedings of the 20th Int'l Conference on Very Large Data Bases*, pp.487-499, Santiago, Chile (1994).

[4] R. Agrawal, T. Imielinski, and A. Swami. Mining association rules between sets of items in large databases. *Proceedings of the ACM SIGMOD int'l Conference on Management of Data*, pp. 207-216, Washington D.C., USA (1993).

[5] S. Brin, R. Motwani, and C. Silverstein. Beyond market baskets: Generalizing association rules to correlations. In Proc. ACM SIGMOD intl. Conf. Management of Data, pages 265-276, Tucson, AZ, 1997.

[6] J. Han, J. Pei, and Y. Yin. Mining frequent patterns without candidate generation, In SIGMOD'00, pages 1-12.

[7] J. S. Park, M. S. Chen, and P. S. Yu. An efficient hash-based algorithm for mining association rules. *SIGMOD Record*, 25(2):175-186, 1995.

[8] J. Pei, J. Han, H. Lu, S. Nishio, S. Tang, and D. Yang. H-Mine: Hyper-Structure Mining of Frequent Patterns in Large Database.

[9] J. Pei, J. Han, and R. Mao. CLOSET: An efficient algorithm for mining frequent closed itemsets. In *Proc. 2000 ACM-SIGMOD Int. Workshop Data Mining and Knowledge Discovery* (*DMKD'00*), pages 11-20.

[10] P. Tan and V. Kumar. Interestingness measures for association patterns: A perspective. In *KDD 2000 Workshop on Postprocessing in Machine Learning and Data Mining*, Boston, MA, August 2000.

[11] P. N. Tan, and V. Kumar. Mining Indirect Associations in Web Data. *In Proc of WebKDD 2001: Mining Log Data Across All Customer TouchPoints*, August (2001)

[12] P. N. Tan, V Kumar, H Kuno. Using SAS for Mining Indirect Associations in Data, *In Proc of the Western Users of SAS Software Conference* (2001).

[13] P. N. Tan, V. Kumar, and J.Srivastava. Indirect Association: Mining Higher Order Dependences in Data. Proceedings of the 4th European Conference on Principles and Practice of Knowledge Discovery in Databases, 632-637, Lyon, France (2000).

[14] Savasere, E. Omiecinski, and S. Navathe. Mining for strong negative associations in a large database of customer transactions. In Proc. of the 14th International Conference on Data Engineering, pages 494-502, Orlando, Florida, February 1998.

[15] Savaswre, E. Omiecinski, and S. Navathe. An efficient algorithm for mining association rules in large databases. *In Proc. of the 21st Int. Conf. on Very Large Databases* (*VLDB'95*), Zurich, Switzerland, Sept., 1995.

[16] Wong and C. J. Butz. *Constructing the Dependency Structure of a Multi-Agent Probability Network.* IEEE Transactions on Knowledge and Data Engineering, Vol. 13, No. 3, 395-415, May 2001.

Case Authoring from Text and Historical Experiences

Marvin Zaluski[1], Nathalie Japkowicz[2], and Stan Matwin[2]

[1]Institute for Information Technology, National Research Council of Canada
Ottawa Ontario, Canada, K1A OR6
marvin.zaluski@nrc.ca
[2] School of Information Technology and Engineering, University of Ottawa
Ottawa, Ontario, Canada, K1N 6N5
{nat,stan}@site.uottawa.ca

Abstract. The problem of repair and maintenance of complex systems, such as aircraft, cars and trucks is a nontrivial task. Maintenance technicians must use a great amount of knowledge and information resources to solve problems that may occur. This paper describes a semi-automated tool that sorts through the mass of information that a maintenance technician must consult in order to make a repair, thus helping him decide how to tackle the problem and thereby increasing his efficiency and, possibly, his reliability. Our tool was developed using state-of-the-art Case-Based Reasoning and Information Extraction technologies. More specifically, we developed a semi-automated Case Authoring method that creates a Case-Base in two steps. It begins by extracting knowledge from readily available resources such as technical documents and follows by complementing those cases using individual experiences in the maintenance organization. The case-base developed is a reflection of the knowledge encoded in the technical documentation and an authentication of the cases with real historical instances. Our case authoring approach is applied to the real world in the aerospace domain.

1 Introduction

A variety of Case-Base Reasoning (CBR) applications have been implemented since the idea of CBR was founded. These applications range from helpdesk [1] to tutorial applications [2]. The most important prerequisite in any CBR application is a collection of experiences in the form of a case-base [3]. Case authoring is the acquisition of new experiences that are not represented in the case-base. These experiences are captured during the case authoring process. A majority of CBR applications use manually intensive approaches to create new experiences for their case-bases. There has been little or no research done to facilitate automatic or semi-automatic approaches to authoring of cases for the case-base [1]. This paper will describe a semi-automated approach to case authoring that utilizes resources that are readily available in an organization.

Y. Xiang and B. Chaib-draa (Eds.): AI 2003, LNAI 2671, pp. 222-236, 2003.

The case-base is a reflection of the experiences that have occurred, but may not be as comprehensive as other knowledge resources such as manufacturers' manuals. Domain experts rely on these other resources to assist them in solving new problems. Our approach to case authoring does not start at the individual experience, but at the documents that contain domain knowledge. It would therefore be useful to develop a case-base in two steps. The first step is to build a generic, comprehensive case-base from technical documentation. In the second, continuing step the case-base grows incrementally with experiences of the organization that uses the CBR system. This approach eliminates the manual processing of previously documented experiences and allows the domain expert to focus their time on authoring cases from the anomalous ones. Finally, the effectiveness of a case can be determined from the historical statistics that have been compiled from past experiences.

This paper outlines the approach taken for authoring cases by using technical manuals and historical experience. This case authoring approach has been implemented within the context of a commercial airline's maintenance and repair facility. The paper establishes the viability of using technical manuals to create cases for a case-base to represent knowledge that is already documented for the aircraft. Also, we demonstrate that case enhancements such as historical statistics could affect the retrieval process from the case-base. The paper shows the results of creating the case-base from technical manuals and the validation of those cases with correlation with historical data. A specific example will be used to demonstrate the steps taken in this case authoring approach.

The paper proceeds as follows. The second section describes the background information for case authoring in CBR applications and the application domain of maintenance and repair. The third section outlines the approach of case authoring from structured documents or manuals. The fourth section describes the results of this approach and discusses issues related to applying this approach. The final section describes conclusions reached from the experimentation and desired future work.

2 Background

2.1 Case Authoring

Case authoring has been implemented with approaches that rely on interaction with the domain expert to handcraft cases. In the case of the aerospace maintenance domain—our domain of interest—several approaches have been sought. The first one used decision tree induction and expert interaction to construct cases for troubleshooting problems on jet engines [4]. Decision tree induction was used to determine relevant slots in the parametric data and use them in the retrieval of cases in the case-base. The textual information in the repair reports had valuable information for constructing cases, but had to be interpreted by the domain experts. The process of interpreting the textual information was time consuming. Further work resulted in the evaluation of the effectiveness of the case-base in their work in troubleshooting jet engines [5]. This helped in the development of a more precise case-base that resulted in more accurate retrieval. The second approach, which results in the *Integrated Di-*

agnostic System (*IDS*), used a custom designed case authoring tool [6]. Due to the limited time available for the domain experts to author cases, their manual approach resulted in a small case-base that was not used to its fullest potential within the maintenance organization. In order for a case authoring to be successful in a CBR application many constraints must be considered. Constraints such as access to domain experts and the time required to author cases are factors that need to be addressed when fielding a successful CBR application. In many maintenance organizations the access to domain experts is very limited and their time is very valuable. Therefore, a manually intensive case authoring approach is not the optimal solution in the maintenance domain.

Information Extraction (IE) has been successfully demonstrated in the construction of cases from the text in the area of court cases [2]. Information recorded in court case documents was extracted using Natural Language Processing (NLP) techniques to construct the case-base. Even though full understanding of the text is not achieved, IE is a useful technique in the identification of information in text and the development of more complex structures from the text. Therefore, IE can be used to process technical manuals to author cases. For instance, preprocessing of a priori knowledge from documentation can benefit the case authoring process. Case authoring approaches for plan creation found that manually eliciting knowledge from a textual doctrine is critical in establishing planning knowledge in case authoring [7].

2.2 Aerospace Maintenance and Repair Domain

Aircraft, cars, trucks, computers, and people have documentation written about them that allow a person to diagnose and repair problems that occur. Domain experts use this documentation to make timely decisions on what actions should be taken to resolve a problem. After the solution has been applied, the domain expert may record this experience in textual form for future reference. Domains such as aerospace and open-pit mining maintenance implement computer applications to track maintenance activities. Other domains such as the medical domain may use more traditional methods such as paper to achieve a similar functionality.

Aircraft are very complex systems with a variety of sensors, computers, and communication equipment. This makes the troubleshooting of aircraft difficult even with the onboard diagnostic capabilities and the extensive documentation developed and provided by the aircraft manufacturer. The diagnostic information and documentation is distributed over many different systems and is consulted before a diagnosis is made. It would be beneficial to automatically collect this information for the maintenance technician in order for them to make more timely accurate decisions.

The majority of knowledge about the aircraft is found in the aircraft's manuals written by the aircraft manufacturer (e.g. *Trouble Shooting Manual* (*TSM*), *Illustrated Parts Catalogue* (*IPC*)). Symptoms to problems related to the TSM are identified as *Fault Event Objects* (*FEOs*) within IDS and stored in a database [6]. Information related to the repair and maintenance of the aircraft is found in the *Aircraft Maintenance Tracking And Control* (*AMTAC*) recording system. The information from these four information resources are critical in documenting reoccurring experiences, which have good potential for cases in a case-base.

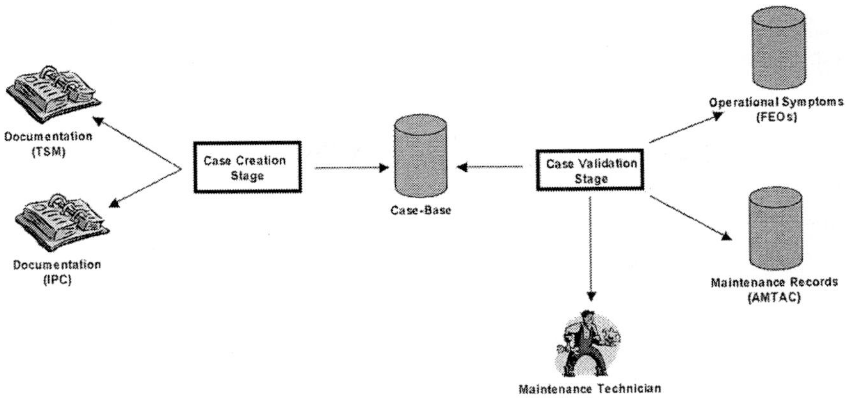

Fig. 1. Case Authoring Process using TSM and AMTAC

3 Case Authoring Approach

Figure 1 describes the overall process of case authoring from the TSM. Our case authoring approach uses readily available resources such as manuals, operational data, and repair data. This case authoring approach differs fundamentally from previous approaches by not considering individual experiences first. Our approach filters out previously documented experiences in the technical documentation and allows other case authoring approaches to concentrate on individual experiences that are undocumented. The first stage is to automatically create cases for the case-base from the manufacturer's documentation using IE techniques. The individual experiences are then used to update the cases within the case-base. This approach to case authoring captures the knowledge encoded in readily available resources and uses it as a starting point to gain further knowledge about the aircraft. This proposed approach to case authoring is a two-stage process: case creation and case validation.

3.1 Case Creation

The case structure used in this case authoring approach is the same as the one used in IDS [6]. The features used for case retrieval are related to the symptoms that describe a problem handled by the case. These symptoms are the automatically generated messages from the built-in test equipment onboard the aircraft. The case separates these symptoms into different aggregations according to textual similarity, time proximity, TSM reference, and human association grouping. The component and action taken on the component is stored in the case as the recommended solution. Additional information such as historical statistics and recorded incidents are also stored in the case. The historical statistics and recorded individual experiences are captured from the organization's historical data in the case validation stage. The case creation stage will focus on automatically extracting TSM reference symptoms for the case and extracting the actions and components used in the solution for the case using the TSM.

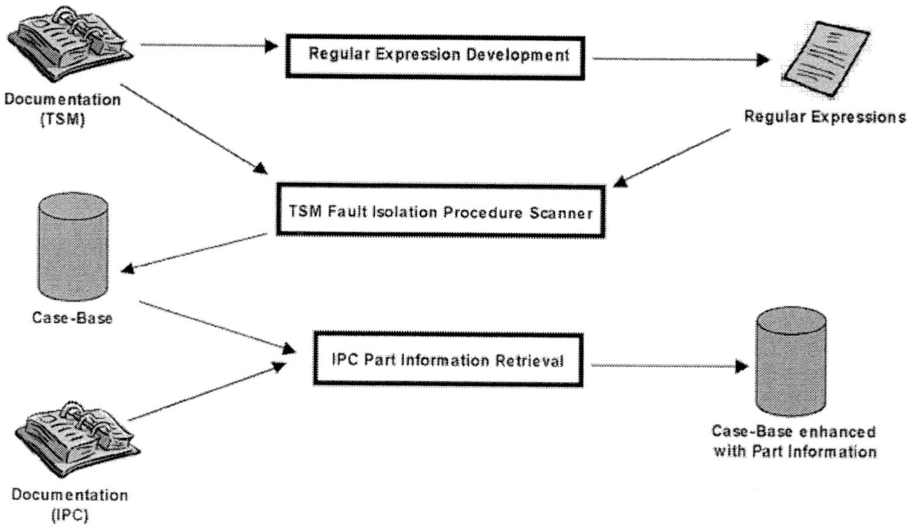

Fig. 2. Case Creation Stage

The case creation stage is the process of automatically extracting knowledge from the TSM in order to create a case-base for the maintenance organization. Identification of symptoms and recommended solutions is critical in the case creation stage. The first part of case creation is to identify the symptom sets for the cases. In IDS, a set of rules was extracted from the TSM [6]. The Left Hand Side (LHS) of these TSM rules describes symptom sets in the form of automatically generated diagnostic message information. These symptom sets described in the LHS of the rules become the TSM reference symptoms in the case. The recommended solution information for the case is found inside the fault isolation procedures described in the Right Hand Side (RHS) of these IDS rules. Using IE techniques, it is possible to extract action and component information from the text in the TSM and correlate it with the symptom set information to create cases.

Our initial approach to IE is very simple and is outlined in Figure 2. We scan the text inside TSM for occurrences of important actions, and extract the surrounding information. Scanning, at this early stage, is performed by regular expressions, which encode what we are looking for, and are matched against the text.

3.1.1 Regular Expression Development

Regular expressions were developed to extract the actions and components found within the TSM fault isolation procedure. After some manual analysis of the text in the fault isolation procedure, the verb 'replace' was identified as the most frequently used action. A set of regular expressions was developed using the most frequently referenced action 'replace'. Table 1 outlines the three expressions used. A text scanner uses these regular expressions to identify the components that are replaced in the TSM. Further regular expression development must be completed to cover other action words used in the solution.

Table 1. Regular Expressions used in the Case Creation from TSM

ID	Regular Expression	Application Frequency
1	/(replace) the (.*)/i.	10,608
2	/do a check of the (.*) and (replace) it/i.	26
3	/make sure that the (.*) is not clogged. If necessary, (replace) it/I	11

3.1.2 TSM Fault Isolation Procedure Scanner

The TSM Fault Isolation Procedure Scanner was developed to create the cases from the TSM. The TSM Fault Isolation Procedure Scanner uses both the IDS rule set and the TSM fault isolation procedures to create the case-base. Each individual IDS rule is processed by the TSM Fault Isolation Procedure Scanner for symptoms located in the LHS of the rule and the corresponding procedure on the RHS. The automatically generated diagnostic messages are extracted from the LHS and then used to create a template case. A template case is created because a symptom set can have more than one recommended solution. The corresponding procedure from the RHS is scanned using the TSM Fault Isolation Procedure Scanner with the regular expressions developed in the previous step. Once an action and component are identified within the TSM fault isolation procedure, a new case is duplicated from the template case. This new case has its component and action fields populated with the action and component information that was identified from the TSM fault isolation procedure. After the IDS rule set has been processed, a case-base is built from the IDS rule set and TSM documentation.

This case-base might be perceived as a duplication of the IDS rule set, but the case-base can be enhanced and updated with supplementary information. Further enhancements can be in the form of additional information gained from other manuals such as the IPC. Another form of enhancement is the recording of individual experiences that validate the case's usefulness. Once the case-base is enhanced with additional information, the cases contain more knowledge and information than the IDS rule set and can be updated easily. This up to date knowledge affects the way the cases are organized and retrieved and represents the current knowledge of the organization.

3.1.3 IPC Part Information Retrieval

The first enhancement of the TSM case-base helps identify components in the case validation stage. The IPC contains information about the specific part number and manufacturers. A correlation between components in the TSM and IPC are established through a code called the *Functional Item Number* (*FIN*). Not all components in the TSM case-base have a FIN number associated with them. If a FIN code is found, it is used to identify IPC part number and manufacturer information and add this component information to the correlated TSM case. Since the identification of components in the AMTAC reports, which will be needed during the case-validation stage (see below), is difficult, any additional part information could be useful in this identification process. The resulting TSM case-base is ready to be validated with related individual historical experiences.

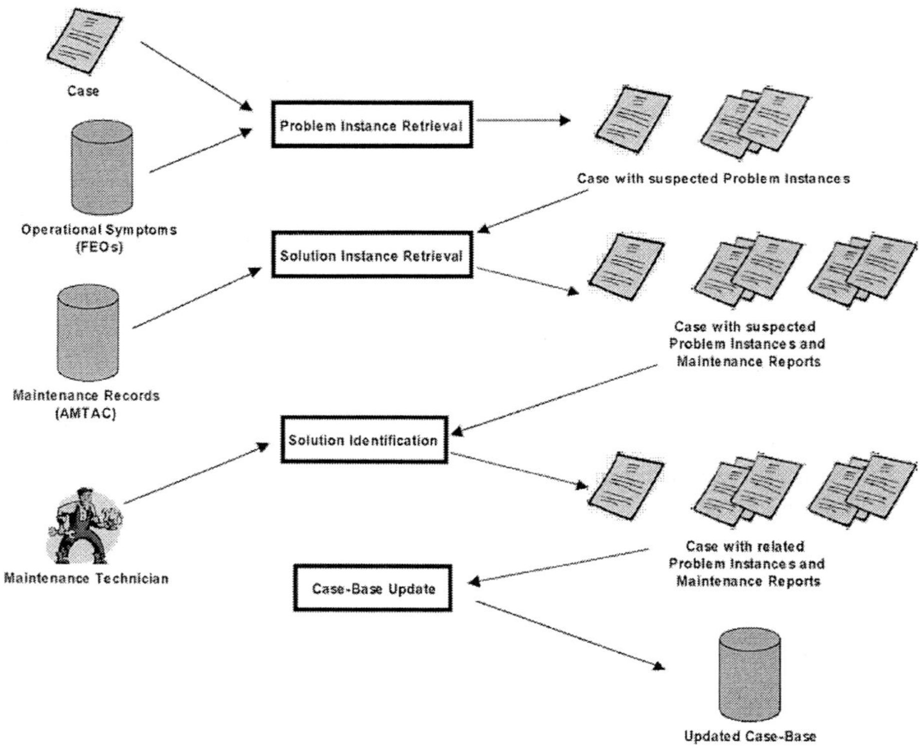

Fig. 3. Case Validation Stage

3.2 Case Validation

The case validation stage is the process that further enhances the case-base by capturing the organization's maintenance history inside the case-base. Even though a large set of cases may have been extracted from the TSM, the aircraft may not have generated all the problem symptoms described by the TSM. For case-base performance, it is desired to minimize the number of cases, but still achieve the same amount of coverage [8]. Since the TSM contains comprehensive information about problems on board the aircraft, an analysis of the aircraft's maintenance history can help reorganize the cases used in the case-base created from the TSM. This reorganization can be done in a hierarchy of cache memory where the most referenced cases are retrieved first before ones that have never been referenced. This applicability metric is established by validating the cases with historical experience. The case validation stage of case authoring can be broken down into four parts: problem instance retrieval, solution instance retrieval, case solution identification, and case-base update. The steps involved in the case validation stage are outlined in Figure 3.

3.2.1 Problem Instance Retrieval

Problem Instance Retrieval uses the symptom set from the case to identify instances of problems that occur in the operation of the aircraft. First, an arbitrary case is retrieved from the case-base to initiate the validation process. Cases describe symptom sets. The symptom sets are used to identify FEO problem instances created by IDS. The FEO database is searched to obtain FEO problem instances related to a specific case. If no FEO problem instances were found then the case would not have been retrieved at any time during the aircrafts' recorded history. Cases record their associated FEO information for later processing. This FEO information includes the aircraft identification and the period of time when the symptoms occurred. Once the FEOs have been retrieved from the FEO database, they are clustered with respect to aircraft identity and time. Two FEOs that happen on the same aircraft within a 24-hour period of each other are considered to be the same problem to eliminate problems that are sporadic in nature. The result at the end of the problem instance retrieval process is a correlation between a case and suspected problem instances where this case could have potentially been applied.

3.2.2 Solution Instance Retrieval

The problem instances retrieved in the Problem Instance Retrieval step contain the aircraft's identity and the period of time when the problem occurred. This information is used to construct a query that will retrieve all the repair documentation for the aircraft during the time of the problem. The repair documentation is in the form of AMTAC reports that are stored in the AMTAC database. The Solution Instance Retrieval process uses the AMTAC database to retrieve suspected AMTAC reports that happened during the time of the problem instance. The query results in a collection of AMTAC reports related to a specific aircraft for the problem instance's period of time. Five fields in the AMTAC report establish its relevance to the problem instance: problem description, solution description, parts installed/removed, and temporal information. These suspected AMTAC reports are correlated to their respective problem instances. Since not all the retrieved AMTAC reports are related to the problem instance, the next step established the relevancy of each of the AMTAC reports to the problem instance.

3.2.3 Case Solution Identification

Case Solution Identification reduces the collection of suspected AMTAC reports to those related to the problem instance. The symptoms, solution, and part information stored in the case is used to establish its relevancy. The first step was to compare the AMTAC part information to the IPC part information stored in the case. The information in the parts removed/installed fields of the AMTAC report helps establish the component replacement with confidence, but this field is not always filled in. Therefore, other fields in the AMTAC report must be processed in order to determine the component and action taken in the solution. The text from the AMTAC report was searched for the words established in the criteria for AMTAC report applicability. The text in these fields was processed using a Bag of Words (BOW) approach to determine similarity to the case's word criteria [9]. A BOW approach was used to determine the existence of terms used in both AMTAC report and the case's word criteria.

In order to improve the accuracy of this second step, a stop list of words was manually created. This stop list contains frequently occurring words such as 'FAULT' and 'MSG'. The presence of a stop word is disregarded unless a nonstop word is present. Automatic processing of the AMTAC reports identifies the AMTAC report(s) that are relevant to the case's suspected problem instances. A final evaluation from the maintenance technician assures that the AMTAC messages are related to the problem instance. This manual evaluation consists of the maintenance technician making a binary decision on whether the solution was applicable or not. After the case solution identification is completed, the case's problem instances contains correlated TSM fault isolation procedures to related AMTAC reports and these problem instances can be used to update the case-base.

3.2.4 Case-Base Update

The case-base update implements a strategy for evaluating the effectiveness of the case solution with respect to the case's problem instances. Each of the case's problem instances contains the solution recommended by the case. The related AMTAC report is used to establish the date and time for the repair. If the repair occurred after the presence of symptoms for the case disappeared then the repair was successful. If not then the repair was unsuccessful. The result of this evaluation is used to update the information inside the case. The case is updated in two ways. The first is the AMTAC report identifier and the results of the repair are added as additional information to the case. The second is the statistical information regarding the result of the application of the case is updated by adding one to the applicable success or failure count. Once the case information is complete, the case is modified in the case-base to reflect these historical experiences.

This semi-automated case authoring approach results in a case-base that is constructed from the TSM manual with enhancements from other manuals and historical experiences. The approach facilitates constructing a case-base from scratch or modifying an existing case-base to reflect changes in the aircraft's documentation. When an update to the TSM is issued, our approach is reapplied to update the existing case-base. Also, this method can be used as a complimentary approach to the other case authoring approaches implemented in IDS. A case-base can be created using this case authoring approach and can later be extended with the Automated Case Creation System in IDS [10]. This method eliminates problems that have solutions in the technical documentation and gives a computationally intensive focus on the undocumented problems that occur on the aircraft.

4 Results and Discussion

The case authoring approach was used to create a case-base for the Airbus A320/A319 aircraft. The latest TSM and IPC manuals were used in the case creation stage. Over six years of historical data from the AMTAC reporting system was used in the case validation stage. This approach resulted in a case-base that could be used by an airline's maintenance technician in IDS. We show three results: two from the stages in the approach and an example using a specific TSM fault isolation procedure.

Table 2. Distribution of Experience with respect to TSM Case Coverage

Case Symptoms Frequency	Number of Cases
0	10085 (81.01%)
> 0 and < 100	1859 (14.97%)
>=100 and < 1000	404 (3.25%)
>=1000	95 (0.77%)
Only ~19% of Case Symptoms have Frequency > 0	

4.1 Case Creation Results

The case creation stage resulted in a case-base from the TSM and IPC with over 10,000 cases. The distribution of the three regular expression frequencies can be seen previously in Table 1. The most frequent applied regular expression was the regular expression '(replace) the *.' with 10,608 occurrences. The other two regular expressions are specialized for specific situations. These regular expressions capture a large number of cases from the TSM, but this scanning approach does not provide complete coverage for extracting cases represented in the TSM. The word 'replace' has 15, 013 occurrences in the TSM, in which 4,332 are not captured using these regular expressions. These specialized instances are outlier situations and additional regular expressions should be developed.

Other regularly used action terms should have similar regular expressions developed for them. This regular expression implementation for IE would quickly become unmanageable and too specialized for the problem domain. A better approach using IE would be to implement an NLP parser to provide more robustness and broader coverage when parsing the TSM. An investigation into the development of a semantic grammar was initiated and the discussion around this investigation is in the future work section.

4.2 Case Validation Results

The results from the case validation stage describe the distribution of the case symptoms with respect to the problems experienced by the maintenance organization. One issue is to determine what amount of the TSM is used in the everyday troubleshooting of aircraft. Table 2 displays the distribution of the number of problem symptom set occurrences with respect to the number of cases with that occurrence. Table 2 shows that a majority of the cases represented by the TSM have never occurred and these cases make up 81% of the case-base. The cases that have their symptoms present in the operational data of the maintenance organization are fewer than 19%. Further investigation is needed to confirm if these cases were actually applied. This result is not surprising because the TSM should possess more comprehensive knowledge than what is experienced in the maintenance organization. Some of these unused cases may be more applicable in different situations, for instance when the aircraft gets older and these constraints must be taken into consideration in case retrieval.

The second result from the case validation stage is the identification of frequently occurring problems on the aircraft. Out of the 19% of cases that have operational experience, 4% of those have symptoms that occur more than a thousand times in a six year period. One could quickly construct a list of problems that have occurred frequently in the past and document these problems for future reference. Also, maintenance technicians and data mining can better focus investigative efforts by using this list of frequently occurring problems. Finally, if no extensive domain expertise exists, this list could be used as a benchmark for the maintenance organization.

Table 3. Results of Cases after Case Validation Stage

Symptoms	Action	Component	Success	Failure
"AFS BSCU2"	Remove/Install	FMGC-1 (1CA1)	1	0
"AFS BSCU2"	Remove/Install	BSCU (10GG)	11	5
"AFS BSCU2"	Remove/Install	FMGC-2 (1CA2)	2	0

4.3 Example

This section presents a detailed example of the extraction procedure. The TSM fault isolation procedure 22-83-00-810-849 is used to demonstrate the viability of our case authoring approach. According to the IDS rule set, this fault isolation procedure must be applied whenever the aircraft generates the failure message "AFS BSCU2". Below is sample text from the fault isolation procedure where the actions and components are highlighted by the applicable regular expression patterns.

A. If the test gives the maintenance message AFS: BSCU2 (ISSUED BY: FG1):
- **replace** the **FMGC-1 (1CA1)**
  AMM TASK 22-83-34-000-001 and AMM TASK 22-83-34-400-001 .
  1. If the fault continues:
     - **replace** the **BSCU (10GG)**
       AMM TASK 32-42-34-000-001 and AMM TASK 32-42-34-400-001.
  2. If the fault continues:
     - do a check and repair the wiring of the BSCU OPP VALID COM and BSCU OPP VALID MON discretes (from the FMGC 1 (1CA1) to the BSCU (10GG)) ASM 22-85/04 .

B. If the test gives the maintenance message AFS: BSCU2 (ISSUED BY: FG2):
- **replace** the **FMGC-2 (1CA2)**

Table 3 displays the three cases that were extracted from the fault isolation procedure 22-83-00-810-849 after the completion of the case extraction process. The symptoms for these cases were used to retrieve 931 problem instances from the FEO database. The problem instance information was used to retrieve 2990 AMTAC reports from the AMTAC database. The case validation stage identified 19 of these AMTAC messages as solutions to 19 problem instances. Table 3 outlines the results after each of the 19 solutions were evaluated against the occurrence of its related problem instance. Even though replacement of the FMGC-2 is referenced after the other two cases in the text, the structure of the troubleshooting logic suggests that this solution occur at the same level as the replacement of the FMGC-1. The maintenance message that results from the test differentiates between the two different troubleshooting paths and any historical statistics recorded from these cases would indicate the troubleshooting path frequency. Currently, the troubleshooting logic recommends the replacement of the FMGC-1 before the replacement of the BSCU, but our case authoring approach uncovers that this historically does not happen. We were thus expecting to see 16 unsuccessful replacements of the FMGC-1, but the results show no unsuccessful applications of that case. Therefore, there must be additional knowledge besides the manuals that the maintenance organization uses to make decisions. This additional information is not reflected within the IDS rule set, but it can be captured in the case-base. The historical statistics on the past applications of a case is additional information that can be used by the maintenance organization to help make decisions on current problems.

Confidence and support measures for association rules were used to reevaluate the ranking of the results in Table 3 [11]. The confidence measure for the cases with replacement of FMGC-1 and FMGC-2 is 100% and better than the case with BSCU replacement, 68.75%. Nonetheless, we should also consider the frequency with which each case occurs. The frequency is reflected in the support measure, which is of 78.57% in the BSCU replacement case, 7.15% in the FMGC-1 and 14.28% in the FMGC-2 cases. We combine confidence and support into an F-like measure and the values are 73.33%, 13.33%, and 25% for the BSCU, FMGC-1, and FMGC-2. This F-like measure suggests that BSCU replacement should be ranked higher than the other two cases, despite its lower confidence. This historical information was influential in the results of the retrieval process by ranking the cases differently than recommended by the TSM. Our case authoring approach compiles statistics on the applicability of the case and adjusts the ranking of similar cases accordingly. Ultimately, the maintenance technician makes the decision once all the information for the problem is evaluated.

The coverage of the solutions with respect to the total number of problem instances is very low and is less than we anticipated. Despite the small coverage, the solutions give a better idea of how the manuals are used in everyday operation. This allows the maintenance organization to focus their attention on the problem instances where the solutions are unknown. In the results, problem symptoms were present and then disappeared without any solution from the TSM been recorded. This can be explained in different ways, but two possibilities have been identified. The first possibility is the problem was resolved as a result of an additional test outlined in the TSM. An example of this is a case where a computer was reset the symptoms were subsequently tested for persistence and the repair action information recorded in the AMTAC report was "CHECKED OK". The second possibility is that there may exist relationships between components and symptoms that have not been documented. For instance, a set of symptoms may disappear because an unrelated component has been replaced. Given the complexity of the equipment and the close relationships between components, this possibility is realistic. These unresolved problem instances, identified by the case authoring approach, could be used as training data for other knowledge discovery techniques to discover new undocumented relationships among different aircraft components. It is unclear and not the purpose of this paper to determine what percentage of cases is related to the two different possibilities.

5 Conclusion and Future Work

The extraction of knowledge from text documents for case authoring is a relatively new idea. Brüninghaus and Ashley [2] were the first authors to discuss it, but they do not address the automation of the process of the creating and validating the cases from textual documentation (ie. manuals). We have developed this semi-automated process using the knowledge encoded in the manufacturer's documentation supplemented with historical experiences from day to day operation. By gaining a better understanding of what is represented in the manufacturer's manual, the domain experts can focus their efforts on the unknown problems. In this paper, we described our experience with authoring cases from the manufacturer's manuals and historical experience. We also present some insights for continued work on the case authoring process using textual documentation and argue in favour of integration of this approach with other knowledge discovery approaches.

Future work can be divided into two different areas: further development of the case-base authoring process using manufacturer's documentation and integration with other knowledge acquisition processes. Better coverage for extracting cases from the TSM could be achieved by the development of a semantic grammar to parse the fault isolation procedures in the TSM. This tool would be useful to further determine the relevance between a subset of cases, as more information becomes available for the problem instance. We performed an initial investigation into the use of a semantic grammar for the TSM fault isolation procedure starting with a randomly chosen fault isolation procedure from the TSM. A lexicon and semantic grammar rules were developed to parse this fault isolation procedure. This new TSM Fault Isolation Procedure parser successfully generated parse trees for 49 out of 50 sentences in the procedure. The parse trees were then converted into cases. A grammar developed for a single fault isolation procedure is unlikely to cover the entire TSM well, and so a more comprehensive lexicon and rule set would need to be developed for the semantic parser to be substantially useful. The resulting semantic grammar is not only useful in parsing TSM fault isolation procedures, but could potentially be used in parsing the AMTAC reports in the case validation stage. Even though the text in the AMTAC reports is cryptic, the dictionary developed for the semantic grammar could be useful in determining the word usage in the AMTAC reports.

Other future work is centered on the integration with other knowledge acquisition systems. This strategy is important to demonstrate the complimentary nature of this case authoring approach to other knowledge acquisition approaches. One possible area of integration for the case-base created from the manufacturer's manuals is with other Knowledge Discovery in Database (KDD) approaches. Once a case-base has been created from the manuals and enhanced with operational experience, this knowledge could become valuable information for other knowledge discovery processes like KDD. KDD has been applied to the aerospace domain and one of the issues is the appropriate use of background knowledge during the different phases of data preprocessing and data analysis [12]. A process for automatically labeling instances is required to successfully field a KDD application. A potential source for automatically labeled instances can be from the case-base created using our case authoring approach. These instances may be useful in determining the models that are created in the data analysis phase. Therefore, further investigation into the TSM case-base being used as training data for building component failure models in aircraft is outlined as a future direction.

Organizations are developing processes to foster knowledge-based activities. The role of a knowledge worker is critical for today's successful organizations [13]. Until recently, knowledge has not been considered as a capital resource, but this intellectual capital has become a very valuable asset within an organization lately [14]. There is no process for directly measuring intellectual capital in an organization, but AI technologies can be used to represent and share knowledge within organizations. This knowledge acquisition and distribution process is demonstrated with the case authoring process using knowledge from textual documents and historical experiences.

Acknowledgments

We would like to thank the people at the National Research Council of Canada for their support, discussion, and valuable assistance. Also, we are grateful to Air Canada for providing us the technical manuals, aircraft fleet maintenance data, and domain expertise. Second and third authors acknowledge the support of the Natural Sciences and Engineering Research Council of Canada.

References

[1] Aha, D. (1998). The Omnipresence of Case-Based Reasoning in Science and Application. Knowledge-Based Systems, 11(5-6), 261-273.

[2] Brüninghaus, S. & Ashley, K. (2001). The Role of Information Extraction for Textual CBR. Proceedings of 4th International Conference on Case-Based Reasoning (ICCBR-01). Vancouver, Canada, July 30 – August 2 2001.

[3] Bartsch-Spörl, B., Lenz, M., Hübner, A. (1999). Case-Based Reasoning – Survey and Future Directions. In the Proceedings of the Fifth Biannual German Conference on Knowledge-Based Systems (XPS), Würtzburg, Germany, March 3-5, 1999.

[4] Heider, R. (1995), Troubleshooting CFM-56-3 Engines for the Boeing 737 - Using CBR and Data Mining. In the Proceedings of the Third European Workshop, EWCBR-96, Advances in Case-Based Reasoning, Lausanne, Switzerland, November 14-16, 1996, pp512-518.

[5] Heider, R. Auriol, E. Tartarin, E. Manago, M. (1997). Improving the Quality of Case Bases for Building Better Decision Support Systems. Proceedings of the 5th German Workshop on Case-Based Reasoning (GWCBR'97), Bad Honnef, March 4-5 1997, p.85

[6] Wylie, R., Orchard,R., Halasz, M., Dubé, F. (1997). IDS: Improving Aircraft Fleet Maintenance. Proceedings of the 14th National Conference on Aritificial Intelligence and Innovative Applications of Artificial Intelligence (IAAI-97), Providence, Rhode Island.: pp. 1078-1085. July 27-31, 1997.

[7] Aha, D.W., Breslow, L.A., & Muñoz-Avila, H. (2001). Conversational case-based reasoning. Applied Intelligence, 14, 9-32.

[8] Lenz, M., Bartsch-Spörl, B., Burkhard, H., Wess, S. (1998). Case-Based Reasoning Technology: From Foundations to Applications. Berlin, Springer.

[9] Craven, M., DiPasquo, D., Freitag, D., McCallum, A., Mitchell, T., Nigam, K., Slattery, S. (1998). Learning to Extract Symbolic Knowledge from the World Wide Web. In the Proceedings of the 15th National Conference on Artificial Intelligence (AAAI-98), Madison, WI, July 26 – 30, 1998.

[10] Yang, C., Orchard, R., Farley, B., Zaluski, M. (2002). Automated Case Base Creation and Management. To appear in the 16th International Conference on Industrial and Engineering Applications of Artificial Intelligence and Expert Systems (IEA/AIE 2003), Loughborough, UK, June 23-26, 2003.

[11] Witten, I. and Frank, E. (2000). Data Mining: Practical Machine Learning Tools and Techniques with Java Implementations. Morgan Kaufmann Publishers, New York.

[12] Létourneau, S., Famili, F, and Matwin, S. (1997). Discovering Useful Knowledge from Aircraft Operation/Maintenance Data. In the Proceedings of the workshop on Machine Learning Applications in the Real World, 14th International Conference on Machine Learning, Nashville, TN, July 8-12, 1997.

[13] Drucker, P. (2001). The Essential Drucker: In One Volume the Best of Sixty Years of Peter Druckers's Essential Writings on Management. New York, Harper Collins.

[14] Stewart, T. (2001). The Wealth of Knowledge: Intellectual Capital and the Twenty-first Century Organization. New York, Doubleday.

Session Boundary Detection for Association Rule Learning Using n-Gram Language Models

Xiangji Huang[1], Fuchun Peng[1], Aijun An[2], Dale Schuurmans[1], and Nick Cercone[3]

[1] School of Computer Science, University of Waterloo
Waterloo, Ontario N2L 3G1 Canada
{jhuang,f3peng,dale}@cs.uwaterloo.ca

[2] Department of Computer Science, York University
Toronto, Ontario M3J 1P3 Canada
aan@cs.yorku.ca

[3] Faculty of Computer Science, Dalhousie University
Halifax, Nova Scotia B3H 1W5 Canada
nick@cs.dal.ca

Abstract. We present a statistical method using n-gram language models to identify session boundaries in a large collection of *Livelink* log data. The identified sessions are then used for association rule learning. Unlike the traditional ad hoc *timeout* method, which uses fixed time thresholds for session identification, our method uses an information theoretic approach that provides a natural technique for performing dynamic session identification. The effectiveness of our approach is evaluated with respect to 4 different interestingness measures. We find that we obtain a significant improvement in each interestingness measure, ranging from a 26.6% to 39% improvement on average over the best results obtained with standard timeout methods.

1 Introduction

The rapidly expanding Web contains a vast amount of data that incorporates useful information waiting to be discovered. Web usage mining is a recently established field that focuses on developing techniques for discovering usage patterns in Web log data, to better serve the needs of Web-based applications. One important Web usage mining problem is to learn interesting association rules from Web logs. Such rules can be used for reorganizing Web sites and making recommendations to facilitate users' browsing activities. However, association rules cannot be conveniently inferred from log entries directly, because these logs usually contain a large amount of irrelevant information and noise. Therefore, to facilitate association rule learning, log entries are usually first grouped into sessions that are defined as a group of user activities related to a common purpose. In this way, session boundary detection forms a useful preprocessing step that itself poses an interesting challenge in Web usage mining.

Y. Xiang and B. Chaib-draa (Eds.): AI 2003, LNAI 2671, pp. 237–251, 2003.

The goal of session identification is to divide a given sequence of page accesses into individual user sessions. The most commonly used session identification method is *Time Out*. Here, a user session is usually defined as a sequence of requests from the same IP address such that no two consecutive requests are separated by an interval more than a predefined threshold. In [7], experiments were conducted on two sets of Web logs: requests logs and Excite (http://www.excite.com). The requests logs from Reuters (Reuters Ltd.) contain searches on a local version of AltaVista (http://www.altavista.com). In these experiments, the session logs were initially cut with a large session interval, which was then gradually decreased while the distribution of session lengths was concurrently recorded. Based on these experiments, the authors concluded that a time range of 10 to 15 minutes was an optimal session interval length. [6] also reports the results of an experiment where a Web browser was modified to record the time interval between user actions on the browser's interface. One result was that the average time interval between each user event was 9.3 minutes, and that 25.5 minutes was subsequently recommended as the threshold for session identification. This amounts to an assumption that most statistically significant events occurred within 1.5 standard deviations (25.5 minutes) from the mean. However, the optimal *timeout* threshold depends on the specific problem. Once a site log has been analyzed and its usage statistics obtained, a timeout that is appropriate for the specific Web site can be fed back into the session identification algorithm. Despite the application dependence of the optimal interval length, most commercial products use 30 minutes as a default timeout.

Obviously, a fixed *timeout* strategy is problematic, because users do not normally take a fixed amount of time (i.e. exactly 10 minutes or 30 minutes) for different purposes purpose. People may stay on one topic for several hours or jump to anther topic immediately. Instead of using a fixed time threshold for detecting session boundaries, we propose a new method for dynamically identifying session boundaries. In this paper, we present a method based on statistical n-gram language modeling that addresses the problem of session boundary detection. Our method is based on information theory and provides a natural mechanism for performing dynamic session boundary detection. We present experimental results on a real world dataset which demonstrates its superiority over the traditional *timeout* method.

The remainder of the paper is organized as follows. Section 2 provides a brief description of n-gram language modeling. We then describe how n-gram language models can provide a natural method for identifying session boundaries in Section 3. Third, we describe our method for mining interesting association rules from session data that has already been segmented (Section 4). The rules that are discovered will be used to evaluate our approach. We then present experimental results that demonstrate the effectiveness of our language modeling session detection technique in Section 5. Finally, we conclude in Section 6.

2 n-Gram Language Modeling

Traditionally, the dominant motivation for language modeling has come from speech recognition. However statistical language models have recently become more widely used in many other application areas, including information retrieval [8, 10, 12], text classification [11], and now we are applying it to Web mining in this paper.

The goal of language modeling is to predict the probability of natural word sequences, or more simply, to put high probability on word sequences that actually occur (and low probability on word sequences that never occur). Given a word sequence $w_1 w_2 ... w_N$ to be used as a test corpus, the quality of a language model can be measured by the empirical perplexity and entropy scores on this corpus [3]

$$Perplexity = \sqrt[N]{\prod_{i=1}^{N} \frac{1}{Pr(w_i|w_1...w_{i-1})}}$$
$$Entropy = \log_2 Perplexity$$

The goal is to obtain small values of these measures.

The simplest and most successful basis for language modeling is the n-gram model. Note that by the chain rule of probability we can write the probability of any word sequence as

$$Pr(w_1 w_2 ... w_N) = \prod_{i=1}^{N} Pr(w_i|w_1...w_{i-1}) \tag{1}$$

An n-gram model approximates this probability by assuming that the only words relevant to predicting $Pr(w_i|w_1...w_{i-1})$ are the previous $n-1$ words; that is, it assumes

$$Pr(w_i|w_1...w_{i-1}) = Pr(w_i|w_{i-n+1}...w_{i-1})$$

A straightforward maximum likelihood estimate of n-gram probabilities from a corpus is given by the observed frequency

$$Pr(w_i|w_{i-n+1}...w_{i-1}) = \frac{\#(w_{i-n+1}...w_i)}{\#(w_{i-n+1}...w_{i-1})} \tag{2}$$

where $\#(.)$ is the number of occurrences of a specified gram in the training corpus. Although one could attempt to use these simple n-gram models to capture long range dependencies in language, attempting to do so directly immediately creates sparse data problems. Using grams of length up to n entails estimating the probability of W^n events, where W is the size of the word vocabulary. This quickly overwhelms modern computational and data resources for even modest choices of n (beyond 3 to 6). Also, because of the heavy tailed nature of language (i.e. Zipf's law) one is likely to encounter novel n-grams that were never witnessed during training in any test corpus, and therefore some mechanism for assigning non-zero probability to novel n-grams is a central and unavoidable issue in statistical language modeling. One standard approach to smoothing probability estimates to cope with sparse data problems (and to cope with potentially missing n-grams) is to use some sort of back-off estimator.

$$Pr(w_i|w_{i-n+1}...w_{i-1}) = \begin{cases} \hat{Pr}(w_i|w_{i-n+1}...w_{i-1}), \\ \qquad \text{if } \#(w_{i-n+1}...w_i) > 0 \\ \beta(w_{i-n+1}...w_{i-1}) \times Pr(w_i|w_{i-n+2}...w_{i-1}), \\ \qquad \text{otherwise} \end{cases} \tag{3}$$

where

$$\hat{Pr}(w_i|w_{i-n+1}...w_{i-1}) = \frac{disc\,\#(w_{i-n+1}...w_i)}{\#(w_{i-n+1}...w_{i-1})} \tag{4}$$

is the discounted probability and $\beta(w_{i-n+1}...w_{i-1})$ is a normalization constant calculated to be

$$\beta(w_{i-n+1}...w_{i-1}) = \frac{1 - \sum_{x \in (w_{i-n+1}...w_{i-1}x)} \hat{Pr}(x|w_{i-n+1}...w_{i-1})}{1 - \sum_{x \in (w_{i-n+1}...w_{i-1}x)} \hat{Pr}(x|w_{i-n+2}...w_{i-1})} \tag{5}$$

The discounted probability (4) could be computed using different smoothing approaches including linear smoothing, absolute smoothing, Good-Turing smoothing and Witten-Bell smoothing [5]. In our experiments, we only used Good-Turing smoothing for a preliminary study, although investigating the effects of different smoothing techniques remains an interesting problem.

3 Session Detection Using n-Gram Language Models

Although the original motivation of language modeling is to estimate the probability of naturally occurring word sequences, language modeling actually provides a general strategy for estimating the probability of *any* sequence—regardless of whether the basic units consist of words, characters, or any other arbitrary alphabet. In this sense, many problems can be formulated as a language modeling problem. In Web usage mining, Web pages (or objects) are visited sequentially in a particular order, similar to the word sequences that occur in a natural language. If we consider each visited object as a basic unit, like a word or character in natural language, we can then attempt to estimate the probability of object sequences using the same language modeling tools described above.

The basic goal of session identification is to group sequential log entries that are related to a common topic, and segment log entries that are unrelated. Language modeling provides a simple, natural approach to segmenting these log sequences. Imagine a set of objects on a common topic that are frequently visited one after another. In this case, the entropy (or perplexity) of the sequence is low. However, when a new object is observed in the sequence that is not relevant to the original topic (but in fact indicates a shift to a new topic), the introduction of this new object causes an increase in the entropy of the sequence because it is rarely visited after the preceding objects. Such an entropy increase serves as a natural signal for session boundary detection. If the change in entropy passes a threshold, a session boundary could be placed before the new object. In other words, the uncertainty (which is measured by entropy) within a session should be roughly constant, allowing for a fixed level of variability within a topic. However, whenever the entropy increases beyond a threshold, this presents a clear signal that the user's activity has changed to another topic. Thus, we should set a session boundary at the place where the entropy changes. The threshold on the entropy change can be tuned to adjust the number of sessions generated. A general principle for setting the threshold is to generate the number of sessions whose average length is in a reasonable range (say, 30 objects). However, more principled ways for setting the threshold could be investigated.

Figure 1 shows the entropy sequence we obtained in our Web log dataset. As one can see, the entropy changes radically at some points, although it remains stable in other places. This figure gives an intuition how entropy could be used for session boundary detection.

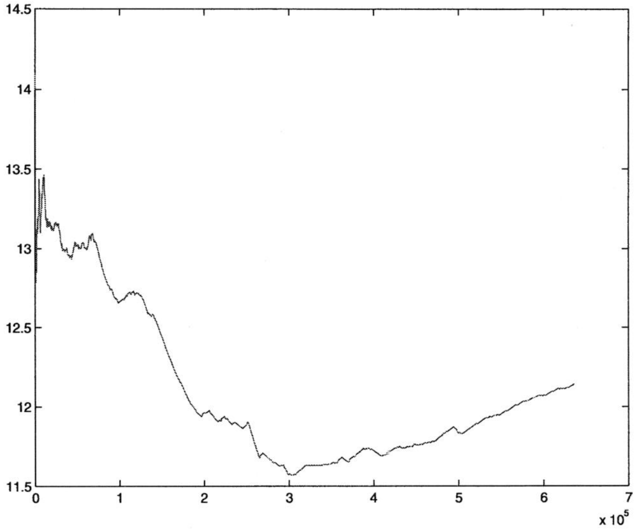

Fig. 1. Entropy evolution in our Web log dataset

Table 1. Number of generated association rules (confidence threshold = 0.5)

Support threshold	0.02	0.01	0.008	0.005	0.003	0.0028	0.0025	0.002	0.001
Number of assoc. rules	2	14	39	88	723	4,556	74,565	4,800,070	>1,000,000,000

4 Mining Interesting Association Rules

We implemented the Apriori algorithm [1] to learn association rules from the pre-segmented Web log data. We then used these discovered association rules to evaluate the quality of our session detection method. As in previous research on Web usage mining, the set of pages to be considered are first identified from all log entries, and then a session file is built upon the identified pages. In our experiments, we initially identified all of the pages involved in the Livelink log files provided to us. Since almost all of the pages in Livelink are actually dynamic, the number of individual pages is huge[1]. However, the problem is not in the number of pages, but in the usefulness of dynamic pages. When we analyzed the discovered patterns that describe access relationships among pages, we found that many of those patterns reveal the *programming patterns* within Livelink. For example, two pages can be found to be always accessed together because one a frame within the other, as defined by the Livelink program. Such patterns were not considered to be interesting by our domain experts. Another feature of this data is that there could be great similarity in the contents of different dynamic pages. That is, in our data two dynamic pages might be considered different, even though they contain the same set of information objects. In order to discover truly interesting and unexpected patterns, we first performed an object identification pass over the dynamic pages captured in the data, and then built the session file based on the objects and not the dynamic pages themselves.

The discovered association rules describe the association relationships between the information objects. For example, an association rule

$$\langle o1, o2, o3\rangle \rightarrow \langle o4, o5\rangle \ [support = 0.01 \ confidence = 0.6]$$

means that 1% of the sessions contain objects $o1, o2, o3, o4$ and $o5$, and that 60% of the sessions containing $o1, o2$ and $o3$ also contain $o4$ and $o5$. The number of association rules that are discovered depends on the *support* and *confidence* thresholds. For our dataset, we found that the number of rules generated is not significantly affected by changing the confidence threshold. However, changing the support threshold affects the number of retrieved rules substantially. Table 1 shows how the number of rules varies with the support threshold. From this table, one can see that a large number of rules can be discovered if the support threshold is set very low. For evaluation purposes, to find interesting rules from a large number of discovered patterns, we rank the discovered rules according to their interestingness measures and prune out redundant rules based on the structural relationship among rules.

[1] We identified nearly 200,000 pages from the two-month data.

We considered four interestingness measures for the purpose of evaluating our new session detection method. These measures were used to measure the interestingness of an association rule $A \rightarrow B$ [2], as shown below. Using support and confidence to measure the interestingness of a discovered rule is straightforward. However, no interesting rules have been found in our experiments by using support as the interestingness measure. So we choose the confidence as one of interestingness methods for evaluation. The reason why we choose the measures IS, MD and $C2$ is that they are among the best interestingness measures according to our earlier work in [9].

1. $C2$ [4]. The C2 formula measures the agreement between A and B. It has been evaluated as a good rule quality measure for learning classification rules [2]. It can be defined as

$$C2 = \frac{P(B|A) - P(B)}{1 - P(B)} \times \frac{1 + P(A|B)}{2}.$$

2. *Confidence (CS).* The confidence of a rule or pattern can be expressed as $P(B|A)$. For association rules, $P(B|A)$ means the probability that objects in B occur in a session conditioned on the occurrence of objects in A. With this measure, rules are ranked according to their confidence value as the main key and their support value as the secondary key. Therefore, this measure is denoted as CS.
3. IS [13]. Derived from statistical correlation, the IS measure is defined as

$$IS = \sqrt{\frac{P(AB)P(AB)}{P(A)P(B)}}.$$

   IS is designed to be better suitable for the scenario in which the support value of the rule is low.
4. *Measure of Discrimination* (MD) [2]. The MD measure was inspired by a query term weighting formula used in information retrieval and has been used to measure the quality of classification rules [2]. We adopt the formula to measure the extent to which an association rule $A \rightarrow B$ can discriminate between B and $\overline{B}$:

$$MD = \log \frac{P(A|B)(1 - P(A|\overline{B}))}{P(A|\overline{B})(1 - P(A|B))}.$$

All the above-listed measures except MD and $C2$ have been used to measure the interestingness of association rules. MD and $C2$ have only been used to measure classification rules. The values from the *MD and C2* measures can be zero or negative, indicating A and B are not correlated or they are negatively correlated, respectively. In our learning programs, rules with this kind of interestingness values are considered uninteresting and are pruned.

[2] In association rule $A \rightarrow B$, A and B are sets of objects.

The use of an interestingness measure can help identify interesting association rules by ranking the discovered rules according to the measure. However, it cannot be used to identify redundant rules. By redundant rules we mean that the same semantic information is captured by multiple rules and hence some of them are considered redundant. We use four pruning methods proposed in [9] for pruning redundant association rules (details omitted here).

5 Empirical Evaluation

We now empirically evaluate the effectiveness of our language modeling based session detection method on the Livelink dataset. We first describe the Livelink dataset in Section 5.1 and how the raw data is preprocessed in Section 5.2. Then in Section 5.4 we present the results of association rule learning given segmentations produced by both the traditional *timeout* and language modeling techniques. We then analyze the results in Section 5.5.

5.1 The Data Set

The log files used in our experiments were extracted from Livelink access data over a period of two months (April and May 2002). Livelink is a Web-based system[3] that provides automatic management and retrieval of a wide variety of information objects over an intranet or extranet. The size of the raw data is 7GB. The data set describes more than 3,000,000 requests made to a Livelink server from around 5,000 users. Each request corresponds to an entry in the log files, where each entry contains: 1, the IP address the user is making the request from; 2, the cookie of the browser the user is making request from, which can be as long as 5,000 bytes; 3, the time the request is made and the time the required page is presented to the user; 4, the name of the request handler in the Livelink program; 5, the name of the method within the handler that is used to handle the request; 6, the query strings that can be used to identify the page and the objects being requested, and some other task relevant information, such as URL addresses for error-handling. A sample log entry of Livelink is shown in Figure 2. For privacy and security reasons, some of the lines are removed.

5.2 Data Preprocessing

The objective of data preprocessing is to transform the raw log data into a form that can be used for learning patterns. The following steps are performed to preprocess the data in our investigation: 1, the user is identified from each log file entry; 2, the requested information objects are identified from each entry; 3, noisy entries are removed (which request no interesting objects); and finally, 4, the log file entries are grouped into sessions according to our language modeling based method outlined above. In this experiment, we use IP addresses to stand

[3] Developed and sold by Open Text Corporation.

```
Wed Apr 10 19:22:52 2002 CONTENT_LENGTH = '0' func = 'll'
GATEWAY_INTERFACE = 'CGI/1.1' HTTPS = 'on' HTTPS_KEYSIZE = '128'
HTTPS_SECRETKEYSIZE = '1024' HTTPS_SERVER_ISSUER = 'C=US, O="RSA
Data Security, Inc.", OU=Secure Server Certi fication Authority'
HTTPS_SERVER_SUBJECT = 'C=CA, S=Ontario, L=Waterloo, OU=Terms of
use at www.cibc.com/verisign/rpa (c)99,
 OU=Authenticated by CIBC, OU="Member, VeriSign Trust Network", O=Open Text Corporation, OU=Network and
 Online Services, CN=intranet.opentext.com'
HTTP_ACCEPT = '*/*' HTTP_ACCEPT_ENCODING = 'gzip, deflate'
HTTP_ACCEPT_LANGUAGE = 'en-us' HTTP_CONNECTION = 'Keep-Alive'
HTTP_COOKIE = 'WebEdSessionID=05CAB314874CD61180FE00105A9A1626; LLInProgress=%2FIOPiE00D4iNz4iMzk3Py8vIA;
 LLCookie=%2FIOPiE00D4iNz4iMzk3MHhvZHd%2Fb28hbW9uaWVifyEkaWFuYW8gAA; LLTZCookie=3600'
HTTP_HOST = 'intranet.opentext.com' HTTP_REFERER =
'https://intranet.opentext.com/intranet/livelink.exe?func=doc.Vie
wDoc&nodeId=12856199' HTTP_USER_AGENT = 'Mozilla/4.0 (compatible;
MSIE 5.01; Windows NT 5.0)' objAction = 'viewheader' objId =
'12856199' PATH_TRANSLATED = 'C:\Inetpub\wwwroot' QUERY_STRING =
'func=ll&objId=12856199&objAction=viewheader' REMOTE_HOST =
'24.148.27.239' REQUEST_METHOD = 'GET' SCRIPT_NAME =
'/intranet/livelink.exe' SERVER_NAME = 'intranet.opentext.com'
SERVER_PORT = '443' SERVER_PROTOCOL = 'HTTP/1.1' SERVER_SOFTWARE =
'Microsoft-IIS/5.0' _REQUEST = 'llweb' Wed Apr 10 19:22:52 2002 -
638968        Func='ll.12856199.viewheader'   Timing:.140
0A<1,0,'Number_of_Dele
te_Statements'=0,'Number_of_Insert_Statements'=0,'Number_of_Other_Statements'=0,'Number_of_Select_Statemen
ts'=7,'Number_of_Update_Statements'=0,'OutputTime'=47,'Total_Execute_Time'=16,'Total_Fetch_Time'=31,'Total
_SQL_Statements'=7,'Total_SQL_Time'=47> 04/10/2002 19:22:52
Done with Request on socket 069DC4B0 04/10/2002 19:22:57
Processing Request on socket 09A87EF8
```

Fig. 2. A Livelink log entry

for users of Livelink. Even though the same user can log into Livelink through different IP addresses, most often a user accesses Livelink from the desktop in his/her office, and therefore most of the accesses are associated with a fixed IP address. This is actually a safer assumption than using cookies to identify users, because cookies are often disabled. Identifying objects from the large number of dynamic Livelink pages is an unique part of the problem. An object could be a document (such as a PDF file), a project description, a task description, a news group message, a picture and so on. Different types of objects have different domains of identities. Based on Livelink domain knowledge we can extract the identities of the objects being requested from the the query string of the log entry. Most entries contain exactly one object, although some entries contain no objects or multiple objects. We ignore all entries that contain no information objects. The total number of different objects identified from the two-month Web log data is 38,679.

5.3 Session Identification

After the users and objects have been identified from the log entries, we grouped the requests into sessions. In our application, a session is an ordered sequence object sets requested by a user during a single visit to Livelink. In most cases, a session is defined as a group a of actions requested by a single user, where that no two consecutive requests are separated by an interval more than a predefined threshold during a limited time of period for a purpose. The method using this definition for identifying sessions is called the *timeout* session detection method.

There are two kinds of session detection methods used in the experiments. The first one uses the *timeout* method to identify sessions, in which we set the fixed time thresholds to be 5, 10, 15, 20, 25, 30, 35 and 40 minutes in the experiments. The second one uses an n-gram language modeling based method to identify sessions. In the experiments, we set n to be 1, 2 and 3 respectively and the corresponding thresholds are set to be 0.005, 0.003 and 0.0025. We will evaluate these two session detection methods by comparing the number of discovered interesting rules in the top 10, top 20 and top 30 lists generated from the two session detection methods.

5.4 Experimental Results

As shown in Table 1, the number of generated rules greatly depends on the support threshold. At low support regions, a very small change in support threshold can lead to a super exponential growth in the number of rules. To avoid missing interesting rules or generating too many rules, we carefully chose the support and confidence thresholds for each method in the experiments. The value of confidence is set to be 0.5 for all the language modeling based methods and the *timeout* methods at different time interval. For example, we set the support and confidence thresholds to be 0.0028 and 0.5 for the *timeout* session detection method at the 10 minutes time threshold in the experiments. The number of rules generated under this setting is 4,556. The support thresholds for the standard methods at the other time interval are set to be values that lead to generation of a similar number of rules.

Results of Timeout Method: Our baseline model is the *timeout* approach, which is the standard method currently used in many Web mining research investigations. For this method, we conducted experiments on time out thresholds of 5, 10, 15, 20, 25, 30, 35 and 40 minute thresholds. The results for the top 10, top 20 and top 30 are shown in Table 2, 3, and 4 respectively. The first row in Table 2 is the number of sessions generated under each threshold. The entries in Table 2, 3 and 4 represent the number of interesting association rules discovered by each interestingness measure with different thresholds among the top 10, 20 and 30 [4]. The last two rows are the total number of interesting rules discovered by the 4 interestingness measures and the percentage of interesting rules discovered, which is computed as the number of total interesting rules discovered divided by the total number of generated rules.

The best performance obtained in top 10, top 20 and top 30 are **62.5%**, **60%** and **65.83%** under time thresholds 25, 40 and 40 minutes.

Results of Language Modeling Based Method: For the language modeling based methods, we experimented with 1-gram, bi-gram, 3-gram models using Good-Turing smoothing. A different threshold is set for each model to generate roughly the same number of sessions, which is 0.0005, 0.0003, 0.00025 respectively. The results are shown in Table 5, 6 and 7 respectively. The first row of

[4] All the discovered association rules were evaluated by our domain experts in Open Text.

Table 2. Top 10 results with timeout method for session boundary detection

time intervals	5 min.	10 min.	15 min.	20 min.	25 min.	30 min.	35 min.	40 min.
C2	3	6	6	6	6	6	6	6
CS	2	1	1	4	4	4	4	4
IS	3	5	5	4	5	6	5	5
MD	6	7	7	10	10	8	8	8
Total	14	19	19	24	**25**	24	23	23
Percentage	35%	47.5%	47.5%	60%	**62.5%**	60%	57.5%	57.5%

Table 3. Top 20 results with *timeout* method for session boundary detection

time intervals	5 min.	10 min.	15 min.	20 min.	25 min.	30 min.	35 min.	40 min.
C2	4	12	11	11	12	11	12	12
CS	3	5	4	8	5	6	6	6
IS	5	10	8	8	8	10	10	12
MD	10	14	14	16	18	18	18	18
Total	22	41	37	43	43	45	46	**48**
Percentage	27.5%	51.25%	46.25%	53.75%	53.75%	56.25%	57.5%	**60%**

the table is the models used (for example, GT1.5 means 1-gram language model with Good-Turing smoothing and the entropy change threshold is 0.0005). Other rows are of the same meaning of Table 2. The values of support for association rule learning are set to be 0.0042, 0.0036 and 0.00336 for the models GT1.5, GT2.3 and GT3.25 respectively. Under this setting, a similar number of rules can be generated for all the three models.

In the language modeling based methods, the results obtained for top 10, top 20 and top 30 are **85%**, **83.75%** and **83.33%**.

Table 4. Top 30 results with *timeout* method for session boundary detection

time intervals	5 min.	10 min.	15 min.	20 min.	25 min.	30 min.	35 min.	40 min.
C2	9	17	16	15	17	19	21	22
CS	5	8	8	12	12	12	12	12
IS	11	18	16	24	18	18	20	19
MD	18	24	24	30	26	26	26	26
Total	43	67	64	74	73	75	**79**	**79**
Percentage	35.83%	55.83%	53.33%	61.67%	60.83%	62.5%	**65.83%**	**65.83%**

Table 5. Experimental top 10 for language modeling methods

LM models	GT1.5	GT2.3	GT3.25
C2	9	9	9
CS	7	2	3
IS	8	10	8
MD	10	10	10
Total	**34**	31	30
Percentage	85%	77.5%	75%

Table 6. Experimental top 20 for language modeling methods

LM models	GT1.5	GT2.3	GT3.25
C2	18	18	18
CS	13	9	4
IS	16	18	18
MD	20	20	20
Total	**67**	65	60
Percentage	**83.75%**	81.25%	75%

Table 7. Experimental top 30 for language modeling methods

LM models	GT1.5	GT2.3	GT3.25
C2	27	28	26
CS	15	14	4
IS	26	28	28
MD	30	30	30
Total	98	**100**	88
Percentage	81.67%	**83.33%**	73.33%

5.5 Analysis and Discussions

Effects of Different Thresholds in Timeout Method: The standard *timeout* session detection method obviously depends on the time threshold. We find that generally time thresholds between 25 minutes and 40 minutes are good. A threshold that is too small (say, 5 minutes) leads to poor performance. Figure. 3 illustrates the influence of different time thresholds in top 10 results.

Effects of Language Modeling Based Method: Table 8 shows the improvements made by the language modeling based method compared to the standard *timeout* method. We choose the best result from each method. We observe that a significant improvement can be made for top 10, 20 and 30 results.

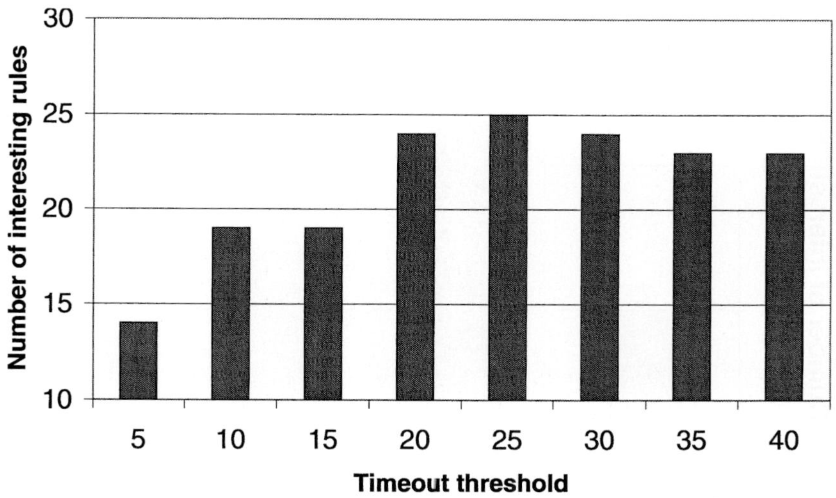

Fig. 3. Timeout method comparison at different thresholds

Table 8. Effects of LM based methods

	Timeout based	LM based	Improvements
top 10	62.5%	85%	36%
top 20	60%	83.75%	39.6%
top 30	65.83%	83.33%	26.6%

It is also interesting to notice that performance of each language modeling based method is much better than the best one obtained in the *timeout* methods. Figure 4 shows the the comparison among the language modeling methods and the best *timeout* method in top 10 results. By looking into each interesting measure, we find that the language modeling based approach consistently outperforms all of the *timeout* methods at the top 10, 20 and 30.

All of these results demonstrate that the language modeling approach is effective at identifying session boundaries for association rule learning.

Effects of Different Order of n-Gram Language Models: We find that in language modeling based approach, better results are obtained on 1-gram and 2-gram models. One reason is that sparse data problems begin to dominate for n-gram language modeling with longer context (see Section 2). Although we do not have to cope with unseen events in this domain (because we are detecting boundaries on the training set) the statistics one obtains from limited training data is not reliable when there are too many parameters being estimated.

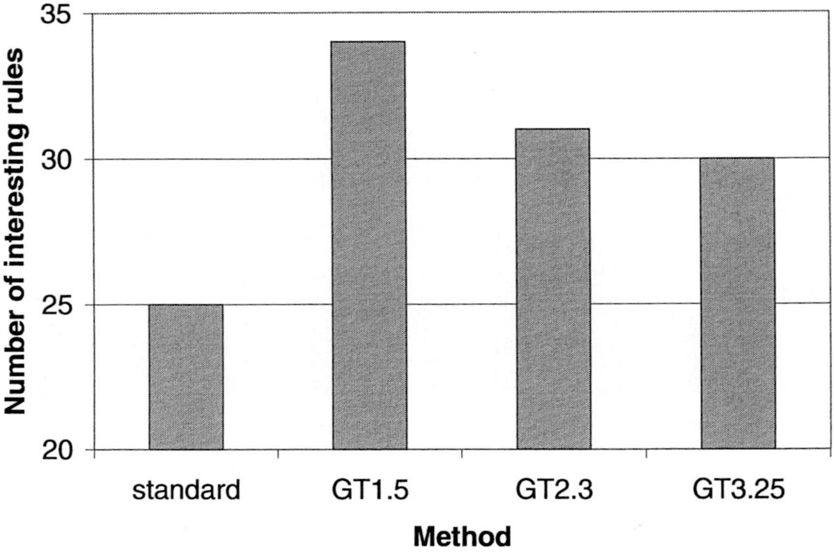

Fig. 4. Comparison of language modeling and timeout methods

6 Conclusions and Future Work

We have proposed a novel approach for dynamic session boundary detection based on statistical n-gram language modeling. This approach is based on information theory and is intuitively understandable. Experiments on learning interesting association rules from the Livelink dataset show that we obtain consistent improvements over the traditional ad-hoc *timeout* methods when preprocessing the data for association rule discovery.

Our future work includes investigating the optimal order of n-gram language models, the influence of different smoothing techniques in language modeling, and the effect of this approach for other Web usage mining problems, such as sequential pattern mining.

Acknowledgements

We would like to thank Gary Promhouse for spending time on evaluating the discovered association rules in the reported experiments. Without his help and useful feedback, this research cannot be fully conducted. We would also like to thank Open Text Corporation for supporting this research and providing us with its Livelink Web log datasets.

References

[1] Agrawal, R. and Srikant, R.; (1994). Fast Algorithms for Mining Association Rules, *Proc. of the 20th International Conference on Very Large Databases*, Santiago, Chile.

[2] An, A. and Cercone, N.; (2001). Rule Quality Measures for Rule Induction Systems: Description and Evaluation, *Computational Intelligence*, Vol. 17 No. 3.

[3] Bahl, L., Jelinek, F. and Mercer, R.; (1983). A Maximum Likelihood Approach to Continuous Speech Recognition *IEEE Transactions on Pattern Analysis and Machine Intelligence*, 5(2), pp. 179-190.

[4] Bruha, I.; (1996). Quality of Decision Rules: Definitions and Classification Schemes for Multiple Rules. In *Nakhaeizadeh, G. and Taylor, C. C. (eds.): Machine Learning and Statistics, The Interface.* Jone Wiley & Sons Inc.

[5] Chen, S. and Goodman, J.; (1998). An Empirical Study of Smoothing Techniques for Language Modeling. *Technical report*, TR-10-98, Harvard University.

[6] Catledge, Lara D. and Pitkow, James E.; (1995) Characterizing Browsing Strategies in the World Wide Web, *Proceedings of the 3rd International World Wide Web Conference*, April 1995, Darmstadt, Germany.

[7] He, D. and Goker, A.; (2000). Detecting session boundaries from Web user logs, *Proceedings of the 22nd Annual Colloquium on Information Retrieval Research (ECIR)*, April 2000, Sidney Sussex College, Cambridge, England.

[8] Hiemstra, D.; (2001). Using Language Models for Information Retrieval. Ph.D. Thesis, Centre for Telematics and Information Technology, University of Twente.

[9] Huang, X., An, A., Cercone, N. and Promhouse, G; (2002) Discovery of Interesting Association Rules from Livelink Web Log Data. In *Proceedings of the IEEE International Conference on Data Mining (ICDM)*, December, 2002, Maebashi TERRSA, Maebashi City, Japan.

[10] Lafferty, J. and Zhai, C.; (2001). Document Language Models, Query Models, and Risk Minimization for Information Retrieval. In *Proceedings of 24th ACM SIGIR Conference on Research and Development in Information Retrieval (SIGIR).*

[11] Peng, F. and Schuurmans, D.; (2003). Combining Naive Bayes and n-Gram Language Models for Text Classification. In *Proceedings of The 25th European Conference on Information Retrieval Research (ECIR).*

[12] Ponte, J. and Croft, W.; (1998). A Language Modeling Approach to Information Retrieval. In *Proceedings of ACM Research and Development in Information Retrieval (SIGIR)*, 275-281.

[13] Tan, P. and Kumar, V.; (2000). Interestingness Measures for Association Patterns: A Perspective, *Technical Report TR00-036*, Department of Computer Science, Univ. of Minnestota.

Negotiating Exchanges of Private Information for Web Service Eligibility

Keping Jia[1,2] and Bruce Spencer[1,2]

[1]National Research Council
46 Dineen Dr., Fredericton, NB, Canada E3B 9W4
[2] Computer Science, University of New Brunswick
Fredericton, NB, Canada E3B 5A3
{Keping.Jia,Bruce.Spencer}@nrc.gc.ca

Abstract. Private information about individuals that engage in e-commerce business transactions is of economic value to businesses for market analysis and for identifying possible future partners. For various reasons, maintaining the privacy of that information is important to these individuals, including avoiding unwelcome communication, *spam*, from those businesses or their associates. In this paper we advocate a negotiation strategy to be used by an individual deciding whether or not to divulge information to a specific electronic business for a specific purpose, such as achieving preferential status with a service provider or a discounted price from a vendor. The strategy makes use of explanation techniques for expert systems that answer "how", "what if" and "why not" questions. We assume that the business practices of the provider or vendor are available as explicit business rules, including the eligibility criteria for preferential status and price discounts. Our prototype allows the user to obtain a proof that the information to be given is both necessary and sufficient for achieving the eligibility / discount – answering "how" eligibility is established. The communication protocol with the prototype also includes "what if" dialogues allowing a user to assess the difficulty and benefits of achieving eligibility, and "why not" dialogues for identifying missing eligibility criteria. The prototype is built upon the emerging standard Web Services architecture. Thus the prototype allows a business to expose its business practices, educating its customers, so it can provide the most appropriate service for a given individual. The prototype engages the customer to assess the benefit of exposing some private information to the business. Through the "what if" interface, the customer can be aware of the complete set of information that will be necessary to achieve the desired eligibility before any private information is actually transmitted. We offer an example where a user is negotiating a car price discount.

Y. Xiang and B. Chaib-draa (Eds.): AI 2003, LNAI 2671, pp. 252-267, 2003.

1 Introduction

In the conventional marketplace we exchange goods and services for money; in the electronic marketplace, where buyers and sellers are often unknown to each other, vendors are often willing to provide goods and services in exchange for a user's private information. This information is of value to a business for profiling the demographics of their clientele and compiling lists of potential future customers, both for itself and for its associated businesses. However, preserving the privacy of that information is often a priority for these users, to avoid receiving unwanted communication from these vendors or their associates. Thus one currency of e-commerce is private information.

Currently and more so in the future, users are asked to divulge increasingly specialized information in exchange for higher levels of services. More specialized information in the hands of the service provider leads to better, customized services, but it makes impositions on a user's privacy. The user may be willing to divulge a private fact if they are informed exactly what it buys them – what new, better service is guaranteed to be provided based on communicating that specific fact.

In the setting of this paper, electronic goods and services are provided within the Web Service architecture. This architecture exposes computational capabilities to consumers across the Internet, and comprises three main facilities: a language for describing such capabilities, a broker for matching an expressed need to a service description and a transport protocol for delivering both the consumer's data to the service provider and the computed results back to the consumer. One set of standards, endorsed by OASIS and by W3C, uses WSDL (Web Services Description Language)[6], UDDI (Universal Delivery, Discovery and Integration)[1] and SOAP (Simple Object Access Protocol)[11], respectively for these three facilities.

Built on top of this Web Service infrastructure, we are beginning to see proposals for more complex access control, based on various rule systems: Common Rules[8], DAML-S [9], N3[2], RuleML[3] and P3P-APPEL[5]. The accessibility is controlled by policies and regulations that are represented as rules. Far more complex and subtle controls can be achieved under this mechanism. In addition, rule technology's ability to explain greatly enhances its usability as a mechanism for the access control. These systems promise more flexible and scalable mechanisms which are needed to work together with traditional ones to satisfy today's usability demands.

We envision that the user is willing to entrust a computerized agent with some of its private information and with the responsibility to communicate that information under conditions specified by the user. This is important for diverting some of the negotiation away from the user's direct attention. There are several proposals for these languages, including RuleML and P3P APPEL. More private information would remain under direct control of the user.

As the access control becomes more complex, the reasons that a service is denied become more varied. It could be that the service requestor is not an eligible user or the service requestor fails to provide enough or correct information to pass the eligibility check. Denials are often caused by the lack of the knowledge on the user's side as to what prerequisites are needed for a service.

Our explanation-capable web service works in conjunction with some given web service where eligibility is governed by rules. Suppose a user requests that his trusted agent establish eligibility with a desired web service but the agent and the web service cannot complete this request. Then the explanation-capable web service interacts directly with the user. At this point the user starts to negotiate an exchange of private information for eligibility for specialized, higher quality web services.

In our example, the user is buying a car and trying to negotiate a price discount. Eligibility for the discount is determined by a set of rules maintained by the vendor and stored in the vendor's computer, and is accessible via a web service that we have developed as part of this work. This web service not only determines the user's discount; it also offers explanations. By interacting with the web service, the user can determine why a specific level of service is offered, and why the user is not eligible for a different level of service. Respectively these are answers to "how" and "why not" questions: "How was that derived?" and "Why was this not derived?"

Returning to the privacy question, a user typically wants assurance that by divulging certain private information as part of a dialog with the system, the expected benefit will actually be achieved. Otherwise it is possible that the user's investment, that of sharing information he would rather have kept private, would satisfy only one of the preconditions, while other conditions are left unmet, and the hoped-for qualification is then not granted. The user's investment would then be spent with no return. Instead our prototype allows the user to answer requests for private information with the response "what if" the information were provided. At the end of the series of questions the user can then decide if the return is worth the investment.

The paper proceeds as follows: Section 2 presents some background on expert systems and web services technologies. Section 3 explains how access control, expressed as rules, is useful for generating specific explanations. It contains a fully worked example and a system overview. Section 4 gives the design of the full system and conclusions are offered in Section 5.

2 Background

Expert Systems (or Knowledge-based systems) are computer programs that are concerned with the concepts and methods of symbolic inference, or reasoning, by a computer, and how the knowledge used to make those inferences will be represented inside the machine. The fields of business rules and expert systems do overlap. Because "[r]ules have been used extensively as a way to represent knowledge" [7]. The technology underlying expert systems is widely used to automate business rules.

The knowledge base and the reasoning engine are the two most important constituent parts of an expert system. The knowledge base is a storage of declarative representation of the expertise or knowledge about an application domain. The reasoning engine is the implementation of logical inference mechanisms. It manipulates the symbolic information and knowledge in the knowledge base and applies them to the deduction rules so that conclusions can be reached. The prototype system of this paper uses j-DREW[15] as the rule engine.

It is often claimed that an important aspect of expert systems is their ability to explain themselves[10]. This means the user can ask the system for justification of conclusions or questions at any point in a consultation with an expert system. On the other hand, by looking at explanations, knowledge engineers can see how the system

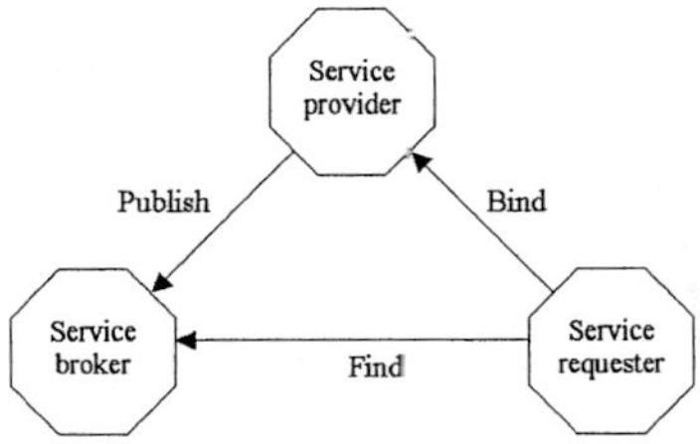

Fig. 1. Web Service Components

is behaving, and how the rules and data are interacting. They serve as the "logical traces for knowledge bases just like program tracing for conventional programs"[13]. Given that the system knows which rules were used during the inference process, it is possible for the system to provide those rules to the user as a means for explaining the results[10]. In fact, most of the existing expert systems follow this way in the implementation of explanation and debugging systems.

Web Services technology is a newly emerging paradigm for building Web-accessible services across Internet. "On the surface, a Web Service is simply an application that exposes a Web-accessible API. That means you can invoke this application programmatically over the Web."[14]

Web Services technology mainly aims at the high-level architectures and protocols of the decentralized system over global network. It is designed to work harmoniously with other existing distributed computing technologies like J2EE, DCOM etc. In addition, Web Service protocols do not restrict the implementation techniques for any individual web service.

The Web Services architecture is a message based, service-oriented architecture that is based on the notion that everything is a service. Two important components constitute the main infrastructure of web services: provider and broker. Together with the service requestor, these three distinct actors compose the lifecycle of a web service.

- Service provider: In one aspect, service provider is the implementer of the web service. As a technical term, service provider also denotes web service itself or the hosting environment that the web service is running on.
- Service broker: Service broker is itself a service provider. Service broker usually has a logically centralized directory of services (UDDI registry) and provides relevant services like intelligent search and business classification or taxonomy.
- Service requester: Service requester is the consumer of the web services. Service requester could be a client side program or another web service.

The life cycle of particular web service starts from the service provider. There are several ways that a service provider can establish a web service. Service providers can build their own web services by first developing the core functionality of the service, then extracting the interface that the service provider wants to expose to the outside world and last wrapping the interface so that it is SOAP accessible. Next the service provider needs to build an XML based web service interface description (WSDL) that includes all the necessary information for invoking a service: the signature of the service, which communication protocol is used, where to locate the web service etc. In addition to deploying the service on a machine that can be accessed through the Internet, the service provider still need to publish the service interface description to a UDDI directory or broker with necessary taxonomy information so that the web service would be easily found by the service requester. Also, a service provider has the freedom of providing his own implementation of a published service interface or wrapping an existing software application or program into a web service.

A service requester needs to find the required web services and invoke them. The UDDI registry provides flexible mechanisms for service discovery. For example, a service requester can find a particular web service interface through one or more taxonomies individually or the combination of all of them. If a requester knows the name of the service or the company that provides this service, he can directly use this information to get the service. Furthermore, if a service requester gets the interface of a web service, he can easily get all the web service implementations for this interface. The interface description is all that a user needs in order to develop client side programs that can integrate the web service functionalities.

Web service broker or UDDI registry acts as an intermedium between web service providers and web service requesters. To carry out this role, a service broker must be publicly known to both service providers and requesters. For web service providers, it provides rich standard taxonomies and flexible mechanisms so that service providers can easily publish their services in a most discoverable way or establish their own information hierarchies. For web service requesters, it provides diverse searching services so that the data stored in the UDDI registry can be accessed easily and in an organizable way. In fact, a service broker is itself a service provider.

The goal of web services is to achieve high web based interoperability and integretability among software applications regardless of their implementing languages and running environments.

3 Rule-Based Access Control and Explanations

Under the web service architecture, we propose a paradigm of accessibility control of level of service that is governed by policies in the form of rules. Under this paradigm, the system makes decisions based on the result of applying static policies (rules) to the user's information under the current context or environment. Questions could be initiated by the system for the information that is relevant for the decision-making yet not volunteered by the user and his agent.

We assume that questions may be asked by the user on aspects of the web services that are governed by rules, such as questions about eligibility, level of service, membership in reward programs, etc. The explanation service can answer three types of questions: "how", "why not" and "what if".

The "how" question is asked by the user to see the proof of some conclusion the system has reached. "How" questions can be asked repeatedly until asked about a fact in the knowledge base. For example, assume that a customer was offered a 5% discount toward the purchase of a Honda car. By asking "how?", he will get the answer that he got 5% discount because (1) he is a premium customer and (2) Honda is categorized as regular car. By continuing asking "how?" on (1), he will get answer that he is a premium customer because he spent more than $5000 at this car dealership last year. Asking "how?" on this answer could result in a list of purchases made by this user, showing the total. No further "how" answer could be offered by the system because this is basic information (facts).

In order to show the user how a goal is achieved, the system will generate a proof tree [12] with the derived goal as the root. Each internal node of the proof tree is itself a goal with a sub-proof tree rooted at it. Each node and its siblings, together with their parent node, will compose an instance of the rule that is used in the proof procedure.

The "why not" question may be asked when the system fails to derive a goal. Repeadedly asking the "why not" question will lead the user through the rules to find out what causes the goal to fail. The customer of the previous example could ask "why did I not get a 7.5% discount on the Honda?". The answer will be that in order to get 7.5% discount, (1) he must be a premium customer and (2) Honda must be categorized as luxury goods. If the client decides to trace this rule, he will be told by the system that (1) is satisfied but (2) failed because "Honda is a luxurious car" is not a fact in database and no other rules can lead to this conclusion. In this case, the user may be asked to consider buying an Acura.

Policy	Rule
An elite customer can get 5% discount on decent or better cars if his payment type is "silver".	discount(V0,V1,'5%percent')←eliteCustomer (V0), decentCarOrAbove(V1), paymentType(silver).
"Silver" payment type is pay by 2 year installments with financial assistance of less than $10000.	paymentType(silver)←payBy(2yearInstallme nt), financialAssistance(lessThan$10000).
"Silver" payment type is pay by 3 year installments with financial assistance of less than $7000.	paymentType(silver)←payBy(3yearInstallme nt), financialAssistance(lessThan$7000).
"Silver" payment type is pay by 5 year installments without financial assistance.	paymentType(silver)←payBy(5yearInstallme nt), financialAssistance($0).
The senior preferred customer who is insurance affiliated automatically becomes an elite customer.	eliteCustomer(V0)←preferedCustomer(V0), senior(V0), insuranceAffiliator(V0).
A customer is a preferred customer if he bought a regular car from this car dealership in the past five years.	preferedCustomer(V0)←purchased(V0, V1, V2), regularCar(V1), withtinLast5Years(V2).
The customer who is older than 60 is the senior customer.	senior(V0)←moreThan60YearsOld(V0).
The customer who buys car insurance in First Rate Co. is insurance affiliated.	insuranceAffiliator(V0)←driverLicenceNo(V0, X), insuredAt('First Rate Co.', X).

Fig. 2. Example Pricing Policy and Corresponding Rule Base

A “why not” question needs a slightly different approach because there is no proof tree when a goal fails. However, the proof tree idea is still useful because a “why not” question is concerned with “why a proof tree cannot be built”. By keeping track of the whole proof procedure and marking down all the failure points that prevent a complete proof tree from being built, we will have gathered enough relevant information to construct partially completed proof tree with gaps.

A “what if” question may be asked together with the “why not” question. “What if” questions give the user a chance to know the consequence of assuming that a condition is true. For example, a client may find out through “why not” questions that he did not get the discount because his purchase value is less than $100. Then he could use a “what if” question to check if this is the only condition that prevents him from getting the discount. If the discount is granted after asking “what if the purchase is more than $100”, the client then has the choice to purchase more than $100 to get the discount. But if after asking that “what if” question, the discount is still not granted because other conditions still need to be satisfied (for example, the user should also be a golden card holder), then the client could again ask “why not” questions to find out other conditions to satisfy.

“What if” questions may be asked only on unsatisfied nodes. The response is an explanation tree in which the node is assumed to be satisfied. An explanation tree is a tree-like structure containing all the updated information the user received so far by asking above three questions. A “how” explanation tree is the same as a proof tree and a “why not” explanation tree is a combination of “why not” and “how” trees and “what if” (assumed) leaf nodes. Assuming to satisfy a goal or undoing such assumptions will make temporary changes to the rule base. In certain situations, these changes will affect the other branches of the explanation tree. So, propagating this effect all over the explanation tree is needed to keep the tree consistent with the rule base.

3.1 Car Purchase Example

The following is an example of a business policy controlling the level of service for car dealerships. In this example, the level of discount for buying a car is governed by a set of rules that makes decisions based on the type of car, payment method, user category and insurance information, etc. In the example, a customer Peter negotiates with the system for a 5% discount on his purchase of Volvo-S60. The rules maintained by the service level control system that are directly related to the example are shown in Fig. 2.

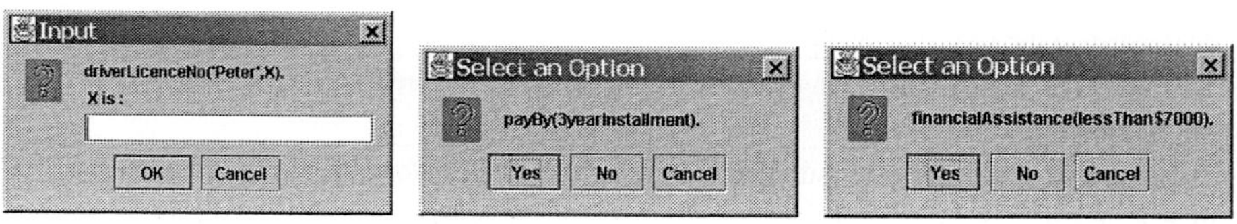

Fig. 3. Questions redirected by Interactive_agent

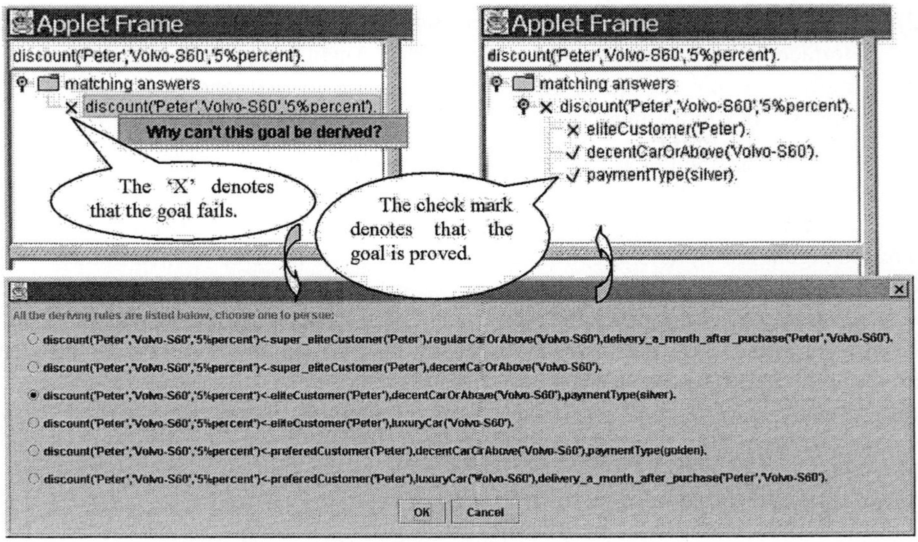

Fig. 4. Interaction on "why not" question

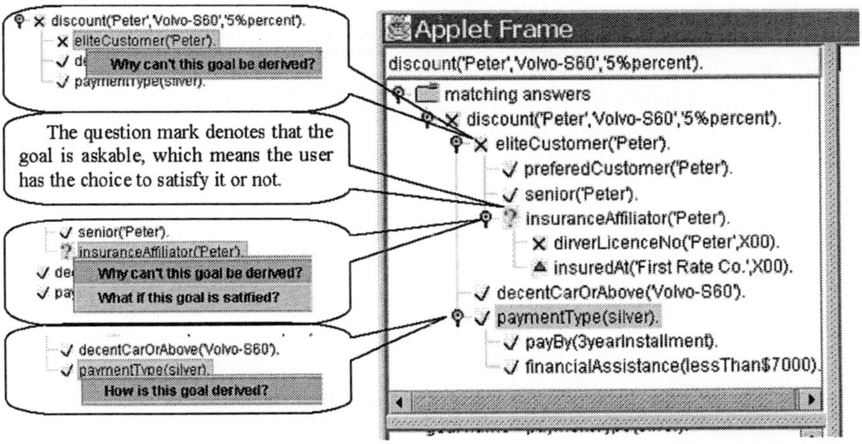

Fig. 5. Interaction on "How" question

The access control system needs to resort to three information sources for the process:

1. Insurance_IS: An information source provided by First Rate Co. in form of web service. The access control system resorts to this information service to get information about whether a people of a particular driver license number is insured in this company.
2. User's Trusted Agent: A personal information service that Peter has registered a an information source. The access control system resorts to this service for th user related information like the driver license number and age.

3. Interactive_agent: A temporary web service that exposes exactly the same interface as Insurance_IS and User's Trusted Agent but processes differently. It simply redirects the query to the user through a GUI and sends the user's response back to the invoker.

As will be described in 3.2, the control system will first resort to the User's Trusted Agent for the user related information and then query the Interactive_agent for any questions that the User's Trusted Agent fails to answer. In the example, the User's Trusted Agent has Peter's age, but does not know Peter's driver licence number and his preference of payment method.

Fig.3 shows some possible questions that may be redirected by the Interactive_agent to the user. We can see that the question itself does not give much hint as to how the answer will help the user towards or hinder the user from obtaining the intended discount level. In this case, the explanation system provides a way for the user to know how the decision is made and also to give user a chance to change his choice.

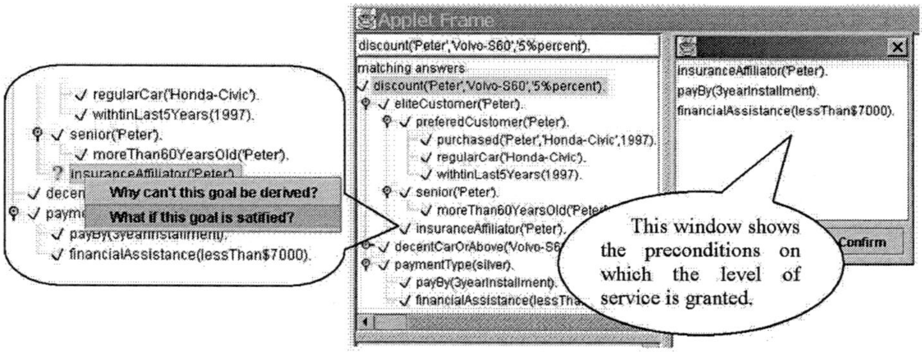

Fig. 6. Interaction on "why" and "why not" question

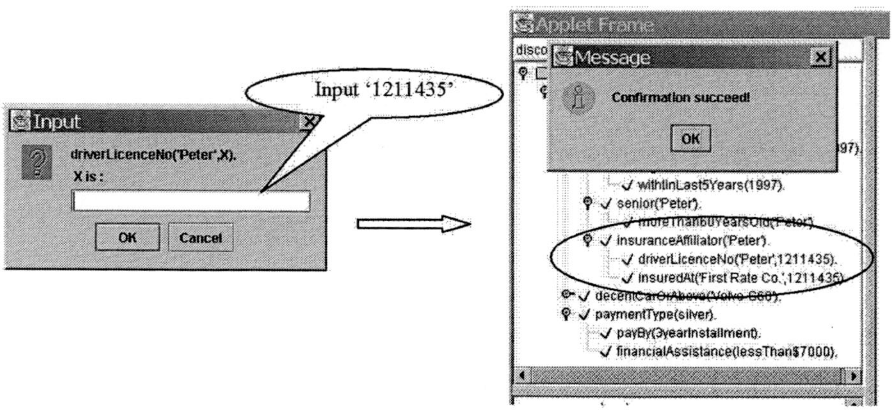

Fig. 7. Confirmation on assumed facts

Fig. 4. shows the interaction model of the “why not” question under the assumption that Peter does not give out his driver license number and answers yes to the payment type questions. This will lead to the denial of his intended discount. By pressing the right mouse button on the item that Peter wants to ask questions about, a menu will pop up showing all the eligible questions for this item, which is only the “why not” question in this example. As a response to this question, the system will display a popup window showing all the possible ways that Peter can get the 5% discount. It is up to Peter to choose a way to continue the process. After selection, the popup window disappears and the explanation window will show the user what preconditions he must satisfy in order to get the intended level of service, what preconditions he already satisfies and what he does not.

The user can continue the process by asking “how” questions on satisfied preconditions and “why not” questions on unsatisfied preconditions. As shown in Fig.5, the user first asks a “why not” question on “eliteCustomer(‘Peter’)”, then another “why not” question on “InsuranceAffiliator(‘Peter’)” and then a “how” question on “paymentType(Silver).”.

Fig. 6. shows how the system responses when the user asks “what if” question on the askable goal on Fig. 5. The system grants Peter 5% discount on the Volvo-S60 under the assumption that Peter is insurance affiliated. Some assumed facts need to be confirmed in order to take effect.

Fig.7 shows a demo confirmation interaction. When Peter clicks the “Confirm” button in the Fig.6, a dialog box will pop up, asking Peter to input his driver license number. After Peter inputs his driver license number, the system will use this information to confirm Peter’s “affiliated” status on Insurance_IS. We should notice that not all the assumed facts could be confirmed online. For those assumed facts that cannot be confirmed online, different application areas have different solutions. For example, the system could simply show an information box to inform the user how to confirm the assumed conditions. When the confirmed information becomes available, Peter can ask for the discount again and it will be granted.

3.2 Architecture Overview

Usually, the information stored in the rule base belongs to one of the two parts: rules or facts. Each rule states that a set of conditions, expressed as atomic predicates, that give rise to a single conclusion, also an atomic predicate. Each fact makes a declaration that a predicate is true. Thus we are using only definite clauses. For the rule-based access control mechanism to work in a distributed environment, we also need to divide the facts into two parts: static facts and case specific facts. Static facts are usually service related facts that apply to all the service requestors for this service and do not change from one case to another. Case specific facts are user related and vary among users.

Since the service designer or service owner maintains most of the rules and static facts, they are easier to configure and deploy. Even though in some cases that information from sources outside the system is needed, the relations between them tend to be stable. We could treat the need for the outsource of this kind as a special “knowledge” in the rule base and, therefore, no extra mechanism is needed for it.

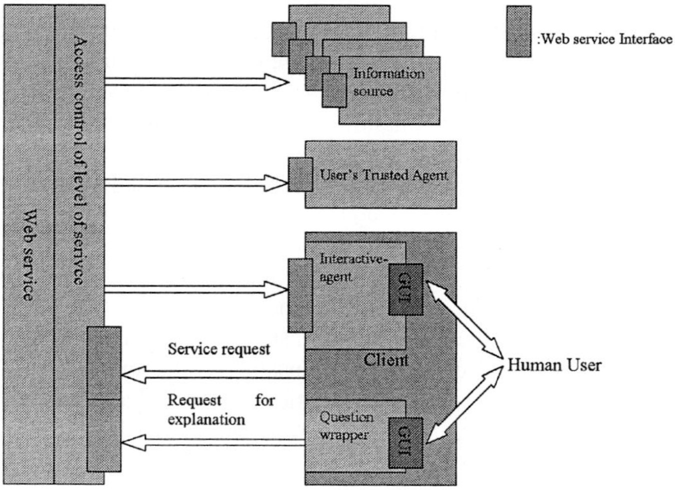

Fig. 8. The interactions between the web services and the information agents

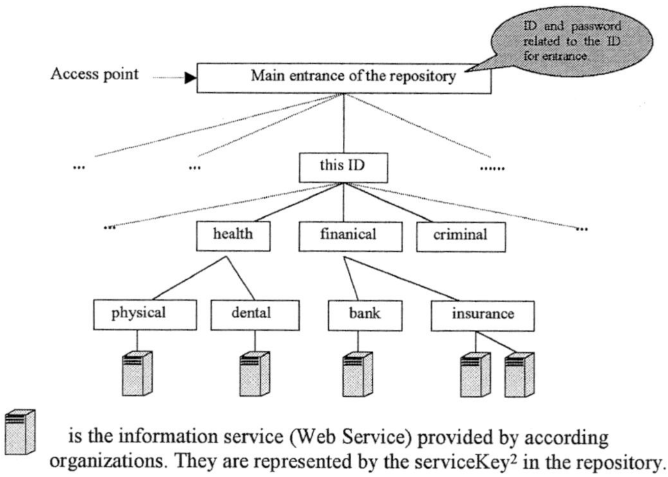

Fig. 9. User information repository

Case specific facts are the most unpredictable factors in this system. The user usually does not know what a service wants from him. Also, the system will not know what information it wants from the beginning because, in many cases, the actual demand for information at a particular point depends on the previous information the user has given. Thus this part of information needs to be requested and given incrementally. This could be done by the access control system interacting with the user for the information or with the user's trusted agent, or both.

Fig. 8. illustrates how the client, access control and all related information services are coordinated to work together. Under this architecture, when a user applies for a service, he must provide the access point of his trusted software agent or the user himself (represented by an interactive agent) or both. The user's trusted software agent is a web service that has preinstalled user knowledge. The interactive agent is a temporary web service that simply provide a GUI for interaction, it is temporary because it need not register itself to UDDI and the access point information is in form of IP:Port rather than bindingKey[1]. The access control will use this information to interact with the agent or the user for the credential check.

In practice, the storage of the user's information tends to be distributed. This is because:

1. Many government or private departments have stored much accurate and detailed information about the user (no mater whether it is a human being or a business entity).
2. Some information about a user is more trustworthy if it is given by a third party. e.g. financial information by bank, health information by hospital etc.
3. A third party is usually more financially sound to build its own credentials than individuals.
4. In order to handle the complexity of the real world, the access point of the User's Trusted Agent could point to the main entrance of a publicly accessible repository instead of a real software agent. This main entrance stores all the possible information services that may provide the information about the user.

We can see that we need a taxonomy, or hierarchical repository with categories for this to work. A hierarchical repository enables the classification of information in a hierarchical way. Categories provide the classification scheme so that the information requester can find out the information in the same way as the information is put into the repository.

Fig.9 illustrates the structure of such a repository. Not all the items under the category must have an information provider. Many of them may be empty (null). In this case, the information requestor could resort to the user for the remaining information or it could fail directly with error messages returned to the user (e.g. the information must to be provided by a service from an authorized organization).

```
Access point
Syntax:
<access_point generic = "1.0" xmlns = "urn:uddi-org:api">
      <User's trusted agent>
              <bindingKey>......</bindingKey>
      </User's trusted agent>
      <interactive_agent>
              <IPAddress>......</IPAddress>
              <port>......</port>
              <tModelKey[3]>......</tModelKey>
      </interactive_agent>
<access_point>
```

Fig. 10. Syntax of Access point

---

[1] BindingKey is an auto-assigned UUID in UDDI that uniquely represents a binding of a service.

4 System Design

Fig. 10 shows the XML data structure used by the client side program for the purpose of informing the control system of the user information source.

The system uses the predefined predicate $askable to denote if a predicate belongs to the user's domain of knowledge. So $askable could also be used to indicate if the system need to go to the access point provided by the user for the proof. In this case, the eligibility checking system acts as a user to the User's Trusted Agent for the proof of the goal. If the User's Trusted Agent cannot provide a satisfactory answer, the system can simply accept it as an unsatisfiable goal or resort to the user (Interactive_agent) for the final answer.

We can generalize the problem of this category into outsourcing the proof of one or more subgoals to external systems. In the prototype system, we introduce a predefined predicate $outsource(query, bindingInfo) to denote where to find service to process the target query. Here, the "query" takes the form of atomic sentence of first order logic and the "bindingInfo" is a XML string that is similar to the accessing point syntax.

We can connect rule-based web services by assigning $outsource facts or rules in the rule base. For static outsource, we could add the fact

1. $outsource (primeRate(X), '***<access_point>*** ***<Info_source>*** ***<bindingKey>*** uuid:51890f8b-eac5-45fe-8aaa-59ca745f0fc3***</bindingKey>*** ***</Info_source >*** ***</access_point>***')

to denote that primate rate information checking will be carried out by a web service with bindingKey of "uuid:51890f8b-eac5-45fe-8aaa-59ca745f0fc3" which is assumed to be a service provided by a national bank. We can also use rules for the control of the conditional outsourcings. For example, the following two rules realize that food product storage queries go to one web service while furniture storage queries go to another one.

2. $outsource(inStore(X, Amount), '***<access_point>*** ***< Info_source >*** ***<bindingKey >*** ...... ***</ bindingKey>*** ***</Info_source >*** ***</access_point>***') ⇐food(X).
3. $outsource(inStore(X, Amount), '***<access_point>*** ***< Info_source >*** ***<bindingKey>*** ...... ***</bindingKey>*** ***</Info_source >*** ***</access_point>***')⇐furniture(X).

The user-related outsourcing is also done with rules, shown here:

4. $outsource(gender(Person), X) ⇐ $userAccessPoint(X).
5. $userAccessPoint('<access_point> < User's trusted agent > <bindingKey> ...... </bindingKey> </User's trusted agent > </access_point>'>
6. $userAccessPoint('<access_point> <interactive_agent> <IPAddress> ...... </IPAddress><port>......</port><tModelKey>......</tModelKey></interactive_agent> </access_point>').

get_bindingDetail

---

[2] TModelKey is an auto-assigned UUID. Here it is used to represent a service interface.

Syntax:
```
<get_bindingDetail generic = "1.0" xmlns = "urn:uddi-org:api">
      <bindingKey> ...</bindingKey>
</get_bindingDetail>
```

Fig. 11. Syntax of get_bindingDetail

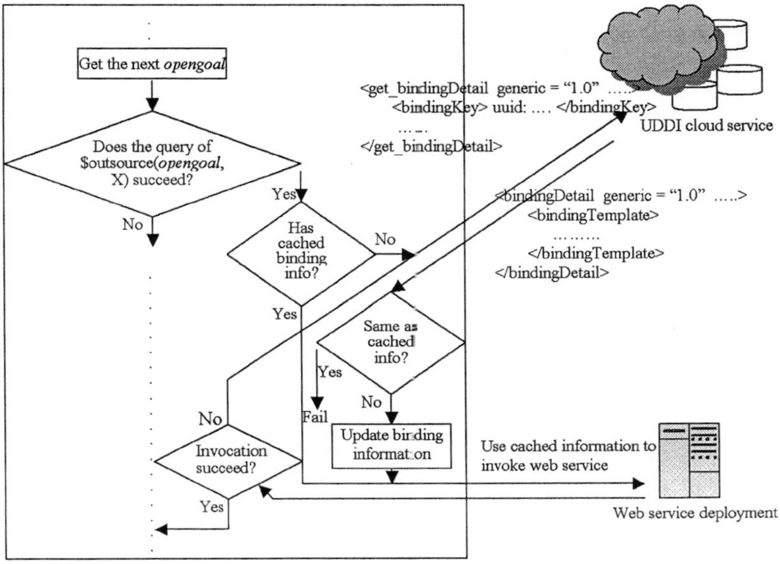

Fig. 12. Operational relationship among inference engine, UDDI and web service

Rule 4 is a static rule that is pre-stored in the rule base. Rule 5 and 6 are dynamically added facts when the user provides access point information as a parameter when applying for a service.

The $outsource predicate acts as a bridge that connects the inference procedures to the universal discovery mechanism of the web services--UDDI. From the endpoint information, the client side program or web service knows where the web service is deployed. In the prototype system, the client side program or web service will use the ***get_bindingDetail*** function for the purpose of searching a web service programmatically at run time. This function will return bindingTemplate information that includes binding port information of the target service. The recommended approach [4] is to cache the bindingTemplate information locally and use the cached information for the repeated calls to the same web service. In the case of the web service invocation failure, the get_bindingDetail function needs to be called again to refresh the binding information. By using the "bindingkey" instead of binding information itself, the system obtains the capacity of tracking web services that might relocate over time.

The operational relationship among inference engine, UDDI and web service is shown in Fig. 12. Based on it, all the participating web services are organized together in a hierarchical way according to their positions in the whole search tree. Each web service is involved in the deduction procedure for the proof of a subgoal and exits when the proof of the subgoal is finished. Also, each web service is autonomous itself and takes the full responsibility to work alone or to involve other services into the local proof procedure. In addition, when the user provides access point of both User's Trusted Agent and Interactive_agent, we may have more than one candidate service for one query. Relating more than one service to a goal is also very useful in many other scenarios. For this kind of query, we need to relate more than one web services to a subgoal and invoke them one at a time during the proof. This invocation mode can be achieved by adding multiple $outsource facts for a query each of which maps to a candidate web service. Of course, this solution needs the collaboration of the inference engine so that all the matching instances are returned instead of just the first one.

5 Conclusion

This paper suggests that privacy of information is a currency, since it is of value to a user to keep it private and of value to a business to access it. It is now common to exchange private information for digital products and services. We perceive that a user will need to choose between privacy and establishing eligibility for a desirable level of service, and that the negotiation will not be entirely straightforward. A business's rules for eligibility commonly have several conditions that a user needs to meet. The user should not divulge any private information for meeting one of these conditions until it is clear that he/she can meet all of the conditions; thus a simple question and answer protocol is not sufficient. In this paper we apply ideas from previous work for generating explanations for expert systems, where the interaction includes "what if", "why not" and "how" questions. We have chosen to deploy our prototype system[4] using the current web services architecture, composed of UDDI, WSDL and SOAP. In response to an initial request from the user, the web service attempts to access some private information by interacting either with the user or with an information agent acting on behalf of the user and entrusted with private information. When the web service asks for more private information to which the user has attached a high value, the interaction is elevated to using the more sophisticated protocols. Through "what if" questions the user may construct an exhaustive list of the valued private information required. The user can also review what information has been accessed via "how" questions, and finally the user can diagnose why the web service did not offer an expected level of service via "why not" questions.

References

[1] Bellwood,T. et al: UDDI Version 3.0. At http://uddi.org/pubs/uddi-v3.00-published- 20020719.htm

[2] Berners-Lee, T.: Ideas about Web Architecture - yet another notation At http://www.w3.org/DesignIssues/Notation3.

---

[3] The prototype system is a 125k package written in JAVA, which has been deployed and tested on the IBM WebSphere Application Server.

[3] Boley, H., Tabet, S.: The Rule Markup Initiative. At http://www.dfki.uni-kl.de/ruleml/.

[4] Cerami, E.: *Web Services Essentials,* O'Reilly & Associates, Inc., Sebastopol, CA, 2002.

[5] Cranor, L., Langheinrich, M., Marchiori, M.: A P3P Preference Exchange Language 1.0 (APPEL1.0), W3C Working Draft 15 April 2002, At http://www.w3.org/TR/P3P-preferences/

[6] Christensen, E., Curbera., F., Meredith, G., Weerawarana, S.: Web Services Description Language (WSDL) 1.1, W3C Note 15 March 2001, At http://www.w3.org/TR/2001/NOTE-wsdl-20010315

[7] Gottesdiener, E.: Business Rules Show Power and Promise. *Application Programming Trends*, vol. 4, n. 3, March, 1997.

[8] Grosof, B.: IBM releases CommonRules 1.0: Business Rules for the Web, At http://www.research.ibm.com/rules/commonrules-overview.html.

[9] Martin, D.: DAML-S: Semantic Markup for Web Services. At http://www.daml.org/services/daml-s/0.7/daml-s.html

[10] Merritt, D.: Building Expert Systems in Prolog. Springer-Verlag, New York, USA, 1989.

[11] Mitra, N.: SOAP Version 1.2 Part 0: Primer, W3C Working Draft, June, 2002, At http://www.w3.org/TR/soap12-part0/.

[12] Poole, D., Mackworth, A., Goebel, R.: *Computational Intelligence – A Logical Approach,* Oxford University Press, New York, 1998.

[13] Russell, S. J., Norvig, P.: *Artificial Intelligence – A Modern Approach*, Prentice Hall, New Jersey, USA, 1995.

[14] Shohoud, Y.: Real World XML Web Services, At http://www.learnxmlws.com/book.

[15] Spencer, B.: The Design of j-DREW: A Deductive Reasoning Engine for the Web, In Proceedings of the First CologNet Workshop on Component-based Software Develoment and Implementation Technology for Computational Logic Systems, Madrid, Spain, Universidad Politécnica de Madrid, Facultad de Informática TR Number CLIP 4/02.0, pages 155-166. Sept 18-19, 2002.

Post-supervised Template Induction for Dynamic Web Sources

Zhongmin Shi, Evangelos Milios, and Nur Zincir-Heywood

Faculty of Computer Science
Dalhousie University
Halifax, N.S., Canada B3H 1W5
{zincir,eem}@cs.dal.ca

Abstract. Dynamic web sites commonly return information in the form of lists and tables. Although hand crafting an extraction program for a specific template is time-consuming but straightforward, it is desirable to automatically generate template extraction programs from examples of lists and tables in html documents. We describe a novel technique, Post-supervised Learning, which exploits unsupervised learning to avoid the need for training examples, while minimally involving the user to achieve high accuracy. We have developed unsupervised algorithms to extract the number of rows and adopted a dynamic programming algorithm for extracting columns. Our system, called TIDE (Template Induction for web Data Extraction), achieves high performance with minimal user input compared to fully supervised techniques.

1 Introduction

Dynamically generated web pages composed of a list or table are becoming widely used. The process is geared towards a human user who employs a web browser to interact with a web site, which is the interface to a database. The process of form filling (to input the query) and viewing the resulting lists or tables is time consuming, and it would be desirable to automate it, especially when this process has to be repeated many times, either to track information over time, or to obtain data for a large number of different queries.

However, the World Wide Web has been dominated for a decade by HTML based on a browsing paradigm [1], which is designed for good look-and-feel and easy reading by a human using a Web browser, instead of facilitating the extraction of information by a program. It is therefore difficult to extract information by HTML parsing. Until more structured representations replace, most web clients rely on existing information extraction techniques, typically Web Wrappers [2].

A wrapper is a program that enables a Web source to be queried as if it were a database [3]. Extraction rules used by the wrapper to identify the beginning and end of the data field to be extracted, form an important part of the wrapper. Quick and efficient generation of extraction rules, so called Wrapper Induction,

Y. Xiang and B. Chaib-draa (Eds.): AI 2003, LNAI 2671, pp. 268–282, 2003.

has been an active area of research in recent years [2, 4]. The first wrapper induction system, WIEN [5] is a supervised learning agent, i.e. it requires manually labelled examples with output information to learn patterns.

A recent wrapper induction algorithm, STALKER, generates high accuracy (80%) extraction rules that accept all positive and reject all negative user-labelled training examples [6], but it still requires manually labelled examples.

To overcome the shortcomings of supervised learning, attention is shifting towards unsupervised learning [2], which needs no manually labelled input. In that work, some general assumptions are made about the structures of lists and tables with a following four-step approach

1. Separators are used to partition the web page.
2. An unsupervised classification algorithm is used to automatically group the web page contents into classes based on separators.
3. Syntactic data patterns, which describe the common start and end of classes [7], are learned by a pattern learning algorithm.
4. A grammar induction algorithm is used to build the finite state automaton of the web page. States that represent the same data contents are then merged, and cycles are generated. The longest circles that correspond to rows are selected [2]

That system was tested on 14 typical examples[2] with about 70% accuracy. It is undoubtedly a significant effort, but it requires several similar web pages to generate the page template in the first step; the general algorithms used, such as DataPro [7] for learning data pattern and AutoClass for unsupervised classification [8, 9], are computationally intensive, a serious problem in Web applications.

Thus, our work aims to improve the performance of information extraction from lists and tables in the web page. Since high-performance unsupervised learning is rather ambitious, the authors have developed a *Post-supervised* learning technique, called TIDE (Template Induction for web Data Extraction), which employs a suite of unsupervised learning algorithms and minimal user interaction on the results. Our system focuses on:

- achieving approximately 100 percent accuracy
- avoiding user labeled training examples
- minimizing the involvement of the user
- improving list/table identification techniques
- the design for non-programmer users

Figure 1 illustrates the whole system at high level.

In the following, identification of rows and columns are described in Sections 2 and 3 respectively. In Section 4 the implementation details of the system and the performance results are given. Finally conclusions are drawn in Section 5.

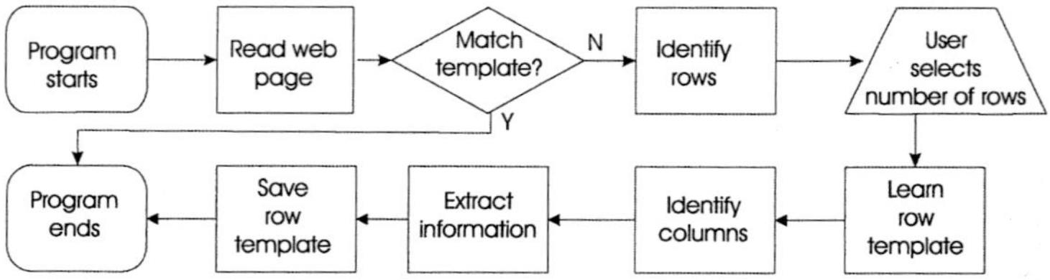

Fig. 1. High level flowchart of the system

2 Identifying Rows

The goal of information extraction is to convert displayed information in the dynamic web page back into structured database format. A standard assumption adopted by the authors is that a dynamic web page including lists and tables is generated by a template, which describes the format of each data field and the visual layout of the whole page[2]. The server-side program fills the template with results of a database query submitted by a Web client (browser). Thus, template extraction is a necessary step in this process. To extract the template, a basic step is identifying common data among a set of dynamic web pages from the same source.

Definition 1 (Page template). *A page template is a set of strings that the web server uses to automatically generate pages and fill them with the results of database query.*

Since the objective of this work is to identify the main list or table in the web page, data that does not belong to the list or table should be ignored. The focus should be on the template that generates the rows of the list or table, the Row Template.

Definition 2 (Row template). *A row template is a set of strings that the web server uses to automatically generate rows of lists or tables in the web page.*

Locating the beginning and the end of each row is a necessary step before identifying the row template. The definition of row template suggests that the number of times that some data are repeated in the web page is equal to the number of rows.

Hence, to track repeating data, we split the content of a web page into individual text chunks. This procedure is called *tokenizing.* The first step in the process is to define special strings that are likely to be found on the boundaries of tokens.

Definition 3 (Separator). *Symbols that separate the web page into individual data fields are called separators.*

Since the data fields we are interested in extracting are visually displayed on the web page, it is intuitive that HTML tags should be treated separately from other data, and punctuation characters are often used to separate data fields. Therefore, a separator is defined as one or more consecutive HTML tags, or any punctuation character excluding the set ”,.(-)’%”, which was selected empirically. The character SPACE is also excluded from the separator list in order to minimize the number of data fields. TABs and NEWLINEs are treated as separators since they are quite likely the separators of the columns and rows.

Definition 4 (Token). *A token is a sequence of characters between separators in the web page. The token includes the separator right after it except for “$<$”, which is included into the token behind it.*

Each token is assigned an index in the web page starting from 0.

Example 1. **1.** A sequence of characters:

$< b > INN\ ON\ THE\ LAKE < /b >< /a >< /td >< td\ align = right > ...$

is separated into six tokens with indices:

$0 :< b >$
$1 : INN\ ON\ THE\ LAKE$
$2 :< /b >$
$3 :< /a >$
$4 :< /td >$
$5 :< td\ align = right >$

Definition 5 (Token Sequence). *A Token Sequence is a sequence of consecutive tokens in the web page. The* length *of a token sequence is the number of tokens it consists of.*

In example 1, “$< b > INN\ ON\ THE\ LAKE < /b >< /a >< /td >< td\ align = right >$” is called a token sequence.

The assumption, on which the definition of row template is based, can be restated using the above definitions as:

Assumption 1. *All rows contain some common token sequences.*

Example 2. **2.** A web page includes two rows like

$... < b > AIRPORT\ HOTEL\ HALIFAX < /b >< /a >< /td >< td\ align = right ...$
$... < b > INN\ ON\ THE\ LAKE < /b >< /a >< /td >< td\ align = right ...$

Two common token sequences, ô$< b >$ö and ô$< /b >< /a >< /td >< td\ align = right$ö, may be parts of the row template.

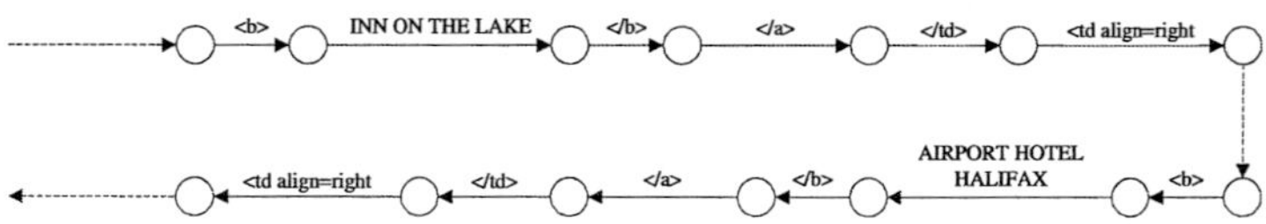

Fig. 2. State diagram of automaton of Example 2

Thus, a grammar induction algorithm [2, 10] is applied to find the repeated data that may correspond to rows. The entire sequence of tokens in the web page is viewed as a string in a language generated by a regular grammar, and the goal is to:

- Construct a Finite State Automaton (FSA) that implements the regular grammar generating the web page.
- Minimize the FSA.
- Learn and use the FSA to recognize the rows.

First a FSA $M = (K, \Sigma, \Delta, s, f)$ of the web page is defined, where:

Σ is an alphabet. Every token in the web page is a symbol of the alphabet.
K is a finite set of states. Each state is between two consecutive tokens.
$s \in K$ is the initial state at the beginning of the web page.
$f \subseteq K$ is the final state at the end of the web page.
Δ, the transition relation, is a subset of $K \times (\Sigma \cup \{e\}) \times K$ [11].

For instance, Figure 2 shows the state diagram of the automaton of Example 2. The minimization procedure consists of state-merging and removal of superfluous transitions.

Two states, i and j, are merged if their incoming transitions, $\delta_{k,i}(a)$ and $\delta_{l,j}(a)$, correspond to the same symbol a, and at least one of the outgoing transitions, $\delta_{i,m}(b)$ and $\delta_{j,n}(b)$, from each state correspond to the same symbol b. Figure 3 illustrates the automaton of Example 2 after state-merging.

Definition 6. *A* ***cycle*** *is a set of consecutive transitions that starts and ends at the same state. A cycle corresponds to a candidate row.*

Definition 7. ***Length of cycle*** *is the number of tokens along the cycle.*

Definition 8. ***Cycle set*** *is a set of cycles that include at least one common state. It corresponds to the candidate list or table.*

Definition 9. ***Overlapping parts*** *are parts of cycles in the cycle set overlapping with each other due to state-merging. They correspond to the common token sequences of candidate rows.*

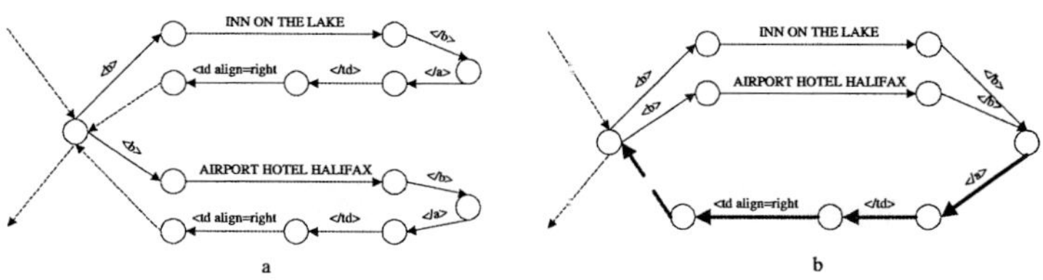

Fig. 3. State diagram of state-merged automaton of Example 2. (a) The automaton with only one pair of states merged. (b) The final automaton after full merging. Thicker lines represent overlapping parts of the cycle set

For a real web page, the automaton is much more complicated than the above example since any repeating tokens will generate cycles, resulting in a large number of cycle sets generated. In order to process all these cycle sets and extract the one that corresponds to the correct rows of the list or table, further processing is required.

The first assumption made is that rows of the same list or table should have similar numbers of tokens. This is a reasonable assumption that applies well to sites generating tables of rows providing the same information about a list of items (for example names, addresses, contact information and pricing of a list of hotels in a city).

Assumption 2. *The number of tokens in a row is close to those of other rows within the same list or table.*

Based on this assumption, a set of cycles should be removed if the lengths of the individual cycles differ greatly from each other. Deviation analysis of a distribution [12] is a general method in statistics to calculate the dispersion degree of a set of data, by normalizing the standard deviation of the data set by its expected value. The coefficient of variation, $Disp(S)$ [13] of a cycle set S is thus defined by the following equation, based on the set L of lengths of cycles in S and assuming that lengths of rows in the list or table are normally distributed.

$$Disp(S) = \sigma(L)/E(L) \tag{1}$$

where $\sigma(L)$ represents the standard deviation of L and $E(L)$ means the expectation of L.

In this work, the acceptable dispersion degree is limited to 1, a rather loose limitation. Any cycle set with dispersion degree larger than 1 will be filtered out.

Since each cycle in the automaton corresponds to a row, the task of identifying rows requires a procedure of evaluating and distinguishing cycle sets that may correctly represent the table. A possible way is to choose the cycle set with the longest cycles [2]. However, our observations show that the longest cycle criterion is not necessary correct, since some trivial data may generate a long cycle. For instance, some web pages have similar data at the beginning and end, like header and footer. Thus, the longest cycles do not always correspond to rows. Compared to the automaton created by real rows, this kind of cycle has the following features:

- Smaller number of cycles in the cycle set, and/or
- Shorter overlapping parts of cycles in the cycle set.

Therefore, to minimize the effect of such cycles, it may be preferable to focus on the number of cycles, and the length of overlapping parts, instead of the total length of cycles in each cycle set. Following this intuition, cycle sets are clustered according to the their number of cycles N into **groups** , and **the sum of lengths $L(N)$ of overlapping cycle parts, i.e. the number of repeated tokens, in each group** is calculated. For example, Table 1 shows descriptions of some cycle sets. They are separated into 2 groups corresponding to the value of N, i.e., 12 and 13. Then we calculate $L(N)$ by summing up the length len of cycle sets in each group. Thus, $L(13) = 2+5+3+9+4+6+3+3$ and $L(12) = 9+8+7+...+16+15+14$. One or more groups are expected to stand out.

An empirical observation related to the number of repeated tokens is that, for a table with n rows, the number of tokens repeated n times is fairly close to the number of tokens repeated $n-1$ times, but much greater than the number of tokens repeated $n+1$ times.

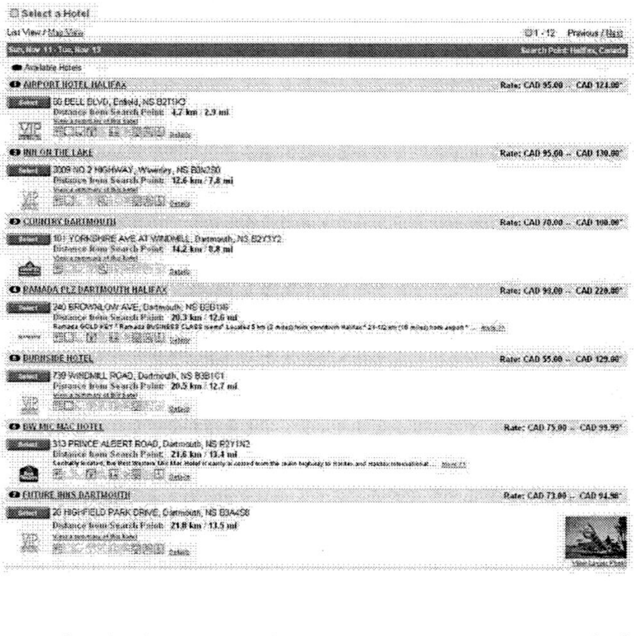

Fig. 4. An example of a dynamic web site, www.Travelocity.com[14]. Web clients can submit queries. The Figure illustrates the response page including a list of search results

Table 1. Examples of Cycle sets with N equal to 12 and 13 of the example in Figure 4. Each row represents one cycle set. N is the the number of repeated cycles in the cycle set. *ind* is the index of the first token of the cycle set, which indicates the location of the cycle set in the web page. *len* is the length of overlapping parts of the cycle set

N	ind	len	N	ind	len
13	690	2	13	880	4
13	866	5	13	992	6
13	868	3	13	995	3
12	999	9	12	1005	3
12	1000	8	12	1018	2
12	1001	7	12	1022	16
12	1002	6	12	1023	15
12	1003	5	12	1024	14

To quantify the above observation as a criterion, a group with cycle sets containing N repeated cycles is very likely to correspond to the correct number of rows if the following condition is satisfied.

$$L(N-1)/L(N) << L(N)/L(N+1) \tag{2}$$

Our system chooses the top 10 groups, ranked by decreasing value of $L(N)/L(N+1)$. This effectively means choosing ten candidate values for the number of rows in the table.

As an example, consider the Travelocity web page [14] with 12 rows shown in Figure 4. Figure 5 shows $L(N)$ for groups of cycle sets with varying N. Figure 6 shows the **Ratio** $L(N)/L(N+1)$ as a function of N. The group with 12 repeated cycles clearly stands out. A similar pattern is observed in several other web sites.

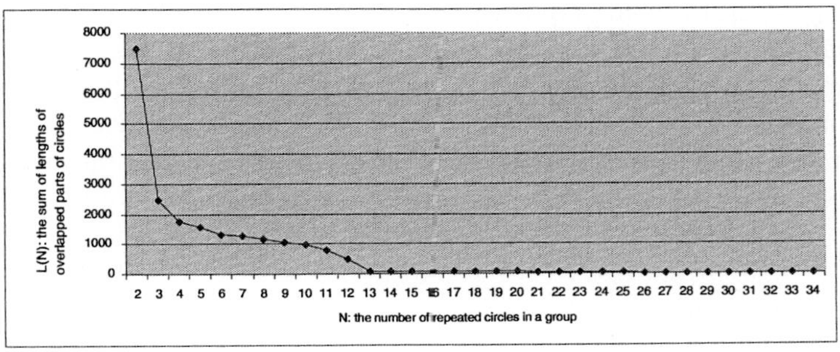

Fig. 5. Sum of lengths of overlapping parts of repeated cycles in each group - Travelocity web page [14] in Figure 4

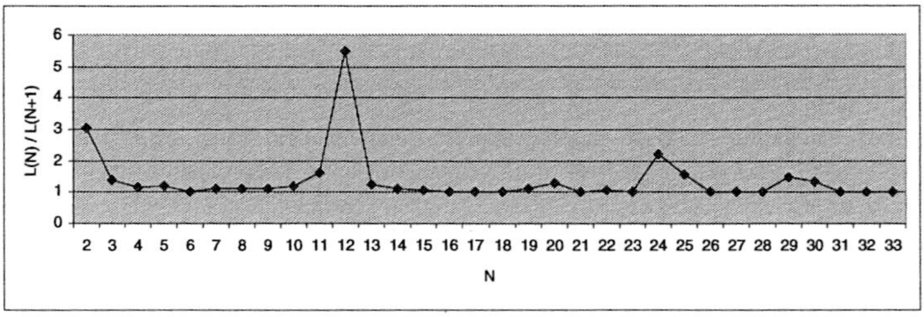

Fig. 6. The ratio L(N) / L(N+1) using the data of Figure 5

The last filtering stage is based on the assumption that, out of the candidate cycle sets, the ones more likely to correspond to the correct number of rows are those that contain the highest number of tokens.

Assumption 3. *The more tokens a candidate list or table has, the more likely it is to be the correct one.*

On the basis of this assumption, the top 5 groups of cluster sets, ranked by number of tokens they contain, are chosen as the finalists in the process of identifying the number of rows in the list or table. The user is then asked to select the group corresponding to the correct number of rows from among them.

The group chosen represents the number of rows, and each cycle set in the group corresponds to a candidate table or list. The system further selects the cycle set with the largest number of tokens. The list or table can then be separated into rows according to the cycles in this cycle set.

3 Identifying Columns

Since all rows in the list and table are properly separated, it is possible to induce a row template from them. The idea behind this is to search for all sequences of tokens that appear in each row. Each induced token sequence becomes part of the page template. Table 2 is a simplified example of a table with 3 rows. From our experiments, to separate the columns correctly, a row template should contain as many token sequences as possible, i.e., the Longest Common Subsequence [15] among rows, since:

- Data fields in the same column are usually close to each other in length, or number of tokens.
- Data fields in the same column are usually close to each other in the relative positions to their own rows. The details are explained later in this section.

Consider sequences of tokens, $X = \{x(1), x(2), ..., x(m)\}$, $Y = \{y(1), y(2), ..., y(n)\}$, $Z = \{z(1), z(2), ..., z(k)\}$. The following definitions formalize subsequences and related concepts.

Table 2. A simplified example of a table in the page. Each character represents a token sequence. B and D are parts of row template, and other characters are data fields

Data field	Template part	Data field	Template part	Data field
A	B	E	D	F
C	B	F	D	A
F	B	A	D	H

Definition 10 (Subsequence). *Sequence Z is a subsequence of X if there exists a strictly increasing sequence* $\{i_1, i_2, ..., i_k\}$ *of indices of X such that for all* $j = 1, 2, ..., k$*, there is a* $x(i_j) = z(j)$.

Definition 11 (Common Subsequence). *Sequence Z is a common subsequence of X and Y if Z is a subsequence of both X and Y. Z is the Longest Common Subsequence (LCS) if it is the maximum-length common subsequence of X and Y [15].*

To solve the LCS problem, a dynamic programming algorithm from [15] can be used.

Denote by X_j the prefix $\{x(1), x(2), ..., x(j)\}$ of X. If Z is a LCS of X and Y, the following conditions are true:

- If $x(m) = y(n)$ then $z(k) = x(m)$, Z_{k-1} is a LCS of X_{m-1} and Y_{n-1}.
- If $x(m), y(n)$ are different and $z(k)$ is not equal to $x(m)$ then Z is a LCS of X_{m-1} and Y.
- If $x(m)$ and $y(n)$ are different and $z(k)$ is not equal to $y(n)$ then Z if a LCS of X and Y_{n-1}.

A recursive algorithm can be constructed from the above three possibilities and eventually reach a LCS of two data sequences. Hence, all rows are successfully separated, from which the row template is generated. The next step is to identify columns.

In order to identify columns, data fields that are not part of the row template need to be extracted. The following features help extract the data fields from the web page:

- Any data field of a column is between two token sequences of the row template.
- Data fields are the actually displayed data on the page.

It is reasonable to assume that most of the data actually displayed consists of everything except HTML tags and control symbols, such as " " and " ". Accordingly, data fields can be extracted by following steps:

1. Pick up all tokens between two consecutive token sequences in all rows and mark as a column.

2. Extract all columns by step 1 and set up as a table.
3. Refine each data field in the table by leaving actually displayed data only.

After identifying columns, the whole list or table in the web page is obtained. Once the row template has been established, it can be used to automatically extract the data fields from the web pages.

4 Implementation and Performance

The system (TIDE) described in this paper works in combination with a web robot [16], which obtains web pages including lists or tables. This web robot automatically queries dynamic web sites on the basis of a script, thus freeing the user from the repetitive form filling and reading of the returned lists and tables associated with activities such as making a car rental or airline flight or hotel reservation. In other words, the web robot system is capable of crawling secure dynamic web sites, and performs the following [16]:

1. Locates target web sites.
2. Establishes network communication.
3. Logs into the site, if required.
4. Obtains environmental variables if necessary.
5. Locates the web pages with inquiry forms.
6. Fills and submits the forms.
7. Obtains and stores the returned web pages for information extraction.

The web robot works as follows:

1. User inputs the address of the web site and links to destination web pages.
2. Robot establishes HTTP or HTTPS (HTTP over Secure Socket Layer) connection.
3. It handles cookies and environmental variables to communicate with server side scripts and log in, if required.
4. It automatically fills and submits the HTML form on the basis of a script containing the required information.
5. It stores response pages from the server for information extraction.

The information extraction and the web robot of [16] have been combined as shown in Figure 7. The information extraction system described in the previous sections receives input from the web robot and outputs the list or table.

TIDE has been tested on web pages from the 14 web sites of Table 3. The web sites cover various application areas, such as hotel reservations, book searches, video rentals, looking for driving directions, searching for people and general search engines. Lists and tables are extracted with 100 percent accuracy in 12 out of 14 examples and more than 90 percent accuracy in remaining 2 examples.

Specifically, our approach concentrates on learning the row template by identifying common data within single web page. Compared to the page template used in [2], the row template has the following advantages:

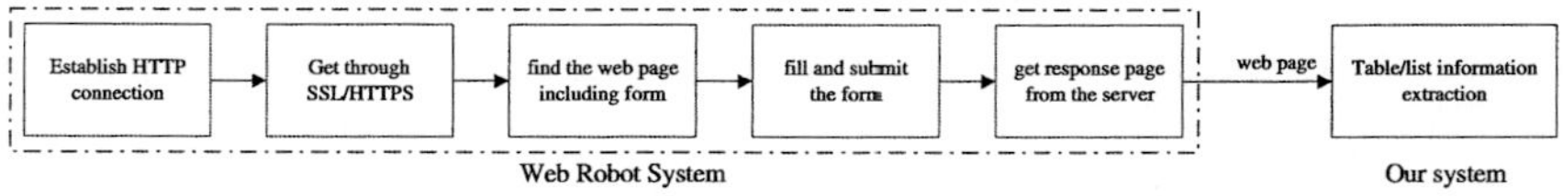

Fig. 7. Combined system

- It can work with a smaller number of pages, even a single page, thus overcoming the potential problem that the number of similar pages available on a particular site at any given time is often quite limited [17].
- Unlike [2], our approach does not require the effort of manually identifying similar web pages as training examples.
- The efficiency is improved by ignoring most of the unrelated web page data outside the lists and tables.
- Rows are identified simultaneously with locating the beginning and end of the row template. This again significantly reduces the complexity of the whole system.
- The row template makes it much easier to identify columns than the page template of [2] by focusing on a single row.
- For all lists generated by the same template, once one of them has been analyzed, others can be successfully extracted in a fully unsupervised manner.

We tested our system on the same web sites as in [2], shown in Table 3. The accuracy is calculated by the percentage of correctly extracted tuples. Lists or tables in most of examples are correctly extracted.

One example, Borders[18], visually consists of three columns, in which we are supposed to extract a book list existing in the middle column as shown in Figure 8. Some advertisement data in the left and right columns, however, are physically present between any two rows of the book list in the HTML file. Therefore, all data fields in the list are successfully extracted but followed by some unnecessary data. We estimate this example as 90 percent correctness by data fields in the list in proportion to all data fields actually extracted.

5 Discussion and Conclusions

A comprehensive performance comparison of the published performance of the systems WIEN, STALKER and Lerman's [2] with TIDE is shown in Table 4. The accuracies of WIEN and STALKER are given as reported in [6]. However, TIDE has only been tested on the same web sites as Lerman's [2] since the web sites, on which WIEN and STALKER were tested, were not specified in [6].

As shown in Table 4, our system has the highest accuracy, almost 100 percent. For practical applications, accuracy is obviously of critical importance.

Moreover, the processing time and the manual labelling overhead are two other critical factors. Comparing these Information Extraction systems, WIEN

Table 3. Performance of the system of [2] and TIDE on the 14 examples of [2]. The second to fourth column show the number of rows, columns and lists/tables respectively. The number of rows/columns is that of the most prominent list/table only. In some cases, the number of columns varies depending on whether some data fields could be combined

Example	rows	cols	lists/tables	**Lerman's system**[2]	**TIDE**
Airport	80	4	2	Correct tuples	Correct tuples
Blockbuster	100	4	2	No tuples extracted	Correct tuples
Borders	25	12	5	Correct	Estimated 90%
cuisineNet	8	-	3	No tuples extracted	Correct tuples
RestaurantRow	10	-	3	Correct tuples	Correct tuples
YahooPeople	10	3	1	Correct tuples	Correct tuples
YahooQuote	30	4	1	18/20 tuples correct	Correct tuples
WhitePapers	10	4	2	Correct tuples	Correct tuples
MapQuest	16	-	2	Tuples begin in the middle of the rows	Correct tuples
Hotel	25	5	1	Correct tuples	Correct tuples
CitySearch	20	-	2	Correct tuples	Correct tuples
CarRental	16	-	3	Correct tuples	Correct tuples
Boston	20	4	3	Correct tuples	Correct tuples
Arrow	10	3	1	No tuples extracted	Correct tuples
Average				**70%**	**99%**

Fig. 8. An example from Borders [18] web site

Table 4. Overall performance comparison of WIEN, STALKER, Lerman's and TIDE

IE System	**WIEN**[6]	**STALKER**[6]	**Lerman's**[2]	**Our System**
Learning Type	Supervised	Supervised	Unsupervised	Unsupervised with minimal user interaction
Training Set	labelled	labelled	Unlabelled	Unlabelled
Accuracy	60%	80%	70%	99%
Computer Processing Time	-	-	-	from several seconds to 1 minute
Human Processing Time	-	-	-	choosing one from 5 items

and STALKER need user labeling of all data fields in several rows for each training example, and therefore they require significant human involvement; the system in [2] employs two general unsupervised learning algorithms, AutoClass and DataPro, which are computationally demanding. On the other hand, algorithms in our system are simpler compared to the other systems; the implementation of the row template greatly decreases the amount of user involvement compared to WIEN and STALKER. Furthermore, in this work, the user is required to make a simple choice among at most 5 options. Since the user decision is based on visual inspection of a web page, it does not require any particular technical or programming skills or expertise. User involvement is only required the first time the information extraction program is applied to a new site, and whenever there is an update to the web site format. The design of a totally unsupervised approach is left for future research.

Our system is designed for all kinds of lists and tables in the web page. Broadly speaking, it is applicable to all data sets with periodical regularity and common features in each period.

Acknowledgements

We thank Dr. M. Heywood for constructive comments, and Jianduan Liang for helpful discussions and technical support. The research was funded by grants from the Natural Sciences and Engineering Research Council of Canada.

References

[1] Deitel, H., Deitel, P., Nieto, T.: Internet and World Wide Web: How to Program. Prentice-Hall, Upper Saddle River, NJ 07458 (2000)

[2] Lerman, K., Knoblock, C., Minton, S.: Automatic data extraction from lists and tables in Web sources. In: Automatic Text Extraction and Mining workshop (ATEM-01), IJCAI-01, Seattle, WA, USA (2001)

[3] Knoblock, C., Lerman, K., Minton, S., Muslea, I.: A machine learning approach to accurately and reliably extracting data from the web. In: IJCAI-2001 Workshop on Text Learning: Beyond Supervision, Seattle, WA, USA (2001)

[4] Kushmerick, N.: Wrapper induction: Efficiency and expressiveness. Artificial Intelligence **118** (2000) 15–68

[5] Kushmerick, N.: Wrapper induction for information extraction. Technical report, Dept. of Computer Science, U. of Washington, TR UW-CSE-97-11-04 (1997)

[6] Muslea, I., Minton, S., Knoblock., C.: Hierarchical wrapper induction for semistructured information sources. Journal of Autonomous Agents and Multi-Agent Systems **4** (2001) 93–114

[7] Lerman, K., Minton, S.: Learning the common structure of data. In: In Proceedings of the 17th National Conference on Artificial Intelligence (AAAI-2000), AAAI Press, Menlo Park (2000) 609–614

[8] Cheeseman, P., Stutz, J.: Bayesian classification (AUTOCLASS): Theory and results. Advances in Knowledge Discovery and Data Mining, AAAI/MIT Press (1996) 153–180

[9] Hanson, J., Stutz, R., Cheeseman, P.: Bayesian classification theory. Technical report, NASA Ames TR FIA-90-12-7-01 (1991)

[10] Carrasco, R., Oncina, J.: Learning stochastic regular grammars by means of a state merging method. In: Proceedings of the Second International Colloquium on Grammatical Inference and Applications (ICGI94). Volume 862 of Lecture Notes on Artificial Intelligence., Berlin, Springer Verlag (1994) 139–152

[11] Lewis, H., Papadimitriou, C.: Elements of the Theory of Computation. Prentice-Hall, Upper Saddle River, NJ 07458 (1998)

[12] Degroot, M., Schervish, M.: Probability and Statistics. Addison-Wesley Pub. Co., Cambridge, Massachusetts (1975)

[13] Rozgonyi, T. G.: Statistics for Engineers. `http://engineering.uow.edu.au/Courses/Stats/File1586.html`, (Accessed on Oct. 28, 2002)

[14] `http://www.travelocity.com/`: Travelocity travel site. (Accessed on Oct. 23, 2002)

[15] Cormen, T., Leiserson, C., Rivest, R.: Introduction to Algorithms. MIT Press, Cambridge, Massachusetts (1989)

[16] Liang, J., Milios, E., Zincir-Heywood, N.: A robot capable of crawling secure dynamic web sites. Technical report, Faculty of Computer Science, Dalhousie University, Halifax, Nova Scotia, Canada (2002)

[17] Cohen, W., Jensen, L.: A structured wrapper induction system for extracting information from semi-structured documents. In: Automatic Text Extraction and Mining workshop (ATEM-01), IJCAI-01, Seattle, WA, USA (2001)

[18] `http://www.borders.com/`: Amazon online shopping site. (Accessed on November 12, 2001)

Summarizing Web Sites Automatically

Yiquing Zhang Zhang, Nur Zincir-Heywood, and Evangelos Milios

Dalhousie University

Abstract. This research is directed towards automating the Web Site summarization task. To achieve this objective, an approach, which applies machine learning and natural language processing techniques, is employed. The automatically generated summaries are compared to manually constructed summaries from DMOZ Open Directory Project. The comparison is performed via a formal evaluation process involving human subjects. Statistical evaluation of the results demonstrates that the automatically generated summaries are as informative as human authored DMOZ summaries and significantly more informative than home page browsing or time limited site browsing.

1 Introduction

The information overload problem [17] on the World Wide Web has brought users great difficulty to find useful information quickly and effectively. It has been more and more difficult for the user to skim over a Web site and get an idea of its contents. Currently, manually constructed summaries by volunteer experts are available, such as the DMOZ Open Directory Project [1]. These human-authored summaries give a concise and effective description of popular Web sites. However, they are subjective, and expensive to build and maintain [8]. Hence in this work, our objective is to summarize the Web site automatically.

The technology of automatic summarization of text is maturing and may provide a solution to this problem [17, 16]. Automatic text summarization produces a concise summary by abstraction or extraction of important text using statistical approaches [9], linguistic approaches [4] or combination of the two [5, 13, 16].

The goal of abstraction is to produce coherent summaries that are as good as human authored summaries [13]. To achieve this, extraction systems analyze a source document to determine significant sentences, and produce a concise summary from these significant sentences [19].

Basically Web page summarization derives from text summarization techniques [9]. However, it is a great challenge to summarize Web pages automatically and effectively [3], because Web pages differ from traditional text documents in both structure and content. Instead of coherent text with a well-defined discourse structure, Web pages often have diverse contents such as bullets and images [6].

Currently there is no effective way to produce unbiased, coherent and informative summaries of Web pages automatically. Amitay et al [3] propose a unique approach, which relies on the hypertext structure. This approach is applied to

Y. Xiang and B. Chaib-draa (Eds.): AI 2003, LNAI 2671, pp. 283–296, 2003.

"generate short coherent textual snippets presented to the user with search engine results".

Garcia-Molina et al [9] compare alternative methods to summarize Web pages for display on handheld devices. They test the performance of these methods by asking human subjects to perform specific tasks using each method, and conclude that the combined *Keyword/Summary* method provides the best performance in terms of access times and number of pen actions on the hand held devices.

Our objective is to automate summarization of Web sites, not simply Web pages. To this end, the "Keyword/Summary" idea of [9] is adopted. However, this methodology is enhanced by applying machine learning and natural language processing techniques. A summary is produced in a sequence of stages: URL & Text extraction are described in Section 2. Sections 3, 4 and 5 detail the narrative paragraph, key-phrase and key-sentence extraction, respectively. Evaluation results are given in Section 6 and conclusions are drawn in Section 7.

2 URL and Text Extraction

Since our objective is to summarize the Web site, we want to focus on top-level pages in order to extract the contents which describe the Web site in a general sense. A module called *Site Crawler* was developed, that crawls within a given Web site using *breadth-first-search*. This means that only Web pages physically located in this site will be crawled and analyzed. Besides tracking the URLs of these Web pages, the Site Crawler also records the depth (i.e. level) and length of each page. Depth represents the number of "hops" from the home page to the current page. For example, if we give the home page depth 1, then all pages which can be reached by an out-link of the home page are assigned depth 2. Length of a Web page is the number of characters in the Web page source file. The Site Crawler only keeps known types of Web pages, such as .htm, .html, .shtml, .php, etc. Handling other types of text and non-text files is a topic for future research.

Normally the Site Crawler crawls the top 1000 pages of a Web site, according to a breadth-first traversal starting from the home page. The number of pages to crawl (1000) is based on the observation after crawling 60 Web sites (identified in DMOZ subdirectories), that there is an average of 1000 pages up to and including depth equal to 4. For each Web site, the Site Crawler will stop crawling when either 1000 pages have been collected, or it has finished crawling depth 4, whichever comes first.

After the URLs of the top 1000 Web pages are collected, the plain text must be extracted from these pages. In this work the text browser *Lynx* [10] is used for this purpose.

3 Narrative Paragraph Classification

The summary of the Web site will be created on the basis of the text extracted by Lynx. However, Web pages often do not contain a coherent narrative structure [6], so our aim is to identify rules for determining which text should be

Table 1. Cross-validation of C5.0 classifier *LONGSHORT*

Fold	1	2	3	4	5	6	7	8	9	10	Mean
Size	2	2	2	2	2	2	2	2	2	2	2.0
Error(%)	5.7	5.7	11.4	4.3	2.9	4.3	4.3	7.1	2.9	10.0	5.9

considered for summarization and which should be discarded. This is achieved in two steps: First, criteria are defined for determining if a paragraph is long enough to be considered for analysis. Then, additional criteria are defined to classify long paragraphs into narrative or non-narrative. Only narrative paragraphs are used in summary generation. The criteria are defined automatically using supervised machine learning.

Intuitively, whether a paragraph is long or short is determined by its length (i.e., the number of characters). However, two more features, number of words, and number of characters in all words, might also play a key role. In order to determine which feature is the most important, a total of 700 text paragraphs is extracted from 100 Web pages. Statistics of three attributes *Length, NumberOfWords* and *NumberOfChars* are recorded from each paragraph. *Length* is the number of all characters in the paragraph. *NumberOfWords* is the number of words in this paragraph, and *NumberOfChars* is the total number of characters in all words. Then each text paragraph is labelled as *long* or *short* manually. The decision tree learning program C5.0 [2] is used to construct a classifier, *LONGSHORT*, for this task.

The training set consists of 700 instances. Among the 700 cases, there are 36 cases misclassified, leading to an error of 5.1%. The cross-validation of the classifier is listed in Table 3. The mean error rate 5.9% indicates the classification accuracy of this classifier.

Not all long paragraphs provide coherent information in terms of generating a meaningful summary. Informally, whether a paragraph is *narrative* or *non-narrative* is determined by the coherence of its text. Our hypothesis is that the frequencies of the part-of-speech tags of the words in the paragraph contain sufficient information to classify a paragraph as narrative. To test this hypothesis, a training set is generated as follows: First, 1000 Web pages were collected from DMOZ subdirectories, containing a total of 9763 text paragraphs, among which a total of 3243 paragraphs were classified as long. Then, the part-of-speech tags for all words in these paragraphs are computed using a rule-based part-of-speech tagger [7].

After part-of-speech tagging, the following attributes are extracted from each paragraph. Let n_i (i = 1, 2, ... , 32) be the number of occurrences of tag i, and S be the total number of tags (i.e. words) in the paragraph. Let P_i be the fraction of S, that n_i represents.

Table 2. Cross-validation of C5.0 classifier *NARRATIVE*

Fold	1	2	3	4	5	6	7	8	9	10	Mean
Size	5	5	3	4	4	5	4	3	4	3	4.0
Error	11.1	9.3	13.6	11.1	9.9	7.4	9.3	16	10.5	14.7	11.3

$$S = \sum_{i=1}^{32} n_i$$
$$P_i = n_i/S \ \ (i = 1, 2, ..., 32) \ . \quad (1)$$

A total of 34 attributes are associated with each paragraph in the training set. The length of the paragraph in characters, and the length of the paragraph in words are added to the 32 attributes P_1, P_2, ..., P_{32}, as defined in (1). Then each paragraph is manually labelled as *narrative* or *non-narrative.* Finally, a C5.0 classifier *NARRATIVE* is trained on the training set of 3243 paragraphs.

Among the 3242 cases, about 63.5% of them are following this rule: if the percentage of *Symbols* is less than 6.8%, and the percentage of *Preposition* is more than 5.2%, and the percentage of *Proper Singular Nouns* is less than 23.3%, then this paragraph is *narrative.* There are 260 cases misclassified, leading to an error of 8.0%. The cross-validation of the classifier *NARRATIVE* is listed in Table 3. The mean error rate 11.3% indicates the predictive accuracy of this classifier.

4 Key-Phrase Extraction

Traditionally, key-phrases (key-words and key-terms) are extracted from the document in order to generate a summary. Key-phrase extraction from a body of text relies on an evaluation of the importance of each phrase [9]. In terms of automatically summarizing a Web site, a phrase is considered as *key-phrase*, if and only if it occurs very frequently in the Web pages of the site, i.e., the total frequency is very high.

In this work, a *key-phrase* can be either *key-word* or *key-term. Key-word* is a single word with very high frequency over the set of Web pages, and *key-term* is a two-word term with very high frequency.

As we discussed in the previous section, Web pages are quite different from traditional documents. The existence of *anchor text* and *special text* contributes much to the difference. *Anchor text* is the text of hyper links, and it "often provides more accurate descriptions of Web pages than the pages themselves" [8]. *Special text* includes title, headings and bold or italicized text. The assumption is that both anchor text and special text may play a key role in describing important topics of Web pages. Therefore a supervised learning approach is applied to test this assumption.

In order to determine the key-words of a Web site, a decision tree is produced. A data set of 5454 candidate key-words (at most 100 for each site) from 60 Web sites are collected. The sites are taken from DMOZ subdirectories. For each

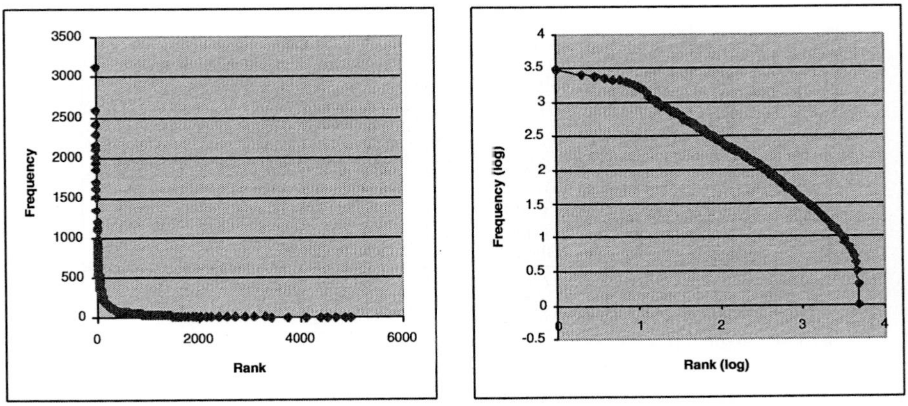

Fig. 1. Rank-Frequency data and Zipf's Law

site, the frequencies of each word in narrative text, anchor text and special text (denoted by fn, fa and fs, respectively), are measured. Then the total frequency, f, of each word over these three categories is computed, where the weight for each category is the same. Moreover, it should be noted that 425 stop words (*a, about, above, across, after, again, against, all, almost, alone, along, already, also, although, always, among, an, and, ...*) [11] are discarded in this stage. Then a simple stemming process was applied to identify each singular noun and its plural form. For example, *product* : 2100 and *products* : 460 yields *product* : 2560.

After this process, on the average there were about 5,100 different words (excluding stop words) within the text body of the top 1000 Web pages. Figure 1 shows that the rank and frequency statistics of these words fit Zipf's Law [15]. The words with the lowest frequencies are obviously not key-words, hence only those words whose frequency is more than 5% of the maximum frequency are kept as *candidate key-words*. This step eliminates about 98% of the original words, leaving about 102 candidate key-words per site. As a result, the top 100 candidate key-words are kept and nine features of each candidate key-word C_i are defined, as shown in Table 3. The feature *Tag* was obtained by tagging candidate key-words with rule-based part-of-speech tagger [7].

Next, each candidate key-word is labelled manually as *key-word* or *non-key-word*. The criterion to determine if a candidate key-word is a true key-word is that a key-word provides important information which is related with the Web site. Based on frequency statistics and part-of-speech feature of these candidate key-words, a C5.0 classifier *KEY-WORD* is constructed.

Among the total 5454 cases, 222 cases are misclassified, leading to an error of 4.1%. In the decision tree, about 35% of cases are following this rule: if R (defined as the ratio of a candidate key-word's frequency to the maximum frequency in Table 3) is less than or equal to 0.1, then this candidate key-word is a non-key-word. Another main stream of cases follows the second rule: if R is greater than

Table 3. Feature list of candidate key-words

No.	Feature	Value	Meaning
1	W	$W_i = f_i / \sum_{i=1}^{100} f_i$	Weight of candidate key-word
2	R	$R_i = f_i / \max_{i=1}^{100} f_i$	Ratio of frequency to max freq.
3	WN	$WN_i = fn_i / \sum_{i=1}^{100} fn_i$	Weight in *narrative* text only
4	RN	$RN_i = fn_i / \max_{i=1}^{100} fn_i$	Ratio in *narrative* text only
5	WA	$WA_i = fa_i / \sum_{i=1}^{100} fa_i$	Weight in *anchor* text only
6	RA	$RA_i = fa_i / \max_{i=1}^{100} fa_i$	Ratio in *anchor* text only
7	WS	$WS_i = fs_i / \sum_{i=1}^{100} fs_i$	Weight in *special* text only
8	RS	$RS_i = fs_i / \max_{i=1}^{100} fs_i$	Ratio in *special* text only
9	Tag	$CC, CD, ..., WRB$	Part-of-speech tag ([7])

Table 4. Cross-validation of C5.0 classifier *KEY-WORD*

Fold	1	2	3	4	5	6	7	8	9	10	Mean
Size	22	20	20	30	23	18	20	27	20	20	22.0
Error(%)	4.0	5.1	5.5	4.4	4.0	5.1	5.1	5.9	5.5	4.0	4.9

0.1, and part-of-speech tag is NN (common singular nouns [7]), and RA (ratio in anchor text) is less than or equal to 0.798, then the candidate key-word is a key-word. This case covers 45% of the data set.

The most important rule here is: if R is greater than 0.1 and part-of-speech tag is NN (common singular nouns) or VBG (verb -ing [7]), then WA (weight in anchor text), RA (ratio in anchor text) and/or WS (weight in special text) will determine if a candidate key-word should be classified as key-word or non-key-word. This demonstrates that our assumption is true, i.e., anchor text and special text do play important roles in determining key-words of a Web site. The cross-validation results of the classifier *KEY-WORD* is listed in Table 4. The mean error rate 4.9% indicates the predictive accuracy of this classifier.

Furthermore, it is observed that terms which consist of two of the top 100 candidate key-words may exist with high frequency. Such a term could be good as part of the description of the Web site. Thus, a similar approach with *automatic key-word extraction* is developed to identify key-terms of the Web site.

The algorithm combines any two of the top 100 candidate key-words and searches for these terms in collocation over narrative text, anchor text and special text. Then these terms are sorted by frequency and the top 30 are kept as *candidate key-terms*. A C5.0 classifier *KEY-TERM* is constructed based on frequency statistics and tag features of 1360 candidate key-terms, which were extracted from 60 Web sites (collected from DMOZ subdirectories). The C5.0 classifier *KEY-TERM* is similar to the KEY-WORD classifier except that it has two part-of-speech tags *Tag1* and *Tag2*, one for each component word.

Table 5. Example of clustering

<table>
<tr><th colspan="4">Candidate Sentence</th></tr>
<tr><td colspan="4">The Software Engineering Information Repository (SEIR) is a Web-based repository of information on software engineering practices that lead to improved organizational performance.</td></tr>
<tr><th>Key-Phrase</th><th>Weight</th><th>Cluster</th><th>Weight</th></tr>
<tr><td>information</td><td>0.021</td><td>1. Software Engineering Information</td><td>0.157</td></tr>
<tr><td>software engineering</td><td>0.293</td><td>2. information on software engineering practices</td><td>0.109</td></tr>
<tr><td>practice</td><td>0.013</td><td colspan="2">Sentence Weight: 0.157</td></tr>
</table>

Once the decision tree rules for determining key-terms have been built, they are applied for automatic key-term extraction to the Web pages of a Web site. The top 10 key-terms (ranked by total frequency) for each site are kept as part of the summary. The frequency of candidate key-words is reduced by subtracting the frequency of top 10 key-terms, which includes them. Then the KEY-WORD classifier is applied. Finally, the top 25 key-words (ranked by frequency) are kept as part of the summary. It is observed that 40% to 70% of key-words and 20% to 50% of key-terms appear in the home page of a Web site.

5 Significant Sentence Extraction

Once the key-words and key-terms are identified, the most significant sentences can be retrieved from all narrative paragraphs. Each sentence is assigned a significance factor or sentence weight. The top five sentences, ranked according to sentence weight, are chosen as part of the summary. In order to achieve this goal, a modified version of the procedure in [9] is applied.

First, the sentences containing any of the list L of key-phrases, consisting of the top 25 key-words and top 10 key-terms identified previously, are selected. Second, all clusters in each selected sentence S are identified. A *cluster* C is a sequence of consecutive words in the sentence for which the following is true: (1) the sequence starts and ends with a key-phrase in L, and (2) less than D non-key-phrases must separate any two neighboring key-phrases within the sentence. D is called the "distance cutoff", and we used a value of 2 as in [9]. Third, the weight of each cluster within S is computed. The maximum of these weights is taken as the sentence weight. As shown in Table 5, a cluster's weight is computed by adding the weights of all key-phrases within the cluster, and dividing this sum by the total number of key-phrases within the cluster. The weight of key-phrase i is defined as $W_i = f_i / \sum_{i=1}^{100} f_i$, where f_i is the frequency of the key-phrase in the Web site (Table 3).

The weights of all sentences in *narrative* text paragraphs are computed and the top five sentences ranked according to sentence weights are included in the

Table 6. Automatically created summary of Software Engineering Institute Web site

Part 1. Top 25 Key-words				
sei	system	software	cmu	product
component	information	process	architecture	organization
course	program	report	practice	project
method	design	institute	development	research
document	management	defense	technology	team
Part 2. Top 10 Key-terms				
software engineering	carnegie mellon	development center	software process	software architecture
maturity model	risk management	software development	process improvement	software system
Part 3. Top 5 Key-sentences				
1. The Software Engineering Information Repository (SEIR) is a Web-based repository of information on software engineering practices that lead to improved organizational performance.				
2. Because of its mission to improve the state of the practice of software engineering, the SEI encourages and otherwise facilitates collaboration activities between members of the software engineering community.				
3. The SEI mission is to provide leadership in advancing the state of the practice of software engineering to improve the quality of systems that depend on software.				
4. The Software Engineering Institute is operated by Carnegie Mellon University for the Department of Defense.				
5. The Software Engineering Institute (SEI) sponsors, co-sponsors, and is otherwise involved in many events throughout the year.				

Table 7. DMOZ summary of Software Engineering Institute Web site

Software Engineering Institute (SEI) - SEI is a federal research center whose mission is to advance the state of the practice of software engineering to improve the quality of systems that depend on software. SEI accomplishes this mission by promoting the evolution of software engineering from an ad hoc, labor-intensive activity to a discipline that is well managed and supported by technology.

summary as *key-sentences*. Finally, a summary is formed consisting of the top 25 key-words, top 10 key-terms and top 5 key-sentences.

Table 6 shows a summary example generated by our system for the Software Engineering Institute (SEI) Web site. This summary gives a brief description of SEI's mission and various activities, whereas Table 7 shows the DMOZ summary for the same Web site.

As we can see, the automatically generated summary basically covers the key contents described by human authors.

Table 8. URL list of the Web sites used in the experiments

Subdirectory	Site URL
Software/ Software Engineering	1. http://case.ispras.ru 2. http://www.ifpug.org 3. http://www.mapfree.com/sbf 4. http://www.cs.queensu.ca/Software-Engineering 5. http://www.sei.cmu.edu
Artificial Intelligence/ Academic Departments	6. http://www.cs.ualberta.ca/~ai 7. http://www.ai.mit.edu 8. http://www.aiai.ed.ac.uk 9. http://www.ai.uga.edu 10. http://ai.uwaterloo.ca
Major Companies/ Publicly Traded	11. http://www.aircanada.ca 12. http://www.cisco.com 13. http://www.microsoft.com 14. http://www.nortelnetworks.com 15. http://www.oracle.com
E-Commerce/ Technology Vendors	16. http://www.adhesiontech.com 17. http://www.asti-solutions.com 18. http://www.commerceone.com 19. http://www.getgamma.com 20. http://www.rdmcorp.com

6 Experiments and Evaluation

In order to measure the overall performance of our approach, four sets of experiments were performed. During these experiments, automatically generated summaries are compared with human-authored summaries, home page browsing and time-limited site browsing, to measure their performance in a specific task.

From the DMOZ Open Directory Project, 20 manually constructed summaries were selected from four subdirectories. As listed in Table 8, sites 1-5 are in the *Software/Software Engineering*[1] subdirectory. Sites 6-10 are in the *Artificial Intelligence/Academic Departments*[2] subdirectory. Sites 11-15 are in *Major Companies/Publicly Traded*[3] subdirectory. And finally sites 16-20 are in *E-Commerce/Technology Vendors*[4] subdirectory. These sites were selected randomly and are of varying size and focus.

Our approach, *W3SS* (World Wide Web Site Summarization), is used to create summaries of these 20 Web sites. Each W3SS summary consists of the top 25 key-words, the top 10 key-terms and the top 5 key-sentences.

[1] http://dmoz.org/Computers/Software/Software_Engineering/

[2] http://dmoz.org/Computers/Artificial_Intelligence/Academic_Departments/

[3] http://dmoz.org/Business/Major_Companies/Publicly_Traded/

[4] http://dmoz.org/Business/E-Commerce/Technology_Vendors/

There are two major types of summarization evaluations: *intrinsic* and *extrinsic* [14, 17]. Intrinsic evaluation compares automatically generated summaries against a gold standard (ideal summaries). Extrinsic evaluation measures the performance of automatically generated summaries in a particular task (e.g., classification). Extrinsic evaluation is also called task-based evaluation and it has become more and more popular recently [18]. In this work, extrinsic evaluation is used.

In extrinsic evaluation, the objective is to measure how informative W3SS summaries, DMOZ summaries, home page browsing and time-limited site browsing are in answering a set of questions [21] about the content of the Web site. Each question is meant to have a well-defined answer, ideally explicitly stated in the summary, rather than being open-ended. Four groups of graduate students in Computer Science (5 in each group) with strong World Wide Web experience were asked to take the test as follows:

The first and second group was asked to read each W3SS and DMOZ summary, respectively and then answer the questions. The third group was asked to browse the home page of each of the 20 Web sites and answer the questions. The last group was asked to browse each Web site for at most 10 minutes (time-limited site browsing) and answer all questions. All answers were then graded in terms of their quality in a scale 0-20. The grades are tabulated in [21].

The average score of the five subjects working with the W3SS summaries is 15.0 out of a possible 20. Moreover, the variance between the average scores of all summaries over five subjects is only 0.213, which shows that all subjects in this experiment evaluated W3SS summaries consistently.

The average score of the five subjects working with the DMOZ summaries is 15.3 out of 20, hence the overall performance of DMOZ summaries is slightly better than that of W3SS ones (with an overall average 15.0). The variance between the average scores of all DMOZ summaries over five subjects is 1.267, much larger than that of W3SS summaries. As indicated in Fig. 2, there are 11 Web sites whose W3SS summaries are better than DMOZ summaries, and 8 sites whose W3SS summaries are worse than DMOZ summaries. The remaining site has the same quality of W3SS and DMOZ summary.

In the *home page browsing* experiment, every subject was allowed to browse only the home page, and there are a few very poor marks as low as 4.4 and 5.0. The average score of the five subjects browsing home pages is 12.7 out of 20, which is less than 15.0 of W3SS summaries and 15.3 of DMOZ summaries. As indicated in Fig. 3, the home page alone is often not sufficiently informative, and that digging deeper into the site conveys more complete information about the site than the home page alone. In order to understand the site better, more browsing beyond the home page alone is needed.

In the fourth test, each subject was allowed 10 minutes to browse each Web site, and look for the answers of all questions. For each site, the average score of all subjects varies from 7.0 to 20.0. This implies that either some Web sites were poorly designed, or there is too much non-text (e.g., flash) in top-level pages, which may confuse the user's understanding of the site. The average

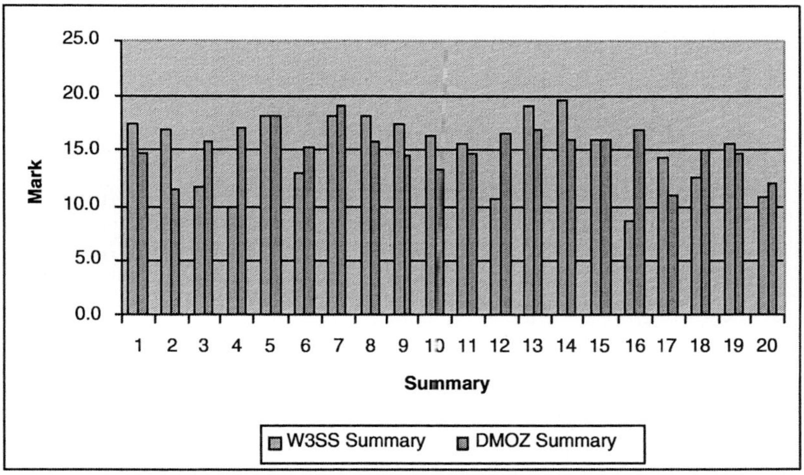

Fig. 2. W3SS summaries vs. DMOZ summaries

Table 9. Pairwise ANOVA results for the four experiments. W3SS, DMOZ, HPB, TLSP is the performance of our summaries, the human-authored summaries, home-page browsing and time-limited site browsing

	W3SS	DMOZ	HPB
DMOZ	$F_{1,190} = 0.18$ $Pvalue = 0.67$		
HPB	$F_{1,190} = 17.42$ $Pvalue < 0.0001$	$F_{1\ 190} = 23.7$ $Pvalue < 0.0001$	
TLSB	$F_{1,190} = 6.13$ $Pvalue = 0.014$	$F_{1,190} = 8.88$ $Pvalue = 0.003$	$F_{1,190} = 1.62$ $Pvalue = 0.20$

score of the five subjects browsing the sites is 13.4 out of 20, which is less than that of both W3SS and DMOZ summaries. As indicated in Fig. 4, it is not so easy to get a good understanding of the site's main contents by browsing within a limited time period. This indicates that our approach of automatically creating summaries is potentially useful because it saves the reader much time.

To confirm the above intuitive conclusions, we perform a two-factor Analysis of Variance with replications on the raw scores from the above experiments. As shown in Table 9, there is no significant difference between our summaries and the human-authored summaries, and between home-page and time-limited site browsing. However, our summaries and the human-authored summaries are significantly better than home-page and time-limited site browsing.

Since the W3SS summaries are as informative as DMOZ summaries, they could be transformed into proper prose by human editors without browsing the

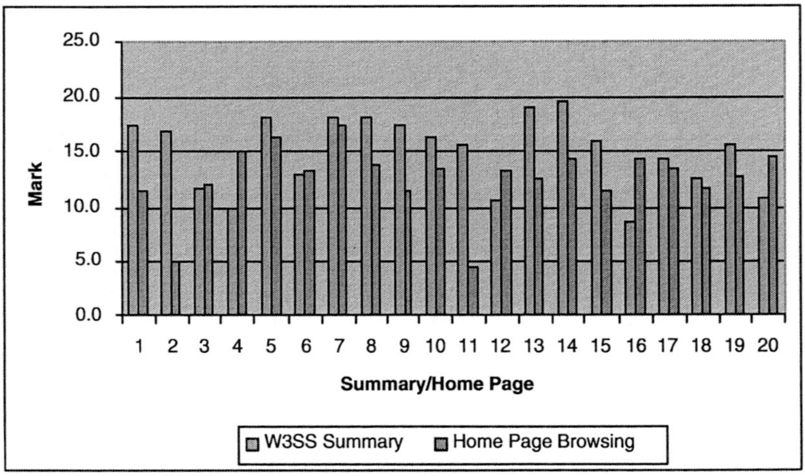

Fig. 3. W3SS summaries vs. Home page browsing

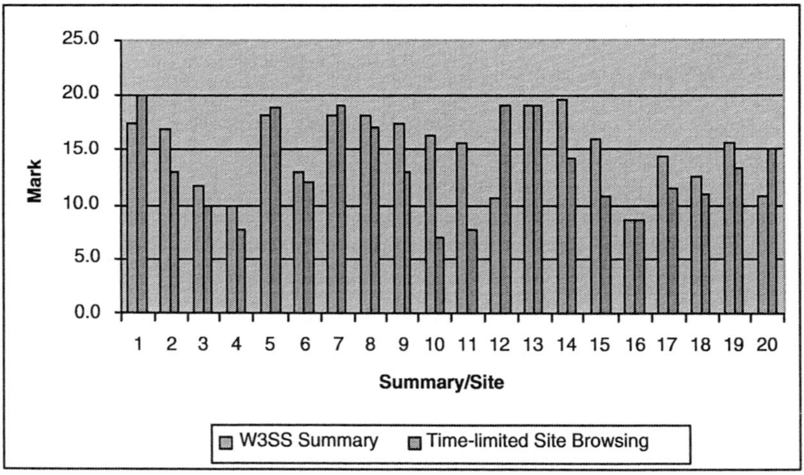

Fig. 4. W3SS summaries vs. Time-limited site browsing

Web site. Automating such a transformation is beyond the state of the art of natural language processing.

7 Conclusion and Discussion

In this work, we developed a new approach for generating summaries of Web sites. Our approach relies on a Web crawler that visits Web sites and summarizes them off-line. It applies machine learning and natural language processing techniques to extract and classify narrative paragraphs from the Web site, from which key-phrases are then extracted. Key-phrases are in turn used to extract key-sentences from the narrative paragraphs that form the summary, together with the top key-phrases. We demonstrate that our summaries, although not in proper prose, are as informative as human-authored summaries, and significantly better than browsing the home page or the site for a limited time. Our approach should be easy to transform into proper prose by human editors without having to browse the Web site. The performance of our method depends on the availability of sufficient narrative content in the Web site, and the availability of explicit narrative statements describing the site.

However, several issues need to be addressed to further improve the performance of our approach. Currently the top 1000 (or all pages between depth 1 and depth 4, inclusively) Web pages of a Web site are crawled for text extraction. Supervised learning may be used instead to determine the most appropriate number of pages to crawl.

In the key-term extraction step, we simply combine any two of top 100 candidate key-words. More sophisticated methods, such as the C-value/NC-value method [12] will be considered to automatically recognize multi-word terms. Also further research is required to determine appropriate weights for the key-phrases from different categories (plain text, anchor text and special text). And redesign of the evaluation process to reduce the inter-rater reliability problem [20] is a topic for future research. Intrinsic evaluation should also be considered.

Acknowledgements

We are thankful to Prof. Michael Shepherd for many valuable suggestions on this work, and to Jinghu Liu for suggesting the use of Lynx for text extraction from Web pages. The research has been supported by grants from the Natural Sciences and Engineering Research Council of Canada.

References

[1] Netscape 1998-2002. *DMOZ - Open Directory Project.* http://dmoz.org, last accessed on Oct. 9, 2002.

[2] RULEQUEST RESEARCH 2002. *C5.0: An Informal Tutorial.* www.rulequest.com/see5-unix.html, last accessed on Oct. 9, 2002.

[3] E. Amitay and C. Paris. Automatically summarising web sites - is there a way around it? In *ACM 9th International Conference on Information and Knowledge Management*, 2000.

[4] C. Aone, M. E. Okurowski, J. Gorlinsky, and B. Larsen. A scalable summarization system using robust NLP. In *Proceedings of the ACL'97/EACL'97 Workshop on Intelligent Scalable Text Summarization*, pages 66–73, 1997.

[5] R. Barzilay and M. Elhadad. Using lexical chains for text summarization. In *Proceedings of the Intelligent Scalable Text Summarization Workshop (ISTS'97), ACL, Madrid, Spain*, 1997.

[6] A. Berger and V. Mittal. Ocelot: a system for summarizing web pages. In *Proceedings of SIGIR*, pages 144–151, 2000.

[7] E. Brill. A simple rule-based part of speech tagger. In *Proceedings of the Third Conference on Applied Natural Language Processing, ACL*, 1992.

[8] S. Brin and L. Page. The anatomy of a large-scale hypertextual web search engine. In *7th International World Wide Web Conference*, 1998.

[9] O. Buyukkokten, H. Garcia-Molina, and A. Paepcke. Seeing the whole in parts: Text summarization for web browsing on handheld devices. In *Proceedings of 10th International World-Wide Web Conference*, 2001.

[10] Internet Software Consortium. *Lynx: a World Wide Web (WWW) client for cursor-addressable, character-cell display devices.* lynx.isc.org, last accessed on Oct. 9, 2002.

[11] C. Fox. *Lexical analysis and stoplists, In W. Frakes and R. Baeza-Yates, editors, Information Retrieval: Data Structures & Algorithms.* Prentice Hall, Englewood Cliffs, NJ, chapter 7, pages 102?30, 1992.

[12] K. Frantzi, S. Ananiadou, and H. Mima. Automatic recognition of multiword terms. *International Journal of Digital Libraries*, 3(2):117–132, 2000.

[13] J. Goldstein, M. Kantrowitz, V. Mittal, and J. Carbonell. Summarizing text documents: Sentence selection and evaluation metrics. In *Proceedings of SIGIR*, pages 121–128, 1999.

[14] S. Jones and J. Galliers. *Evaluating Natural Language Processing Systems: an Analysis and Review.* Springer, New York, 1996.

[15] Wentian Li. *Zipf's Law.* linkage.rockefeller.edu/wli/zipf, last accessed on Oct. 9, 2002.

[16] I. Mani. Recent developments in text summarization. In *ACM Conference on Information and Knowledge Management, CIKM'01*, pages 529–531, 2001.

[17] I. Mani and M. Maybury. *Advances in Automatic Text Summarization.* MIT Press, ISBN 0-262-13359-8, 1999.

[18] D. R. Radev, H. Jing, and M. Budzikowska. Centroid-based summarization of multiple documents: sentence extraction, utility-based evaluation, and user studies. In *Summarization Workshop*, 2000.

[19] IBM Research Laboratory Tokyo. *Automatic Text Summarization.* www.trl.ibm.com/projects/langtran/abst_e.htm, last accessed on Oct. 9, 2002.

[20] Colorado State University. *Writing Guide: Interrater Reliability.* writing.colostate.edu/references/research/relval/com2a5.cfm, last accessed on Oct. 9, 2002.

[21] Y. Zhang, N. Zincir-Heywood, and E. Milios. World Wide Web site summarization. Technical Report CS-2002-8, Faculty of Computer Science, Dalhousie University, October 2002.

Cycle-Cutset Sampling for Bayesian Networks*

Bozhena Bidyuk and Rina Dechter

Information and Computer Science
University of California - Irvine
Irvine, CA 92697-3425, USA
{bbidyuk,dechter}@ics.uci.edu

Abstract. The paper presents a new sampling methodology for Bayesian networks called *cutset sampling* that samples only a subset of the variables and applies exact inference for the others. We show that this approach can be implemented efficiently when the sampled variables constitute a cycle-cutset for the Bayesian network and otherwise it is exponential in the induced-width of the network's graph, whose sampled variables are removed. Cutset sampling is an instance of the well known Rao-Blakwellisation technique for variance reduction investigated in [5, 2, 16]. Moreover, the proposed scheme extends standard sampling methods to non-ergodic networks with ergodic subspaces. Our empirical results confirm those expectations and show that cycle cutset sampling is superior to Gibbs sampling for a variety of benchmarks, yielding a simple, yet powerful sampling scheme.

1 Introduction

Sampling methods for Bayesian networks are commonly used approximation techniques, applied successfully where exact inference is not possible due to prohibitive time and memory demands. In this paper, we focus on Gibbs sampling, a member of the Markov Chain Monte Carlo sampling methods group for Bayesian networks [6, 7, 17]. Given a Bayesian network over the variables $X = \{X_1, ..., X_n\}$, and evidence e, Gibbs sampling [6, 7, 17] generates a set of samples $\{x^t\}$ from $P(X|e)$ where each sample $x^t = \{x_1^t, ..., x_n^t\}$ is an instantiation of all the variables in the network. It is well-known that a function $f(X)$ can be estimated using the generated samples by:

$$E[f(X)|e] \cong \frac{1}{T} \sum_t f(x^t) \quad (1)$$

where T is the number of samples. Namely, given enough samples, the estimate converges to the exact value. The central query of interest over Bayesian networks is computing the posterior marginals $P(x_i|e)$ for each value x_i of variable X_i. For this query, the above equation reduces to counting the fraction of occurrences

* This work was supported in part by NSF grant IIS-0086529 and MURI ONR award N00014-00-1-0617.

Y. Xiang and B. Chaib-draa (Eds.): AI 2003, LNAI 2671, pp. 297–312, 2003.

of $X_i = x_i$ in the samples. A significant limitation of all existing sampling schemes, including Gibbs sampler, is the increase in the statistical variance for high-dimensional spaces. In addition, standard sampling methods fail to converge to the target distribution when the network is not ergodic.

In this paper, we present a sampling scheme for Bayesian networks that addresses both of these limitations by sampling from a subset of the variables. It is rooted in the well established Rao-Blakwellisation methodology for sampling that was developed in the past years by various authors, most notably [5, 2, 16]. Based on the Rao-Blackwell theorem ([8]), it is easy to show that sampling from a subspace (if feasible computationally) can reduce the variance and therefore yield faster convergence to the target function.

The basic Rao-Blackwellisation scheme can be described as follows. Suppose we partition the space of variables X into two subsets C and Z. It can be shown that if we can efficiently compute $P(c|e)$ and $E[f(C,Z)|c,e]$ (by summing out Z in both cases), then we can perform sampling only on C generating $c^1, c^2, ..., c^T$ and approximate the quantity of interest by:

$$E[f(X)|e] \cong \frac{1}{T}\sum_t E[f(c^t,Z)|c,e] \tag{2}$$

If function $f(X)$ is a posterior marginal of node X_i, then $f(X)|e = P(x_i|e)$ and $f(c^t,Z)|c,e = P(x_i|c^t,e)$, then Equation (2) instantiates to:

$$P(x_i|e) \cong \frac{1}{T}\sum_t P(x_i|c^t,e) \tag{3}$$

In this paper, we propose to use the above scheme when the subspace C is such that conditioning on C yields a sparse Bayesian network where exact inference is polynomial, such as when C is a cycle-cutset. The proposed scheme is called *cutset sampling.* This yields a special application of Rao-Blackwellisation for sampling in Bayesian networks that offers two-fold benefits over regular sampling: 1. improved convergence and 2. convergence in non-ergodic networks.

Indeed, we show empirically that cycle-cutset sampling converges faster not only in terms of number of samples, as dictated by theory, but it is also time-wise cost-effective on all the benchmarks tried (CPCS networks, random networks, and coding networks). We also demonstrate the applicability of this scheme to non-ergodic networks such as Hailfinder network and coding networks.

The approach we propose is simple, however, to the best of our knowledge, it was not yet presented for general Bayesian networks except for the special case of Dynamic Bayesian networks [4]. In that paper, the authors apply Rao-Blackwellisation to particle filtering that iterates along the timeline, by selecting a specific sampling set C. Hence, the current paper extends the work of [4] to general Bayesian networks. Following background (Section 2), the paper presents cutset-sampling and analyzes its complexity (Section 4), provides empirical evaluation in Section 6 and concludes in Section 7.

2 Background

Definition 1 (Belief Networks). *Let $X = \{X_1, ..., X_n\}$ be a set of random variables over multi-valued domains $D(X_1), ..., D(X_n)$. A* belief network (BN) *is a pair (G, P) where G is a directed acyclic graph on X and $P = \{P(X_i|pa_i)|i = 1, ..., n\}$ is the set of conditional probability matrices associated with each X_i. A belief network is ergodic if any assignment $x = \{x_1, ..., x_n\}$ has non-zero probability, defined by $P(x_1, ..., x_n) = \Pi_{i=1}^{n} P(x_i|x_{pa(X_i)})$. An evidence e is an instantiated subset of variables E. The moral graph of a belief network is obtained by connecting the parents of the same child and eliminating the arrows. Figure 1 shows a belief network(left) and its moral graph(center).*

Definition 2 (Induced-Width). *The* width *of a node in an ordered undirected graph is the number of the node's neighbors that precede it in the ordering. The width of an ordering d, denoted w(d), is the width over all nodes. The induced width of an ordered graph, w*(d), is the width of the ordered graph obtained by processing the nodes from last to first. When node X is processed, all its preceding neighbors are connected. The resulting graph is called induced graph or triangulated graph.*

Definition 3 (Induced-Width, Cycle-Cutset). *A* cycle *in G is a path whose two end-points coincide. A* cycle-cutset *of undirected graph G is a set of vertices that contains at least one node in each cycle in G. A graph is* singly connected *(also called a* polytree*), if its underlying undirected graph has no cycles. Otherwise, it is called* multiply connected. *A* loop *in D is a subgraph of D whose underlying graph is a cycle. A vertex v is a* sink *with respect to loop $\mathcal{L}$ if the two edges adjacent to v in $\mathcal{L}$ are directed into v. A vertex that is not a sink with respect to a loop $\mathcal{L}$ is called an* allowed *vertex with respect to $\mathcal{L}$. A* cycle-cutset *of a directed graph D is a set of vertices that contains at least one allowed vertex with respect to each loop in D.*

2.1 Gibbs Sampling

Gibbs sampling generates samples from $\hat{P}(X|e)$ which converges to $P(X|e)$ as the number of samples increases [18, 17] as long as the network is ergodic. Given a Bayesian network $\mathcal{B}$, Gibbs sampling generates a set of samples x^t where t

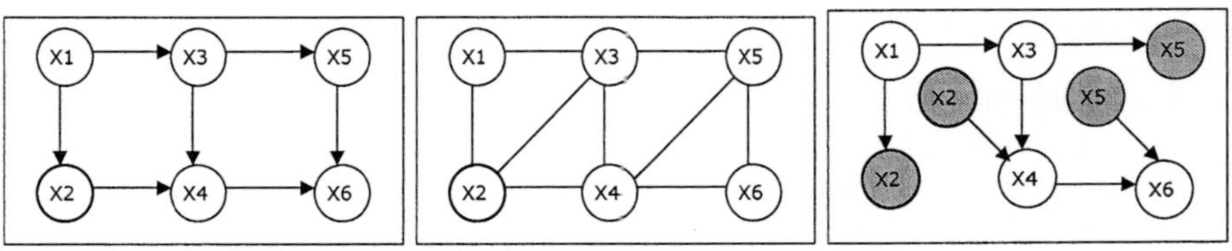

Fig. 1. Bayesian network (left), its moral graph(center), and conditioned polytree (right) (conditioned on $C = \{X_2, X_5\}$)

denotes a sample and and x_i^t is the value of X_i in sample t. Given a sample $x^{t-1} = \{x_1^{t-1}, x_2^{t-1}, ..., x_n^{t-1}\}$ (evidence variables remain fixed), a new sample x^t is generated by assigning a new value x_i^t to each variable X_i in some order. Value x_i^t is computed by sampling from the conditional probability distribution: $P(x_i) = P(x_i|x_1^t, x_2^t, x_{i-1}^t ..., x_{i+1}^{t-1}, ..., x_n^{t-1}) = P(x_i|markov^t(x_i))$, where $markov^t(x_i)$ is the assignment in sample t to the Markov blanket of variable X_i which includes its parents, children, and parents of its children.

Once all the samples are generated, we can answer any query over the samples. In particular, computing a posterior marginal belief $P(x_i|e)$ for each variable X_i can be estimated by counting samples where $X_i = x_i$:

$$\hat{P}(x_i|e) = \frac{1}{T}\sum_{t=1}^{T} \delta_{x_i}(x^t) \tag{4}$$

(here $\delta_{x_i}(x^t) = 1$ if $x_i^t = x_i$ and equals 0 otherwise) or by averaging the conditional marginals (known as mixture estimator):

$$\hat{P}(x_i|e) = \frac{1}{T}\sum_{t=1}^{T} P(x_i|markov^t(x_i)) \tag{5}$$

This method is likely to converge faster than simple counting [18]. The Markov blanket of X_i ([18]) is given explicitly by:

$$P(x_i|markov^t(x_i)) = \alpha P(x_i|x^t_{pa(X_i)}) \prod_{\{j|X_j \in ch_j\}} P(x_j^t|x^t_{pa_j}) \tag{6}$$

Thus, generating a complete new sample requires $O(n \cdot r)$ multiplication steps where r is the maximum family size and n is the number of variables. Subsequently, computing the posterior marginals is linear in the number of samples.

3 Augmentation Schemes

Variable augmentation schemes exist that allow to improve the convergence properties of simple Gibbs sampler. The two main approaches are blocking (grouping variables together and sampling simultaneously) and Rao-Blackwellisation (integrating out some of the random variables). Given Bayesian network with three random variables: X, Y, and Z, we can schematically describe those three sampling schemes as follows:

1. Rao-Blackwellised: sample x from $P(x|y)$, sample y from $P(y|x)$ integrating out random variable z.
2. Blocking Gibbs: samples values from $P(x|y,z)$, $P(y,z|x)$
3. Standard Gibbs: samples values from $P(x|y,z)$, $P(y|x,z)$, $P(z|x,y)$

As shown in [16], the blocking Gibbs sampling scheme, where several variables are grouped together and sampled simultaneously, is expected to converge faster than standard Gibbs sampler. Variations to this scheme have been investigated in [10, 13]. Still, in a blocking Gibbs sampler a sample is an instantiation of all the variables in the network, same as standard Gibbs sampler. The Rao-Blackwellised sampling scheme actually allows to integrate some of the random variables out, thus reducing sampling space, and it is expected to converge the fastest [16]. Thus, of the two basic data augmentation scheme, namely Rao-Blackwellisation and Blocking, Rao-Blackwellisation is generally preferred.

The caveat in the utilization of the Rao-Blackwellised sampling scheme is that computation of the probabilities $P(x|y)$ and $P(y|x)$ must be efficient. In case of Bayesian networks, the task of integrating variables out equates to performing exact inference on the network where evidence nodes and sampling nodes are observed and its time complexity is exponential in the network size. Taken *a priori* that performance of the sampler will be severely impacted when many variables are integrated out, Rao-Blackwellisation has been applied only to a few special cases of Bayesian networks. In particular, it has been applied to the Particle Filtering (using importance sampling) method for Dynamic Bayesian networks [4] in cases where some of the variables can be integrated out easily either because they are conditionally independent given the sampled variables (plus evidence) or because their probability distribution permits tractable exact inference (for example, using Kalman filter).

In this paper, we define a general scheme for Rao-Blackwellised sampling for Bayesian networks (see Section 4) and show that Rao-Blackwellisation can be done efficiently when sampling set is a cycle-cutset of the Bayesian network. We demonstrate empirically for several networks that we can compute a new sample faster using cutset sampling scheme than standard Gibbs sampler. The gain is easily explained. In a Bayesian network of size $|X| = N$, Gibbs sampler maybe able to compute individual probabilities $P(x|markov^t(x))$ fast, but it has to repeat this computation N times. In Rao-Blackwellised scheme, where most variables are integrated out and sampling set $C \in X$ is of size $|C| = K$, $K < N$, it may take longer to compute $P(x|c, e)$, but we only have to repeat this computation K times (potentially, K can be much smaller than N). Most importantly, fewer samples are needed for convergence.

4 Cutset Sampling

This section presents the cutset sampling method. As noted in the introduction, the basic scheme partitions variables X into two subsets C and Z. If we can efficiently compute $P(c|e)$ and $P(x_i|c^t, e)$, then we can sample only values of C efficiently and approximate the quantity of interest via equation (3).

4.1 Cutset Sampling Algorithm

The cutset sampling algorithm is given in Figure 2. Given a subset of cutset variables C=$\{C_1, C_2, ..., C_m\}$, it generates samples c^t, t=1...T, over subspace C. Here, c^t is an instantiation of the variables in C. Similarly to Gibbs

Cutset Sampling
Input: A belief network ($\mathcal{B}$), cutset $C = \{C_1, ..., C_m\}$, evidence e.
Output: A set of samples c^t, $t = 1...T_c$.
1. **Initialize:** Assign random value c_i^0 to each $C_i \in C$ and assign e.
2. **Generate samples:**
For t = 1 to T, generate a new sample c^t:
For i = 1 to m, compute new value c_i^t for variable C_i as follows:
1. Using algorithm **join-tree clustering** $JTC(C_i, c_{(i)}^t, e)$, compute:

$$P(c_i) = P(c_i | c_{(i)}^t, e) \tag{7}$$

2. Sample a new value c_i^t for C_i, from (7).
End For i
End For t

Fig. 2. *Cutset sampling* Algorithm

sampling, we generate a new sample c^t by sampling a value c_i^t from the probability distribution $P(c_i | c_1^{t+1}, c_2^{t+1}, ...c_{i-1}^{t+1}, c_{i+1}^t, ..., c_m^t, e)$ for each C_i. We will denote $c_{(i)}^t = c_1^{t+1}, c_2^{t+1}, ...c_{i-1}^{t+1}, c_{i+1}^t, ..., c_m^t$ for conciseness.

The key idea is that the relevant conditional distributions (eq. (7)) can be computed by exact inference algorithms whose complexity is tied to the network's structure and is improved by conditioning. We use $JTC(X, e)$ as a generic name for a class of variable-elimination or join tree-clustering algorithms that compute the exact posterior beliefs for a variable X given evidence e [15, 3, 11]. It is known that the complexity of $JTC(X, e)$ is time and space exponential in the induced-width of the network's moral graph whose evidence variables E are removed.

4.2 Computing the Posterior Marginals

Once the samples over the cutest C are available, we can compute the posterior beliefs of all variables as follows. For each cutset variable $C_i \in C$ (excluding evidence variables), the posterior marginals can be computed as in Gibbs sampling:

$$\hat{P}(c_i | e) = \frac{1}{T} \sum_t P(c_i | c_{(i)}^t, e) \tag{8}$$

If we record the distributions computed during sample generation (equation (7)), these quantities will be readily available for summation.

For each non-cutset variable $X_i \in X \backslash E, C$, and every sample c^t, $P(x_i | c^t, e)$ can be computed over the Bayesian network conditioned on c^t and e, by $JTC(X_i, c^t, e)$:

$$\hat{P}(c_i | e) = \frac{1}{T} \sum_t P(x_i | c^t, e) \tag{9}$$

Note that the probability distribution $P(x_i | c^t, e)$ can be computed as soon as sample c^t is generated. Namely, it is sufficient to keep a running sum (eq. 3) (relative to samples c^t) for each value x_i of each variable X_i.

We provide a proof of the convergence of this general scheme in Section 5. Namely, computing $P(x_i|e)$ by cutset sampling is (1) guaranteed to converge to the exact quantities. In general, cutset sampling requires fewer samples to converge than full sampling as a result of Rao-Blackwell theorem

Example. Consider again a belief network shown in Figure 1. When sampling from set $C = \{X_2, X_5\}$ (although there is a better cutset $C = \{X_3\}$), we will have to compute for each sample t the probabilities $P(x_2|x_5^{t-1})$ and $P(x_5|x_2^t)$. These probabilities can be computed using belief propagation over the singly connected network (Figure 1, right) or bucket elimination in linear time. For each new value of variables X_2 and X_5, we profane the updated messages through the (singly-connected) network. The desired joint $P(x_2', x_5', e)$ can be computed at any variable and then normalized to yield the conditional distribution.

4.3 Complexity

Cutset sampling uses the *adjusted induced width* w, to control the size of the sampling set and thus can adjust the trade-off between sampling and inference. Given an undirected graph $G = (V, E)$, if C is a subset of V such that when removed from G, the induced width of the resulting graph is less or equal w, then C is called a *w-cutset* of G and the *adjusted induced width* of G relative to C is w. The cycle-cutset of a graph is a 1-cutset.

Clearly, computing a new sample c^t in cutset-sampling is more complex (step 1) than Gibbs sampling. However, it is still very efficient when the cutset C is a cycle-cutset of the Bayesian network (w=1). In this case, JTC reduces to belief propagation algorithm [18, 19] that can compute the joint probability $P(c_i, c_{(i)}^t, ..., c_m^t, e)$ in linear time and then normalize it relative to C_i yielding equation (7) (details are omitted). When C is a w-cutset, the complexity of JTC (equation 7) is exponential in w and will dominate the complexity of generating the next sample. Therefore:

Theorem 1 (Complexity of Sample Generation). *The complexity of generating a sample by cutset sampling with cutset C is $O(m \cdot d \cdot n \cdot d^w)$ where C is a w-custet of size m, d bounds the variables domain size, and n is the number of nodes.*

Corollary 1. *If C is a cycle-cutset, the complexity of generating a sample by cycle-cutset sampling is linear in the size of the network.*

Computing $P(X_i|e)$ using equation (3) requires computing $P(x_i|c^t, e)$ for each variable. The complexity of this computation by $JTC(X_i, c^t, e)$ is also exponential in w, the adjusted induced width relative to cutset:

Theorem 2. *Given a w-cutset C, the complexity of computing the posterior of all the variables using cutset sampling over T samples is $O(T \cdot n \cdot d^w)$.*

Corollary 2. *If C is a cycle-cutset, the complexity of computing the posterior of all the variables by cycle-cutset sampling is linear in the size of the network.*

In conclusion, when sampling over a cycle-cutset C, both sampling and estimating the marginal posterior are linear in the size of the network and the number of samples.

5 Convergence of Cutset-Sampling

In this section we will show that $\hat{P}(c_i|e)$ and $\hat{P}(x_i|e)$ as defined in equations (8) and (9) converge to the correct probabilities $P(c_i|e)$ and $P(x_i|e)$ respectively.

Theorem 3 (Cutset Convergence). *Given a network $\mathcal{B}$ over X and a subset of evidence variables E, and given a cutset C, assuming $\hat{P}(c_i|e)$ and $\hat{P}(x_i|e)$ were computed by equations (8) and (9) over the cutset sample, then $\hat{P}(c_i|e) \rightarrow P(c_i|e)$ and $\hat{P}(x_i|e) \rightarrow P(x_i|e)$ as the number of samples T_c increses.*

While the result of theorem 3 is implied by the Rao-Blackwell theorem, the proof from first principles is simple enough.

Proof. Let $|C| = m$. Let $|X| = n$. The computation of $\hat{P}(c_i|e)$ is done exactly in the same way as in Gibbs sampling. There are several different ways to prove convergence of Gibbs sampling and we will not repeat them here. Therefore, based on the correct convergence of Gibbs sampling we can conclude that $\hat{P}(c_i|e) \rightarrow P(c_i|e)$ as the number of samples increases.

Consider now a variable X_i not in C and not in E. We could write the posterior distribution of variable X_i as follows: $P(x_i|e) = \sum_c P(x_i|c,e)P(c|e)$.

Assume that we have generated a collection of samples $c^1, c^2, ..., c^T$ from the correct distribution $P(C|e)$. Let $m(c)$ be the number of times c occurs in the samples. Then, for each tuple $C = c$:

$$P(c|e) = \frac{m(c)}{T} \tag{10}$$

After we substitute the right hand side of the equation 10 in the expression for $P(x_i|e)$:

$$P(x_i|e) = \sum_c P(x_i|c,e)\frac{m(c)}{T} \tag{11}$$

Factoring out $\frac{1}{T}$ we get:

$$P(x_i|e) = \frac{1}{T}\sum_c P(x_i|c,e)m(c). \tag{12}$$

Clearly, $\sum_c m(C) = T$. Therefore, we can sum over T instead of summing over instantiations of C, yielding:

$$\sum_c P(x_i|c,e)m(c) = \sum_{t=1}^{T} P(x_i|c,e) \tag{13}$$

After replacing the sum over C in (12) with the sum over T, we get:

$$P(x_i|e) = \frac{1}{T}\sum_{t=1}^{T} P(x_i|c,e) \tag{14}$$

Therefore we obtained expression (14), assuming that $\frac{m(c)}{T}$ converges to the exact $P(C|e)$. Since $\hat{P}(c_i|e)$ converges to $P(c_i|e)$ in cutset-sampling, as we have already shown, then we can conclude that $\hat{P}(x_i|e) \rightarrow P(x_i|e)$. □

6 Experiments

We compared cycle-cutset sampling with full Gibbs sampling on several CPCS networks, random networks, Hailfinder network, and coding networks. Generally, we are interested in how much accuracy we can achieve in a given period of time. Therefore, we provide here figures showing accuracy of the Gibbs and cycle-cutset sampling as a function of time. For comparison, we also show the accuracy of Iterative Belief Propagation algorithm (IBP) after 25 iterations. IBP is an iterative message-passing algorithm that performs exact inference in Bayesian networks without loops ([18]). It can also be applied to Bayesian networks with loops to compute approximate posterior marginals. The advantage of IBP as an approximate algorithm is that it is very efficient. It requires linear space and usually converges very fast. IBP was shown to perform well in practice ([9, 12]) and is considered the best algorithm for inference in coding networks where finding the most probable variable values equals the decoding process.

For each Bayesian network $\mathcal{B}$ with variables $X = \{X_1, ..., X_n\}$, we computed exact posterior marginals $P(x_i|e)$ using bucket-tree elimination and computed the mean square error (MSE) in the approximate posterior marginals $\hat{P}(x_i|e)$ for each approximation scheme:

$$MSE = \frac{1}{\sum_i |D(x_i)|} \sum_i \sum_{D(x_i)} (P(x_i|e) - \hat{P}(x_i|e))^2$$

and averaged MSE over the number of instances tried. In all networks, except for coding networks, evidence nodes were selected at random. The cutset was always selected so that evidence and sampling nodes together constitute a cycle-cutset of the network using the mga algorithm ([1]).

CPCS Networks. We considered four CPCS networks derived from the Computer-based Patient Case Simulation system. The largest network, cpcs422b, consisted of 422 nodes with induced width w*=23. With evidence, its cycle-cutset size was 42. The results are shown in Figures 3-4. Each chart title specifies network name, number of nodes in the network N, the size of evidence set $|E|$, size of cycle-cutset (sampling set) $|C|$, and induced width w* of the network instance. For all four CPCS networks, we observed that the cutset sampling is far better than Gibbs sampling. In case of cpcs179 (Figure 6, middle),

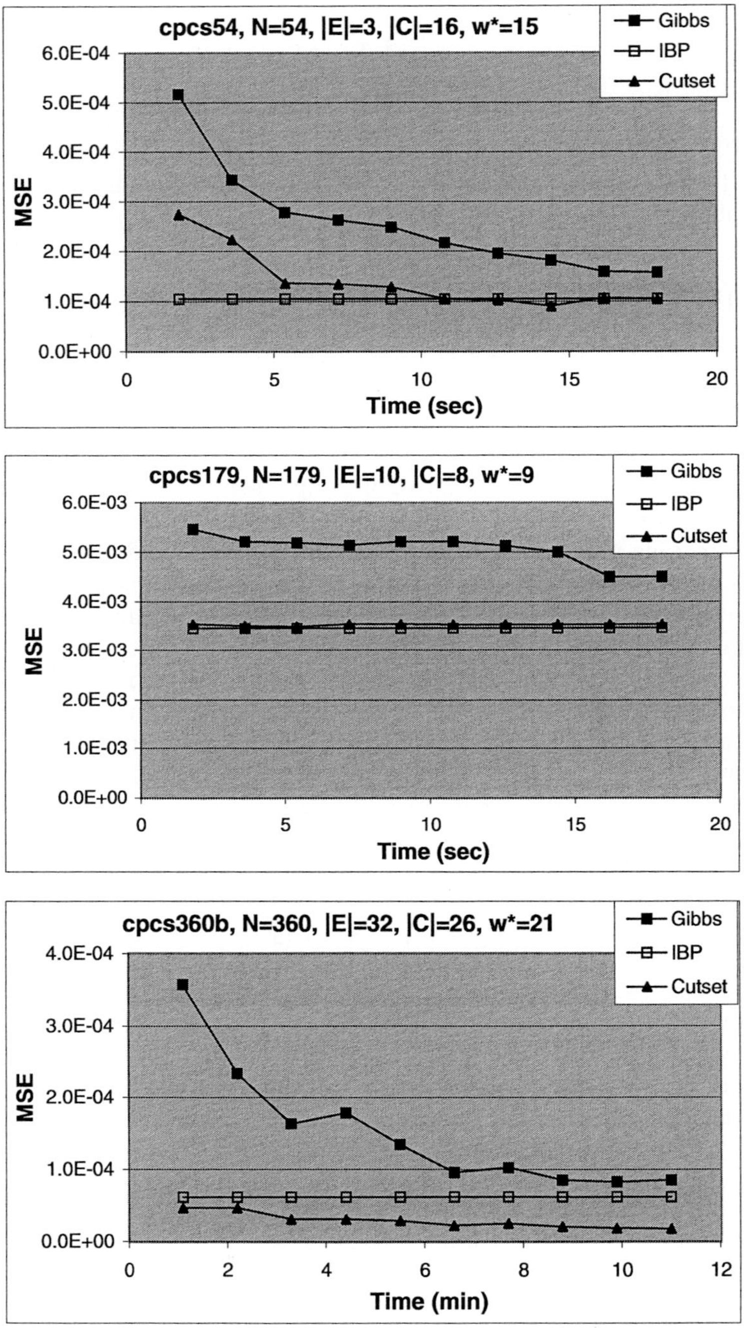

Fig. 3. Comparing cycle-cutset sampling, Gibbs sampling and IBP on CPCS networks averaged over 3 instances each. MSE as a function of time

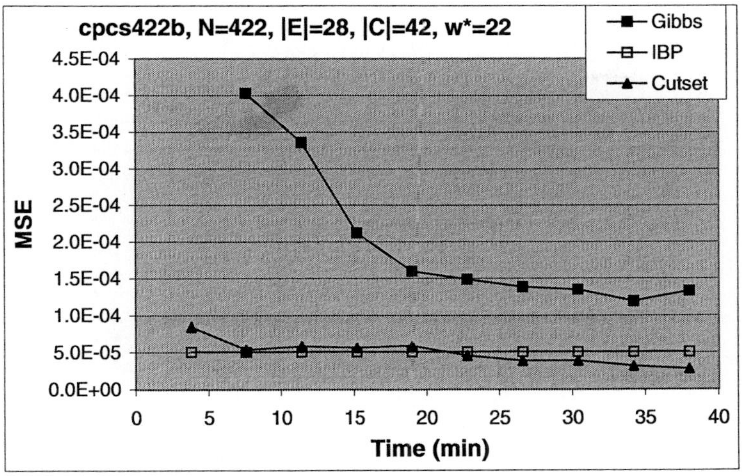

Fig. 4. Comparing cycle-cutset sampling, Gibbs sampling and IBP on cpcs422b network averaged over 2 instances. MSE as a function of time

cpcs360b (Figure 6, bottom), and cpcs422b (Figure 6) cutset sampling achieves even greater accuracy than IBP. Gibbs sampling does not converge on cpcs179 due to non-ergodic properties of the network. The cutset sampling overcomes this limitation because the cycle-cutset selected is an ergodic subspace.

Random Networks. We generated a set of random networks with bi-valued nodes. Each network contained total of 200 nodes. The first 100 nodes, $\{X_1, ..., X_{100}\}$, were designated as root nodes. Each non-root node X_i was assigned 3 parents selected randomly from the list of predecessors $\{X_1, ..., X_{i-1}\}$. The conditional probability table values $P(X_i = 0|pa(X_i))$ were chosen randomly from a uniform distribution. We collected data for 10 instances (Figure 5, top). Cutset sampling always converged faster than Gibbs sampling.

2-Layer Networks. We generated a set of random 2-layer networks with bi-valued nodes. Each network contained 50 root nodes (first layer) and a total of 200 nodes. Each non-root node (second layer) was assigned a maximum of 3 parents selected at random from the root nodes. The conditional probability table values $P(X_i = 0|pa(X_i))$ were chosen randomly from uniform distribution. We collected data for 10 instances (Figure 5, middle). On those types of networks, Iterative Belief Propagation often does not perform well. And, as our experiments show, cutset sampling outperfoms both Gibbs sampling and IBP (although it takes longer time to converge than IBP).

Coding Networks . We experimented with coding networks with 100 nodes (25 coding bits, 25 parity check bits). The results are shown in Figure 5, bottom. Those networks had cycle-cutset size between 12 and 14 and induced width

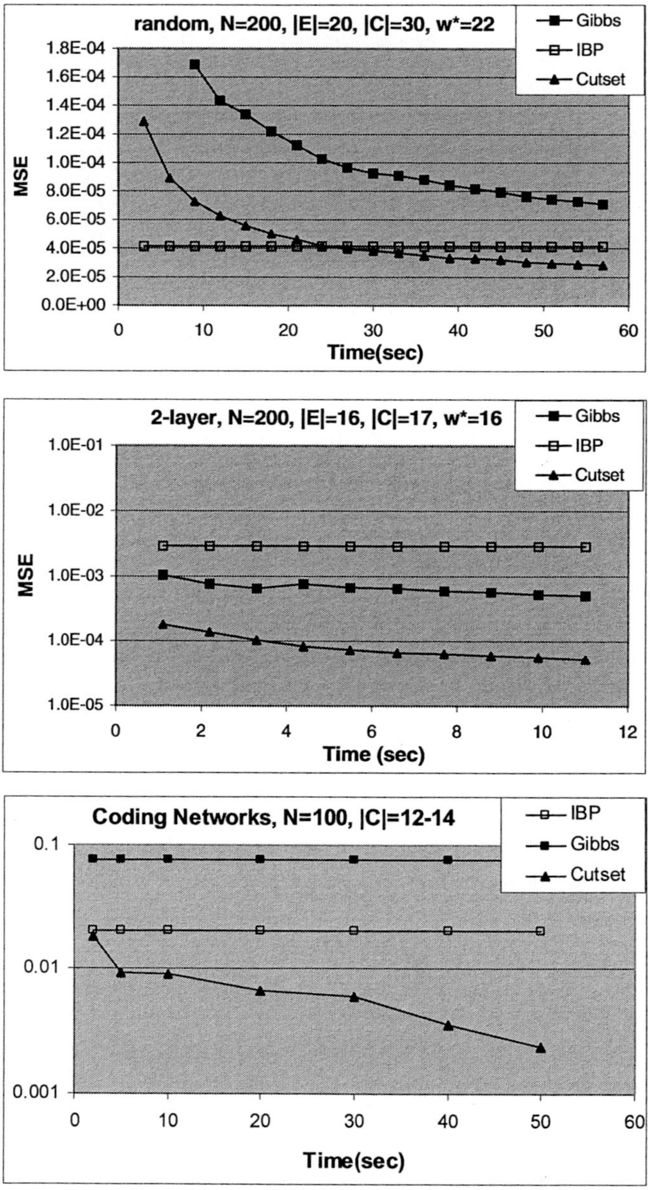

Fig. 5. Comparing cycle-cutset sampling, Gibbs sampling and IBP on random networks (top), 2-layer random networks (middle), and coding networks, σ=0.4 (bottom), averaged over 10 instances each. MSE as a function of time

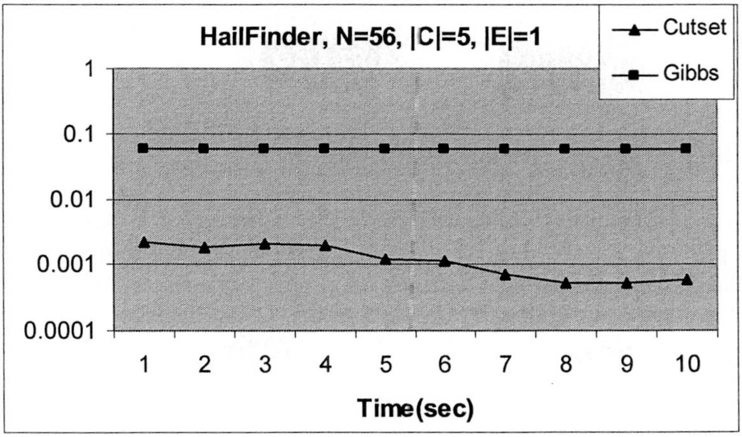

Fig. 6. Comparing cycle-cutset sampling and Gibbs sampling on Hailfinder network, 1 instance. MSE as a function of time

between 13 and 16. The parity check matrix was randomized; each parity check bit had three parents. We computed MSE over all coding bits and averaged over 10 networks. Coding networks are not ergodic due to the deterministic parity check function. As a result, Gibbs sampling does not converge. At the same time, the subspace of code bits only is ergodic and cutset sampling, that samples a subset of coding bits, converges and generates results comparable to those of IBP. In practice, IBP is certainly preferable for coding networks since the size of the cycle-cutset grows linearly with the number of code bits.

Hailfinder Network. Hailfinder is a non-ergodic network with many deterministic relationships. It has 56 nodes and cycle-cutset of size 5. Indeed, this network is easy to solve exactly. We used this network to compare the behavior cutset sampling and Gibbs sampling in non-ergodic networks. As expected, Gibbs sampling fails while cycle cutset sampling computes more accurate marginals and its accuracy continues to improve with time (Figure 6).

In summary, the empirical results demonstrate the cycle-cutset is cost-effective time-wise and is superior to Gibbs sampling. We measured the ratio $R = \frac{M_g}{M_c}$ of the number of samples generated by Gibbs M_g to the number of samples generated by cycle-cutset sampling M_c in the same time period. For cpcs54, cpcs179, cpcs360b, and cpcs422b the ratios were correspondingly 1.4, 1.7, 0.6, and 0.5. We also obtained R=2.0 for random networks and R=0.3 for random 2-layer networks. While cutset sampling algorithm often takes more time to generate a sample, it produced substantially better results overall due to its variance reduction. In some cases, cutset sampling could actually compute samples faster than Gibbs sampler. in which case the improvement in the accuracy was due to both large sample set and variance reduction. Cutset sampling also achieves better accuracy than IBP on some CPCS and random networks although takes more time to achieve same or better accuracy. In 2-layer networks and coding networks, cycle-cutset sampling achieves the IBP level of accuracy very quickly and is able to substantially improve with time.

7 Related Work and Conclusions

We presented a sampling scheme called cutset sampling for Bayesian networks that samples only a subset of variables in the network. The remaining nodes are marginalised out (by inference) which is an instance of a technique known as Rao-Blackwellisation. As we showed theoretically and empirically, cutset sampling: (1) improves convergence rate due to sampling from lower-dimensional space and (2) allows sampling from non-ergodic network that have ergodic subspace. The resulting scheme is a simple yet powerful extension of sampling in Bayesian networks that is likely to dominate regular sampling for any sampling method. While we focused on Gibbs sampling, other sampling techniques, with better convergence characteristics, can be implemented with cutset sampling as long as they permit to exploit Bayesian network structure in a similar manner.

Previously, sampling from a subset of variables was successfully applied to particle sampling for Dynamic Bayesian networks (DBNs) [4]. Indeed, the authors demonstrated that sampling from a subspace combined with exact inference yields a better approximation. Our scheme offers an elegant way of extending [4] and combining inference and sampling in Bayesian networks.

A different combination of sampling and exact inference for join trees was described in [14] and [13]. Both papers proposed to use sampling to estimate the probability distribution in each cluster from which they compute messages sent to the neighboring clusters. In this approximation scheme, sampling is always performed locally (within the cluster) and thus, the algorithm must rely on the approximated messages received from neighbors when generating new samples. In [14], the authors attempt to remedy this problem by iterative refinement. Our cutset-sampling algorithm does not encounter such problems since it takes into account the global state of the network when generating a new sample. Cutset sampling can also be seen as an approximation to cycle-cutset coditioning ([18]).

In [10], exact inference was used in combination with blocking Gibbs sampling. The major differences between our cutset sampling approach and one proposed in [10] are that first, in the proposed blocking Gibbs sampling, a sample consists of all the variables in the network (as usual) while cutset sampling never assigns values to those variables that are integrated out; second, in [10], exact inference is used to perform joint sampling step for a group of variables while cutset sampling uses exact inference to integrate variables out.

The direction of our future work is to investigate methods for finding a sampling set with good convergence properties. Some of the factors that strongly affect convergence of MCMC methods are the sampling set size, the complexity of sample generation, and the correlations between variables. Reducing sampling set size generally leads to a reduction in the sampling variance due to Rao-Blackwellisation, but it also results in the increased complexity of exact inference when generating a new sample. Another factor is strong correlations between sampled variables (deterministic probabilities, present in non-ergodic networks, are an extreme example of strong correlation). If two variables are strongly dependent, it is preferred to either integrate one of them out or group them together and sample jointly (as in blocking Gibbs sampler) (see [16]). Taking above into consideration, a good sampling set could be defined as a minimal w-cutset with a small w and with all strongly-correlated variables removed.

References

[1] A. Becker, R. Bar-Yehuda, and D. Geiger. Random algorithms for the loop cutset problem. In *Uncertainty in AI (UAI'99)*, 1999.

[2] G. Casella and C. P. Robert. Rao-blackwellisation of sampling schemes. *Biometrika*, 83(1):81–94, 1996.

[3] R. Dechter. Bucket elimination: A unifying framework for reasoning. *Artificial Intelligence*, 113:41–85, 1999.

[4] A. Doucet, N. de Freitas, K. Murphy, and S. Russell. Rao-blackwellised particle filtering for dynamic bayesian networks. In *Uncertainty in AI*, pages 176–183, 2000.

[5] A. E. Gelfand and A. F. M. Smith. Sampling-based approaches to calculating marginal densities. *Journal of the American Statistical Association*, 85:398–409, 1990.

[6] S. Geman and D. Geman. Stochastic relaxations, gibbs distributions and the bayesian restoration of images. *IEEE Transaction on Pattern analysis and Machine Intelligence (PAMI-6)*, pages 721–42, 1984.

[7] W. Gilks, S. Richardson, and D. Spiegelhalter. *Markov chain Monte Carlo in practice.* Chapman and Hall, 1996.

[8] M. H. De Groot. *Probability and Statistics, 2nd edition.* Addison-Wesley, 1986.

[9] K. Kask I. Rish and R. Dechter. Empirical evaluation of approximation algorithms for probabilistic decoding. In *Uncertainty in AI (UAI'98)*, 1998.

[10] C. Jensen, A. Kong, and U. Kjaerulff. Blocking gibbs sampling in very large probabilistic expert systems. *International Journal of Human Computer Studies. Special Issue on Real-World Applications of Uncertain Reasoning.*, pages 647–666, 1995.

[11] F. V. Jensen, S.L Lauritzen, and K. G. Olesen. Bayesian updating in causal probabilistic networks by local computation. *Computational Statistics Quarterly*, 4:269–282, 1990.

[12] Y. Weiss K. P. Murphy and M. I. Jordan. Loopy belief propagation for approximate inference: An empirical study. In *Uncertainty in AI (UAI'99)*, 1999.

[13] Uffe Kjærulff. Hugs: Combining exact inference and gibbs sampling in junction trees. In *Uncertainty in AI*, pages 368–375. Morgan Kaufmann, 1995.

[14] D. Koller, U. Lerner, and D. Angelov. A general algorithm for approximate inference and its application to hybrid bayes nets. In *Uncertainty in AI*, pages 324–333, 1998.

[15] S. L. Lauritzen and D. J. Spiegelhalter. Local computation with probabilities on graphical structures and their application to expert systems. *Journal of the Royal Statistical Society, Series B*, 50(2):157–224, 1988.

[16] W. H. Wong Liu, J. and A. Kong. Covariance structure of the gibbs sampler with applications to the comparison of estimators and augmentation schemes. *Biometrika*, pages 27–40, 1994.
[17] D. J.C MacKay. Introduction to monte carlo methods. In *Proceedings of NATO Advanced Study Institute on Learning in Graphical Models. Sept 27-Oct 7*, pages 175–204, 1996.
[18] J. Pearl. *Probabilistic Reasoning in Intelligent Systems.* Morgan Kaufmann, 1988.
[19] M. A. Peot and R. D. Shachter. Fusion and proagation with multiple observations in belief networks. *Artificial Intelligence*, pages 299–318, 1992.

Learning First-Order Bayesian Networks

Ratthachat Chatpatanasiri and Boonserm Kijsirikul

Department of Computer Engineering, Chulalongkorn University
Pathumwan, Bangkok, 10330, Thailand.
Ratthachat.C@Student.chula.ac.th
Boonserm.K@chula.ac.th

Abstract. A first-order Bayesian network (FOBN) is an extension of first-order logic in order to cope with uncertainty problems. Therefore, learning an FOBN might be a good idea to build an effective classifier. However, because of a complication of the FOBN, directly learning it from relational data is difficult. This paper proposes another way to learn FOBN classifiers. We adapt Inductive Logic Programming (ILP) and a Bayesian network learner to construct the FOBN. To do this, we propose a feature extraction algorithm to generate the significant parts (features) of ILP rules, and use these features as a main structure of the induced the FOBN. Next, to learn the remaining parts of the FOBN structure and its conditional probability tables by a standard Bayesian network learner, we also propose an efficient propositionalisation algorithm for translating the original data into the single table format. In this work, we provide a preliminary evaluation on the mutagenesis problem, a standard dataset for relational learning problem. The results are compared with the state-of-the-art ILP learner, the PROGOL system.

Keywords: First-Order Bayesian Networks, Inductive Logic Programming, Overfitting Problem, Feature Extraction, Propositionalisation.

1 Introduction

Because of the ability to employ background knowledge and the representation power of first-order logic, Inductive Logic Programming (ILP) has been widely accepted as a very powerful machine learning technique for learning concepts from relational data [6,15,17]. However, first-order rules induced by ILP still have some limitations on the flexibility in handling imperfect data in real-world problems such as noisy or sparse training examples. This usually makes ILP rules struggle with the *overfitting* problem (cf. [15]). Although there are a number of extended ILP methods proposed to prevent the rules from overfitting the training examples, e.g. [15,16], but the obtained rules are still first-order and thus not flexible enough to handle the problem (see Example 1). Also, there are other methods improving the obtained rules to efficiently predict an unseen imperfect data, but those methods usually lose the expressive power of first-

Y. Xiang and B. Chaib-draa (Eds.): AI 2003, LNAI 2671, pp. 313-328, 2003.

order logic such that it is hard to understand the meaning of induced rules (see e.g. [12]).

Recently, extensions of first-order logic are proposed by Koller et al. [13,9], Kersting and De Raedt [11,10] and Poole [19] in the names of *Probabilistic Relational Model (PRM)*, *Bayesian Logic Program (BLP)* and *Independent Choice Logic (ICL)*, respectively. All models are extensions of the original first-order model that cope with uncertainty problems of relational data in imperfect domains. On the other hand, they can also be viewed as extensions of regular Bayesian networks that learn concepts from relational data. For simplicity, in this paper we will call all these models *first-order Bayesian networks (FOBNs)*. The model of the FOBN is very powerful to handle noisy data by the power of probabilistic theories, and also a superbly expressive model by the power of the first-order model combining with a Bayesian network. However, because of complication of the model, directly learning the FOBN from relational data is more complicated than learning regular Bayesian networks or first-order rules (see [9,10]). Moreover, the FOBN learning algorithms proposed in [9,10] centrally concern only in discovery tasks whereas the algorithm to learn the FOBN as a classifier (to learn concepts in the FOBN format) has not been well discussed.

In this paper, we propose another method to learn the FOBN as a classifier. We adapt ILP and a (propositional) Bayesian network learner to construct the FOBN. In the learning process, our method splits each ILP rule into significant parts (called *features*). All features are extracted by our proposed algorithm called MCAFEE, and will be used as the main structure of the induced FOBN. To learn the remaining parts of the FOBN structure, together with its conditional probability tables (CPTs) by a standard Bayesian network learner, we also propose an efficient *ground-substitutions-as-examples propositionalisation* algorithm called GRASP inspired by [7] to translate the original (relational) input data into the single table format. Moreover, because of the space complexity problem while translating the relational into propositional data (cf. Section 4), we will use the *minimal valid chains* and *non-duplicate maximal specific bindings* techniques performed by MCAFEE and GRASP, respectively, to alleviate the problem.

The main contributions of this paper can be summarized as follows:

- We propose a learning framework to learn FOBN as classifier. The main advantages of the FOBN learned by our framework are (1) it can efficiently classify an unseen data in noisy domains, (2) its model is easily understandable by humans, and (3) our framework can employ background knowledge to build the FOBN as ILP systems do.
- We present a feature extraction algorithm which efficiently generates significant features from first-order rules, especially for constructing the FOBN as a classifier.
- The use of "ground-substitution-as-examples" as the propositionalisation algorithm is reinvestigated, and we will show that this algorithm is very appropriate to construct the FOBN classifier.

The rest of this paper is organized as follows. We explain the problem and the overview of our framework in Section 2. In Section 3 and 4 we describe the details of the MCAFEE and GRASP algorithms, respectively. Then, the experimental results are given in Section 5, and finally, we discuss and compare our approach to other related works in Section 6.

2 The Framework Overview

In this paper, we address two main problems. The first one is the overfitting problem that we propose to solve by using FOBN rules instead of standard first-order rules, and the second one is the complexity problem of learning the FOBN itself. First, to illustrate an overfitting problem, consider the following example.

Example 1 (An Overfitting Problem). Assume that we have two simple rules of `rich(X)`, the target class, learned by ILP:

```
rich(X)  :- diligent(X),genius(X).
rich(X)  :- work_in(X,Y),big_company(Y),good_company(Y).
```

And we have an unseen data case of `ann` as follows:

```
diligent(ann). work_in(ann,ibm). big_company(ibm).
```

From the above rules, we conclude that `rich(ann)` is false. □

In an overfitting problem, we usually get the induced rules that are more specific than the real concept. Too many specific rules do not match well with an unseen data. As we can see, we cannot conclude that `rich(ann)` is true from the rules though she is diligent and works in a big company. Notice that these two properties *partially match* both of rules. The partially matching property is the key idea of our proposed method inspired by [12] together with the FOBN's inference method for solving the overfitting problem. To illustrate this, consider FOBN of Example 1 in Figure 1 and 2. Significant properties or features extracted from the rules now construct the main structure of the FOBN. With this FOBN (together with its corresponding CPTs), given matched properties of `ann`, we can solve the overfitting problem in Example 1 by calculating posterior probability to predict the most appropriate class for `ann` (whether she is rich) by the inference method of FOBN (see [13]). In this paper, we will call an FOBN centrally learned for the classification tasks, like the FOBN of Example 1, as *FOBN classifier*. The definition of an FOBN classifier which will be constructed by our method is formally defined as follows.

Definition 1 (FOBN classifier). Any FOBN is said to be FOBN classifier iff (1) the class attribute(s) is always output node(s) in the network, and (2) the class attribute is directed influenced by all extracted features.

In other words, our method always gives two additional constraints while learning FOBN as classifier. First, the class attribute always has no children node, and, second, we will use all features to construct a *support network* [10] of the class attribute. The reason to do this is because we want to retain the core knowledge of the first-order rules induced by the ILP system. Note that an FOBN classifier can have more than one output node if we are concerned with multi-class problems. We will discuss the FOBN that is centrally concerned with discovery tasks, but may not be efficient to predict an unseen data in Section 6.

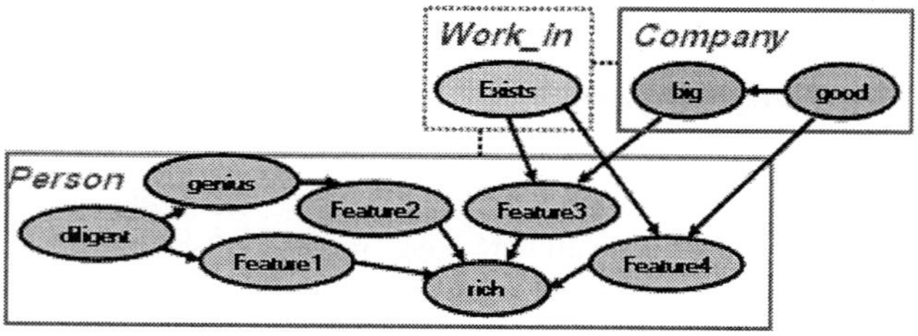

Fig. 1. FOBN of Example 1 (PRM format)

Main Structure:
```
rich(X) | fea-
ture1(X),feature2(X),feature3(X,Y),feature4(X,Y)
feature1(X)  | diligent(X).
feature2(X)  | genius(X).
feature3(X,Y)  | work_in(X,Y), big_company(Y).
feature4(X,Y)  | work_in(X,Y), good_company(Y).
```

Remaining Structure:
```
big_company(X)  | good_company(X).
genius(X)  | diligent(X).
```

Fig. 2. FOBN of Example 1 (BLP format)

The next problem we address in this paper is about the learning complexity of FOBN. Botta et al. [2] have recently shown that the relational learning problem is linked to the exponential complexity of matching, and the learner could hardly search in practice for target concepts having more than four *non-determinate variables* (cf. Section 4). Chickering [4] has also shown that learning a Bayesian network from (raw) data is an NP-complete problem. Therefore, the methods which directly learn the FOBN proposed in [9,10] are very complicated in practice. This is the main reason that our framework adapts a standard Bayesian network learner and an ILP system to learn the FOBN from the original data. Other benefits of using the standard ones are that we can select, from existing algorithms already built in each standard learner, the most appropriate search strategy, heuristic function, and other methods which can masterly handle other kinds of imperfect data such as missing value data (cf. [15]). All processes to construct the FOBN classifier and predict unseen data are shown in Figure 3.

To build an FOBN classifier (the training step), our framework first receives the relational examples and background knowledge as inputs like standard ILP systems, and then we induce ILP rules as usual. Next, we use the MCAFEE algorithm described in Section 3 to extract the features from the rules. We then use these extracted features as *the main structure* of the output FOBN. The main structure of FOBN, in our context, consists of all nodes and links described in Definition 1. Each feature will become a parent node of the target class node, and all literals of each feature will become parent nodes of that feature (see Figure 1 and 2). After that, we are ready to learn *the remaining parts of the FOBN structure* and their CPTs by a standard Bayesian network learner. The remaining parts of the structure mean additional nodes and links those fit the training data but are not explored by our feature extraction algorithm. Note that the remaining parts, which are appropriately learned, would make the induced FOBN more efficient, but in practice we let the user choose whether to learn those parts or not. In order to use a standard Bayesian network learner to learn the rest of the FOBN classifier, we have to translate relational data into the propositional representation, i.e. the single database table. Such a transformation is so-called *propositionalisation* [5,7,14,15]. This propositionalisation process is done by our proposed algorithm named GRASP. Inspired by [7], GRASP uses *variable bindings (ground substitutions) as examples* instead of the original examples, and we will show in Section 4 that using this method makes the learning process more appropriate and much easier than learning from the original examples. The testing process in Figure 3 will also be described in Section 4.

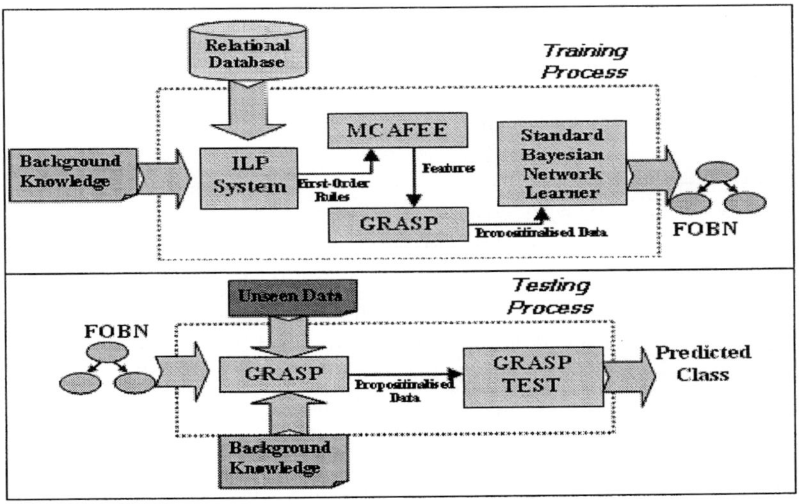

Fig. 3. All processes of the framework

3 MCAFEE (Minimal ChAin FEature Extraction Algorithm)

In this section, we use the notion of *chain* to be a part of a first-order rule. A part of rule means a subset of literals in the body of that rule. MCAFEE is an algorithm that extracts only *significant chains* or, namely, *features* from induced ILP rules. This kind of algorithm is also known as *constructive induction* algorithm (see [14,17]). In practice, any chains of a rule could be selected as features, but for our method the selected significant ones should not be *meaningless* or *redundant*. A meaningless chain occurs when some variables occuring in the chain are not introduced by any other literal of that chain before (see [12,14]). For instance, consider rule `rich(X) :-`

`dad(Y,X),rich(Y),good_company(W)`. While variable `Y` is introduced by `dad(Y,X)`, variable `W` occurring in the body is not introduced by any literal before, so `good_company(W)` is meaningless. Thus any chains generated from this rule and containing `good_company(W)` will not be selected as features.

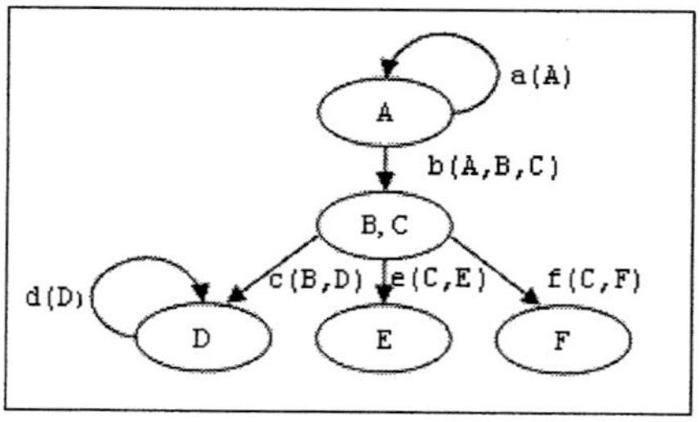

Fig. 4. The dependency graph for the rule in Example 2

The main idea of MCAFEE to extract only meaningful chains is based on [12]. This idea is best understood by viewing each rule as a directed dependency graph. To illustrate, consider the following example.

Example 2 (Dependency Graph of ILP Rule). Suppose that we have the following rule:

```
r(A) :- a(A),b(A,B,C),c(B,D),d(D),e(C,E),f(C,F).
```

This rule has a corresponding dependency graph as shown in Figure 4. The root node of the graph is a set of variables occurring in the head of the rule. Each of the other nodes represents a set of new variables introduced by a literal in the body, and an edge to the node represents the body literal. □

MCAFEE intends to extract only meaningful chains that are based on the notion of *valid chain* defined as follows.

Definition 2 (Valid Chain). In a directed dependency graph of each rule, any path in the graph is called *valid chain* iff that path satisfies one of the two following conditions: (1) some edge(s) of the path connects to any node which is already in the path, *or* (2) some edge(s) of the path connects to a *leaf* node of the graph.

More precisely, the first kind of valid chain will occur when some edge(s) causes loop to occur in the path, and the second will occur when the path terminates at any leaf node. In our context, leaf node is a node that has no edge leaving out of itself. Since every edge connecting to a new node that contains new variable(s) is a literal which introduces the new variable(s), every valid chain guarantees to be meaningful. However, recall that all features extracted by MCAFEE are the parents of the class attribute (see Definition 1). This makes some valid chains redundant if we select them all as features. This is because every combination of all parent nodes will be used to construct the CPT of the class attribute. For instance, from the Example 2, the valid chain "`b(A,B,C),e(C,E),f(C,F)`" is redundant because it can be constructed by the combination of two valid chains "`b(A,B,C),e(C,E)`" and "`b(A,B,C),f(C,F)`".

MCAFEE, therefore, will extract only meaningful and non-redundant chains as features. This kind of chains is called *minimal valid chain*, and can be formally defined as follows.

Definition 3 (Minimal Valid Chain). Any valid chain r is a *minimal valid chain* iff there is no any other valid chain r'' such that $r'' \subseteq r$.

In other words, a path is a minimal valid chain whenever it is *a shortest path* of the rule dependency graph that satisfies condition (1) or (2) of Definition 2. Let R be the set of all valid chains. By the partial order properties of poset(R, $\subseteq$) [20], every other valid chain can be constructed by the union of two or more minimal valid chains. All extracted features, therefore, now guarantee to be non-redundant and meaningful. The obtained features of Example 2 are shown in Figure 5. Notice that all variables occurring in the features are set to be global. This makes the combination of two or more minimal valid chains to construct other valid chains possible. The obtained features, as well as the original data are then used in the propositionalisation process in order to construct the remaining parts of the FOBN structure and its CPTs as described in the previous section.

```
f1(A)  :- a(A).
f2(A,B,C,D)  :- b(A,B,C),c(B,D),d(D).
f3(A,B,C,E)  :- b(A,B,C),e(C,E).
f4(A,B,C,F)  :- b(A,B,C),f(C,F).
```

Fig. 5. The extracted features of Example 2 by MCAFEE

4 GRASP (GRound-substitutions-AS-examples Propositionalisation)

As we described in Section 2, we adapt a standard (propositional) Bayesian network learner to construct the remaining structure and the CPTs of the output FOBN. A standard Bayesian network learner receives the single (flat) table as its input. The columns of the table will be used as nodes in the obtained FOBN, and each row is corresponding to one example. Therefore, we have to translate the original (relational) data into the flat one. However, some relational problems cannot be simply translated or solved by propositional learners, especially for relational problems containing *non-determinate literals*. As described in [14], literals are non-determinate if they introduce new variables that can be bound in several alternative ways, e.g., `work_in` in Example 1 is non-determinate if we know that `ann` also works in another company such as `work_in(ann,dell)`. The transformation of non-determinate relational data to propositional data exists theoretically, but the output table size will be unacceptable in practice (see [5]). We, therefore, propose GRASP, an alternative way, to translate the original data into the single table format. GRASP limits the number of attributes (columns) in the output table by the features extracted by MCAFEE as well as all parents of the features. We can formally define the table columns in Definition 4.

Definition 4 (Attributes/Table Columns). Given the set of extracted features $\mathcal{F}$, the attributes (columns) of the propositionalised table are (1) all features in $\mathcal{F}$ themselves, and (2) all literals in the set $\{ \ell \mid \exists f\ (f \in \mathcal{F} \text{ and } \ell \in \text{body}(f)) \}$.

Because of non-determinate literals, in the translation process each training example may have many different variable bindings so that it may correspond to more than one row in the translated table. Following [7], we then regard each *variable binding (ground substitution)* θ *as a new example* (we simply call example) instead of the original example. More precisely, each original training example is split into new examples such that each new example corresponds to one variable binding of the original example. For simple instance, from Example 1 if we have other facts of `ann` such as `work_in(ann,dell)` and `good_company(dell)`, we will have two new examples of `ann` corresponding to two variable bindings {`X/ann,Y/ibm`} and {`X/ann,Y/dell`}. Suppose we know that in fact `ann` is rich and use her as a training example. In this case, the propositionalised table of Example 1 corresponding to the features in Figure 2 can be shown in Table 1. For simplicity, we refer to `feature1(X)`, `feature2(X)`, `feature3(X,Y)` and `feature4(X,Y)` as F_1, F_2, F_3 and F_4, respectively.

Table 1. The propositionalised table of Example 1 (with additional information described above)

Example	class	θ	F_1	F_2	F_3	F_4
ann	+	`X/ann,Y/ibm`	1	0	1	0
		`X/ann,Y/dell`	1	0	0	1

Using each binding as an example has two main advantages when constructing FOBN. First, obviously, with the new definition of the data cases, we can learn FOBN from a standard Bayesian network learner *directly* because the translated data, at this time, is absolutely in the propositional form. This contrasts with multi-instance based propositionalisation (see e.g. [1,14]) in which a new example in the output table may correspond to more than one rows, and thus the output table cannot be learned by the propositional learner directly. Second, when dealing with the non-determinate problem, some methods try to select the best binding of each original example to be a new example (see e.g. [12]). However, when taking a closer look at the constructing process of FOBN, the rules obtained by using all bindings as examples are more reasonable. This property is what [7] calls *strong completeness*. To illustrate, consider the following example.

Example 3 (Strong Completeness). Suppose that we have simple translated data shown in Table 2.

As shown in the table, the translated data consists of original five examples, and each example can be bound by two ground substitutions, so that now we have ten new examples. From the table, we know that the prior probability of class to be positive is P(+) = 0.6. Using GRASP, without any constraint, since the posterior probabilities of the positive class given F_2 and F_4 are $P(+ \mid F_2) = 1.0$ and $P(+ \mid F_4) = 1.0$, respectively, we will get the support network of the class attribute such as `class | F2, F4` (suppose we have an inductive bias that 1.0 >> 0.6). However, for those methods which use only the best binding (θ_{E11}, θ_{E22}, and θ_{E31} if we greedily select the binding that gives the maximum number of true features as the best binding), those methods may get an incorrect support network of the class attribute such as `class | F4`. □

Table 2. Simple translated data of Example 3.

Example	class	θ	F_1	F_2	F_3	F_4
E_1	+	θ_{E11}		0	0	1
		θ_{E12}		1	0	0
E_2	+	θ_{E21}		1	0	0
		θ_{E22}		0	0	1
E_3	+	θ_{E31}		0	1	1
		θ_{E32}		0	1	0
E_4	-	θ_{E41}		0	1	0
		θ_{E42}		0	0	0
E_5	-	θ_{E51}		0	1	0
		θ_{E52}		0	0	0

There are two points needed to be considered from the example above. First, notice that θ_{E32} is a positive example which contradicts wrt other negative examples. In this case, we regard this example like a noisy data, and let the standard Bayesian network learner handle it. Second, from Definition 1, the support network of the class attribute always consists of all features as the parent, so the support network of class attribute is always fixed and correct (with our definition). However, our method for strong completeness is still necessary to prevent the occurrence of incorrect support networks of other attributes those are defined in Definition 4 (the remaining parts of FOBN structure).

Nonetheless, the use of the "ground-substitution-as-example" method can cause two problems. The first problem is about the size of the translated table. Despite the fact that we limit the number of columns as defined in Definition 4, in some non-determinate (real world) problems, the table size is still very large. Another problem is that this method, in some cases, still causes incorrect support networks. To illustrate, see the example below.

Example 4 (Incorrect Support Network). In addition to the original examples in Example 3, suppose we have additional two original examples shown in Table 3.

Table 3. Additional data cases added into the table in Example 3

E_6	+	θ_{E61}	0	0	0	1
E_7	-	θ_{E71}	0	0	0	1
		θ_{E72}	0	0	0	1
		θ_{E73}	0	0	0	1
		θ_{E74}	0	0	0	1

At this time, by our method (every binding as example) we get a posterior probability P(+ | F_4) = 0.5 and a prior probability P(+) = 0.47, so, by our method, the Bayesian network learner would not choose F_4 as a parent node of the class attribute. This is a wrong result because, actually, only one negative example contradicts four positive examples (in fact, P(+ | F_4) = 0.8). The wrong result in this case is because of duplicate bindings which are produced several times in the same original negative example. Conversely, duplicate bindings in the same original positive example also lead to incorrect a Bayesian network (too many parent nodes). □

Fortunately, both the size and incorrect support network problems can be solved concurrently by the technique proposed in [1,21]. In order to use this technique, first of all, we give a definition of *maximal specific binding*.

Definition 5 (Maximal Specific Binding). Given a set of all original examples $\mathcal{E}$, for each $e \in \mathcal{E}$, a maximal specific binding of e is any variable binding θ such that there is no other variable binding α of e whose set of all true attributes is a superset of the set of all true attributes of θ.

As shown in Example 4, we have a problem about the duplicate bindings that lead to an incorrect support network problem. Therefore, GRASP will select only *non-duplicate maximal specific bindings* in each original example as new examples. To illustrate, consider the following example.

Example 5 (Non-duplicate Maximal Specific Binding). Suppose that we have the translated table shown in Table 4.

Table 4. Simple translated data of Example 5

Example	class	θ	F_1	F_2	F_3	F_4
E_1	+	θ_{E11}		1	0	1
		θ_{E12}		1	0	1
		θ_{E13}		1	1	0
		θ_{E14}		1	0	1
E_2	-	θ_{E21}		1	0	1
		θ_{E22}		0	1	0
		θ_{E23}		0	1	0
		θ_{E24}		1	0	0

From the table above, the maximal specific bindings of E_1 are θ_{E11}, θ_{E13}, θ_{E14}, and the maximal specific bindings of E_2 are θ_{E21}, θ_{E22}, θ_{E23}, but the new examples generated by GRASP are only θ_{E11}, θ_{E13} and θ_{E21}, θ_{E22}, because θ_{E14} is the same as θ_{E11} and also θ_{E23} is the same as θ_{E22}. □

Notice that although θ_{E21} is the same as θ_{E11}, these two bindings are not generated from the same original example, so GRASP still uses θ_{E21} as a new example. By the technique described above, not only we guarantee that no duplicate binding in the same original example occurs, but, in practice the size of the output table is dramatically decreased also. Therefore, both size and incorrect support network problems are solved by GRASP. Moreover, the important information of the original data still remains in the translated table (for more details see [1,21]). Now, we formally give the definition of new examples used by GRASP in Definition 6. Note that, for simplicity, we give a definition only for binary classification, but it is easy to extend Definition 6 for multi-class problems.

Definition 6 (Examples/Table Rows). Given a class literal *p*, and a set of original training examples $\mathcal{E}$ containing sets $\mathcal{E}^+$ and $\mathcal{E}^-$ corresponding to sets of original positive and negative examples, respectively. *Each (new) positive and negative examples* in the translated table is a maximal specific binding θ such that (1) θ is not the same as other previous maximal specific bindings in the same original example, and (2) $p\theta \in \mathcal{E}^+$ (new positive example), or $p\theta \in \mathcal{E}^-$ (new negative example).

Since we use all non-duplicate maximal specific bindings as the examples in the training process (constructing the FOBN), it is reasonable to use this kind of bindings in the predicting process of unseen data also. As shown in Figure 3, our testing framework gets the induced FOBN and background knowledge as inputs to predict the appropriate class of an unseen data. The data will also be propositionalised by GRASP to get all of its non-duplicate maximal specific bindings. However, there are many ways to predict the class of the unseen data which is now extracted into many new data cases by GRASP. The predicting method depends on the system bias. For example, we can use the simple method such that we first calculate all posterior probability for each new data (binding), and then use only the maximum one to predict the most appropriate class (as well as other methods such as using the average probability or the majority vote of new data cases to predict the class). Hence, in our framework, we use GRASP-TEST which allows the user to specify the best bias for the problem.

5 Preliminary Experiments

We have evaluated our framework by performing experiments on the Mutagenesis dataset, a well-known ILP problem. As described in [1,23], in this dataset, each example consists of a structural description of a molecule as a definite clause. The molecules have to be classified into mutagenic (active) and non-mutagenic (inactive) ones. The representation language used has been defined from background knowledge $\mathbf{B}_2$ (see [23] for a deeper explanation). In a few words, 138 positive and 92 negative examples of the target class are molecules described in terms of *atoms*, *bonds* between some of these atoms and the interesting molecular properties, a measure of hydrophobicity of the compound (logP) and the energy of the compounds lowest unoccupied molecular orbital (LUMO). In the experiments, we selected PROGOL (CProgol version 4.2) [18], the state-of-the-art ILP system, for learning first-order rules, and WinMine [4] as a standard Bayesian network learner. The experiments are contributed in two fields of data mining tasks, the discovery and classification tasks. To the best of our knowledge, our framework is the first one adapting FOBN to cope with well-known ILP classification problems. Although our method is intended to construct

FOBN for classification task, the obtained FOBN is still valuable in discovery task (cf. below).

In the following classification experiments, we used three-fold cross-validation for all testing processes, and for bias in GRASP-TEST, we simply used the maximum posterior probability of all bindings in each original example to predict the most appropriate class as described in Section 4. In addition to the original mutagenesis problem, to see how well our learner handles noisy data, we also added 10% and 15% of random class noise into the mutagenesis dataset in these preliminary experiments. In fact, PROGOL also has an ability to handle noisy data as its option, so in our experiments we tried to set this option with many different values to compare with our learner. The average results over three-fold data of all systems are shown in Table 5.

Table 5. Compared accuracy of our framework with PROGOL on the mutagenesis dataset

Noise Level in Dataset	PROGOL 0% noise setting	PROGOL 5% noise setting	PROGOL 10% noise setting	PROGOL 15% noise setting	PROGOL +FOBN
0%	84.58	82.99	77.14	77.14	84.34
10%	64.23	65.42	69.72	71.29	78.67
15%	60.56	59.02	61.54	65.31	74.33

"x% noise setting" in the table indicates that noise was set to x% as an option of PROGOL. As shown in the table, when there was no noise in the dataset, we see that our learner was comparable to PROGOL, but when 10% and 15% of noise was added into the dataset, the accuracy of our framework (shown in the last column) was much higher than PROGOL (with all different values of the noise option). The better results are according to the disadvantage of first-order rules directly induced by ILP systems as we described in previous sections. There are two main reasons that the FOBN rules induced by our framework are more robust against noise than original first-order rules. The first reason is due to partial matching technique as Kijsirikul et al. [12] have shown that even using the partial matching technique with the extracted features alone (without using another technique such as the probabilistic theory like our method), the predicting performance still outperforms the classical technique (matching ILP rules straightforwardly) especially for data in noisy domains and multi-class problems. The second reason is because of the power of the probabilistic theory which makes the use of the features more flexible by assigning appropriate weight into each feature.

As the discovery task, a sample of the learned FOBN classifier of the mutagenesis problem can be demonstrated in Figure 6 and 7. Note that with the method described in [11] every FOBN in PRM representation can be easily translated into BLP representation.

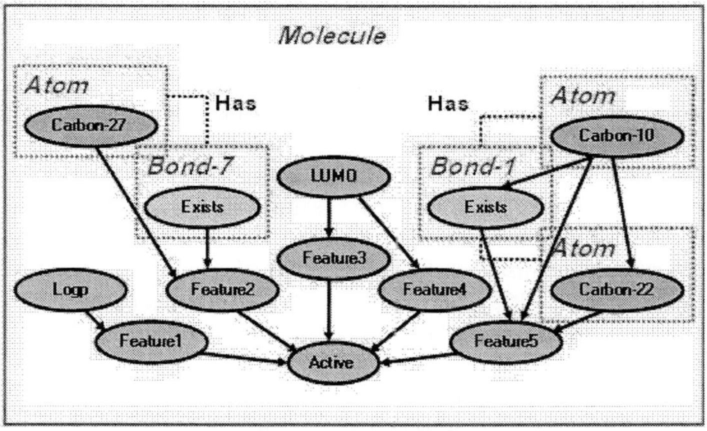

Fig. 6. The example of PRM learned from the mutagenesis problem

Main Structure:

```
active(A) | feature1(A,LP),feature2(A,Atom1),feature3(A,LM),
feature4(A,LM),feature5(A,Atom2,Atom3).

feature1(A,LP)      | logp(A,LP), gteq(LP, 4.23).
feature2(A,Atom1)  | atm(A,Atom1,carbon,27, ),
bond(A,Atom1, ,7).
feature3(A,LM)      | lumo(A,LM), lteq(LM,-2.14).
feature4(A,LM)      | lumo(A,LM), lteq(LM,-1.74).
feature5(A,Atom2,Atom3) | atm(A,Atom2,carbon,22, ),
bond(A,Atom2,Atom3,1), atm(A,Atom3,carbon,10, ).
```

Remaining Structure:

```
atm(A,Atom3,carbon,22, )    | atm(A,Atom3,carbon,10, ).
bond(A,Atom2,Atom3,1) | atm(A,Atom3,carbon,10,_).
```

Fig. 7. The example of BLP learned from the mutagenesis problem

6 Related Works

There are few classification techniques which upgrade first-order rules to handle noisy data. BANNAR [12] upgrading the rules by the backpropagation neural network achieves one of the best results for the classification tasks in many well-known ILP datasets. As we introduced in the first section, this method, however, lost the expressive ability of first-order logic which is central to discovery data mining. 1BC [8] is also a model for first-order Bayesian network classifiers, but the model is only a naïve one (every node in the network except the target node is mutually independent to the others, and directly influences to the target node) which is the specialization of a FOBN classifier learned by our framework. To construct an efficient classifier in 1BC, moreover, users have to provide *structural predicates* and *properties* for generating atomic features, in contrast with our method in which users are not necessary to provide all features since the MCAFEE algorithm uses the ILP rules to automatically generate the significant features. Some methods [9,10] have been proposed to directly learn FOBN from relational data by using the greedy heuristic. However, those methods are not intended to learn the *concept* of the target attribute (learn the FOBN to classify data) as our method. They proposed the algorithms mainly for discovery tasks. The obtained structure will be selected for the best fit to all attributes but not specially for the class attribute as our method. Therefore, in some cases the class attribute would be independent from some important features, and thus the obtained FOBN is not efficient to classify an unseen data.

Related to propositionalisation and feature extraction methods, are LINUS and its extension named DINUS [15] which are the very first systems proposing propositionalisation techniques for relational problems. However, LINUS and DINUS use very strong bias such that they allow no non-determinate literal in their learning framework (see [14]). Those systems straightforwardly generate features from background knowledge, and do not determine in advance whether the features are useful (significant) in classification tasks or not. Kijsirikul et al. [12] have shown that the extracted features similar to our method are much more efficient than LINUS's features in all of their experimental results. Kramer et al. [14] reviewed many useful techniques to extend a propositionalisation algorithm to handle non-determinate literals, e.g., stochastic propositionalisation and Turney's RL-ICET algorithm. Although those techniques do not concern about the redundant features (see Section 3), it is still interesting to take a closer look and compare those techniques with our method.

Acknowledgements

We would like to thank Sukree Sinthupinyo for many useful discussions about the propositionalisation process. We thank David Maxwell Chickering and Daniel Lowd for their help on problems of the WinMine toolkit used as a standard Bayesian network learner in this paper. We also thank anonymous reviewers for the suggestion about Poole's works. This work is supported by the Thailand Research Fund.

References

[1] E. Alphonse and C. Rouveirol. Lazy Propositionalisation for Relational Learning, In Horn W., editor, *Proc. of 14th European Conference on Artificial Intelligence*, Berlin, Allemagne , pages 256-260, IOS Press, 2000.

[2] M. Botta and A. Giordana and L. Saitta and M. Sebag. Relational learning: Hard Problems and Phase transition. *Selected papers from AIIA'99*, Springer-Verlag, 2000.

[3] D. M. Chickering. Learning Bayesian Networks is NP-Complete. In D. Fisher and H. J. Lenz, editors, *Learning from Data: Artificial Intelligence and Statistics* V, 1996.

[4] D. M. Chickering. The WinMine Toolkit. *Technical Report MSR-TR-2002-103*, Microsoft, 2002

[5] L. De Raedt. Attribute value learning versus inductive logic programming: The missing links (extended abstract). In D. Page, editor, *Proc. of the 8th Int. Conference on Inductive Logic Programming*, LNAI 1446, pages 1-8. Springer-Verlag, 1998.

[6] S. Dzeroski. Relational Data Mining Applications: An Overview. *Relational Data Mining*, S. Dzeroski and N. Lavrac, editors, Springer-Verlag, 2001.

[7] D. Fensel, M.Zickwolff, and M. Weise. Are substitutions the better examples ? In L. De Raedt, editor, *Proc. of the 5th International Workshop on ILP*, 1995.

[8] P.A. Flach and N. Lachiche. 1BC: A first-order Bayesian classifier. In S. Dzeroski and P.A. Flach, editors, *Proc. of the 9th International Workshop on Inductive Logic Programming*, LNAI 1634, pages 92–103. Springer-Verlag, 1999.

[9] L. Getoor, N. Friedman, D. Koller, and A. Pfeffer. Learning Probabilistic Relational Models. *Relational Data Mining*, S. Dzeroski and N. Lavrac, editors, 2001

[10] K. Kersting, L. De Raedt. Basic Principles of Learning Bayesian Logic Programs. Technical Report No. 174, Institute for Computer Science, University of Freiburg, Germany, June 2002

[11] K. Kersting, L. De Raedt. Bayesian Logic Programs. In J. Cussens and A. Frisch, editors, *Work-in-Progress Reports of the Tenth International Conference on Inductive Logic Programming (ILP -2000)*, London,U.K., 2000.

[12] B. Kijsirikul, S. Sinthupinyo, and K. Chongkasemwongse. Approximate Match of Rules Using Backpropagation Neural Networks. *Machine Learning Journal*, Volume 44, Issue 3, September, 2001

[13] D. Koller and A. Pfeffer. Object-Oriented Bayesian Networks. *Proc. of UAI*, 1997.

[14] S. Kramer, N. Lavrac and P. Flach. Propositionalization Approaches to Relational Data Mining, in: Dzeroski S., Lavrac N, editors, *Relational Data Mining*, 2001.

[15] N. Lavrac and S. Dzeroski. *Inductive Logic Programming : Techniques and Applications*. Ellis Horwood, New York, 1994

[16] E. McCreath and A. Sharma. ILP with Noise and fixed Example Size: a Bayesian Approach. *Proc. of the 15th International Joint Conference on Artificial Intelligence (IJCAI)*, Nagoya, Japan, August 1997

[17] S. Muggleton and L. De Raedt. Inductive Logic Programming: Theory and Methods. *Journal of Logic Programming*, 12:1-80, 1994.

[18] S. Muggleton. Inverse entailment and Progol. *New Generation Computing*, Special issue on Inductive Logic Programming, 13(3-4):245–286, 1995.

[19] D. Poole. The Independent Choice Logic for modeling multiple agents under uncertainty. *Artificial Intelligence*, 94 (1-2), special issue on economic principles of multi-agent systems: 7-56, 1997.

[20] K. H. Rosen. *Discrete Mathematics and its Applications*. 4th Edition, Mcgraw-Hill, 1998.

[21] M. Sebag and C. Rouveirol. Constraint Inductive Logic Programming. In L. De Raedt, editor, *Advances in Inductive Logic Programming*, 277-294, IOS-Press, 1996.

[22] Srinivasan and R.D. King. Feature construction with Inductive Logic Programming: a study of quantitative predictions of biological activity aided by structural attributes. *Data Mining and Knowledge Discovery*, 3(1):37-57, 1999

[23] Srinivasan, R.D. King, and S. Muggleton. The role of background knowledge: using a problem from chemistry to examine the performance of an ILP program. *Technical Report PRG-TR-08-99*, Oxford University Computing Laboratory, Oxford, 1999.

AUC: A Better Measure than Accuracy in Comparing Learning Algorithms

Charles X. Ling[1], Jin Huang[1], and Harry Zhang[2]

[1] Department of Computer Science, The University of Western Ontario
London, Ontario, Canada N6A 5B7
{ling,jhuang}@csd.uwo.ca

[2] Faculty of Computer Science, University of New Brunswick
Fredericton, NB, Canada E3B 5A3
hzhang@unb.ca

Abstract. Predictive accuracy has been widely used as the main criterion for comparing the predictive ability of classification systems (such as C4.5, neural networks, and Naive Bayes). Most of these classifiers also produce probability estimations of the classification, but they are completely ignored in the accuracy measure. This is often taken for granted because both training and testing sets only provide class labels. In this paper we establish rigourously that, even in this setting, the area under the ROC (Receiver Operating Characteristics) curve, or simply AUC, provides a better measure than accuracy. Our result is quite significant for three reasons. First, we establish, for the first time, rigourous criteria for comparing evaluation measures for learning algorithms. Second, it suggests that AUC should replace accuracy when measuring and comparing classification systems. Third, our result also prompts us to re-evaluate many well-established conclusions based on accuracy in machine learning. For example, it is well accepted in the machine learning community that, in terms of predictive accuracy, Naive Bayes and decision trees are very similar. Using AUC, however, we show experimentally that Naive Bayes is significantly better than the decision-tree learning algorithms.

1 Introduction

In classification, the goal of a learning algorithm is to build a classifier from a set of training examples with class labels. The predictive ability of the algorithm is typically measured by its predictive accuracy (or error rate, which is 1 minus the accuracy) on the testing examples. However, most classifiers (including C4.5 and Naive Bayes) can also produce probability estimations or "confidence" of the class prediction. Unfortunately, this information is completely ignored in accuracy. That is, the accuracy measure does not consider the probability (be it 0.55 or 0.99) of the prediction; as long as the class with the largest probability estimation is the same as the target, it is regarded as correct. This is often taken for granted since the true probability is unknown for the testing examples anyway.

Y. Xiang and B. Chaib-draa (Eds.): AI 2003, LNAI 2671, pp. 329–341, 2003.

In many applications, however, accuracy is not enough. For example, in direct marketing, we often need to promote the top X% of customers during gradual roll-out, or we often deploy different promotion strategies to customers with different likelihood of buying some products. To accomplish these tasks, we need more than a mere classification of buyers and non-buyers. We need (at least) a ranking of customers in terms of their likelihoods of buying. Thus, a ranking is much more desirable than just a classification [1], and it can be easily obtained since most classifiers do produce probability estimations that can be used for ranking (testing) examples.

If we want to achieve a more accurate ranking from a classifier, one might naturally expect that we must need the true ranking in the training examples [2]. In most scenarios, however, that is not possible. Instead, what we are given is a dataset of examples with class labels only. Thus, given only classification labels in training and testing sets, are there better methods than accuracy to evaluate classifiers that also produce rankings?

AUC (area under the curve) of the ROC (Receiver Operating Characteristics) curve has been recently used as an alternative measure for machine learning algorithms [3, 4, 5]. The ROC curve compares the classifiers' performance across the entire range of class distributions and error costs. See [3, 5] for more details. Figure 1 shows a plot of four ROC curves, each representing one of the four classifiers, A through D. A ROC curve X is said to *dominate* another ROC curve Y if X is always above and to the left of Y. This means that the classifier of X always has a lower expected cost than that of Y, over all possible error costs and class distributions. In this example, A and B dominate D. However, often there is no clear dominating relation between two ROC curves. For example, curves A and B are not dominating each other in the whole range. In those

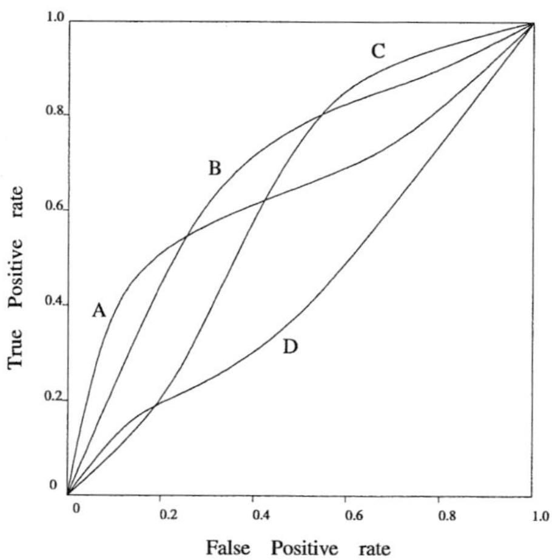

Fig. 1. An example of four ROC curves

Table 1. An example for calculating AUC with r_i

	−	−	−	−	+	−	+	+	+	+
i					1		2	3	4	5
r_i					5		7	8	9	10

situations, the area under the ROC curve, or simply AUC, is a good "summary" for comparing the two ROC curves.

Hand and Till [6] present a simple approach to calculating the AUC of a classifier G below.

$$\hat{A} = \frac{S_0 - n_0(n_0+1)/2}{n_0 n_1}, \tag{1}$$

where n_0 and n_1 are the numbers of positive and negative examples respectively, and $S_0 = \sum r_i$, where r_i is the rank of i_{th} positive example in the ranked list. Table 1 shows an example of how to calculate AUC from a ranked list with 5 positive examples and 5 negative examples. The AUC of the ranked list in Table 1 is $\frac{(5+7+8+9+10)-5\times6/2}{5\times5}$, which is 24/25. It is clear that AUC obtained by Equation 1 is a measure for the quality of ranking, as the more positive examples are ranked higher (to the right of the list), the larger the term $\sum r_i$. AUC is also shown to be equivalent to the Wilcoxon statistic rank test [7].

Bradley [7] has compared popular machine learning algorithms using AUC, and found that AUC exhibits several desirable properties compared to accuracy. For example, AUC has increased sensitivity in Analysis of Variance (ANOVA) tests, is independent to the decision threshold, and is invariant to *a priori* class probability distributions [7]. However, no formal arguments or criteria have been established. How can we compare two evaluation measures for learning algorithms? How can we establish that one measure is better than another? In this paper, we give formal definitions on the consistency and discriminancy for comparing two measures. We show, empirically and formally, that AUC is indeed a statistically consistent and more discriminating measure than accuracy.

Our work is quite significant for several reasons. First, we establish rigourously, for the first time, that even given only labelled examples, AUC is a better measure (defined in Section 2.1) than accuracy. Second, our result suggests that AUC should replace accuracy in comparing learning algorithms in the future. Third, our results prompt and allow us to re-evaluate well-established results in machine learning. For example, extensive experiments have been conducted and published on comparing, in terms of accuracy, decision tree classifiers to Naive Bayes classifiers. A well-established and accepted conclusion in the machine learning community is that those learning algorithms are very similar as measured by accuracy [8, 9, 10]. Since we have established that AUC is a better measure, are those learning algorithms still very similar as measured by AUC? We perform extensive experimental comparisons to compare decision trees and Naive Bayes, and we conclude that Naive Bayes is significantly better than decision tree algorithms in AUC. These kinds of new conclusions are very useful to the machine learning community, as well as to machine learning applications (e.g., data mining). Fourth, as a new measure (such as AUC) has been found and proved to be better than a previous measure (such as accuracy), we can re-design most learning algorithms to optimize the new measure. This would produce classifiers that not only perform well in the new measure, but also in the previous measure, compared to the classifiers that optimize the previous measure, as shown in [1]. This would further improve the performance of our learning algorithms.

2 Comparing Evaluation Measures for Learning Algorithms

Intuitively, we can see why AUC is a better measure than accuracy from the following example. Let us consider two classifiers, Classifier 1 and Classifier 2, both producing probability estimates for a set of 10 testing examples. Assume that both classifiers classify 5 of the 10 examples as positive, and the other 5 as negative. If we rank the testing examples according to increasing probability of being + (positive), we get the two ranked lists as in Table 2.

Table 2. An Example in which two classifiers have the same classification accuracy, but different AUC values

Classifier 1	$- - - - +\mid - + + + +$
Classifier 2	$+ - - - -\mid + + + + -$

Clearly, both classifiers produce an error rate of 20% (one false positive and one false negative), and thus the two classifiers are equivalent in terms of error rate. However, intuition tells us that Classifier 1 is better than Classifier 2, since overall positive examples are ranked higher in Classifier 1 than 2. If we calculate AUC according to Equation 1, we obtain that the AUC of Classifier 1 is $\frac{24}{25}$ (as seen in Table 1), and the AUC of Classifier 2 is $\frac{16}{25}$. Clearly, AUC does tell us that Classifier 1 is indeed better than Classifier 2.

Unfortunately, "counter examples" do exist, as shown in Table 3 on two other classifiers: Classifier 3 and Classifier 4. It is easy to obtain that the AUC of Classifier 3 is $\frac{21}{25}$, and the AUC of Classifier 4 is $\frac{16}{25}$. However, the error rate of Classifier 3 is 40%, while the error rate of Classifier 4 is only 20% (again we assume that the threshold for accuracy is set at the middle so that 5 examples are predicted as positive and 5 as negative). Therefore, a larger AUC does not always imply a lower error rate.

Another intuitive argument for why AUC is better than accuracy is that AUC is more discriminating than accuracy since it has more possible values. More specifically, given a dataset with n examples, there is a total of only $n + 1$

Table 3. A counter example in which one classifier has higher AUC but lower classification accuracy

Classifier 3	$- - - + -$ | $- - + + +$
Classifier 4	$+ - - - -$ | $+ + + + -$

Table 4. A counter example in which two classifiers have same AUC but different classification accuracies

Classifier 5	$- - + + -$ | $+ + - - +$
Classifier 6	$- - + + +$ | $- - + - +$

different classification accuracies ($0/n$, $1/n$, ..., n/n). On the other hand, assuming there are n_0 positive examples and n_1 negative examples ($n_0+n_1 = n$), there are $n_0n_1 + 1$ different AUC values ($0/n_0n_1$, $1/n_0n_1$, ..., n_0n_1/n_0n_1), generally more than $n+1$. However, counter examples also exist in this regard. Table 4 illustrates that classifiers with the same AUC can have different accuracies. Here, we see that Classifier 5 and Classifier 6 have the same AUC($\frac{3}{5}$) but different accuracies (60% and 40% respectively). In general, a measure with more values is not necessarily more discriminating. For example, the weight of a person (having infinitely many possible values) has nothing to do with the number of siblings (having only a small number of integer values) he or she has.

How do we compare different evaluation measures for learning algorithms? Some general criteria must be established.

2.1 (Strict) Consistency and Discriminancy of Two Measures

Intuitively speaking, when we discuss two different measures f and g on evaluating two learning algorithms A and B, we want at least that f and g be *consistent* with each other. That is, when f stipulates that algorithm A is (strictly) better than B, then g will not say B is better than A. Further, if f is more *discriminating* than g, we would expect to see cases where f can tell the difference between algorithms A and B but g cannot.

This intuitive meaning of consistency and discriminancy can be made precise as the following definitions.

Definition 1 (Consistency) *For two measures f, g on domain Ψ, f, g are (strictly) consistent if there exist no a, $b \in \Psi$, such that $f(a) > f(b)$ and $g(a) < g(b)$.*

Definition 2 (Discriminancy) *For two measures f, g on domain Ψ, f is (strictly) more discriminating than g if there exist a, $b \in \Psi$ such that $f(a) > f(b)$ and $g(a) = g(b)$, and there exist no a, $b \in \Psi$ such that $g(a) > g(b)$ and $f(a) = f(b)$.*

As an example, let us think about numerical marks and letter marks that evaluate university students. A numerical mark gives 100, 99, 98, ..., 1, or 0 to students, while a letter mark gives A, B, C, D, or F to students. Obviously, we regard A > B > C > D > F. Clearly, numerical marks are consistent with letter marks (and vice versa). In addition, numerical marks are more discriminating than letter marks, since two students who receive 91 and 93 respectively receive different numerical marks but the same letter mark, but it is not possible to have students with different letter marks (such as A and B) but with the same numerical marks. This ideal example of a measure f (numerical marks) being strictly consistent and more discriminating than another g (letter marks) can be shown in the figure 2(a).

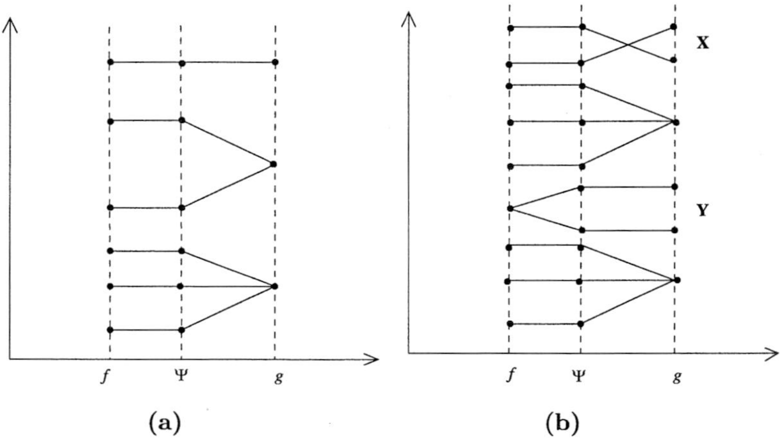

Fig. 2. Illustrations of two measures f and g. A link between two points indicates that the function values are the same on domain Ψ. In (a), f is strictly consistent and more discriminating than g. In (b), f is not strictly consistent or more discriminating than g. Counter examples on consistency (denoted by X in the figure) and discriminancy (denoted by Y) exist here

2.2 Statistical Consistency and Discriminancy of Two Measures

As we have already seen in the beginning of Section 2, counter examples on consistency and discriminancy do exist for AUC and accuracy. Therefore, it is impossible to prove the consistency and discriminancy on AUC and accuracy based on Definitions 1 and 2. What we will define and prove is the *probabilistic version* of the two definitions. Figure 2(b) illustrates a situation where one measure f is not completely consistent with g, and is not strictly more discriminating than g. In this case, we must consider the probability of being consistent and degree of being more discriminating. We extend the previous definitions on strict consistency and discriminancy to degree of consistency and degree of discriminancy, as follows:

Definition 3 (Degree of Consistency) *For two measures f and g on domain Ψ, let $R = \{(a,b)|a,b \in \Psi, f(a) > f(b), g(a) > g(b)\}$, $S = \{(a,b)|a,b \in \Psi, f(a) > f(b), g(a) < g(b)\}$. The degree of consistency* [1] *of f and g is $\mathbf{C}$ ($0 \leq \mathbf{C} \leq 1$), where $\mathbf{C} = \frac{|R|}{|R|+|S|}$.*

Definition 4 (Degree of Discriminancy) *For two measures f and g on domain Ψ, let $P = \{(a,b)|a,b \in \Psi, f(a) > f(b), g(a) = g(b)\}$, $Q = \{(a,b)|a,b \in \Psi, g(a) > g(b), f(a) = f(b)\}$. The degree of discriminancy for f over g is $\mathbf{D} = \frac{|P|}{|Q|}$.*

There are clear and important implications of these definitions of measures f and g in evaluating two machine learning algorithms, say A and B. If f and g are consistent to degree $\mathbf{C}$, then when f stipulates that A is better than B, there is a probability $\mathbf{C}$ that g will stipulate A is better than B. If f is $\mathbf{D}$ times more discriminating than g, then it is $\mathbf{D}$ times more likely that f can tell the difference between A and B but g cannot than that g can tell the difference between A and B but f cannot. Clearly, we require that $\mathbf{C} > 0.5$ and $\mathbf{D} > 1$ if we want to conclude a measure f is "better" than a measure g. This leads to the following definition:

Definition 5 *The measure f is* statistically consistent and more discriminating *than g if and only if $\mathbf{C} > 0.5$ and $\mathbf{D} > 1$. In this case, we say, intuitively, that f is a better measure than g.*

For the example of numerical and letter marks in the student evaluation discussed in Section 2.1, we can obtain that $\mathbf{C} = 1.0$ and $\mathbf{D} = \infty$, as the former is strictly consistent and more discriminating than the latter.

To prove AUC is statistically consistent and more discriminating than accuracy, we substitute f by AUC and g by accuracy in the definition above. To simplify our notation, we will use AUC to represent AUC values, and acc for accuracy. The domain Ψ is the ranked lists of testing examples (with n_0 positive and n_1 negative examples). Since we require $\mathbf{C} > 0.5$ and $\mathbf{D} > 1$ we will essentially need to prove:

Theorem 1. *Given a domain Ψ, let $R = \{(a,b)|AUC(a) > AUC(b), acc(a) > acc(b), a,b \in \Psi\}$, $S = \{(a,b)|AUC(a) < AUC(b), acc(a) > acc(b), a,b \in \Psi\}$. Then $\frac{|R|}{|R|+|S|} > 0.5$ or $|R| > |S|$.*

Theorem 2. *Given a domain Ψ, let $P = \{(a,b)|AUC(a) > AUC(b), acc(a) = acc(b), a,b \in \Psi\}$, $Q = \{(a,b)|acc(a) > acc(b), AUC(a) = AUC(b), a,b \in \Psi\}$. Then $|P| > |Q|$.*

We have proved these two theorems formally (submitted), and due to space limitation, the proofs are omitted.

[1] It is easy to prove that this definition is symmetric; that is, the degree of consistency of f and g is same as the degree of consistency of g and f.

2.3 Empirical Verification on AUC and Accuracy

We conduct experiments with two kinds of (artificial) testing sets to verify the statistical consistency and discriminancy between AUC and accuracy. The first kind is the balanced datasets with equal numbers of positive and negative examples, and the other kind is the unbalanced datasets with 25% positive and 75% negative examples. For the balanced dataset, we test ranked lists with 4, 6, 8, 10, 12, 14, and 16 examples. For the unbalanced dataset, we test ranked lists with 4, 8, 12, and 16 examples (so we can have exactly 25% of positive examples and 75% of negative examples). For each number of examples, we enumerate all possible ranked lists of positive and negative examples. For the balanced dataset with $2n$ examples, there are $\binom{2n}{n}$ such ranked lists.

We exhaustively compare all pairs of ranked lists to see how they satisfy the consistency and discriminating propositions probabilistically. To obtain degree of consistency, we count the number of pairs which satisfy "$AUC(a) > AUC(b)$ and $acc(a) > acc(b)$", and the number of pairs which satisfy "$AUC(a) > AUC(b)$ and $acc(a) < acc(b)$". We then calculate the percentage of those cases; that is, the degree of consistency. To obtain degree of discriminancy, we count the number of pairs which satisfy "$AUC(a) > AUC(b)$ and $acc(a) = acc(b)$", and the number of pairs which satisfy "$AUC(a) = AUC(b)$ and $acc(a) > acc(b)$".

Tables 5 and 6 show the experiment results for the balanced dataset. For consistency, we can see (Table 5) that for various numbers of balanced testing examples, given $AUC(a) > AUC(b)$, the number (and percentage) of cases that satisfy $acc(a) > acc(b)$ is much greater than those that satisfy $acc(a) < acc(b)$. When n increases, the degree of consistency (**C**) seems to approach 0.94, much larger than the required 0.5. For discriminancy, we can see clearly from Table 6 that the number of cases that satisfy $AUC(a) > AUC(b)$ and $acc(a) = acc(b)$ is much more (from 15.5 to 18.9 times more) than the number of cases that satisfy $acc(a) > acc(b)$ and $AUC(a) = AUC(b)$. When n increases, the degree of discriminancy (**D**) seems to approach 19, much larger than the required threshold 1.

Table 5. Experimental results for verifying statistical consistency between AUC and accuracy for the balanced dataset

#	$AUC(a) > AUC(b)$ & $acc(a) > acc(b)$	$AUC(a) > AUC(b)$ & $acc(a) < acc(b)$	**C**
4	9	0	1.0
6	113	1	0.991
8	1459	34	0.977
10	19742	766	0.963
12	273600	13997	0.951
14	3864673	237303	0.942
16	55370122	3868959	0.935

Table 6. Experimental results for verifying AUC is statistically more discriminating than accuracy for the balanced dataset

#	$AUC(a) > AUC(b)$ & $acc(a) = acc(b)$	$acc(a) > acc(b)$ & $AUC(a) = AUC(b)$	D
4	5	0	NA
6	62	4	15.5
8	762	52	14.7
10	9416	618	15.2
12	120374	7369	16.3
14	1578566	89828	17.6
16	21161143	1121120	18.9

Table 7. Experimental results for verifying statistical consistency between AUC and accuracy for the unbalanced dataset

#	$AUC(a) > AUC(b)$ & $acc(a) > acc(b)$	$AUC(a) > AUC(b)$ & $acc(a) < acc(b)$	C
4	3	0	1.0
8	187	10	0.949
12	12716	1225	0.912
16	926884	114074	0.890

Tables 7 and 8 show the experimental results for the unbalanced dataset (25% positive examples and 75% negative examples). We can draw similar conclusions that the degree of consistency (from 0.89 to 1.0) is much greater than 0.5, and the degree of discriminancy (from 15.9 to 21.6) is certainly much greater than 1.0.

These empirical experiments show clearly that AUC is indeed a statistically consistent and more discriminating measure than accuracy for balanced or unbalanced datasets, as a measure for learning algorithms.

3 Comparison of Naive Bayes and Decision Trees

We have established in Section 2 that AUC is a statistically consistent and more discriminating evaluation measure than accuracy. But most previous works only focussed on comparing the learning algorithms by accuracy. A well-accepted conclusion in the machine learning community is that the popular decision tree learning algorithm C4.5 [11] and Naive Bayes are very similar in predictive accuracy [8, 9, 10]. How do popular learning algorithms, such as decision trees and Naive Bayes, compare in terms of the better measure AUC? In this section, we will answer this question experimentally.

Table 8. Experimental results for verifying AUC is statistically more discriminating than accuracy for the unbalanced dataset

#	$AUC(a) > AUC(b)$ & $acc(a) = acc(b)$	$acc(a) > acc(b)$ & $AUC(a) = AUC(b)$	**D**
4	3	0	NA
8	159	10	15.9
12	8986	489	18.4
16	559751	25969	21.6

3.1 Representational Capacity

We first discuss some intuitions regarding the representational capacity of ranking in decision trees and Naive Bayes. In decision trees, the posterior probability of an example is the probability distribution of the leaf that the example falls into. Thus, all examples in the same leaf have the same probability, and they will be ranked randomly. This weakens substantially the capacity of decision trees in representing accurate ranking. This is because two contradictory factors are in play at the same time. On one hand, decision tree algorithms (such as ID3 and C4.5) aim at building a small decision tree. This results in more examples in the leaf nodes. Therefore, the many examples in the same leaves will be ranked randomly. In addition, a small tree implies a small number of leaves, and thus a small number of different probabilities. Thus, a small trees limits the discriminating power of the tree to rank examples. On the other hand, if the tree is large, the tree may not only overfit the data, but the number of examples falling into the leaf nodes becomes small, and thus the probability estimations of examples in the leaves would not be reliable. This would also produce poor ranking of testing examples.

This kind of contradiction does not exist in Bayesian networks. Naive Bayes calculates the posterior probability $p(c|e)$ based on $p(a_i|c)$, where a_i is the value of attribute A_i of example e with class c. Although Naive Bayes has only $2n+1$ parameters, the number of possible different posterior probabilities can be as many as 2^n. Therefore, intuitively speaking, even Naive Bayes has a significant advantage over decision trees in the capacity of representing different posterior probabilities.

3.2 Empirical Comparison

The fact that C4.5 produces poor probability estimations or AUC was recognized recently by some researchers [12]. Provost and Domingos [12] make the following improvements on C4.5 in an effort to improve its AUC scores:

1. **Turn off Pruning.** C4.5 builds decision trees in two steps: building a large tree, and then pruning it to avoid the overfitting which results in a small tree with a higher predictive accuracy. However, Provost and Domingos show

Table 9. Descriptions of the datasets used in our experiments

Dataset	Attributes	Class	Instances
Australia	14	2	690
breast	10	2	683
cars	6	4	700
dermatology	34	6	366
ecoli	7	8	336
hepatitis	4	2	320
import	24	2	205
iris	4	3	150
pima	8	2	392
segment	19	7	2310
vehicle	18	4	846
vote	16	2	232

that pruning also reduces the quality of the probability estimation, as discussed above. For this reason, they choose to build the tree without pruning, resulting in substantially large trees.

2. **Smooth Probability Estimations by Laplace Correction.** Because pruning has been turned off, the decision tree becomes large and has more leaves, and there are fewer examples falling into one leaf. The leaves with a small number of examples (e.g., 2) may produce probabilities of extreme values (e.g., 100%). In addition, it cannot provide reliable probability estimations. For this reason, Laplace correction was used to smooth the estimation and make it less extreme.

Provost and Domingos [12] called the resulting algorithm C4.4, and they showed that C4.4 produces decision trees with significantly better probability estimations than C4.5.

We conduct experiments to compare Naive Bayes, C4.5, and its recent improvement C4.4, using AUC as the evaluation criterion. We use 12 datasets with a relatively large number of examples from the UCI repository [13] as shown in Table 9. Our experiments follow the procedure below:

1. The continuous attributes in the dataset are discretized by the entropy-based method described in [14].
2. For each dataset, run Naive Bayes and C4.4 with the 5-fold cross-validation, and obtain the AUC on the testing set unused in the training.
3. Repeat Step 2 above 6 times and obtain an average AUC on the testing data.

Notice that we use the generalization of the AUC [6] for those datasets with more than two classes. Since Laplace correction has been used in C4.4 and significantly improves the AUC [12], we also use it in Naive Bayes.

The results are shown in Table 10. As we can see, in most datasets, Naive Bayes produces better AUC than C4.4, and C4.4 produces better AUC than C4.5

Table 10. Experimental results of the AUC values of Naive Bayes, C4.4, and C4.5

Dataset	NB	C4.4	C4.5
Australia	75.8±0.8	73.1±0.1	72.0±0.1
breast	97.7±1.2	97.0±1.1	94.7±1.5
cars	93.6±0.3	94.3±0.0	90.3±0.1
dermatology	98.8±1.1	98.3±0.0	95.6±0.0
ecoli	99.3±0.1	99.2±0.0	98.5±0.0
hepatitis	62.1±1.1	59.5±0.1	60.8±0.1
import	99.2±0.2	100.0±0.0	100.0±0.0
iris	97.3±0.3	97.4±0.0	97.9±0.0
pima	77.6±0.9	75.6±0.1	75.7±0.1
segment	95.5±0.1	95.3±0.0	87.2±0.0
vehicle	91.3±0.9	88.1±0.1	84.3±0.1
vote	86.4±0.8	83.1±0.1	78.8±0.1
Average	**89.55**	**88.41**	**86.32**

(as observed by [12]). We conduct a paired two-tailed t-test on the average AUC values of the 12 datasets, and conclude that Naive Bayes is significantly better than C4.4 in terms of AUC (with a 97.5% confidence level), and is certainly significantly better than C4.5 in terms of AUC (with a 99.6% confidence level). We also verify results in [12]: C4.4 is significantly better than C4.5 in terms of AUC (with a 98.0% confidence level).

Previous research have concluded that Naive Bayes and decision trees are very similar in prediction measured by accuracy [8, 9, 10]. As we have established in this paper, AUC is a better measure than accuracy. Our empirical comparisons between Naive Bayes and the decision tree algorithm C4.5 and its recent improvement C4.4 clearly show that Naive Bayes outperforms decision trees in terms of AUC.

4 Conclusions

In this paper, we argued that AUC is a better measure than accuracy based on formal definitions of discriminancy and consistency. Since AUC is applied under the same setting as accuracy — examples with only class labels — it allows us to re-evaluate many well-established conclusions based on accuracy in machine learning (such as the conclusion that decision trees, Naive Bayes, and neural networks are virtually equivalent in terms of accuracy). We have shown via extensive experimental comparisons that in terms of AUC, Naive Bayes predicts significantly better than the decision tree learning algorithms. Our results recommend AUC as a preferred "single number" evaluation measure over accuracy when evaluating and comparing classifiers. Many previous, well-accepted conclusions based on accuracy should also be re-evaluated using AUC.

Such new conclusions will be very useful for machine learning and its applications (e.g., data mining for direct marketing).

Acknowledgements

We gratefully thank Foster Provost for kindly providing us with the source codes of C4.4, which is a great help to us in the comparison of C4.5 and C4.4 to other algorithms.

References

[1] Ling, C. X., Zhang, H.: Toward Bayesian classifiers with accurate probabilities. In: Proceedings of the Sixth Pacific-Asia Conference on KDD (to appear). Springer (2002)

[2] Cohen, W. W., Schapire, R. E., Singer, Y.: Learning to order things. Journal of Artificial Intelligence Research **10** (1999) 243–270

[3] Provost, F., Fawcett, T.: Analysis and visualization of classifier performance: comparison under imprecise class and cost distribution. In: Proceedings of the Third International Conference on Knowledge Discovery and Data Mining. AAAI Press (1997) 43–48

[4] Swets, J.: Measuring the accuracy of diagnostic systems. Science **240** (1988) 1285–1293

[5] Provost, F., Fawcett, T., Kohavi, R.: The case against accuracy estimation for comparing induction algorithms. In: Proceedings of the Fifteenth International Conference on Machine Learning. Morgan Kaufmann (1998) 445–453

[6] Hand, D. J., Till, R. J.: A simple generalisation of the area under the ROC curve for multiple class classification problems. Machine Learning **45** (2001) 171–186

[7] Bradley, A. P.: The use of the area under the ROC curve in the evaluation of machine learning algorithms. Pattern Recognition **30** (1997) 1145–1159

[8] Kononenko, I.: Comparison of inductive and naive Bayesian learning approaches to automatic knowledge acquisition. In Wielinga, B., ed.: Current Trends in Knowledge Acquisition. IOS Press (1990)

[9] Langley, P., Iba, W., Thomas, K.: An analysis of Bayesian classifiers. In: Proceedings of the Tenth National Conference of Artificial Intelligence. AAAI Press (1992) 223–228

[10] Domingos, P., Pazzani, M.: Beyond independence: conditions for the optimality of the simple Bayesian classifier. In: Proceedings of the Thirteenth International Conference on Machine Learning. (1996) 105 – 112

[11] Quinlan, J.: C4.5: Programs for Machine Learning. Morgan Kaufmann: San Mateo, CA (1993)

[12] Provost, F., Domingos, P.: Tree induction for probability-based ranking. Machine Learning (2003) To appear.

[13] Merz, C., Murphy, P., Aha, D.: UCI repository of machine learning databases. In: Dept of ICS, University of California, Irvine. http://www.ics.uci.edu/~mlearn/MLRepository.html (1997)

[14] Fayyad, U., Irani, K.: Multi-interval discretization of continuous-valued attributes for classification learning. In: Proceedings of Thirteenth International Joint Conference on Artificial Intelligence. Morgan Kaufmann (1993) 1022–1027

Model-Based Least-Squares Policy Evaluation

Fletcher Lu and Dale Schuurmans

School of Computer Science, University of Waterloo
Waterloo, ON, Canada, N2L 3G1
{f2lu, dale}@cs.uwaterloo.ca

Abstract. A popular form of policy evaluation for large Markov Decision Processes (MDPs) is the least-squares temporal differencing (TD) method. Least-squares TD methods handle large MDPs by requiring prior knowledge *feature vectors* which form a set of basis vectors that compress the system down to tractable levels. Model-based methods have largely been ignored in favour of model-free TD algorithms due to two perceived drawbacks: slower computation time and larger storage requirements. This paper challenges the perceived advantage of the temporal difference method over a model-based method in three distinct ways. First, it provides a new model-based approximate policy estimation method which produces solutions in a faster computation time than Boyan's least-squares TD method. Second, it introduces a new algorithm to derive basis vectors without any prior knowledge of the system. Third, we introduce an iteratively improving model-based value estimator that can run faster than standard TD methods. All algorithms require model storage but remain computationally competitive in terms of accuracy with model-free temporal differencing methods.

1 Background

In the field of reinforcement learning, a subset of machine learning, we represent the environment as a collection of states. We transition from a state s_i to another state s_j given some action a_i according to a probability distribution $P(s_j|s_i, a_i)$. The process is Markov because moving to a next state is dependent only on the current state and action taken in that state, not on any previous states visited. A reward is obtained for entering a state. The objective is to optimize the amount of rewards obtained during navigation through the system. This can be done by developing a policy π, for navigating states, where π is a function that maps states to actions. An optimal policy will maximize rewards obtained over the long run of navigating through the system. In order to determine if a policy π_i is better than a policy π_j, we need to perform policy evaluation. Whenever one enters a state, we obtain an immediate reward. But the true value for being in a state should not only be measured by the immediate reward, but also by the future rewards that may be obtained through future states that may be reached from the current state. Determining this 'value', is the process known as value estimation. Since this value estimation is dependent on a given policy for navigating the system, it is also known as policy evaluation. Essentially, value

Y. Xiang and B. Chaib-draa (Eds.): AI 2003, LNAI 2671, pp. 342–352, 2003.

estimation assigns an numerical value to each state in the system according to the policy for navigating the system. The ultimate goal is to obtain an optimal policy that will maximize the overall state values. However, one step removed from that goal is to simply be able to perform value estimation for a given policy, which is what this paper deals with.

Methods for performing value estimation can be divided into two general categories: model-based and model-free methods. Model-based methods, as the name suggests, keep a model of the state-to-state probability transitions obtained through sampling a system and use this information to produce a value estimate of states. Model-free methods generally obtain value estimates during sampling without forming any model of the probability transitions.

The study of value estimation in a Markov reward process has been dominated by research in model-free approaches such as Monte Carlo and temporal differencing [1]. The general reasoning behind this preference is that model-free methods are considered to run faster than model-based approaches. Also, avoiding a model saves on storage space. In contrast, model-based methods are generally understood to produce considerably more accurate results. An excellent summary of these advantages and disadvantages was given in [2]. The model-based approach produces the best solution because it forms a maximum likelihood estimate of the value function minimizing approximation error. Recent work has shown that the perception of greater computational efficiency by model-free methods is based on some oversimplifications. A finer analysis has shown that model-based approaches such as maximum likelihood under many circumstances can be computationally competitive with their model-free counterparts [3]. That work principally dealt with polynomial size state spaces.

However, most practical problems deal with exponentially large state spaces. Temporal differencing methods deal with such large MDPs by using a form of compression which reduces the system to a polynomial size based on some set of state assumptions [4]. This form of compression assumes a relation between states whereby some set of states will act in a manner similar to other states. Based on this assumption, least-squares temporal differencing reduces the state space to a tractable problem size. In practical applications, the transition probabilities are formed from a simulation model or from actual experience collected through an agent. The problem with TD methods is that they do not take full advantage of knowledge gained through this data collection. By storing the data in a model, model-based methods can exploit relations not gathered by model-free methods.

This paper exploits a model based approach in several ways. First, based on a model, we provide an alternative least-squares policy evaluation formula to the standard least-squares temporal difference formula (LSTD) introduced in [5] and modified in [4]. We demonstrate that the proposed method runs in faster time than the LSTD method and uses approximately the same storage space. When no model is built from the system, methods such as TD can only form a compression by having prior knowledge which they then exploit. The compression uses a set of basis vectors to reduce the system size. Without prior knowledge the LSTD method cannot be applied. By constructing a model, this paper provides a systematic way to create basis vectors. Assuming that the system can be compressed considerably, we demonstrate that a model-based method of policy evaluation will run faster than temporal differencing. Because it is a model-based method, the value estimates will be more accurate. We further enhance the algorithm to perform iterative improvements in our value estimates allowing early termination for shorter execution time when a certain residual tolerance level is reached.

Although we are able to demonstrate advantages to using a model-based approach to policy evaluation in terms of computational speed and accuracy, greater storage requirements remain a drawback to this method. However, with the advent of greater amounts of cheap memory storage, the trade-off of greater speed and accuracy for extra storage space may be one which is preferable to some users.

2 Least-Squares Policy Evaluation

A discrete time Markov reward process [6] on a finite set of N states, $n = 1, ..., N$ can be described by a transition model $\mathrm{P}(S_{i+1} = m|S_i = n)$, where S_i represents the state we are in at time period i. We move from state n to state m during time transition from time period i to $i+1$. We assume the transition probabilities do not change over process time i to $i+1$ (stationarity assumption). Such a transition model can be represented by an $N \times N$ matrix P, where $P(n,m)$ denotes $\mathrm{P}(S_{i+1} = m|S_i = n)$ for all process times i. We obtain rewards R_i at time period i for entering state S_i. The reward R_i observed at time i is independent of all other rewards and states. We assume a stationary reward model. Let $\mathbf{r}(n)$ denote $\mathrm{E}[R_i|S_i = n]$ and $\boldsymbol{\sigma}^2(n)$ denote $\mathrm{Var}(R_i|S_i = n)$ for all process times i. Thus, $\mathbf{r}$ and $\boldsymbol{\sigma}^2$ represent the vectors (of size $N \times 1$) of expected rewards and reward variances respectively over the different states $n = 1, ..., N$.

Table 1. Notation used in complexity analysis

N	Number of states
M	Total number of steps taken over all sampling trajectories
ϕ_i	A basis/feature vector
Φ	Matrix of basis/feature vectors
k	Number of feature vectors. Φ is of size $N \times k$
l	Size of a subset of feature vectors. $l \leq k$.
P	Probability transition matrix
T	Number of nonzeros in P

The value function $\mathbf{v}(n)$ is defined to be the expected sum of discounted future rewards obtained by starting in a state $S_0 = n$. That is, $\mathbf{v}$ is a vector given by

$$\begin{aligned}\mathbf{v} &= \mathbf{r} + \gamma P\mathbf{r} + \gamma^2 P^2\mathbf{r} + \cdots \\ &= \mathbf{r} + \gamma P\mathbf{v}.\end{aligned} \tag{1}$$

Therefore, if P and $\mathbf{r}$ are known then $\mathbf{v}$ can be solved by

$$(I - \gamma P)\mathbf{v} = \mathbf{r}. \tag{2}$$

The LSTD method modifies equation 2 by using a set of k *feature vectors* ϕ_i each of size $N \times 1$ where $k \leq N$. These feature vectors capture similar properties among states. The LSTD method lets $\Phi\mathbf{w} = \mathbf{v}$ where $\Phi = [\phi_1, ...\phi_k]$. Thus, equation 2 becomes

$$(I - \gamma P)\Phi\mathbf{w} = \mathbf{r}. \tag{3}$$

The matrix $\gamma P\Phi$ is an over-determined matrix. LSTD finds a solution by using a least-squares approach which multiplies both sides of equation 3 by the transpose of Φ

$$\Phi^T(I - \gamma P)\Phi\mathbf{w} = \Phi^T\mathbf{r}. \tag{4}$$

The elegance of this approach, first introduced by Bradtke and Barto [5], is that when performing policy value estimation, it allows for online updating of state values without waiting for termination of data collection in the same way that regular TD does. The complete probability transition matrix is never explicitly represented. Boyan improved the accuracy of the solution by storing a $k \times k$ matrix and iteratively updating that matrix during sampling [4]. Then he solved for the matrix equation of equation 4. Lagoudakis and Parr extended this idea to a policy iteration method [7]. Boyan's LSTD method actually implicitly captures the complete, estimated transition probabilities $\hat{P}$, but just in a compressed $\Phi^T\hat{P}\Phi$ form.

The alternative model-based least-squares (MBLS) form of policy value estimation we propose is to use the transpose of the matrix $(I - \gamma P)\Phi$ instead of Φ to minimize the residual errors in equation 3 to produce

$$\Phi^T(I - \gamma P)^T(I - \gamma P)\Phi\mathbf{w} = \Phi^T(I - \gamma P)^T\mathbf{r}. \tag{5}$$

The benefit of this approach is that it will minimize any residual errors of the vector specified by $(I - \gamma P)\Phi\mathbf{w}$ by projecting this vector onto the vector $\mathbf{r}$ [8]. The LSTD approach only minimizes the residuals if the matrix P happens to be symmetric. The reason why equation 5 is not used in LSTD is that the matrix-matrix multiplication $(I - \gamma P)^T(I - \gamma P)$ cannot be performed online. The $P \times P$ multiplication can only be performed after the probability estimates have been completely collected. For this reason, equation 5 can only be used in a model based method while equation 4 can be used in a model-free TD approach. A second improvement we have made is that we build only an $N \times k$ matrix, $\hat{P}\Phi$, instead of the full $N \times N$ matrix, $\hat{P}$. By storing a $N \times k$ matrix instead of the $k \times k$ matrix that LSTD does, we avoid the k^2 computation LSTD incurs at every sampling step in order to update its $\Phi^T \hat{P}\Phi$ matrix. We build $\hat{P}\Phi$ by

$$(\hat{P}\Phi)_{i*} \leftarrow (\hat{P}\Phi)_{i*} + \Phi_{j*} \tag{6}$$

at each transition step observation from state i to state j. Essentially, equation 6 is a transformation of a $\hat{P}_{ij}$ update to an update of the $\hat{P}\Phi$ matrix. Updating an $N \times k$ matrix costs only k additions. We therefore reduce the computation time of MBLS relative to LSTD. The trade-off is storage of an $N \times k$ matrix. But if the LSTD method stores its Φ basis vectors and since Φ is $N \times k$, then the LSTD will use O(Nk) space already. Under that circumstance MBLS will improve on the computation time of LSTD without any storage increase. An important caveat to Boyan's approach is that as long as the order of states for the rows is kept the same as the order of states of the columns, then the matrix can be considered symmetric. Under this circumstance, Boyan's LSTD method will produce solutions that are as accurate as the MBLS method since both minimize residuals and both are actually forms of model-based methods.

2.1 Comparing Algorithm Efficiency

LSTD differs from TD by updating values of $\hat{\mathbf{w}}$ rather than the values of $\hat{\mathbf{v}}$ directly during each sampling step of a trajectory. Boyan showed that a single update of weight $\hat{\mathbf{w}}_t$ at some time t costs O(k^2) where k is the number of feature/basis vectors for LSTD. Since this update must be performed at each

```
Initialize an N × N matrix Â = 0, column vectors T = 0 &
r = 0 and set γ & basis Φ,
Repeat for each trajectory:
   Draw an initial state i according to π
   Repeat for each step of trajectory:
      Observe next state j
      Â_i* ← Â_i* + φ_i
      T_i1 ← T_i1 + 1
      r_j1 = observed reward at state j
      i ← j
   Until state i is terminal
Repeat for each row i of T:
   Â_i* ← Φ_i* − γÂ_i*/T_i1
Solve for ŵ in Â^T Âŵ = Â^T r
```

Fig. 1. Model-Based Least-Squares (MBLS) policy value estimation

step during sampling, then if M is the total number of sample steps taken, the complete runtime for policy value estimation of LSTD would be $O(Mk^2)$.

For our MBLS method we use a maximum likelihood (ML) approach to collect probability transition values to form the transition matrix, but instead of updating $\hat{P}_{ij} \leftarrow \hat{P}_{ij} + 1$ we build and update the $\hat{P}\Phi$ by $(\hat{P}\Phi)_{i*} \leftarrow (\hat{P}\Phi)_{i*} + \Phi_{j*}$ which costs k for each sampling step for a total of $O(Mk)$. Forming equation 5 from $\hat{P}$ and Φ and solving it costs $O(Nk^2)$ time. When using feature vectors for large MDPs, we assume $k << N$. Since $N \leq T$ and $T \leq M$, then it is reasonable to assume $M \geq Nk$. Thus, the overall runtime of MBLS is $O(Mk)$. Therefore, MBLS runs faster than LSTD's $O(Mk^2)$.

2.2 Comparing Storage Requirements

MBLS is more fault tolerant than LSTD since it does not need to maintain row and column order to minimize its residuals and it produces solutions faster. However, MBLS may use more space than LSTD if features/basis vectors are not stored. If LSTD does store feature/basis vectors, then storage is equivalent.

Figure 1 illustrates the MBLS algorithm. The matrix $\hat{A}$ is a single matrix that represents the matrix product $\hat{P}\Phi$. The vector T is used to normalize $\hat{A}$ so that the rows of $\hat{P}$ sum to 1.

3 Determining Basis Vectors

LSTD is able to deal with large MDPs by using a linear function approximator in the form of basis vectors which compact the system into unique independent states [9]. The LSTD method requires that the feature vectors be known prior to any processing. Therefore, in problems where no prior knowledge is available, the LSTD method cannot be applied.

```
Initialize Φ' = 0, e = 0,
Repeat for each nonzero column of matrix Â:
  Let a be the chosen column of A at some column position i
  Choose a nonzero element in a, call it Â_ij
  e_i = 1
  Repeat for each nonzero column l of Â:
    Â_*l ← Â_il Â_*j − Â_ij Â_*l
    ifÂ_*l = 0 then
      e_l = 1
  Append column e_l to Φ
(Φ on termination is a matrix composed of k e_i vectors [e_1e_2...e_k].)
```

Fig. 2. Model-based basis vector determination

MBLS does not require a prior set of basis vectors. However, when no basis matrix Φ exists, the algorithm degenerates to a maximum likelihood (ML) estimation method where the probability transition matrix update becomes: $\hat{P}_{ij} \leftarrow \hat{P}_{ij} + 1$ when a sampling step transitions from state i to state j. We simply solve for $(I - \gamma\hat{P})\hat{\mathbf{v}} = \hat{\mathbf{r}}$ directly. But with the transition matrix model, it is also possible to determine a minimal spanning set of column vectors of $\hat{P} = [\hat{P}_{*1}, \hat{P}_{*2}, ..., \hat{P}_{*k}]$. This minimal spanning set forms a set of basis vectors of $\hat{P}$. By finding the basis vectors of $\hat{P}$ we can build a set of feature vectors ϕ_i from it to compress our ML model. ϕ_i is the i'th column vector of Φ composed of only zeros and ones. If $\phi_{ij} = 1$ then the j'th column of $\hat{P}$ is a member of our basis vector set for $\hat{P}$.

Figure 2 illustrates a model-based basis vector (MBBV) determination algorithm for finding basis/feature vectors of Φ of an arbitrary matrix $\hat{A}$.[1] It does so by choosing a column vector $\hat{A}_{*j}$ of $\hat{A}$ and then choosing one nonzero row position i of $\hat{A}$ ($\hat{A}_{ij} \neq 0$). It then eliminates all nonzero elements in row i for all other l columns in $\hat{A}$ by: $\hat{A}_{*l} \leftarrow \hat{A}_{il}\hat{A}_{*j} - \hat{A}_{ij}\hat{A}_{*l}$. This row elimination eliminates all remaining column vectors that are linearly dependent on vector $\hat{A}_{*j}$. We then choose another vector in the remaining set of unselected column vectors and repeat the process. Since we eliminate all vectors linearly dependent on $\hat{A}_{*j}$ from our remaining set of column vectors, each iteration step increases our basis set by one linearly independent vector. Assuming a maximum of $k \leq N$ linearly independent column vectors in $\hat{A}$, MBBV will run in $O(N^2k)$ time.

Aside from the advantage of being able to use the derived Φ feature vectors for future computation compression, the upper bound of k independent column vectors of $\hat{P}$ means that we can perform a model-based estimation by first applying ML and then using the MBBV algorithm on $\hat{P}$ to find a Φ which produces a solution in $O(N^2k)$ time.

3.1 Comparing Algorithm Efficiency

Assuming no prior knowledge exists and one wished to use a temporal differencing approach, only standard TD methods and not LSTD methods may be applied to find a solution to a large MDP network. Standard TD equations run in $O(MN)$ time where every sampling step updates all state value estimates. Without prior knowledge, MBLS degenerates to ML which takes $O(M)$ time for data collection. With k linearly independent states, MBBV runs in $O(N^2k)$ time. Once we have the basis vectors of Φ, we can compute $(I - \gamma\hat{P})\Phi$ in $O(N^2k)$ time. We produce $\Phi^T(I - \gamma\hat{P})^T(I - \gamma\hat{P})\Phi$ in $O(Nk^2)$ time to find the weight vector $\hat{\mathbf{w}}$ which can be used to derive $\hat{\mathbf{v}} = \Phi\hat{\mathbf{w}}$. The overall worst case runtime of ML with MBBV with no prior information is $O(N^2k)$. Except in trivial systems, $M > Nk$. Therefore, ML with MBBV will run faster than TD.

[1] This algorithm finds basis vectors for any arbitrary matrix, not just probability matrices, we therefore use the more general symbol $\hat{A}$ instead of $\hat{P}$.

```
Repeat for each nonzero of r̂:
   Find the largest nonzero r̂_i of r̂
   Find the column j of Â such at Â_ij ≠ 0
   v_i ← r̂_i/Â_ij
   Repeat for each nonzero column m of Â:
      Â_*m ← Â_im Â_*j − Â_ij Â_*m
   r̂ ← r̂_i Â_*j − Â_ij r̂
```

Fig. 3. Minimal basis search for $\hat{\mathbf{v}}$ (MBSV)

3.2 Comparing Storage Requirements

Standard TD algorithms still require less storage, since they only store $O(N)$ state value estimates. MBLS requires the storage of the the $N \times N$ probability transition matrix. Computing the basis vectors of Φ will potentially use up $O(N^2)$ amount of memory space.

4 Finding a Minimal Basis Set for State Value Estimates

If we are only interested in finding an estimate of $\hat{\mathbf{v}}$ and do not care to collect information on Φ, then it is possible to improve our $O(N^2k)$ time to an $O(N^2l)$ time, where $l \leq k$. The basic idea is that some minimal linear combination of l independent column vectors of $\hat{P}$ will sum to the reward vector $\hat{\mathbf{r}}$:

$$\hat{\mathbf{r}} = \hat{P}_{1*}v_1 + ... + \hat{P}_{l*}v_l.$$

All other columns of $\hat{P}$ are assumed to have negligible contribution to the value of the reward vector $\hat{\mathbf{r}}$. Let l be that minimal set of column vectors of $\hat{P}$. Since there are at most k independent columns in $\hat{P}$, then $l \leq k$. We can find the set $\{\hat{P}_{1*}v_1, ..., \hat{P}_{l*}v_l\}$ and the coefficients $\{v_1, ..., v_l\}$ by using a method similar to MBBV, but instead of arbitrarily choosing a nonzero vector from our set of $\hat{P}$, we first find a nonzero element $\hat{\mathbf{r}}_j$ in $\hat{\mathbf{r}}$. Choose only a column vector $\hat{P}_{i*}$ where $\hat{P}_{ij} \neq 0$. Set $\hat{\mathbf{v}}_i \leftarrow \hat{\mathbf{r}}_i/\hat{P}_{ij}$. Perform row elimination as in MBBV and on the reward vector $\hat{\mathbf{r}}$. By choosing a column vector $\hat{P}_{*j}$ that has a nonzero component in i, then eliminating that component in all other column vectors, we make $\hat{P}_{*j}$ essential to the solution $\hat{\mathbf{v}}$ of $\hat{\mathbf{r}}$ since it is the only vector that can produce a nonzero value in position i. The row elimination is performed on $\hat{\mathbf{r}}$ to remove $\hat{P}_{*j}$'s effect on $\hat{\mathbf{r}}$. Figure 3 illustrates this minimal basis search for $\hat{\mathbf{v}}$ (MBSV) on a matrix $\hat{A}$. Similar to MBBV the row elimination step takes $O(N^2)$. With l independent column vectors of $\hat{P}$ which form $\hat{\mathbf{r}}$, MBSV runs in only $O(N^2l)$ time. One additional improvement made to MBSV is that we choose the largest $|\mathbf{r}_i|$ for elimination at each step in order to try and reduce the residual error $= |\hat{\mathbf{v}}_i - \hat{\mathbf{v}}|$ as early as possible so that a user may stop the iteration process early and still get a minimal residual solution.

Table 2. Residual and Complexity Observations

LSTD vs MBLS[2]

N	Traj	M_{LSTD}	M_{MBLS}	r_{LSTD}	r_{MBLS}	f_{LSTD}	f_{MBLS}
20	100	967	1131	0.1582	0.1490	9814	4499
50	100	2739	1990	0.2122	0.2034	25605	7067
100	200	10267	9832	0.1713	0.1667	95213	43388
1000	2000	65990	65528	0.3439	0.2829	612917	288516

TD vs ML with MBBV[2]

N	Traj	M_{TD}	M_{ML}	r_{TD}	r_{ML}	f_{TD}	f_{ML}
20	100	652	747	0.6296	0.2186	43784	20984
50	100	2766	2929	0.4232	0.1871	434362	126033
100	200	9028	8462	0.3191	0.1633	2771796	475971
1000	3000	26502	26962	0.6311	0.5075	186952190	1812695

5 Experimental Results

In these experiments, we attempt to confirm our theoretical derivations. Since none of the theoretical results depended on any specific network structure, we used randomly generated transition matrices for our MDP network. We implemented a limited linear dependence on a subset of states in order to allow for compression. The number of linearly *independent* states ranged between 10 and 100 states. All numerical results used a discount factor of $\gamma = 0.8$. All networks had at least one absorbing state which every state could reach by at least one path.

The residual errors in the tables are calculated by finding the true value estimate vector $\mathbf{v}$ by using the true transition matrix P and solving $(I - \gamma P)\mathbf{v} = \mathbf{r}$. The residual is then found by: residual $= \frac{|\hat{\mathbf{v}} - \mathbf{v}|}{|\mathbf{v}|}$. If the method being analysed generates a compressed solution $\hat{\mathbf{w}}$ of weights, then $\hat{\mathbf{v}}$ is calculated by $\hat{\mathbf{v}} = \Phi\hat{\mathbf{w}}$ and then a residual is computed. The TD algorithm updated value estimates of all states. The LSTD algorithm only produced a value estimate at termination of sampling.

Table 2 confirms our main assertions that both LSTD and MBLS will have the same relative accuracy assuming that the matrices are symmetric. The r_{LSTD} and r_{MBLS} columns both show comparable residual errors. When the matrix is symmetric, the main advantage of the MBLS method is a runtime savings. The floating point operations of f_{LSTD} and f_{MBLS} consistently show that MBLS requires between one half and one third the amount of processing time of LSTD.

[2] N: # of states, Traj: # of trajectories, M: # of transition steps, r: residual error, f: floating point operations, for TD $\alpha = .5$, $\lambda = .9$

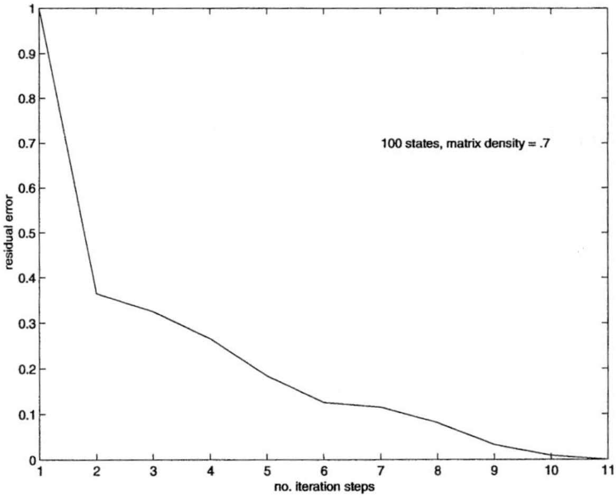

Fig. 4. Residual error $= \frac{|\hat{v}-\hat{v}_i|}{|\hat{v}|}$ vs. iterations of MBSV applied to a 100x100 matrix averaging over 100 samples.

Table 2 also compares the standard temporal differencing method with a ML method which then applies the MBBV algorithm to find basis compression vectors and then produces a value estimate using the compression basis vectors. Our residual computations support the general belief that model-based methods produce more accurate solutions than a model-free method such as TD. We also verify that when states can be compressed by some basis matrix Φ, the model-based method with MBBV can be competitive computationally with TD. The floating point columns of f_{TD} and f_{ML} show consistently that model-based methods with basis compression always run faster than TD when $k << N$.

Figure 4 plots the change in normalized residual error $\frac{|\hat{v}-\hat{v}_i|}{|\hat{v}|}$ of the estimated value function $\hat{\mathbf{v}}$ over each iteration step i of the MBSV algorithm. As expected, each step provides a nontrivial improvement since each iteration improves the estimate by one independent column vector of $\hat{A}$. Figure 4 also confirms that the residuals decrease fastest in the early iterations as MBSV was designed to do.

6 Conclusions

This paper introduced an alternative policy evaluation method called model-based least-squares (MBLS), an algorithm for finding feature vectors to compress a MDP network called model-based basis vector (MBBV) determination and an iteratively improving estimator for model-based value estimation called minimal basis search for value (MBSV) estimates. The MBLS policy evaluation equation modifies the traditional least-squares temporal differencing (LSTD) equation, improving on the computation time at no extra storage cost when feature vectors are stored by LSTD. Under the assumption that a nontrivial MDP system is

Table 3. Summary of computational differences[3]

	Prior		No prior		
	LSTD	MBLS	TD	ML w MBBV	ML w MBSV
runtime	Mk^2	Nk^2	MN	N^2k	N^2l
storage	k^2 or Nk	Nk	N	N^2	N^2
accuracy	same	same	less	more	more

compressable from a set of N states to some small set of k states, but no prior feature vectors are available, then a maximum likelihood (ML) estimator with the MBBV algorithm can find the k feature/basis vectors that will compress the system and produce a policy value estimate faster than TD. If no feature/basis vectors are desired, we can run an alternate MBSV algorithm instead of MBBV which will run as fast or faster than ML with MBBV. Table 3 summaries the advantages and costs of the various methods.

In future work, we will attempt to reduce storage costs with sparse matrix methods without detrimentally affecting the improvements in accuracy and time complexity. We also plan to investigate the issue of over-fitting that can result from choosing basis vectors based on a *estimate* of the true probability transition matrix.

References

[1] Sutton, R. S., Barto, A. G.: Reinforcement Learning: An Introduction. MIT Press, Cambridge, Massachusetts (1998)

[2] Singh, S. P., Sutton, R. S.: Reinforcement Learning with Replacing Eligibility Traces. Machine Learning **22** (1996) 123-158

[3] Lu, F., Patrascu, R., Schuurmans, D.: Investigating the Maximum Likelihood alternative to TD(λ). Proceedings of the 19th ICML (2002) 403-410

[4] Boyan, J. A.: Least-squares Temporal Difference learning. Proc. of 16th ICML (1999) 123-158

[5] Bradtke, S. J., Barto, A. G.: Linear Least-Squares Algorithms for Temporal Difference Learning. Machine Learning **22** (1996) 33-57

[6] Bellman, R. E.: A Markov decision process. J. of Mathematical Mechanics **6** (1957) 679-684

[7] Lagoudakis, M. G., Parr, R.: Model-Free Least Squares Policy Iteration. NIPS **14** (2001)

[8] Lawson, C. L., Hanson, R. J.: Solving Least Squares Problems. Prentice-Hall, Englewood Cliffs, New Jersey (1974)

[9] Koller, D., Parr, R.: Computing factored value functions for policies in structured MDPs. 16th Intl. Joint Conference on Artificial Intelligence (1999) 1332-1399

[3] Table 1 provides a list of definitions of all variables. $LSTD_{MBBV}$ & $MBLS_{MBBV}$: LSTD & MBLS with MBBV applied.

DIAGAL: A Tool for Analyzing and Modelling Commitment-Based Dialogues between Agents

M. A. Labrie[1], B. Chaib-draa[1], and N. Maudet[2]

[1] Dépt. Informatique et Génie Logiciel, Université Laval
Ste-Foy, PQ, Canada
{chaib,labrie}@iad.ift.ulaval.ca
[2] IRIT, Université Paul Sabatier
Toulouse, France
maudet@irit.fr

Abstract. This paper overviews our currently in progress agent communication language simulator, called DIAGAL, by describing its use in analyzing and modelling automated conversations in offices. Offices are modelled here as systems of communicative action based on dialogue games. Through such games, people in office engage in actions by making promises, stating facts, asking for information, and so on. And through these actions they create, modify, discharge, cancel, release, assign, delegate commitments that bind their current and future behaviors. To make apparent such commitments, we consider here Agent Communication Language (ACL) from the dialectic point of view, where agents "play a game" based on commitments. Such games based on commitments are incorporated in DIAGAL tool, which has been developed having in mind the following questions: (1) What kind of structure has the game? How are rules specified within the game?; (2) What kind of games' compositions are allowed?; (3) How participants in conversation reach agreement on the current game? How are games opened or closed?

1 Introduction

Dialogue games reflects interactions between different participants in dialogue or conversations. In such interactions, each participant intervenes by making utterances, according to a pre-defined set of rules. Typically, the rules define how the dialogue may or must start, what statements may or must be uttered in a given context and, how the dialogue may or must terminate. Such games have found many applications during our history. Thus, they have been used, in ancient and medieval philosophy, for the argumentation and more generally for logical thinking. In modern philosophy, they have been used for the argumentation theory related to the contextual analysis of fallacious reasoning.

Dialogue games have also been applied in computational linguistics, computer science and cognitive science. In computational linguistics, dialogue games have been introduced to explain sequences of human utterances in conversations. Thus, the pioneering work of Levin and Moore [10] introduced the notion

Y. Xiang and B. Chaib-draa (Eds.): AI 2003, LNAI 2671, pp. 353–369, 2003.

of dialogue game as a way of initiating an interaction of a specified type, and of controlling it with a partially ordered set of subgoals. The participants in this game take each her role and attempt to achieve it in the given temporal time. This influential work has found subsequent applications in machine-based natural language processing and generation [9, 11], in human-computer interactions [3, 15]. Recently, dialogue games have been proposed as the basis for "conversation policies" for autonomous software agent communication. To this end, work has focussed on Persuasion dialogues [1]; Negotiation dialogues [2, 17]; agent-team formation dialogues [5]; Commitment dialogues [13]; Dialogues for rational interactions [14], etc. However, none of these approaches has addressed an applicative area with some implementation. This paper attempts to fill this gap by proposing a method for modelling offices as systems of communicative actions based on dialogue games. Through such dialogue games, people in office engage in actions by making promises, stating facts, asking for information, and so on. And through these actions they create, modify, discharge, cancel, release, assign, delegate commitments that bind their current and future behaviors. This paper presents our currently in progress agent communication language DIAGAL (*DIAlogue-Game based Agent Language*) by describing its use in analyzing and modelling automated conversations based on dialogue games.

2 A Dialogue Game Tool Based on Commitments

Commitment-based conversations policies (i.e., general constraints on the sequences of semantically coherent messages leading to a goal) aims at defining semantics of the communicative acts in terms of public notions, e.g. social commitments. In this paper we take a further step in our investigation of this approach by proposing a tool, called DIAGAL (*DIAlogue-Game based Agent Language*) which helps to analyze and model conversations between agents. We have developed this tool having in mind the following questions: (1) What kind of structure has the game? How are rules specified within the game?; (2) What kind of games' compositions are allowed?; (3) How are games grounded? in other words, how participants in conversation reach agreement on the current game? How are games opened or closed? Then, we went further to see how our tool can be used.

2.1 Commitments

As our approach is based on commitments, we start with some details about the notion of commitment. The notion of commitment is a social one, and should not be confused with some psychological notion of commitment. Crucially, commitments are contracted towards a partner or a group. They are expressed as predicates with an arity of 6:

$$C(x, y, \alpha, t, s_x, s_y)$$

meaning that x is committed towards y to α at time t, under the sanctions s_x and s_y. The first sanction specifies conditions under which x reneges its commitment, and the second specifies conditions under which y can withdraw from the considered commitment. In these conditions, the following commitment

$$c_1 = C(Al, Bob, sing(Al, midnight), now, 10, 20)$$

states that agent *Al* is committed towards agent *Bob* to *sing* at *midnight*. If *Al* eventually decides to renege its commitment he will pay the penalty 10. If *Bob* decides to withdraw from this commitment, he will pay 20. We concede that this account of penalties is extremely simple in this version. A more complete account could be similar to the one of Toledo et al. [7]

The notation is inspired from [18], and allows us to compose the actions involved in the commitments: $\alpha_1|\alpha_2$ classically stands for the choice, and $\alpha_1 \Rightarrow \alpha_2$ for the conditional statement that the action α_2 will occur in case of the occurrence of the event α_1. Finally, the operations on the commitments are just creation and cancellation.

$$c_2 = C(Al, Bob, sing(Al, midnight)|dance(Al, midnight), now, 10, 20)$$

and

$$c_3 = C(Al, Bob, music(Bob, midnight) \Rightarrow create(c_2), now, 10, 20)$$

The commitment c_2 captures that the agent *Al* is committed towards *Bob* to *sing* or *dance* at midnight. The commitment c_3 captures that the agent *Al* is committed to contract the preceding commitment (c_2) if agent *Bob* plays *music*. All commitments hold a time concerning when they were contracted (*now*). From now, for the sake of readability, we will ignore the *create* operation. We also permit propositional commitments, that we regard as collections of commitments centering on some proposition p, in the line of [19]. Such commitments are typically the result of assertive moves.

Now we need to describe the mechanism by which the commitments are discussed and created during the dialogue. This mechanism is precisely captured within our game structure. To account for the fact that some commitments are established within the contexts of some games *and only make sense within this context* [11, 14], we make explicit the fact that this commitments are specialized to game g. This will typically be the case of the dialogue rules involved in the games, as we will see below.

2.2 Game Structure

We share with others [4, 8, 14] the view of dialogue games as structures regulating the mechanism under which some commitments are discussed through the dialogue. Unlike [4, 14] however, we adopt a strict commitment-based approach within game structure and express the dialogue rules in terms of commitments. Unlike [8] on the other hand, we consider different ways to combine the structures of the games.

In our approach, games are considered as bilateral structures defined by *entry conditions* (which must be fulfilled at the beginning of the game, possibly by some accommodation mechanism), *success conditions* (defining the goals of the participants when engaged in the game), *failure conditions* (under which the participants consider that the game reached a state of failure), and *dialogue rules*. As previously explained, all these notions, even dialogue rules, are defined in terms of (possibly conditional) commitments. Technically, games are conceived as structures capturing the different commitments created during the dialogue.

To sum up, we have Entry conditions (E), Success conditions of initiator (SI) and partner (SP), Failure conditions of initiator (FI) and partner (FP), and dialogues Rules (R) for each game. Within games, conversational actions are time-stamped as "turns" (t_0 being the first turn of dialogue within this game, t_f the last).

2.3 Grounding the Games

The specific question of how games are grounded through the dialogue is certainly one of the most delicate [12]. Following [16], we assume that the agents can use some meta-acts of dialogue to handle game structure and thus propose to enter in a game, propose to quit the game, and so on. In this case, agents can exchange messages as

$$propose.enter(Al, Bob, g_1)$$

where g_1 describes a well-formed game structure (as detailed above). This message is a proposal of the agent *Al* to agent *Bob* to enter the game g_1. This means that games can have different status: they can be *open*, *closed*, or simply *proposed*. How this status is discussed in practice is described in a *contextualization* game which regulates this meta-level communication. As a simple first account of this game, we could adopt the intuitive view of games simply opened through the successful exchange of a propose/accept sequence. However, things are getting more complicate if we want to take account different kinds of combinations. All these kinds of structures are considered within a contextualization game that we do not detail here. Readers interested by these fine aspects can refer to Maudet's thesis [11].

2.4 Composing the Games

As explained before, the possibility to combine the games is a very attractive feature of the approach. The seminal work of [19] and the follow-up formalization of [16] have focused on the classical notions of *embedding* and *sequencing*, but recent works extend this to other combinations [14]. We now detail the games' compositions that we use in our framework. To this end, we precise the conditions under which they can be obtained, and their consequences. Ultimately, such conditions and consequences should be included in the contextualization game we are working on [12].

Sequencing noted $g_1; g_2$, which means that g_2 starts immediately after termination of g_1.
Conditions: game g_1 is *closed.*
Effects: termination of game g_1 involves entering g_2.

Choice noted $g_1|g_2$, which means that participants play either g_1 or g_2 non-deterministically. Not surprisingly, this combination has no specific conditions nor consequences.

Pre-sequencing noted $g_2 \rightsquigarrow g_1$, which means that g_2 is opened while g_1 is proposed.
Conditions: game g_1 is *proposed.*
Effects: successful termination of game g_2 involves entering game g_1.
Such pre-sequencing games can be played to ensure that entry conditions of a forthcoming game are actually established —for instance to make public a conflicted position before entering a persuasion game. Notice that in the case where the first game is not successful, the second game is simply ignored.

Embedding noted $g_1 < g_2$, which means that g_1 is now opened while g_2 was already opened.
Conditions: game g_1 is *open.*
Effects: (conversational) commitments of the embedded games are considered having priority over those of the embedding game.
Much work needs to be done to precisely define this notion within this framework, but this may be captured by constraining the sanctions related to the embedded game to be greater than those of the embedding game ($s_{g2} > s_{g1}$).

Notice that if we want make explicit Initiator and Partner, compositions can be written under the following: $[x, y]g_1; [y, x]g_2$ or $[x, y]g_1|[y, x]g_2$ or $[x, y]g_2 \rightsquigarrow [y, x]g_1$ or $[x, y]g_1 < [y, x]g_2$. In this case $[x, y]g_1$ means that the initiator of g_1 is x and the partner is y.

3 Basic Games

Up to now we have introduced four basic building dialogue games : (1) a "request" game (rg); (2) an "offer" game (og), (3) an "inform" game (ig) and (4) an "ask" game (ag). Sanctions were omitted in our games specifications just for better readability.

3.1 Request Game (rg)

This game captures the idea that the initiator (I) "request" the partner (P) and this latter can "promise" or "reject". The conditions and rules are:

$$
\begin{array}{r|l}
E_{rg} & \neg C(y, x, \alpha, t_0) \\
SI_{rg} & C(y, x, \alpha, t_f) \\
SP_{rg} & \text{Nil} \\
FI_{rg} & C(y, x, \neg\alpha, t_f) \\
FP_{rg} & \text{Nil} \\
R_{rg} & C_g(x, y, \textit{request}(x, y, \alpha), t_0) \\
 & C_g(y, x, \textit{request}(x, y, \alpha) \Rightarrow \\
 & C_g(y, x, \textit{promise}(y, x, \alpha) | \textit{refuse}(y, x, \alpha), t_1), t_0) \\
 & C_g(y, x, \textit{promise}(y, x, \alpha) \Rightarrow C(y, x, \alpha, t_2), t_0) \\
 & C_g(y, x, \textit{refuse}(y, x, \alpha) \Rightarrow C(y, x, \neg\alpha, t_2), t_0)
\end{array}
$$

Fig. 1. Conditions and rules for the request game

3.2 Offer Game (*og*)

An offer is a promise that is conditional upon the partner's acceptance. To make an offer is to put something forward for another's choice (of acceptance or refusal). To offer then, is to perform a conditional commissive. Precisely, to offer α is to perform a commissive under the condition that the partner accept α. Conditions and rules are in this case:

$$
\begin{array}{r|l}
E_{og} & \neg C(x, y, \alpha, t_0) \\
SI_{og} & C(x, y, \alpha, t_f) \\
SP_{og} & \text{Nil} \\
FI_{og} & C(x, y, \neg\alpha, t_f) \\
FP_{og} & \text{Nil} \\
R_{og} & C_g(x, y, \textit{offer}(x, y, \alpha), t_0) \\
 & C_g(y, x, \textit{offer}(x, y, \alpha) \Rightarrow \\
 & C_g(y, x, \textit{accept}(y, x, \alpha) | \textit{refuse}(y, x, \alpha), t_1), t_0) \\
 & C_g(x, y, \textit{accept}(y, x, \alpha) \Rightarrow C(x, y, \alpha, t_2), t_0) \\
 & C_g(x, y, \textit{refuse}(y, x, \alpha) \Rightarrow C(x, y, \neg\alpha, t_2), t_0)
\end{array}
$$

Fig. 2. Conditions and Rules for the offer game

3.3 Inform Game (*ig*)

Notice that a partner can be in the disposition of being in accord or agreement with someone without uttering any word. He can also agree by doing a speech act. In this case, he agrees when he can assert a proposition p while presupposing that the initiator has previously put forward p and while expressing his accord or agreement with this initiator as regards p. To disagree is to assert $\neg p$ when the other has previously put forward p. In this game, we assume that the successful termination is when an agreement is reached about the proposition p. The conditions and rules for this couple is the following:

$$
\begin{array}{l|l}
E_{ig} & C(y,x,p,t_0) \text{ or } C(y,x,\neg p,t_0) \\
SI_{ig} & C(y,x,p,t_f) \text{ and } C(x,y,p,t_f) \\
SP_{ig} & \text{Nil} \\
FI_{ig} & \text{Nil} \\
FP_{ig} & \text{Nil} \\
R_{ig} & C_g(x,y,assert(x,y,p),t_0) \\
 & C_g(y,x,assert(x,y,p) \Rightarrow \\
 & C_g(y,x,assert(y,x,p)|assert(y,x,\neg p),t_1),t_0) \\
 & C_g(x,y,assert(x,y,p) \Rightarrow C(x,y,p,t_1),t_0) \\
 & C_g(y,x,assert(y,x,p) \Rightarrow C(y,x,p,t_2),t_0)
\end{array}
$$

Fig. 3. Conditions and rules for the inform game

3.4 Ask Game (*ag*)

We use "ask" in the sense of asking a question, which consists to request the partner to perform a future speech act that would give the initiator a correct answer to his question. According to these remarks, we propose for the *ask* game the following structure:

$$
\begin{array}{l|l}
E_{ag} & \text{Nil} \\
SI_{ag} & C(y,x,p,t_f) \text{ or } C(y,x,\neg p,t_f) \\
SP_{ag} & \text{Nil} \\
FI_{ag} & \text{Nil} \\
FP_{ag} & \text{Nil} \\
R_{ag} & C_g(x,y,question(x,y,p),t_0) \\
 & C_g(y,x,question(x,y,p) \Rightarrow \\
 & C_g(y,assert(y,x,p)|assert(y,x,\neg p),t_1),t_0) \\
 & C_g(y,x,assert(y,x,p) \Rightarrow C(y,x,p,t_2),t_0)
\end{array}
$$

Fig. 4. Conditions and rules for the ask game

3.5 A Simple Use Case Example

To make things more concrete, let us illustrate previous considerations with a request game presented in Fig. 1.

Suppose that agent *Al* and agent *Bob* have entered the request game. *Al* is committed to play a request move towards agent *Bob*, and *Bob* is committed to create a commitment to play a promise or a refuse if *Al* honors his commitment. If *Bob* plays the promise, this will lead to the success condition of *Al* (SI_{rg}) or to failure condition (FI_{rg}) if *Bob* plays a refuse. When the game expires (successfully or not), the commitments that were specialized to this game, those which are dependent on the context "*g*", are automatically cancelled. The others remain as "persistent" commitments.

4 DIAGAL a Dialogue Game Simulator

We have developed a tool (called DIAGAL) which simulates dialogue as a game based on commitments as presented in the previous section while allowing the integration of some future concepts. DIAGAL (*DIAlogue-Game based Agent Language*) aims to be an effective tool of validation as well as a means of analyzing dialogues between agents, diagrams and structures concerning the various games. In this section, we describe the various components of DIAGAL.

4.1 Game Files

As mentioned previously, a game is composed of entry conditions, success conditions, failure conditions and rules of the game. Each of these elements is defined in its own file, adding to the possible information re-use while facilitating the maintainability of the files.

All the files concerning the games are written in XML. That has a major advantage of being easily manageable in liaison with JAVA and the Object-Oriented programming language used to code the simulator. Using XML offers a good way of describing information. The DTD (Document Type Definition), associated with XML files, describes the precise way in which the game designer must create his files. That gives designers and users a mean of knowing if a game is in conformity with its specifications and if it is manageable by the simulator.

The games are loaded when the simulator starts. These games are placed in a list and all the agents can use them to build their dialogues. Note that a game whose files do not answer the criteria specified in DTD will not be loaded.

4.2 Agenda

The agenda is the principal component of DIAGAL. With it, agents and users can follow the effects of the actions on each move on the conversation i.e., check the creation, cancellation, fulfillment, . . . of commitments between the agents. More particularly, an agent's agenda is used by this agent mainly in its process of deliberation on the continuation of the operations to carry out. This structure contains commitments in action as well as propositional commitments deduced from dialogue rules when an action is played. An agenda is in fact a kind of "Commitment Store" where commitments are classified according to time they were contracted.

Each agent has his own agenda which does not contain commitments of all agents which are created in the simulator, but only commitments concerning the agent owner of the agenda being the debtor or creditor. Note that an agenda is private and only its owner has the rights of accessing it.

Because no agent can have access to the agenda of another, whether for writing or reading, we can mention that the agent owner of the agenda is "responsible" for the contents which are found in its own agenda. More particularly, it is the module "Dialogue Manager", intern to the agent, who controls commitments which are added or removed according to various rules of the dialogue games. Concerning commitments in action, a commitment is fulfilled when an action played by an agent corresponds exactly to its description which is in the agenda i.e. all the parameters of this commitment are also present in the action. For example, if an agent is commit to $C(x, y, CloseWindow(x, 9h00))$, action $CloseWindow(x, 9h00)$ does satisfies this commitment, but $CloseWindow(x, 10h00$ does not. In fact, it is the "Dialogue Manager" of the agent which should fulfill or not a commitment when an action is executed.

4.3 Action Board and Game Stack

The action board is mainly a representation of the actions which were played during simulation. It is modelled as a UML sequence diagram. Each workspace has its own board where users can observe the exchanges of messages between agents as well as the time which is attached to these actions. It is represented as an history of the actions carried out relating to each initiated dialogue. In fact, such a board acts as a visual component for the simulator user, to help him understand and analyze what occurred in a dialogue between two agents. Moreover, an agent could use it to remember what actions were played by other agents who communicated with him, and to deliberate thus about the next actions he can play.

The stack is used to keep track of the embedded games during a conversation. Each time a new game is opened, it is placed on the top of the stack inside the related workspace and it becomes the current game of this workspace.

The stack makes it possible to know which game will become active when the top one is closed and withdrawn from the stack. This stack is also used to manage the priority between the games: the top element having more priority over the bottom element.

4.4 Dialogue Workspace

The workspace is an environment which contains all the data which are specific to a dialogue between two agents: games stack, hierarchical relations between agents as well as the actions board. The agenda of an agent is not even found in the workspace since its owner can be implied in several different dialogues and, according to this, in several workspaces.

In Fig. 5, we present an overview of how dialogues work in DIAGAL. As presented in this diagram, we have two communicating agents interacting via the "Dialogue Workspace". They communicate by sending each other some messages (communicative actions) and as such messages are produced, the simulator place them into "Actions Board". In accordance with the current game on the "Game Stack", the "Dialogue Manager" of the agent who sends the message and the agent which received it deduces the appropriate commitments and places them into the appropriate agendas.

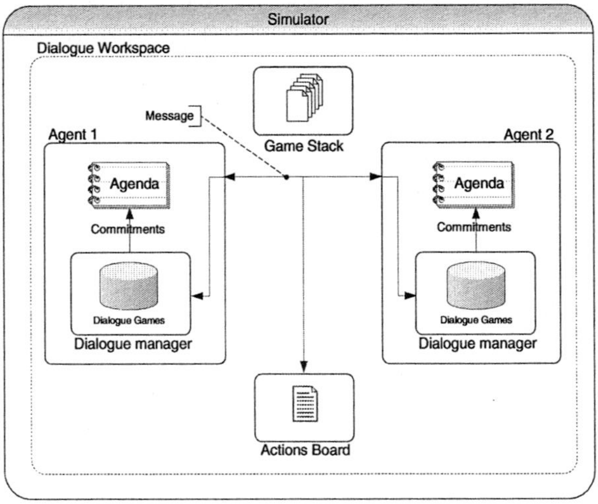

Fig. 5. Simulator overview

In its current form, DIAGAL simulates conversations between a pair of software agents and these conversations are based on dialogue games as presented in the previous sections.

5 Test Case Study: A Summer Festival Organization

We present now an illustrative example which is a first part of an ongoing work on a method for modelling offices as systems of communicative actions based on dialogue games. Through such games, participants engage in actions by making promises, asking for information, stating facts, etc. .... And through these actions, they create, modify, discharge, cancel, release, fulfill, ... commitments that bind their current and future behavior. The illustrative example on which we focus here concerns the organization of a summer festival. This festival which lasts several days consists of a group of artists coming from various areas. We want that all the management task necessary to manage such an event is done between software agents.

5.1 Specific Agents in the Summer Festival Organization

Five various types of agents having some resources to manage were defined for this scenario:

- *AgArtist*: A type of agent representing an artist in the system. An instance is represented by a_i where i is used to indicate that potentially several artists will be present in the simulation. He can accept or refuse invitation regarding the requested fee.

- *AgPlanner*: An instance of *AgPlanner* (*pl*) is an interface between an agent of type *AgArtist* and the remainder of the system. He is responsible to find the artists to be invited, to manage a budget as well as a schedule. He delegates also some tasks to the agent *AgSecretary*.
- *AgSecretary*: An instance of *AgSecretary* (*sc*) is an interface between an agent of type *AgPlanner* and the resources agents (of type *AgHotels* and *AgTravelAgency*).
- *AgHotels*: An instance of *AgHotels* (*ht*) is an agent which represents a conglomerate of hotels. He manages a list of rooms, those being able to be reserved by the artists for the duration of the festival.
- *AgTravelAgency*: An instance of *AgTravelAgency* (*ta*) is an agent which represents a conglomerate of airline companies. He seeks plane tickets for artists.

5.2 A Methodology of Analysis for Commitments Based Task

The method is based on "Partial-Order Planning" to describe the management process of tasks which implies commitments. The principal advantage of this methodology lies in the way of describing efficiently and simply the effects of actions or tasks seen in the form of creation or fulfillment of commitments. The creation of such diagram helps the programmer in his phase of analysis and design of agents as is the case of the coordination of plans for agents of BDI type. It would be possible to use effects as useful preconditions in the relevance of plans as it is case for the plans that JACK agents use, facilitating thus the conceptualization of such agents.

There is a remark which is necessary to bring in connection with the method. The dialogue tasks do not always involve the effects definite on the diagram. For example, the task "Ask artist ar_i for FlightReservation" (c.f. Fig. 6) will not commit ar_i on $C(ar_i, WantTicket(ar_i, date))$ if he refused the request for reservation of a plane ticket. Therefore, if the closing of a dialogue task does not involve the effects hoped, all the actions forming the causal chain rising from this task must be removed. Thus in our example, the causal chain rising from the task "Ask artist ar_i for FlightReservation" should be removed. That corresponds to the suppression of task "FlightReservation for artist ar_i" and the actions *PayTicket* and *SendTicket* as well as the suppression of the effects of these actions. However, the action *ComeToFestival* is not removed since it is protected by an active causal link coming from the invitation of the artist to the festival.

5.3 An Overview of the Dialogue

In our summer festival example, an agent of type *AgPlanner* is the leader of the discussion. It carries out invitations to the agents of type *AgArtist* by taking into account the constraints imposed by its budget. Then he asks artists if: (a) they accept the invitation; (b) they want plane tickets; (c) they want hotel rooms. This agent also transmits the artists' preferences to an agent of type

AgSecretary which is responsible to carry out these reservations with an agent of type *AgHotels* and an agent of type *AgTravelAgency*. After that, the *AgSecretary* agent transmits results of the reservations to *AgPlanner* agent which transmits them, as a confirmation, to the *AgArtist* agent concerned.

Now, we define the meaning of the various tasks presented in Fig. 6.

1. Invitation of artist ar_i:
   Here, the agent of type $AgPlanner$ wishes to invite an artist for the Summer Festival. This task consists in opening a "request game" introduced by *pl* towards ar_i. The request concerns the action $ComeToFestival(ar_i, date)$. It is possible that the agents enter some negotiation cycle about the requested action. This means that we could find a sequence of different request-offer

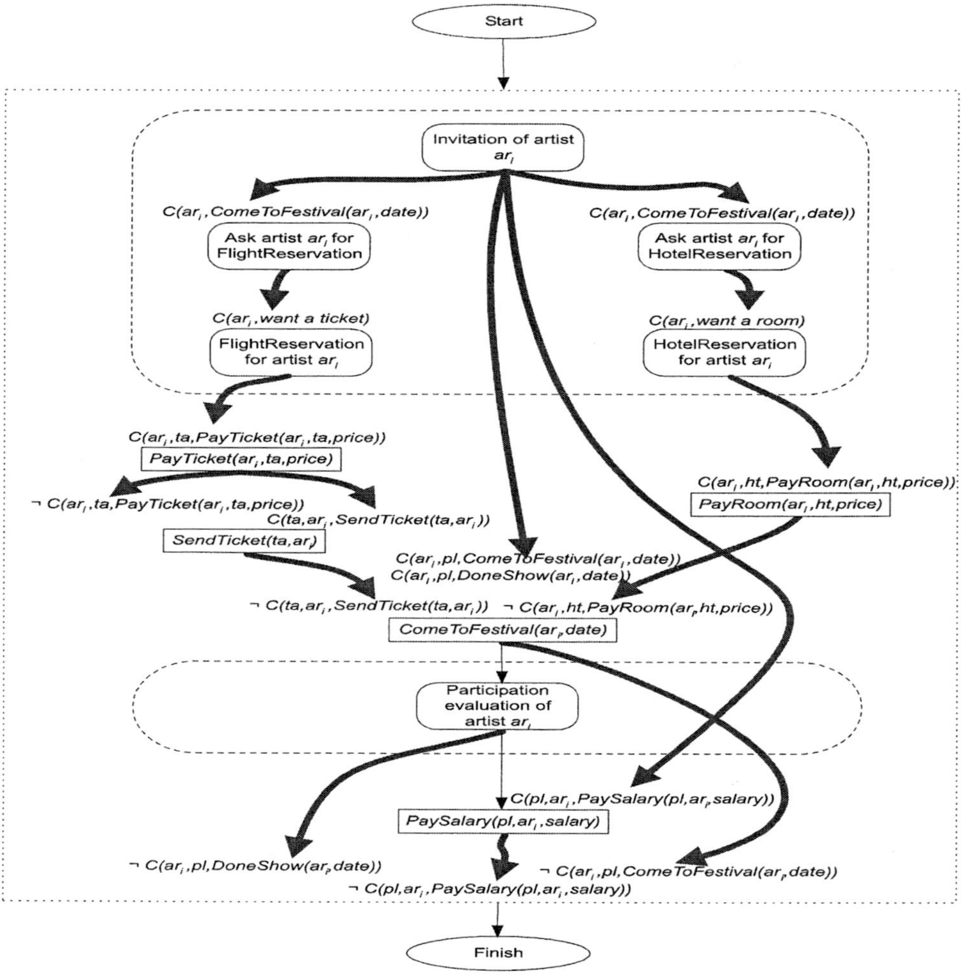

Fig. 6. Summer Festival Analysis

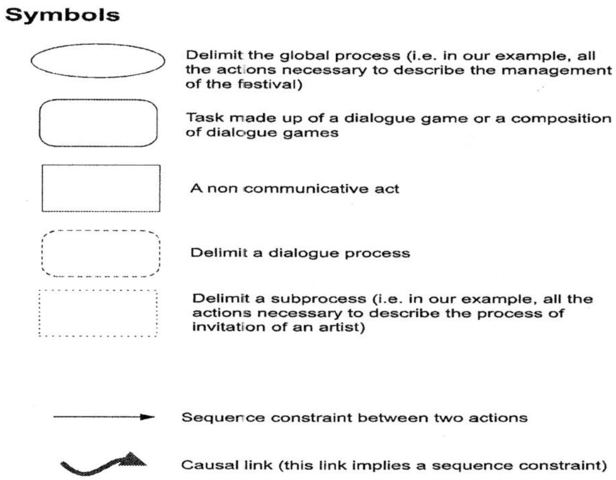

Fig. 7. Legend for the Summer Festival Analysis

made by the agents about the requested date. This first phase pre-sequences an offer-request phase were *pl* offers $PayFee(pl, ar_i, fee)$ and ar_i can counter by requesting an other fee. We use the pre-sequence because the second phase will be ignored if the first one is not successful. Note, that we use the shortcut $(*)$ to stipulate that a sequence can be repeated a number of times, with different games parameters.
Specification: $([pl, ar_i]rg; [ar_i, pl]og)^* \rightsquigarrow ([pl, ar_i]og; [ar_i, pl]rg)^*$

2. Ask artist ar_i for FlightReservation:
   The goal of this task is to know if an agent of type *AgArtist* wants to have a flight reservation. This task simply consists in the opening of an "ask game" by *pl* towards ar_i or the opening of an "inform" game by ar_i towards *pl*. These two games concern the proposition $WantTicket(ar_i, date)$.
   Specification: $[pl, ar_i]ag|[ar_i, pl]ig$
3. FlightReservation for artist ar_i:
   If agent ar_i wants a plane ticket reservation, then this requires a reservation. A "request game" is then addressed by *pl* to *sc* about the action $ReserveFlight(sc, ar_i, date)$. Thereafter, *sc* opens a "request game" with *ta* concerning the action $ReserveFlight(ta, ar_i, date)$. After this, a request game is addressed by *sc* to ar_i about the action $PayTicket(ar_i, ta, price)$.
   Specification: $[pl, sc]rg$ and $[sc, ta]rg$ and $[sc, ar_i]rg$
4. Ask artist ar_i for HotelReservation:
   The goal of this task is to know if an agent of type *AgArtist* wants to have a room reservation. This task consists in the initiation of an "ask game" by *pl* towards ar_i or the initiation of an "inform game" by ar_i towards *pl* about the proposition $WantRoom(ar_i, date)$.
   Specification: $[pl, ar_i]ag|[ar_i, pl]ig$
5. HotelReservation for artist ar_i:
   If agent ar_i wants a room reservation, this requires a reservation.

A "request game" is then addressed by pl to sc about the action $ReserveRoom(sc, ar_i, date)$. Thereafter, the secretary sc opens a "request game" with ht concerning the action $ReserveRoom(ht, ar_i, date)$. After that, a request game is addressed by sc to ar_i about the action $PayRoom(ar_i, ht, price)$.
Specification: $[pl, sc]rg$ and $[sc, ht]rg$ and $[sc, ar_i]rg$

6. Participation evaluation of artist ar_i:
To complete the global process of invitation, it is necessary for pl to do an evaluation of the action $DoneShow(ar_i, date)$. To do this, pl can initiate an "ask game" with ar_i about the proposition $DoneShow(ar_i, date)$. In an other way, ar_i can open an "inform game" towards the *AgPlanner pl* also about this same proposition. Thus, one of this two games will trigger the evaluation process.
Specification: $[pl, ar_i]ag \| [ar_i, pl]ig$

Note that our model analysis offers some features as represented in Fig. 7. These features are as follows: light arrows show general time constraints between actions. Bold arrows show causal links and implies more specific constraints over actions, specified by commitments. This last type of arrows present the effects of an action or a task on the dialogue at its extremity. These effects are preconditions on the action or task which follow them.

The modelling method, used in this paper, facilitates not only coordination at the level of actions but also coordination at the level of commitments. Indeed, with such method, we can easily follow the evolution of commitments as actions are played.

Each precondition of each step is satisfied by another step. If it is not the case, the causal chain derived from the first one is removed. Every linearization is a possible solution carrying out the goals. Generally, goals in our framework are presented as commitments in action which were fulfilled by the some actions expected by the initiator of the global process, and propositional commitments which hold at the end of the process.

As mentioned in Fig. 7, "dialogue tasks" imply a dialogue game or possibly a composition of some. In our model, DIAGAL, a dialogue game is an interaction mechanism which occurs between two participants. We can see in Fig. 8 between the different pairs of agents which intervenes in our festival example and whose the respective dialogues has been tested using DIAGAL.

6 Conclusion and Further Direction

We have sketched our commitment-based approach for the agent communication language by explaining (1)what is a game in our approach and how this game is structured, what are the rules specified within the game; (2) the kind of games' compositions which are allowed; (3) the ways that participants in conversation reach agreement on the current game and how are games opened or closed. Then we have presented in details our DIAGAL simulator through

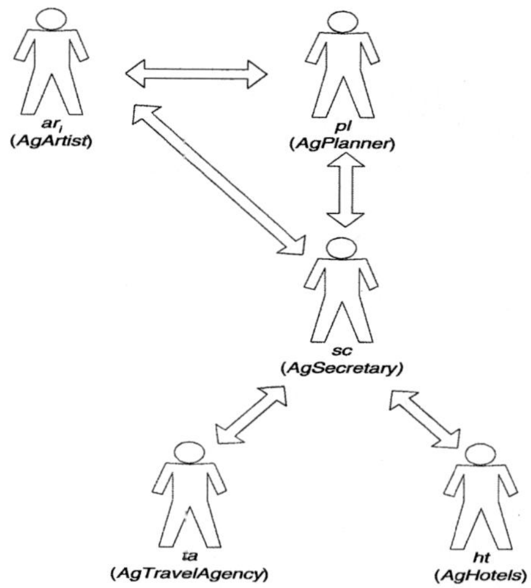

Fig. 8. Communication flow between the different pairs of agents in the Festival Example

the example of summer festival where participants should manage their commitments. We have presented to this end, an approach based on "Partial-Order Planning" which allows designers to describe the management process of tasks implying commitments. We have explained that the principal advantage of this methodology lies in the way of describing efficiently and simply the effects of actions or tasks seen in the form of creation or fulfillment of commitments.

In the future, the simulator will be an indispensable tool allowing at the same moment to simulate conversations among software agents as well as to evaluate metrics on conversations. Among the metrics that we want to address:

1. **Task metrics:**
   - Task completion : i.e., the success rate of a task
   - Task complexity : The minimal number of required interactions for task completion
2. **Commitment metrics:**
   - Commitments release ratio
   - Commitments withdrawn ratio
   - Commitments renege ratio
3. **Qualitative measures:**
   - Agent response delay
   - Dialogue completion delay
   - Utterance accuracy
   - Inappropriate utterance ratio

Acknowledgment

This research is partially supported by Social Sciences and Humanities Research Council of Canada (SSHRC/CRSH).

References

[1] L. Amgoud, N. Maudet, and S. Parsons. Modelling dialogues using argumentation. In *Proceedings of the 4th Conference on Multi-Agent Systems (ICMAS)*, Boston, 2000.

[2] L. Amgoud, S. Parsons, and N. Maudet. Arguments, dialogue, and negotiation. In *Proceedings of the European Conference on Artificial Intelligence (ECAI)*, Berlin, 2000.

[3] T. Bench-Capon, P. E. S. Dunne, and P. H. Leng. Interacting with knowledge-based systems through dialogue games. In *11th International Conference on Expert Systems and Applications Avignon*, pages 123–140, 1991.

[4] M. Dastani, J. Hulstijn, and L. V. der Torre. Negotiation protocols and dialogue games. In *Proceedings of the BNAIC*, 2000.

[5] F. Dignum, B. Dunin-Keplicz, and R. Vebrugge. Agent theory for team formation by dialogue. In C. Castelfranchi and Y. Lespérance, editors, *Intelligent Agent VII: Proceedings of the Seventh International Workshop on Agent Theories, Architectures and Languages (ATAL 2000)*, pages 150–166, LNAI, 1986, Berlin, Germany, Springer, 2000.

[6] F. Dignum and M. Greaves, editors. *Issues in agent communication*, volume 1916 of *Lecture Notes in Computer Science*. Springer-Verlag, 2000.

[7] C. Excelente-Toledo, R. A. Bourne, and N. R. Jennings. Reasoning about commitments and penalties for coordination between autonomous agents. In *Proceedings of Autonomous Agents*, 2001.

[8] R. F. Flores and R. C. Kremer. A formal theory for agent conversations for actions. *Computational intelligence*, 18(2), 2002.

[9] J. Hulstijn. *Dialogue models for inquiry and transaction.* PhD thesis, University of Twente, The Netherlands, 2000.

[10] J. Levin and J. Moore. Dialogue-games: meta-communication structure for natural language interaction. *Cognitive science*, 1(4):395–420, 1978.

[11] N. Maudet. *Modéliser les conventions des interactions langagières: la contribution des jeux de dialogue.* PhD thesis, Université Paul Sabatier, Toulouse, 2001.

[12] N. Maudet. Negociating games —a research note. *Journal of autonoumous agents and multi-agent systems*, 2002. (submitted).

[13] N. Maudet and B. Chaib-draa. Commitment-based and dialogue-game based protocols–new trends in agent communication language. *The Knowledge Engineering Review*, 17(2):157–179, 2002.

[14] P. McBurney, S. Parsons, and M. Wooldridge. Desiderata for agent argumentation protocols. In *Procceedings of the First International Conference on Autonomous Agents and Multi-Agents*, 2002.

[15] D. Moore. *Dialogue game theory for intelligent tutoring systems.* PhD thesis, Leeds Metropolitan University, England, 1993.

[16] C. Reed. Dialogue frames in agent communication. In *Proceedings of the Third International Conference on MultiAgent Systems (ICMAS)*, 1998.

[17] F. Sadri, F. Toni, and P. Torroni. Logic agents, dialogues and negotiation: an abductive approach. In M. Schroeder and K. S. A. 2001), editors, *Symposium on Information Agents for E-Commerce, AI and the Simulation of Behaviour Conference*, York, UK, 2001. AISB.

[18] M. P. Singh. A social semantics for agent communication language. In *[6]*, pages 31–45. 2000.

[19] D. Walton and E. Krabbe. *Commitment in dialogue.* State University of New York Press, 1995.

Situation Event Logic for Early Validation of Multi-Agent Systems

Sehl Mellouli, Guy Mineau, and Bernard Moulin

Département d'Informatique et de Génie Logiciel, Faculté des Sciences et Génie, Université Laval, G1V 7P4, Québec, Canada
{sehl.mellouli,guy.mineau,bernard.moulin}@ift.ulaval.ca

Abstract. Nowadays agent-oriented software engineering methodologies emphasize the importance of the environment in which a multi-agent system (MAS) operate. Meanwhile, they do not propose any diagram to represent the environment and its effects on the MAS. So, we propose two diagrams that can be introduced in agent-oriented methodologies: an environment diagram representing environment evolution over time, and an agent diagram showing the MAS organization according to the agents' roles and their relationships. Furthermore, many model checking techniques were defined to validate whether a MAS will solve the problem for which it is designed. However, these techniques do not consider the environment in their checking procedure. We propose a Situation Event Logic, an extension of modal logic, in which modal operators have a well defined scope over a set of situations. This logic is used to represent and infer knowledge from the environment and agent diagrams.

1 Introduction

A multi-agent system (MAS) can be viewed as an agent organization (by analogy with human organization) or as some artificial society or organization [14]. It evolves in a certain environment, has objectives to achieve and its agents operate together to achieve these objectives. So we think that the design of MAS should be inspired by our knowledge of human organizations (based on organization theories) [9]. Studying human organizations, we identified five aspects to consider when designing them, that we adapt to the design of an agent organization [9]. These aspects are: the nature of the environment, the tasks to be performed, the control, communication and collaboration relationships between agents. The environment can be thought of as a set of situations that can occur during the organization life cycle, each situation having an influence on the organization structure. We think that modelling the environment and its influence on the MAS organization structure, according to the roles played by the agents and their relationships (control, communication and collaboration) [9], is vital to the usefulness of the system.

Y. Xiang and B. Chaib-draa (Eds.): AI 2003, LNAI 2671, pp. 370-382, 2003.

Considering agent-oriented methodologies such as Gaia [14], AUML [11] and MAS-CommonKADS [4], we find that they do not integrate any mechanism to explicitly model the environment, its evolution and its impact on the MAS structure [9]. They have no formal representation of the specifications of the MAS, and therefore, there is no way to implement any early validation process of the MAS behaviour [10].

The representation of the environment leads to the representation of its influence on the control, communication and collaboration relationships between agents. We propose to add two diagrams to MAS modelling methodologies in order to conceptualize and represent the environment and its influence on the MAS organization structure [10]: the environment and agent diagrams. In the environment diagram the environment is represented as a set of situations and transitions (events) between them [10].The agent diagram, defined in relation to the environment diagram, represents the agents structure (roles, and functions) and their relationships (control, collaboration and communication relationships), and how the environment affects them [10]. These diagrams are created during the early stages of a MAS development process .

The environment diagram helps us to identify situations that influence the MAS organization structure. Some of these situations could lead the MAS to a failure. So, we propose a situation event logic, an extension of modal logic, to explicitly model the environment as defined in this paper. The formal representation of the environment and its influence on the MAS can be captured and used to validate its behaviour under different situations. This logic system aims at providing a platform to test potential failure situations. For our demonstration, we choose to model a soccer team, a domain that is largely used nowadays in many AI research fields [13].

This paper is organized as follows. Section 2 presents the environment diagram. Section 3 presents the agent diagram. Section 4 presents certain limits of existing logics. Section 5 introduces situation event logic. Section 6 concludes.

2 The Environment Diagram

A MAS is operating in an environment with which it interacts. We claim that a MAS must have a representation or a model of its environment. *how the environment can be modelled?*. For McCarthy, in situation calculus [8], the environment (or world) is composed of situations. A situation is the complete state of the world at an instant of time; a snapshot of the world at some instant. Each situation can be followed by an event that leads to a new situation. Situation calculus allows us to infer something about future situations. It defines a result function such that s' = result(e,s) where s' is a situation that can be reached from situation s when event e occurs. Situation calculus is specifically designed to represent dynamically changing worlds.

Several approaches take into account the environment when designing a Multi-Agent System [12, 1]. Nevertheless, no formal representation has been built to model the environment; in this paper, we propose such a formal representation . When modeling the environment, it is difficult to consider all the different situations and events that can occur in it. Consequently, we only consider macro-situations and critical events. A *macro-situation* is a set of situations characterized by certain key parameters those values do not change during a certain period of time. If the value of a key parameter changes, the environment enters in a new macro-situation. This change can influence the MAS' organization and possibly prevent it to achieve its objectives. The event that induces the value change of one of these key parameters is called a *critical event*. We define the environment as *a set of macro-situations, each being described by a set of critical parameters and a set of critical events. These critical parameters correspond to specific information those value changes affect the MAS' organization structure. They can characterize the external environment of the MAS or the MAS itself.*

Formally, the environment structure S is defined as S = <I, W, E, R, F> where I is the set of initial macro-situations, W is the set of all identified possible macro-situations ($I \subseteq W$), E is the set of all identified possible critical events, R is a relation that represents transitions between sets of macro-situations with $R \subseteq \wp(W) \times E \times \wp(W)$ where $\wp(W)$ is the power set of W. R is a triplet (S_i, e, S_j) where S_i and S_j are in $\wp(W)$ and e is in E. The triplet (S_i, e, S_j) means that from any macro-situation of S_i, if event e occurs, the system will evolve in any macro-situation of S_j. The set F is the set of the final macro-situations that can be reached by the environment ($F \subseteq W$). There are no possible situations after the elements of F, i.e., no triplet of R has the structure (S_i, e, S_j) for whatever e in E and there is a macro-situation f in F and f in S_i. The macro-situations and their transitions define the environment diagram [10] which is a state transition diagram. It is a graph representing R such that the nodes represent elements in W. An arc e between two situations s_i and s_j in W exists if there exists two sets $S_i \in \wp(W)$ and $S_j \in \wp(W)$ such that $s_i \in S_i$, $s_j \in S_j$ and $< S_i, e, S_j> \in R$. Each macro-situation is identified by a unique name and characterized by the values of its parameters.

Our study will be illustrated by the design of a MAS controlling a team of agents playing soccer. We identified three parameters (for simplicity reasons) which, together, characterize macro-situations that may influence the agents' roles. They are: the Score Difference (SD), the Remaining Time (RT) and the Deployment TactiC (TC) of the agents' team. If SD = $+v$, for $v \in N^*$, it means that the team is leading by v goals. If SD = $-v$, then it is loosing by v goals. The RT parameter can take values of the form: op t, where $t \in N^*$, and op $\in \{=, <, >, \leq, \text{or} \geq\}$. Finally, TC is of the form 'n_1-n_2-n_3' such that $n_1+n_2+n_3$ is equal to the number of players on the field (for the same team), where n_1 is the number of defenders, n_2 is the number of midfielders and n_3 is the number of strikers.

For the soccer example, we restrict our study to only eight macro-situations (see Figure 1). Among these macro-situations, s_0, s_1, s_3, s_5 and s_6. s_0 is the initial macro-situation identified by a bold rectangle. It is the first macro-situation that could occur and represents the environment when the game starts. s_1, s_3, s_5 and s_6 are final macro-situations; There are no possible macro-situations after them.

Considering this set of micro-situations of Figure 1, we can define the environment S by the sets I, W, E, R, and F which compose it. I = $\{s_0\}$, W = $\{s_0, s_1, s_2, s_3, s_4, s_5, s_6, s_7\}$, E = {box_goal, scores_goal, time_<_25, injured_player, recovered_player), R = {({s_0}, box_goal, {s_1}), ({s_0}, scores_goal, {s_2}), ({s_0}, time_<_25, {s_4}), ({s_2}, box_goal, {s_5}), ({s_4}, scores_goal, {s_3}), ({s_4}, injured_player, {s_7}), ({s_7}, recovered_player, {s_6})} and F = $\{s_1, s_3, s_5, s_6\}$.

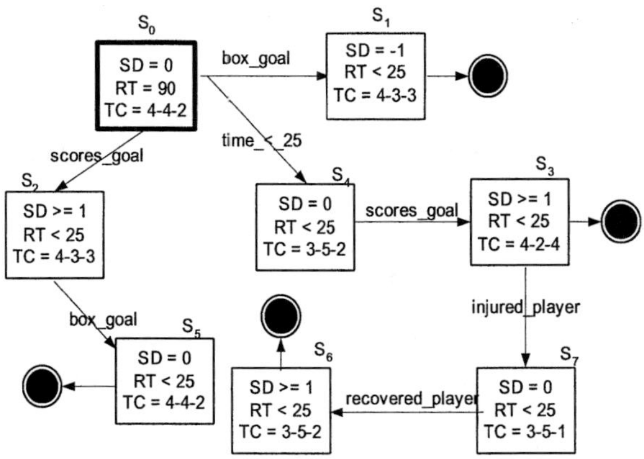

Fig. 1. The environment diagram of a soccer game

Once the macro-situations are identified, it is interesting to see their influence on the MAS structure, more specifically on the roles played by the agents and their relationships. For this purpose, we use an agent diagram [10] to represent agents, and describe their roles and relationships. This is what we present in the next section.

3 The Agent Diagram

The environment diagram is composed of macro-situations that could have an influence on the MAS organization structure according to the roles played by the agents and their relationships (control, communication and collaboration). The agent diagram shows the influence of any macro-situation on the MAS organization structure. In this diagram, each agent is specified by its name and roles. Since control and communication relations (for now, we will consider collaboration as a kind of communication) are at the centre of a MAS architecture [9, 10], it is important to represent them. Their explicit representation favours knowledge elicitation (more semantics is added to the agent diagram); their formal representation favours (partial) automatic validation of the system. Furthermore, the maintenance of the system will be facilitated by such an explicit representation.

Each agent diagram (or subpart of it) is attached to an environment macro-situation, which is identified by the label *macro-situation name* in the agent diagram. To illustrate how the agent diagram is related to the environment, we now continue with the soccer example. In the initial state s_0, the team is organized according to a 4-4-2 deployment tactic: four defenders, four midfielders and two strikers. Any player can communicate with any other player. Of course the volume of communication is more abundant between players who have the same roles. The agent diagram associated with the macro-situation s_0 is represented in Figure 2. In this figure, we have not represented communication or control relationships between agents which have little communication. For example, we suppose that since agent A_8 controls the midfielders team mates, he is the only agent responsible for this task, and hence no control or communication relations are necessary between A_7, A_6 and A_9. Its is clear that is a simplification when considering real soccer games. But, this simplification is acceptable for our illustration purposes.

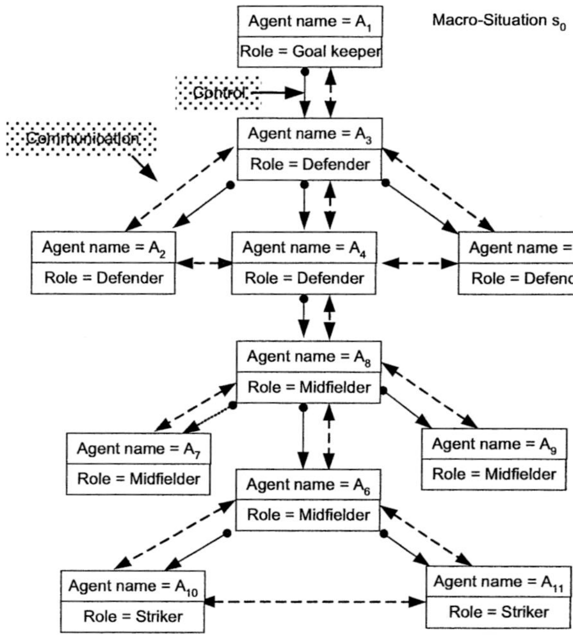

Fig. 2. The agent diagram D_1 in associated with situation s_0

In macro-situation s_2, the team is organized in a 4-3-3 tactic. The A_6 player changes its role to become a striker. The volume of communication between him and the other strikers will increase but decreases between him and other midfielders. Figure 3 represents how the MAS structure changes in macro-situation s_2 where the role of A_6 has changed to become a striker (the changes are in bold) .

The agent diagram structure is defined as $D_a = \{A, C, R_a\}$ where A is the set of agent instances, C is the set of relationships that can be defined between agents, and R_a is a relation that determines the relationships between agents; $R_a \subseteq A \times C \times A$. Each agent diagram is related to a particular macro-situation in the environment diagram. We define D as a set of agent diagrams D_a, so $D = \{D_a\}$.We define a function f: W → D that relates a macro-situation from W to some agent diagram. In the soccer game example, according to Figure 3, we have $f(s_2) = D_2$. The agent diagram D_2 is defined as $D_2 = \{A, C, R_a\}$ where $A = \{A_4, A_6, A_7, A_8, A_9, A_{10}, A_{11}\}$, C = {control, communication} and R_a = {(A_4, control, A_8), (A_4, communication, A_8), (A_8, communication, A_4), (A_8, control, A_7), (A_8, communication, A_7), (A_7, communication, A_8), (A_8, control, A_9), (A_8, communication, A_9), (A_9, communication, A_8), (A_8, control, A_{10}), (A_8, communication, A_{10}), (A_{10}, communication, A_8), (A_8, control, A_6), (A_8, communication, A_6), (A_6, communication, A_8), (A_8, control, A_{11}), (A_8, communication, A_{11}), (A_{11}, communication, A_8), (A_6, communication, A_{10}), (A_{10}, communication, A_6), (A_6, communication, A_{11}), (A_{11}, communication, A_6), (A_{10}, communication, A_{11}), (A_{11}, communication, A_{10})}.

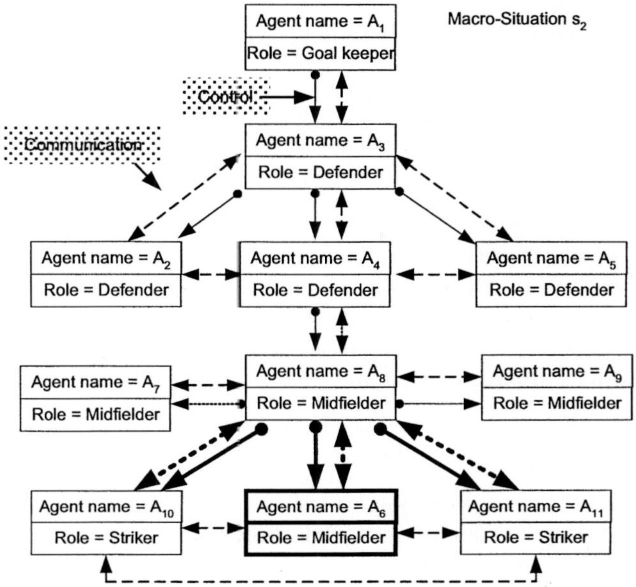

Fig. 3. Part of the agent diagram D_2 associated with situation s_2: (the role of A_6 as well the relationships with the neighbouring agents have changed)

Since each macro-situation of the environment diagram is associated to an agent diagram, we can observe the evolution of the MAS' organization structure in reaction to the environment changes. Meanwhile, we want to check whether the MAS could reach its objectives under all these different macro-situations or not. We aim at deriving a computational model from the environment and the agent diagrams, which could be used to check the validity of the possible executions of the MAS. This model should be able to detect incoherencies, and designers could revise the MAS specifications accordingly. To this end, we propose a situation event logic system that will offer model checking capabilities (section 5) based on environment and agent diagrams.

4 Limits of Existing Logics

In the following subsections, we review three existing logics, modal logic [3], state event logic [2] and ConGoLog logic [5, 6] and show why they cannot be used to express the knowledge contained within the environment and agent diagrams.

4.1 Modal Logic

Modal logic [3] is based on the modal operators that define the necessity ($\Box$) and the possibility ($\Diamond$) of a proposition. Each proposition can be true in a context and false in another one. Each context can be seen as a world (situation). The different situations may be connected by relations that trigger a situation change. A situation s_j is accessible from another situation s_i if there exists an accessibility function that leads from s_i to s_j. The modal operators are applied in each world of the system. The interpretation given to the operators is:

$\Box_\alpha p$ is true, means that p is true in any world that is accessible from world α.
$\Diamond_\alpha p$ is true, means that p is true in at least one world accessible from world α.

The environment diagram is composed of a set of macro-situations that can be considered as possible worlds that the system can access. These situations are connected by events. Modal logic does not deal with events. In fact, transitions between worlds (situations) need to be expressed when modeling environment diagram otherwise we lose knowledge from our diagram. So, modal logic is not well suited to deal with environment diagram..

4.2 State Event Logic

State event logic [2] is a modal logic used to reason about events and causality between events. It is quite common to represent the behavior of a dynamic system by a sequence of states (situations). Two subsequent states are connected by the occurrence of some event. An event can be instantaneous or lasts during a period of time. State event logic defines a set of possible worlds in which propositions are evaluated. The set of possible worlds is $T \subseteq W \times E$, where W is the set of states and E is the set of events. Each element of T is a pair which has a state and an event component. Thus, instead of reasoning about states connected by events, we reason about pairs of states and events. Any proposition is evaluated in the state and during the event that occurs after that state. There is an accessibility relation R that leads from one world of T to another world of T such that $R \subseteq T \times T$. Any modal rule will be applied in a world identified by a state and an event. The necessitation rule $\Box p$ is true in a pair (w, e) where w is a state and e is an event and (w, e) belongs to T, if p is true in all the pairs $(w', e') \in T$ such that $[(w, e), (w', e')] \in R$. The possibility rule $\Diamond p$ is true in a pair (w, e) if p is true at least in one pair $(w', e') \in T$ such that $[(w, e), (w', e')] \in R$. All the rules defined in modal logic holds in event logic.

Consider the environment diagram of Figure 1. In this diagram, we have one player missing between macro-situations s_3 and s_7 since he is injured. In this case, we deduce, from this diagram, that "it is necessarily true that the player is missing between s_3 and s_7". Doing so, modal operators have a well defined scope over a set of macro-situations. State event logic cannot handle modal expressions in which a proposition is necessarily (possibly) true between two situations, since the necessity (possibility) operator is evaluated in all possible reachable situations, from a particular one. In our case, we introduce a limit to the application of the necessity (possibility) operator. This is what we propose in section 5.

4.3 ConGoLog

ConGoLog [5, 6] is an agent-oriented framework for modeling processes in organizations and requirements engineering. It is based on situation calculus [8]. Two components are involved in a ConGoLog domain; the first component is a specification of the different states of the system, the actions to be performed by the agents, their preconditions, their effects and what is known about the initial state of the system. The second component is a specification of the behavior of the agents in the domain. The ConGoLog approach is applied to a MAS as a system to be checked whether it executes well or not. There is no way of specifying the MAS' environment, nor the influence of this environment on the MAS' organization structure. Only the actions performed by the agents are considered. The events that lead the environment to evolve from one situation to another are not considered in the ConGoLog approach.

In section 5, we present Situation Event Logic. Our proposition aims at extending the expressivity of modal, state event and ConGoLog logics so that we could check whether the MAS will well function according to a precise semantics of the environment and agent diagrams. We need to extend these logics so that the semantics of these diagrams can easily be captured. State Event Logic will allow us to handle modal operators by restricting their scope over situations in which the propositions will be evaluated.

5 Situation Event Logic

In this section, we define a situation event logic that will help us capture the semantic represented by our environment and agent diagrams as illustrated in figures 1, 2 and 3. We exemplify our definition using assertions that modal, state event and ConGoLog logics do not take into account.

In situation calculus [8], a binary predicate symbol $\sqsubset$ defines an ordering relation on situations [7]. If s $\sqsubset$ s', then s' is reachable from s; there exists a sequence of events, occurring after situation s, that leads to situation s'. Meanwhile, for relation R defined in the environment system S = (I, W, E, R, F), there could be several paths to go from s to s' according to different sequences of events. So, we introduce the predicate s $\sqsubset_e$ s' to state that s' is reachable from s when event e occurs while in s. This new predicate will be used to define our situation event logic.

Situation event logic, that we call *system S* thereafter, proposes an extension to modal logic. It is based on the formal definition of modal logic as presented in [3]. We propose to deal with formulae of the form $\Box_{(s_i, e, s_j)}p$ where $\Box$ is the necessity modal operator, p is a proposition and the triplet (s_i, e, s_j) indicates that p will be evaluated in any situation between s_i and s_j, that is accessible from situation s_i when event e occurs in s_i. Situation event logic is based on the following definitions (assertions) (S_i, S_j and S_k are elements of $\wp(W)$).

1. $\Box_{(s_i, \varnothing, s_i)}p$: proposition p is true in s_i (assertion 1) which can also be written $\Box_{s_i}p$ in short.
2. $\Box_{(s_i, e, s_j)}p$: p is necessarily true in all situations s_k between s_i and s_j, when event e occurs in s_i. $(s_i \sqsubset_e s_j) \wedge (s_i \sqsubset_e s_k) \wedge (s_k \sqsubset s_j) \wedge \Box_{s_k}p \wedge \Box_{s_j}p \mid s_i \in S_i, s_j \in S_j, (S_i, e, S_j) \in R, \forall s_k \in S_k, (S_i, e, S_k) \in R, \exists e' \in E\ (S_k, e', S_j) \in R$. (assertion 2).

3. $\Box_{(s_i, \forall e, s_j)}p$: p is necessarily true in all situations s_k between s_i and s_j. $(s_i \sqsubset s_j) \wedge (s_i \sqsubset s_k) \wedge (s_k \sqsubset s_j) \wedge \Box_{s_k}p \wedge \Box_{s_j}p \mid s_i \in S_i, s_j \in S_j, \forall s_k \in S_k, \exists e, e' \in E, (S_i, e, S_j) \in R, (S_i, e, S_k) \in R, (S_k, e', S_j) \in R$ (assertion 3).
4. $\Box_{(s_i, e, \forall s_j)}p$: p is necessarily true in all situations s_j reached from s_i, when event e occurs in s_i. $(s_i \sqsubset_e s_j) \wedge \Box_{s_j}p \mid s_i \in S_i, \forall s_j \in S_j, (S_i, e, S_j) \in R$ (assertion 4).
5. $\Box_{(s_i, \forall e, \forall s_j)}p$: p is necessarily true in all situations s_j that can be reached from s_i independently of the events that could occur in s_i. $(s_i \sqsubset s_j) \wedge \Box_{s_j}p \mid s_i \in S_i, \forall s_j \in S_j, \exists e \in E, (S_i, e, S_j) \in R$. (assertion 5).
6. $\Box_{(\forall s_i, e, s_j)}p$: p is necessarily true in all situations s_k, occurring between a situation s_i (when event e occurs in s_i) and s_j. $(s_i \sqsubset_e s_j) \wedge (s_i \sqsubset_e s_k) \wedge (s_k \sqsubset s_j) \wedge \Box_{s_k}p \wedge \Box_{s_j}p \mid \forall s_i \in S_i, s_j \in S_j, (S_i, e, S_j) \in R, \forall s_k \in S_k, (S_i, e, S_k) \in R, \exists e' \in E\ (S_k, e', S_j) \in R$ (assertion 6).
7. $\Box_{(\forall s_i, e, \forall s_j)}p$: proposition p is necessarily true in all situations s_j reachable from a situation s_i (when event e occurs in s_i): $(s_i \sqsubset_e s_j) \wedge \Box_{s_j}p \mid \forall s_i \in S_i, \forall s_j \in S_j, (S_i, e, S_j) \in R$ (assertion 7).
8. $\Box_{(\forall s_i, \forall e, s_j)}p$: p is necessarily true in all situations s_i leading to s_j. $(s_i \sqsubset s_j) \wedge \Box_{s_i}p \wedge \Box_{s_j}p \mid \forall s_i \in S_i, s_j \in S_j, \exists e \in E, (S_i, e, S_j) \in R$. (assertion 8). The modal operators have a future view; we introduce in this case a past view. In fact, sometimes we need to verify if a property is true in any situation that precedes another one. Classical modal logic has no operator or mechanism to express this kind of formula.

These assertions can be adapted to the possibility modal operator ($\Diamond$); but are not presented in this paper. We define relations between the necessity and the possibility operators. For example: $\Box_{(s_i, e, s_j)}p \Rightarrow \Diamond_{(s_i, e, s_j)}p$: if p is necessarily true then it is possibly true.

Situation event logic is based on modal logic; however, we redefine the modus ponens rule in order to take into account our new formalism. For this, we need two axioms:

A1: $(s_i \sqsubset_{e_1} s_j) \wedge (s_j \sqsubset_{e_2} s_k) \Rightarrow s_i \sqsubset_{e_1} s_k$ (A_1): this rule means that if s_j is reachable from s_i by event e_1, and s_k is reachable from s_j by event e_2, by transitivity s_k is reachable from s_i by event e_1.

A2: $\Box_{(s_i, e_1, s_j)}p \Rightarrow \Box_{(s_k, e_2, s_l)}p$ if $(s_i \sqsubset_{e_1} s_k) \wedge (s_k \sqsubset_{e_2} s_l) \wedge (s_l \sqsubset s_j)$ (A_2): if p is necessarily true in all situations between s_i and s_j when event e_1 occurs in s_i, then it is necessarily true in all situations between s_k and s_l . This rule is valid if event e_2 occurs in s_k, s_k is reachable from s_i when e_1 occurs while in s_i, s_l is reachable from s_k when event e_2 occurs while in s_k, s_j is reachable from s_l.

Based on these two axioms, the modus ponens rule is defined as follows (equation 1):

$$\frac{\Box_{(s_i, e_1, s_j)}p,\ \Box_{(s_k, e_2, s_l)}p \Rightarrow \Box_{(s_m, e_3, s_p)}q}{\Box_{(s_m, e_3, s_p)}q} \qquad \text{if } \Box_{(s_i, e_1, s_j)}p \Rightarrow \Box_{(s_k, e_2, s_l)}p \text{ (see Figure 4):}$$

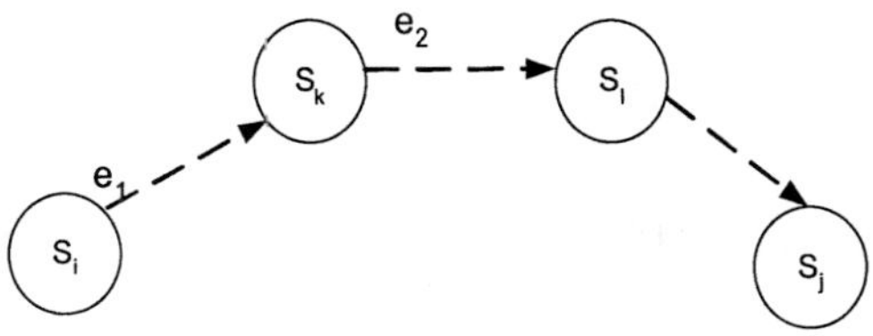

Fig. 4. Relations between s_i, s_k ,s_l and s_j

In the classical modus ponens rule, a proposition is evaluated in a particular situation therefore in *system S* modus ponens rule, a proposition is evaluated taking into account a set of macro-situations. This modus ponens rule allows us to express the classical modus ponens rule (special case of equation 1):

$$\frac{p,\ p \Rightarrow q}{q} \quad \text{becomes} \quad \frac{\Box_{s_i}p,\ \Box_{s_i}p \Rightarrow \Box_{s_i}q}{\Box_{s_i}q}$$

After defining the different assertions of situation event logic, we now define the validity of a proposition in *System S*. We define the semantic rules of the form S ⊩ $\Box_{(s_i\ e,\ s_j)}p$, as follows:

- S ⊩ $\Box_{(s_i,\ e,\ s_j)}p$ iff $\Box_{(s_i,\ e,\ s_j)}p$
- S ⊩ $\Box_{(s_i,\ e,\ s_j)}\neg p$ iff not S ⊩ $\Box_{(s_i,\ e,\ s_j)}p$
- S ⊩ $\Box_{(s_i,\ e,\ s_j)}(p \vee q)$ iff $\Box_{(s_i,\ e,\ s_j)}(p) \vee \Box_{(s_i,\ e,\ s_j)}(q)$

These rules are also defined for the different forms of assertions that we have introduced previously. So, in *system S*, a formula p is S-valid (written S ⊩ p) if S ⊩ $\Box_{(*s_i,\ *e,\ *s_j)}$ p, where * is either a space character or the ∀ character.

Situation event logic can be used to infer new information from the knowledge contained in environment and agent diagrams and to check whether the MAS could reach its objectives. This is what we illustrate with the soccer example. The team has the objective to win the game, which can be expressed by the proposition SD_>=_1. To reach this objective, many preconditions, must be verified. Here is an example:

Precondition P_1: If the score difference (SD) is superior or equal to 1 (SD_≥_1), and the remaining time (RT) is inferior to 25 minutes (RT_<_25), the tactic (TC) adopted is 4-3-3 (TC_=_433) and there is a goal keeper (goal_keeper) then the team wins the game (SD_≥_1). This rule is translated in proposition logic as: (SD_≥_1) ∧ (RT_<_25) ∧ (TC_=_433) ∧ (goal_keeper) ⇒ (SD_≥_1).

Using Situation Event Logic, we need to check whether for each macro-situations the MAS would win the game, considering the evolution of the environment and the MAS' organization structure,. In macro-situation s_2, we need to check whether the precondition P_1 is satisfied. We find that (from the environment and agent diagram associated to s_2):

- $\square_{s_2}$ (SD_≥_1) = true
- $\square_{s_2}$ (RT_<_25) = true
- $\square_{s_2}$ (TC_=_433) = true
- $\square_{s_2}$ (goal_keeper))= true

The precondition P_1 is verified. We deduce that, the MAS will win the game while in s_2. But in situation s_5 the MAS could not win the game because P_1 is not verified. Situation event logic is also used to extract knowledge from the environment and agent diagrams. For example, we have $\Diamond_{(s_4,\ \forall e,\ s_6)}$ (SD_>=_1) since for any event that can occur after s_4, there are macro-situations where proposition (SD_>=_1) is true.

Also, using the modus-ponens rule as defined in Equation 1, and knowing that:

$\square_{(s_4,\ scores\_goal,\ s_6)}$(RT_<_25), $\square_{(s_3,\ injured\_player,\ s_6)}$(RT_<_25) $\Rightarrow$ $\Diamond_{(s_3,\ injured\_player,\ s_6)}$ (SD_=_0)

we deduce : $\Diamond_{(s_3 injured\_player,\ s_7)}$ (SD_=_0) because according to axiom A2 $\square_{(s_4,\ scores\_goal,\ s_6)}$(RT_<_25) $\Rightarrow$ $\square_{(s_3,\ injured\_player,\ s_6)}$(RT_<_25) (from the environment diagram illustrated in Figure 1). This deduction cannot be made by classical modus-ponens rule.

6 Conclusion and Future Work

A MAS behavior is affected by the evolution of the environment over time. We proposed to model the environment as a set of macro-situations. Each macro-situation is described by a set of critical parameters. A change in value of one of these parameters will lead the environment to a new macro-situation. The evolution of the environment can effect the system behavior. Hence, we propose to attach to each environmental macro-situation, a subpart of the agent diagram that shows the impact of this state on the MAS organization.

Furthermore, the MAS is designed to achieve objectives. It is important to verify whether the MAS will achieve its objectives or not. We propose Situation Event Logic, a system of logic which introduces a new semantic to the possibility and necessity modal operators. It allows us to express assertions of the form: the proposition is necessarily true between two particular situations that the classical necessity operators cannot express as shown in previous sections. To show the relevance of our logic, we made a comparison with several logics: modal, state event and ConGoLog logics. Situation Event Logic is more expressive than these logics when it comes to specifying the MAS environment. It is used to check whether a MAS will well function taking into account the environment in which it is placed, and the evolution of its organization structure.

Several issues are still open for future investigation. Since the environment is unpredictable, we are not able to predict which macro-situation will occur after a given one. Consequently, we have to use a probabilistic approach in the representation of the state transition diagram. Doing so, we can transform the environment diagram into a probabilistic one. Hence, we will need to extend situation event logic to probabilistic situation event logic. It is also important to represent the agent beliefs in the agent diagram. The agents' beliefs will be considered in situation event logic so that the MAS model checking procedure will be more complete. Finally, the final purpose of our work is to define an incremental approach to build the environment and agent diagrams and to simplify the model checking process. Doing so, we will reduce the complexity of building the diagrams and validating the system by identifying macro-situations that could lead the MAS to a failure.

References

[1] Bernon., C., Gleizes., G., Peyruqueou., S., Picard., G. ADELF, a Methodology for Adaptive Multi-Agent Systems Engineering. Workshop Notes of the Third International Workshop Engineering Societies in the agents world, 16-17 September 2002, Madrid, Spain, pp. 21-34.

[2] Groe., G. State Event Logic. Phd thesis, Technical University Darmstadt. Darmstadt, Germany, 1996.

[3] Hughes. G. E. et Cresswell. M. J.. An Introduction to Modal Logic. Eds. Methuen and Co Ltd, 1968.

[4] Iglesias., C. A., and Garijo., M., and Gonzales., J. C., and Velasco., R. Analysis and Design of Multi-Agent Systems using MAS-CommonKADS. In proceedings of the AAAI'97 Workshop on agent Theories, Architectures and Languages, Providence, USA, July, 1997.

[5] Lespérance., Y., and Shapiro., S. On Agent-Oriented Requirements Engineering. Position paper for the Agent Oriented Information Systems (AOIS'99), Heidelberg, June 99, Germany.

[6] Lespérance., Y., Kelley., T. G., Mylopoulos., J., and Yu., E. S. K. Modeling Dynamic Domains with ConGoLog. Advanced Information Systems Engineering. Proceedings of the 11th International Conference, CAiSE-99, Heidelberg, Germany, June 1999, LNCS vol. 1626, Springer-Verlag, Berlin. pp. 365-380.

[7] Levesque., H., and Pirri., F., and Reiter., R. Foundations for the Situation Calculus. Linkoping Electronic Articles in Computer and Information Science, volume 3, 1998. http://www.ep.liu.se/ea/cis/1998/018.

[8] McCarthy., J. Situation Calculus With Concurrent Events and Narrative. http://www-formal.stanford.edu/jmc/narrative/narrative.html, 2000.

[9] Mellouli., S., Mineau., G., and Pascot., D. The Integrated Modeling of Multi-agent Systems and their Environment. In Proceedings of the First International Conference on Autonomous Agents and Multi-Agent Systems 2002 (AAMAS 2002), 15-19 July 2002, Bologna, Italy. (to appear).

[10] Mellouli., S., Mineau., G., and Pascot., D. Multi-Agent System Design. In workshop notes of the Third International workshop Engineering Societies in the Agents World, 16-17 September 2002, Madrid, Spain. pp 127-138.

[11] Odell., J., Parunak., V. D. H., and Bauer., B. Extending UML for Agents. Proceedings of the Agent-Oriented Information Systems Workshop at the 17th National Conference on Artificial Intelligence, Austin, Tx, pp 3-17, AOIS Workshop at AAAI 2000.
[12] Omicini., A. SODA : Societies and Infrastructures in the Analysis and Design of Agent-based systems. Agent Oriented Software Engineering Workshop, 10 June 2000, Limerick, Ireland, pp 185-193.
[13] Stone., P., Balch., T. and Kreatzschmarr., G. RoboCup-2000: Robot Soccer World Cup IV. SpringerVerlag, Berlin, 2001.
[14] Wooldridge., M., and Jennings., N. R., and Kinny., D. The Gaia Methodology for Agent-Oriented Analysis and Design. Journal of Autonomous Agents and Multi-Agent Systems 3 (3).

Understanding "Not-Understood": Towards an Ontology of Error Conditions for Agent Communication

Anita Petrinjak and Renée Elio

Department of Computing Science, University of Alberta
Edmonton, Alberta, Canada T6G 2H1
{anita,ree}@cs.ualberta.ca

Abstract. This paper presents the notion of an agent interaction model, from which error conditions for agent communication can be defined—cases in which an agent generates a *not-understood* message. Such a model specifies task and agent interdependencies, agent roles, and predicate properties at a domain-independent level of abstraction. It also defines which agent beliefs may be updated, revised, or accessed through a communication act from another agent in a particular role. An agent generates a *not-understood* message when it fails to explain elements of a received message in terms of this underlying interaction model. The reason included as content for the *not-understood* message is the specific model violation. As such, *not-understood* messages constitute a kind of 'run-time error' that signals mismatches between agents' respective belief states, in terms of the general interaction model that defines legal and pragmatic communication actions. The interaction model can also set policies for belief revision as a response to a *not-understood* message, which may be necessary when task allocation or coordination relationships change during run time.

1 Introduction

One cornerstone of the software agent paradigm has been the effort to define and standardize a high-level language for agent communication. The Federation for Intelligent Physical Agents (FIPA) offers one such standard for an agent communication language (ACL) [9]. This standard defines core message types (e.g., *inform*, *request*, and *query*) with associated semantics based on an underlying theory of communication as rational action [3, 20]. To be compliant with this standard, an agent need not be able to process all the predefined core messages. But there is a *single* core message that all agents must be able to generate and interpret. This message is *not-understood.* The form of this message is *(not-understood :sender j :receiver i :content c),* where *i* and *j* are agents. The *not-understood* message is *j*'s response to *i* in the context of some previous message from *i* to *j*. The message content *c* is defined as a tuple con-

Y. Xiang and B. Chaib-draa (Eds.): AI 2003, LNAI 2671, pp. 383-399, 2003.

sisting of an action or event (e.g., a just-received *inform* message from *i* to *j*) and a 'reason.' The occasion for sending *not-understood* is described as follows:

> The sender of the not-understood communicative act has received a communication act it did not understand. There may be several reasons. [An agent] may not have been designed to process a certain act or class of acts, or it may have been expecting a different message. For example, it may have been strictly following a predefined protocol, in which the possible message sequences are predetermined. The not-understood message indicates to the receiver that nothing has been done as a result of the message....The second term of the [content] tuple is a proposition representing the reason for the failure to understand. There is no guarantee that the reason is represented in a way that the receiving agent will understand. However, a cooperative agent will attempt to explain the misunderstanding constructively. [9]

The *not-understood* message is pragmatically quite important for agent communication. The basic premise of speech act theory [1,21], and its adoption in computational accounts of communication as planning [3,4] is that communication acts are actions upon a world. By FIPA's formal semantics, if agent *i* informs agent *j* of some proposition α, agent *i*'s intended effect is that *j* adopt belief in α. Agent *j* may not do so for a number of reasons, and hence the intended effect is just that—intended but not guaranteed. Thus, in making a communication act, a speaker is aiming to change an aspect of a non-deterministic world that is not directly accessible, namely the mental state of the hearer or receiving agent. Hence, *not-understood* is a quite pointed response back to agent *i* from that inaccessible world, indicating that the action was not (merely) unsuccessful but, to put it crudely, dead on arrival for some other reason. Our interest here is in defining those conditions that must be met before *j* would even attempt to assimilate α into its informational state.

The work we describe here proposes the notion of an interaction model for defining and structuring reasons for generating a *not-understood* message type, and also for defining possible responses to receiving a *not-understood* message. Our approach is to use an interaction model to define expected, legal, and pragmatic messages in ways that are more general than predefined protocols. Deviations from this interaction model are occasions for generating a not-understood. An ontology of error conditions for agent communication flows directly from an interaction model and the different ways in which messages might constitute deviations from this model.

There are several reasons why we think it is theoretically and pragmatically useful to take a serious look at *not-understood.* First, thinking about *not-understood* is a different way of thinking about what it means to *understand.* We can think of understanding as the message's extended perlocutionary effects, i.e., how that message affects an agent's internal state, such that it behaves differently for having received and assimilated the message [see 8, 18]. Second, the considerable effort in specifying the syntax and semantics for agent communication languages does not address the matter of what agents actually communicate *about*, i.e., what fills the *:content* field of a message, even when there is a shared ontology and a shared content language. It seems that, for some applications, what cooperating or coordinating agents 'talk about' is their problem-solving progress. The abstract specification of task interdependencies and what constitutes task progress can serve as part of a jointly held conversation policy [8, 10]. Finally, if we seriously regard the notion of agent as a kind of programming abstraction [22], then *not-understood* can be viewed as signaling a 'run-time error.' The analogy is this: a communication action generates an error when its effect would constitute an illegal or impossible action on the receiving agent's internal (mental) state. The matter at hand, then, is to define that set of illegal or impossible actions, and for that some kind of model is needed.

Generally speaking, our view is that an interaction model defines what agents can, must, or might talk about during their joint problem solving, and how this may be further constrained through the specification of agent roles. A *not-understood* is the detection of a discrepancy between the messages that are allowed by that model and what messages are encountered. The 'constructive reason' used in the *:content* field is a specific type of violation, stated at the same abstract level as the interaction model. Now, if agent *i* receives a *not-understood* concerning one of its messages, it would be good if agent *i*'s internal state changed, so that it did not send that very same message again. The inclusion of a 'constructive reason' that is interpretable by agent *i* opens the possibility for belief revision, and this is a complicated matter. We discuss our initial ideas about how an interaction model might set some policies for this as well.

2 Occasions for Not-Understanding an Inform

Our current interaction model has three main elements: (a) the ontology of predicates that are interpretable by the agents, (b) what kinds of propositions using those predicates can be used in the *:content* field of particular message types (i.e., the object of particular illocutionary forces); and (c) which agents are permitted to send particular message types, with particular content, to which other agents. Together, (a) and (b) define what kinds of beliefs in agent *j*'s mental state could be updated, revised, or accessed through an external communication action from agent *i*. Element (c) further constrains these operations to be legal only when agent *i* holds a particular role to agent *j*, in the context of some cooperative or coordinated behavior.

To illustrate the general intuitions behind our approach, the top portion of Table 1 presents a schema for *inform*, which takes a proposition α as its content. The schema includes FIPA's feasibility preconditions and rational effects for *inform*. We also include contextual relevance conditions, i.e., that the receiver of the *inform* wishes to know α [3, 13, 21]. Finally, we specify certain success conditions [21] that stipulate (some) conditions that must hold for the *inform* action to be successful. There are six conditions in total for our *inform* schema. An *inform* is legal to send—and understandable to receive— when these conditions are holding. Conversely, an *inform* is *not-understood* if, from the receiver's perspective, one or more of these conditions ought not to be holding in the sender's internal state. This is what the lower part of Table 1 shows.

Specifically, the lower portion of Table 1 illustrates six types of *not-understood* that are defined by the six conditions in the upper part of the table. The first three are concerned with the propositional content of the message itself, the particular illocutionary force applied to the content, and the role of the sender to the receiver. Case (i)

Table 1. An *inform* schema that defines six cases for *not-understood*

<inform i, j, α>		
success conditions:	i.	α is interpretable by *j*
	ii.	*j*'s state concerning α can be updated
	iii.	*j*'s state concerning α can be updated by *i*
feasibility preconditions:	iv.	*i* knows α
	v.	*i* believes *j* has no position on α
contextual relevance conditions:	vi.	*i* believes *j* desires to know α
intended effect		*j* adopts belief in α

<*inform i, j, α*> is not-understandable to *j* wrt an interaction model *m* if by that model

i) α's predicate is not in a commonly shared ontology
- the intuition: "I don't know what α means."
- model component: public vs. private predicates

ii) *j*'s position on α cannot be updated/revised
- the intuition: "My belief about α cannot be changed."
- model component: static vs. defeasible predicates

iii) *j*'s position on α cannot be updated/revised by a communication act from *i*
- the intuition: "*You* cannot change my belief about α."
- model component: external vs. internally defeasible predicates; agent roles derived from shared task model

iv) *j* cannot explain why *i* would know α
- the intuition: "How is it that *you* know α?"
- model component: agent models derived from shared task model

v) *j* cannot explain why *i* believes *j* has no position on α.
- the intuition: "Why do you believe I do not *already* know α?"
- model component: agent models from shared task model and run-time updating

vi) *j* does not desire to know α
- the intuition: "*Why* are you telling me α? It would have no impact on my behavior."
- model component: agent models derived from shared task model

is a simple matter of whether the predicate of proposition α is in the shared ontology of the agents. Such predicates are classed as *public* and are allowable in the propositional content of a message. The interaction model designates *private* predicates as those used to construct belief state propositions that might be idiosyncratic to particular agents, or that ought not to be exchanged. Case (ii) stipulates what propositions that involve public predicates are defeasible, and which are not, by classifying public predicates as either *static* or *defeasible*. Case (iii) covers which defeasible beliefs are changed through *internal* reasoning actions only or through an *external* communicative act of another agent. For example, an interaction model could specify that agent *i* may not *inform* agent *j* what agent *j* believes, intends or desires, to embody the constraint that revisions to *j*'s mental attitudes are the province of agent *j*. (These cases loosely correspond to canonical examples such as "I insult you." "I convince you of α." [1]). But this distinction can apply more widely to other propositions in *j*'s belief state, namely any proposition for which only *j* can determine a truth status.

Cases (iv) through (vi) focus on *not-understanding* as violations of agent models—beliefs about other agents, their capabilities, their responsibilities, their realm of knowledge, and so forth. Systems of coordinating or cooperating agents often implicitly or explicitly rely on such acquaintance models, derived from a global or partial model of interdependencies among tasks and the agents assigned to those tasks [6,11, 14]. In these cases, a *not-understood* message signals a mismatch between agent *i* and *j*'s respective models of each other. For example, cases (iv) and (v) correspond to *j*'s inability to explain why—given its beliefs about agent *i* and what agent *i* ought to know about agent *j*— the feasibility conditions for *inform* are holding for *i*. Finally, case (vi) covers an important pragmatic case, from the viewpoint of a message's extended perlocutionary effects. Presumably, *i* intends that *j* adopt belief α so that *j*'s behavior will change. If belief in α would not impact any of *j*'s behaviors, there is no consequence of adopting it. In this instance, *j*'s *not-understood* signals a mismatch between *j*'s own model of contextual relevance, and agent *i*'s model of what is contextually relevant to *j*. In some situations, it might be quite important for agent *i* to learn that the *inform* it sent to agent *j* would have no impact on anything that agent *j* does. Agent *j* might not coordinate its activities with *i* any differently, release resources any differently, and so on, if *j* cannot understand the *inform* message in terms of its task or agent models. This could result in a domain-level error situation, brought about because an *inform* action did not have its intended effect.

We wish to make a few additional points at this juncture. First, we have not explicitly included the case of protocol violation, which is the typical situation used to motivate or define a *not-understood* scenario. A predefined protocol can be viewed as a special instance of case (vi). We readily acknowledge that protocol violations are more easily recognized as syntactic violations, but that is a matter of processing convenience. Second, we use the term 'explain' in Table 1 to emphasize that a received message must be consistent with the receiver's model. We have no particular investment in how simple or complex this consistency-checking process might be nor do we expect that agents will necessarily discover a discrepancy by means of some theorem proving procedure applied to formulas in the semantic language that represents their mental states. Finally, it is natural at this juncture to speculate whether agent *i*, having received a *not-understood* message from agent *j*, would itself generate a *not-understood* message back to agent *j*. And on *infinitum*. This can be a difficult issue. Our initial approach for avoiding this is to appeal again to the interaction model, and we address this in a later section.

We have focused to date on FIPA message types that take propositions as message content, namely *inform* and *disconfirm*. Our treatment also handles a variation of *query* (namely, *query-ref*), whose semantics under the FIPA specification are (composed of) a *request* for an *inform* action. FIPA includes *refuse* as a possible response to a request for an action, although a *query* might generate a *not-understood* by our analysis in Table 1. For brevity's sake, we limit our discussions and examples to *inform* in the remainder of this paper.

3 Elements of an Interaction Model

One purpose of an interaction model is to define the space of possible intentions that cooperating or coordinating agents can have. A second purpose is to define the occasions on which it is expected or likely that those intentions would arise. A third purpose, related to these first two, is to delimit message content, i.e., what appears in the *:content* field of a particular message.

There are three main components to defining an interaction model that would support the generation of *not-understood* messages illustrated in Table 1. The first is a language to describe tasks and interdependencies among tasks, and hence interdependencies among agents assigned to those tasks. TÆMS [7] is an example of such a language and we adopted several of its distinctions. The second is a set of axioms and inference rules that agents can use, together with a model of task dependencies, to derive initial and run-time propositional beliefs about other agents and other tasks. It is these propositions that agents will exchange, update, or revise through communication actions during a problem solving episode. Particular exchanges, revisions, and updates are then understood as required, expected or plausible, *given* these task and agent models. The third component concerns definitions of particular predicate classes, that define what types of message content can be exchanged under various circumstances (e.g., the static vs. defeasible, internal vs. external distinctions described in Section 2). The remainder of this section aims to present just enough detail about our current interaction model framework, to ground our examples from Section 2 and our later discussion about replies to receiving a *not-understood.*

3.1 Task Structures

We model a task as an abstract specification of a problem to be solved that has a number of defining properties. Following [7], the solution method for a task is specified as either a directly executable *method* or via the achievement of a set of *subtasks.* A (sub)task is related to another task through either an *and*-decomposition or an *or*-decomposition. Tasks may also be related to each other via an enables/enabled-by relationship: if task i enables task j, then task i must be completed before task j can begin. A *task-structure* specifies a hierarchical decomposition of a task into a set of subtasks whose leaf nodes are executable methods. In our modeling assumptions, each task and method in a task structure is assigned to exactly one agent, although a given agent may be responsible for more than one task or method. Figure 1 shows a fragment of an (abstract) task structure to illustrate these properties.

A task definition also includes pre and post conditions, which are used to define its initial state and its goal state. Pre and post conditions are stated as Boolean constraints on domain-specific variables relevant to initiating a task and deeming it successful, respectively. In our airline ticket reservation application, a simple precondition to the task of obtaining user information would include that the departure and return dates are unknown; a post condition is that both such dates are known and that the former occurs before the latter. Any kind of domain-dependent check can be specified in this way; we assume that agents have the domain-dependent code to determine if the constraint is holding. In our more abstract domain-independent language, the preconditions are regarded as resources that an agent requires to begin work on a task. Similarly, to declare that a task is completed and successful, an agent must acquire beliefs that a task's results have been achieved (i.e., that the post condition constraints are holding). That brings us to the matter of abstract task operators.

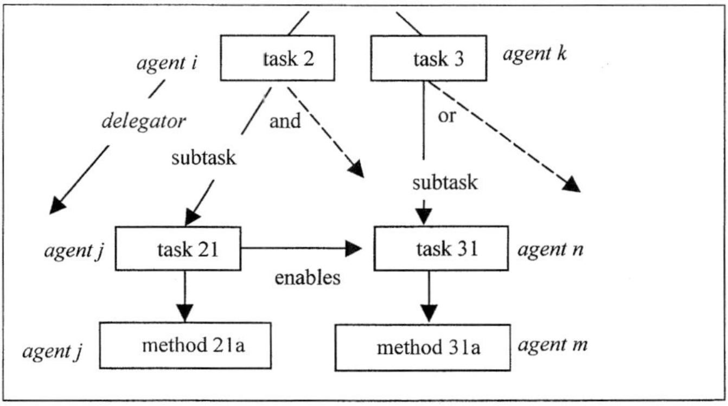

Fig. 1. Elements of task structure and derived agent roles

3.2 Task Progress and Agent Beliefs

Our interaction model also uses a domain-independent vocabulary for task progress. A task can be in one of these states: *not-attempted, possible, not-possible, irrelevant, failed,* or *succeeded.* An agent is designed to move its task from its initial state (*not-attempted*) to a final state (*irrelevant, failed,* or *succeeded*). It does so by applying what we call abstract task operators. An example abstract task operator, using English gloss, is:

If I intend task *t*, and status of task *t* is currently not-attempted
& I have all the resources and information specified for task *t's* initial state
& all semantic constraints on those preconditions are satisfied
then change task *t*'s status to possible

This operator essentially captures the notion that problem solving on a task can commence, i.e., the constraints that constitute its preconditions have been met and therefore progress on the task can commence. Application-specific code is used to instantiate the preconditions in these operators. These operators thus serve to bridge task dependent constraints with a task independent ontology that agents can use in their communication acts.

All agents have access to the entire task structure (the complete decomposition of a root task and the assignment of subtasks and methods to other agents), although this is not strictly necessary for our purposes. An agent's belief state is initialized and modified during run time by the agent's use of the shared task structure coupled with a set of axioms and inference rules. This is the second, major component of the interaction model, which serves to unite a model of task interdependencies with a traditional belief-desire-intention perspective for modeling an agent's internal state. Some examples of these rules (stated in English) are: "*Every task has an assigned agent and only one such agent.*" "*Only the agent assigned to a task can intend it*". "*An agent desires resources for its assigned task iff the agent intends it.*" The further explication of our axioms and inference rules is outside the scope of this short paper and not central to our concern. However, the general character of these rules is that they define and constrain task properties on the one hand and agent properties (e.g., roles, attitudinal states) on the other. The role of agent *i* to agent *j* in Figure 1 as *delegator* is derived from such inference rules applied to the jointly held task model. Similarly, the belief that agent *n* desires the results from task-21 is derived from beliefs that agent *n* is the agent assigned to that task, and that task-21 enables agent *n*'s task. These ultimately serve as the states that correspond to preconditions for communication acts. Table 2 shows a subset of the beliefs that would follow from these sorts of inference rules, coupled with the task structure in Figure 1.

Table 2. Illustrative belief state elements for agent j, Fig. 1

beliefs about self	(agent-for j task-21) (relevant task-21) (intend j task-21) (agent-for j method-21a) (desire (j (result-for (task-21 result-a))) (enables task-21 task-31) (subtask-of task-21 task-2) ...
beliefs about others	(agent-for n task-31) (agent-for i task-2) (intend n task-31) (relevant task-31) (desire (n (result-of (task-21 result-b))))….
beliefs about tasks	(relevant task-21) (status task-21 possible) (have-all-resources task-21) (valid-all-resources task-21) (decomposition task-21 method-21) ... (status method-21 not-attempted) ….

At the implementation level, we allow one level of nesting for belief propositions, and drop the outer most *believe*. *(Desire agent α)* is used to signify that an agent will aim to achieve a belief state in which proposition α is true. The *intend* predicate signifies an attitude towards a task by an agent; *intend (agent-i task-23*) is shorthand for signifying a behavioral commitment on agent *i*'s part to bring task-23 to a final state. In using this kind of vocabulary, it is important to specify axioms to define the semantics of these concepts. From our viewpoint, domain-specific computations on domain-specific information states can be carried out in any fashion, as long as they ultimately create beliefs in the agent that are represented using this (or some other) abstraction vocabulary. The implementation must ensure that, during execution, agent belief states are internally consistent with the axioms defining the semantics.

3.3 Communication Plans

Within each agent, a communication plan module handles the generation and assimilation of *inform, disconfirm* or *query* messages. Communication plans are triggered in two ways. First, an agent may select a particular communication plan as the means for satisfying the preconditions of an abstract task operator. For example, an agent may execute a *query* plan to receive information about resources that are necessary to move its task from *not-attempted* to *possible.* Second, an agent may proactively generate an *inform* or a *disconfirm* message to exchange information it believes will be useful to other agents. For example, an agent that determines its own task has failed may immediately inform other agents who require its results or resources. The communication plans implement the kind of schema illustrated in the top panel of Table 1. An agent's communication module also creates the necessary data structures for maintaining conversations between itself and several agents. Incoming messages are recognized as either completing or continuing an on-going conversation or as initiating a new conversation, provided that such messages pass the *not-understood* filters (described below).

3.4 Declarative and Procedural Forms of the Interaction Model

In our framework, agents share a declarative form of the interaction model represented in XML, with document type definitions for the key components that follow. The first component is the definition of a task structure using the general task description language, with agents assigned to specific tasks and methods within this structure. The second component is the set of allowable message types. In our sample model, this set has the members *inform, disconfirm, query-ref,* and *not-understood.* The third component is the set of allowable predicates that can comprise a proposition in an agent's belief set. Each of these predicates must be classified along three dimensions, defined generally in Section 2: public or private, static or defeasible, internal or external. Only propositions that involve public predicates may appear in any message content. Propositions involving defeasible predicates may be revised during run-time; those involving static predicates may not. External predicates may appear in the propositional content of inform or disconfirm messages; internal predicates may not. The fourth component is a specification of agent roles. In our current interaction model, there are two types of agent roles which are isomorphic to task dependencies: delegator—delegatee (isomorphic to task—subtask) and enabler-enablee (isomorphic to task dependencies of enables—enabled-by). However, an interaction model could include agent roles that are not isomorphic to task structure. The fifth component of the interaction model defines what combinations of message type, agent-role, and predicate type are allowable, i.e., which illocutionary forces can be applied to particular public, external, defeasible predicates by an agent having a particular role relative to another agent. Here is a portion of model that captures these last two components:

public:	{relevance resource task-status task-relevance intend agent-for...}
defeasible:	{relevance resource task-status task-relevance intend ...}
external:	{relevance resource}
inform	[sender-role: delegator] [predicate-class: external] [object: task-of(receiver)]
query	[sender-role: any] [predicate-class: public] [object: task-of(receiver)]

This model fragment indicates that agent *j*'s beliefs about the relevance of its task can be updated via an *inform* act from agent *i*, if agent *i* had delegated that task to agent *j*. (This is just one specification for *inform*—the model would specify several of these.) This particular specification also permits any public predicate to be the content of a query, regardless of the respective roles of the sender and receiver. A different specification could constrain queries as a function of agent roles. We have mentioned the importance of axioms and inference rules that unite these abstract interaction elements; these are not in our XML representation, although a more expressive modeling language [e.g. 5] might allow such axioms to be part of a declarative representation.

inform-messages ⇒	inform-1 | inform-2
inform-1 ⇒	(inform sender receiver role-of$_{s\text{-}to\text{-}r}$ (task-subject))
task-subject ⇒	task-of$_{sender}$ | task-of$_{receiver}$
role-of$_{s\text{-}to\text{-}r}$ ⇒	delegator | delegatee | enabler | enablee
external ⇒	relevant | resource
modality ⇒	intend | believe | desire
[delegator] [task-subject] ⇒	[delegator] [task-subject] [external]
[delegatee] [task-of$_{sender}$]⇒	[delegatee][task-of$_{sender}$][result]
[role-of$_{s\text{-}to\text{-}r}$][task-of$_{sender}$]⇒	[role-of$_{s\text{-}to\text{-}r}$][task-of$_{sender}$][status]
inform-2 ⇒	(inform sender receiver role$_{s\text{-}to\text{-}r}$ (sender modality)

Fig. 2. A grammar for legal inform messages allowable by an interaction model (*s-to-r* = *sender-to-receiver*)

Upon reflection, it is clear that the interaction model could be used to enumerate the set of all messages that adhere to its constraints. Indeed, the point of the model is to define a finite set of intentions and hence a finite set of messages that could (in principle) be sent between agents. It is convenient and useful to re-represent this functionality as a grammar that an agent can use to generate (or validate) messages. Figure 2 shows such a grammar for generating schematic versions of an *inform* message, created (by hand) from an interaction model specification.

In Figure 2, *Task-of* is a function that takes a particular agent as an argument and returns the task(s) to which that agent is assigned. For convenience, we defined two types of *informs* and the grammar generates schematic templates for each type. An example of an *inform-1* that this grammar generates is:

(inform sender receiver delegator (task-of$_{sender}$ relevant))

This *inform* is consistent with the interaction constraints that it is legal and *pragmatic* for an agent *i* (as sender) to inform agent *j* (as receiver) of agent *i*'s own task relevance, if agent *j* is performing a subtask for agent *i* (i.e., *i* stands as delegator to *j*). Using the Figure 1 task structure, the grammar allows *i* to inform *j* that task-2 is, for example, not relevant. It is legal, because agent *i* can send messages with propositional content about task relevance (relevance is public) and relevance can be updated via communication acts (it is defeasible and external). It is pragmatic, because agent *j* might infer its own task should be initiated (or stopped) by receiving messages about agent *i*'s task relevance. This grammar would not generate the following *inform-1:*

X (inform sender receiver delegatee (task-of$_{receiver}$ relevant))

Using the structure in Figure 1, agent *j* cannot inform agent *i* anything about the relevance of agent *i*'s task (task-2): agent *j*'s role to agent *i* is delegatee, not delegator. Such a communication act is disallowed by the interaction axioms and that is captured in this grammar.

An example of a schematic *inform-2* that this grammar generates is:

(inform sender receiver delegatee (sender believe))

This second type of *inform* captures the notion that a sender can inform a receiver about (only) the sender's attitudes towards propositions. Note that this particular grammar is based on an interaction model that requires that *some* direct role exist between the sender and receiver for such a message in the first place (e.g., the grammar would not generate this message from agent *i* to agent *m* in Fig. 1).

Any agent in our system can run this grammar by first binding *sender* to itself and *receiver* to some particular other agent. The grammar implicitly embodies constraints about public, defeasible, and external predicates *as well as* pragmatic considerations about what constitute plausible *informs* from one agent to another. The latter are captured through reference to the role that the sender plays to the receiver. We implement grammars like this one for *inform*, *disconfirm* (similar to inform) and *query*. This alternative representation of the interaction model is useful because it gives an agent the procedural capability of (a) generating all legal and pragmatic messages between itself and another agent, and (b) checking whether the general form of an incoming message passes various types of understandability filters. The grammars also serve an important function for us, namely to forbid certain kinds of replies *to* a not-*understood* message. We discuss this in the next section.

4 Not-Understood Responses and Conversations

Having both declarative and procedural specifications for an agent interaction model, it is possible to define a general message assimilation routine. Such a routine parses an incoming message and determines whether a *not-understood* response is warranted, by essentially asking these four questions:

1. Is the predicate in the content proposition a public predicate?
2. Is the illocutionary force applied to this predicate allowed?
3. Does the sender hold the proper role relative to the hearer, in order to apply this illocutionary force to the proposition?
4. Are the feasibility, relevance, and success preconditions (assumed to hold on the speaker's part) consistent with the receiver's interaction model and its current belief state about the sender and the task?

Recall that the general form of *not-understood* is *(not-understood :sender j :receiver i :content (m reason)),* where *m* is a just-received message from *i.* Any of the four checks listed above could generate a *not-understood* with a *reason* that takes one of four possible corresponding forms:

```
(not-understood :sender :receiver
    :content (m (not (public <predicate p of m's content>)) |
             (m (not (external <predicate p of m's content >)) |
             (m (not (permissible-role sender receiver)) |
             (m (not α)))
```

The first three of these cases can be handled by using the grammar. The last case includes a proposition α that will describes the mismatch between the receiver's model and the sender's model of what feasibility and relevance conditions are thought to be holding. For example, this case might correspond to "It is false that I desire the result of task-23." This could occur if tasks are dynamically reallocated and agent models about task responsibilities are out of sync.

At this point, we could consider the matter of generating and structuring *not-understood* messages as done. This is especially true if we regard *not-understood* messages as true run-time errors, i.e., errors that would bring an agent system to a halt, or at least stop further interaction between two agents.

However, things become more interesting, and complicated, if we try to allow some further resolution of a *not-understood* through additional message exchange. Recall that the reason included with *not-understood* is supposed to be a 'constructive explanation' about the matter. It would be *most* constructive if it caused some change to the internal state of the agent who sent the original message *m*, such that the agent would not simply regenerate message *m* all over again. In this sense, we can interpret the reason in a *not-understood* as an opportunity to bring two disparate models into alignment: the reason constitutes the content of an *inform*.

But this immediately raises the question of whose model is to be taken as true—the sender who generated message *m* or the receiver who asserts it is not understandable? We do not, of course, have a general answer for this, but we believe that the underlying interaction model could be used to represent application-specific policies about this. Consider this possible message exchange scenario:

	message 1	(inform *i j* (intend (*j* ....)))
	message 2	(not-understood *j i* (<message 1> (not (external intend))))
?	message 3	(disconfirm *i j* (not (external intend)))
X	message 3'	(not-understood *i j* (<message 2> (external intend))))

In message 2, *j*'s reason is that *j* believes that *intend* is not an external defeasible predicate, i.e., one whose truth status can be updated by a communication action from another agent. Hence *i*'s message 1 is not allowed under *j*'s interaction model. Now, there are two possible responses that *i* could make. In message 3, *i* aims to revise *j*'s model about whether the *intend* predicate is external. Is message 3 allowable? It depends solely on the underlying interaction model: if the predicate *external* is itself an external, defeasible predicate, then message 3 is allowed. Otherwise, it is not. (This does not settle the more general matter of whose model should be taken as correct, but perhaps that can be stipulated via agent roles that make sense within the realm of a given application). The second possible response is message 3', namely that *i* tells *j* that *j*'s *not-understood* message is not understandable to *i*. Within our framework, this cannot happen, because to do so is tantamount to *i* informing *j* what *j* already knows from message 1 (that *i* believes that *intend* was an external predicate). This would violate a feasibility precondition for *inform* (again regarding the reason as the content of an *inform*) and would not be allowed by the model.

The next message exchange illustrates a case where agent *i*'s model of task and agent interdependencies is incorrect, and *i* informs *j* of some result *j* does not need:

message 4 (inform *i j* (result-of (task-23 ....)))
message 5 (not-understood *j i* (<message 4>
(not (desire (*j*, result-of (task-23...))))
X message 6 (disconfirm *i j* (desire (*j*, result-of (task-23)))

According to the interaction model, message 4 is not understood because, from *j*'s viewpoint, the contextual relevance conditions for this *inform* should not be holding for *i*: *j* does not need to know the result of task-23 and *i* apparently believes otherwise. The *not-understood* reason, taken as an *inform* from *j* to *i* about *j*'s beliefs, is legal under the interaction model. This can cause agent *i* to update its model of agent *j*'s responsibilities. But agent *i* cannot try to revise agent *j*'s belief state with message 6, because by the interaction model, *i* cannot change *j*'s state about what *j* desires.

In this last scenario, there could be a different reason why agent *j* does not understand message 4. It might not (according to its own model of agent *i*) believe that an *inform* feasibility precondition holds for agent *i*, e.g., that agent *i* has reason to know the results of task-23. If only agents assigned to a task can know task results and *j* does not believe *i* is the agent assigned to task-23, then it might generate message 5' in response to message 4:

message 5' (not-understood *j i* (<message 4> (not (agent-for (*i* task-23)))
? message 6' (disconfirm *i j* (not (agent-for (i task-23)))

Message 6' could be a legal continuation of this exchange, *iff* the interaction model defines *agent-for* to be an external, defeasible predicate and (by the associated axioms) that an agent is the final authority on its task assignments (i.e., it can update beliefs held by others about its task assignments).

We have not considered message exchanges involving *query*, but many of the same issues arise. In the simple scenarios considered here, an agent may reply with a *refuse* to a *query* concerning α if it cannot resolve, by its underlying interaction model, that the inquiring agent has reason to know α. In this way, an interaction model can be used to enforce certain privacy constraints on information exchanged in a multi-agent system. In general, many issues remain about if and how agents use *not-understood* as a means for aligning disparate belief states. Belief states of cooperating agents could diverge during problem solving, through lost messages or, say, through task reallocation during run time. So it is not unreasonable to consider that this simple belief revision—triggered through communication exchanges—might be necessary for agents to adjust to a changing task environment.

5 Related Work and Themes

There has been general recognition that error conditions need to be specified for agent communication [9]. However, to our knowledge, there has not been work done either in defining such error conditions or in structuring *not-understood* messages through an explicit interaction model for software agents. The framework we present here adopts a number of the pragmatic assumptions that emerge from theoretical notions developed in the discourse understanding community [11, 14, 15, 19]. Explicit representations of tasks and task plans are used in such frameworks to define plausible or expected communication. As we have noted earlier, various approaches to coordinating distributed agents employ rich task environment modeling languages [6, 7] and such languages are central to specifying an interaction model. But the primary focus in that work has not been the motivation and resolution of communication actions *per se.* More recently, there is an effort to link conversation protocols directly to task interaction patterns [23]. Our interaction model requires the specification of axioms that link task interdependencies to agent properties. Such axioms provide the bridge from coordination information to BDI approaches for agent behavior and communication that support to abstract conversations about joint agent goals, envisioned in[23]. Our use of agent roles in specifying interaction conventions is also related to models of social problem solving. Such models describe agents in terms of the actions they are committed to executing, the resources they will need to meet those commitments, and their expectations and beliefs about the actions, commitments, and resource needs of others [2]. [24] uses roles for describing the expectations about individual behavior. Here, we are using agent roles as part of an interaction model for defining the pragmatic as well as legal communication actions that may be taken by one agent upon another agent's internal state.

Our working assumption is that understanding and hence not-understanding can only be resolved through appeal to *some* sort of model. By our view, such a model requires a shared task specification that describes task and agent interdependencies and a set of axioms that relate these specifications to BDI elements for characterizing an agent's internal state. What this means is that a set of cooperating or coordinating agents have a 'deep model' of their joint work and each other. This is easy to achieve in a closed agent system, in which a system designer can impart such models to a set of homogeneous and stable agents. But in such a system, one can argue that there is no real need to adhere to a high level ACL in the first place, because the agents can be programmed to communicate with each other in whatever way the system designer decides is best. A good part of the motivation for a high level standardized ACL was for communication among heterogeneous agents, who most likely have *shallow* models of each other. And that is where we come up against the matter of just what such agents will 'talk about'. There is considerable work on specifying ontologies that can support certain web-motivated types of interactions (e.g., service brokering [16]), but it still seems to us that such agents must subscribe to some kind of underlying interaction model. Fixed conversation protocols can certainly be regarded as a simple interaction model, but —as it is generally recognized — such protocols do not constrain message content, only sequences of message types. Some of the interaction model components we have advocated here (e.g., restrictions on whether particular beliefs can be updated or revised through communication actions taken by agents in particular roles) can add a level of semantic check, even without a deeper shared problem solving model.

In either open or closed agent systems, we think that a case can be made for explicit interaction models of the kind we have considered here. It might seem that providing such models is too much overhead. However, there has been increasing interest in extending and applying software engineering methodologies to the agent paradigm [12, 17, 25] and many of the interaction model components we have advocated here emerge 'for free' in the course of specifying a system design in, say, UML.

6 Conclusions and Future Work

The main contribution of this work is the perspective that messages are *not-understood*, and hence understood, with reference to a shared, declarative interaction model. We have also outlined the kinds of elements that such an interaction model might minimally include. A good portion of agent message types have intended effects that are essentially manipulations, updates, or revisions of the mental (informational) state of the receiving agent. We have considered here how *not-understood* messages can be viewed as replies to illegal instances of such actions on an agent's mental state. The model is the means by which legality and illegality is defined. In our framework, the model includes what feasibility preconditions, success conditions, and relevance conditions ought to be holding for the sender, to take a particular communicative action. We have also included the idea that some kinds of agent beliefs are not revisable by communicative acts, or indeed cannot even be the content of communication acts. When these constraints are combined with agent roles, the interaction model can become even richer and more complex (e.g., *some* agents get to revise *some* sorts of beliefs held by other agents, depending on their relative roles). The general point is that any and all such elements can be used to define a principled approach to constraining message content, message exchange patterns, and thereby a set of error conditions for agent communication.

We have employed the interaction model in a multi-agent solution to a simple domain task (making airline reservations through different web sites) as our test application. Our system framework instantiates and deploys agents that follow the interaction model as they interact to execute this task. We test the framework's ability to generate and assimilate *not-understood* messages by perturbing the individual agent models and generating messages to other agents that are illegal or non-pragmatic, from their viewpoints. The *not-understood* message exchange scenarios described earlier are handled within our implemented system. As we considered in Section 4, interesting issues emerge when we move beyond the error ontology *per se* and consider *not-understood* messages themselves as opportunities for belief revision during problem-solving. Agent roles are crucial to our analysis, because they so strongly influence the legal and pragmatically expected belief revision and updates that can take place through *informs* and *disconfirms*. If agent task assignment (and roles) are permitted to change during a problem solving episode, there must be consistent and reliable means for synchronizing agents' respective models of each other in the task context. This is an important consideration, since it relaxes the assumption that agents systems are stable and task allocation does not change during coordinated or cooperative problem solving. Our on-going work is aimed at a more careful consideration of using the *not-understood* conversations to synchronize mismatching agent models.

Acknowledgements

This work was supported by an NSERC research grant to R. Elio.

References

[1] Austin, J.: How to do Things with Words. Harvard University Press (1962)
[2] Bond, A. H.: Commitment: Some DAI Insights from Symbolic Interactionist Society. In: Proceedings of 9th Workshop on Distributed Artificial Intelligence. (1989)
[3] Breiter, P., Sadek, M.: A Rational Agent as the Kernal of a Cooperative Spoken Dialogue System. In: Intelligent Agents III (LNAI Vol. 1193). Springer-Verlag (1997) 189-204
[4] Cohen, P., Pernault, R.: Elements of a Plan-Based Theory of Speech Acts. Cognitive Science 3 (1979) 177-212
[5] DAML Agent Markup Language, www.daml.org
[6] Decker, K., Lesser, V.: Designing a Family of Coordination Algorithms. In: Proc. 5th Intl. Conference on Multi-agent Systems. MIT Press (1995) 73-80
[7] Decker, K., Lesser, V.: Quantitative modeling of complex computational task environments. In: Proc. of AAAI-93. AAAI Press (1993) 217-224
[8] Elio, R., Haddadi, A.: On abstract models and conversation protocols. In F. Dignum and M. Greaves (eds.): Issues in Agent Communication. (LNAI 1916). Springer-Verlag (2000) 301-313
[9] FIPA: "Agent Communicative Act Library Specification" available at http://www.fipa.org/specs
[10] Greaves, M., Holmback, H., Bradshaw, J.: What is a conversation policy? In F. Dignum and M. Greaves (eds.): Issues in Agent Communication. (LNAI 1916). Springer-Verlag (2000) 118-131
[11] Grosz, B. J., Sidner, C. L.: Plans for Discourse. In: P. R. Cohen, J. Morgan, & M. E. Pollack (eds.): Intentions in Communication. MIT Press (1990) 417-444
[12] Jennings, N.R.: On agent-based software engineering. Artificial Intelligence 117 (2000) 277-296
[13] Labrou, Y., Finin, T.: A semantics approach for KQML. In: Proc. of the Third International Conference on Information and Knowledge Management, ACM Press (1994) 447-455
[14] Lochbaum, K.E., Grosz, B. J., Sidner, C. L.: Models of Plans to Support Communication. In: Proc. 8th Nat. Conf. on Artificial Intelligence. AAAI Press (1990) 485-490

[15] Lochbaum, K.E.: The use of knowledge preconditions in language processing. In Proc. IJCAI-95 (1995) 1260-1266
[16] Nodine. M., Fowler, J., Ksiezyk, T., Perry, B., Taylor, M., Unruh, A.: Active Information Gathering in InfoSleuth. Intl. Journal of Cooperative Information Systems 9 (2000) 3-28
[17] Odell, J., Parnunak, H.V.D., Bauer, B.: Extending UML for Agents. In: Proc. Agent-Oriented Information Systems Workshop at the 17th Natl. Conference on Artificial Intelligence. AAAI Press (2000)
[18] Pitt, J., Mamdani, A.: Communication protocols in multi-agent systems. In F. Dignum and M. Greaves (eds.): Issues in Agent Communication. (LNAI 1916). Springer-Verlag (2000) 160 - 177
[19] Rich, C., Sidner C. L.: COLLAGEN: When agents collaborate with people. In M. H. Huhns & M. P. Singh (eds.): Readings in Agents. Morgan Kaufmann (1994) 814-819
[20] Sadek, M. D.: A Study in the Logic of Intention. In Proc. 3rd Conf. on Principles of Knowledge Representation and Reasoning. Morgan Kaufmann (1992) 462-473
[21] Searle, J.: What is a Speech Act. In: Black, M. (ed.): Philosophy in America. Cornell Univ Press (1965) 221-239
[22] Shoham, Y.: Agent Oriented Programming. Artificial Intelligence (1993) 51-92
[23] Wagner, T., Benyo, B., Lesser, V., Xuan, P.: Investigating Interactions between Agent Conversations and Agent Control Components. In F. Dignum and M. Greaves (eds.): Issues in Agent Communication. (LNAI 1916). Springer-Verlag (2000) 301-314-330.
[24] Werner, E.: Cooperating Agents: A Unified Theory of Communication and Social Structure. In: L. Gasser and M. H. Huhns (eds.): Distributed Artificial Intelligence Vol II. Pitnam Publishing (1989) 3-36
[25] Wooldridge, M., Jennings, N.J., Kinny, D.: The Gaia Methodology for Agent-oriented analysis and design. Autonomous Agents and Multi-agent Systems 3. Kluwer (2000) 285-312

An Improved Ant Colony Optimisation Algorithm for the 2D HP Protein Folding Problem

Alena Shmygelska and Holger H. Hoos*

Department of Computer Science, University of British Columbia
Vancouver, B.C., V6T 1Z4, Canada
{oshmygel,hoos}@cs.ubc.ca
http://www.cs.ubc.ca/labs/beta

Abstract. The prediction of a protein's structure from its amino-acid sequence is one of the most important problems in computational biology. In the current work, we focus on a widely studied abstraction of this problem, the 2-dimensional hydrophobic-polar (2D HP) protein folding problem. We present an improved version of our recently proposed Ant Colony Optimisation (ACO) algorithm for this $\mathcal{NP}$-hard combinatorial problem and demonstrate its ability to solve standard benchmark instances substantially better than the original algorithm; the performance of our new algorithm is comparable with state-of-the-art Evolutionary and Monte Carlo algorithms for this problem. The improvements over our previous ACO algorithm include long range moves that allows us to perform modification of the protein at high densities, the use of *improving* ants, and selective local search. Overall, the results presented here establish our new ACO algorithm for 2D HP protein folding as a state-of-the-art method for this highly relevant problem from bioinformatics.

1 Introduction

Ant Colony Optimisation (ACO) is a population-based approach for solving combinatorial optimisation problems that is inspired by the foraging behaviour of ants. The fundamental approach underlying ACO is an iterative process in which a population of simple agents ("ants") repeatedly construct candidate solutions; this construction process is probabilistically guided by heuristic information on the given problem instance as well as by a shared memory containing experience gathered by the ants in previous iterations ("pheromone trails"). Following the seminal work by Dorigo *et al.* [5], ACO algorithms have been successfully applied to a broad range of hard combinatorial problems (see, *e.g.*, [6, 7]).

In this paper, we present a substantially improved version of the ACO algorithm first proposed in [19] for solving an abstract variant of one of the most challenging problems in computational biology: the prediction of a protein's

* To whom correspondence should be addressed.

Y. Xiang and B. Chaib-draa (Eds.): AI 2003, LNAI 2671, pp. 400–417, 2003.

structure from its amino-acid sequence. Genomic and proteomic sequence information is now available for an increasing number of organisms, and genetic engineering methods for producing proteins are well developed. The biological function and properties of proteins, however, are crucially determined by their structure. Hence, the ability to reliably and efficiently predict protein structure from sequence information would greatly simplify the tasks of interpreting the sequence data collected, of designing drugs with specific therapeutic properties, and of developing biological polymers with specific material properties. Currently, protein structures are primarily determined by techniques such as NMRI (nuclear-magnetic resonance imaging) and X-ray crystallography, which are expensive in terms of equipment, computation and time. Additionally, they require isolation, purification and crystallization of the target protein. Computational approaches to protein structure prediction are therefore very attractive. In this work, we focus on one of the most studied simple protein models — the two dimensional Hydrophobic-Polar (2D HP) Model. Even in this simplified model, finding optimal folds is computationally hard ($\mathcal{NP}$-hard).

The remainder of this paper is structured as follows. In Section 2, we introduce the 2D HP model of protein structure, and give a formal definition of the 2D HP Protein Folding Problem as well as a brief overview of existing approaches for solving it. Our improved ACO algorithm for the 2D HP Protein Folding Problem is described in Section 3. (More information on our previous Ant Colony Optimisation algorithm can be found in [19]). An empirical study of our new algorithm's performance and the role of various algorithmic features is presented in Section 4. In Section 5 we draw some conclusions and point out several directions for future research.

2 The 2D HP Protein Folding Problem

Since the processes involved in the folding of proteins are very complex and only partially understood, simplified models like Dill's Hydrophobic-Polar (HP) model have become one of the major tools for studying proteins [12]. The HP model is based on the observation that hydrophobic interaction is the driving force for protein folding and the hydrophobicity of amino acids is the main force for development of a native conformation of small globular proteins [12, 15].

In the HP model, the primary amino-acid sequence of a protein (which can be represented as a string over a twenty-letter alphabet) is abstracted to a sequence of hydrophobic (H) and polar (P) residues, *i.e.*, amino-acid components. The protein conformations of this sequence are restricted to self-avoiding paths on a lattice; for the 2D HP model considered here, a 2-dimensional square lattice is used. An example for a protein conformation under the 2D HP model is shown in Figure 1.

One of the most common approaches to protein structure prediction is based on the thermodynamic hypothesis which states that the native state of the protein is the one with the lowest Gibbs free energy. In the HP model, based on the biological motivation given above, the energy of a conformation is defined as

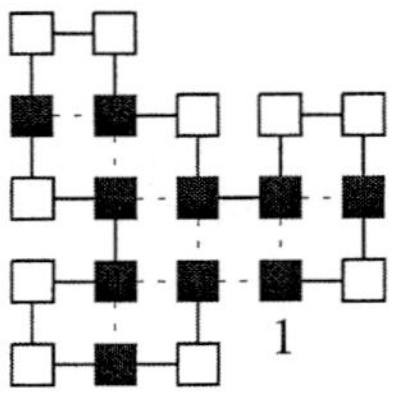

Fig. 1. A sample protein conformation in the 2D HP model. The underlying protein sequence (Sequence 1 from Table 1) is HPHPPHHPHPPHPHHPPHPH; black squares represent hydrophobic amino-acids while white squares symbolise polar amino-acids. The dotted lines represents the H-H contacts underlying the energy calculation. The energy of this conformation is -9, which is optimal for the given sequence

a number of topological contacts between hydrophobic amino-acids that are not neighbours in the given sequence. More specifically, a conformation c with exactly n such H-H contacts has free energy $E(c) = n \cdot (-1)$; *e.g.*, the conformation shown in Figure 1 has energy -9.

The 2D HP Protein Folding Problem can be formally defined as follows: Given an amino-acid sequence $s = s_1 s_2 \ldots s_n$, find an energy-minimising conformation of s, *i.e.*, find $c^* \in C(s)$ such that $E^* = E(c^*) = \min\{E(c) \mid c \in C\}$, where $C(s)$ is the set of all valid conformations for s. It was recently proved that this problem and several variations of it are $\mathcal{NP}$-hard [11].

Existing 2D HP Protein Folding Algorithms

A number of well-known heuristic optimisation methods have been applied to the 2D HP Protein Folding Problem, including Evolutionary Algorithms (EAs) [10, 11, 21, 20] and Monte Carlo (MC) algorithms [1, 3, 9, 13, 14, 17]. The latter have been found to be particular robust and effective for finding high-quality solutions to the 2D HP Protein Folding Problem [9].

An early application of EAs to protein structure prediction was presented by Unger and Moult [20, 21]. They presented a nonstandard EA incorporating characteristics of Monte Carlo methods, which was able to find high-quality conformations for a set of protein sequences of length up to 64 amino-acids (see Table 1). Unfortunately, it is not clear how long their algorithm ran to achieve these results.

Various Monte Carlo methods are among the best known algorithms for the 2D HP Protein Folding Problem, including the Pruned Enriched Rosenbluth Method (PERM) of Grassberger *et al.* [1, 9]. PERM is a biased chain growth algorithm. Using this method, the best known solution for Sequence 7 ($E^* = -36$), Sequence 9 ($E^* = -53$) and Sequence 11 ($E^* = -48$) from Table 1 were found; however, it took 30 hours on a 500 MHz DEC 21264 CPU to obtain the best-known conformation for Sequence 8 [9].

Seq.No.	*Length*	E^*	*Protein Sequence*
1	20	**-9**	$(HP)_2PH_2PHP_2HPH_2P_2HPH$
2	24	**-9**	$H_2P_2(HP_2)_6H_2$
3	25	**-8**	$P_2HP_2H_2P_4H_2P_4H_2P_4H_2$
4	36	-14	$P_3H_2P_2H_2P_5H_7P_2H_2P_4H_2P_2HP_2$
5	48	-23	$P_2HP_2H_2P_2H_2P_5H_{10}P_6H_2P_2H_2P_2HP_2H_5$
6	50	-21	$H_2(PH)_3PH_4PHP_3HP_3HP_4HP_3HP_3HPH_4(PH)_3PH_2$
7	60	-36	$P_2H_3PH_8P_3H_{10}PHP_3H_{12}P_4H_6PH_2PHP$
8	64	-42	$H_{12}(PH)_2(P_2H_2)_2P_2H(P_2H_2)_2P_2H(P_2H_2)_2P_2HPHPH_{12}$
9	85	-53	$H_4P_4H_{12}P_6(H_{12}P_3)_3HP_2(H_2P_2)_2HPH$
10	100	-50	$P_3H_2P_2H_4P_2H_3(PH_2)_3H_2P_8H_6P_2H_6P_9HPH_2PH_{11}P_2H_3PH_2$ $PHP_2HPH_3P_6H_3$
11	100	-48	$P_6HPH_2P_5H_3PH_5PH_2(P_2H_2)_2PH_5PH_{10}PH_2PH_7P_{11}H_7P_2H$ $PH_3P_6HPHP_2$

Table 1. Benchmark instances for the 2D HP Protein Folding Problem used in this study with optimal or best known energy values E^*. (E^* values printed in bold-face are provably optimal.) The first eight instances can also be found at http://www.cs.sandia.gov/tech_reports/compbio/tortilla-hp-benchmarks.html, Sequence 9 is taken from [10], and the last two instances are taken from [14]. (H_i, P_i, and $(\ldots)_i$ indicate i-fold repetitions of the respective symbol or subsequence)

Other methods for this problem include the dynamic Monte Carlo algorithm by Ramakrishnan *et al.* [14], which found conformations with energies -46 and -44 for Sequence 10 and 11, respectively. Liang *et al.* [13] introduced the evolutionary Monte Carlo (EMC) algorithm which works with population of individuals that each performs Monte Carlo (MC) optimisation. They also implemented a variant of EMC which reinforces certain secondary structures (α-helices and β-sheets). EMC found the best-known conformation (with energy -42) for Sequence 8 and a conformation with energy -52 for Sequence 9 (with secondary structure constraints), but failed to find the best known conformation for Sequence 7. Chikenji *et al.* introduced the Multi-self-overlap ensemble (MSOE) Monte Carlo method [3], which considers overlapping chain configurations; it found a best-known configuration for Sequence 10 ($E^* = -50$) and a sub-optimal configuration for Sequence 11 ($E^* = -47$).

Finally, the Core-directed Chain Growth (CG) method of Beutler *et al.* approximates the hydrophobic core of the protein with a square (this is a very restrictive heuristic that finds only certain native states). CG was able to find optimal or best known conformations for Sequences 1 through 8, except for Sequence 7 [2].

Currently, none of these algorithm appears to completely dominate the others in terms of solution quality and run-time.

```
procedure ACO-for-static-optimisation
   input: problem instance
   output: candidate solution
   initialise pheromone trails
   while (termination condition not met) do
      construct candidate solutions
      perform local search
      update pheromone trails
   end while
   return(best found solution)
end procedure
```

Fig. 2. Algorithmic outline of a generic ACO algorithm for a static combinatorial optimisation problem

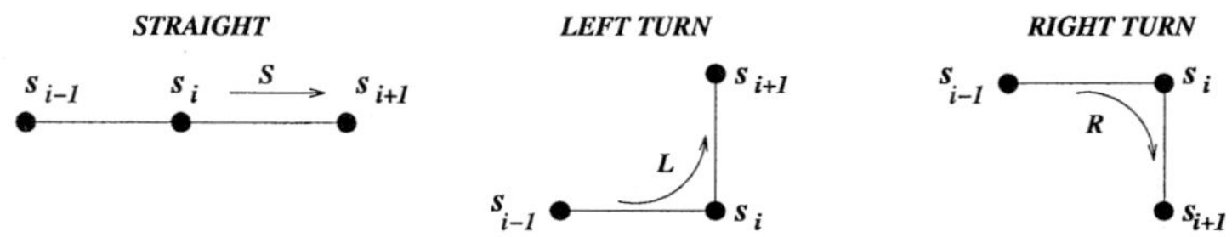

Fig. 3. The local structure motifs that form the solution components underlying the construction and local search phases of our ACO algorithm

3 The Improved ACO Algorithm

The ants in our ACO algorithm construct candidate conformations for a given HP protein sequence, apply local search to achieve further improvements, and update the pheromone trails based on the quality of the solutions found, as seen in the outline Figure 2.

As in [11], candidate conformations are represented using local structure motifs (or relative folding directions) *straight* (S), *left* (L), and *right* (R) which for each amino-acid indicate its position on the 2D lattice relative to its direct predecessors in the given sequence (see Figure 3).

Since conformations are invariant with respect to rotations, the position of the first two amino-acids can be fixed without loss of generality. Hence, we represent candidate conformations for a protein sequence of length n by a sequence of local structure motifs of length $n-2$. For example, the conformation of Sequence 1 shown in Figure 1 corresponds to the motif sequence LSLLRRLRLLSLRRLLSL.

Construction Phase, Pheromone and Heuristic Values

In the construction phase of our ACO algorithm, each ant first randomly determines a starting point within the given protein sequence. From this starting point, the given protein sequence is folded in both directions, adding one amino-acid symbol at a time. The relative directions in which the conformation is extended in each construction step are determined probabilistically using heuristic values $\eta_{i,d}$, as well pheromone values $\tau_{i,d}$ (also called trail intensities), where where i is a sequence position and $d \in \{S, L, R\}$ is the direction of folding at position i. These relative directions correspond to local structure motifs between triples of consecutive sequence positions $s_{i-1}s_is_{i+1}$ that form the solution components used by our ACO algorithm; conceptually, these play the same role as the edges between cities in the Traveling Salesperson Problem, a classical application domain of ACO.

Likewise, pheromone values $\tau'_{i,d}$ and heuristic values $\eta'_{i,d}$ are used when extending a conformation from position i to the $i-1$. In our algorithm, we use $\tau'_{i,L} = \tau_{i,R}$, $\tau'_{i,R} = \tau_{i,L}$, and $\tau'_{i,S} = \tau_{i,S}$ and analogous equalities for the respective η' values. This reflects a fundamental symmetry underlying the folding process: Extending the fold from sequence position i to $i+1$ by placing s_{i+1} right of s_i (as seen from s_{i-1}) or extending it from position i to $i-1$ by placing s_{i-1} left of s_i (as seen from s_{i+1}) leads to the same local conformation of $s_{i-1}s_is_{i+1}$.

The heuristic values $\eta_{i,d}$ should guide the construction process towards high-quality candidate solutions, *i.e.*, towards conformations with a maximal number of H-H interactions. In our algorithm, this is achieved by defining $\eta_{i,d}$ based on $h_{i+1,d}$, the number of new H-H contacts achieved by placing s_{i+1} in direction d relative to s_i and s_{i-1} when folding forwards (backwards folding is handled analogously). Note that if $s_{i+1} = \text{P}$, this amino-acid cannot contribute any new H-H contacts and hence $h_{i+1,S} = h_{i+1,L} = h_{i+1,R} = 0$. Furthermore, for $1 < i < n-1$, $h_{i+1,d} \leq 2$ and $h_{n,d} \leq 3$; the actual $h_{i+1,d}$ values can be easily determined by checking the seven neighbours of the possible positions of s_{i+1} on the 2D lattice (obviously, the position of s_i is occupied and hence not included in these checks). The heuristic values are then defined as $\eta_{i,d} = h_{i+1,d} + 1$; this ensures that $\eta_{i,d} > 0$ for all i and d which is important in order to not exclude *a priori* any placement of s_{i+1} in the construction process.

When extending a partial conformation $s_k \dots s_i$ to s_{i+1} during the construction phase of our ACO algorithm, the relative direction d of s_{i+1} w.r.t. $s_{i-1}s_i$ is determined based on the heuristic and pheromone values according to the following probabilities:

$$p_{i,d} = \frac{[\tau_{i,d}]^\alpha [\eta_{i,d}]^\beta}{\sum_{e \in \{L,R,S\}} [\tau_{i,e}]^\alpha [\eta_{i,e}]^\beta} \tag{1}$$

The case of extending partial conformation $s_i \dots s_m$ to s_{i-1} is handled analogously.

In the previous version of the ACO algorithm [19], when folding from a randomly determined starting point l (independently chosen for each ant), first, the partial conformation $s_l \dots s_1$ is constructed, followed by the partial conformation $s_l \dots s_n$. Here, we consider a new, physically more plausible mechanism, in which folds are probabilistically extended in both directions; more precisely, in each step an extension in each direction is performed with a probability equal to the number of residues left to fold at the respective end divided by the sum of the number of unfolded residues at both ends. As in previous work [19], we also studied variants of our algorithm in which all ants start their construction process at the same point (left end, middle, or right end of the protein sequence). Performance results for these alternative mechanisms are reported in Section 4. As in our first ACO algorithm for 2D HP Protein Folding [19], we use a backtracking mechanism in the construction process to recover from infeasible conformations, which are frequently encountered when folding long protein sequences.

Local Search

Similar to other ACO algorithms known from the literature, our algorithm for the 2D HP Protein Folding Problem incorporates a local search phase. In this work, we modified the local search mechanism from our previous ACO algorithm by using a new type of *long range move*, *selective local search*, and *improving ants* that perform *probabilistic iterative improvement* on the best conformations seen so far.

Long range moves in the local search phase allow for chain reconfigurations even when the protein conformation is very compact. Similar attempts were previously undertaken but different from our approach these involve disconnection of the chain [14]. Conventional short range moves, such as point mutations (*i.e.*, random modifications of the direction of a single residue, which correspond to a rotations) and macro-mutations (sequences of point mutations between two sequence positions) — both types of moves have been employed in EAs for HP Protein Folding — result in infeasible conformation when the protein is already dense. Likewise, standard Monte Carlo moves, such as the end-move, crankshaft move, and corner move [14], are not powerful enough to change a given configuration significantly.

Therefore, we designed a new type of long range move that closely models the movement of real proteins. First, a sequence position at which the move is going to originate is chosen uniformly at random.[1] Then we randomly modify the direction of the chosen amino-acid and adjust the location of the remaining residues probabilistically as follows. For each subsequent residue, we first attempt to place it using its previous folding direction. If this is infeasible, we refold the residue probabilistically using the same heuristic values as during the initial folding (but ignoring the pheromone values). This initiates a chain reaction that continues until all the residues have found feasible directions. Intuitively, this mechanism mimics the fact that in real proteins, a moving residue will typically push its neighbours in the chain to different positions.

Since these long range moves are computationally quite expensive, our new algorithm applies local search selectively. More precisely, local search is only applied to the best conformations constructed in a given iteration of the algorithm;

[1] We also tested a probabilistic selection of the origin (based on the constrainedness of the residue position), but results were not significantly different from those for uniform random choice.

```
procedure II-LS
   input: conformation c
   output: conformation c′
   while (termination condition not met) do
      choose sequence index i uniformly at random from 1..n
      c′ = longRangeMove(i)
      if E(c′) ≤ E(c) then
         return (c′)
      else
         return (c)
      end if
   end while
end procedure
```

Fig. 4. The iterative improvement local search performed by *forager* ants after the construction phase

the fraction of ants that are allowed to perform local search is a parameter of our algorithm. This *selective local search mechanism* is based on the intuition that the improvement in solution quality that can be achieved by the local search procedure strongly depends on the energy of the given starting conformation; in particular, bad starting conformations can rarely be improved to high quality solutions.

In our original ACO algorithm for 2D HP Protein Folding [19], we only considered *forager* ants that perform heuristic conformation construction followed by iterative improvement ("greedy") local search. Here, we additionally introduce *improving* ants that take the global best solution found so far (or best solution in the current iteration) and apply *probabilistic iterative improvement* ("randomised greedy") local search to it. Iterative improvement accepts a new conformation generated via long range moves only when the energy of the new conformation c' improves over the energy of the current conformation, c. Our probabilistic iterative improvement mechanism accepts worsening steps depending on the respective deterioration of the evaluation function with probability $p = E(c')/E(c)$. Algorithm outlines for the iterative improvement and probabilistic iterative improvement local search procedures are given in Figures 4 and 5. The number of improving ants used in each iteration of our algorithm is specified as a fraction of the total number of ants; empirical results on the impact of this parameter on the performance of our algorithm are reported in Section 4.

```
procedure PII-LS
   input: conformation c
   output: conformation c'
   while (termination condition not met) do
      choose sequence index i uniformly at random from 1..n
      c' = longRangeMove(i)
      if E(c') ≤ E(c) then
         return (c')
      else
         with probability p = E(c')/E(c) do
            return (c')
         otherwise
            return (c)
         end whith
      end if
   end while
end procedure
```

Fig. 5. The probabilistic iterative improvement local search procedure performed by the *improving* ants on the best configuration seen so far in the optimisation process

Update of the Pheromone Values

After each construction and local search phase, selected ants update the pheromone values in a standard way:

$$\tau_{i,d} \leftarrow (1-\rho)\tau_{i,d} + \Delta_{i,d,c} \tag{2}$$

where $0 < \rho \leq 1$ is the pheromone persistence, a parameter that determines how fast the information gathered in previous iterations is "forgotten", and $\Delta_{i,d,c}$ is the relative solution quality of the given ant's candidate conformation c if that conformation contains a local structure motif d at sequence position i and zero otherwise. We use the relative solution quality, $E(c)/E^*$, where E^* is the known minimal energy for the given protein sequence or an approximation based on the number of H residues in the sequence, in order to prevent premature search stagnation for sequences with large energy values.

4 Empirical Results

To assess its performance, we applied our improved ACO algorithm to the eleven standard benchmark instances for the 2D HP Protein Folding Problem shown in Table 1; these instances have been widely used in the literature [1, 2, 3, 11, 13, 19, 20, 21]. Experiments were conducted by performing a number of independent runs for each problem instance (500 runs for sequence length $n \leq 50$, 300 for $50 < n \leq 64$, and 100 runs for $n > 64$). Unless explicitly indicated otherwise, we used parameter settings $\alpha = 1$, $\beta = 2$, $\rho = 0.8$ for all experiments; furthermore, a population of 500 ants was used for small sequences ($n \leq 48$) while 1500 ants were used for larger sequences ($n > 48$); 1% of these were allowed to perform local search, and the number of improving ants was set to 0.5% of the total colony size. The local search procedure was terminated if no solution improvement had been obtained while scanning through the protein sequence once (for $n \leq 48$) or twice (for $n > 48$). Furthermore, we used elitist pheromone update in which only the best 1% of the total colony size were used for updating the pheromone values. Run-time was measured in terms of CPU time and all experiments were performed on PCs with 1GHz and Pentium III CPUs, 256KB cache and 1GB RAM.

In the following, we report results from several series of experiments that highlight the impact of various features of our new ACO algorithm on its performance. In these experiments we used primarily two test sequences: Sequence 4 (short sequence, length 36) and Sequence 5 (longer sequence, length 48); these sequences were chosen since the CPU time required to find the best known solutions was sufficiently small to perform a large number of runs (300–500 per instance). We also tested other benchmark sequences from Table 1 and generally obtained results similar to the ones described below.

ACO algorithms exploit heuristic information as well as information learned over multiple iterations (the latter is reflected in the pheromone matrix). In a first experiment, we investigated the impact of these two components and their relative importance for the performance of our algorithms. Following the methodology of Hoos and Stützle [8], we measured run-time distributions (RTDs) of our ACO algorithm, which represent the (empirical) probability of reaching (or exceeding) a given solution quality within a given run-time; the solution qualities used here and in the following experiments are provably optimal or best known energies for the respective sequences. All RTDs are based on 100–500 successful runs; we generally show semi-log plots to give a better view of the distribution over its entire range.

As can be seen from the results shown in Figure 6, both, the pheromone values and the heuristic information are important; when ignoring either of them ($\alpha = 0$ or $\beta = 0$, respectively), the algorithm performs substantially worse, especially for larger sequences. The optimal settings for α and β depends on the problem instance; as shown in Figure 6, the heuristic information seems to be more important than the pheromone information for small sequences. For longer sequences, the pheromone information appears to become more important than the heuristic information. These observations were confirmed for other benchmark instances.

Secondly, we tested how the colony size, *i.e.*, the number of ants that construct candidate solutions in each iteration affects the performance of our ACO algorithm. The proportion of ants that perform local search, the proportion of elitist ants, and the proportion of improving ants was chosen such that in all

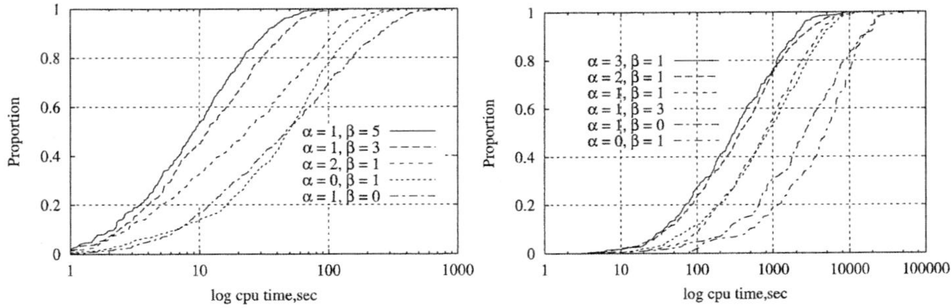

Fig. 6. Effect of the α and β weights for pheromone and heuristic information respectively on the average CPU time required for reaching optimal confirmations. Left side: Run-time distributions (RTDs) for Sequence 4 (length 36), right side: RTDs for Sequence 5 (length 48)

cases the number of local search ants, elitist ants, and improving ants, remains the same for all colony sizes. (Colony sizes tested were between 15 and 2000 ants.)

As can be seen from the results shown in Figure 7, there appears to be a single optimal colony size for each problem instance; optimal performance for longer sequences is achieved using larger colonies (1000 – 1500 ants) than for shorter sequences (500 – 1000). It may be noted that using a single ant only (not shown here) was found to result in extremely poor performance. These results can be intuitively explained as follows. For very few ants, the probability of constructing high quality initial solutions is very small and local search requires substantial amounts of CPU time for finding conformations of the desired quality. Beyond a certain colony size, on the other hand, the computational expense incurred for constructing additional conformations cannot be amortised by reductions in local search cost. The longer the given sequence, the more conformations need to be constructed to obtain the coverage (or exploration) of the corresponding more extensive search spaces required to find good starting points for the subsequent local search phase.

Our next experiment was designed to analyse the effectiveness of the selective local search mechanism used in our new ACO algorithm, in which local search is only performed by a certain fraction of all ants that constructed high quality conformations. The results shown in Figure 8 indicate that there is a small optimal interval for the fraction of local search ants; this optimal fraction depends on colony size and on the given problem instance. Essentially, if the fraction of local search ants is too small, the search process has difficulties in finding high quality conformations (lack of search intensification). On the other hand, if too many ants perform local search, the benefit of the additional local search does not amortise the higher computational cost. Our results indicate that longer sequences require a lower fraction of local search ants than shorter sequences;

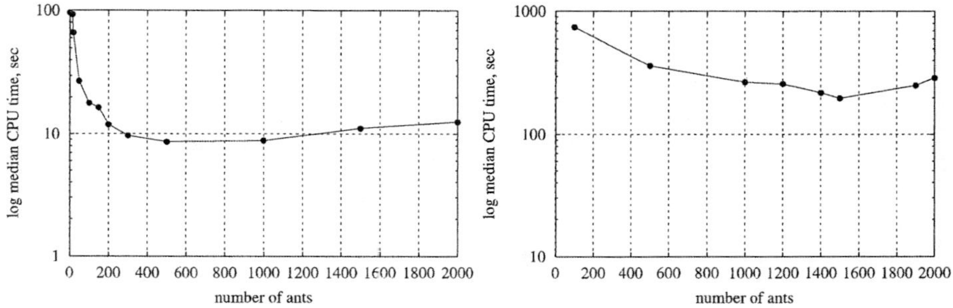

Fig. 7. Median CPU time required to obtain the best known solution quality as a function of the colony size (number of the ants on which construction is performed) for Sequence 4 (left side) and Sequence 5 (right side)

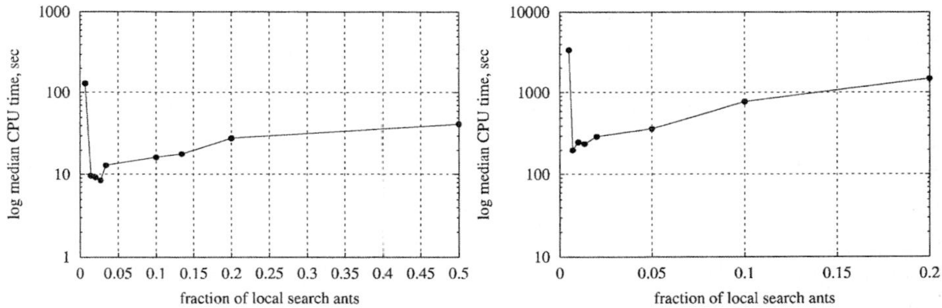

Fig. 8. Median CPU time required to obtain the best known solution quality as a function of the proportion of the ants on which local search is performed for Sequence 4 (left side, colony size 500) and Sequence 5 (right side, colony size 1500)

however, given the the larger optimal colony size, the optimal number of local search ants increases with sequence size. This is consistent with the interpretation that larger sequences require a more diversified search process, as provided by locally optimising a larger number of candidate solutions in each iteration. It is worth noting that without a local search phase, the performance of our ACO method is abysmal.

The use of improving ants that, instead of iteratively constructing conformations, use probabilistic iterative improvement local search on the best conformations seen so far is an important new feature of our new ACO algorithm. Figure 9 illustrates the results from our empirical analysis of the effectiveness of this feature in terms of the impact of the fraction of improving ants on the performance of our algorithm. Overall, the use of improving ants results in an

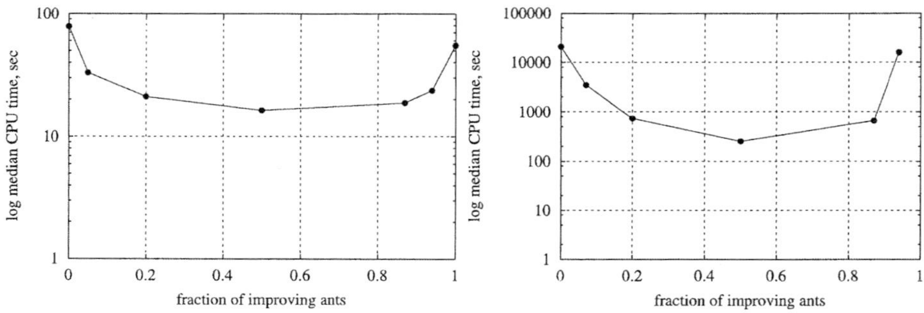

Fig. 9. Median CPU time required to obtain the optimum as a function of the proportion of the improving ants for Sequence 4 (left side) and Sequence 5 (right side)

performance increase of our algorithm for all sequences; this effect is especially pronounced for long sequences.

It is interesting to note that the optimal ratio between the number of (forager) ants that perform iterative improvement local search and the number of improving ants performing probabilistic iterative improvement appears to be 1 : 1 for all sequences.

Finally, we studied the effect of the starting point for the construction of conformations on the performance of our improved ACO. It has been shown that real proteins fold by hierarchical condensation starting from folding nuclei; the use of complex and diverse folding pathways helps to avoid the need to extensively search large regions of the conformation space [16]. This suggests that the starting point for the folding process can be an important factor in searching for optimal conformations. We tested four strategies for determining the starting point for the folding process performed in the construction phase of our algorithm: all ants fold forwards, starting at the N-terminus of the given sequence (position 1); all ants fold backwards, starting at the C-terminus (position n); all ants fold forwards and backwards, starting at the midpoint of the given sequence; and all ants fold forwards and backwards, starting at randomly determined sequence positions. As can be seen from Figure 10, the best choice of the starting folding point depends on the given sequence, and in general, most consistent performance on all sequences is obtained by allowing all ants start the folding process from randomly chosen sequence positions. This is particularly the case for longer sequences, which require to a larger extent the added search diversification afforded by multiple and diverse starting points.

After studying the influence of various parameters on our algorithm we conducted a performance comparison with existing algorithms for the 2D HP Protein Folding Problem. As can be seen from the results reported in Table 2, our new ACO algorithm found optimal or best known solutions for benchmark sequences 1–8, while our previous ACO algorithm [19] had failed to find optimal solutions

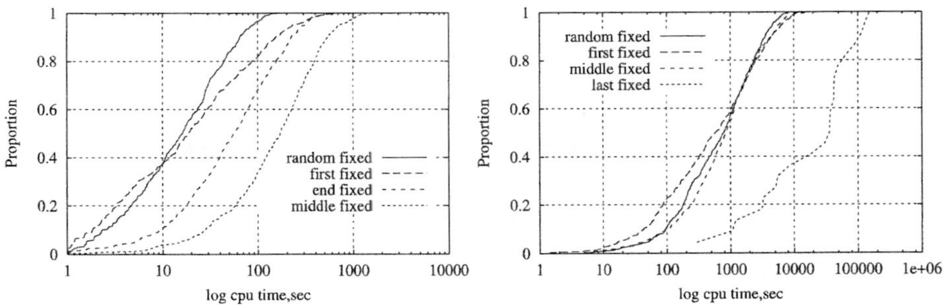

Fig. 10. Impact of various strategies for choosing the starting point for constructing candidate conformations. Left side: RTDs for Sequence 4, right side: RTDs for Sequence 5

for the longer sequences 7 and 8. Moreover, the new algorithm finds best-known solutions in every run, and in cases where both algorithms have a success rate of 100%, it requires substantially less time for finding optimal solutions.

For most GA and MC methods found in literature, including [11, 13, 20, 21], only the number of valid conformations scanned during the search is reported. This makes a performance comparison difficult, since run-time spent for backtracking and the checking of partial or infeasible conformations may vary substantially between different algorithms. Table 3 illustrates the solution quality

Table 2. Performance comparison of the original and the improved ACO algorithm, where $\hat{E}$ is the best solution quality over all runs, sr is the success rate of the algorithm reported due to the fact that some of the runs of older algorithm were unsuccessful, t_{avg} is the average run-time (in CPU sec on a 1GHz Intel Pentium III machine) required by the algorithm to reach energy $\hat{E}$. Measurements are based on $20 - 700$ runs for the original ACO algorithm and $300 - 500$ tries for the improved algorithm. Energies indicated in bold-face are currently best-known values

Instances			*Original ACO from [19]*			*New ACO (this paper)*		
No	*Length*	E^*	$\hat{E}$	$sr[\%]$	$t_{avg}[CPU sec]$	$\hat{E}$	$sr[\%]$	$t_{avg}[CPU sec]$
1	20	-9	**-9**	100	23.90	**-9**	100	3.33
2	20	-9	**-9**	100	26.44	**-9**	100	2.52
3	25	-8	**-8**	100	35.32	**-8**	100	10.62
4	36	-14	**-14**	16.4	(4,746.12)	**-14**	100	11.81
5	48	-23	**-23**	0.6	(1,920.93)	**-23**	100	405.79
6	50	-21	**-21**	41.9	(3,000.28)	**-21**	100	4,952.92
7	60	-36	-34	0.8	(4,898.77)	**-36**	100	6,2471.24
8	64	-42	-32	4.5	(4,736.98)	**-42**	100	5,844.93

Table 3. Comparison of the solution quality obtained by the genetic algorithm (GA), the evolutionary Monte Carlo (EMC), Multi-Self-Overlap Ensemble (MSOE) and new ACO. For GA and EMC, the reported energy values are the lowest among five independent runs, and the values shown in parentheses are the numbers of valid conformations scanned before the lowest energy values were found. Gaps in the table indicate that particular method has not been tested on the respective instance. The CPU times on a 500 MHz CPU are reported in parenthesis for MSOE (where available) and CPU times on a 1 GHz CPU are reported in parenthesis for the new ACO. Energies indicated in bold are currently best known values

No	*Length*	*Energy*	*GA*	*EMC*	*MSOE*	*New ACO*
1	20	-9	**-9** (30,492)	**-9** (9,374)		**-9**
2	24	-9	**-9** (30,491)	**-9** (6,929)		**-9**
3	25	-8	**-8** (20,400)	**-8** (7,202)		**-8**
4	36	-14	**-14** (301,339)	**-14** (12,447)		**-14**
5	48	-23	**-23** (126,547)	**-23** (165,791)		**-23**
6	50	-21	**-21** (592,887)	**-21** (74,613)		**-21**
7	60	-36	-34 (208,781)	-35 (203,729)		**-36**
8	64	-42	-37 (187,393)	-39 (564,809)	**-42** (30 hrs)	**-42** (2 hrs)
9	85	-53		-52 (44,029)		-51 (6 hrs)
10	100	-50			-50 (50 hrs)	-47 (9 hrs)
11	100	-48			-47	-47 (3 hrs)

reached by various algorithms on the test instances. These results indicate that our new ACO algorithm is competitive with GA and MC methods described in literature; it works very well on sequences of sizes up to 64 amino acids and produces high quality suboptimal configurations for the longest sequences (85 and 100 amino acids) considered here.

We also compared our improved implementation to the best performing algorithm from the literature for which performance data in terms of CPU time is available — PERM [9] (we used the most recent implementation, which was kindly provided by P. Grassberger). PERM is an iterated heuristic construction algorithm; it evaluates partially folded conformations, and creates copies of those partial configurations that have high statistical weight (enrichment, based on energy achieved and folded length), and it eliminates partial conformations with low weight (pruning). After completing the folding of the current configuration, PERM performs backjumping to the next partial configuration that was put on the stack during enrichment (or starts a new chain). It should be noted that tries in PERM are not entirely independent, since some statistical information, including upper and lower thresholds on weights and statistical averages, are kept between tries. Although the PERM algorithm is randomised, as seen from empirical observations the time it takes to find the first optimal conformation has very low variation. The only fair comparison of the new ACO and PERM is

Table 4. Comparison of the improved ACO algorithm and PERM, where $\hat{E}$ is the best solution quality over all runs, t_{avg} is the average run-time required by the algorithm to reach energy $\hat{E}$ on 1GHz CPU machine (both for ACO and PERM), t_{first} is the time required to reach energy $\hat{E}$ in the first run (reported for PERM since only the first run is independent of the others and can be compared with ACO). Measurements are based on $100 - 500$ tries for ACO algorithm, PERM reports $20 - 200$ tries. Energies indicated in bold are currently best-known values.
* After running PERM for 2 days wall clock time, -38 was the best energy reached

Instances			*New ACO*		*PERM*		
No	*Length*	E^*	$\hat{E}$	$t_{avg}[CPUsec]$	$\hat{E}$	$t_{first}[CPUsec]$	$t_{avg}[CPUsec]$
1	20	-9	**-9**	3.33	**-9**	0.01	0.01
2	20	-9	**-9**	2.52	**-9**	0.02	0.02
3	25	-8	**-8**	10.62	**-8**	80.01	16.29
4	36	-14	**-14**	11.81	**-14**	0.05	0.21
5	48	-23	**-23**	405.79	**-23**	1,762.69	881.67
6	50	-21	**-21**	4,952.92	**-21**	0.48	1.61
7	60	-36	**-36**	62,471.24	**-36**	0.52	4.43
8	64	-42	**-42**	5,844.93	-38*	(6.07)	(7.90)
9	85	-53	-51	(21,901.34)	**-53**	31.95	11.74
10	100	-50	-47	(29,707.22)	**-50**	19,962	14,432.10
11	100	-48	-47	(10,835.51)	**-48**	152.71	144.41

by considering time it takes to reach first optimum. As can be seen from Table 4, our improved ACO algorithm requires less CPU time on average for finding best known conformations for Sequences 5 (slightly) and 8 (significantly); but PERM performs better for Sequences 6 and Sequence 7 (significantly). Sequence 8 has a very symmetrical optimal conformation that, as argued in [9], would be difficult to find for any chain growth algorithm; our ACO algorithm is able to handle it quite well, since a number of ants folding from different starting points can produce good folding motives with respect to various starting folding points. For the longest sequences (85 and 100 amino acids), our algorithm finds high quality configurations, but does not reach the solution quality obtained by PERM.

5 Conclusions and Future Work

In this paper we introduced an improved ACO algorithm for the 2D HP Protein Folding Problem that has shown promising performance for an extremely simplified but widely studied and computationally hard protein structure prediction problem. An empirical study of our algorithm demonstrated the effectiveness of the improved ACO approach for solving this problem and highlighted the impact of its new features, including long range moves, improving ants, and selective local search. Long range moves in combination with the non-greedy local search performed by improving ants allows for the relaxation of compact conformations, which helps the search to escape from local optima encountered by greedy local search. Selective local search reduces the time complexity of the local search phase by performing this time critical operation only on promising, low energy conformations (which provide the best starting points for the optimisation *via* local search).

In general, we expect that the improvements introduced in this work for an ACO algorithm for the 2D HP Protein Folding Problem can be utilised for solving more traditional artificial intelligence problems (such as constraint satisfaction problems [18]). For example, the use of improving ants provides a general means of intensifying the search around high quality solutions, while long range moves in local search can be useful for escaping from local optima by considering higher order neighbourhoods relevant to the particular problem.

There are many directions for future research on ACO algorithms for protein folding problems. It might be fruitful to consider ACO approaches based on more complex solution components than the simple local structure motifs used here. Furthermore, separate pheromone matrices could be used for independently reinforcing secondary and tertiary interactions. Finally, it would be interesting to develop and study ACO algorithms for other types of protein folding problems, such as the 3-dimensional HP model [4].

Overall, we strongly believe that ACO algorithms offer considerable potential for solving protein structure prediction problems robustly and efficiently and that further work in this area should be undertaken.

Acknowledgements

This work has been supported by an NSERC Postgraduate Scholarship (PGS-A) to AS and by HH's NSERC Individual Research Grant #238788. We thank Peter Grassberger for kindly providing us with his PERM implementation.

References

[1] Bastolla U., H. Frauenkron, E. Gestner, P. Grassberger, and W. Nadler. *Testing a new Monte Carlo algorithm for the protein folding problem.* Proteins: Structure, Function & Genetics 32 (1): 52-66, 1998.

[2] Beutler T., and K. Dill. *A fast conformational search strategy for finding low energy structures of model proteins.* Protein Science 5: 2037–2043, 1996.

[3] Chikenji G., M. Kikuchi, and Y. Iba. *Multi-Self-Overlap Ensemble for protein folding: ground state search and thermodynamics.* Phys. Rev. Let. 83(9): 1886–1889, 1999.

[4] Dill, K. A., S. Bornberg, K. Yue, K. Fiebig, D. Yee, P. Thomas, and H. Chan. *Principles of protein folding - a perspective from simple exact models.* Protein Science, 4: 561-602, 1995.

[5] Dorigo, M., V. Maniezzo, and A. Colorni. Positive feedback as a search strategy. Technical Report 91–016, Dip. Elettronica, Politecnico di Milano, Italy, 1991.

[6] Dorigo, M. and G. Di Caro. The ant colony optimization meta-heuristic. In D. Corne, M. Dorigo, and F. Glover, eds., *New Ideas in Optimization*, pp. 11–32. McGraw-Hill, 1999.

[7] Dorigo, M., G. Di Caro and L. M. Gambardella. *Ant Algorithms for Discrete Optimization.* Artificial Life 5(2): 137–172, 1999.

[8] Hoos, H. H., and T. Stützle. *On the empirical evaluation of Las Vegas algorithms.* Proc. of UAI-98, Morgan Kaufmann Publishers, 1998.

[9] Hsu, H. P., V. Mehra, W. Nadler, and P. Grassberger. *Growth Algorithm for Lattice Heteropolymers at Low Temperatures.* e-print cond-mat/0208042, 2002.

[10] Konig, R., and T. Dandekar. *Improving genetic algorithms for protein folding simulations by systematic crossover.* BioSystems 50: 17–25, 1999.

[11] Krasnogor, N., W. E. Hart. J. Smith, and D. A. Pelta. *Protein structure prediction with evolutionary algorithms.* Proceedings of the Genetic & Evolut. Comput. Conf., 1999.

[12] Lau, K. F., and K. A. Dill. *A lattice statistical mechanics model of the conformation and sequence space of proteins.* Macromolecules 22: 3986–3997, 1989.

[13] Liang F., and W. H. Wong. *Evolutionary Monte Carlo for protein folding simulations.* J. Chem. Phys. 115 (7): 3374–3380, 2001.

[14] Ramakrishnan R., B. Ramachandran, and J. F. Pekny. *A dynamic Monte Carlo algorithm for exploration of dense conformational spaces in heteropolymers.* J. Chem. Phys. 106 (6): 2418–2424,1997.

[15] Richards, F. M. *Areas, volumes, packing, and protein structures.* Annu. Rev. Biophys. Bioeng. 6: 151–176, 1977.

[16] Rose, G. D. *Hierarchic organization of domains in globular proteins.* J. Mol. Biol. 134: 447–470, 1979.

[17] Sali, A., E. Shakhnovich and M. Karplus. *How Does a Protein Fold?* Nature, 369: 248–251, May 1994.

[18] Solnon, C. *Ants Can Solve Constraint Satisfaction Problems.* IEEE Transactions on Evolut. Comput., 6 (4): 347-357, August 2002.

[19] Shmygelska, A., R. Hernandez and H. H. Hoos. *An Ant Colony Algorithm for the 2D HP Protein Folding Problem.* In Proc. of ANTS 2002, LNCS, Vol. 2463,p. 40.

[20] Unger, R., and J. Moult. *A genetic algorithm for three dimensional protein folding simulations.* In Proc. 5th Intl. Conf. on Genetic Algorithms, pp. 581–588, 1993.

[21] Unger, R., and J. Moult. *Genetic algorithms for protein folding simulations.* J. of Mol. Biol. 231 (1): 75–81, 1993.

Hybrid Randomised Neighbourhoods Improve Stochastic Local Search for DNA Code Design

Dan C. Tulpan and Holger H. Hoos*

Department of Computer Science, University of British Columbia
Vancouver, B.C., V6T 1Z4, Canada
{dctulpan,hoos}@cs.ubc.ca
http://www.cs.ubc.ca/labs/beta

Abstract. Sets of DNA strands that satisfy combinatorial constraints play an important role in various approaches to biomolecular computation, nanostructure design, and molecular tagging. The problem of designing such sets of DNA strands, also known as the DNA code design problem, appears to be computationally hard. In this paper, we show how a recently proposed stochastic local search algorithm for DNA code design can be improved by using hybrid, randomised neighbourhoods. This new type of neighbourhood structure equally supports small changes to a given candidate set of strands as well as much larger modifications, which correspond to random, long range connections in the search space induced by the standard (1-mutation) neighbourhood. We report several cases in which our algorithm finds word sets that match or exceed the best previously known constructions.

1 Introduction

DNA codes, *i.e.*, sets of DNA strands that satisfy combinatorial constraints, play an important role in various approaches to biomolecular computation [7, 8], nanostructure design [16, 18], and molecular tagging [1, 2, 6]. Good code design is important in order to minimise errors due to non-specific hybridization between distinct strands and their complements, to obtain a higher information density, and to obtain large sets of strands for large-scale applications.

For the types of combinatorial constraints typically desired, there are no known efficient algorithms for DNA code design. Techniques from coding theory have been applied to the design of DNA codes [2, 8]; while valuable, this approach is hampered by the complexity of the combinatorial constraints on the sets of DNA strands ("code words"), which are often hard to reason about theoretically. For these reasons, heuristic approaches such as stochastic local search offer much promise in design of DNA codes.

Stochastic local search (SLS) algorithms strongly use randomised decisions while searching for solutions to a given problem. They play an increasingly important role for solving hard combinatorial problems from various domains of

* To whom correspondence should be addressed.

Y. Xiang and B. Chaib-draa (Eds.): AI 2003, LNAI 2671, pp. 418–433, 2003.

Artificial Intelligence and Operations Research, such as satisfiability, constraint satisfaction, planning, and scheduling. Over the past few years there has been considerable success in developing stochastic local search algorithms as well as randomised systematic search methods for solving these problems, and to date, stochastic search algorithms are amongst the best known techniques for solving problems from many domains. Detailed empirical studies are crucial for the analysis and development of such high-performance stochastic search techniques.

Stochastic search methods have already been applied to the design of DNA codes. Deaton *et al.* [3, 4] and Zhang and Shin [19] used genetic algorithms for designing DNA codes, and provide some small sets of code words that satisfy well-motivated combinatorial constraints. However, some details of their algorithms are not specified in these papers. Faulhammer *et al.* [6] also use a stochastic search approach and provide an implementation of their algorithm. In all cases, while small sets of code words produced by the algorithms have been presented (and the papers make other contributions independent of the word design algorithms), little or no analysis of algorithm performance is provided. As a result it is not possible to extract general insights on the design of stochastic algorithms for DNA code design or to do detailed comparisons of their approaches with other algorithms. Our goal is to understand which algorithmic principles are most effective in the application of SLS methods to the design of DNA or RNA word sets (and more generally, codes over other alphabets, particularly the binary alphabet).

Our previous work [17] presents results on the performance of a new SLS algorithm for the design of DNA codes fulfilling different combinations of combinatorial constraints, the same as the ones described in Section 2. In that work, we reported empirical results that characterised performance of the SLS algorithm and indicated its ability to find high-quality sets of DNA codes.

In this paper, we describe an improved version of the simple stochastic local search algorithm for DNA code design presented in [17]. In particular, we describe how by using hybrid randomised neighbourhoods, substantial performance improvements can be achieved. To our best knowledge, this type of neighbourhood has not been previously described and may well be applicable to SLS algorithms for other problems.

In this study, we have chosen to design word sets that fullfil the following three constraints: Hamming distance (**HD**), GC content (**GC**), and reverse complement Hamming distance (**RC**). We define these constraints precisely in Section 2. Our reason for considering these constraints is that there are already some constructions for word sets satisfying these constraints, obtained using both theoretical and experimental methods, with which we can compare our results.

Our algorithm, described in detail in Section 4, performs local search in a space of DNA codes of fixed size (= number of strands) that may violate the given constraints. The underlying search strategy is based on a combination of randomised iterative improvement and conflict-directed random walk. The basic algorithm is initialised with a randomly selected set of DNA words. Then, repeatedly a conflict, that is, a pair of words that violates a constraint, is selected and resolved by modifying one of the respective words. The modification step is based on different neighbourhoods which will be further described in Section 4. The algorithm terminates when a set of DNA strands that satisfies all given constraints is found, or after a specified number of iterations has been completed.

The performance of this algorithm is primarily controlled by a so-called noise parameter that determines the probability of greedy vs. random conflict resolution. Optimal settings for this parameter have been reported in [17] and we will show how these are affected by different choices of neighbourhoods.

Our empirical results, reported in Section 5, show that compared to our previous, simple SLS algorithm, our new SLS algorithm shows dramatically improved performance on hard DNA code design problems. In particular, by empirically analysing its run-time distributions, we show that for DNA code design problems studied in [17], the new algorithm does not suffer from the previously reported severe stagnation behaviour.

We compared the sizes of the word sets obtainable by our algorithm with previously known word sets, starting with the previously studied case of word sets that satisfy all three constraints. Out of a total of 30 comparisons with previous results (see Tables 1 and 2), we found word sets that equal or improved on previous constructions in all but one case. In this particular case, while our algorithm was not able to meet the previous best construction when starting from a random initial set of words, we were still able to improve on the best previous construction by initializing our algorithm with the best previously known word set plus additional random words.

2 Problem Description

The DNA code design problem that we consider is: given a target k and word length n, find a set of k DNA words, each of length n, satisfying certain combinatorial constraints. A DNA word of length n is simply a string of length n over the alphabet $\{A, C, G, T\}$, and naturally corresponds to a DNA strand with left end of the string corresponding to the 5' end of the DNA strand. We consider the following constraints:

- **Hamming Distance Constraint (HD):** For all pairs of distinct words w_1, w_2 in the set, $H(w_1,w_2) \geq d$. Here, $H(w_1,w_2)$ represents the Hamming distance between words w_1 and w_2, namely the number of positions i at which the ith letter in w_1 differs from the ith letter in w_2.
- **GC Content Constraint (GC):** A fixed percentage of the letters within each word is either G or C. Throughout, we assume that this percentage is 50%.
- **Reverse Complement Hamming Distance Constraint (RC):** For all pairs of DNA words w_1 and w_2 in the set, where w_1 may equal w_2, $H(w_1,wcc(w_2)) \geq d$. Here, $wcc(w)$ denotes the Watson-Crick complement of DNA word w, obtained by reversing w and then by replacing each A in w by T and vice versa, and replacing each C in w by G and vice versa.

Motivation for considering these constraints can be found in many sources; see for example Frutos *et al.* [8].

The total number of code words of length n defined over any quaternary alphabet is 4^n. The number of possible word sets of size k that can be formed with 4^n code words is:

$$\binom{4^n}{k} = \frac{(4^n)!}{k! \times (4^n - k)!}$$

For the particular example of code words with $n = 8$ and $k = 100$, the number of all possible word sets is approximately 1.75×10^{267}. The huge number of possible sets that must be explored in order to find a big set of words suggests the use of non-exhaustive search algorithms for solving this type of problems. One class of such methods are stochastic local search algorithms and they have been used with success for many years in code design as well as in other combinatorics areas [11].

3 Related Work

Stochastic search methods have been used successfully for decades in the construction of good binary codes [5, 10]. Typically, the focus of this work is in finding codes of size greater than the best previously known bound, and a detailed empirical analysis of the search algorithms is not presented.

Deaton *et al.* [3, 4] and Zhang and Shin [19] describe genetic algorithms for finding DNA codes that satisfy much stronger constraints than the HD and RC constraints, in which "frame shifts" are taken into account. However, they do not provide a detailed analysis of the performance of their algorithms. Hartemink *et al.* [9] used an algorithm for designing word sets that satisfy yet other constraints, in which a large pool (several billion) of strands were screened in order to determine whether they meet the constraints. Several other researchers have used computational methods to generate word sets (see for example [1]), but provide no details on their algorithms. Some DNA code design programs are publicly available. The DNASequenceGenerator program [15, 7] designs DNA sequences that satisfy certain subword distance constraints and, in addition, have melting temperature or GC content within prescribed ranges. The program can generate DNA sequences *de novo*, or integrate partially specified words or existing words into the set. The PERMUTE program was used to design the sequences of Faulhammer *et al.* [6] for their RNA-based 10-variable computation.

4 The Improved Stochastic Local Search Algorithm

Our basic stochastic local search algorithm, which is subject to further improvement and development, performs local search in a space of code word sets of fixed size which violate the given constraints. Figure 1 shows the outline of the simple SLS algorithm as described in [17].

The underlying search strategy is based on a combination of randomised iterative improvement and conflict-directed random walk. The search is initialised

```
procedure StochasticLocalSearch for DNA Code Design
  input: Number of words (k), word length (n), set of combinatorial constraints (C)
  output: Set S of m words that fully or partially satisfies C
  for i := 1 to maxTries do
     S := initial set of words
     Ŝ := S
     for j := 1 to maxSteps do
        if S satisfies all constraints then
           return S
        end if
        Randomly select words w1, w2 ∈ S that violate one of the constraints
        M := N(w1) ∪ N(w2), i.e. all words from the neighbourhoods of w1 and w2
        with probability θ do
           select word w' from M uniformly at random
        otherwise
           select word w' from M such that
           number of constraint violations in S is maximally decreased
        end with probability
        if w' ∈ N(w1) then
           replace w1 by w' in S
        else
           replace w2 by w' in S
        end if
        if S has no more constraint violations than Ŝ then
           Ŝ := S;
        end if
     end for
  end for
  return Ŝ
end StochasticLocalSearch for DNA Code Design
```

Fig. 1. Outline of the stochastic local search procedure for DNA code design; $\mathcal{N}(w)$ denotes the neighbourhood of code word w

with a randomly selected set of DNA strands. Then, repeatedly a conflict, that is, a pair of words that violates a constraint, is selected and resolved by modifying one of the respective words. The selection process for conflicting code words is done uniformly at random from the pool of candidate code words involved in one or more conflicts. The modification process is based on replacing a code words w that is currently involved in a conflict, with a new code word w' chosen from a pool of related DNA words called the neighbourhood of w. With probability $(1-\theta)$, we select w' such that the number of conflicts in the set of code words, S, is maximally reduced; otherwise we select a neighbour of w uniformly at random. (θ is a parameter of our algorithm.) Here, we propose different types of neighbourhoods (mostly based on randomisation), which lead to performance improvements of the basic SLS algorithm. If after a user specified number of steps no valid code (*i.e.*, set of DNA words satisfying all given constraints) has been found, the search process is re-initialised and new attempt at finding a solution is made (outer loop in Figure 1). The algorithm terminates when a valid code is found, or a given number of unsuccessful tries have been completed.

It should be noted that our algorithm considers only words with the prescribed GC content during the search, and the neighbourhoods are restricted accordingly. In this paper, we consider the following neighbourhoods:

ν-Mutation Neighbourhood. The ν-mutation neighbourhood of a given code word w_0 consists of all code words that can be obtained from w_0 by modifying up to ν bases, except w_0 itself. Our previous SLS algorithm was based on the 1-mutation neighbourhood; for a given pair of code words of length n (as considered in each step of our algorithm), there are $2 \times n$ 1-mutation neighbours that fulfill the GC constraint. The 3-mutation neigbourhood of a pair of code words, in contrast, consists of $n \times (n \times n + 5)/3$ code words satisfying the GC content constraint.

Pure Random Neighbourhoods. Another simple way of defining the neighbourhood of a given word w is by choosing a fixed number of random code words with the same length and GC-content as w. Note that this pure random neighbourhood will differ between search steps in which the same w is chosen. This type of neighbourhood increases the mobility of the algorithm within the search space and supports search steps that are equivalent to several search steps in a ν-neighbourhood with small ν. Somewhat surprisingly, using this rather simplistic neighbourhood mechanism leads to substantial improvements in the performance of our algorithm, as we will document in Section 5.

Hybrid Randomised Neighbourhoods. These are obtained by adding elements of the pure random neighbourhood to a ν-mutation neighbourhood. This effectively enables the algorithm to explore regions of the search space that could not be reached easily using pure ν-mutation neighbourhoods, while still keeping the search focussed on local regions of the space of candidate sets of code words. The additional randomisation of the search achieved by adding random code words to the set of ν-mutation neighbours enhances the ability of the SLS algorithm to escape from local minima regions and eventually find solutions faster. As our empirical results show, this novel type of neighbourhood leads to substantial improvements in the performance of our SLS algorithm.

In the next section we will discuss the impact of these neighbourhoods on the performance of our SLS algorithm for DNA code design. In particular, we will see that the use of randomised neighbourhoods helps to avoid search stagnation and allows the algorithm to find bigger DNA codes.

5 Results and Discussion

To evaluate the performance of our improved SLS algorithm, we performed two types of computational experiments. First, detailed analyses of the run-time and run-length distributions (RTDs and RLDs) of our algorithm on individual problem instances were used to study the behaviour of the algorithm and the impact of parameter settings. For these empirical analyses, the methodology of [12] for measuring and analysing RTDs and RLDs was used. Run-length was measured in terms of search steps, and absolute CPU time per search step was measured to obtain a cost model of these search steps. Then, in a second type of

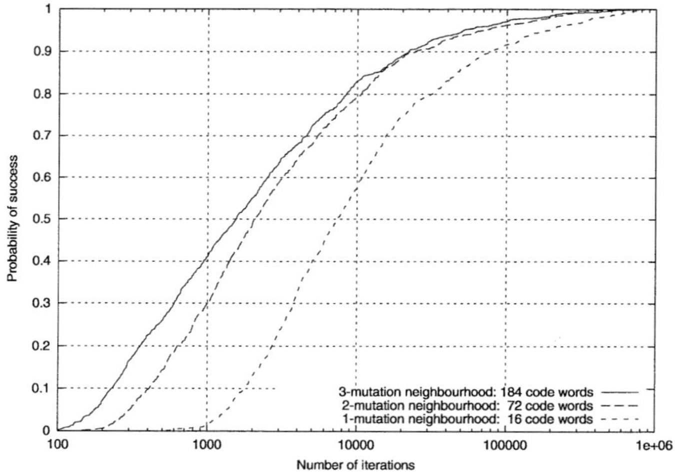

Fig. 2. RLDs for different ν-mutation neighbourhoods, set size $k = 70$, word length $n = 8$, Hamming distance $d = 4$, all 3 constraints

experiment, we used the optimised parameter settings obtained from the detailed analyses for obtaining DNA code sets of maximal size for various word lengths and combinatorial constraints.

5.1 Neighbourhoods

To study and characterise the behaviour of the new proposed neighbourhood mechanisms for the simple SLS algorithm, we measured RTDs and RLDs from 1000 successful runs of the algorithm applied to a representative problem instance with set size $k = 70$, words length $n = 8$, Hamming distance $d = 4$ and all 3 constraints (HD, RC, and GC). Experiments with other problem instances gave analogous results (not reported here) to the ones observed for this instance. Using extremely high settings of the cutoff parameter ensured us that a solution was found in each individual run without using random restarts. For each neighbourhood, we performed a number of independent runs of the algoritm in which we measured the number of search iterations required for finding a solution. The empirical run-length distribution that can be easily obtained from this data gives the probability of finding a solution as a function of the number of search iterations performed. Run-time distributions are obtained by multiplying the number of search steps represented in the respective RLD with the corresponding CPU time per step.

ν-Mutation Neighbourhoods. The 1-mutation neighbourhood has been successfully used in the simple version of the SLS algorithm described in [17]. While one would expect that using ν-mutation neighbourhoods with $\nu > 1$ decreases the number of search steps required for finding certain word sets, it is not clear whether the increased computational cost of scanning these larger neighbourhoods can be amortised. Figure 2 shows RLDs for different types of ν-mutation neighbourhoods for the problem instance described above. The time required for obtaining a set of words of size $k = 70$ with a fixed probability p increases with ν and p. For high p, this increase is much more dramatic than for low p values. The right 'fat' tails of the RLDs emphasise this phenomenon. As can be seen from Figure 3, the higher time complexity of the search steps using ν-mutation neighbourhoods with $\nu > 1$ is not amortised by the reduction in the number of search steps. Similar results were obtained for other problem instances.

Pure Random Neighbourhoods. Interestingly, using pure random neighbourhoods leads to better performance of our algorithm than any of the ν-mutation neighbourhoods. For our representative problem instance, this can be seen when comparing the medians of the RTDs for ν-mutation neighbourhoods in Figure 3 with the median run-times for pure random neighourhoods for varying sizes shown in Figure 6. At the same time, using pure random neighbourhoods leads to RTDs that do not have the same "fat" right tails that indicated the stagnation behaviour of our SLS algorithm for the ν-mutation neighbourhoods. This leads to even more substantial performance advantages of pure random neighbourhoods over the ν-mutation neighbourhoods when comparing the mean CPU times for solving a given problem instance or high percentiles of the respective RTDs.

When varying the size of the pure random neighbourhoods, *i.e.*, the number of code words considered for replacing a given word in a candidate word set, we found that typically there is an optimal range of neighbourhood sizes. When using smaller neighbourhoods, the performance of the algorithm decreases since intuitively a higher number of "shorter" search steps is required for covering the same distance in the search space (*e.g.*, to the nearest solution). For larger neighbourhoods, the time complexity for each search step increases, and at some point the reduction in the number of search steps required for finding a solution no longer amortises this higher cost. This is illustrated for our representative problem instance in Figure 6.

Hybrid Neighbourhoods. We noticed that adding random code words to ν-mutation neighbourhoods leads to improved performance of our SLS algorithm. This raises the following question: is there any reason to keep the ν-mutation neighbourhood as part of a bigger, hybrid randomised neighbourhood?

We investigated this question in an experiment in which we compared three hybrid neighbourhoods of 200 words that include the 1-mutation, 2-mutation, and 3-mutation neighbours of a given word, respectively, as well as a purely random neighbourhood of size 200. From Figures 4 and 5 we can see that for our representative problem instance, including the 1-mutation neighbourhood

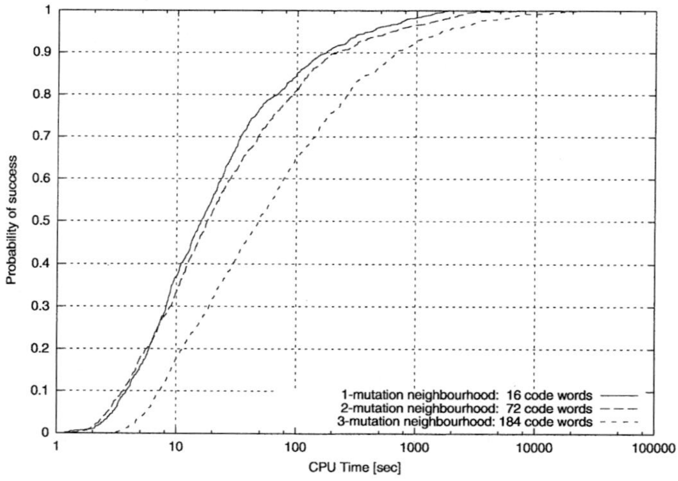

Fig. 3. RTDs for different ν-mutation neighbourhoods, set size $k = 70$, word length $n = 8$, Hamming distance $d = 4$, all 3 constraints

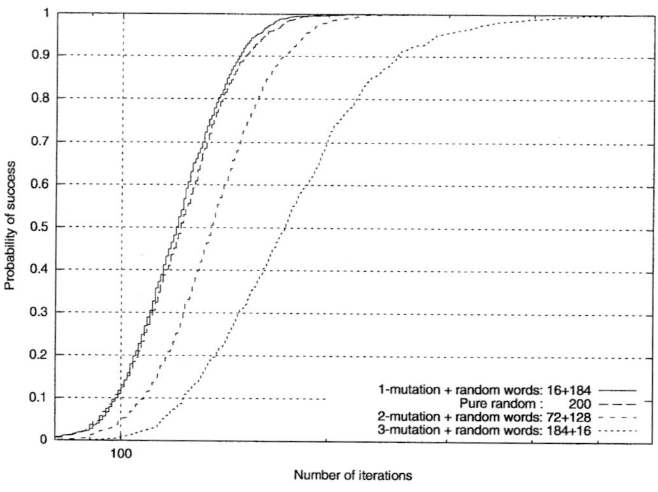

Fig. 4. RLDs for pure random and hybrid neighbourhoods of size 200, set size $k = 70$, word length $n = 8$, Hamming distance $d = 4$, all 3 constraints

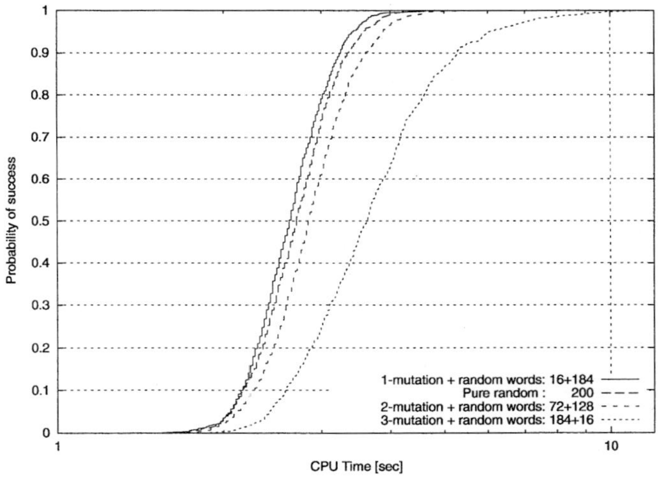

Fig. 5. RTDs for pure random and hybrid neighbourhoods of size 200, set size $k = 70$, word length $n = 8$, Hamming distance $d = 4$, all 3 constraints

in a bigger, hybrid randomised neighbourhood results in slight performance improvements in terms of iterations as well as CPU time, while including the 2- or 3-mutation neighbourhoods is disadvantageous.

In a second experiment we tested whether this result also holds for different neighbourhood sizes. As can be seen from Figure 6, hybrid neighbourhoods obtained by adding random neighbours to the 1-mutation neighbourhood generally leads to improved performance compared to using pure random neighbourhoods of the same size. One intuitive explanation for the efficiency of using hybrid neighbourhoods is based on the fact that 1-mutation neighbours can be easily mutated back into the original word. This mechanism allows the algorithm to easily and cheaply reverse problematic search steps that, *e.g.*, lead into a local minimum of the underlying search space.

Further experiments have been performed for different (k, n, d) combinations (*e.g.*, (102,10,5), (10,10,7), (15,12,8), (25,6,3)) as well as for different set sizes and GC content fractions (*e.g.*, $k = 56$ and GC-content $= 3$, $k = 28$ and GC-content $= 2$, and $k = 8$ and GC-content $= 1$). Our algorithm found solutions faster when we used hybrid neighbourhoods than when using pure random neighbourhoods, considering the total size of the neighbourhood as being fixed in both cases. The CPU time per step is roughly the same for hybrid and pure random neighbourhoods of the same size, but when using the hybrid neighbourhood, a smaller number of steps is required for reaching the same solution quality than when using pure random neighbourhoods. Overall, in all the cases we examined, using hybrid neighbourhoods consisting of all 1-mutation neighbours and additional random code words lead to better performance than using pure random or ν-mutation neighbourhoods.

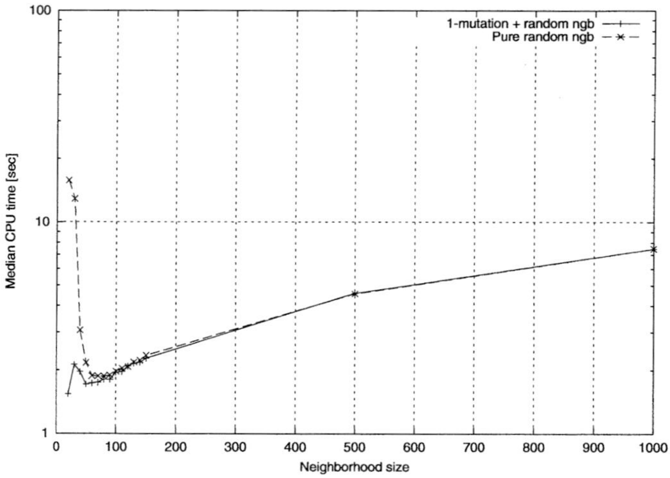

Fig. 6. Median number of CPU seconds for different neighbourhood sizes, set size $k = 70$, word length $n = 8$, Hamming distance $d = 4$, GC-content = 50%, all 3 constraints

5.2 Noise Parameter

Introducing noise in the simple SLS algorithm, *i.e.*, using probabilistic moves when taking decisions, provides robustness to the algorithm and allows it to escape from local minima. Using the previous 1-mutation neighbourhood, we found an optimal setting for this noise parameter θ around 0.2 (Figure 7) for different problem instances and sizes, as described in [17]. When considering randomised neighbourhoods, the optimal value for the noise parameter appears to be 0 as can be seen in Figure 8.

One possible explanation for this phenomenon may reside in the added need of greediness in the search algorithm when searching bigger neighbourhoods. Furthermore, the additional diversification provided by random neighbours can apparently compensate and even substitute for the effect of the noise mechanism – both provide mechanisms for escaping from local optima in the underlying search space.

5.3 New DNA Codes and Empirical Bounds

After studying the impact of neighbourhood type and size as well as the noise parameter setting, we used the enhanced SLS algorithm (based on hybrid randomised neighbourhoods) to solve a number of challenging instances of our DNA code design problem.

For the DNA code design problem with all three constraints (HD, GC, RC) and 50% GC-content, we compared the sizes of the word sets obtained with our

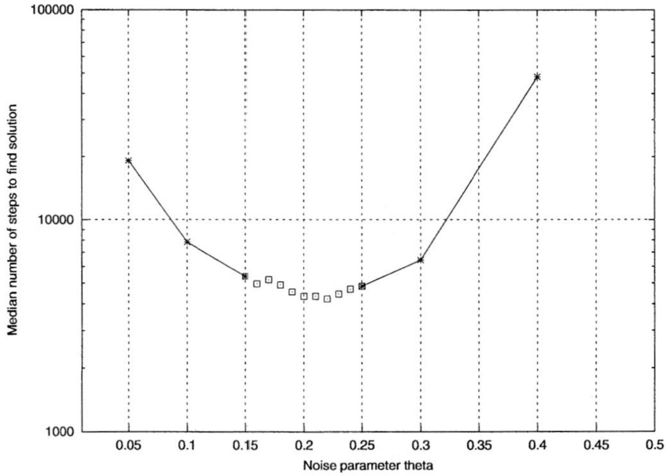

Fig. 7. Median number of iterations as a function of noise parameter values: 1-mutation neighbourhood, all three constraints, $n = 8$, $d = 4$, and $k = 70$

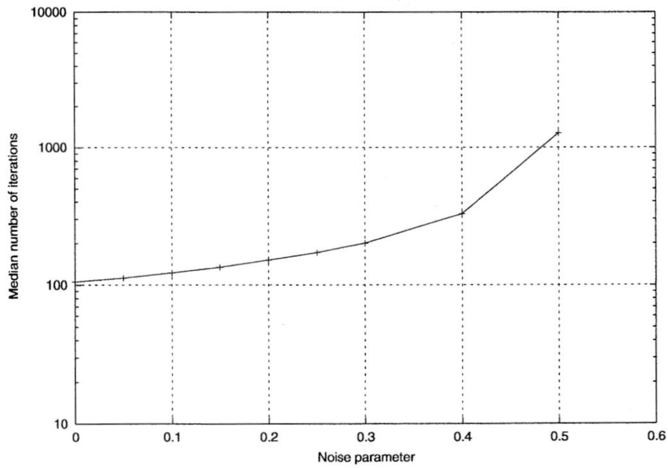

Fig. 8. Number of iterations as a function of noise parameter values: hybrid neighbourhood, all three constraints, $n = 8$, $d = 4$, and $k = 70$

new SLS algorithm with previously known word sets [17]. Out of a total of 31 comparisons with previous results (see Tables 1 and 2), we found word sets that equal or improved on previous constructions in all but one case. In this particular case ($n = 8$ and $d = 4$), we obtained a code of size 107 when initialising the search with a random set of code words. This is a substantial improvement over our simple SLS algorithm, which only found codes sizes of 92. However, for the same

Table 1. Set sizes for **(HD, RC, GC)** DNA codes obtained with the simple SLS algorithm presented in [17]. 1-mutation neighbourhood have been used for all the results. The numbers in square brackets represent the average number of iterations spent by the algorithm to obtain the set with the specified size

n/d	2	3	4	5	6	7	8	9	10
4	20 [.03k]	5 [.02k]	2 [.001k]	-	-	-	-	-	-
6	282 [1k]	37 [19k]	11 [3k]	2 [.003k]	2 [.006k]	-	-	-	-
8	3981 [20k]	350 [119k]	92* [4000k]	19 [1.2k]	7 [10k]	2 [.01k]	2 [.02k]	-	-
10	X	3700 [287k]	640 [406k]	127 [170.5k]	37 [38k]	11 [134k]	5 [1.3k]	2 [.02]	1 [.005k]
12	X	X	5685 [455k]	933 [531k]	210 [121.5k]	59 [77k]	21 [217k]	9 [341.5k]	3 [1.5k]

Table 2. Set sizes for **(HD, RC, GC)** DNA codes obtained with the improved SLS Algorithm. 1-mutation+random code words neighbourhoods have been used. The number of random code words used here are $\{10, 100, 1000, 5000\}$. For $n = 8$, $d = 4$ we found a better bound, namely 112 code words by initializing our algorithm with the best previously known word set (108 code words) plus an additional random word. Bold-face numbers represent improved set sizes compared with the previous ones obtained in [17]. The numbers in square brackets represent the average number of iterations spent by the algorithm to obtain the set with the specified size

n/d	2	3	4	5	6	7	8	9	10
4	**24** [.03k]	**6** [.01k]	2 [.001k]	-	-	-	-	-	-
6	**310** [.7k]	**41** [1.5k]	**15** [.3k]	**4** [.005k]	2 [.002k]	-	-	-	-
8	**4022** [16.7k]	**390** [3.4k]	**107*** [40k]	**26** [64k]	**12** [4.8k]	2 [.002k]	2 [.002k]	-	-
10	X	**4007** [25.7k]	**790** [9.4k]	**158** [2k]	**41** [1.2k]	**15** [.6k]	**6** [2.6k]	2 [.002]	**2** [.002k]
12	X	X	**6100** [256k]	**988** [23.3k]	**240** [3.1k]	**70** [1.7k]	**25** [1.2k]	9 [3.2k]	**4** [.2k]

case, Frutos *et al.* [8] constructed a set of 108 words. But even with our simple algorithm we have obtained sets of 112 code words by initialising the search with the best known set containing 108 code words and by iteratively expanding this set with one additional code word at a time (initialised at random) [17]. The same code size of 112 is also achieved by our new SLS algorithm with randomised neighbourhoods. It may be noted that Frutos *et al.* used a theoretical approach to design the 108 set. Their map-template construction relies on symmetries and other mathematical properties of this specific code design problem and, different from our SLS algorithm, it cannot be used for iteratively improving or expanding a given code.

It may be noted that, to our best knowledge, there are no theoretical bounds for DNA codes fulfilling the HD, RC, and GC constraints known from the literature. Some theoretical upper and lower bounds have been published by Marathe *et al.* [14] for codes satisfying the HD and RC constraints. We compared our results with their bounds, keeping also in mind that our codes have a fixed GC content. For the $(n, d) = (8, 4)$ case, our best result (code size 112) is quite close to the lower bound of 128 from Marathe *et al.*, but of course it is not clear whether that bound applies for codes that additionally have to satisfy the 50% GC content constraint we used. In other situations, our results improved on the Marthe *et al.* bounds. For example, for $(n, d) = (10, 5)$, their lower bound is 32 code words, while our simple and enhanced SLS algorithm reach code sizes of 127 and 158, respectively. It is also worth noting in most cases, the ranges between the theoretical lower and upper bounds from Marateh *et al.* are very large. For example, for the (10,5) case, the the upper bound is 1202, compared to a lower bound of 32. This provides some indication that there might be room for substantial improvements in the code sizes achievable for these and related code design problems.

Finally, it is worth mentioning that based on a very limited initial investigation, our new SLS algorithm based on randomised neighbourhoods achieves performance improvements similar to the ones reported here for the (HD, GC, RC) constraint combination for other code design problems that include the GC content constraint (*e.g.*, HD and GC constraints). We are currently performing an in-depth analysis of our algorithm's performance on these closely related code design problems, the results of which we plan to present in the near future.

6 Conclusions

We presented an improved version of the simple SLS algorithm for DNA Code Design proposed in [17], based on a new neighbourhood generation mechanism, along with empirical results that characterise its performance. New insights on the role of the neighbourhood type and size have been described and we showed evidence that by using hybrid randomised neighbourhoods, the performance of our original SLS algorithm can be significantly improved. Intuitively, the use of randomised ν-mutation neighbourhoods enhances the ability of the SLS algorithm to escape from local minima regions, and facilitates the exploration of regions in the underlying search space that are very far apart with respect to the traditional 1-mutation neighbourhood.

In future work, we plan to examine further ways for improving the algorithm. The existing theoretical bounds on combinations of constraints (see Section 5.3) similar to the ones considered here, indicate that there should be sustantial room for further improvements. One possibility to improve the SLS algorithm is to consider more complex SLS strategies, which are expected to achieve improved performance that hopefully will lead to larger word sets. In another direction of future work, we plan to use hybrid randomised neighbourhood mechanisms for DNA code design problems with different constraint combinations as well as for the design of binary codes.

Search space analysis may provide more insight on the hidden mechanisms that make it difficult to computationally solve DNA code design problems and shed more light on the precise reasons for the efficiency of the hybrid neighbourhoods studied here. Finally, it would be interesting to see if better theoretical design principles can be extracted from the codes that are empirically obtained from high-performance SLS algorithms for DNA code design.

Acknowledgments

This work has been supported by NSERC Individual Research Grant #238788; it builds on previous research in collaboration with Anne Condon, who also provided valuable feedback on the ideas presented here.

References

[1] R. S. Braich, C. Johnson, P. W. K. Rothemund, D. Hwang, N. Chelyapov, and L. M. Adleman, "Solution of a satisfiability problem on a gel-based DNA computer", Preliminary Proc. Sixth International Meeting on DNA Based Computers, Leiden, The Netherlands, June, 2000.

[2] S. Brenner and R. A. Lerner, "Encoded combinatorial chemistry", Proc. Natl. Acad. Sci. USA, Vol 89, pages 5381–5383, June 1992.

[3] R. Deaton, R. C. Murphy, M. Garzon, D. R. Franceschetti, and S. E. Stevens, Jr., "Good encodings for DNA-based solutions to combinatorial problems," Proc. DNA Based Computers II, DIMACS Workshop June 10-12, 1996, L. F. Landweber and E. B. Baum, Editors, DIMACS Series in Discrete Mathematics and Theoretical Computer Science, Vol. 44, pages 247–258, 1999.

[4] R. Deaton, M. Garzon, R. C. Murphy, J. A. Rose, D. R. Franceschetti, and S. E. Stevens, Jr., "Genetic search of reliable encodings for DNA-based computation," Koza, John R., Goldberg, David E., Fogel, David B., and Riolo, Rick L. (editors), Proceedings of the First Annual Conference on Genetic Programming 1996.

[5] A. A. El Gamal, L. A. Hemachandra, I. Shperling, and V. K. Wei, "Using simulated annealing to design good codes," IEEE Transactions on Information Theory, Vol. IT-33, No. 1, January 1987.

[6] D. Faulhammer, A. R. Cukras, R. J. Lipton, and L. F. Landweber, "Molecular computation: RNA solutions to chess problems," Proc. Natl. Acad. Sci. USA, 97: 1385-1389, 2000.

[7] U. Feldkamp, W. Banzhaf, H. Rauhe, "A DNA sequence compiler," Poster presented at the 6th International Meeting on DNA Based Computers, Leiden, June, 2000. See also http://ls11-www.cs.uni-dortmund.de/molcomp/Publications/publications.html (visited November 11, 2000).

[8] A. G. Frutos, Q. Liu, A. J. Thiel, A. M. W. Sanner, A. E. Condon, L. M. Smith, and R. M. Corn, "Demonstration of a word design strategy for DNA computing on surfaces," Nucleic Acids Research, Vol. 25, No. 23, pages 4748-4757, December 1997.

[9] A. J. Hartemink, D. K. Gifford, and J. Khodor, "Automated constraint-based nucleotide sequence selection for DNA computation," 4th Annual DIMACS Workshop on DNA-Based Computers, Philadelphia, Pennsylvania, June 1998.

[10] I. S. Honkala, and P. R. J. Ostergard, "Code design," In Local Search In Combinatorial Optimization (E. Aarts and J. K. Lenstra, eds.), Wiley-Interscience Series in Discrete Mathematics and Optimization, 1997.

[11] H. H. Hoos, "Stochastic Local Search - Methods, Models, Applications", infix-Verlag, Sankt Augustin, Germany, ISBN 3-89601-215-0, 1999.

[12] H. H. Hoos and T. Stützle, "Evaluating Las Vegas Algorithms — Pitfalls and Remedies," In *Proceedings of the Fourteenth Conference on Uncertainty in Artificial Intelligence (UAI-98)*, pages 238-245, 1998.

[13] M. Li, H-J. Lee, A. E. Condon, and R. M. Corn, "DNA Word Design Strategy for Creating Sets of Non-interacting Oligonucleotides for DNA Microarrays," Langmuir, 18, pages 805-812, 2002.

[14] A. Marathe, A. Condon, and R. Corn, "On combinatorial DNA word design," J. Computational Biology, 8:3, pages 201-220, 2001.

[15] Programmable DNA web site, **http://ls11-www.cs.uni-dortmund.de/molcomp/Downloads/downloads.html**. Visited November 11, 2000.

[16] J. H. Reif, T. H. LaBean, and N. C. Seeman, "Challenges and Applications for Self-Assembled DNA Nanostructures", Proc. Sixth Inter.l Workshop on DNA-Based Computers, Leiden, The Neth., June, 2000. DIMACS Ed. by A. Condon and G. Rozenberg, Lecture Notes in CS, Springer-Verlag, Berlin Heidelberg, vol. 2054, pages 173-198, 2001.

[17] D. C. Tulpan, H. H. Hoos, A. Condon, "Stochastic Local Search Algorithms for DNA Word Design", DNA 8 Conference, Japan, March 2002.

[18] B. Yurke, A. J. Tuberfield, A. P.Jr Mills, F. C. Simmel and J. L. Neumann, "A DNA-fuelled molecular machine made of DNA." Nature 406, pages 605-608, 2000.

[19] B-T. Zhang and S-Y. Shin, "Molecular algorithms for efficient and reliable DNA computing," Proc. 3rd Annual Genetic Programming Conference, Edited by J. R. Koza, K. Deb, M. Doringo, D. B. Fogel, M. Garzon, H. Iba, and R. L. Riolo, Morgan Kaufmann, pages 735-742, 1998.

A Strategy for Improved Satisfaction of Selling Software Agents in E-Commerce

Thomas Tran and Robin Cohen

School of Computer Science, University of Waterloo
Waterloo, ON, N2L 3G1, Canada
{tt5tran,rcohen}@math.uwaterloo.ca

Abstract. In this paper, we present a model for buying and selling agents in electronic marketplaces, based on reputation modelling and reinforcement learning. We take into account the fact that multiple selling agents may offer the same good with different quality and that selling agents may alter the quality of their goods in order to satisfy individual buyers. In our approach, buying agents learn to maximize the expected value of goods by dynamically maintaining sets of reputable and disreputable sellers. Selling agents learn to maximize their expected profits by adjusting prices and optionally altering the quality of their goods. In this paper, we focus on presenting experimental results that confirm the improved satisfaction of selling agents following the proposed selling algorithm. This work therefore demonstrates a valuable strategy for selling agents to follow in marketplaces where buyers model reputation.

1 Introduction

Artificial intelligence researchers have been interested for some time in developing models for buying and selling agents in electronic marketplaces, allowing these agents to reason about their actions [2, 12]. In our research, we are especially interested in allowing buying and selling agents to learn from past experiences, using reinforcement learning. In particular, we have buyers model the reputation of sellers in order to learn how to make good purchases and we have sellers adjust the quality of their goods in order to meet the demands of buyers and make more sales.

The marketplace we envisage is one that is populated by self-interested agents whose goal is to maximize their own benefit. These buying and selling agents are free to enter or leave the market as well. In addition, we allow agents free access to all other agents in the marketplace. The process of buying and selling goods is realized via a *contract-net* like protocol [3, 9], which consists of three elementary phases: *(i)* A buyer announces its request for a good. *(ii)* Sellers submit bids for delivering such goods. *(iii)* The buyer evaluates the submitted bids and selects a suitable seller. The buyer then pays the chosen seller and receives the good from that seller. Thus, the buying and selling process can be viewed as an *auction* where a seller is said to be *winning the auction* if it is able to sell its good to the buyer. Fig. 1 illustrates the three basic phases of this process.

Y. Xiang and B. Chaib-draa (Eds.): AI 2003, LNAI 2671, pp. 434–446, 2003.

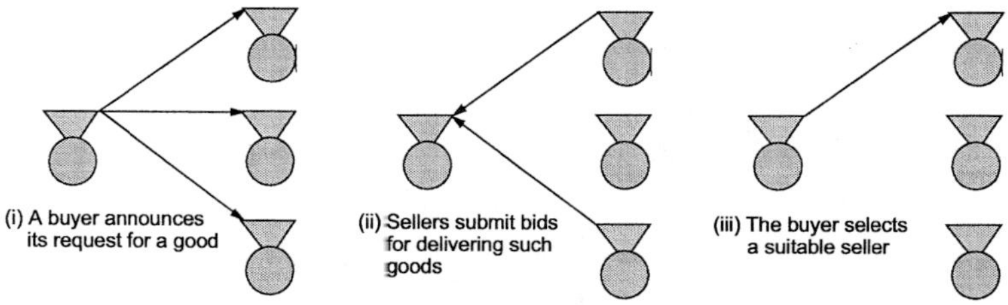

Fig. 1. Three basic phases of the buying and selling process

In this paper, we first present the algorithms proposed for buying and selling agents. We assume that the quality of a good offered by multiple sellers may not be the same, and a seller may alter the quality of its goods. We also assume that a buyer can examine the quality of the good it purchases only after it receives that good from the selected seller. Each buyer has some way to evaluate the good it purchases, based on its price and quality. Thus, in our market environment a buyer tries to find those sellers whose goods best meet its expected value, while a seller tries to maximize its expected profit by setting suitable prices for and providing more customized values to its goods, in order to satisfy the buyers' needs. In our approach, buyers are designed to be reputation-oriented to avoid the risk of purchasing low quality goods. They each dynamically maintain sets of reputable and disreputable sellers, and learn to maximize their expected value of goods by selecting appropriate sellers among the reputable sellers while avoiding the disreputable ones. Sellers learn to maximize their expected profits by not only adjusting product prices but also by optionally altering the quality of their goods.

We go on to discuss how our algorithms provide a detailed modelling of reputation and how they improve the satisfaction of both buyers and sellers. We then focus on presenting experimental results confirming the value of adjusting product quality for sellers, an important extension to the design of selling agents using reinforcement learning in market environments, such as [11]. In focusing on this part of our experimental work, we aim to show that our model therefore provides a valuable strategy for designing selling agents that operate in a marketplace where buying agents are modeling reputation.

The paper is organized as follows: The next section, section 2, introduces our proposed strategies, followed by a discussion on important extensions and potential advantages of the strategies. Section 3 presents the experimental results demonstrating the improved satisfaction for sellers. Section 4 remarks on related work. Section 5 concludes the paper with some future research directions.

2 The Proposed Learning Strategies

This section proposes the reputation-oriented reinforcement learning strategies for buyers and sellers, respectively. The strategies are aimed at maximizing the expected values of goods and avoiding the risk of purchasing low quality goods for buyers, and maximizing the expected profits for sellers.

2.1 Buying Strategy

Consider the scenario where a buyer b requests for some good g. Let G, P, and S be finite sets of goods, prices, and sellers in the market, respectively.

Buyer b maintains reputation ratings for sellers using function $r^b : S \mapsto (-1, 1)$, called the *reputation function* of b. Initially, buyer b sets $r^b(s) = 0$ for every seller $s \in S$. After each transaction with a seller s, buyer b will update $r^b(s)$ depending on whether or not s has satisfied b in the transaction. A seller s is considered *reputable* by buyer b if $r^b(s) \geq \Theta$, where Θ is buyer b's *reputation threshold* $(0 < \Theta < 1)$. A seller s is considered *disreputable* by buyer b if $r^b(s) \leq \theta$, where θ is buyer b's *disreputation threshold* $(-1 < \theta < 0)$. A seller s with $\theta < r^b(s) < \Theta$ is neither reputable nor disreputable to buyer b. In other words, b does not have enough information to decide on the reputation of s. Let S_r^b and S_{dr}^b be the sets of reputable and disreputable sellers to buyer b respectively, i.e.,

$$S_r^b = \{s \in S \mid r^b(s) \geq \Theta\} \subseteq S, \tag{1}$$

and

$$S_{dr}^b = \{s \in S \mid r^b(s) \leq \theta\} \subseteq S. \tag{2}$$

To avoid low quality goods, buyer b will focus its business on the reputable sellers and stay away from the disreputable ones.

Buyer b estimates the expected value of the goods it purchases using the *expected value function* $f^b : G \times P \times S \mapsto \mathbb{R}$. Hence, the real number $f^b(g, p, s)$ represents buyer b's expected value of buying good g at price p from seller s.

Since multiple sellers may offer good g with different qualities and a seller may alter the quality of its goods, buyer b puts more trust in the sellers with good reputation. Thus, it chooses among the reputable sellers in S_r^b a seller $\hat{s}$ that offers good g at price p with maximum expected value:

$$\hat{s} = \arg \max_{s \in S_r^b} f^b(g, p, s), \tag{3}$$

where arg is an operator such that $\arg f^b(g, p, s)$ returns s.

If no sellers in S_r^b submit bids for delivering g or if $S_r^b = \emptyset$, then buyer b will have to choose a seller $\hat{s}$ from the non-reputable sellers provided that $\hat{s}$ is not a disreputable seller:

$$\hat{s} = \arg \max_{s \in (S - (S_r^b \cup S_{dr}^b))} f^b(g, p, s). \tag{4}$$

In addition, with a small probability ρ, buyer b chooses to explore (rather than exploit) the marketplace by randomly selecting a seller $\hat{s} \in (S - S_{dr}^b)$. This gives buyer b an opportunity to discover new reputable sellers. Initially, the value of ρ should be set to 1, then decreased over time to some fixed minimum value determined by b.

After paying seller $\hat{s}$ and receiving good g, buyer b can examine the quality $q \in Q$ of good g, where Q is a finite set of real values representing product qualities. It then calculates the true value of good g using the *true product value function* $v^b : G \times P \times Q \mapsto \mathbb{R}$. For instance, if buyer b considers the quality of good g to be twice more important than its price, it may set $v^b(g,p,q) = 2q - p$.

The expected value function f^b is now incrementally learned in a reinforcement learning framework:

$$\Delta = v^b(g,p,q) - f^b(g,p,\hat{s}), \tag{5}$$

$$f^b(g,p,\hat{s}) \leftarrow f^b(g,p,\hat{s}) + \alpha\Delta, \tag{6}$$

where α is called the *learning rate* ($0 \leq \alpha \leq 1$). The learning rate should be initially set to a starting value of 1 and, similar to ρ, be reduced over time to a fixed minimum value chosen by b.

Thus, if $\Delta = v^b(g,p,q) - f^b(g,p,\hat{s}) \geq 0$ then $f^b(g,p,\hat{s})$ is updated with the same or a greater value than before. This means that seller $\hat{s}$ has a good chance to be chosen by buyer b again if it continues offering good g at price p in the next auction. Conversely, if $\Delta < 0$ then $f^b(g,p,\hat{s})$ is updated with a smaller value than before. So, seller $\hat{s}$ may not be selected by buyer b in the next auction if it continues selling good g at price p.

In addition to updating the expected value function, the reputation rating $r^b(\hat{s})$ of seller $\hat{s}$ also needs to be updated. Let $\vartheta^b(g) \in \mathbb{R}$ be the product value that buyer b demands for good g. We use a reputation updating scheme motivated by [13] as follows:

If $\delta = v^b(g,p,q) - \vartheta^b(g) \geq 0$, that is, if seller $\hat{s}$ offers good g with value greater than or equal to the value demanded by buyer b, then its reputation rating $r^b(\hat{s})$ is increased by

$$r^b(\hat{s}) \leftarrow \begin{cases} r^b(\hat{s}) + \mu(1 - r^b(\hat{s})) \text{ if } r^b(\hat{s}) \geq 0, \\ r^b(\hat{s}) + \mu(1 + r^b(\hat{s})) \text{ if } r^b(\hat{s}) < 0, \end{cases} \tag{7}$$

where μ is a positive factor called the *cooperation factor*[1] ($0 < \mu < 1$).

Otherwise, if $\delta < 0$, that is, if seller $\hat{s}$ sells good g with value less than that demanded by buyer b, then its reputation rating $r^b(\hat{s})$ is decreased by

$$r^b(\hat{s}) \leftarrow \begin{cases} r^b(\hat{s}) + \nu(1 - r^b(\hat{s})) \text{ if } r^b(\hat{s}) \geq 0, \\ r^b(\hat{s}) + \nu(1 + r^b(\hat{s})) \text{ if } r^b(\hat{s}) < 0, \end{cases} \tag{8}$$

where ν is a negative factor called the *non-cooperation factor* ($-1 < \nu < 0$).

To protect itself from dishonest sellers, buyer b may require $|\nu| > |\mu|$ to implement the traditional assumption that reputation should be difficult to build up, but easy to tear down. Moreover, buyer b may vary μ and ν as increasing functions of v^b to reflect the common idea that a transaction with higher value should be more appreciated than a lower one (i.e., the reputation rating of a seller offering higher true product value should be better increased).

[1] Buyer b will consider seller $\hat{s}$ as being *cooperative* if the good $\hat{s}$ sells to b has value greater than or equal to that demanded by b.

The set of reputable sellers to buyer b now needs to be updated based on the new reputation rating $r^b(\hat{s})$, as in one of the following two cases:

- If $(\hat{s} \in S_r^b)$ and $(r^b(\hat{s}) < \Theta)$ then buyer b no longer considers $\hat{s}$ as a reputable seller, i.e.,
$$S_r^b \leftarrow S_r^b - \{\hat{s}\}. \tag{9}$$
- If $(\hat{s} \notin S_r^b)$ and $(r^b(\hat{s}) \geq \Theta)$ then buyer b now considers $\hat{s}$ as a seller with good reputation, i.e.,
$$S_r^b \leftarrow S_r^b \cup \{\hat{s}\}. \tag{10}$$

Similarly, the set of disreputable sellers also needs to be updated:

- If $(\hat{s} \notin S_{dr}^b)$ and $(r^b(\hat{s}) \leq \theta)$ then buyer b now considers $\hat{s}$ as a disreputable seller, i.e.,
$$S_{dr}^b \leftarrow S_{dr}^b \cup \{\hat{s}\}. \tag{11}$$

2.2 Selling Strategy

Consider the scenario where a seller $s \in S$ has to decide on the price to sell some good g to a buyer b. Let B be the finite set of buyers in the market and let function $h^s : G \times P \times B \mapsto \mathbb{R}$ estimate the expected profit for seller s. Thus, the real number $h^s(g, p, b)$ represents the expected profit for seller s if it sells good g at price p to buyer b. Let $c^s(g, b)$ be the cost of seller s to produce good g for buyer b. Note that seller s may produce various versions of good g, which are tailored to meet the needs of different buyers. Seller s will choose a price $\hat{p}$ greater than or equal to cost $c^s(g, b)$ to sell good g to buyer b such that its expected profit is maximized:

$$\hat{p} = \arg \max_{\substack{p \in P \\ p \geq c^s(g,b)}} h^s(g, p, b), \tag{12}$$

where in this case arg is an operator such that $\arg h^s(g, p, b)$ returns p.

The expected profit function h^s is learned incrementally using reinforcement learning:

$$h^s(g, p, b) \leftarrow h^s(g, p, b) + \alpha(\phi^s(g, p, b) - h^s(g, p, b)), \tag{13}$$

where $\phi^s(g, p, b)$ is the actual profit of seller s if it sells good g at price p to buyer b, and is defined as follows:

$$\phi^s(g, p, b) = \begin{cases} p - c^s(g, b) & \text{if seller } s \text{ wins the auction,} \\ 0 & \text{otherwise.} \end{cases} \tag{14}$$

Thus, if seller s does not win the auction then $(\phi^s(g, p, b) - h^s(g, p, b))$ is negative, and by (13), $h^s(g, p, b)$ is updated with a smaller value than before. This reduces the chance that price $\hat{p}$ will be chosen again to sell good g to buyer b in future auctions. Conversely, if seller s wins the auction then price $\hat{p}$ will probably be re-selected in future auctions.

If seller s succeeded in selling good g to buyer b once, but subsequently fails for a number of auctions, say for m consecutive auctions (where m is seller s specific constant), then it may not only because s has set a too high price for good g, but probably also because the quality of g does not meet buyer b's demand. Thus, in addition to lowering the price via equation (13), seller s may optionally add more quality to g by increasing its production cost[2]:

$$c^s(g,b) \leftarrow (1 + Inc)c^s(g,b), \tag{15}$$

where Inc is seller s specific constant called the *quality increasing factor.*

In contrast, if seller s is successful in selling good g to buyer b for n consecutive auctions, it may optionally reduce the quality of good g, and thus try to further increase its future profit:

$$c^s(g,b) \leftarrow (1 - Dec)c^s(g,b), \tag{16}$$

where Dec is seller s specific constant called the *quality decreasing factor.*

2.3 Discussion

The algorithms presented here offer a detailed modelling of reputation in electronic marketplaces, extending the ideas first presented in [10].

First, aside from the set of reputable sellers, a buyer in our approach also dynamically maintains the set of disreputable sellers. These are sellers who constantly and greatly disappoint the buyer with such low value transactions that their reputation ratings fall below the buyer's disreputation threshold. The buyer then learns to maximize the expected value of goods by focusing its business on the reputable sellers while avoiding interaction with the disreputable ones. This strategy protects the buyer from the risk of purchasing low quality goods from the disreputable sellers and therefore brings better satisfaction to the buyer.

Second, we introduce the demanded product value $\vartheta^b(g)$, which serves as a product value threshold that buyer b would like good g at least to have. The reputation rating of seller $\hat{s}$ is updated based on whether or not the true value of good g that it offers meets the buyer's demand. Modelling the demanded product value allows the buyer to specify clearly the conditions under which a seller deserves to have its reputation rating increased or reduced, namely when the buyer's demanded product quality is or is not being met by the seller.

Third, we suggest to vary the cooperation factor μ and the non-cooperation factor ν as as increasing functions of the true product value v^b to support the common agreement that a transaction with higher value should be more appreciated than a lower one (e.g., a one-thousand-dollar transaction should be considered more important than a one-dollar one). This idea is implemented in our experiments, and so is the traditional assumption that reputation should be difficult to build up, but easy to tear down.

[2] This supports the common assumption that it costs more to produce high quality goods.

Our approach also provides an important strategy for a seller in an electronic marketplace. The seller learns to maximize its expected profit by tailoring its goods to meet specific needs of buyers. In particular, the proposed algorithm allows the seller to keep track of individual buyers and adjust both the price and quality of its goods to satisfy the buyers (equations (13) and (15)). This strategy therefore provides the seller with more opportunities to win auctions and accordingly brings better satisfaction to the seller.

Our algorithms allow buyers to explore the marketplace, with probability ρ. Accordingly, it is possible for new sellers to enter the marketplace and to be considered by buyers, even though they are not currently in those buyers' reputable sets. It also gives sellers an opportunity to become reputable and to continue to be successful, after past failures with buyers, by including appropriate adjustment of the quality of their goods.

The contract-net protocol [3, 9] that facilitates our agents in buying and selling goods works well in small and moderate-sized environments; however, as the problem size increases, it may run into difficulties due to the slow and expensive communication. Our buying strategy suggests a potential solution to this problem: A buyer may just send the requests for goods to its reputable sellers instead of all sellers[3], hence reducing the communication load and increasing the overall system performance.

In our proposed buying strategy, a buyer selects a seller based on its own experience without communicating with other buyers. This type of learning has certain advantages: Buyers can act independently and autonomously without being affected by communication delays, the failure of other buyers, or the reliability of the information received. The resultant system, therefore, should be robust [8].

3 Experimentation

We have performed a number of experiments to measure the value of our model on the microscopic and macroscopic levels. On the micro level, we were interested in examining the individual benefit of agents, particularly their level of satisfaction. Our experimental results confirm that in both modest and large-sized marketplaces, a buyer will obtain higher true product values (therefore better satisfaction) if it models sellers' reputation, and a seller will have more opportunities to win an auction (hence greater satisfaction) if it considers improving the quality of its goods, according to the proposed strategies. On the macro level, we studied how a market populated with our buyers and sellers would behave as a whole. Our experimental results show that such a market can reach an equilibrium state where the agent population remains stable (as some sellers who repeatedly fail to sell their goods will decide to leave the market), and this equilibrium is optimal for the participant agents.

[3] The buyer would send requests for goods to all sellers a certain percentage of the time in order to meet new sellers, but would only communicate with reputable sellers the remainder of the time.

Our focus in this paper is to present the modest-sized marketplace experiments that confirm the satisfaction of sellers following the proposed selling strategy. In particular, we would like to show that in a marketplace where buyers make use of a learning strategy, sellers following the proposed selling strategy should achieve better satisfaction than sellers following a simplified version where they use reinforcement learning but do not consider adjusting the quality of their goods. Since the more often a seller is successful in selling its goods, the higher profit it makes and the better satisfied it is, we record and compare the number of sales made by a seller following the proposed strategy with that made by a seller following the simplified version. Alternatively, we also compare the actual profits made by these two sellers after they have participated in the same number of auctions in the same marketplace.

We simulate a modest sized marketplace populated with 8 sellers and 4 buyers using Java 2. We let the first seven sellers, namely s_0, s_1, s_2, s_3, s_4, s_5, and s_6, follow the the simplified version and offer goods with fixed qualities of 38.0, 38.5, 39.0, 39.5, 40.0, 40.5, and 41.0, respectively. We let seller s_7 follow the proposed selling strategy and offer goods with an initial quality of 38.0. All the four buyers, namely b_0, b_1, b_2, and b_3, are designed to follow the proposed buying strategy. Other parameters are as follows:

- The learning rate α and the exploration probability ρ are both set to 1 initially and decreased over time (by factor 0.995) down to $\alpha_{min} = 0.1$ and $\rho_{min} = 0.1$.
- The quality q of a good is chosen to be equal to the cost for producing that good. This supports the common assumption that it costs more to produce high quality goods.
- The true product value function $v^b(p, q) = 3.5q - p$, where p and q represent the price and quality of the good, respectively.
- The reputation threshold $\Theta = 0.5$ and the disreputation threshold $\theta = -0.9$.
- The demanded product value $\vartheta^b(g) = 102$. Thus, even when a seller has to sell at cost, it must offer goods with quality of at least 40.8 in order to meet the buyers' requirement [4].
- If $v^b - \vartheta^b \geq 0$, we define the cooperation factor μ as

$$\mu = \begin{cases} \dfrac{v^b - \vartheta^b}{v^b_{max} - v^b_{min}} & \text{if } \frac{v^b - \vartheta^b}{v^b_{max} - v^b_{min}} > \mu_{min}, \\ \mu_{min} & \text{otherwise,} \end{cases}$$

  where $\mu_{min} = 0.005$, $v^b_{max} = 3.5q_{max} - p_{min}$, $v^b_{min} = 3.5q_{min} - p_{max}$, $q_{max} = p_{max} = 49.0$, and $q_{min} = p_{min} = 1.0$. In this definition, we vary μ as an increasing function of v^b to reflect the idea that the reputation rating of a seller that offers goods with higher product value should be better increased. we also prevent μ from becoming zero when $v^b = \vartheta^b$ by using value μ_{min}.

[4] Because $v^b(p, q) = 3.5q - p$ and $3.5(40.8) - 40.8 = 102$.

– If $\upsilon^b - \vartheta^b < 0$, we define the noncooperation factor ν as

$$\nu = \begin{cases} \lambda(\frac{\upsilon^b - \vartheta^b}{\upsilon^b_{max} - \upsilon^b_{min}}) \text{ if } & \lambda(\frac{\upsilon^b - \vartheta^b}{\upsilon^b_{max} - \upsilon^b_{min}}) > \nu_{min} \\ \nu_{min} & \text{otherwise,} \end{cases}$$

where $\nu_{min} = -0.9$ and $\lambda = 3$. In this definition, ν is also varied as an increasing function of υ^b to support the idea that the lower product value a seller offers, the more its reputation rating should be decreased. The use of factor $\lambda > 1$ indicates that a buyer will penalize a non-cooperative seller λ times greater than it will award a cooperative seller. This implements the traditional assumption that reputation should be difficult to build up, but easy to tear down. We prevent ν from moving out of the required lower bound -1 by using value ν_{min}.
– The number of consecutive unsuccessful auctions (after which a seller following the proposed algorithm may consider improving the quality of its goods) $m = 10$, and the number of consecutive successful auctions (after which a seller following the proposed algorithm may consider reducing the quality of its goods) $n = 10$.
– The quality increasing factor $Inc = 0.05$, and the quality decreasing factor $Dec = 0.05$.

All experimental results presented in this section are based on the average of 100 runs, each of which has 5000 auctions.

Table 1 presents the number of sales made by each seller to the four buyers. It can be seen clearly from the table that seller s_7 (the seller that follows the proposed selling strategy) makes the greatest number of sales among all sellers, and therefore achieves better satisfaction. In particular, the number of sales made by seller s_7 is about 2.33 times greater than that made by seller s_6, the most successful seller among those using the simplified version. The success of seller s_7 is due to the fact that, although s_7 initially offers goods with relatively low quality (of 38.0), it learns to improve the quality of its goods according to the proposed selling strategy, and therefore becomes reputable to the buyers.

Table 1. Number of sales made by each seller to the four buyers

	b_0	b_1	b_2	b_3
s_0	104.78	111.50	113.13	103.25
s_1	107.22	113.26	115.06	105.41
s_2	108.96	116.00	117.98	107.11
s_3	113.49	120.24	120.81	111.09
s_4	119.21	122.87	125.12	115.53
s_5	131.94	137.51	133.34	131.45
s_6	172.79	165.62	162.63	157.93
s_7	**391.61**	**363.00**	**361.93**	**418.23**

The fact that seller s_7 obtains greater satisfaction than seller s_6 can also be seen by comparing the actual profits made by these two sellers. Fig. 2 displays the actual profit values made by seller s_6 (graph (i)) and by seller s_7 (graph (ii)), respectively. It is clearly shown in the figure that the profit made by seller s_7 is much higher than that made by s_6. In fact, the mean profit value of seller s_7 is 1.2391, which is approximately 2.40 times greater than seller s_6's mean profit value of 0.5153. This is because after the first few hundred auctions, seller s_7 is able to learn to improve the quality of its goods to meet the buyers' demand, and therefore constantly makes successful sales to the buyers.

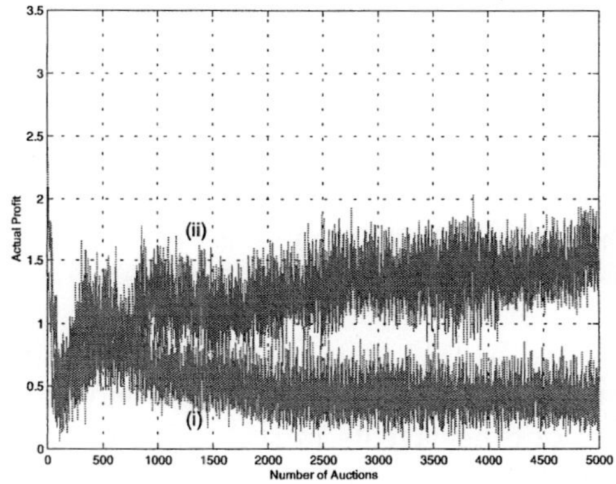

Fig. 2. Comparison of actual profits made by seller s_6, the most successful seller among those that use the simplified version (graph(i)), and by seller s_7, the seller that follows the proposed selling strategy (graph (ii))

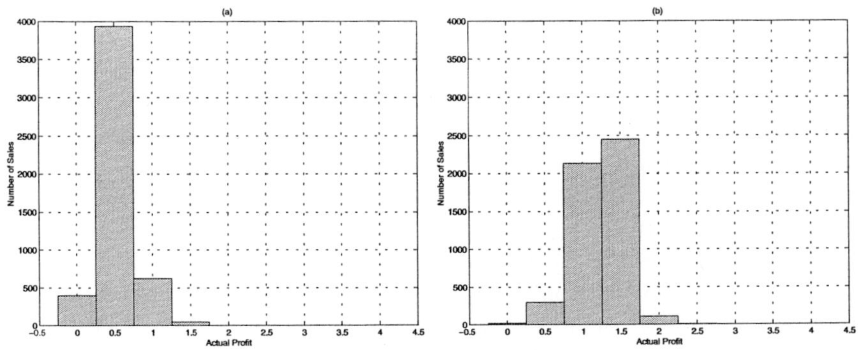

Fig. 3. Histograms of actual profits made by seller s_6, the seller that uses the simplified version (a), and by seller s_7, the seller that follows the proposed selling strategy (b)

Alternatively, figure 3(a) and (b) display the histograms of actual profit values made by seller s_6 and by seller s_7, respectively. We notice that seller s_6 makes very few sales in which the mean profit value is 1.5, and only about 650 sales in which the mean profit value is 1.0; while seller s_7 is able to make almost 2500 sales with mean profit value of 1.5, and over 2000 sales with mean profit value of 1.0. Seller s_6 makes almost 4000 sales with very low mean profit value of 0.5, while seller s_7 makes only about 250 sales with that low mean profit value. In other words, seller s_7 is able to make more sales with higher profits and fewer sales with lower profits, and therefore obtains better satisfaction.

4 Related Work

Reinforcement learning has been studied in various multi-agent problems such as pursuit games [5], soccer [4], the prisoner's dilemma game [7], and coordination games [8]. However, the agents and environments studied in these works are not economic agents and market environments. The reinforcement learning based strategies proposed in this paper are, on the contrary, aimed at application domains where agents are economically motivated and act in open market environments.

Our work is motivated by [11]. This research, however, focuses on the question of when an agent benefits from having deeper models of others, resorting to recursive modelling of other agents in the marketplace. In contrast, we believe that reputation of sellers is an important factor that buyers can exploit to reduce the risk of purchasing low quality goods, and sellers may increase their sales by not only adjusting the prices but also by altering the quality of their goods to meet the buyers' needs. Thus, instead of having agents deal with the computational costs of maintaining recursive models of others, we use a reputation mechanism to protect buyers from purchasing undesired goods, and give sellers the option to alter the quality of their goods.

A number of researchers have investigated the modelling of reputation. Yu and Singh [13] develop a general model for trust, focusing on acquiring information from other agents in an agent community. They use specific values to update the trust ratings of agents. In contrast, we have variable cooperative and non-cooperative factors, to allow for agents who greatly disappoint to be more seriously penalized. We also outline specifically the strategies for adjusting the model of reputation within a setting of electronic marketplaces.

Other researchers, such as Sabater and Sierra [6], do not elaborate on strategies for initiating and updating reputation models, but do offer more extensive representations for reputation. They consider the reputation of an agent not as a single and abstract concept, but rather a multi-facet concept. This idea may be useful to implement our strategies with deeper models of quality in which the quality of a product can be judged according to a combination of various factors such as the physical product characteristics, whether the product is distributed on time, whether the product is supported after purchase, etc.

5 Conclusion and Future Work

In this paper we proposed feasible reinforcement learning and reputation based strategies for buyers and sellers in market environments. According to the strategies, buyers learn to optimize their expected product values by selecting appropriate sellers to do business with among their reputable sellers and avoiding interaction with the disreputable ones. Sellers learn to maximize their expected profits by both adjusting the prices and optionally altering the quality of their goods. We discussed that the proposed strategies should lead to improved satisfaction for both buyers and sellers, reduced communication load, and more robust systems. In addition, we focussed on presenting the experimental results that confirm the improved satisfaction for sellers following the proposed selling strategy. This work therefore demonstrates the value of adjusting product quality for sellers in electronic marketplaces, offering an advantage over algorithms where sellers simply use reinforcement learning to improve their behaviour over time. Our algorithms are designed to operate in environments where buyers are modelling the reputation of sellers. They therefore allow sellers to continue to be successful, modelling past success with individual buyers to adjust the quality of their goods accordingly. In addition, our work shows that reputation modelling can be used in combination with reinforcement learning to design intelligent agents that participate in market environments.

For the next step, we plan to investigate more sophisticated learning strategies that allow agents in electronic markets to cooperate with other agents and/or take advantage of their knowledge about other agents to maximize their local utility. One interesting case to consider is allowing buyers in the market to form neighborhoods (as in [13]) such that within a neighborhood they inform one another of their knowledge about sellers. These buyers can then use their own knowledge combined with the informed knowledge to make decisions about which sellers to select. We predict that this form of transferring knowledge may be beneficial to new buyers, who can use the experience of existing buyers to make satisfactory purchase decisions without having to undergo several trials to build up enough experience for themselves. In this kind of environment, sellers may then need to be sensitive to the decisions being made by a group of buyers in the marketplace. This research may lead us into investigating more carefully the concept of coalitions in multi-agent societies. Breban and Vassileva [1], for instance, have studied the benefits for vendors to participate in coalitions in order to engender and maintain the trust of a set of buyers. This is another strategy for surviving in an environment where reputation of sellers is being modelled. In our proposed future work where buyers exist in neighbourhoods, vendors could endeavour to be considered reputable to all buyers in a neighbourhood, for instance, to achieve the effect of the buyer-vendor coalitions discussed in [1].

In general, the aim of our research is to develop a set of strategies for designing buying and selling agents in electronic marketplaces and to then characterize the conditions under which the different models are preferable. By accomplishing this objective, we hope to provide a principled framework for building effective economic agents and desirable market environments.

References

[1] S. Breban, and J. Vassileva. Using Inter-agent Trust Relationships for Efficient Coalition Formation. In *Proceedings of the Fifteenth Conference of the Canadian Society for Computational Studies of Intelligence*, pages 221-236, May 2002.

[2] A. Chavez, and P. Maes. Kasbah: An Agent Marketplace for Buying and Selling Goods. In *Proceedings of the First International Conference on the Practical Application of Intelligent Agents and Multi-Agent Technology*, 1996.

[3] R. Davis, and R. G. Smith. Negotiation as a Metaphor for Distributed Problem Solving. In *Artificial Intelligence*, 20(1): 63-109, January 1983.

[4] M. L. Littman. Markov Games As Framework for Multi-Agent Reinforcement Learning. In *Proceedings of the Eleventh International Conference on Machine Learning*, pages 157-163, 1994.

[5] N. Ono, and K. Fukumoto. Multi-Agent Reinforcement Learning: A Modular Approach. In *Proceedings of the Second International Conference on Multi-Agent Systems*, pages 252-258, 1996.

[6] J. Sabater, and C. Sierra. REGRET: A Reputation Model for Gregarious Societies. In *Papers from the Fifth International Conference on Autonomous Agents Workshop on Deception, Fraud and Trust in Agent Societies*, pages 61-69, 2001.

[7] T. W. Sandholm, and R. H. Crites. Multi-Agent Reinforcement in the Iterated Prisoner's Dilemma. In *Biosystems*, 37: 147-166, 1995.

[8] S. Sen, M. Sekaran, and J. Hale. Learning to Coordinate without Sharing Information. In *Proceedings of the Twelfth National Conference on Artificial Intelligence*, pages 426-431, 1994.

[9] R. G. Smith. The Contract Net Protocol: High Level Communication and Control in a Distributed Problem Solver. In *IEEE Transactions on Computers*, C-29(12): 1104-1113, December 1980.

[10] T. Tran, and R. Cohen. A Learning Algorithm for Buying and Selling Agents in Electronic Marketplaces. In *Proceedings of the Fifteenth Conference of the Canadian Society for Computational Studies of Intelligence*, pages 31-43, May 2002.

[11] J. M. Vidal, and E. H. Durfee. The Impact of Nested Agent Models in an Information Economy. In *Proceedings of the Second International Conference on Multi-Agent Systems*, pages 377-384, 1996.

[12] P. R. Wurman, M. P. Wellman, and W. E. Wash. The Michigan Internet AuctionBot: A Configurable Auction Server for Humans and Software Agents. In *Proceedings of the Second International Conference on Autonomous Agents*, pages 301-308, 1998.

[13] B. Yu, and M. P. Singh. A Social Mechanism of Reputation Management in Electronic Communities. In M. Klusch and L. Kerschberg, editors, *Cooperative Information Agents IV*, Lecture Notes in Artificial Intelligence, Vol. 1860, pages 154-165. Springer-Verlag, Berlin, 2000.

Pre-negotiations over Services – A Framework for Evaluation

Petco E. Tsvetinov

Queensland University of Technology, School of Information Systems
GPOBox 2434, Brisbane, QLD 4001, Australia
p.tsvetinov@qut.edu.au

Abstract. A framework for evaluation and selection of service offers during the *pre-negotiation* phase in automated negotiations over services is proposed. The pre-negotiation problem for a buyer of services is regarded as essentially a decision making problem, related to a set of possible scenarios, involving a number of pre-negotiation choices – identifying suitable service offers, establishing a common criteria scheme, evaluating the offers and choosing the best alternatives to proceed negotiations on. The concept of Alternative Focused Thinking (AFT) during pre-negotiations is introduced. Since the comparison of service packages involves multiple criteria, it is argued that it may be beneficial to use an integrated approach for evaluation, involving different weighting methods. The use of multiple criteria decision aid software in supporting the pre-negotiation interactions is illustrated through a HIPRE model, involving three weighting techniques – the Analytic Hierarchy Process (AHP), the Multi-Attribute Rating Technique (SMART) and a simple weighting function. The application of hybrid multi-criteria decision making (MCDM) methods in pre-negotiations is proposed as a direction for future research.

1 Introduction

The electronic commerce of services is a vastly expanding area and especially suitable for automation. Numerous negotiating agents of varying complexity are already in place. Advanced models of negotiation reasoning engines have been developed. Very few studies, however, have addressed the reasoning and actions that may take place during the pre-interaction phase of an automated negotiation, the *pre-negotiation* [1]. Although the computational complexities of automating negotiations over multidimensional goods like services have been identified, the concept of preempting some of the decision-making problems and shifting part of the reasoning and deliberations to the pre-negotiation phase has not yet been clearly formulated.

The reasoning during pre-negotiations may be regarded as largely a MCDM evaluation problem. Such problems involve uncertainties related both to the values of the criterion variables and to the weights of the criteria. There exists no

Y. Xiang and B. Chaib-draa (Eds.): AI 2003, LNAI 2671, pp. 447–457, 2003.

'best' method for evaluation. Different methods allow different problem formulation options and possibilities. Each method can give some additional 'flavor' to an evaluation scheme.

The reasoning process during pre-negotiations has also a behavioral aspect. The currently overwhelming way of thinking among buyers of services is the Value Focused Thinking (VFT).

The purpose of this paper is to set a framework for pre-negotiations over services and to focus on possible evaluation methodologies facilitating the selection of optimal service offers.

On the first place, an Alternative Focused Thinking (AFT) approach is proposed to complement the VFT one since the consideration of alternatives may help identify and define criteria, while criteria are shown to help identify and define alternatives.

Secondly, the paper discusses and demonstrates an integrated evaluation approach with the simultaneous use of three MCDM weighting methods in support of a pre-interaction selection of service providers. The main aim in applying different methods in combination is to use their advantages in a compatible manner. The AHP is applied in order to bring qualitative analysis capacity into an evaluation scheme, SMART in cases where the AHP method causes rank reversal, etc. Such an integrated evaluation approach is possible with the current availability of suitable decision analysis software.

2 Negotiation over Services

During negotiations over services the bargaining parties are engaged in multi-criteria decision making, where the decision variables may be both discrete and continuous in value, quantitative and qualitative in nature. Since the trading in services is unique in a number of ways due to their intangible character, complex properties and spatio-temporal constraints, the need for decision support enhancing the processes of search and transactions raises a number of problems, among them the evaluation of the set of issues to be resolved and the assessment and selection of the best service offers.

Service properties and their representation are of major importance in building evaluation models and designing automated negotiation mechanisms [2]. Among the major properties are price, method of payment, service quality, availability, security and trust. Building a utility function as a measure of the goodness of a service package is far from being a straightforward task due to a number of reasons:

Price and Pricing: The intangible nature of services offer opportunities for flexibility and customization. Since demand for services may fluctuate, demand fluctuating pricing may be employed. Bundling together services is another marketing approach with great potential in services. Thus evaluating the perceived cost is rather difficult in contrast with the trade in goods.

Charging Techniques: They may vary, depending on the type of delivery of the service, the granularity of the service, etc.

Settlement Methods: They may be transactional, rental, escrow agreements, swap agreements.

Service Quality: Largely domain specific, measured often along five dimensions - reliability, responsiveness, assurance, empathy and tangibles. These criteria being of different importance, their evaluation is further complicated by the subjective character of some.

This substantial diversity and complexity in service properties means that a decision maker, potential buyer of a service, has to use a complex assessment scheme in selecting a particular offer. With service providers trying to differentiate their product from those of their competitors, the eventual mapping of service properties of diverse nature and different providers with the buyer's requirements is a challenging problem.

3 Pre-negotiations

Durfee [3] contends that *"In many domains, a substantial part of the negotiation effort is involved in figuring out what needs to be settled. As our computational agents are increasingly applied in dynamically evolving worlds (like on the Internet), capabilities for identifying who needs to negotiate and over what, rather than having these predefined by the system developers or users, will come to the fore."*

Authors agree [4],[1],[5] that the local problem of agents is defined in the *pre-negotiation phase*[1] where decision variables describing the deal offer and the preferred satisfaction constraints are enumerated. The possibility of assisting decision makers at that preliminary stage of negotiations is a challenging design problem. With a large number of decision variables that interact in a non-linear way, the decision space can become exponentially large. Some preference elicitation and representation problems arise as well. Most existing negotiation models only partially address the problem of how to reason and communicate during the pre-negotiation phase. The possibilities to set an optimal framework and implement an intelligent pre-assessment of possible scenarios for the negotiation itself are either underestimated or simply not addressed.

Faratin et al. [6] think that it is impossible to pre-compute an optimal strategy at design time. Rather the agents need to adopt an heuristic and satisficing approach in choosing their strategy 'on the fly'.

4 Framework for Evaluation and Selection

The assessment of the initial multidimensional service property packages as early as the pre-negotiation phase require at least two stages:

[1] The pre-negotiation phase is sometimes referred to as a *meta-negotiation* phase, i.e. negotiating over negotiations. For example, a buyer or seller of services may negotiate which negotiation rules to accept before the start of the actual negotiation

Property Discovery and Comparison of the Services. The process of property discovery presumes pre-negotiation deliberations between the buyer and sellers of services. Services today are typically described by a large range of properties, thus their accurate representation and description is of major importance both for the service provider and service requestor. Due to the difficulty of describing complex services, some service providers may not always outline specific details. *The current study proposes a new approach in this early pre-negotiation phase involving the application of an Alternative Focused Thinking concept, where the buyer should be able to build and refine the preliminary request for service.* The interactions between the service requestor and service providers may lead to updating some service representations and the iteration process may result in an evolution in the service offer at this early stage of negotiations.

Using Appropriate Evaluation Methods. There are many techniques to elicit attribute weights. Using appropriate evaluation methods in the case of multidimensional goods like services requires the application of techniques that address several unsolved problems, the major one being how to build a common evaluation scheme for qualitative and quantitative criteria (attributes). Another major issue to be addressed is the difficulty in modeling relationships that may exist among service properties. Existing evaluation methods used in isolation may solve one type of problems, while leave another unresolved.

The Multi-attribute Value Theory (MAVT) [7]uses an additive value function to aggregate the component values. The weights indicate the relative importance of an improvement of one attribute from its worst level to its best level compared with changes in other attributes. While the MAVT provides a way of ranking service provision offers, it requires preferential and utility independence among the attributes, conditions that are often not met in service package offers.

The Analytic Hierarchy Process (AHP) [8] uses a simpler and theoretically sound multiple-criteria methodology for evaluation that can complement the MAVT. The strengths of the AHP, namely its ability to structure complex, multi-attribute problems hierarchically and then model the decision-maker's preferences by pairwise comparisons, are ideally suited to the above requirements.

Several other MCDM weighting methods have been applied to problems of various complexity, each one with its advantages and shortcomings. The simultaneous application of different methods seems suitable in refining the evaluation process during the pre-negotiation stage. It has become possible lately with the proliferation of suitable, multi-facet software.

4.1 Alternative Focused Thinking

Multi-criteria decision-making is based on conceptualization in terms of criteria and alternatives. The problem of first identifying the alternatives and then applying value information (issue weightings, etc.) in order to make a decision

is commonly referred to as *Alternative-Focussed Thinking* (AFT). With *Value-Focused Thinking* (VFT) the explicit consideration of values is the starting point to the structuring process [9].
March [10] argues that values and criteria are formed out of experience with alternatives. Further Corner et al. [11] suggest that consideration of alternatives helps identify and define criteria, while criteria are shown to help identify and define alternatives. Such interaction seems to improve the decision-making process and as the authors note that *'thinking about alternatives helps generate criteria and vice versa'*. Thus during the pre-negotiation phase a buyer may notice, analyzing the offers of a number of sellers of services, that there are service providers that address not only the core criteria, but provide new features as well, thus introducing new criteria. The buyer might be tempted to rethink his requirements at this stage and restructure her preference scheme. The buyer might send further queries to the vendors requiring more information regarding new issues. Such a dynamic iteration (Fig.1) between criteria and alternatives illustrates the notion that *buyers cannot decide what they want until they can see what they can get.* In the case of multi-issue multi-vendor negotiations that means that the buyer will benefit by using a multi-stage pre-negotiation protocol, where an initial query is sent to all potential sellers of services, and only after receiving the various initial offers a comprehensive and extended evaluation scheme should be designed. We have already suggested such an approach during the pre-negotiation phase [13].

Further iterations may also be possible based on further queries to the sellers regarding additional attributes of the proposed service. Thus the alternative focused approach may complement the value focused one during the pre-negotiation phase.

4.2 Using an Integrated Evaluation Approach

In a recently published book Belton et al. [14] stress the need for an integrated approach to multiple criteria decision aid, including the use of multiple methods. The same conclusion can be drawn from other studies as well [15],[16].

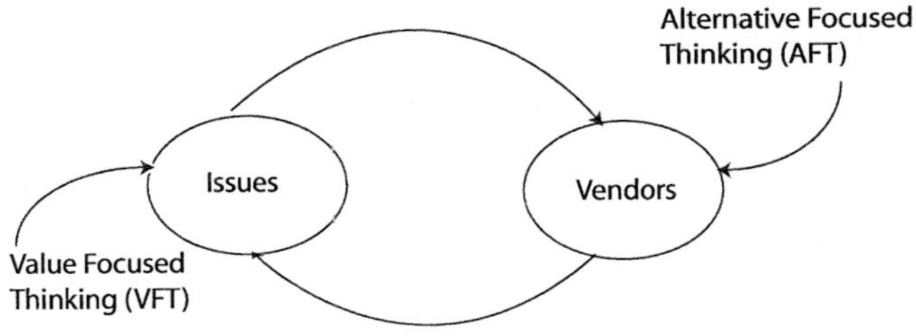

Fig. 1. AFT and VFT in pre-negotiations

The evaluation and weighting of the attributes of service offers in this study have been done using three weighting methods - the AHP, SMART and simple value functions, in various combinations and at different levels and nodes of the decision hierarchy. This integrated approach has been chosen because the AHP and SMART are better suited for quality evaluation, while the application of simple value functions seems the best suited method at the lowest value of a hierarchy (determining the scores of the alternatives).

The Analytic Hierarchy Process [8] allows users to assess the relative weight of multiple criteria (or multiple alternatives against a given criterion) in an intuitive manner. It involves the use of *pairwise comparisons*, thus solving a problem in cases when quantitative ratings are unavailable. In such cases research has shown that humans are still adept at recognizing whether one criteria is more important than another. The AHP provides a consistent way of converting such pairwise comparisons into a set of numbers representing the relative priority of each criteria. Each criterion can be broken down into individual parameters whose values are either estimated or determined by measurement or experimentation. Once the hierarchy has been structured, local priorities must be established on a given level with respect to each factor on the level immediately above it. This is done by making pairwise comparisons between the criteria to develop the relative weights. Since the approach is basically qualitative, it is arguably easier to implement from both a data requirement and validation point of view than using the multiattribute value theory approach. Not all MAVT independence conditions need to be verified, nor functions derived.

A potential drawback of the AHP method, however, is the so called *Rank Reversal* phenomenon [17]. Since judgments using the AHP are relative by nature, changing the set of alternatives may change the decision scores of all the alternatives. It has been shown that even if a new, very poor alternative is added to a completed model, those alternatives with top scores sometimes reverse their relative ranking. In such cases, however, the *The Simple Multi-Attribute Rating Technique (SMART)* can be applied. When using SMART, ratings of alternatives are assigned directly, in the natural scales of the criteria (where available). In order to keep the weighting of criteria and rating of alternatives as separate as possible, the different scales of criteria need to be converted to a common internal scale. In AHP this is taken care of by the relative nature of the rating technique. In SMART, it is done mathematically by the decision maker by means of a value function. The simplest choice of a value function is a linear function, and in most cases this is sufficient. However, to better allow for human psychology in decision making, it is often advantageous to use non-linear functions. The advantage in using the SMART method is that the decision model is independent of the alternatives. While the introduction of value functions makes the decision modeling process much more difficult to implement, using the SMART method ensures that the ratings of alternatives are not relative, so that changing the number of alternatives considered will not in itself change the decision scores of the original alternatives.

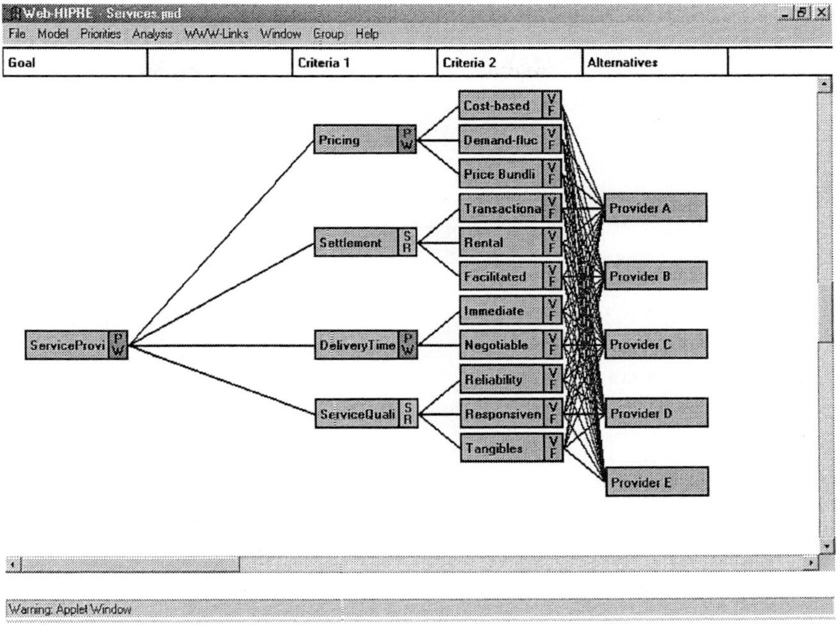

Fig. 2. An AHP three level hierarchy for choosing a service provider

5 Results

The model presented illustrates the application of the AHP method and SMART in combination with a simple multi-attribute weighting technique using Web-HIPRE (HIPRE, software for decision analytic problem structuring, multi-criteria evaluation and prioritization, has been created at the System Analysis Laboratory, Helsinki University of Technology by R. Hamalainen and H. Lauri, http://www.hipre.hut.fi). The software supports several weighting methods including AHP, SMART, SWING[2], SMARTER[3] and simple value functions that map the ratings of alternatives directly to their values. The advantage of this approach is that different methods may be applied at different levels and nodes of the decision hierarchy.

The model demonstrates an evaluation scheme for pre-negotiation service offers involving four major criteria and their respective sub-criteria – pricing (cost based, demand fluctuating, price bundling), settlement (transactional, rental, facilitated), delivery time (immediate or negotiable) and service quality (reliability, responsiveness, tangibles). Five service providers (alternatives) were to

[2] Using the SWING technique you are asked first to give 100 points to the most important attribute change from the worst criterion level to the best level.

[3] In the SMARTER-technique you are asked to rank the attributes in the order of importance for the attribute changes from their worst level to the best level.

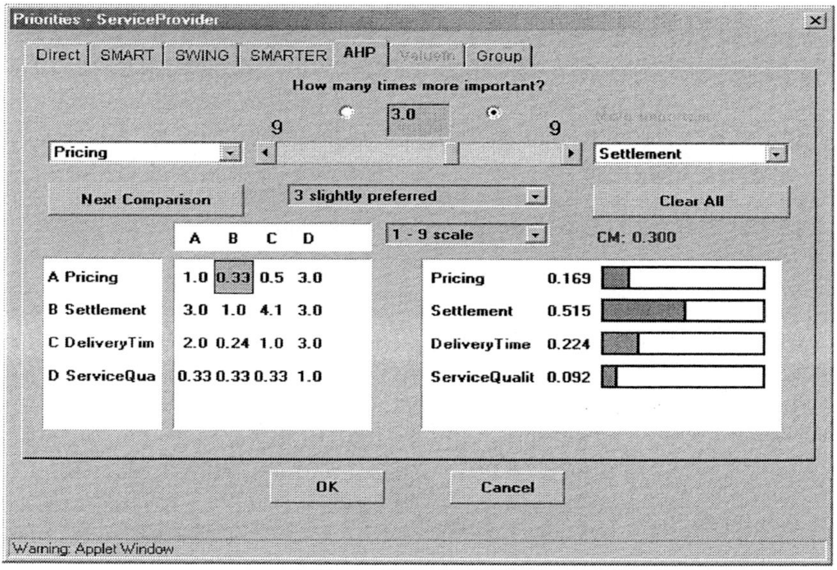

Fig. 3. Pairwise comparisons in HIPRE

be evaluated (ranked). An example of the three level hierarchy for deciding on a suitable service provider is shown on Fig.2.

As can easily be seen, some of the criteria are qualitative and related, thus the application of a simple multi-attribute value approach alone was not sufficient. We used a combination of weighting methods – *PC* on the Figure stands for Pairwise Comparison (AHP), *SR* – for SMART and at the last level – *VF* – for simple value functions. The evaluation methods at the different levels of the hierarchy and at different nodes were also selectively applied according to the type of criteria. For example the preferred method at Level 1 on the Figure is AHP since some of the criteria are interdependent (Pricing and Service Quality). A ratio scale was applied to quantify the decision maker's ranking on any two alternatives with respect to a given criterion. The derived weights were interpreted as the degree to which one alternative is preferred to another. The AHP comparison engine of HIPRE is shown on Fig.3.

With four factors to be compared, the matrix has $n(n-1)/2 = 6$ elements (answers). The total weights of the alternatives (named 'composite priorities') are shown in Fig.4 by a bar graph. The bars, divided into segments, indicate the contribution of each criterion.

One of the aims of the experiments was to observe the effects of using various evaluation methods at different levels of the hierarchy and at different nodes. We tested three different configurations:

1. Using SMART at Level 1(the highest level), AHP (pairwise comparisons) at Level 2 and simple value functions at the lowest Level 3.

2. Using AHP at both Level 1 and Level 2, and simple value functions at the lowest level.
3. Using AHP at Level 1, SMART and and AHP at selected nodes of Level 2, and simple value functions at the lowest level.

While using SMART, the weights were elicited in two steps – first, ranking the importance of the changes in the attributes from the worst attribute levels to the best levels, and second – making ratio estimates of the relative importance of each attribute relative to the one ranked lowest in importance. We started with assigning 10 points to the least important attribute. The relative importance of the other attribute(s) were then evaluated by giving them points from 10 upwards.

We observed different composite priorities in all three configurations, although no rank reversal among the alternatives (service providers) was established for the set of data (preferences) used. The difference in values in the composite priorities for the same set of initial preference data, however, was substantial in some cases.

Our results show that using various evaluation methods at different levels of the hierarchy and at different nodes does influence the overall weightings and further research should be conducted in that direction. While some authors [18] have seen different methods yielding different results to be a major disadvantage

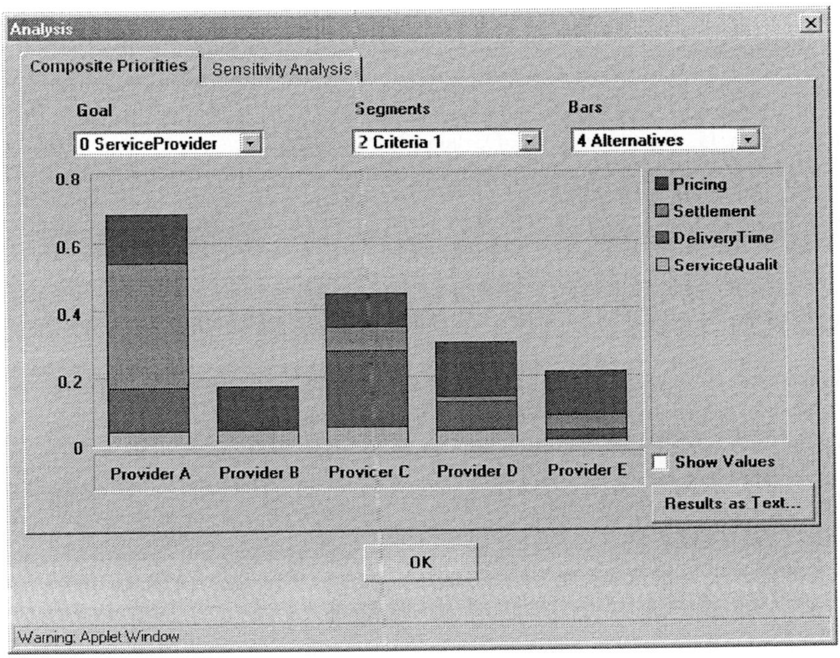

Fig. 4. Composite priorities in HIPRE

of the MCDM approach, we think that the integration of various methods may be the way to a more comprehensive multi-attribute analysis. Hybrid applications, similar to HIPRE, may provide practitioners in various areas with the possibility of tailoring and fine tuning suitable tools for decision support.

6 Conclusions

Integrative evaluation schemes using a combination of weighting methods and suitable hybrid software packages may provide flexibility in decision making during pre-negotiations. While methodological extensions in existing MCDM methods may enable more sophisticated analysis, research around differences among methods becomes increasingly important as the currently available software allows the combination of different weighting methods easily. Developing hybrid methods that make use not only of MCDM methods, but combine also other decision support approaches like the outranking method (PROMETHEE II and ELECTRE III), seems a promising avenue for future research.

References

[1] Faratin, P.: Automated Service Negotiation Between Autonomous Computational Agents. University of London. PhD thesis (2000)

[2] O'Sullivan, J., Edmond, D., ter Hofstede, A.: What's in a Service? Towards Accurate Description of Non-functional Service Properties.In:Distributed and Parallel Databases Journal - Special Issue on E-Services, 12, (2002)

[3] Durfee, E.: Practical Negotiation Strategies. In: Proceedings of the International Workshop on MultiAgent Systems (IWMAS98). MIT, Massachusetts, (1998)

[4] Kersten, G., Szpakowicz., S.: Decision Making and Decision Aiding. Defining the Process, its Representations and Support. In: Group Decision and Negotiation , Vol 3, (1994), 237-261

[5] Jennings, N., Parsons, S., Sierra, C., Faratin, P.: Automated Negotiation. In: Proc. of the Conference on Pratical Applications of Intelligent Agents and Multi-agent Systems (PAAM), Manchester, UK (2000)

[6] Faratin, P., Klein, M.: Automated Contract Negotiation and Execution as a System of Constraints. MIT, Cambridge (2001)

[7] Keeney, R. and Raiffa, H.: Decisions with multiple objectives - preferences and value tradeoffs. John Wiley and Sons, (1976)

[8] Saaty, T.: Multicriteria Decision Making - The Analytic Hierarchy Process. RWS Publications (1992)

[9] Keeney, R.: Value Focused Thinking. Harvard University Press, Cambridge, Massachusetts, (1992)

[10] March,J.: Decisions and Organisations. Blackwell, Oxford, (1988)

[11] Corner, J., Buchanan, J., Henig, M.: Dynamic Decision Problem Structuring, In: J. Multi-Crit. Decis. Anal., bf 10, (2001) 129-141

[12] van Leeuwen, J. (ed.): Computer Science Today. Recent Trends and Developments. Lecture Notes in Computer Science, Vol. 1000. Springer-Verlag, Berlin Heidelberg New York (1995)

[13] Tsvetinov, P.: MCDM in E-Negotiations Protocols, In: XVIth MCDM Conference Proceedings, Semmering, Austria, (Feb 16 - 20, 2002)

[14] Belton, V., Stewart, TJ.: Multiple Criteria Decision Analysis – An Integrated Approach. Kluwer Academic Publishers:Dordrecht (2001)

[15] Schmoldt, D., Kangas, J. Mendoza GA, Pesonen M. (eds): The Analytic Hierarchy Process in Natural Resource and Environmental Decision Making. Kluwer Academic Publishers:Dordrecht, The Netherlands, (2001)

[16] Kangas,J., Kangas, A., Leskinen, P.,Pykalainen, J. : MCDM Methods in Strategic Planning of Forestry on State-Owned Lands in Finland: Application and Experiences. In: J.MultiCrit. Decis. Anal. 10, (2001), 257-271

[17] Salo, A. and Hamalainen,R.: On the Measurement of Preferences in the Analytic Hierarchy Process. In: Journal of Multi Criteria Decision Analysis, 6, (1997)

[18] Zanakis, SH, Solomon, A., Wishart, N., Dublish, S. : Multi-attribute Decision Making : A Simulation Comparison of Select Methods. In: European Journal of Operational Research, 107, (1998), 507-529

A Formal Theory for Describing Action Concepts in Terminological Knowledge Bases

Christel Kemke

Department of Computer Science
562 Machray Hall, University of Manitoba, Winnipeg, Manitoba, R3T 2N2, Canada
ckemke@cs.umanitoba.ca

Abstract. This paper introduces a formal theory for describing actions in terminological knowledge bases, closely related to description logics. It deals in particular with the problem of adapting the subsumption/specialization relations and the definition of inheritance from the well-formulated notions for static object concepts to dynamic action concepts. The description of action concepts integrates a formal notation of preconditions and effects similar to STRIPS planning systems. The approach suggested here anchors action descriptions in the object-concept part of the taxonomy. Object-concepts, their attributes, and relations are integrated as parameters in action descriptions, and are used in precondition and effect formulae, which specify changes in the object-concept part of the taxonomy. The definition of action concepts and their extensional semantics is based on the view of actions as transformers between world states, where preconditions and effects describe constraints on world states. This view allows a definition of inheritance and the subsumption/specialization relation for action concepts in parallel to the respective definitions for object concepts.

1 Introduction

Since the upcoming of taxonomical or terminological knowledge bases in the eighties, which lead later to the development of the more formal area of description logics, several researchers have investigated the integration of action concepts as dynamic entities into taxonomical representation languages which were originally only used for static object concepts [1]-[8][19][20]. Most of these approaches, however, turned to extending standard description logic languages with representations of time concepts [2]-[7], or integrated planning and plan recognition methods [8][19][20] instead of dealing in detail with action concepts. Other approaches [18] were oriented towards the practical integration of action representations into terminological representation languages like LOOM or CLASSIC, and did not focus on formalizing inheritance and subsumption for action concepts. Terminological languages and

Y. Xiang and B. Chaib-draa (Eds.): AI 2003, LNAI 2671, pp. 458-465, 2003.

Description Logics is thus still lacking a clear conceptualization of inheritance and specialization/ subsumption for action concepts.

In this paper, we outline a framework which grounds the description of action concepts on a functional view of actions as transformers between world states where these world states relate to the underlying object-concept part of the taxonomy. A key issue in this approach is an anchoring of action concept definitions in the object part of the respective taxonomy such that object concepts, their attributes, and relations between object concepts are integrated into action definitions as parameters which are then used in the notation for precondition and effect formulae which are attached like attributes to action concepts. This is the basis for defining an extensional semantics of action concepts which provides the basis for defining a subsumption relation for action concepts. The representation of actions includes precondition and effect descriptions as logical formulae and is thus suitable for use in planning methods. The hierarchical arrangement of action concepts can be used in addition for efficient storing and search of actions and action concepts in planning and other applications like natural language processing.

2 Outline of the Theory

The approach to representing actions suggested in this paper focuses on developing a concise and efficient representation of action concepts in taxonomical hierarchies, with a definition of inheritance and the subsumption/specialization of action concepts.

The notion of specialization and subsumption of action concepts is based on the view of actions as transformers between world states. A concrete world state is determined by a set of object instances which are specified in accordance with the conceptual object taxonomy, i.e. with feature values and roles or relations to other objects. A set of world states corresponds to a set of possible instantiations of the respective object taxonomy. Action concepts determine in addition constraints through preconditions and effects which restrict the set of possible instantiations related to the application or instantiation of a generic action defined as action concept.

The semantics of action concepts and their subsumption/specialization can informally be defined as follows. A concrete action transforms a concrete world state W_1 into another concrete world state W_2 where world state W_1 has to satisfy the precondition formulae of the action, and world state W_2 the effect formula of the action. A generic action is described by a set of world states, in which the precondition formula is well-defined and satisfied, and another set of world states, which potentially result from the action, in accordance with the effect formula. This leads to a formal definition of the subsumption-relation for action concepts which states that an action concept *a* subsumes an action concept *a'* if the set of world states $W_{a,pre}$ specified by the precondition formula of *a* and the set of world states $W_{a,post}$ specified by the effect formula, respectively, subsume the related set of world states $W_{a',pre}$ and $W_{a',post}$ of *a'*.

3 General Concept Terminology

3.1 The Concept Terminology Language

For simplicity, we chose a simplified concept language which contains the following basic elements (with correspondence to First-Order Predicate Logic):

Concept Language		Predicate Logic	Interpretation
Concept	C, D, …	unary Predicate	Set of Domain Objects
Instance	c, d, …	Constant	Singleton Set of Domain Objects
Feature	f, g, …	Function	Function from Domain Objects to Domain Objects
Role	R, S, …	Predicate	Relation between Domain Objects

Concepts are assumed to correspond to unary predicates, i.e. they consist of simple sets of elements. Features correspond to functions $f: C \rightarrow D$, which have the concept C as domain and another concept D as range. Roles correspond to (in general binary) predicates or relations between concepts $R \subseteq C \times D$.
Notational convention: In order to refer to the range/value of a feature f of a concept C, or an element $c \in C$, we use the dot-notation C.f and c.f.

3.2 Fluents

In order to define the semantics of action concepts in a suitable way, we assume a distinction of roles and features into those which are static, and cannot be changed or modified, and those which are dynamic and changeable. The second class corresponds to the general notion of Fluents as introduced in Situation Calculus. The separation into these two distinct classes allows a distinction between roles and features which can / cannot be changed by an action. Which roles and features fall into the class of Fluents and non-Fluents depends of course on the domain and application for which the knowledge base is modeled. The formal model in this paper assumes that roles evaluate to truth values, and their dynamic existence as Fluents is defined through a possible change of the truth value, whereas Fluents which are based on features are defined through a change of the respective feature value.

This approach allows the modeling of dynamic, non-persistent features and properties of objects, e.g. spatial relations like ‘in’ or ‘on’ as part of the concept terminology. Actions can modify these properties through changing their value (in case of features) or their truth status (in case of relations) for individual concept instantiations. This parallels the concept of add- and delete-lists in the STRIPS planning methodology.

3.3 Defining the Object Concept Taxonomy

Object concepts are in general described by a set of roles and features.[1] Roles and features are inherited from the subsuming concept(s) and additional ones can be

[1] Various types of filler specifications based on general mathematical notions like sequences, sets, ordered sets etc. are described in [13].

specified for the concept. Instances are associated with concepts and each instance instantiates a specific concept through substituting general concepts specifying role or feature filler sets with concrete specific values.

The general subsumption / specialization relation for object concepts is given by

$$C \textit{ subsumes } C' \,/\, C' \textit{ specializes } C :\Leftrightarrow \forall x: (x \in C' \Rightarrow x \in C)$$

Thus, subsumption between concepts is also written in the form $C' \subseteq C$.

One way to specialize a concept is by constraining the set of possible fillers for a role or feature by specializing the respective range concept, i.e. a concept C with a role $R \subseteq C \times D$ is specialized to a concept $C' \subseteq C$ if the role is modified to $R' \subseteq C \times D'$ with $D' \subseteq D$ and $R' \subseteq R$; equivalently, a feature $f: C \rightarrow D$ can be restricted to $f': C \rightarrow D'$.

4 Defining Action Concepts

Action concepts are described by a set of parameters or object variables which refer to concepts in the object taxonomy, and a precondition formula as well as an effect formula describing how the world changes through the action, which are stored as features of the action concept, similar to object-features but with formulae instead of concepts as filler constraints.[2]

4.1 General Notion of Action Semantics and Subsumption

We consider first as a paradigmatic example the general action 'change-feature-value', which can be described as follows:

change-feature-value(c,d,f)

c	object-concept C	* *the concept whose feature value changes*
d	feature-value-concept D	* *the concept for the feature values*
f	feature $f: C \rightarrow D$	* *the feature whose value is to be modified*
pre	$\exists x$: feature-value-concept(x) $\wedge$ c.f = x	* *the old feature-value*
effect	c.f = d	* *the new feature-value*

This action concept comes with three parameters: the object to be modified as $c \in C$, the feature f whose value is changed, and the new value $d \in D$. In which way the precondition is defined depends on issues of the specific domain modeling. In this case, it would actually not be necessary to specify a precondition, since the old feature value will be overwritten with the new value. For the same reason, a delete-operation is unnecessary. In order for the action to be instantiated, the respective type-constraints given through the parameter-concepts, have to be satisfied, and then, the action is well-defined and applicable.

4.2 Action Concepts and World States

We regard action concepts in a traditional view as generic transformers between world states, similar to functions, where the domain of the transformation function is

---

[2] The idea to describe action concepts by including parameter objects has been first described by the author in [11][13], and not in [9] as cited in [2].

the set of worlds fulfilling the precondition of an action, and the range or image of the transformation function is specified by the effect formula of the action concept.

In taxonomical knowledge bases or terminologies, a possible world state refers to a set of object-concept instances adhering to the concept definitions specified in the terminology. A terminological knowledge base on the generic level thus describes a set of world states, in accordance with the terminology. On the extensional, interpretation level a single world state is a model of the knowledge base given an interpretation of the concept descriptions.

4.3 The Subsumption Relation for Action Concepts

For defining the subsumption relation for actions, we consider - in the traditional manner - the set inclusion of the extensions of the concepts $C' \subseteq C$. In the case of action concepts, their extension is defined as the sets of worlds specified through precondition and effect formulae, which reflect the domain and the range of the transforming function, when we regard actions as transformers between world states.

We now define the subsumption relation for action concepts *a, a'* via a subsumption relation between the corresponding world sets

$$a' \text{ specializes } a \ (a \text{ subsumes } a') :\Leftrightarrow W_{a',pre} \subseteq W_{a,pre} \text{ and } W_{a',post} \subseteq W_{a,post}$$

where $W_{a,pre}$ denotes the set of worlds specified through the precondition formula of *a* and $W_{a,post}$ denotes the set of worlds specified by the effect formula of action *a* (equivalent for *a'*). Note that a complete world state to a state of a KB also integrates the object-concept definitions, which can also be formulated as FOPL formulae, but we consider here only the additional constraints specified through the action concepts.

Since the notion of world states is equivalent to the notion of models of the corresponding First-Order Predicate Calculus (FOPL) expressions, we can now relate the definition of the subsumption relation for world states related to action definitions in a terminological KB to the notions of logical consequence and formal inference of FOPL formulae.

Let α, α' be FOPL formula describing preconditions or effects of action concepts a, a', and $W_\alpha, W_{\alpha'}$ the set of possible interpretations of α, α'. Then

$$\alpha' \text{ specializes } \alpha \ (\alpha \text{ subsumes } \alpha') :\Leftrightarrow W\alpha' \subseteq W\alpha$$

which leads to

$$\alpha' \text{ specializes } \alpha \ (\alpha \text{ subsumes } \alpha') \Leftrightarrow \alpha' \models \alpha$$

Now, we use the correspondence of logical consequence and formal inference $\alpha' \models \alpha \Leftrightarrow \alpha' \vdash \alpha$ and integrate this with the subsumption definition for action concepts:

$$a' \textit{ specializes } a \ / \ a \textit{ subsumes } a' \Leftrightarrow \alpha' \vdash \alpha$$

This is a generalized notion of the specialization of action concepts based on the notion of inference between precondition and effect formulae, respectively. For action concepts, this is a new way of dealing with the subsumption and specialization relations, based on the introduced definition of the extensional semantics of action concepts as the set of world states specified through precondition and effect formulae, in coherence with the terminology. This conceptualization integrates various forms of specializing action concepts e.g. suggested in [11][13][18][19][20].

4.4 Specializing Action Concepts

In parallel to the standard forms of specializing object concepts, we can define specialization forms for action concepts, by specializing parameter-objects and precondition and effect formulae. As paradigmatic examples, based on the concept of Fluents as explained in section 3.2, we take the two general actions 'change-feature-value' (see section 4.1) and 'change-role' (see below) as paradigmatic examples, and specialize them by constraining the set of possible fillers for a parameter concept.

<u>change-colour-feature (c,d,f)</u>

is-a	change feature-value-action	
c	coloured-thing	*coloured-thing-concept*
d	colours	*colour-concept*
f	has-colour	*colour-feature*
pre	$\exists$x: colours(x) $\wedge$ c.has-colour = x	
effect	c.has-colour = d	

The action-definition 'change-colour-feature' above is derived from the generic 'change-feature-value' action by substituting the original concept restrictions with the new concept constraints 'coloured-thing', 'colours', and 'has-colour', respectively, and substituting the respective symbols in the precondition- and effect-formulae.

An equivalent approach is taken in case of roles/relations between concepts, like R(c,d) or ON(c,d). Consider the following general 'change-role' action:

<u>change-role (c,d,R)</u>

c	object-concept C	*parameter1*	
d	range-concept D	*parameter2*	
R	role R$\subseteq$ C$\times$D	*parameter3*	
pre	(c,d) $\notin$ R	*alternatively:*	$\neg$ *R(c,d)*
effect	(c,d) $\in$ R	*and*	*R(c,d)*

We can specialize this general action by reducing the set of possible fillers for the parameter-object, and otherwise inherit and modify the precondition- and effect-descriptions accordingly.

<u>put-in (c,d,R)</u>

is-a	change-role-status-action
c	containee-object-concept C
d	container-object-concept D
R	IN$\subseteq$ C$\times$D
pre	(c,d) $\notin$ R
effect	(c,d) $\in$ R

Since R in the generic action-description subsumes all possible combinations of C and D, the role IN is a sub-concept of R. The modified action has fewer instantiations and thus interpretations then the original one, due to the restriction of parameter-object concepts, and subsequently the relation IN.

5 Conclusion and Outlook

This paper outlines and explains a framework for describing actions in terminological or taxonomical knowledge bases which focuses on a more sophisticated definition of the subsumption relation between action concepts. For this purpose, it has been argued that action concepts can in general be defined as transformers between world states, where these world states are specified by the given terminology. The subsumption relation between actions has been based on a model-theoretic semantic, conform with the subsumption between world states as specified in the precondition and effect formulae of the subsumed and subsuming concept. This conceptual framework leads to a generalized form of the subsumption relation for action concepts in which subsumption is paralleled with logical inference of precondition or effect formula of a subsuming concept from the respective formulae of a subsumed concept. This is coherent with the view that a more specialized action is described by more restrictive formulae and operates on more constrained world models than the subsuming concept.

The framework outlined here is currently being implemented as part of a knowledge representation language with a focus on action representations. The connection with a planning system is envisaged.

References

[1] Allen, J. F., Temporal Reasoning and Planning, In: Allen, Kautz, Pelavin, Tenenberg (eds.), *Reasoning about Plans*, Morgan Kaufmann, 1991

[2] Artale A. and E. Franconi, A Temporal Description Logic for Reasoning about Actions and Plans, *Journal of Artificial Intelligence Research,* 9,pp. 463-506, 1998

[3] Artale A. and E. Franconi, A Computational Account for a Description Logic of Time and Action, *Proceedings of the Fourth International Conference on Principles of Knowledge Representation and Reasoning*, pp. 3-14, Bonn, Germany, 1994

[4] Artale A. and E. Franconi, Time, Actions, and Plans Representation in a Description Logic, *International Journal of Intelligent Systems*, 1995

[5] Artale A. and E. Franconi, Hierarchical Plans in a Description Logic of Time and Action,

[6] Bettini, C. A Formalization of Interval-Based temporal Subsumption in First-Order Logic, In: *Lecture Notes in Artificial Intelligence*, LNAI-810, Springer, 1994

[7] Bettini, C. Time Dependent Concepts: Representation and Reasoning Using Temporal Description Logics, *Data and Knowledge Engineering*, 22(1), pp.1-38, 1997

[8] Devanbu, P. T. and D. J. Litman, Taxonomic Plan Reasoning, *Artificial Intelligence*, 84, pp. 1-35, 1996

[9] Heinsohn, J., D. Kudenko, B. Nebel, and H.-J. Profitlich, *RAT: Representation of Actions Using Terminological Logics,* DFKI Technical Report, 1992

[10] Heinsohn, J., D. Kudenko, B. Nebel, and H.-J. Profitlich, An Empirical Analysis of Terminological Representation Systems, *Artificial Intelligence* 68(2):367-397, 1994

[11] Kemke, C. Die Darstellung von Aktionen in Vererbungshierarchien. In: Hoeppner (ed.), *GWAI-88, Proceedings of the German Workshop on Artificial Intelligence*, Springer, 1988

[12] Kemke, C. *What Do You Know about Mail? Representation of Commands and Concepts in the SINIX Consultant.* Invited talk & paper presented at the Workshop `Help Systems for UNIX Derivatives', UCB Berkeley, December 1987. Reprinted as Report No. 44, Computer Science Department, University of the Saarland, 1987

[13] Kemke, C. Representation of Domain Knowledge in an Intelligent Help System. In *Proceedings of the Second IFP Conference on Human-Computer Interaction INTER-ACT'87*, pp. 215-200, Stuttgart, FRG, 1987

[14] Kemke, C. What Do You Know about Mail? Knowledge Representation in the SINIX Consultant. *Artificial Intelligence Review*, 14: 253-275, Kluwer Academic Publishers, 2000. Reprinted in Stephen J. Hegner, Paul Mc Kevitt, Peter Norvig, Robert Wilensky (eds.): ***Intelligent Help Systems for UNIX.*** Kluwer Academic Publishers, Boston, USA & Dordrecht, The Netherlands, 2000

[15] Kemke, C. ***About the Ontology of Actions.*** Technical Report MCCS-01-328, Computing Research Laboratory, New Mexico State University, 2001

[16] Lifschitz, V. On the Semantics of STRIPS, In: *The 1986 Workshop on Reasoning about Actions and Plans*, pp.1-10, Morgan Kaufmann, 1987

[17] Patel-Schneider, P. F., B. Owsnicki-Klewe, A. Kobsa, N. Guarino, R. MacGregor, W. S. Mark, D. L. McGuiness, B. Nebel, A. Schmiedel, and J. Yen, Term Subsumption Languages in Knowledge Representation, *AI Magazine*, 11(2): 16-23, 1990

[18] Liebig, T. and D. Roesner, Action Hierarchies in Description Logics, Workshop on Description Logics, 1995

[19] Weida R. and D, Litman, Terminological Reasoning with Constraint Networks and an Application to Plan Recognition, *Proc. Third International Conference on Principles of Knowledge Representation and Reasoning*, pp. 282-293, Cambridge, MA, 1992

[20] Weida R. and D, Litman, Subsumption and Recognition of Heterogeneous Constraint Networks, Proceedings of CAIA-94, 1994

Improving User-Perceived QoS in Mobile Ad Hoc Networks Using Decision Rules Induction*

Juan A. Botía, Pedro Ruiz, Jose Salort, and Antonio Gómez-Skarmeta

Departamento de Ingeniería de la Información y las Comunicaciones
Universidad de Murcia. Spain
juanbot@um.es
pedro.ruiz@agoratechnologies.com
jsrn99ip@teleline.es, skarmeta@um.es

Abstract. Internetworking multimedia over mobile and wireless ad hoc networks, usually requires real-time multimedia applications to include some intelligent adaptive capabilities. These capabilities allow these applications to adapt to the constantly and unpredictable changing network conditions, making the user perceive a good quality rather than a variable quality with continuous blackouts. Modeling the end-user perception of the quality that the multimedia application delivers, is a crucial issue to take into account when deciding when to change the application settings in terms of codecs, frame rates, video sizes, etc. We present our inductive approach to obtain a decision rule set to take such decisions.

1 Introduction

The main focus of traditional multimedia applications is the reduction of the data rate when the network bandwidth becomes scarce, and the increase of the data rate whenever more resources become available. Of course, this behavior improves the QoS perceived by the user. However, the relation between user-perceived QoS and the data-rate required to achieve that QoS is not linear. So, when the network conditions become very bad, a correct change in the internal application settings, could greatly reduce the data rate, while keeping the QoS to an acceptable level. The main problem, is that for these applications to do that, they have to be aware of the user-perception of QoS. This modeling is very complex because it usually has subjective components which cannot be modeled analytically.

We propose in this work the use of decision rule induction [6] to model an user perception of quality given a concrete application settings (i.e. audio codec, video codec, etc) and concrete network conditions (i.e. bandwidth, network delay, etc). Learning data has been produced in the laboratory trying to cover the most important range of cases. Each one of the examples has been scored by an expert. Once data is available, we have used SLIPPER [3] to obtain an acceptable model

* Work supported by CICYT by means of the projects ISAIAS TIC2000-0198-P4-04 and SAM TIC2002-04531-C04-04.

Y. Xiang and B. Chaib-draa (Eds.): AI 2003, LNAI 2671, pp. 466–471, 2003.

of the user's perception of quality. The process developed to obtain this model is presented in section 2. Results are explained in section 3. Finally, conclusions and future works are given in section 4.

2 Modeling the User by SLIPPER

2.1 The Data from the User

In order to inductively model the QoS perception of an user, we have to produce a learning data set. And this has to be compound by examples of situations referring to a particular network condition and a particular multimedia application sending to and receiving data from the networks. Network conditions have been reproduced by using a reflector. This is a software tool collocated in the middle of a dedicated link between two communicating nodes that will be in charge of simulating different levels of available bandwidth and packet losses. The multimedia application used, ISABEL-Lite, is a reduced version of ISABEL [1] which allows both manual and automatic changes of its settings. Following, we present all attributes and the corresponding range of values, which compound the data set used to model the user. The BW parameter with values in $\{33, \ldots, 384\}$, refers to the limit of network bandwidth. The LOSS parameter with values from 0 to 100 refers to packet losses. AUDCOD, which can be one of {PCM, G711-u, G722, GSM} refers to the audio codec. And VIDCOD, {MJPEG, H.263} to the video codec. FSIZE is the video frame size and its possible values are {CIF, QCIF, 160x128}. QFVIDEO is the quality factor for video data taking values in {5, 10, 15, 30, 60}. FPS is the number of frames per second sent between 0 and 12. Finally, QoS with values in {1, 2, 3, 4, 5} is the score given by the user. The data set consists of 864 instances, each one scored by an user. It can be considered to be balanced with the following distribution of examples by score: 241 (27.8%) examples with score 1, 83 (10.4%) for score 2, 181 (20.9%) examples with score 3, 233 (26.9%) with 5 and finally, 125 (14.46%) for the highest score.

2.2 The Learning Experiments

Learning experiments have been performed using SLIPPER [3]. This algorithm does not directly use the classic search bias of divide an conquer for rule induction. Instead, it bases its strategy on boosting [4]. It uses a weak learner (i.e. a very simple rule induction algorithm) which boost by modifying learning instances probability each iteration to focus in instances not correctly classified yet. In fact, we also tested IREP, IREP* [5] and RIPPER [2]. Former algorithms which do not use boosting and all of them under-performed SLIPPER.

Two configuration parameters must be set for SLIPPER. They are the growing factor and the count of rounds to boost the weak learner we mentioned above. The growing factor is the proportion of instances from the data set used for growing a rule, meanwhile the rest is left for pruning it. We used a 80% of data for growing and the remaining 20% for pruning. Concerning the value of the

```
if matchConfidence {
        [QFVIDEO >= 60, VIDCOD = MJPEG, FSIZE = QCIF, LOSS <= 10, FPS >= 6] -> 2.8792
        [AUDCOD = GSM, BW >= 80, QFVIDEO >= 30, FSIZE = QCIF, FPS <= 6] -> 1.4357
        [AUDCOD = GSM, BW >= 128, LOSS = 0, QFVIDEO >= 30, FPS >= 3, VIDCOD = MJPEG]
                                                                              -> 1.7013
        [] -> -2.4188
} > 0 then 5 else if matchConfidence {
        [BW >= 384, QFVIDEO >= 40, FSIZE <= 2] -> 2.7121
        [QFVIDEO >= 30, VIDCOD = MJPEG, LOSS <= 3, AUDCOD = G722, BW >= 80] -> 1.1756
        [FSIZE = CIF, QFVIDEO >= 30, LOSS <= 3, AUDCOD = G722, BW >= 80] -> 1.4437
        [] -> -1.5044
} > 0 then 4 else if matchConfidence {
        [LOSS >= 30] -> 2.1188
        [QFVIDEO <= 5] -> 1.4142
        [LOSS >= 16, FPS <= 3] -> 1.5438
        [] -> -1.0984207275826066
} > 0 then 1 else if matchConfidence {
        [LOSS >= 16] -> 1.9109
        [QFVIDEO <= 10, FSIZE = QCIF] -> 1.5861
        [FSIZE = 160X128, QFVIDEO <= 40, VIDCOD = H.263] -> 1.2546
        [] -> -0.3953
} > 0 then 2 else 3
```

Fig. 1. SLIPPER model used to decide when to change application configuration

second parameter, let it be denoted with t, the higher its value (from 1 to n), the higher the model accuracy and its complexity. We developed experiments with values in $\{1, 2, \ldots, 15\}$. Results have Finally, the model we have selected from among the whole bunch of possible data sets is the one appearing at figure 1. It corresponds to $t = 5$ and has a total of 12 rules.

An instance is classified as belonging to a class if the sum of confidence value of all rules of the class matching the instance is higher than its negative value. The rule set extracted by SLIPPER allows us to identify which parameters are most important for the user-perception of QoS and which is the relation between ones and the others. For example, the rules imply that the higher the frame rate the better quality, but the user prefers changing from a higher frame rate to a lower one, provided that the video size is increased. Although there are big differences in bandwidth consumption between the different audio codecs, the rule set has identified that provided that there are no losses in the network, the better option is to use GSM only when the network resources are scarce, and using G.722 is enough to guarantee a good user-perception. This information given by the rule set, has allowed us to generate a concrete combination of settings among which, the application will change depending on the network conditions, and guaranteeing a good user-perceived QoS.

3 Results

In order to evaluate the effectiveness of our proposal, we have set up a real ad hoc testbed, on which we will compare the performance of real-time videoconferencing both with traditional applications and with *adaptive applications*. The

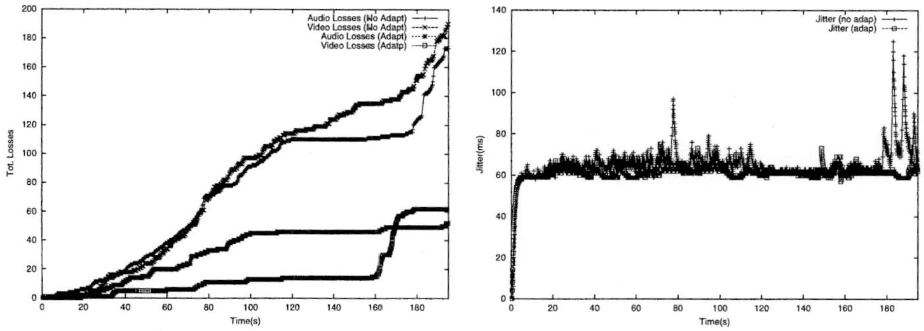

(a) (b)

Fig. 2. Total Losses (a) and Audio Jitter (b)

testbed has been deployed in the basement of the CS Faculty at the Univ. of Murcia. The route at the ad hoc testbed has been specifically selected so that link breaks and route changes take place during the videoconferencing session. Furthermore, the signal strength changes due to the variation of the distance to network nodes and the number of intermediate walls to traverse. This makes the available bandwidth vary during the session. The results which we present are extracted from control packets which are generated by the videoconferencing application. We have used the same route, at the same speed and in the same network conditions for the adaptive and non-adaptive trials.

The results presented in figure 2(a) show that the use of adaptive applications is able to reduce the overall packet losses both for audio and video to approximately 1/3. As expected, the differences are higher in the periods in which there is less bandwidth available. This is also noticed in the variation of the delays depicted in figure 2(b). In the same critical periods, the non-adaptive approach is not able to control the growing of the end-to-end delay, whereas the adaptive one is able to quickly restore the original state.

The overall packet losses is a good reference to identify the points of the trial in which the network conditions are most critical. This is identified by an increase in the slope of the total packet loss curve. However, what really affects the user perception of QoS is the instantaneous loss-rate, which is what causes the service disruptions.

In figure 3(a), we compare the statistical histogram for the distribution of the audio loss-rate for both approaches. The same statistical analysis is performed for the video flow in figure 3(b). For example, for the audio flow, the adaptive application approach is able to keep the loss-rate below 10% all the time. In fact, it keeps the loss-rate below 5% during the 91% of the time. For the video flow, the loss-rate is kept under the 5% the 64% of the time, and its has been under the 10% the 78% of the time.

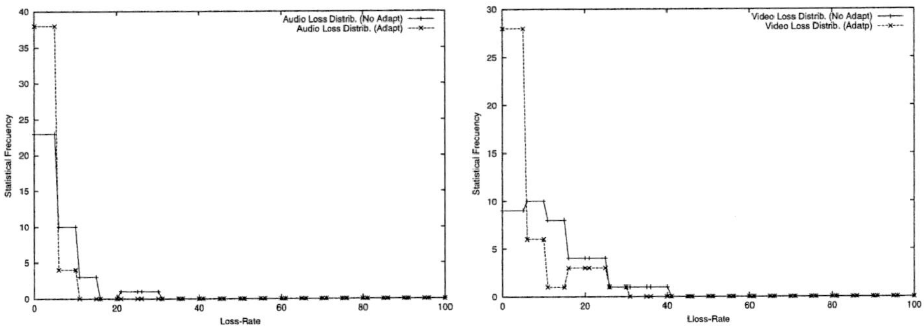

(a) (b)

Fig. 3. Audio Loss-rate distribution (a) and video loss-rate distribution (b)

These figures clearly demonstrate that the adaptive application approach driven by our induced rule set has been able to offer a very good user-perceived QoS in a scenario in which traditional solutions offer less performance.

4 Conclusions

In this work, we have demonstrated the validity of rule induction as a mechanism to extract user knowledge, in the form of decision rules, from a set of different cases. Machine learning tasks related to rule induction have been performed by using a software tool developed in our research group. It is called METALA and allows performing multiple learning experiments (i.e. definition, execution and analysis) with little effort, provided the learning algorithm (i.e. SLIPPER) and induced model (i.e. crisp decision rules) are previously integrated in the tool. The rule-based adaption logic we propose allows real time multimedia applications, used in ad hoc networks to maintain the quality perceived by the user at an acceptable level, while moving through different network conditions.

References

[1] *The ISABEL CSCW application.* [On line] http://www.agora2000.com/productos/isabel.html.

[2] W. Cohen. Fast effective rule induction. In *Proceedings of the Twelfth International Conference on Machine Learning*, pages 115–123, Lake Tahoe, CA, 1995.

[3] William W. Cohen and Yoram Singer. A simple, fast, and effective rule learner. In *Proceedings of the Conference of American Asociation for Artificial Ingelligence*, 1999.

[4] Yoav Freund and Robert E. Schapire. A short introduction to boosting. *Journal of Japanese Society for Artificial Intelligence*, 14(5):771–780, September 1999.

[5] J. Furnkranz. Separate and conquer rule learning. Technical report, Austrian Research Institute for Artificial Intelligence, 1996.

[6] Ryszard S. Michalski. A theory and methodology of inductive learning. In R. S. Michalski, J. G. Carbonell, and T. M. Mitchell, editors, *Machine Learning: An Artificial Intelligence Approach*, volume 1, pages 83–129. Springer, 1983.

Risk Neutral Calibration of Classifiers

Ron Coleman

Computer Science Department, Marist College
Poughkeepsie, New York, 12601, United States
ron.coleman@marist.edu

Abstract. In this paper we introduce a new, non-invasive approach to calibrating classifiers in a risk neutral setting based on the *worthwhile index*, W. We employ a simple Markov chain classifier and show through exhausted tests on data sets from the UCI machine-learning repository how to use the worthwhile index to significantly reduce the incidence of misclassification false positives. We hypothesize our approach to calibration may be applied to other classifier systems with few or no changes since the method involves observing the classifier's external behavior, not its internal mechanisms.

1 Introduction

Classifier systems play a key role in knowledge discovery in data warehouses. However, classifier systems are not typically well-calibrated in that the predicted performance learned on training data sets departs from the empirical performance on validation data sets [8]. This discrepancy exposes the data miner because accepting classification results may commit the individual or organization, either contractually or otherwise and thus, introduce financial, legal, operational, etc. risks. For instance, a mortgage company may face litigation and public relations (e.g., critical press) risks if its sales practices, guided by data mining analysis, appear to discriminate illegally.

Since commercial and administrative databases are often so large and complex and volatile, a human analyst, or other "intelligent" arbiter, may need to assess and ultimately validate the classifier's recommendations so as to mitigate misclassification risks. Yet this process can be costly and itself, error-prone. The goal of classifier calibration, then, is to support such interventions, to make them more reliable and cost-effective—that is, *worthwhile*.

In this paper, we present a new, non-invasive approach to calibration method based decision theoretic principles of risk neutrality. That is, an arbiter accepts a classification if the expected loss, $R(a|\omega^k)$, is zero for classification a in the feature vector, ω^k. Otherwise, the arbiter rejects the classification. To provide a formal estimate of what we mean by "worthwhile," we also introduce a new measure, the *worthwhile index*, W.

In the balance of the paper, we review related work and discuss our basic approach in further detail. Finally, we present of results calibrating a simple Markov chain clas-

Y. Xiang and B. Chaib-draa (Eds.): AI 2003, LNAI 2671, pp. 472-478, 2003.

sifier [6,8] on databases from the UCI machine-learning repository [9]. We show in a risk neutral setting how to significantly reduce misclassification false positives.

2 Related Work

A classifier system is *calibrated* if, given classification scores s_x and s_y such $s_x < s_y$, we have the probability distribution, $P(s_x) < P(s_y)$ [12]. A classifier system is *well-calibrated* if furthermore the predicted distribution, P(s), converges to the empirical distribution, $\pi(s)$, namely, lim $P(s)=\pi(s)$ for $n\rightarrow\infty$. Note that in either case the probability is nominal. That is, the goal of calibration is not specifically to maximize P(s), although this might be achieved as a side effect. No, the goal is to maximize the structure, cor[P(s),π(s)]. Early studies of calibration for classifier systems were rooted in weather forecasting [2]. Murphy and Winkler [10] analyzed forecasts using reliability diagrams in which predicted probabilities and empirical probabilities of well-calibrated classifiers follow a straight-line in an x-y scatter plot. DeGroot and Fienberg [4] investigate classifiers in terms of calibration and *refinement* which is a measure how close probability estimates comes to zero or one, that is, whether the prediction is unequivocal. More recently naïve Bayes and other classifiers [1,5,11] have been the focus of calibration research efforts. Of particular interest are cost-based methods [7,11] which are related to ours in that they also consider the expected loss or risk, $R(a|\omega^k) = \Sigma\lambda(a|b)P(b|\omega^k)$, given the conditional probability distribution, $P(b|x)$, and the loss function, $\lambda(a|b)$, of class a when the true class is b [6]. In our approach, however, the goal is not to minimize $R(a|\omega^k)$ using $P(b|w^k)$ and $\lambda(a|b)$ which may be unknown or difficult to estimate. Rather, we assume $R(a|\omega^k)=0$. Yet since there is no guarantee we'll find scenarios of $P(b|\omega^k)$ and $\lambda(a|b)$ compatible with $R(a|\omega^k)=0$, we may reject the classification, or even the classifier. The risk for our purposes is the opportunity costs, rather than the realized costs, of rejection.

3 Calibration in a Risk Neutral Setting

During the "calibration phase" which follows the training phase but precedes the validation phase we measure the correlation structure, $\mathbb{B}:\alpha\rightarrow r$, between the predicted probability of error, $P(e|\alpha)$, and the conditional Bernoulli error, $e|\alpha$, over a set of acceptance criteria, $\{\alpha_j\}$. This structure, $\mathbb{B}$, a surjective mapping called the *blocking curve*, also gives a W index for each α according to (1) below. Using W and r, we analyze $\mathbb{B}$ for possibly non-unique rejection thresholds, α, compatible with $R(a|\omega^k)=0$.

3.1 Worthwhile Index

The worthwhile index, W, is a measure of relative benefit founded on the risk neutral assumption, namely, when $R(a|w^k)=0$. Intuitively, if an arbiter is *a priori* risk neutral and rejects q percent of classifications as being inherently unreliable, this loss or opportunity cost, is offset by at least q percent reduction in false positives, namely,

$$W = \frac{\%\ reduction\ \ in\ \ f.p.}{\%\ classification\ rejection}\ . \tag{1}$$

More formally, we have:

$$W = (1 - P(e\,|\,\alpha) / P(e)) / \int_{\alpha}^{1} P(e\,|\,\theta)\ P(\theta)\ d\theta\ \cdot \tag{2}$$

When W < 1, we are rejecting more classifications than reducing the incidence of false positives. According to decision theory, this scenario is only worthwhile for a *risk-prone* arbiter, that is, $R(a|w^k)>0$. When W≥1 we are reducing the incidence of false positives faster than we are rejecting classifications. This setting is worthwhile for *risk neutral* and *risk adverse* arbiters, that is, $R(a|w^k)\leq 0$. We also note that if we apply *ex post facto* the empirical probability, π, instead of P, in (2), we have the empirical worthwhile index. We could similarly employ the "cross" worthwhile index by comparing two different classifiers. This idea is discussed in [3].

3.2 Choosing α

In a calibrated classifier if $s_x < s_y$ we have $P(s_x) < P(s_y)$ in which case $P(s_x|\alpha)<P(s_y|\alpha)$ must also hold. But by definition we have the error distribution is $P(e_x|\alpha)=1-P(s_x|\alpha)$. Thus, we state the lemmas, which follow from Murphy-Winkler reliability diagrams:

Lemma 1. If, $P(e|\alpha)<P(e)$, the classifier system is calibrated..

Lemma 2. If, $\pi(e|\alpha)=\beta_0+\beta_1\ P(e|\alpha)$ for $\beta_0\approx 0$ and $\beta_1\approx 1$, the classifier system is well-calibrated.

In the simplest scenario we select the value of α that maximizes r. We do not, however, recommend choosing a single *r* as such since, among other things, the level and significant (or p-value) of r may be unacceptable. Alternatively, we can use a more flexible, two-step approach that takes all available information into consideration, including worthwhile index, W, (discussed below):

Step 1. Start with the set, $\{\alpha_{W\geq 1}\}$. If we have $\{\alpha_{W\geq 1}\}=\varnothing$, we scrub the classifier completely regardless of r since the calibration tells us there's not like to be any worthwhile classifications. Typically, however, we have $\alpha_{\max(r)}\in \{\alpha_{W\geq 1}\}$.

Step 2. Proceed with $\{\alpha_{W\geq 1}:p\leq\tau\}$, namely, only statistically significant r. If, of course, $\{\alpha_{W\geq 1}:p\leq\tau\}=\varnothing$, we again reject the classifier. If on the other hand $|\alpha_{W\geq 1}:p\leq\tau|>1$, we suggest considering each α separately if it is practical to do so.

3.3 Markov Chain Classifier

We employ a simple Markov chain classifier of whose score is given by

$$s_x = \arg\max(\omega^k \in \Omega)\ \{P(x\,|\,\omega^k \backslash x)\ P(\omega^k \backslash x)\}\ \cdot \tag{3}$$

In this situation x is the goal attribute representing the next state; $\omega^k\backslash x$ are the non-goal attributes representing the current state; and ω^k is the "state of knowledge" from the training knowledgebase, Ω, that gives the most probable classification state $\{a,b,\ldots\}\in x$.

Table 1. Blocking curve for The Insurance Company Benchmark

α	r	p	P(e|α)	a.r.	W	π(e|α)
70%*	0.20	0.00	3.42%	21%	1.03	3.06%
75%*	0.23	0.00	3.92%	27%	1.08	3.37%
80%*	0.33	0.00	4.18%	45%	1.40	3.77%
85%*	0.34	0.00	6.49%	56%	1.46	5.38%
90%*	0.20	0.00	14.97%	86%	1.22	12.83%
95%*	0.06	0.00	18.05%	<100%	3.60	15.28%
100%	0.00	1.00	18.14%	100%	∞	15.65%

4 Results

In this section we present results calibrating the Markov chain classifier. We note that our tests are exhaustive Bernoulli trials. In other words, we classify *every* attribute in turn, not just the "class" attribute. These tests are thus substantially more rigorous and comprehensive compared to conventional tests on these datasets in the literature. The columns in each table have the following meaning: α is the nominal reject threshold; r is the Pearson correlation coefficient of between the predictive false positives, P(e|α), and the Bernoulli error distribution, (e|α), observed during the calibration phase; a.r. is the accept ratio, i.e., we reject (1-a.r.) at α; W is the predictive worthwhile index; and π(e|α) is the empirical false positives observed during validation. The * rows in each table represent α's selected the during the calibration phase according to the steps in Section 3.2. Following Murphy-Winkler, we also give the regression coefficients, β_0 and β_1, to further assess the degree of calibration.

4.1 The Insurance Company Benchmark Data Set

This is the first data set we consider from the UCI repository. We used only the training set which has nearly 6,000 rows and 86 attributes. We used the second 1,000 rows for the classifier training phase, the first 100 rows for the calibration phase, and the second 100 rows for validation phase. We mined the data over all 86 attributes, not just the one "caravan" class attribute. Thus, the calibration and validation phases each consist of n=8,600 classifications. We note by inspection that this classifier is well-calibrated according to Lemma 2 since β_0=0.00 and β_1=0.84.

4.2 Audiology Data Set

This is the second data set we consider from the UCI repository. It has 70 attributes. The training set has 76 rows and we split the original validation set into calibration (50 rows) and validation (100 rows) sets. Thus, for calibration and validation we have n=3,500 and n=7,000 classifications respectively.

In Table 2, we note the classifier is well-calibrated (β_0=0.01 and β_1=1.03) with substantial reductions in false positives. Although this classifier appears to get better with fewer tests it rejects, we must be careful in these situations. At α=95% the classifier rejects just three classifications, i.e., a.r. is 99.9134%.

4.3 Soybeans Data Set

This is the third data set we consider from the UCI repository. It has 36 attributes. The training set has 228 rows and we split the original validation set into calibration (50 rows) and validation (405 rows) sets. Thus, for calibration and validation we have n=1,800 and n=14,580 tests respectively.

In Table 3, we can note the reason we might not want to simply consider α's which maximize r since in this case the corresponding W (not shown) is less than one. Nevertheless, for the selected α's the classifier is less well-calibrated (β_0=0.04 and β_1=0.66) yet in some cases, the reductions in false positives are substantial.

4.4 Pittsburgh Bridges Data Set

This is the fourth data set we consider from the UCI repository. The bridges data set has 11 attributes. The training set has 54 rows and we split the original validation set into calibration (30 rows) and validation (24 rows) sets. Thus, for calibration and validation we have n=330 and n=264 tests respectively. This test represents the first negative case in which there are no scenarios compatible with $R(a|\omega^k)=0$ and consequently we reject the classifier as a whole. We note that that the peak correlation, r=0.17, is not predicted to be worthwhile since W=-0.29, a risk prone scenario. Indeed, the empirical false positives are higher (48%) than the predicted false positives (35%).

Table 2. The blocking curve for Audiology

α	R	p	P(e|α)	a.r	W	π(e|α)
75%*	0.15	0.00	5.24%	81%	1.40	6.13%
80%*	0.16	0.00	6.21%	95%	2.67	6.83%
85%*	0.19	0.00	6.77%	99%	7.81	7.66%
90%*	0.17	0.00	6.96%	<100%	11.53	7.88%
95%*	0.11	0.00	7.12%	<100%	12.90	7.98%
100%	0.00	1.00	7.20%	100%	∞	8.01%

Table 3. Blocking curve for Soybeans data set

α	r	P	P(e|α)	a.r.	W	π(e|α)
65%*	0.22	0.00	6.84%	57%	1.13	8.94%
70%*	0.20	0.00	8.93%	70%	1.10	9.86%
75%*	0.19	0.00	10.75%	86%	1.39	11.02%
80%*	0.19	0.00	11.70%	95%	2.16	12.09%
85%*	0.08	0.00	13.01%	99%	2.12	12.71%
90%*	0.05	0.03	13.20%	<100%	2.77	13.08%
95%	0.00	1.00	13.28%	100%	∞	13.25%
100%	0.00	1.00	13.28%	100%	∞	13.28%

Table 4. Blocking curve for the vote database

α	r	p	P(e|α)	a.r.	W	π(e|α)
65%*	0.25	0.00	17.31%	87%	1.47	22.87%
70%*	0.26	0.00	17.86%	91%	1.77	23.36%
75%*	0.26	0.00	18.33%	93%	1.90	24.67%
80%*	0.22	0.00	19.40%	96%	2.18	26.96%
85%*	0.20	0.00	19.97%	98%	2.53	27.54%
90%*	0.08	0.02	20.93%	99%	1.70	28.03%
95%*	0.04	0.32	21.18%	<100%	1.36	28.55%
100%	0.00	1.00	21.25%	100%	∞	28.83%

4.5 Vote Data Set

This is the fifth and final data set we consider from the UCI repository. It has 16 attributes. The training set has 300 rows and we split the original validation set into calibration (50 rows) and validation (80 rows) sets. Thus, for calibration and validation we have n=800 and n=1,280 classifications respectively. In Table 4 we see again a situation in which the empirical performance is better than the predicted performance. The empirical W=1.59 (not shown) is better than the predicted W=1.47, at α=65%. The classifier is less well-calibrated (β_0=-0.03 and β_1=1.51) yet the reductions in false positives are substantial in some cases.

5 Conclusions

In this paper we introduced new approach to calibrating classifiers that also significantly reduces the incidence of false positives. As our approach is both risk neutral and non-invasive—it does not depend on knowledge of the internal workings of the classifier—we hypothesize it can be readily applied to other classifier systems with possibly even better results. The only requirement is that classification scores can be calibrated at some threshold(s). This modest criterion, however, would seem to cover many systems, for instance, probabilistic and "possibilistic" classifiers.

The non-invasive nature also suggests the approach can be applied to classification systems, which generate asymptotically low probability scores. This is the case, for instance, for the Naïve Bayes classifier whose scores can be small since the independence assumptions mean many probabilities may have to be multiplied. Since our method does not depend on the level of probability, we do not expect this to be an issue. Future work needs to confirm this. Future work also need to address the rescaling the α's consistent with the predicted probabilities.

References

[1] P.N. Bennett. Assessing the calibration of naïve Bayes' posterior estimates. Dept. Comp Sci, CMU, Sep 12, 2000

[2] G.W. Brier. "Verification of forecasts expressed in terms of probability," *Monthly Weather Review*, 78:1-3, 1950

[3] R. Coleman, Analysis of Non-Calibrated and Risk Neutral Calibrated Classifier Systems, Unpublished manuscript

[4] M.H. DeGroot and A.E. Fienberg. The comparison and evaluation of forecasters. Statistician, 32(1):12-22, 1982

[5] J. Drish, Obtaining Probability Estimates from Support Vector Machines, http://citeseer.nj.nec.com/cs

[6] R.O. Duda and P.E. Hart. Pattern Classification, Wiley-Interscience, 2nd ed, 2001

[7] P. Domingos, MetaCost: A general method for making classifiers cost sensitive. Proceedings of the Fifth International Conference on Knowledge Discovery and Data Mining, ACM Press, 1999

[8] T. Mitchell. Machine Learning, McGraw-Hill, 1997

[9] P.M. Murphy and D. Aha, UCI Repository of Machine Learning Databases, ftp://ics.uci.edu/pub/machine-learning-databases, 1994

[10] Murphy and R. Winkler. Reliablity of subjective forecasts of precipitation and temperature., JRSS Series C, vol 26, p41-47, 1977

[11] Zadrozny and C. Elkan, Obtaining calibrated probability estimates from decision tress and naïve Bayes classifiers, Proc. 18 International Conf. On Machine Learning, 2001

[12] Zadrozny and C. Elkan, Transforming Classifier Scores into Accurate Multiclass Probability Estimates, Proc 8th Intl Conf on Knowledge Discovery and Data Mining, 2002

Search Bound Strategies for Rule Mining by Iterative Deepening

William Elazmeh

Department of Computing and Information Science
University of Guelph, Guelph, Ontario, Canada N1G 2W1
welazmeh@cis.uoguelph.ca

Abstract. Mining transaction data by extracting rules to express relationships between itemsets is a classical form of data mining. The rule evaluation method used dictates the nature and the strength of the relationship, eg. an association, a correlation, a dependency, etc. The widely used `Apriori` algorithm employs breadth-first search to find frequent and confident association rules. The Multi-Stream Dependency Detection (`MSDD`) algorithm uses iterative deepening (`ID`) to discover dependency structures. The search bound for `ID` can be based on various characteristics of the search space, such as a change in the tree depth (`MSDD`), or a change in the quality of explored states. This paper proposes an `ID`-based algorithm, $ID_{G_{max}}$, whose search bound is based on a desired quality of the discovered rules. The paper also compares strategies to relax the search bound and shows that the choice of this relaxation strategy can significantly speed up the search which can explore all possible rules.

1 Introduction & Problem Definition

Mining rules from data has been the focus of extensive research [1, 7, 12, 13] which requires searching an exponentially sized space of all rules involving combinations of itemsets present in the data. A measure of interest indicates the strength and the nature of the relationship (eg. an association, a correlation, a dependency, etc.). The rule mining problem can be very complex, for instance, mining optimized rules with constraints from data is NP-hard [4, 10]. The `Apriori` algorithm uses breadth-first search to explore a potentially explosive space, which can be costly [2, 5]. `Apriori` relies on a minimum support to prune candidate itemsets which limits the algorithm to discovering only frequent association rules [6]. The `MSDD` algorithm searches for rules of the k highest G-scores by using depth-first iterative deepening (`ID`) with a search bound based on the depth of states in the tree [12]. `MSDD` estimates candidate itemsets involved in desired rules which cannot be guaranteed to converge to an actual itemsets in the desired rules [12]. Korf et al., in [15], show that the search bound can be based on a change in quality of states being explored.

In this work, we present a rule mining algorithm $ID_{G_{max}}$ which uses `ID` search bounded by the quality of discovered rules and guarantees to discover the N rules of the highest G-scores. We present and compare three search bound relaxation

Y. Xiang and B. Chaib-draa (Eds.): AI 2003, LNAI 2671, pp. 479–485, 2003.

strategies (Conservative, Dynamic, and Exhaustive) to an implementation of `MSDD`. Our results show that the choice of a relaxation strategy can significantly speed up the search.

The problem of discovering the highest quality N rules can be reduced to a search for the set of N states which yield the highest evaluation scores, where each state contains a relationship rule. In a database T containing R transactions, let I be the set of all items present in all transactions. A relationship rule has the form $X \Rightarrow Y$ where $X = \{x_1, x_2, \cdots, x_n\}$, $Y = \{y_1, y_2, \cdots, y_m\}$, $x_i \in I$, $y_j \in I$, $X \cup Y \subseteq I$, and $X \cap Y = \phi$. For efficiency, a transaction $t \in T$ is a binary vector of binary items where each item $t[k] = 1$ or 0 indicates the presence or absence of the item k in t respectively. For a relationship rule $X \Rightarrow Y$, X and Y are represented as binary vectors where the binary bit $X[i] = 1$ or $*$ indicates the presence or the indifference of presence of item i in X. This "indifference" of presence restricts the rule to a positive interpretation excluding relationships which involve the absence of items. The search space is generated starting at the most general rule $[*, *, \cdots, *] \Rightarrow [*, *, \cdots, *]$, then, successors are generated by specializing one additional bit once in X or once in Y but never in both. This space forms a Directed Acyclic Graph (a DAG) containing duplicate rules. However, by eliminating duplicates, the search space becomes a finite state tree with the root being the most general relationship rule with a number of states $= 3^{|I|}$ because every item $\in I$ is specialized once in X, once in Y, or never.

2 Rule Evaluation G with an Upper Bound G_{max}

Research has focused on the quality of discovered rules quantified by a measure of interest [4]. However, quantifying "interestingness" is subject to the rule evaluation test. Classical statistics may be used to interpret relationships such as associations [4], correlations [3, 6, 9], causalities [14], dependencies [11], etc. The `MSDD` algorithm searches for dependencies measured by the G measure [11], a statistical measure of non-independence. `MSDD` also uses G_{max} as an upper bound on the G scores of all descendants of a rule for pruning [4].

For a relationship rule $S = X \Rightarrow Y$, we count the number of transactions n_1, n_2, n_3, n_4 containing $X \wedge Y$, $X \wedge \bar{Y}$, $\bar{X} \wedge Y$, or $\bar{X} \wedge \bar{Y}$ respectively. We compute their expected values $\hat{n}_1 = (n_1+n_2)(n_1+n_3)/T$, $\hat{n}_2 = (n_1+n_2)(n_2+n_4)/T$, $\hat{n}_3 = (n_3 + n_4)(n_1 + n_3)/T$, and $\hat{n}_4 = (n_3 + n_4)(n_2 + n_4)/T$ where $T = n_1 + n_2 + n_3 + n_4$. Then, G can be computed by $G = 2\sum_{i=1}^{4} n_i log(\frac{n_i}{\hat{n}_i})$. It is shown [11] that the G scores of all descendants of S are maximized by computing the G_{max} value. An important property is that G_{max} is monotone with non-increasing values for descendants in the tree space. Detailed analysis and computations of G and G_{max} are presented in [11]. Our algorithm, $ID_{G_{max}}$, evaluates a rule S using G and computes a heuristic upper bound on G scores of all descendants of S using G_{max}. Additionally, $ID_{G_{max}}$ uses the G_{max} values for the search bound of `ID`, for pruning rules whose G–scores are guaranteed by G_{max} to be low, and for ordering candidate rules for further exploration.

Algorithm $ID_{G_{max}}(S = root, SearchBound = \infty)$:
while not done **do**
  Perform a recursive depth–first search starting at S, limited by $SearchBound$;
  {This records observed G_{max} before pruning states $G_{max} < SearchBound$}
  if ($SearchBound <$ lowest G found || no more observed G_{max}) **then**
    Done
  else
    $T \leftarrow Relaxation\_Factor \times$ number of states expanded so far
    $SearchBound \leftarrow$ observed G_{max} {guarantees additional fringe states $\leq T$}
  end if
end while

Fig. 1. The $ID_{G_{max}}$ algorithm using the dynamic relaxation strategy. The conservative or the exhaustive relaxation selects the highest or lowest observed G_{max} respectively

3 $ID_{G_{max}}$ Algorithm, Results, and Discussion

The search algorithm $ID_{G_{max}}$ employs a classical search technique known as depth-first iterative deepening (ID) [8]. ID performs series of depth–first searches (DFS) each is limited to a depth cutoff known as the search bound. Over many iterations, ID progressively relaxes the search bound until it reaches the set of desired states. Traditionally, the search bound is based on the depth of states in the tree but for $ID_{G_{max}}$, we use a heuristic estimate of the quality of states reflected by G_{max} values observed in the space. $ID_{G_{max}}$ relaxes the search bound in a decreasing sequence of the observed G_{max} values (Fig. 1). In a single DFS iteration and starting at the root, $ID_{G_{max}}$ generates and searches states within the search bound while recording frequencies and G_{max} values of those states outside the search bound before pruning them. Every DFS iteration explores previously explored states plus states found within the current search bound. After an iteration is completed, the search bound for next iteration is relaxed to a selected G_{max} value observed from the fringe states according to a particular relaxation strategy. Such strategy can be **conservative** which selects the highest observed G_{max}, **exhaustive** which selects the lowest observed G_{max}, or **dynamic** which selects an observed G_{max} score which grows the search space sufficiently to balance work–load and performance. This attempt is based on imposing a threshold (proportional to the number of states expanded) on the number of additional fringe states to be included in the space. This proportion of growth is controlled by the `Relaxation_Factor`, a user-supplied parameter.

MSDD explores high G_{max} scoring rules relating frequent itemsets under the assumption that frequently appearing items continue to be useful in the successor rules [12]. To ensure a justified comparison between $ID_{G_{max}}$ and MSDD, we produce ID_{Depth}, an implementation of MSDD, which uses ID limited by the tree depth and explores states which are expected to produce higher G scores early on in the search but with few alterations from MSDD. First, unlike MSDD, ID_{Depth} does not approximate itemsets involved in rules to guarantee the discovery of the strongest N rules. Second, MSDD returns a set of rules of the highest k values of the G scores, hence, it may discard rules of the same G scores. ID_{Depth} and $ID_{G_{max}}$ return the set of N rules that have the highest G scores including rules of the same G scores. Third, MSDD alters the search strategy to a single unlimited DFS due to the consistent behavior of the combinatorial increase followed by a decrease in the size of the tree [11]. ID_{Depth} continuously performs DFS iterations limited by the tree depth search bound without altering the search method for consistency.

We compare the performance of the conservative, the dynamic, and the exhaustive search bound relaxation strategies used by $ID_{G_{max}}$ to each other and to ID_{Depth}. We present results from two datasets. The **Solar Flare** dataset contains 323 records and 40 features and is obtained from UC Irvine repository (Fig. 2). The **Flight Errors** dataset consists of 22433 records of failure messages reported by 30 aircraft subsystems and is provided by Air Canada (Fig. 3). All four algorithms are run twice on every dataset, once with a varying **Relaxation_Factor** (Fig. 2.i, 3.i) and a second with a varying number of desired rules N (Fig. 2.ii, 3.ii). The size of the datasets influences CPU time because records are consulted by the search algorithms whenever a state is evaluated. Each algorithm performs a complete pass on a dataset when it evaluates every state it generates. Thus, for every run, we report the CPU time and counts of expanded states and generated states. The increasing **Relaxation_Factor** is rel-

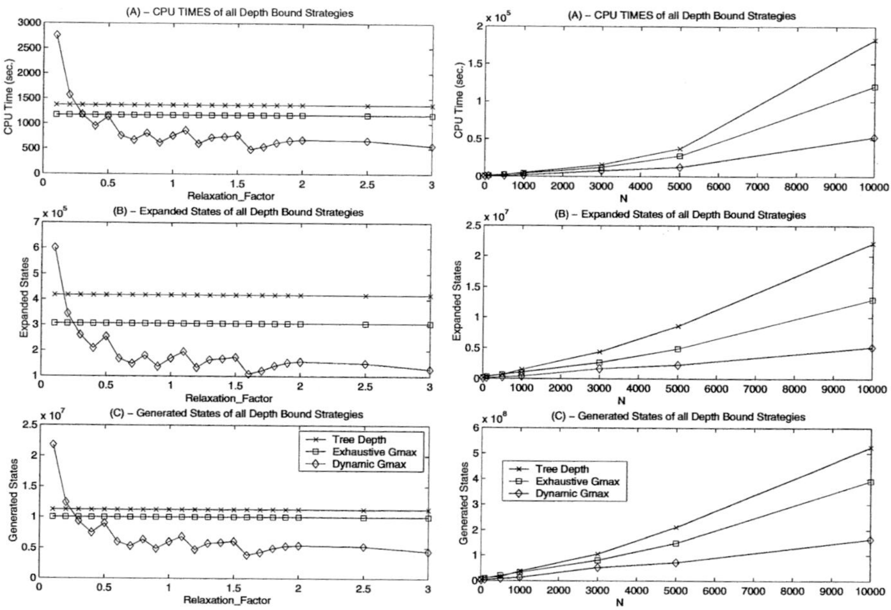

(i) (ii)

Fig. 2. Solar Flare: 323 records, 40 items. (i) N=100. (ii) Relaxation_Factor=3.0. (A) CPU time. (B) Expanded states. (C) Generated states

evant only to the $ID_{G_{max}}$ using the dynamic strategy exhibiting an improved performance (Fig. 2.i, 3.i), while a variable N may increase beyond the number of rules in the space whose $G_{max} > 0$, which causes all four algorithms to explore the same space in subsequent runs and flattens out their performance curves (Fig. 3.ii).

Since ID_{Depth} is bound by the depth of states in the space regardless of quality, it explores the tree with disregard to the location of desired states relying on pruning to be effective. Alternatively, $ID_{G_{max}}$ is bound by G_{max} scores, hence, states are generated and expanded based on their estimated quality. Therefore, when G_{max} is close to G, the space is explored with focus on desired quality. However, G_{max} is a heuristic function and can fail to reflect the actual G, leaving the search algorithm faced with an explosive or misleading space where depth–first search deficiencies become costly [15]. For our datasets, the G_{max} failed to accurately estimate the G scores for most of the discovered rules but our results show that G_{max} failure does not affect the performance of $ID_{G_{max}}$. However, the conservative strategy (Fig. 3.i) suffers significantly from the cost of re-exploring previously explored states, therefore, it was excluded from some experiments.

The exhaustive strategy consistently outperforms ID_{Depth} and can perform as good as the dynamic strategy which improves its performance as the value of the `Relaxation_Factor` increases. Hence, for an appropriate `Relaxation_Factor`

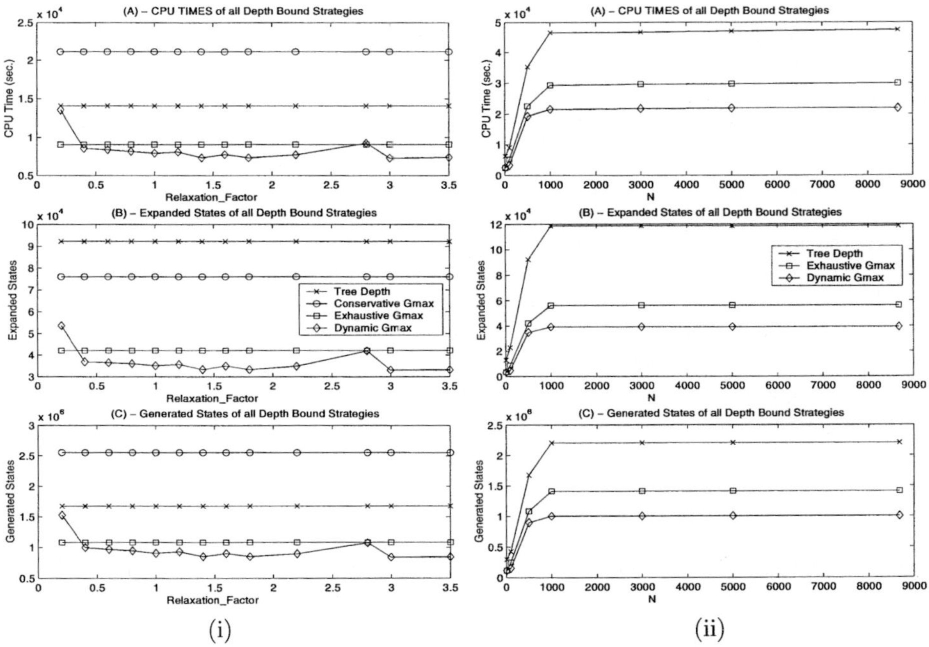

Fig. 3. Flight Errors: 22433 records, 30 items. (i) N=500. (ii) Relaxation_Factor=2.2. (A) CPU time. (B) Expanded states. (C) Generated states

value, the dynamic strategy consumes significantly less CPU time while exploring and generating fewer states.

4 Conclusions and Future Work

Mining for the strongest rules by iterative deepening while using an estimation of quality (G_{max}) is more suitable than using the state depth to limit the search provided the algorithm uses a non-conservative relaxation strategy. Both exhaustive and dynamic strategies perform well compared to ID_{Depth}. The dynamic strategy can perform significantly better than all other strategies given an appropriate `Relaxation_Factor`. Future work includes determining an appropriate `Relaxation_Factor` value systematically, allowing $ID_{G_{max}}$ to modify the search bound value during a depth–first iteration, and possibly using advanced memory management methods to avoid restarting every search iteration.

References

[1] R. Agrawal, T. Imielinski, and A. Swami. Mining associations between sets of items in massive databases. In *ACM-SIGMOD Int. Conf. on Management of Data*, pages 207–216, 1993.
[2] R. Agrawal and R. Srikant. Fast algorithms for mining association rules. In *The Twentieth VLDB Int. Conf.*, pages 487–499, 1994.
[3] A. Agresti. *Categorical Data Analysis.* John Wiley & Sons, New York 1990.
[4] R. J. Bayardo and R. Agrawal. Mining the most interesting rules. In *The Fifth Int. Conf. on Knowledge Discovery and Data Mining*, pages 145–154, 1999.
[5] R. J. Bayardo, R. Agrawal, and D. Gunopulos. Constraint-based rule mining in large, dense databases. In *The Fifteenth Int. Conf. on Data Engineering*, pages 188–197, 1999.
[6] S. Brin, R. Motwani, and C. Silverstein. Beyond market baskets: Generalizing association rules to correlations. In *ACM-SIGMOD Int. Conf. on The Management of Data.*, pages 265–276, 1997.
[7] U. M. Fayyad, G. Piatetsky-Shapiro, P. Smyth, and R. Uthurusamy. *Advances in Knowledge Discovery and Data Mining.* AAAI Press / The MIT Press, 1996.
[8] R. E. Korf. Depth-first iterative deepening: An optimal admissible tree search. In *Artificial Intelligence*, volume 27, pages 97–109, 1985.
[9] W. Mendenhall, R. Scheaffer, and D. Wackerly. *Mathematical Statistics with Applications.* Duxbury Press, 3rd edition, 1986.
[10] S. Morishita. On classification and regression. In *The First Int. Conf. on Discovery Science – Lecture Notes in Artificial Intelligence.*, volume 1532, pages 40–57, 1998.
[11] T. Oates and P. R. Cohen. Searching for structure in multiple streams of data. In *The Thirteenth Int. Conf. on Machine Learning*, pages 346–354, 1996.
[12] T. Oates, M. D. Schmill, and P. R. Cohen. Efficient mining of statistical dependencies. In *The Sixteenth Int. Joint Conf. on Artificial Intelligence.*, pages 794–799, 1999.
[13] G. Piatetsky-Shapiro and W. J. Frawley. *Knowledge Discovery in Databases.* AAAI Press / The MIT Press, 1991.

[14] C. Silverstein, S. Brin, R. Motwani, and J. Ullman. Scalable techniques for mining causal structures. In *Data Mining and Knowledge Discovery*, pages 163–192, 2000.

[15] N. R. Vempaty, V. Kumar, and R. E. Korf. Depth-first versus best-first search. In *The 9th National Conf. on Artificial Intelligence*, pages 434–440, 1991.

Methods for Mining Frequent Sequential Patterns

Linhui Jiang and Howard J. Hamilton

Department of Computer Science
University of Regina, Regina, SK, Canada S4S 0A2

Abstract. We consider the problem of finding frequent subsequences in sequential data. We examine three algorithms using a trie with K levels. The $O(K^2n)$ breadth-first (BF) algorithm inserts a pattern into the trie at level k only if level k-1 has been completed. The $O(Kn)$ depth-first (DF) algorithm inserts a pattern and all its prefixes into the trie before examining another pattern. A threshold is used to store only frequent subsequences. Since DF cannot apply the threshold until the trie is complete, it makes poor use of memory. The heuristic depth-first (HDF) algorithm, a variant of DF, uses the threshold in the same manner as BF. HDF gains efficiency but loses a predictable amount of accuracy.

1 Introduction

Data mining is the analysis of (often large) observational data sets to find unsuspected relationships and to summarize the data in novel ways that are both understandable and useful to the data owner [HMS2001]. ***Pattern discovery***, or the search for frequently occurring subsequences in sequences, is a well-known data-mining task. Sequences of events occur naturally in many domains.

In this paper, we address an abstract version of the problem of finding frequent sequences of page accesses in a log file by considering the problem of finding frequent subsequences in a sequence dataset. In the abstract problem, each web page in a website is represented by a symbol from a finite alphabet letter. We use the 26 uppercase letters to represent the possible web pages, and examine the problem of finding frequently occurring subsequences of items in very long sequences. The particular problem studied is to find all frequently occurring substrings of length K or less in a very long string. In our experiments, we generate synthetic test data containing subsequences with known properties, and then test the effectiveness of various algorithms at finding the frequently occurring substrings.

We examine a specific problem where the events in the sequence are restricted to the 26 uppercase letters and the maximum length of the subsequences is restricted to K. This restricted problem is equivalent to finding all frequently occurring substrings of length K or less in a very long string. Although the number of possible subsequences in a single-sequence dataset of length n is $n+(n-1)+\ldots+1=(n^2+n)/2$,

Y. Xiang and B. Chaib-draa (Eds.): AI 2003, LNAI 2671, pp. 486-491, 2003.

the maximum number of possible subsequences of at most length K in such a sequence is $nK - K(K-1)/2$.

Generally, frequent sequences are sought in two types of datasets: single-sequence datasets and multiple-sequence datasets. A ***single-sequence dataset*** consists of only one sequence. A ***multiple-sequence dataset*** consists of one or more sequences. A ***sequential pattern*** is a consecutive or nonconsecutive ordered subset of an event sequence. A ***subsequence pattern*** is a consecutive sequential pattern. A ***frequent sequential pattern*** occurs more than a specified number of times (the threshold) in a dataset. When searching for patterns in a multiple-sequence dataset, the general idea is to seek sequential patterns that exist in a high proportion of the sequences. Candidate-generation algorithms, such as AprioriAll [AS1995] and SPADE [Zak1997], are useful for finding common patterns within multiple-sequence datasets. For a single-sequence dataset, the problem can be simplified to discovering all frequent sequential patterns in a long sequence. Search windows are used and only subsequence patterns are considered. When searching for subsequence patterns, generating candidates reduces neither the number of patterns to seek nor the time required to scan the dataset. Thus, direct search without candidate generation is sufficient to find subsequence patterns.

Since finding subsequences in a single-sequence dataset is equivalent to finding substrings in a string, recent research on the latter topic is of interest. The ***frequent substring generation algorithm*** [Vil1998] discovers frequently occurring substrings in DNA and protein sequences. As described in their paper, the algorithm constructs a pattern trie in a breadth first fashion. A simplified version of the frequent substring generation algorithm is the basis for the breadth-first algorithm we introduce in the next section.

2 Methods for Mining All Frequent Subsequences

We describe three methods for finding frequent subsequences. All three methods are based on a data structure called a trie. We consider two methods of searching the data, which result in two different ways of inserting into the trie, namely bread-first insertion and depth-first insertion. Once the trie has been constructed, we can readily find all frequent subsequences with length less than or equal to K in the trie. A threshold is used with these algorithms to specify the minimum number of occurrences required to be "frequent". We also propose an additional heuristic method based on depth-first insertion. The threshold is used speed up depth-first insertion by ignoring longer subsequences until their initial subsequences have been determined to be frequent.

```
LET = 26;
struct TNode
{
  int      IArray[LET];
  TNode* PArray[LET];
};
```

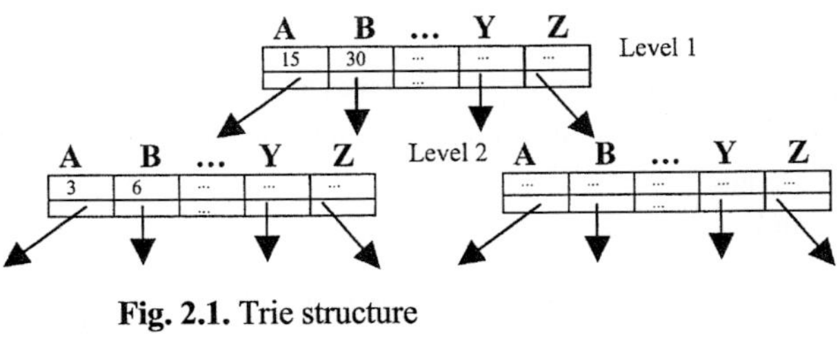

Fig. 2.1. Trie structure

A ***trie*** is a tree where every edge-label has length exactly one. In our trie representation, each node in the trie has 26 buckets, one for each of the 26 uppercase letters. A partial trie structure is shown in Figure 2.1. For a full trie, there are 26^{k-1} nodes at the kth level, but we are most interested in non-full tries.

The **Breadth-First (BF) algorithm** makes *K* passes over the data to construct a trie. On the kth pass, all subsequences with length *k* are added to the trie. For example, on the first pass through the data, all subsequences with length 1 are inserted. During insertion, the threshold plays a major role. After all patterns of length *k* have been inserted, an additional check is made to prune all newly generated nodes that have counts less than the threshold.

The **Depth-First (DF) algorithm** reads the dataset only once, using a window of size *K*. The subsequence *s* in the first window consists of the first through K^{th} letters of the dataset, and the ith window consists of ith through $(i+k\text{-}1)^{th}$ letters. When a subsequence *s* with length *K* is processed, it and all its prefixes are inserted into the trie. After the whole trie is constructed, any node with all counts less than the threshold is pruned. Although DF is fast compared to BF, it can use significantly more space for the same threshold setting. With DF, pruning cannot be performed until all subsequences have been inserted into the trie. Since every node has 26 buckets (which would be much larger for a less restricted alphabet), each with 2 fields of say 4 bytes each, space requirements rise rapidly for larger values of *K*; e.g. *K*=4, $(26*2*4)^4$ bytes = 1,871,773,696 bytes. A subsequence is kept during the trie construction, even if it only occurs once.

The **Heuristic Depth-First (HDF) algorithm** is based on DF. To apply pruning before the trie has been completely constructed, the number of occurrences of a subsequence's prefixes is compared to the threshold before inserting the subsequence. If any prefix of a subsequence has not yet been shown to be frequent, then we choose not to start counting the occurrences of the subsequence itself.

Input: Dataset *s*, maximum length *K*, and threshold *t*.

```
Root ← new node
for i = 1 to (dataset length – K + 1)  // all subsequences
    s = S[i...i + K – 1]
    InsertAllPrefixes(Root, K)
end
if t > 0
    PruneTrie(Root, K)
end
```

Fuction InsertAllPrefixes (Root, *K*)

```
for k = 1 to K
    if subsequence s[1...k – 1] is present in the trie with root R with count ≥ t
        Insert the subsequence s[1...k] into the trie with root R
    end
end
```

Fig. 2.2. The Heuristic Depth-First (HDF) algorithm

HDF is shown in Figure 2.2. During insertion, if the prefix of a subsequence is not present, the subsequence itself is not inserted. Thus, occurrences of a subsequence of length 4 are ignored until first its prefixes of length 1, and then length 2, and finally length 3 are found to be frequent. The maximum number of occurrences of a subsequence that will be lost is the product of the threshold and the subsequence's length. HDF is appropriate when $Kt << n$, i.e., when the product of the threshold and the maximum sequence length is small compared to the length of the dataset.

3 Results

All three methods for finding frequently occurring subsequences were tested on a variety of large synthetic datasets. The comparison is based on two aspects, elapsed time and memory utilization. The lengths of the synthetic datasets were 10^4, 10^5, 10^6, and 10^7. For all experiments, every value reported or shown in a graph is the average value from ten newly generated datasets. Four parameters were used: dataset length, maximum sequential pattern length K (which corresponds exactly to the maximum number of levels in the trie), algorithm (BF, DF or HDF), and threshold value.

We observed memory utilization (maximum nodes), with K fixed and the thresholds varying, as shown in Figure 3.1. All methods generate fewer nodes as the threshold increases. Since patterns randomly appear in the datasets, it is unlikely that the threshold and the number of trie nodes will have a straight inverse ratio. Instead, nodes are dropped sooner and more quickly for longer datasets than shorter ones. As well, as the threshold is increased, some nodes no longer have high enough counts and are dropped. If plotted on a graph, the number of nodes appears to be a flat line, with a vertical decrease when some nodes no longer meet the threshold, followed by another flat line.

We compared the elapsed time with thresholds of 0 and 10 and varying lengths of datasets. With a threshold of 0, as shown in Figure 3.2(a), the elapsed time for building the trie is directly proportional to the dataset length for all three methods. BF spends more time than DF and HDF because it has $O(K^2n)$ time complexity instead of $O(Kn)$. HDF always requires slightly more time than DF for threshold checking. With a threshold of 10, the elapsed time is still directly proportional to the data length. DF generally requires more time than BF, except for datasets with length 10^7. In all these cases, HDF requires less time than BF or DF.

The observed difference between the behavior of BF and DF is consistent with their worst-case time complexities. This difference is caused by the placement of the threshold check in the two methods. For DF, the threshold is only checked after all patterns have been inserted into the trie, and as a result, it spends more time than without threshold. As shown in Figure 3.2(b), for generating a trie for a dataset with length 10^7, BF requires more time than DF with a threshold of 10. Possibly the dataset is so large and the threshold is so small that the threshold has little effect.

DF and HDF require significantly less time than BF when no threshold is set. When a threshold is set, DF is not able to use it effectively, since it prunes the trie after all subsequences have been inserted. By pruning after each level of the trie has been constructed, BF responds better to the frequencies in a particular dataset. Longer patterns are only inserted into the trie if their prefixes are frequent. By combining the efficiency of depth first insertion and level-by-level response to the threshold, HDF obtains excellent results on very large datasets.

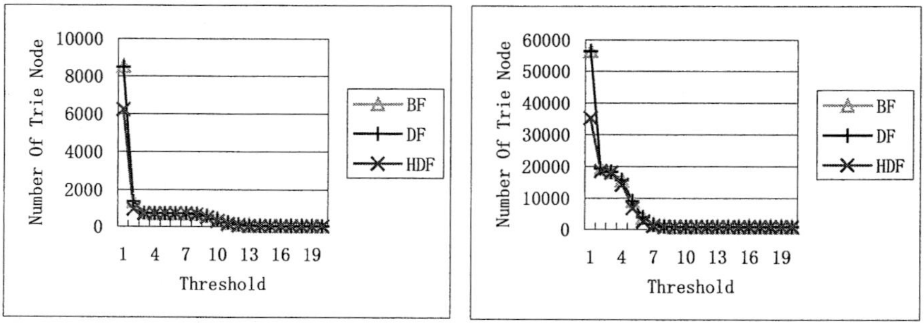

(a) Dataset with length 10^5 (b) Dataset with length 10^6

Fig. 3.1. Memory utilization for various thresholds

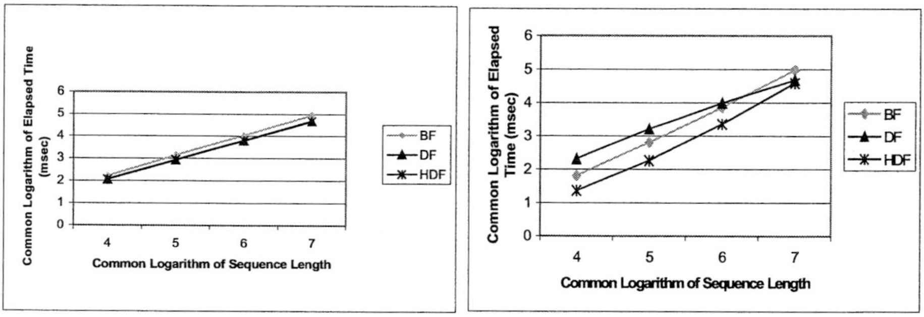

(a) threshold $t = 0$. (b) threshold $t = 10$

Fig. 3.2. Dataset length versus elapsed time

4 Conclusion

The problem of finding sequential patterns that occur frequently in a large dataset was addressed in this paper. Experiments were conducted to compare the performance of the three methods, BF, DF, and HDF on a variety of synthetic datasets. Each synthetic dataset was created based on specified constraints and pseudo-random number generation. We measured the elapsed time and memory utilization. HDF may miss a few longer patterns that are present only near the beginning of the dataset, but it is more efficient and better able to find long patterns than BF or DF. It sacrifices completeness for efficiency. For long patterns more details are given in [Jia2003].

References

[AS1995] Agrawal, R., and Srikant, R., "Mining Sequential Patterns." *Proceedings IEEE International Conference on Data Engineering*, Taipei, Taiwan, 1995.

[HMS2001] Hand, D.J., Mannila, H., and Smyth, P., *Principles of Data Mining*, MIT Press, Cambridge, Massachusetts, 2001.

[Jia2003] Jiang, L., "A Quick Look at Methods for Mining Long Subsequences", *Proceedings AI'2003*, this volume.

[SA1995] Srikant, R., and Agrawal, R., *Mining Sequential Patterns: Generalizations and Performance Improvements*. Research Report RJ9994, IBM Almaden Research Center, San Jose, California, December 1995.

[Vil1998] Vilo, J., *Discovering Frequent Patterns from Strings*, Technical Report C-1998-9, Department of Computer Science, University of Helsinki, FIN-00014, University of Helsinki, May 1998.

[Zak1997] Zaki, M.J., *Fast Mining of Sequential Patterns in Very Large Databases*, Technical Report 668, Computer Science Department, University of Rochester, Rochester, New York, Nov. 1997.

Learning by Discovering Conflicts

George V. Lashkia[1] and Laurence Anthony[2]

[1] Dept. of Information Science, Chukyo University
101 Tokodachi, Kaizu-cho, Toyota, Japan
lashkia@sccs.chukyo-u.ac.jp

[2] Dept of Inf. & Comp. Eng., Okayama University of Science
1-1 Ridai-cho, Okayama 700-0005, Japan
anthony@ice.ous.ac.jp

Abstract. The paper describes a novel approach to inductive learning based on a 'conflict estimation based learning' (CEL) algorithm. CEL is a new learning strategy, and unlike conventional methods CEL does not construct explicit abstractions of the target concept. Instead, CEL classifies unknown examples by adding them to each class of the training examples and measuring how much noise is generated. The class that results in the least noise, i.e., the class that least conflicts with the given example is chosen as the output. In this paper, we describe the underlying principles behind the CEL algorithm, a methodology for its construction, and then summarize convincing empirical evidence that suggests that CEL can be a perfect solution in real-world decision making applications.

1 Introduction

The task studied in this paper is supervised learning or learning from examples. Several different representations have been used to describe the concepts used in supervised learning. Many learning algorithms such as decision trees [1], neural networks [2] and decision rules [3] derive generalizations from training instances and construct explicit abstractions, which are then used to classify subsequent test instances. Instance-based learning algorithms [4], on the other hand, use the training instances themselves as explicit abstractions, and compute a distance between the input vector and the stored examples when generalizing.

In this paper we propose a novel strategy for learning. Instead of computing explicit abstractions that characterize the unknown target concept we simply measure how well an input example is fitted to the known training examples. In other words, we place an input example in a set of training examples of a class and measure the noise that it produces. The class that least conflicts with the input example, i.e., the class that results in the least amount of noise, is selected as the outcome. We demonstrate our learning strategy by a simple real world example. Imagine that we are asked to predict the nationality of a person. The prediction can be carried out by detecting

Y. Xiang and B. Chaib-draa (Eds.): AI 2003, LNAI 2671, pp. 492-497, 2003.

characteristic properties of each country and constructing abstractions that capture the decision structure in an explicit way. Our approach is different. We place the person in a group of people from each country and look at what conflicts emerge in the group. In general, we have less conflicts with people from our home country, and so by detecting the amount of conflicts (noise) that emerge, a decision can be made.

The CEL approach is inspired by the work [5], where a new noise filtering method that resembles frequency domain filtering in signal and image processing was proposed. This method explicitly detected and eliminated noisy examples from the training data by filtering the so-called *pattern frequency domain* of the training examples. Noise instances generated patterns with low frequency (opposite to high frequency in signal and image processing), and therefore by preserving high pattern frequencies and suppressing low pattern frequencies, noise cleaning could be achieved. It is important to note that the term noise is used as a synonym for outliers: it refers to exceptional cases as well as incorrect examples.

The ability to detect noise is an essential feature of CEL. CEL places an unknown example in a set of training examples of a class and then counts how many low frequency patterns will be generated. If the example is placed in an incorrect class, it will appear as noise and therefore result in an increase in the number of low frequency patterns. Although CEL is not based on distance calculations, it acts like an instance-based learning algorithm, in that it uses examples from the training set to calculate pattern frequencies. A major limitation of CEL is that in principle it can only operate on discrete attributes. This limitation is not rare in machine learning. Many algorithms, including decision trees, require a discrete attribute space. Although there are ways to handle continuous attributes in CEL (in the same way as in [5]), in this paper we assume that all attributes are discrete.

2 CEL

We consider the problem of automatically inferring a target concept c defined over X from a given training set of examples D. Following standard practice, we identify each domain instance with a finite vector of attributes $\tilde{x} = (x_1,...,x_n)$. Suppose that a training set D is formed from positive instances P, and negative instances N. For simplicity, we consider a two-class problem, although it is easy to extend the concept to many classes. Let us define a set of binary patterns $S = P \oplus N$, where $P \oplus N = \{\tilde{a} \oplus \tilde{b} \mid \tilde{a} \in P,\ \ \tilde{b} \in N\}$, $\tilde{a} \oplus \tilde{b} = (a_1 \oplus b_1,..., a_n \oplus b_n)$, and $a \oplus b$ is 0 if $a = b$ and 1 otherwise. The *pattern frequency domain* of D is a set of pairs $(\tilde{x}, m)$, where $\tilde{x} \in S$ and m is an integer which represents the frequency of appearance of the pattern $\tilde{x}$ when calculating $P \oplus N$. Note that one pattern can be generated by many pairs of positive and negative examples. Low frequency patterns are patterns that have low m values. The presence of low frequency patterns indicates the presence of noise in the database [5].

During the learning phase, CEL calculates the pattern frequency domain with an $O(|P||N|\, n)$ time complexity. Storage reduction is conducted here if necessary. The only parameter value that should be assigned to CEL during the learning phase is a threshold value tr, which indicates the number of low frequency patterns that will be monitored for changes. We call such patterns *indicators*. When presented with an example $\tilde{t}$ for classification, CEL first treats $\tilde{t}$ as a negative example and calculates the pattern frequency domain $\tilde{t} \oplus P$, which is generated by $\tilde{t}$ and positive examples. Then, CEL treats $\tilde{t}$ as a positive example and calculates the pattern frequency domain $\tilde{t} \oplus N$, generated by $\tilde{t}$ and negative examples. These calculations take $O(|P|+|N|)$ time. For each calculated pattern frequency domain, CEL counts how many indicator patterns, as well as new patterns appear. Let us denote $C_{tr}(W)$ the number of indicators and new patterns in W. If $C_{tr}(\tilde{t} \oplus P) > C_{tr}(\tilde{t} \oplus N)$ then $\tilde{t}$ is outputted as a positive example. If $C_{tr}(\tilde{t} \oplus P) < C_{tr}(\tilde{t} \oplus N)$ then $\tilde{t}$ is outputted as a negative example. The possible 'tie' case $C_{tr}(\tilde{t} \oplus P) = C_{tr}(\tilde{t} \oplus N)$ is solved by choosing a class according to the a priori class probability of the training data.

The proposed CEL monitors low frequency patterns. We can also consider a similar method which we denote as CEL-H, that monitors high frequency patterns. In this case if an example is placed in the correct class it results in an increase in the number of high frequency patterns. We assume that an example that participates in the generation of high frequency patterns is a typical non-noisy example. In some cases the detection of typical non-noisy examples can be more effective than the detection of noisy examples. We demonstrate this by considering the pima database in the following section.

The general approach for optimizing parameters of the classifier is to employ the classifier itself on the training data, and use an n-fold cross-validation approach repeated multiple times. The number of repetitions can be determined on the fly by looking at the standard deviation of the accuracy estimate, assuming they are independent. While this approach works well in practice we have not found this necessary on the databases we used. To choose an optimal threshold value, we simply use the one holdout method on the training data, and employ CEL itself to estimate recognition accuracies for different values of tr. The threshold value that results in the highest recognition rate is used on the test data. We show in the next section that this simple approach for threshold selection gives quite reasonable results.

3 Empirical Results

We use three induction algorithms as a basis for comparisons. These are the decision tree (C4.5), a backpropagation artificial neural network (ANN), and kNN. All are well known in the machine learning community and represent completely different approaches to learning. Hence, we hope that the results here are of a general nature. In our experiments we optimize each individual induction algorithm with respect to selecting “good” parameter values that govern its performance. For brevity we will omit the details. For the kNN classifier a value k=3 was chosen. For ANN, the number of nodes in the hidden layer was selected to be equal to the number of attributes plus the number of classes.

Estimating the generalization ability of the classifier is the most critical issue at the design stage. An empirical approach to this task consists of splitting available samples into training and testing sets and conducting a series of experiments. In our experiments, we used the house votes (*votes*), tic-tac-toe (*tictac*), pima-indians (*pima*) and *monk2* databases from the Machine Learning Database Repository at the University of California. All databases except *pima* are discrete, and since in this paper we are considering only discrete databases, the *pima* database was also discretized in preprocessing. We randomly selected 80% of each database as a training set and the remaining 20% as a test set, and 5 such trials were carried out. Table 1 shows the recognition results on the *votes*, *tictac*, *pima* and *monk2* databases. The reported accuracies are the mean of the five accuracies from the five trials. We also show the standard deviation from the mean. As seen in Table 1, CEL shows an improved performance over the conventional classifiers in many cases. Although CEL is successful on the *votes*, *tictac*, and *monk2* databases, it fails to improve on the recognition rates of conventional classifiers for the *pima* database. One possible reason for the poor performance of CEL is a large number of outliers presented in the *pima* database. Although noise cleaning can be done in preprocessing, in this paper we concentrate only on the CEL performance itself. In the case of the *pima* database, however, a CEL-H approach that operates on high frequency patterns is more successful. CEL-H achieves 75.1±5.0% recognition rate and improves on the recognition rates of the conventional classifiers. This example suggests that there could be many effective variations of the proposed learning method.

Table 1. Recognition results of classifiers on the votes, tictac, pima, and monk2 databases

	kNN	ANN	C4.5	CEL
Votes	91.0 ± 2.8	93.8 ± 2.5	92.7 ± 2.4	95.2 ± 2.0
Tictac	90.6 ± 2.7	95.6 ± 5.5	88.6 ± 2.1	99.8 ± 0.4
Pima	72.4 ± 2.1	74.7 ± 2.2	73.9 ± 1.5	70.2 ± 5.0
Monk2	57.0 ± 2.8	70.5 ± 1.6	67.4 ± 0.0	73.7 ± 3.5

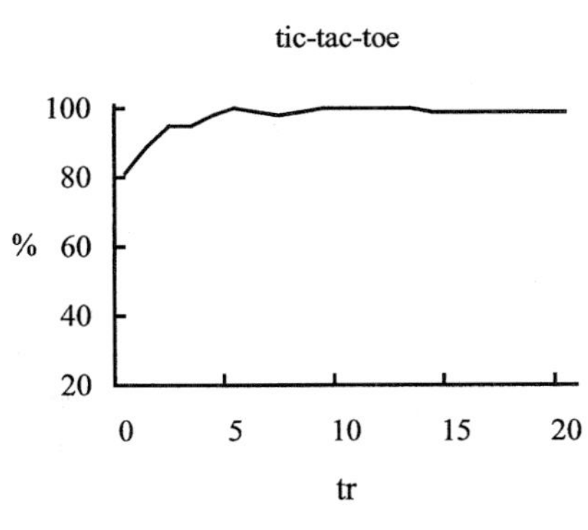

Fig. 1. Recognition rate vs. tr on the tic-tac toe data

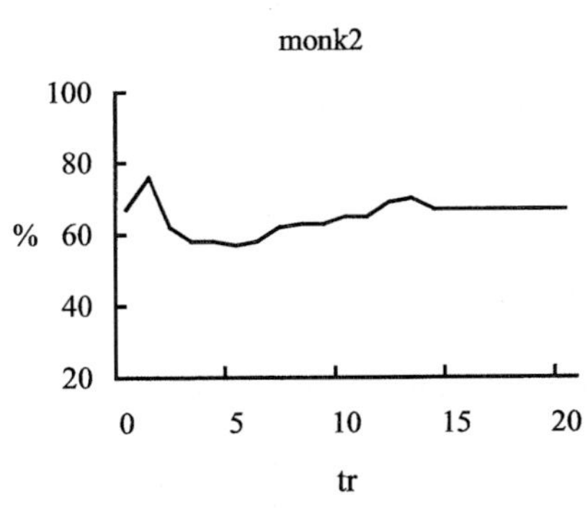

Fig. 2. Recognition rate vs. tr on the monk2 data

Our selection approach for the optimal *tr* value showed success in all experiments. Three of the tested databases have a wide range of optimal threshold values. In Fig. 1, we show CELs recognition rates on the *tic-tac* test data for different threshold values. In such cases, the selection of the optimum *tr* value is not difficult. Fig. 2 shows that in the case of the *monk2* database, optimal threshold values are located at a very narrow interval. Despite this, in all trials on the *monk2* data, the proposed method selected optimal threshold values.

4 Conclusions

In the field of pattern recognition, there is much interest in trainable pattern classifiers, as seen, for example, in the growth of research in data mining [7] and statistical learning theory [8]. The goal of designing pattern classification systems is to achieve the best possible classification performance for the task at hand. There are several factors to be considered when selecting a classifier for a specific task. These are: time sufficiency, memory size, complexity and generalization ability. Many classifiers in the learning phase require optimization methods, and have problems with convergence, stability and time efficiency [9]. Statistical and structural methods learn badly when exact statistical or structural knowledge is not available [10]. Any method based on metrics uses the hypothesis that proximity in the data space expresses membership in the same class, and therefore, when a data set does not satisfy this condition it cannot be treated by such an approach.

In this paper, we present a new learning approach that avoids many drawbacks of conventional classifiers. The proposed CEL is based on a new learning approach that first estimates the conflict between a given example and each training class, and then classifies the example into the least conflicting class. The proposed method is simple and easy to implement. It can also be used to structure data into typical, noisy, and outlier types. As we described in Section 2, typical examples generate high frequency patterns, and noisy examples result in low frequency patterns. Outliers are examples that have no representatives in the training data, and they can belong to any class. Therefore, the pattern frequency domain will not be altered significantly by placing such examples into different classes. This property can be used for their detection. The strongest advantage of CEL is its generalization ability, which is the most important property of a classifier in most applications. Empirical results showed that CEL could generate improved classification accuracy over several popular, conventional classifiers. This demonstrates the effectiveness of the proposed method as a practical solution to many difficult problems.

The CEL method has some limitations, which dictated the choice of datasets in our experiments. In principle, it can only operate on discrete attributes. It can also become meaningless for domains containing only a few instances each with a large number of attributes. Such databases are likely to generate only patterns with low frequencies. To deal with such cases, it will be necessary to apply a feature selection procedure in preprocessing.

References

[1] Quinland, J. Q., Induction of decision trees, Machine Learning, 1 (1986) 81-106.

[2] Lippmann, R., Pattern Classification Using Neural Networks, IEEE Commun. Mag., Nov. (1989) 47-64.

[3] Rivest, R., Learning decision lists, Machine Learning, 2 (1987) 229-246.

[4] Aha, D., Kibler, D., and Albert, M., Instance-based learning algorithms, Machine Lerning 7 (1991) 37-66.

[5] Lashkia, G., A Noise Filtering Method for Inductive Concept Learning, Proc. of Artificial Intelligence, AI'02, (2002) 79-89.

[6] Wilson, D., and Martinez, T., Reduction techniques for instance-based learning algorithms, Machine Learning, 38 (2000) 257-286.

[7] Hand, D., Mannila, H., Smyth, P., Principles of data mining, The MIT Press (2001).

[8] Vapnik, V., An overview of statistical learning theory, IEEE Trans. Neural Networks, Vol. 10, No. 5, (2001) 988-999.

[9] Gazula S., and Kabuka, M., Disign of Supervised Classifiers Using Boolean Neural Networks, IEEE Trans. PAMI, Vol. 17, No. 12 (1995) 1239-1245.

[10] Denceux, T., Analysis of Evidence-Theoretic Decision Rules for Pattern Classification, Pattern Recognition, Vol. 30, No. 7, (1997) 1095-1127.

Enhancing Caching in Distributed Databases Using Intelligent Polytree Representations

Ouerd Messaouda[1], John B. Oommen[2], and Stan Matwin[1]

[1] School of Information Technology and Engineering
University of Ottawa, Ottawa, Canada K1S 5B6
{ouerd,stan}@site.uottawa.ca

[2] School of Computer Science
Carleton University, Ottawa, Canada K1S 5B6
oommen@scs.carleton.ca

Abstract. In this paper we study the issue of utilizing polytree structures in a real-life application namely that of enhancing caching in distributed databases. Specifically, in this application, the only data or learning cases available is a huge trace of a set of queries of the type of "*Select*" statements made by different users of a distributed database system. This trace is considered as a sequence containing repeated patterns of queries. The aim is to capture the *repeated patterns* of queries so as to be able to perform anticipated caching. By introducing the notion of caching, we try to take advantage of performing local accesses rather than remote accesses, because the former significantly reduces the communication time, and thus improves the overall performance of a system. We utilize polytree-based machine learning schemes to detect sequences of repeated queries made to remote databases. Once constructed, such networks can provide insight into probabilistic dependencies that exist among the queries, and thus enhance distributed query optimization.

1 Introduction & Related Work

We consider a problem of significant importance, namely that of increasing performance in systems involving distributed databases. As the usage of wide areas networks increases, the need for enhancing the systems' performance becomes apparent. The traditional way of dealing with query optimization is to find an execution strategy, which is optimal, or close to optimal, considering the fact that communication cost is involved. In this paper we approach the problem of query optimization in distributed databases in a completely different way, one which is inspired by the fact that communication time is the main factor considered by the database management system in distributed databases. In our approach we reduce the communication time by minimizing the number of queries made to remote databases by caching the repeated que-

Y. Xiang and B. Chaib-draa (Eds.): AI 2003, LNAI 2671, pp. 498-504, 2003.

ries. Anticipated caching is also achieved by learning the workflow of the data given a trace of queries made to the databases. Using learning principles we show that we can build causal structures, primarily because causality is important to our caching process, since it allows the anticipated caching mechanism.

Although it is impossible to review the state of the art here (such a review is found in [10]), we mention briefly, the Netcache *s*oftware. Netcache is a partial solution to the problem of access to distributed databases. It has been addressed by the Netcache [8] software from King Systems Limited (KSL). Our system can be seen to be a continuation and improvement of their software. It is able to make **decisions** on which queries are to be cached, and which queries to be discarded, rather than caching all the queries. Netcache is a network caching software package, which stores all the answers to previously resolved queries up to the capacity of the memory, and then, whenever a new query is presented, the system compares it to the ones which are already cached in local memory and returns the answer to the user. Thus, our solution fits into the general field of machine learning [5], which is, concerned with the question of how to construct computer programs that automatically improve with experience, and into the type of inductive learning associated with sequence prediction.

2 Our Solution

Over the last decade Bayesian learning principles have received a fair amount of attention. Although they are elegant, they usually involve summations or integrals along all possible instantiations of the parameters, and along all possible models. In the case of learning of Bayesian networks this can be perceived as a discrete optimization problem. Precise solutions of this can be obtained by using search techniques, if we assume that there are only a few relevant models. This has proven to be the method of choice in many real-life applications [2]. Many of the studied Bayesian models are intractable [4], and so, the challenge is to find general-purpose, tractable approximation algorithms for reasoning with these elegant and expressive models. For example, if we are to use Bayesian learning to improve performance of distributed database applications, where there can be millions of transactions every day, we will need an efficient technique to build a model of the use of the database. The belief network that underlies the Bayesian learning is at the heart of the approach.

It is clear that the learning benefits if a more comprehensive and causal *model* of interaction between the variables is available. Such a model, represented as a Bayesian network, plays the role of a restricted hypothesis bias. The method allows us to obtain the approximating probability distribution P(X) by a well-defined and easily computable density function $P_a(X)$. Our goal is to build a probabilistic network from the distribution of the data, which adequately represents it. Once constructed, such a network can provide insight into probabilistic dependencies that exist between the variables. Chow and Liu [4] used the Kullback-Leibler cross-entropy metric to approximate discrete distributions by collecting the entire first and second order marginals. A Maximum Weight-Spanning Tree (MWST) called the "Chow Tree" [4,11,12] was built using the information measure between the variables forming the nodes of the tree. A subsequent work due to Rebane and Pearl [12] used the Chow Tree as the starting point of an algorithm which builds a polytree (singly connected network) from a probability distribution [6]. This algorithm orients the Chow tree by assuming the availability of independence tests on various multiple parent nodes. As opposed to assuming that the components of the random vector are statistically independent, one can also assume that every variable is dependent on every other variable, making the model both cumbersome, and intractable. The first attempt to strike a happy medium was the one due to Chow [3] in which the model assumed that there was a tree-based dependence between the variables. This dependence has been exhaustively studied for discrete and continuous vectors using various error norms including the entropy and Chi-square norms. This model has been successfully generalized to specify the dependence using polytrees, which is the model of interest used in this study. The question: "Why Polytrees ?" is thus not rhetorical. Indeed, in his Doctoral thesis, Dasgupta (See Section V.1 titled "*Why Polytrees*" in [4]) argued, that while it is easy to learn branchings of *trees* in the structured learning problem, it is NP-Hard to learn probabilistic nets even if the degrees are bounded. As opposed to this, de Campos and his colleagues presented an experimental proof of their proposed techniques in Acid *et al* [1].

2.1 Description of the Queries and the Process of Parsing

We consider our database queries to be SQL-like (Structured Query Language) queries. These queries involve only *Select* statements, which fetch data from databases. A *Select* statement has the following syntax:

Select <attribute list> **from** < table list> **where** <condition>,

in which:

<attribute list>	:	is a list of attributes whose values are to be retrieved by the query.
<table list>	:	is a list of the relation names required to process the query.
<condition>	:	is a conditional (Boolean) search expression that identifies the tuples to be retrieved by the query.

A trace of these *Select* statements constitutes our data for the real-life application considered in this paper. This data is first parsed and then generalized into other *Select* statements as described below. The data or the input file to the project is a file containing a real trace of the *Select* statements (queries) made to the distributed databases for a period of 24 hours. The size of the trace file is 36MB. There are 32 clerks making use of these databases. After examining the trace data, we observed that these clerks put 121,181 queries against the database in the duration of the trace, which, in our case, was 24 hours. Concurrent accesses are made to this database 24 hours per day and 7 days per week. The query system uses the notion of a *Cursor* to declare a *Select* statement, which can be invoked from any location. The data used in the *Select* statement, represented by the given cursor, is fetched at any time by invoking the command "Fetch" with the cursor number. The parsing process analyzes the cursor statements and stores every declaration of a cursor to access the data used by the *Select* statement defined in that cursor. The examples below give a portion of data from the initial trace of the accesses to the database. Here, two cursors, cursor #1 and cursor

#3, were declared. To aid in explanation, a small sub-file of this file is given in Table 1. In Table 2, the numbers assigned to the fetching command "fetch(#)" represent the addresses of the locations where the actual queries are saved and stored.

2.2 Generalizing the Queries

For our application, since the *Select* statements are simple expressions, we merely use the term "generalization" for the process of obtaining a reduced representation of the data. The generalization process takes two *consecutive* queries and generalizes them into one single query. We say that two consecutive queries are "**generalizable**" if they have the same arguments i.e., the same columns and the same tables in their query form. When we generalize the queries, the column and table names will be considered equal for the respective queries, and will thus remain the same after the generalization. The generalization is achieved by dropping the condition argument found in consecutive "where" clauses. The non-consecutive "where" clauses are dropped in the final stage when the dictionary of queries itself is built. The motivation for this generalization process is that when accessing remote data, whether we retrieve one or more tuples from the databases, the most important feature is that we are processing that particular column of data found in that specific table. In our real-life application, we reduced the number of queries in the trace from 121,181 queries to a sequence of 31,978 queries. A portion of data taken from the parsed file of the trace, which includes candidates for generalization, is given below. After the generalization process every query is assigned two given addresses. The first one is the address already assigned in the parsing process, which is the address of the initial query. The second address is the address of the location for the generalized query in the dictionary of the generalized queries.

Table 1. Example of a Trace of *Select* Statements as it is Given in the Initial Data

```
PARSING IN CURSOR #1 len=147 dep=1 uid=0 oct=3 lid=0 tim=4092015242
Select privilege#,level from sysauth$ connect by grantee#=prior privilege# and
Privilege#>0 start with (grantee#=:1 or grantee#=1) and privilege#>0
END OF STMT
PARSE #1:c=1,e=1,p=0,cr=0,cu=0,mis=0,r=0,dep=1,og=4,tim=4092015242
EXEC #1:c=0,e=0,p=0,cr=0,cu=0,mis=0,r=0,dep=1,og=4,tim=4092015242
FETCH #1:c=0,e=0,p=0,cr=4,cu=0,mis=0,r=1,dep=1,og=4,tim=4092015242
PARSING IN CURSOR #3 len=36 dep=1 uid=0 oct=3 lid=0 tim=4092015244
Select text from view$ where obj#=:1
END OF STMT
PARSE #3:c=0,e=0,p=0,cr=0,cu=0,mis=0,r=0,dep=1,og=4,tim=4092015244
EXEC #3:c=0,e=0,p=0,cr=0,cu=0,mis=0,r=0,dep=1,og=4,tim=4092015245
FETCH #3:c=1,e=0,p=1,cr=4,cu=0,mis=0,r=1,dep=1,og=4,tim=4092015245
```

Table 2. Example of a Parsed Portion of a Trace of *Select* Statements (Fetching)

```
Cursor: #1
Select: select level, privilege# from sysauth$ connect by grantee# =prior privilege# and
privilege# > 0 start with ( grantee# = : 1 or grantee#=1 ) and privilege# > 0
Select key string: level, privilege# from sysauth$
Fetch(#1) = 1
```

Table 3. Example of a Generalized Portion of the Trace

```
280     3156
Select account_bill_num, account_holder_uic, comm_group_id, cost_centre_code,
Facility_number, facility_type, gl_acct_code, item_completion_date, item_seq_num,
Quantity, rate_group, recoverable_code, recoverable_mrc, rowid, tso_equipment_code,
User_stn_seq_num, vendor_equip_code, vendor_ident From equipment_item Where
( comm_group_id = '76' ) and ( account_holder_uic = '0001' ) and ( account_bill_num =
' 1061' ) and ( facility_type = 'LOCAL' ) and ( facility_number = '9957848' ) and
( user_stn_seq_num = '001' ) order by item_seq_num
```

Table 4. Example of a Portion of the Learning Trace

```
(1) fetch(cursor #69) == 2389
(1) fetch(cursor #70) == 2390
(2) fetch(cursor #71) == 1243
(2) fetch(cursor #72) == 1669
(2) fetch(cursor #73) == 510
(2) fetch(cursor #34) == 1668
(1) fetch(cursor #74) == 1671
```

2.3 Getting the Learning Trace

After the generalization process some statistics are derived. The following example is a portion of data taken from the file containing these results. The first number in every line represents the number of consecutive generalized statements, the fetch command includes the number of the cursor it is fetching from, and the index of the generalized query, which corresponds to that cursor.

2.4 Building the Chow Tree and Orienting the Polytree

After the parsing and the generalization processes, the initial trace of the *Select* statements is reduced to a sequence of numbers. The number of the *Select* statements in the processed dataset was 31,978, which is mainly the sequence of the repeated generalized *Select* statements in the trace. This sequence contains numbers that represent indexes in the dictionary where the generalized *Select* statements are stored. The total number of these generalized queries in the dictionary was 624, which represents also the number of the nodes in the structure built. Using the sequence of the queries, we computed the conditional probabilities of the nodes, and then from these probabilities we derived the information measures between every pair of nodes. The orientation of the polytree was based on the independence of the nodes measured by a "thresholded" correlation coefficient as explained in [10]. Figure 1 shows a portion of the undirected Chow tree and the final polytree ; the details of the computations are given in [10].

3 Verification of the Polytree

As in any real-life application, the verification of the results is the most difficult part of the entire exercise. In this case, the verification of the quality of the polytree obtained is a problem in itself. We achieved the "testing" by requesting the expert in the field, to subjectively study the input and the polytree that we had obtained. Indeed, the expert from whom the data was obtained was pleased with our results [7], even though he stated that "this verification problem could be a project in its own right". One possible approach for such a testing strategy would be cross-validation, but even here, the method by which this can be achieved is open. To estimate the effect of our strategy on performance, one would require implementation of the system in conjunction with NetCache. Apart from the problem being conceptually difficult, there are numerous other anticipated difficulties of such a project, which are explained in [10].

4 Conclusion

In this paper we have described the problem of query optimization in distributed databases. We showed that learning the workflow of the data could reduce the communication time. Specifically, in this application, the only data or learning cases available is a huge trace of a set of queries of the type of "*Select*" statements made by different users of a distributed database system. This trace is considered as a sequence containing repeated patterns of queries. The aim was to capture the *repeated patterns* of queries so as to be able to perform anticipated caching. By introducing the notion of caching, we attempted to take advantage of performing local accesses rather than remote accesses, because the former significantly reduces the communication time, and thus improves the overall performance of a system. Polytree-based learning schemes were utilized to detect sequences of repeated queries made to the databases.

Acknowledgements

The authors are grateful to the Natural Sciences and Engineering Research Council of Canada for supporting their research, including this project. Dr. D. King's input and advice are greatly appreciated.

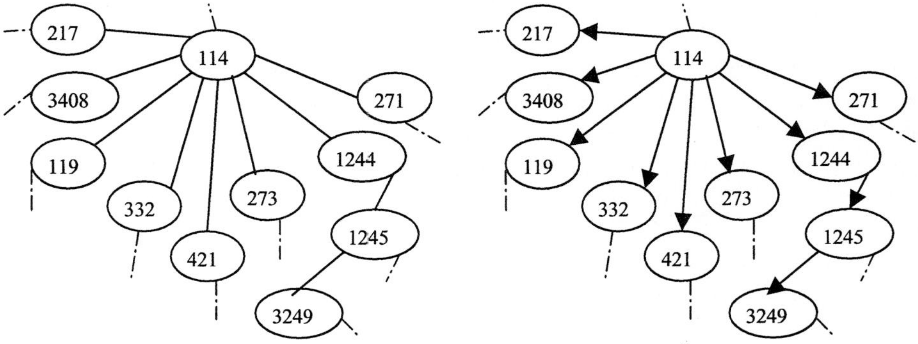

Fig. 1. A portion of the Chow tree on the left, and the corresponding portion of the oriented polytree on the right, as obtained from the trace of the data

References

[1] Acid, S. and de Campos, L.M., (1994): Approximations of Causal Networks by Polytrees: An Empirical Study. Proceedings of the Fifth IPMU Conference, 972-977.

[2] Cooper, G.F. and Herskovits, E.H., (1992): A Bayesian Method for the Induction of Probabilistic Networks from Data. Machine Learning, Vol. 9: 309-347.

[3] Chow, C.K. and Liu, C.N., (1968): Approximating Discrete Probability Distributions with Dependence Trees". IEEE Trans. on Information Theory, Vol. 14: 462-467.

[4] Dasputa, S. (2000): Learning Probability Distributions. Doctoral Dissertation, University of California at Berkeley, 2000.

[5] Dietterich, T.G, and Michalski, R.S., (1983): Learning to Predict Sequences. Machine Learning II: An Artificial Intelligence Approach. Edited by Michalski, Carbonell and Mictchell.

[6] Geiger, D., Paz, A., and Pearl, J. (1990): Learning Causal Trees from Dependence Information. Proceedings of the Eighth National Conference on Artificial Intelligence, AAAI Press, pp. 770-776.

[7] King, D., (1999). Personal Communication. President and CEO, KSL King Systems Limited, 28 Newton Street, Ottawa, Ontario, Canada, K1S 2S7.

[8] KSL King Systems Limited. (1995): The NetCache Software Manual, The Remote Database Performance, NC01.

[9] Ouerd, M., Oommen, B.J., and Matwin, S. (2000): A Formalism for Building Causal Polytree Structures using Data Distributions. Proceedings of the Int'l Symposium on Intelligent Systems, Charlotte, NC: pp. 629-638.

[10] Ouerd, M., (2000): Building Probabilistic Networks and Its Application to Distributed Databases. Doctoral Dissertation, SITE, University of Ottawa, Ottawa, Canada.

[11] Pearl, J. (1988): Probabilistic Reasoning in Intelligent Systems: Networks of Plausible Inference. Morgan Kaufmann, San Mateo, CA.

[12] Rebane, G. and Pearl, J. (1987): "The Recovery of Causal Polytrees from Statistical Data". Proceedings of the Third Workshop on Uncertainty in Artificial Intellig*ence.* Seattle, Washington, 222- 228.

Feature Selection Strategies for Text Categorization

Pascal Soucy[1,2] and Guy W. Mineau[2]

[1]Copernic Research, Copernic Inc., Québec, Canada
psoucy@copernic.com
[2]Department of Computer Science, Université Laval, Québec, Canada
{Pascal.Soucy,Guy.Mineau}@ift.ulaval.ca

Abstract. Feature selection is an important research issue in text categorization. The reason for this is that thousands of features are often involved, even when the simplest document representation model, the so-called bag-of-words, is used. Among the many approaches to feature selection, the use of some scoring function to rank features to filter them out is an important one. Many of these functions are widely used in text categorization. In past feature selection studies, most researchers have focused on comparing these measures in terms of accuracy achieved. For any measure, however, there are many selection strategies that can be applied to produce the resulting feature set. In this paper, we compare some such strategies and propose a new one. Tests have been conducted to compare five selection strategies on four datasets, using three distinct classifiers and four common feature scoring functions. As a result, it is possible to better understand which strategies are suited to particular classification settings.

1 Introduction

Most text categorization (TC) approaches use bag-of-words to represent documents. Feature selection (FS) is the process of identifying what words are best suited for this task. Most of FS approaches for TC use a feature scoring function, that is, a function that estimates a feature relevancy for the categorization task.

In past FS studies, most researchers have focused on comparing scoring functions to determine those yielding the best feature sets in terms of classification accuracy. For any scoring function, however, there are many feature selection strategies (FSS) that can be applied to produce the resulting feature set. In this paper, we define and report results conducted with five FSS on four datasets, using three classifiers and four common feature scoring functions.

Y. Xiang and B. Chaib-draa (Eds.): AI 2003, LNAI 2671, pp. 505-509, 2003.

2 Experimental Settings

The FSS determine an appropriate set of features given their ranking by a feature scoring function. We have tested, in our study, four of them that are commonly used in TC experiments: Information Gain, Cross Entropy, Chi-Square and Document Frequency.

Each FSS has an associated threshold *thr* that have been tested using an adequate range of values (more or less than 10 values by strategy; for instance, the FSS that consists of selecting a predefined number of features has been tested with 100, 250, 500, 1000, 2500, 5000, 7500, 10000, 25000 and 50000 features). Overall, these experiments comprise more than 3500 runs that have been conducted almost continuously over a period of 4 months on two PIII computers. For this reason, we believe this study to be rather exhaustive.

2.1 Data Sets

Reuters-21578. Reuters-21578 [1] consists of categorized business news reports. These reports are written in a telegraphic style, using a very specific vocabulary that includes almost no misspell. There are 90 unevenly balanced categories. Each document might be assigned to one or many categories. ModApte split has been used.

Ohsumed. Ohsumed is another well known TC task. We have used the 49 "Heart Diseases" sub-categories as described in [2]. All these categories contain at least 75 documents in the training set. Each document is tagged using a set of MeSH terms Only the 49 MeSH terms from "Heart Diseases" are used in this setting. Documents that contain none of these 49 MeSH terms are discarded.

LingSpam. The LingSpam text collection is very interesting, yet a little bit too small to be used alone. There are only 2 categories: e-mails posted in a mailing-list during a period of time and spam emails. As there is no standard to split this collection into training and testing sets, we randomly divided Ling and Spam in approximately two halves, giving 1443 documents in the training set and 1445 in the testing set. Generally speaking, this task is considered to be easy, as proved in [3].

DigiTrad. DigiTrad (The Digital Tradition Collection) have been introduced as a TC task in [4] and is not yet widely used. The vocabulary of this collection is very particular: it is often made of metaphoric, rhyming, archaic and unusual language [4] and less restricted than in Reuters and Ohsumed. We used a slightly modified version of the DT100 split defined in [4]. The result was 3475 training documents and 1736 testing documents.

2.2 Classifiers

The classifiers we have included in our experiments are Bayes, KNN and SVM. Due to a lack of space, we will only describe results obtained with SVM.

SVM is a recent learning method that has been applied to TC for the first time by Joachims in 1997 [5]. Since then, it is accepted as being a very strong model for TC. Using SVM, one has to create n classifiers for an n-categories problem. Each ith

classifier thus solves a binary task, where the positive class comprises documents from the ith category and the negative class any document not assigned to this i^{th} category. We did use the SVM^{light} package[1] with TFIDF document representation (See [6] for a complete description).

2.3 Feature Scoring Functions

Four feature scoring functions have been included in this study. They all have been commonly studied in TC problems, which in part explain this choice. Moreover, all these functions can return a score for a given category. Therefore, that score can be used to order the feature set for each category. The 4 scoring functions that we have used in this paper are: Information Gain, Chi-Square, Cross-Entropy and Document Frequency. The reader is invited to read [7] and [8] for further information about these functions.

2.4 Strategies to Determine Feature Set Size

Predefined Feature Count (PFC). This FSS has been widely used. Simply, the *thr* best features are selected.

Threshold on Feature Score (THR). This is another common FSS. Any feature whose score is over *thr* is kept.

Proportional to Category Initial Feature Set Size (Mladenic's Vector Size, MVS). This approach has been proposed by Mladenic in [8]. For each category, a list of words occurring in the training documents is built. Then, *thr* is used to determine the proportion of features to keep. For instance, if *thr* = 0.5, half the features (the bests according to the scoring function) that occurred in a category training set are kept.

Mladenic's Sparsity (SPA). Sparsity also has been proposed by Mladenic [9], more recently. This strategy is quite different from the other FSS presented in this paper. Sparsity measures the average document vector size (not to confuse with the previous vector size definition; here vector size refers to non-zero values in document vectors). The higher that value is the more non-zero values in document vectors. Thus, choosing frequent words increases the sparsity value faster than choosing rare words.

Proportional to Category Size (PCS). This is a new approach we propose in this paper. Intuitively, large categories (those containing many training documents) should have more words significantly related to them. As a result, more features associated with these categories could be kept.

Similarly to MVS, a list of features is built for each category. However, instead of keeping a fraction of the feature set, the product between *thr* and the category size (in terms of the number of documents in this category training set) determine the number of features to keep for that category. For instance, suppose a category c_1 containing 1000 documents, a category c_2 containing 100 documents and *thr* = 0.1. The final feature set will be the merge of the 100 best features in c_1 and the 10 best in c_2.

---

[1] http://svmlight.joachims.org/

Table 1. Maximum accuracy by text collection with SVM

	PFC	**THR**	MVS	**SPA**	**PCS**
Spam	0.994	0.994	0.995	0.994	0.994
Reuters	0.877	0.877	0.884	0.879	0.883
Digitrad	0.474	0.473	0.483	0.471	**0.483**
Ohsumed	0.695	0.695	0.697	0.696	0.696

2.5 Evaluation

Text categorization evaluations are mainly related to classification accuracy. For this reason, Micro-average F1, a common TC evaluation measure [10], has been chosen. We report the maximum micro-average F1 (using the best `thr`) obtained for a particular setting. Recall that for each FSS, a full range of `thr` values have been tested. We report only the result obtained by the best `thr` in the range.

3 Results

The following table summarizes results obtained. Each cell contains classification micro-F1 for the corresponding experiment. The ordering is obtained by ranking each FSS for each collection and measuring their average position.

Ordering: MVS > PCS > SPA > PFC > THR. THR and PFC (two very common approaches) are underperformers according to this report, while MVS is clearly better (despite not by a large proportion) than any other approach.

4 Conclusion

This paper has presented a comparative study of feature selection strategies that are intended to determine the resulting set of features given their ordering by a feature scoring function. Tests allowed the observation of the following:

- MVS seems to be the best strategy for SVM;
- The two mostly used FSS (PFC and THR) are underperformers compared to the other approaches;
- SPA has been particularly designed to be used with feature scoring functions that do not favor common words [9]. All the four feature scoring functions tested in this study favor frequent words, which could explain why no significant improvement has been observed in this study.

Other avenues still remain in the field studied in this paper. For instance, MVS selects features according to a linear proportion of the number of features (found in a particular category). However, studies have shown that the behavior of word occurrence in texts follows other scaling laws, as depicted by Zipf's Law, for instance. Therefore, instead of selecting a fraction of the vocabulary, MVS could be extended to select a number of features proportional to the log of the size of the vocabulary. Other such variations could be tested as well.

References

[1] D.D. Lewis (1997), Reuters-21578 text categorization test collection, Distrib. 1.0, Sept 26.

[2] D. Lewis, R. Schapire, J. Callan, and R. Papka (1996), Training Algorithms for Linear Text Classifiers, In *Proc. of ACM SIGIR*, 298-306.

[3] I. Androutsopoulos, G. Paliouras, V. Karkaletsis, G. Sakkis, C. D. Spyropoulos & P. Stamatopoulos (2000). Learning to Filter Spam E-Mail : A Comparison of a Naive Bayesian and a Memory-Based Approach. In *Proc. of the workshop Machine Learning and Textual Information Access*, PKDD-2000, Lyon, 1-13.

[4] S. Scott and S. Matwin. (1999) Feature engineering for text classification. In *Proc. of ICML 99*, San Francisco, 379-388.

[5] T. Joachims (1997), Text Categorization with Support Vector Machines: Learning with Many Relevant Features. *LS8-Report 23*, Universität Dortmund.

[6] Thorsten Joachims (2002), Learning to Classify Text Using Support Vector Machines. Dissertation, Kluwer.

[7] Yang, Y., Pedersen, J.O. (1997), A Comparative Study on Feature Selection in Text Categorization, In *Proc. of the ICML97*, 412-420.

[8] Mladenic, D (1998). *Machine Learning on non-homogeneous, distributed text data*. PhD thesis, University of Ljubljana, Slovenia, October.

[9] Janez Brank, Marko Grobelnik, Natasa Milic-Frayling, Dunja Mladenic (2002). Interaction of Feature Selection Methods and Linear Classification Models, In *Proc. of Nineteenth Conf. on Machine Learning (ICML-02)*, Workshop on Text Learning.

[10] Y. Yang and X. Liu (1999). A re-examination of text categorization methods. In *SIGIR-99*.

Learning General Graphplan Memos through Static Domain Analysis

M. Afzal Upal

OpalRock Technologies
42741 Center St, Chantilly, VA
afzal@opalrock.com

1 Introduction & Background

Graphplan [1] is one of the most efficient algorithms for solving the classical AI planning problems. Graphplan algorithm as originally proposed [1] repeatedly searched parts of the same space during its backward solution extraction phase. This suggested a natural way of speeding up Graphplan's performance by saving memos from a previously performed search and reusing them to avoid traversing the same part of the search tree later on in the search for the solution of the same problem. Blum and Furst [1] suggested a technique for learning such *memos*. Kambhampati [2] suggested improvements on this algorithm by using a more principled learning technique based on explanation-based learning (EBL) from failures. However, these and other [3] learning techniques for Graphplan, learn rules that are valid only in the context of the current problem and do not learn *general rules* that can be applied to other problems. This paper reports on an analytic learning technique that can be used to learn general memos that can be used in the context of more than a single planning problem.

Graphplan has two interleaved processes; graph expansion and solution extraction. The graph expansion process incrementally expands the planning-graph structure while the solution extraction performs a backward search through the planning-graph to find a valid plan. Planning-graph is a multilayered data structure used by Graphplan to keep track of dependencies between actions, their preconditions, and effects. Each planning-graph layer consists of two sublayers: the proposition sublayer, and the action sublayer. Each action node is linked to its precondition propositions in the previous layer and its effect propositions in the next layer as shown in Fig. 1. An important part of the planning graph expansion phase is the maintenance and propagation of binary mutual exclusion relationships (called "mutexes" henceforth) between actions and propositions. The expansion phase is interleaved with the solution extraction phase when a proposition layer containing all the problem goals gets created. The solution extraction process starts by checking if any two goals are mutex with each other. If that is not the case, then its searches backward on the preconditions of the actions supporting the goals to see if any of them are mutex at the previous level. This process continues until it reaches the initial conditions of the problem. If goal propositions are mutex at any level, then (1) solution extraction is stopped, (2) a memo is stored, (3) the planning graph is expanded one more level, and (4) solution extraction is invoked from the newly expanded level. This process continues until either a valid

Y. Xiang and B. Chaib-draa (Eds.): AI 2003, LNAI 2671, pp. 510-514, 2003.

plan is found or expansion has nothing new to add (in which case no solution for the planning problem exists. We illustrate the Graphplan algorithm and its inefficiencies with the help of the following example.

Example 1: Given the following domain operators:

Operator *O*:	preconditions: *a*	Effects: *e*
Operator *P*:	preconditions: *a*	Effects: $\neg e$, *f*
Operator *Q*:	preconditions: *b*	effects: *f*

and a planning problem with Initial Conditions = {*a*}, and Goals = {*e*, *f*}, Graphplan expands the planning graph to proposition layer 2 as shown in Fig. 1. Since all the problem goals (*e*, *f*, and *g*) are present in the proposition layer 2, the solution extraction process kicks in. It discovers that goal *e* is mutex with goal *f* because all actions supporting *e* are mutex with all actions supporting *f*. Graphplan stores the conjunction of *e*, *f*, and *h* as a memo at level 2. Next, Graphplan expands the graph one more level and restarts solution extraction. Solution extraction search recurses on the preconditions of all the no-op actions (which are the propositions *e*, *f*, and *g* themselves), finds the previously stored memo and abandons the search at this level to try other actions supporting the goals at level 3 thereby saving some computational effort. The problem, however, is that the memo learned by Graphplan is too specific and can only be used in the same problem. When faced with the same or slightly different planning situation (such as the one shown in Example 2) in the future, Graphplan must relearn the memo.

Example 2: The same domain operators as in Example 1.
Initial conditions: {*a*, *c*}
Goals: {*e*, *f*}

Graphplan essentially reconstructs exactly the same planning-graph as it did for Example 1 including relearning the memo. Had it learned a general memo, it would have been able to save the effort required to (1) search for subgoals *e* and *f* at level 2, and (2) relearn the memo. However, the naïve approach of simply not forgetting the memos after a problem is over so that they can be reused in subsequent problem will not work because soundness of a memo depends upon the problem context from which it was learned. The learning challenge then is to remember just enough context that is needed to ensure soundness of a memo but no more.

2 The Problem

Given a failed solution extraction search at a level `l`, the learning problem is to compute the necessary and sufficient set of context conditions under which a search will always fail at the level `l`. A problem's context conditions include:

1. assertions about the goals being searched for,
2. assertions about the initial conditions of the problem, and
3. assertions about the domain operators.

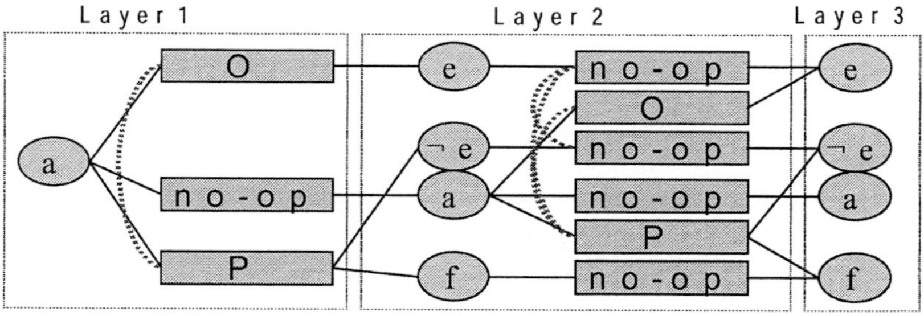

Fig. 1. Planning graph constructed by Graphplan for Example 1. Actions are shown by rectangular boxes whereas propositions are shown as ovals. Solid straight lines show precondition and effect dependencies between actions and their preconditions and effects. The mutex links between actions are shown by curved broken lines

Graphplan's memos take the goals into account but assume that the initial conditions and the domain operators remain unchanged and hence do not need to be stored. In this paper, we also assume that the domain operators do not change hence we can ignore them but we have to include assertions about the initial conditions of the problem in order to use memos learned from one problem in the solution extraction search for another problem. For instance, the memo learned from search level 2 in Example 1 is reusable at search level 2 in Example 2 because the two examples share the initial conditions.

3 The Learning Algorithm

The algorithm proposed in this paper performs a static analysis of the domain before starting the planning process to learn general memos. The general memos are instantiated when solving a problem in the context of that problem. The key idea is to create a number of *general goal sets* covering all possible goals of a problem and performing a backwards goal directed search from a level to find the conditions under which a valid plan cannot exist at that level. This process is repeated for all possible levels (say from a level L downto level 1). The learning algorithm is illustrated with the help of the following example.

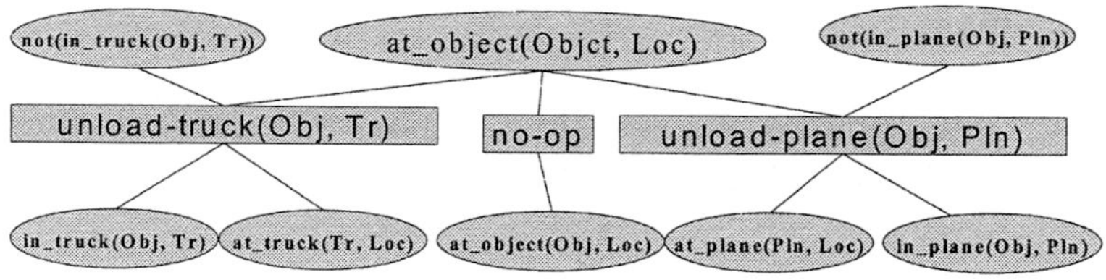

Fig. 2. One level planning graph drawn by backwards search from Goal Set {at_object(Obj, Loc)}

Example 4:
In the logistics transportation domain a goal literal can only be of the form at_object(Object, Location). A planning problem from the logistics transportation may be a conjunction of an n such goals, then the general Goal Set {at_object(Object, Location)} covers all one-goal logistics transportation problems. Our learning algorithm starts by conducting a goal-directed search from the covering goal set. A planning graph similar to a planning graph is constructed through this process. The one-level planning graph constructed by goal directed search performed on the Goal Set {at_object(Object, Location)} is shown in **Fig. 2**. The goal can be supported by any of the three actions of unload_truck(Obj, Tr), unload_plane(Obj, Pln) or no-op. In order for goal level at_object(Obj, Pln) to succeed at this level, either one of the three actions must succeed or conversely for goal at_object(Obj, Pln) to fail all three actions must fail. The actions can fail if any of their preconditions are not satisfied. This knowledge can be translated into the following memo:

Goals : {at_object(Obj, Loc)}
Initial Conditions that must be present : {}

Conditions that must be absent from Init Conds: {(in_truck(Obj, Tr) ∨ at_truck(Tr, Loc)) ∧ (at_plane(Pln, Loc) ∨ in_plane(Obj, Pln)) ∧ (at_object(Obj, Loc)))}

If we are given the extra domain knowledge (i.e., domain knowledge beyond that assumed by classical AI planning system) that the literals in_truck and in_plane are never part of the initial conditions then the above memo can be simplified to

Goals : {at_object(Obj, Loc)}
Initial Conditions that must be present : {}
Conditions that must be absent from Init Conds: {at_object(Obj, Loc)}.

4 Experiments & Results

We have conducted preliminary experiments to see if the rules learned by our analytic learning system actually improve Graphplan's performance on benchmark problems. We allowed our system to learn memos for covering goal sets of size one, two, and three from level 20 downto 1. These memos were used to solve 100 randomly generated logistics problems and the amount of time it took to solve 100 problems was recorded. We also ran Graphplan without the extra memos and recorded the time it took to solve the same 100 problems. Ten trials were conducted and the times averaged. The results show that the general memos do not speed up Graphplan. Instead, they slow down its performance (from 15% to 20%). This meant that the cost of matching and retrieving the general memos exceeded the savings obtained by pruning the search. The cost of retrieving the general memos is much larger than the cost of retrieving the instantiated memos that the original Graphplan learns. In order to see if the memos learned by our learning system are useful in an instantiated form, we implemented a module that uses the initial conditions and the goal of a problem to instantiate the memos before starting planning. This does two things, first it reduces the number of memos by eliminating those memos that cannot be instantiated by the top level goals and initial conditions. Second, it allows us to forget the initial conditions leaving the memos in the same form as those learned by Graphplan. We reran the experiments described earlier with the instantiation engine and measured the amount of time it took Graphplan with instantiated memos and the original Graphplan to plan for 100 randomly generated problem. The results show that the instantiated memos significantly improve Graphplan's performance ranging from 5% to 33%.

Table 1. Results of running Java version of Graphplan with and without general memos on a 366 MHz Pentium II machine

	Graphplan	Graphplan+GenMemos
1-goal	29 seconds	35 seconds
2-goals	51 seconds	60 seconds
3-goals	89 seconds	101 seconds

Table 2. Results of running Java version of Graphplan with and without general memos on a 366 MHz Pentium II machine

	Graphplan	Graphplan+GenMemos
1-goal	29 seconds	27.5 seconds
2-goals	51 seconds	45 seconds
3-goals	89 seconds	60 seconds

5 Conclusion

This paper has presented a static domain analysis technique that can be used to learn general memos that can be used in a broad range of problems. Preliminary results show that the general memos are too costly to match and retrieve. However, when instantiated and pruned they lead to improvements in planning efficiency on small problems from the logistics domain. We are currently conducting experiments to see if these techniques can scale up to the larger problems and to problems from other domains.

References

[1] Blum, A., Furst, M.: Fast Planning Through Graph Analysis. Artificial Intelligence 1997 (15) 281-300.

[2] Kambhampati, S.: Planning Graph as a (dynamic) CSP: Exploiting EBL, DDB, and other CSP search techniques in Graphplan. Lecture Notes in Computer Science, Vol. 1000. Springer-Verlag, Berlin Heidelberg New York (1995)

[3] Fox, M. and Long, D. The Automatic Inference of State Invariants in TIM, Journal of Artificial Intelligence Research, 9 (1998), 367-421.

Classification Automaton and Its Construction Using Learning

Wang Xiangrui[1] and Narendra S. Chaudhari[2]

[1] School of Computer Engineering, Block N4-02a-32, Nanyang Avenue
Nanyang Technological University, Singapore 639798
xray@pmail.ntu.edu.sg

[2] School of Computer Engineering, Block N4-02a-32, Nanyang Avenue
Nanyang Technological University, Singapore 639798
asnarendra@ntu.edu.sg

Abstract. A method of regular grammar inference in computational learning for classification problems is presented. We classify the strings by generating multiple subclasses. A construction algorithm is presented for the classification automata from positive classified examples. We prove the correctness of the algorithm, and suggest some possible extensions.

1 Introduction

The theories of learning languages such as context free language (CFL) and regular language from sample data help us to get an insight into the structural aspects of the data. Many approaches have been investigated in this direction [1, 2].

In this paper, we modify the well-known approach by Dana Angluin, for inferring regular languages [1]. In short, Dana Angluin's method first constructs the prefix tree of the given positive strings for a given language, and then it uses mergence to get a consistent automaton that accepts the target language. It is based on a special language called reversible language. A *0*-reversible language is a language, which can be accepted by a DFA with only one start state and one final state, and when reversed, it is also a DFA. This method classifies input strings as either "accept" or "reject", which are only two classes. We generalize this technique to classify strings into a finite number of classes. We modify the method by adding class symbols to the end of every input string as its classification suffix. We present an algorithm to construct an automaton, which can classify a given string in multiple classes.

We denote an algorithm for constructing zero-reversible automata of Dana Angluin [3] by *ZR*. We give the concept of classification symbol extension in section 2. We call our extension of Dana Angluin's algorithm for classification as *cl-ZR*, and it is given in section 3. Next, we prove the correctness of our *cl-ZR* algorithm in section 4. Concluding remarks are given in section 5.

Y. Xiang and B. Chaib-draa (Eds.): AI 2003, LNAI 2671, pp. 515-519, 2003.

2 Notations

We use the definitions and notations from Hartmanis [4] and Angluin [3]. Let U be an alphabet. Let S be a finite set of strings in a language L over U. If π is a partition of S, then for any element $s \in S$ there is a unique element of π containing s, which we denote by $B(s,\pi)$ and call it as the block of π containing s. An acceptor (over U) is a quadruple $A=(Q, I, F, \delta)$ such that Q is a finite set of states, I and F are subsets of Q, and δ maps from QxU to subsets of Q. Let A be a deterministic acceptor with initial state set I. Define the partition π_A by $B(w_1, \pi_A) = B(w_2, \pi_A)$ iff $\delta(I, w_1) = \delta(I, w_2)$. The prefix tree acceptor for a given sample set S, is denoted as $PT(S)$. Let $A = (Q, I, F, \delta)$ be an acceptor, and let $L=L(A)$. The reverse of δ, denoted by δ^r (and corresponding acceptor, denoted by A^r) is defined by

$$\delta^r(q, a) = \{q' \mid q \in \delta(q', a)\}, \text{ for all } a \in U, q \in Q.$$

The acceptor A is said to be *0*-reversible iff both A and A^r are deterministic.

3 Classification Algorithm: *cl-ZR*

We consider an extended alphabet $U \cup \{\$_1, \$_2, \$_3, \dots \$_n\}$. We append the string s_i a symbol called classification symbol $\$(s_i)$, denoting the class of string s_i. Formally, a sample string set S' for classification is defined as:

$$S' = \{s'_i \mid s'_i = s_i \, \$(s_i), \text{ where } \$(s_i) \text{ is the classification symbol of } s_i, \, s_i \in S\}$$

We now construct automaton for S'. Let A be a deterministic acceptor with initial state set I. Define the classification state set of A as $CS(A)$, such that:

$$CS(A) = \{ qc_i \mid qc_i \in Q, \text{ there exists } \$_i, \ \delta(q, \$_i) \in F, \text{ where } i \text{ is the class number}\}.$$

For all $qc_i \in CS(A)$, we denote qc_i as classification state in class i.

The algorithm *ZR* of Dana Angluin [3] can be applied on our extended strings. However, since the algorithm *ZR* works with merging states, some of the states that are connected to different classification symbol may be merged in the resultant automata in *ZR*.

We now explain our solution to the problem of merging of such states. In the algorithm *ZR*, the states are merged in an order, so that it is possible for us to get the merging chain that causes a mergence. The algorithm ZR merges B_1 and B_2, if $\delta(B_1, a) = \delta(B_2, a) = B_3$. When we have multiple classes, we should avoid merging of states that lead to different classes. To achieve this, we find out the mergence that forms the block B_3, and then find out this chain recursively, until we get the first mergence of two classification states that in the same class. Then we split the two classification states by our algorithm. After the splitting, the classification symbols in the class i, for instance, will be changed in to $\$_{i,1}$ and $\$_{i,2}$.

The method we use for finding the corresponding mergence is *find mergence method*:

1. Find B_3 such that $\delta(B_1, a) = \delta(B_2, a) = B_3$.
2. Search the merging log, until we find which mergence resulted in B_3 .
3. Do 1 and 2 recursively, until B_3= {final state of A}.
4. Find all states with the same alphabet symbol pointing to B_3.

After we use the *find mergence* method, to prevent the unwanted mergence chain, we have to *split* the corresponding states so that they will not be merged. This method is relatively simple. The *split* method is to replace original classification symbols with new split classification symbols as $\$_{i,\ 1}$ and $\$_{i,\ 2}$. Then we run the algorithm again, with the changed symbols.

In the algorithm *cl-ZR*, *s(B, b)* and *p(B, b)* is defined as in the *ZR* [3]: for each block *B* of the current partition and each symbol $b \in U$, we maintain two quantities, *s(B, b)* and *p(B, b)*, indicating the *b*-successors and *b*-predecessors of *B*. If there exists some state $q \in B$ such that $\delta_0(q, b)$ is defined, then $s(B, b)$ is some such $\delta_0(q, b)$; otherwise $s(B, b)$ is the empty set. The $p(B, b)$ is defined on $\delta_0{}^r$, similar to $s(B, b)$.

```
Algorithm cl-ZR
do{                                              //Initialization
Let A=(U,Q0,I0,F0,δ0) be PT(S).
Let π0 be the trivial partition of Q0.
For each b ∈ U, and q ∈ Q0, let s({q},b)=δ0(q,b) and
p({q},b) = δ0^r(q,b).
Choose some q' ∈ F0
Add all pairs (q',q) such that q ∈ F0-{q'}to the LIST.
Let i=0          //Merging
error=False
  While LIST ≠ Ø and error == False do
  {     Remove some element (q1,q2) from LIST.
        Let B1 = B(q1,πi), B2 = B(q2,πi).
          If B1 ≠ B2 then
          { If B1 and B2 contain classification states
            belonging to different class then
               { error = True
                 Find mergence that causes the
                 terminal mergence. Split the terminal
                 mergence.}
               else
               { Let πi+1 be πi with B1 and B2 merged.
                 For each b ∈ U, s-UPDATE (B1,B2,b) and
                 p-UPDATE (B1,B2,b).
                 Increase i by 1. }
        }
  }
} While error ==True                             //Termination
Let f = i, and output the acceptor A0/πf
End Algorithm cl-ZR
```

After we get the acceptor A, we make the following modification: omit the final state, mark all those classification states as new final states with their split classification symbols. As a result, we get the classification automata, which can now be used for predicting the class for a new string. Its class will be the final state the automata reaches in the end. Since we have no final state with more than one class attached, we can always get the string classified if the automaton accepts it. If not, class of the string can be called as "unknown".

Fig.1 to Fig. 4 illustrate the working of algorithm *cl-ZR* for the set of strings *S*.

S = { λ.class 1, 00.class2, 0000.class1, 0101.class3, 0110.class3, 1010.class3, 1.class3, 100.class1}

4 Correctness of *cl-ZR*

The correctness of *cl-ZR*, is expressed in the form of following lemmas and theorems.

Lemma 1 In any stage of *cl-ZR*, for any final state block B_1, non-final state block B_2, and any block B_3, the following are never satisfied:

(*i*) $\delta(B_1, a) = \delta(B_2, a) = B_3$

(*ii*) $\delta^r(B_1, a) = \delta^r(B_2, a) = B_3$.

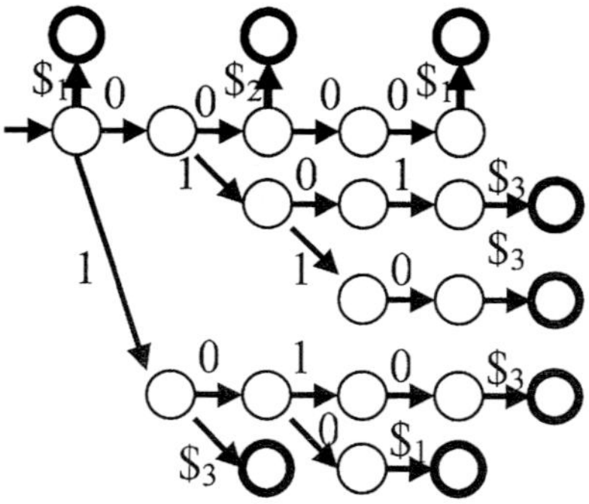

Fig. 1. Extension prefix-tree

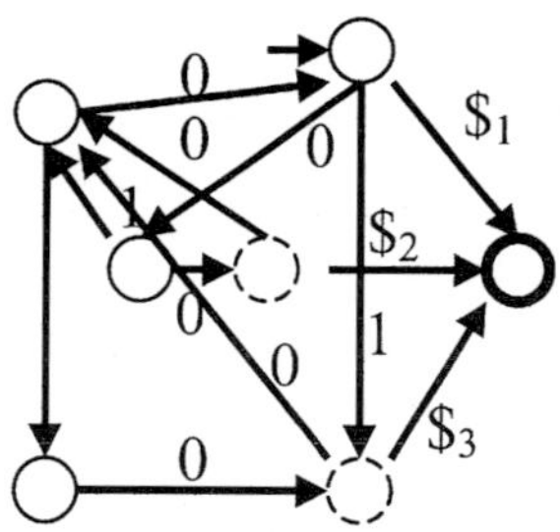

Fig. 2. Merging of states

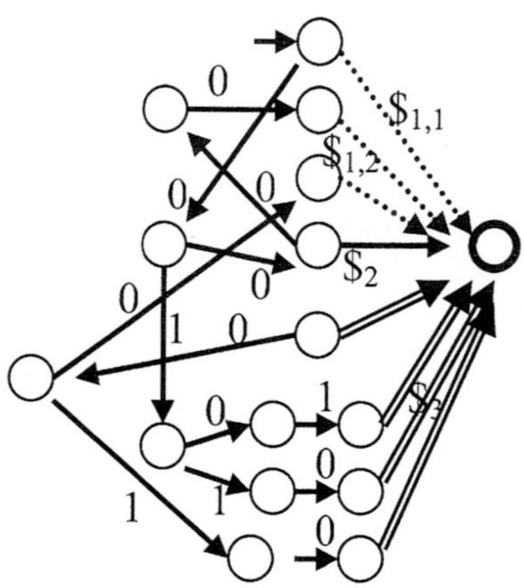

Fig. 3. Splitting of states

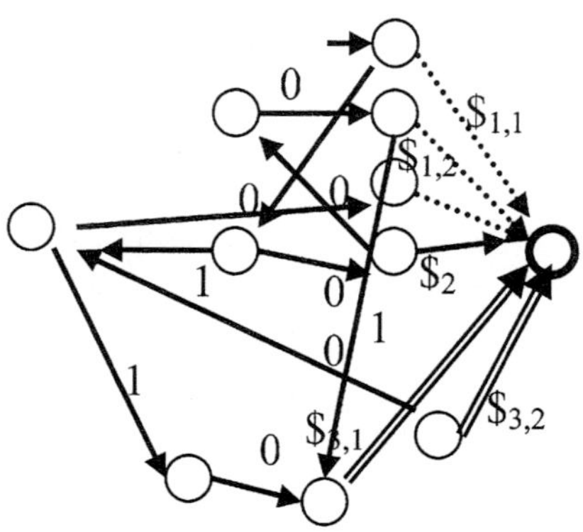

Fig. 4. Resultant Automaton

Theorem 1 During the merging in the algorithm, final state and non-final state are never merged.

Lemma 2 After the mergence of the final states, all blocks B_1 and B_2 satisfying $\delta(B_1, a) = \delta(B_2, a) = B_3$ are classification states, and no such blocks B_1 and B_2 satisfying $\delta^r (B_1, a) = \delta^r (B_2, a) = B_3$ exist.

Theorem 2 For any non-final state blocks B_1 and B_2, the first mergence found by *find mergence method* must be a mergence of two classification symbols with the same class.

PROOF

In cl-ZR, the mergences are done in a sequential order. Some mergences must be done after other mergences, as the later mergences need the result of earlier mergences. For a given mergence, we can get the previous mergence from the LIST (maintained in algorithm *cl-ZR*, section 3). Suppose we have $\delta(B_1, a) = \delta(B_2, a) = B_3$, and it is the first mergence; hence B_3 must be a block which contains a single state; let this state be q_3. That is, we have $\delta(q_1, a) = \delta(q_2, a) = q_3$, $B_3 = \{q_3\}$, $q_1 \in B_1$, $q_2 \in B_2$. If q_1, q_2 are not classification states and q_3 is not the merged final state, then it will lead to a contradiction to lemma 2. Hence Theorem 2 follows. Q.E.D.

Theorem 3 The algorithm *cl-ZR* needs $O(mn\alpha(n))$ operations, where m is the number of strings, n is one more than the sum of the lengths of the input strings and α is a very slowly growing function [3, 5].

5 Concluding Remarks

We presented an extension of Dana Angluin's zero-reversible algorithm, *ZR*, for classification into multiple classes. We call our algorithm by *cl-ZR*. We proved the correctness of the algorithm, and stated that its time complexity as $O(mn\alpha (n))$. In our algorithm *cl-ZR*, additional splitting strategies can be introduced, especially to make it efficient for the task of classification in multiple classes.

References

[1] I. H. Witten. Learning structure from sequences, with applications in a digital library. In Algorithmic Learning Theory, 13th International Conference, ALT 2002, L"ubeck, Germany November 2002, Proceedings, volume 2533 of Lecture Notes in Artificial Intelligence, pages 42-56. Springer, 2002.

[2] L. Miclet. Regular inference with a tail-clustering method. IEEE Trans. on Systems, Man, and Cybernetics, SMC-10:737-743, 1980.

[3] D. Angluin, (1982), Inference of Reversible Languages, *Journal of the Association for Computing Machinery*, Vol. 29 No. 3, July 1982, pp. 741-765

[4] Hartmanis, J. , Stearns, R.E. (1966), *Algebraic Theory of Sequential Machines, Prentice-Hall*, Englewood Cliffs, N.J., 1966.

[5] Tarjan, R. E. (1975) Efficiency of a good but not linear set union algorithm. *J. ACM* 22,2 (Apr. 1975) 215-225.

A Genetic K-means Clustering Algorithm Applied to Gene Expression Data

Fang-Xiang Wu[1], W. J. Zhang[1], and Anthony J. Kusalik[2]

[1] Division of Biomedical Engineering, University of Saskatchewan
Saskatoon, SK, S7N 5A9, CANADA
faw341@mail.usask.ca
zhangc@engr.usask.ca
[2] Department of Computer Science, University of Saskatchewan
Saskatoon, SK, S7N 5A9, CANADA
kusalik@cs.usask.ca

Abstract. One of the current main strategies to understand a biological process at genome level is to cluster genes by their expression data obtained from DNA microarray experiments. The classic K-means clustering algorithm is a deterministic search and may terminate in a locally optimal clustering. In this paper, a genetic K-means clustering algorithm, called GKMCA, for clustering in gene expression datasets is described. GKMCA is a hybridization of a genetic algorithm (GA) and the iterative optimal K-means algorithm (IOKMA). In GKMCA, each individual is encoded by a partition table which uniquely determines a clustering, and three genetic operators (selection, crossover, mutation) and an IOKM operator derived from IOKMA are employed. The superiority of the GKMCA over the IOKMA and over other GA-clustering algorithms without the IOKM operator is demonstrated for two real gene expression datasets.

1 Introduction

The development of DNA microarray techniques and genome sequencing has resulted in large amount of gene expression data for many biological processes. Gene expression of tissue sample can be quantitatively analyzed by co-hybridizing cDNA fluor-tagged with Cy5 and Cy3 (Cy5 for those from a treatment sample and Cy3 for those from a reference sample) to genes (called targets) on a DNA microarray [1]. Fluorescence intensity ratios are extracted via image segmentation for all target genes. A series of ratios collected at different time points in a biological process comprise a gene expression pattern. Gene expression data from many organisms are available in publicly-accessible databases [2]. One of the main goals of analyzing these data is to find correlated genes by searching for similar gene expression patterns. This is usually achieved by clustering them [3-6].

Y. Xiang and B. Chaib-draa (Eds.): AI 2003, LNAI 2671, pp. 520-526, 2003.

Clustering methods can be divided into two basic types: hierarchical and partitional clustering [7]. They have both been widely applied to analysis of gene expression data [3~6]. Genetic algorithms have also been applied to many clustering problems [8-11]. However, these methods are not suitable for the analysis of gene expression data because of (typical) size of a dataset. To our best knowledge, there have been no reports of the application of genetic algorithms to clustering gene expression data yet.

In this paper, we propose a genetic K-means clustering algorithm (GKMCA), which is a hybrid approach to combining a genetic algorithm with the iterative optimal K-means algorithm (IOKMA). In our GKMCA, the solutions are encoded by a partition table. GKMCA contains three genetic operations -- natural selection, crossover and mutation-- and one IOKM operation derived from IOKMA.

The remainder of the paper is organized as follows. In section 2 the K-means clustering problem and the IOKMA are introduced. In section 3, the operators incorporated into GKMCA are described in detail, and GKMCA is presented. In section 4 two DNA microarray datasets are introduced. GKMCA is compared to classic K-means clustering algorithms (i.e. IOKMA) and other GA-clustering algorithms on these two datasets. Finally, some conclusions are drawn in section 5.

2 IOKMA

In general, a K-partitioning algorithm takes as input a set $D=\{x_1,x_2\cdots,x_n\}$ of n objects and an integer K, and outputs a partition of D into exactly K disjoint subsets $D_1, D_{2,}, \cdots, D_K$. In the context of clustering gene expression data, each object (gene) is expressed by a real number row vector (called the expression pattern) of dimension d, where d is the number of ratios in the expression pattern. We will not distinguish an object from its expression pattern. Each of the subsets is a cluster, with objects in the same cluster being somehow more similar to each other than they to objects in any other cluster. Of a number of K-partition algorithms, K-means is the best-known one. We will not distinguish an object from its expression pattern.

Let x_{ij} denote the j th component of expression pattern x_i. For the predefined number K of clusters, define the partition table as the following matrix $W=[w_{ik}]$ $(i=1,\cdots,n; k=1,\cdots,K)$.

$$w_{ik}=\begin{cases}1, & \text{if } i\text{th object belongs to } k\text{th cluster,}\\ 0, & \text{otherwise.}\end{cases} \quad (1)$$

Obviously, the matrix W has property that

$$\sum_{k=1}^{K} w_{ik}=1 \quad (i=1,\cdots,n) \; . \quad (2)$$

Let the centroid of the k th cluster be $m_k=(m_{k1},\cdots,m_{kd})$ $(k=1,\cdots,K)$. Then

$$m_k=W*X/\Sigma_{i=1}^{n}w_{ik} \; . \quad (3)$$

where $X=[x_{ij}]$ is the expression matrix determined by the component x_{ij}'s of all expression patterns in the dataset. A sum-of-squared-error (the cost function of a K-partition) is defined by

$$J(W)=\sum_{k=1}^{K} J_k(W)=\sum_{k=1}^{K}\sum_{i=1}^{n} w_{ik}\left\|x_i-m_k\right\|^2 . \tag{4}$$

where $J_k(W)=\sum_{i=1}^{n} w_{ik}\left\|x_i-m_k\right\|^2$, and $\|\bullet\|$ is Euclidean distance measure of a vector. The objective of K-means algorithms is to find an optimal partition expressed by $W^*=[w_{ik}^*]$ which minimizes $J(W)$, i.e.

$$J(W^*)=\min_{W}\{J(W)\} . \tag{5}$$

The optimization problem (5) is NP-hard and may be solved by a heuristic algorithm called the iteratively optimal K-means algorithm (IOKMA) [12].

3 GKMCA

GKMCA shown in Figure 1 is a hybrid algorithm of GA to IOKMA, including the three genetic operators in GA and an IOKM operator derived from IOKMA. In this section we specify coding, selection operator, crossover operator and mutation operator and IOKM operator before we present GKMCA.

Coding: A partition table is used to express a solution to a clustering. Thus, the search space consists of all W matrices that satisfy (1) ~(2). Such an W is coded by an integer string s_W consisting of n integers from the set $\{1,\cdots,K\}$. Each position in the string corresponds to an object and the value in the position represents the cluster number where the corresponding object belongs. In the following, we will not distinguish W from its code s_W. A population is expressed by a set of partition tables representing its individuals, denote by $\widetilde{W}p$ or Wp.

Selection operator-- $\widetilde{W}p=Selection(Wp,X,K,N)$: For convenience of the manipulation, GKMCA always assigns the best individual found over time in a population to individual 1 and copies it to the next population. Operator $\widetilde{W}p=Selection(Wp,X,K,N)$ selects $(N-1)/2$ individuals from the previous population according to the probability distribution given by

$$Ps(W_i)=F(W_i)/\sum_{i=1}^{N} F(W_i) \tag{6}$$

where N (an odd positive integer) is the number of individuals in a population, W_i is the partition table of individual i, and $F(W_i)$ represents the fitness value of individual i in the current population defined as $F(W_i)=TJ-J(W_i)$, where $J(W)$ is calculated by (4), and TJ is the total squared error incurred in representing the n

objects $x_1, x_2 \cdots, x_n$ by their center $\overline{m} = \sum_{i=1}^{n} x_i / n$, i.e. $TJ = \sum_{i=1}^{n} \|x_i - \overline{m}\|^2$. Note that there are $(N-1)/2+1$ individuals in $\widetilde{W}p$.

Crossover operator-- $Wp = Crossover(\widetilde{W}p, ROW, N)$: The intention of the crossover operation is to create new (and hopefully better) individuals from two selected parent individuals. In GKMCA, of two parent individuals, one is individual 1 (i.e. the optimal individual found over time), and another is one of the selected $(N-1)/2$ individuals from the parent population other than individual 1 by selection operator. Here crossover operator adopts single-point crossover methods for simplicity. Note that after crossover operation population Wp has N individuals.

Genetic K-means Clustering Algorithm (GKMCA)

Input: Expression matrix, X; Number of objects, ROW; Number of attributes, COL; Number of clusters, K; Mutation probability, Pm; Population size, N; Number of generation, GEN;

Output: Minimum sum-of-squared-errors of clustering found over evolution, JE.

1. Initialize the population, Wp; /* Wp is a set of partition table of a population */
2. Re-order individuals such that the first one is the optimal in population Wp, and set $W^* = Wp(1)$, $JE(0) = J(W^*)$, and $g = 1$.
3. While ($g \le GEN$)
4. $\widetilde{W}p = Selection(Wp, X, K, N)$;
5. $Wp = Crossover(\widetilde{W}p, ROW, N)$;
6. $Wp = Mutation(Wp, Pm, ROW, COL, K, N)$;
7. $[Wp, J(Wp)] = IOKM(Wp, X, ROW, COL, K, N)$;
8. Find the optimal individual in population Wp, denote by W^O;
9. If ($J(W^*) > J(W^O)$), then $W^* = W^O$, and set $JE(g) = J(W^O)$ else $JE(g) = JE(g-1)$;
10. Re-arrange individuals such that $Wp(1) = W^O$;
11. $g = g + 1$;
12. End while
13. Return JE corresponding to the partition table W^* by (4).

Figure 1. Genetic K-means Algorithm (GKMCA)

Mutation operator-- $Wp = Mutation(Wp, Pm, ROW, COL, K, N)$: Each position in a string is randomly selected with a mutation probability P_m, and the value of the selected position is uniformly randomly replaced by another integer from the set $\{1, \cdots, K\}$. In [8], the value of the position is changed depending on the distance of the cluster centoids from the corresponding object. Actually such a complex technique may not be necessary because IOKM operator is used. To avoid any singular partition (containing an empty cluster), after previous operation, mutation operator also randomly assigns K different objects to K different clusters in order to assure that every cluster has at least one object.

IOKM operator--$[Wp, J(Wp)] = IOKM(Wp, X, ROW, COL, K, N)$: IOKM operator is obtained by IOKMA [11] where each individual W in population Wp is an initial partition. In [8-10], several different K-means operators were employed, and their functions are similar to that of IOKMA. However, those K-means algorithms are not iteratively optimal.

4 Experiments and Discussion

4.1 Datasets

Experiments on two datasets are performed to demonstrate the performance of GKMCA, compared to IOKMA and other GA-clustering algorithms. The first dataset (α factor) contains 612 genes which were identified as cell-cycle regulated in the α factor-synchronized experiment [4], with no missing data in the 18 arrays. It may be created from the related data at http://genome-www.staforrd.edu/SVD. The second dataset (Fibroblast) contains 517 gene expressions selected by authors from an experiment studying the response of human fibroblasts to serum [5]. The original data may be obtained at http://genome-www.stanford.edu/serum.

4.2 Experiment Results

According to cell-cycle division process [4, 5], we took 4 = k for number of clusters in both datasets in experiments. In GKMCA, we took population size $N = 21$, mutation probability $Pm = 0.02$, and number of generations $GEN = 20$. Experiment results (not exhibited here because of space limitations) shows that the inclusion of the IOKM operator greatly improves the convergence rate of the algorithms. In fact, GAs without this type of operator [11] converge slowly, or not at all. Thus such GAs are not applicable to DNA microarray datasets of practical size.

Table 1. Performance comparisons of GKMCA and IOKMA. GKMCA: the sum-of-squared-errors of the final clustering from GKMCA; the K -Means Average and STD: the average of the sum-of-squared-errors and the standard derivation of the resultant clusterings for 420 independent runs, respectively

Datasets	K-Means		GKMCA
	Average	STD	
α factor	367.5253	3.0080	358.4712
Fibroblast	215.1420	0.5720	213.8420

In order to compare GKMCA and IOKMA, GKMCA was run again on two datasets 5 times (results from them are the same for each dataset) while IOKMA was run on two datasets 420 ($= N * GEN$) times. In these experiments, for each individual IOKM operator in GKMCA only performs two repeat-loops while each IOKMA performed much more than two repeat-loops to reach its convergence. Experiment results are listed in Table 1. From the Table, it can be observed that GKMCA clearly outperforms the IOKMA in that GKMCA is less sensitive to the initial conditions, and in that the sum-of-squared-errors of the resultant clusterings from GKMA is less than the average of the sum-of-squared-errors of the clusterings from 420 runs of IOKMA .

5 Conclusion

In this study, a genetic K-means clustering algorithm (GKMCA) is proposed for clustering tasks on large-scale datasets such as gene expression datasets from DNA microarray experiments. GKMCA is a hybrid algorithm of the iterative optimal K-means algorithm and a genetic algorithm. Some special techniques were employed in GKMCA to avoid any singular clustering (in the mutation operator) and to speed up the rate of convergence (in the IOKM operator). GKMCA was run on two real gene expression datasets. Experiments results show that not only can GKMCA fulfil the clustering tasks on gene expression datasets, but also its performance is better than that of IOKMA and some existing GA-clustering algorithms.

References

[1] Eisen, M. B. and Brown, P. O. DNA Arrays for Analysis of Gene Expression. *Methods Enzymol* 303: 179-205, 1999.

[2] Sherlock, G., *et al.* David Botstein and J. Michael Cherry, The Stanford Microarray Database, *Nucleic Acids Research*, 29: 152-155, 2001.

[3] Eisen, M. B., *et al.* Cluster Analysis and Display of Genome-Wide Expression Patterns. *Proc Natl. Acad. Sci. USA*, 95: 14863-8, 1998.

[4] Spellman, P. T., *et al.* Comprehensive Identification of Cell Cycle-regulated Genes of the Yeast Saccharomyces cerevisiae by Microarray Hybridization. *Mol. Biol. Cell.*, 9: 3273-97, 1998.

[5] Iyer, V R., *et al.* The transcriptional program in the response of human fibroblasts to serum. *Science*. 283: 83-87, 1999

[6] Chen, G., *et al.* Cluster analysis of microarray gene expression data: application to and evaluation with NIA mouse 15K array on ES cell differentiation. *Statistica Sinica*, 12: 241-262, 2001.

[7] Hartigan, J. (1975) Clustering Algorithms. Wiley, New York, NY.

[8] Krishna, K. and Murty, M. M. Genetic K-means algorithm, IEEE Transactions on Systems, Man, and Cybernetics---Part B: Cybernetics, 29: 433-439, 1999.

[9] Maulik, U. and Bandyopadhyay, S. Genetic algorithm-based clustering technique, *Pattern Recognition*, 33: 1455-1456, 2000.

[10] Franti, P. et al. Genetic algorithms for large-scale clustering problems, *The compuer Journal*, 40: 547-554, 1997.

[11] Hall, L. O., Ozyurt, I. B., and Bezdek, J. C. Clustering with a genetically optimized approach, *IEEE Transactions on Evolutionary Computation*, 3: 103-112, 1999.

[12] Richard, O. D., Peter, E. H., and David, G. S., Pattern Classification, New York: Wiley, 2001.

Explanation-Oriented Association Mining Using a Combination of Unsupervised and Supervised Learning Algorithms

Yiyu Yao Yao, Yan Zhao, and Robert Brien Maguire

Department of Computer Science, University of Regina
Regina, Saskatchewan, Canada S4S 0A2
{yyao,yanzhao,rbm}@cs.uregina.ca

Abstract. We propose a new framework of explanation-oriented data mining by adding an explanation construction and evaluation phase to the data mining process. While traditional approaches concentrate on mining algorithms, we focus on explaining mined results. The mining task can be viewed as unsupervised learning that searches for interesting patterns. The construction and evaluation of mined patterns can be formulated as supervised learning that builds explanations. The proposed framework is therefore a simple combination of unsupervised learning and supervised learning. The basic ideas are illustrated using association mining. The notion of conditional association is used to represent plausible explanations of an association. The condition in a conditional association explicitly expresses the plausible explanations of an association.

1 Introduction

Data mining is a discipline concerning theories, methodologies, and in particular, computer systems for exploring and analyzing a large amount of data. A data mining system is designed with an objective to automatically discover, or to assist a human expert to discover, knowledge embedded in data [2, 6, 21]. Results, experiences and lessons from artificial intelligence, and particularly intelligent information systems, are immediately applicable to the study of data mining.

By putting data mining systems in the wide context of intelligent information systems, one can easily identify certain limitations of current data mining studies. In this paper, we focus on the explanation facility of intelligent systems, which has not received much attention in data mining community. We present a new explanation-oriented framework for data mining by combining unsupervised and supervised learning.

For clarity, we use association mining to demonstrate the basic ideas. The notion of conditional association is used to explicitly state the conditions under which the association occurs. An algorithm is suggested. Conceptually, it consists of two parts and uses two data tables. A transaction data table is used to learn an association in the first step. An explanation table is used to construct an explanation of the association in the second step.

Y. Xiang and B. Chaib-draa (Eds.): AI 2003, LNAI 2671, pp. 527–531, 2003.

2 Motivations

In the development of many branches of science such as mathematics, physics, chemistry, and biology, the discovery of a natural phenomenon is only the first step. The important subsequent tasks for scientists are to build a theory accounting for the phenomenon and to provide justifications, interpretations, and explanations of the theory. The interpretations and explanations enhance our understanding of the phenomenon and guide us to make rational decisions [22].

Explanation plays an important role in learning and is an important functionality of many intelligent information systems [5, 8, 9, 11, 15]. Dhaliwal and Benbasat argue that the role of constructing explanation is to clarify, teach, and convince [5]. Human experts are often asked to explain their views, recommendations, decisions or actions. Users would not accept recommendations that emerge from reasoning that they do not understand [9].

In an expert system, an explanation facility serves several purposes [17]. It makes the system more intelligible to the user, helps an expert to uncover shortcomings of the system, and help a user to feel more assured about the recommendations and actions of the system. Typically, the system provides two basic types of explanations: the *why* and the *how*. A why type question is normally posed by a user when the system asks the user to provide some information. A how type question is posed by a user if the user wants to know how a certain conclusion is reached. Wick and Slagle [19] proposed a journalistic explanation facility which include the six elements *who*, *what*, *where*, *when*, *why*, and *how*.

A data mining system may be viewed as an intermediate system between a database or data warehouse and an application, whose main purpose is to change data into usable knowledge [21]. To achieve this goal, the data mining system should provide necessary explanations of mined knowledge. A piece of discovered knowledge is meaningful and trustful only if we have an explanation. An association does not immediately offer an explanation. One needs to find explanations regarding *when*, *where*, and *why* an association occurs. If a data mining system is an interactive system, it must also provide explanations for its recommendations and actions. For a knowledge-based data mining systems, explanation of the use of knowledge is also necessary to make the mining process more understandable by a user. The observations and results regarding explanations in expert systems are applicable to data mining systems. In order to make data mining a well-accepted technology, more attention must be paid to the needs and wishes for explanations from its end users. Without the explanation functionality, the effectiveness of data mining systems is limited.

On the other hand, studies in data mining have been focused on the preparation, process and analysis of data. Little attention is paid to the task of explaining discovered results. There is clearly a need for the incorporation of an explanation facility into a data mining process.

It is commonly accepted that a data mining process consists of the following steps: data selection, data preprocessing, data transformation, pattern discovery, and pattern evaluation [6]. Several variations have been studied by many authors [7, 10, 16]. By adding an extra step, explanation construction and evaluation, we can obtain a framework of explanation-oriented data mining. This leads to a significant step from detecting the *existence* of a pattern to searching for the underlying *reasons* that explain the existence of the pattern.

3 Explanation-Oriented Association Mining

Association mining was first introduced using transaction databases and deals with purchasing patterns of customers [1]. A set of items are associated if they are bought together by many customers. Some authors extended the original associations to negative associations [20].

3.1 Conditional Associations and Explanation Evaluation

The reasons for the occurrence of an association can not be provided by the association itself. One needs to construct and represent explanations using other information. More specifically, if one can identify some conditions under which the occurrence of the association is more pronounced, the condition may provide some explanation. By adding time, place, customer features (profiles), and item features as conditions, we may identify *when*, *where* and *why* an association occurs, respectively.

The notion of conditional associations has been discussed by many authors in different contexts [4, 14, 18]. Typically, conditions in conditional associations mining are used as constraints to restrict a portion of the database to mine useful associations. For explanation-oriented association mining, we take a reverse process. We first mine association and then search for conditions.

We can profile transactions by customers, places, and time ranges. Domain specific knowledge is used to select a set of profiles and to form an explanation table. Different explanation tables can be constructed, which lead to different explanations. Each explanation table may or may not be able to provide a satisfactory explanation. It may also happen that each table may be able to explain only some aspects of the association.

Let $\phi\psi$ denote an association discovered in a transaction table. Let χ denote a condition expressible in the explanation table. A conditional association is written by $\phi\psi \mid \chi$. Suppose s is a measure that quantifies the strength of the association. An example of such measures is the *support* measure used in association mining [1]. Plausible explanations may be obtained by comparing the values $s(\phi\psi)$ and $s(\phi\psi \mid \chi)$. If $s(\phi\psi \mid \chi) > s(\phi\psi)$, namely, the association $\phi\psi$ is more pronounced under the condition χ, we say that χ provides a plausible explanation for $\phi\psi$, otherwise, χ does not. We may also introduce another measure g to quantify the quality of conditions [22]. Explanations are evaluated jointly by these two measures.

3.2 Explanation Construction

Construction of explanations is equivalent to finding conditions in conditional associations from an explanation table.

Suppose $\phi\psi$ is an association of interest. We can classify transactions into two classes, those that satisfy the association, and those that do not satisfy the association. With this transformation, searching for conditions in conditional associations can be stated as learning of classification rules in the explanation table. Any supervised learning algorithm, such as ID3 [12], its later version C4.5 [13], or PRISM [3], may be used to perform this task.

3.3 An Algorithm for Explanation-Oriented Association Mining

Explanation-oriented associating mining consists of two steps. In the first step, an unsupervised learning algorithm, such Apriori [1] or a clustering algorithm, is used to discover an association. In the second step, an association of interest is used to create a label in the explanation table. Any supervised learning algorithm, such as ID3 [12] or PRISM [3], is used to learn classification rules, which are in fact conditional associations.

The framework of explanation-oriented association mining is thus a simple combination of existing unsupervised and supervised learning algorithms. As an illustration, the combined Apriori-ID3 algorithm is described below:

Input: A transaction table and explanation profiles.
Output: Conditional associations (explanations).

1 Use the Apriori algorithm to generate a set of frequent itemsets in the transaction table. For each $\phi\psi$ in the set, $support(\phi\psi) \geq minsup$.

2 If $\phi\psi$ is interesting

- **2.a** Introduce a binary attribute named *Decision*. Given a transaction $x \in U$, its value on *Decision* is "+" if it satisfies $\phi\psi$ in the transaction table. Otherwise, its value is "-".
- **2.b** Construct an information table by using the attribute *Decision* and explanation profiles. The new table is called an *explanation table.*
- **2.c** By treating *Decision* as the target class, we can apply the ID3 Algorithm to derive classification rules of the form: $\chi \Rightarrow Decision =$ "+", which corresponds to the conditional association $\phi\psi \mid \chi$. The condition χ is a formula in the explanation table, which states the condition χ under which the association $\phi\psi$ occurs.
- **2.d** Evaluate conditional associations based on statistical measures.

4 Conclusion

By drawing results from artificial intelligence in general and intelligent information systems in specific, we demonstrate the needs for explanations of mined results in a data mining process. We show that explanation-oriented association mining can be easily achieved by combining existing unsupervised and supervised learning methods. The main contribution is the introduction of a new point of view to data mining research. An explanation facility may greatly increase the effectiveness of data mining systems.

References

[1] Agrawal, R. and Srikant, R., Fast algorithms for mining association rules in large databases, *Proceedings of VLDB*, 487-499, 1994.

[2] Berry, M. J. A. and Linoff, G. S., *Mastering Data Mining: The Art and Science of Customer Relationship Management*, John Wiley & Sons, New York, 2000.

[3] Cendrowska, J., PRISM: An algorithm for inducing modular rules, *International Journal of Man-Machine Studies*, **27**, 349-370, 1987.

[4] Chen, L., *Discovery of Conditional Association Rules*, Master thesis, Utah State University, 2001.

[5] Dhaliwal, J. S. and Benbasat, I., The use and effects of knowledge-based system explanations: Theoretical foundations and a framework for empirical evaluation, *Information Systems Research*, **7**, 342-362, 1996.

[6] Fayyad, U. M., Piatetsky-Shapiro, G. and Smyth, P., From data mining to knowledge discovery: An overview, *Advances in Knowledge Discovery and Data Mining*, Fayyad, U. M., Piatetsky-Shapiro, G., Smyth, P. and Uthurusamy, R. (Eds.), 1-34, AAAI/MIT Press, Menlo Park, California, 1996.

[7] Han, J. and Kamber, M., *Data Mining: Concept and Techniques*, Morgan Kaufmann, Palo Alto, CA, 2000.

[8] Hasling, D. W., Clancey, W. J. and Rennels, G., Strategic explanations for a diagnostic consultation system, *International Journal of Man-Machine Studies*, **20**, 3-19, 1984.

[9] Haynes, S. R., *Explanation in Information Systems: A Design Rationale Approach*, Ph.D. Dissertation, The London School of Economics, University of London, 2001.

[10] Mannila, H., Methods and problems in data mining, *Proceedings of International Conference on Database Theory*, 41-55, 1997.

[11] Pitt, J., *Theory of Explanation*, Oxford University Press, Oxford, 1988.

[12] Quinlan, J. R., Learning efficient classification procedures, *Machine Learning: An Artificial Intelligence Approach*, Michalski, J. S., Carbonell, J. G., and Mirchell, T. M. (Eds.), Morgan Kaufmann, Palo Alto, CA, 463-482, 1983.

[13] Quinlan, J. R., *C4.5: Programs for Machine Learning*, Morgan Kaufmann, Palo Alto, CA, 1993.

[14] Rauch, J., Association rules and mechanizing hypotheses formation, *Proceedings of ECML Workshop: Machine Learning as Experimental Philosophy of Science*, 2001.

[15] Schank, R. and Kass, A., Explanations, machine learning, and creativity, *Machine Learning: An Artificial Intelligence Approach*, Kodratoff, Y. and Michalski, R. (Eds.), Morgan Kaufmann, Palo Alto, CA, 31-48, 1990.

[16] Simoudis, E., Reality check for data mining. *IEEE Expert*, **11**, 1996.

[17] Turban, E. and Aronson, J. E., *Decision Support Systems and Intelligent System*, Prentice Hall, New Jersey, 2001.

[18] Wang, K. and He, Y., User-defined association mining, *Proceedings of PAKDD*, 387-399, 2001.

[19] Wick, M. R. amd Slagle, J. R., An explanation facility for today's expert systems, *IEEE Expert*, **4**, 1989, 26-36.

[20] Wu, X., Zhang, C. and Zhang, S., Mining both positive and negative association rules, *Proceedings of ICML*, 1997.

[21] Yao, Y. Y., A step toward foundations of data mining, manuscript, 2003.

[22] Yao, Y. Y., Zhao, Y. and Maguire, R. B., Explanation oriented association mining using rough set theory, *Proceedings of International Conference on Rough Sets, Fuzzy Sets, Data Mining and Granular Computing*, to appear, 2003.

Motion Recognition from Video Sequences*

Xiang Yu and Simon X. Yang

Advanced Robotics and Intelligent Systems (ARIS) Lab
School of Engineering, University of Guelph
Guelph, ON N1G 2W1, Canada
{yux,syang}@uoguelph.ca

Abstract. This paper proposes a method for recognizing human motions from video sequences, based on the hypothesis that there exists a repertoire of movement primitives in biological sensory motor systems. First, a content-based image retrieval algorithm is used to obtain statistical feature vectors from individual images. A decimated magnitude spectrum is calculated from the Fourier transform of the edge images. Then, an unsupervised learning algorithm, self-organizing map, is employed to cluster these shape-based features. Motion primitives are recovered by searching the resulted time serials based on the minimum description length principle. Experimental results of motion recognition from a 37 seconds video sequence show that the proposed approach can efficiently recognize the motions, in a manner similar to human perception.

1 Introduction

The analysis of human actions by a computer is gaining more and more interest [1, 2, 4, 5, 6]. A significant part of this task is the recognition and modelling of human motions in video sequences, which provides a basis for applications such as human/machine interaction, humanoid robotics, animation, video database search, sports medicine. For human/machine interaction, it is highly desirable if the machine can understand the human operator's action and react correspondingly. The work for the remote control of camera view is a good example. The recognition of human motions is also important for humanoid robotics research. For example, imitation is a powerful means of skill acquisition for humanoid robots, i.e., a robot learns its motions by understanding and imitating the action of a human model. Another application is video database search. The increasing interest in the understanding of action or behaviour has led to a shift in computer vision from static images to video sequences [2, 3].

A conventional solution to human motion recognition is based on a kinematics model. For example, Ormoneit et al. [5] introduced a human body model in which the human body is represented by a collection of articulated limbs. One problem of this approach is how to decompose a time series into suitable temporal primitives in order to model these body angles. Hidden Markov models (HMMs)

* This work was supported by Natural Sciences and Engineering Research Council (NSERC).

Y. Xiang and B. Chaib-draa (Eds.): AI 2003, LNAI 2671, pp. 532–536, 2003.

have also been well used for recognition of human action. However, the topology of the HMMs is obtained by learning a hybrid dynamic model on periodic motion and it is difficult to be extended to other types of motions, which could be more complex [6].

In this work, we propose a unsupervised learning based approach to model and represent human motion in video sequences. We use self-organizing maps (SOM) to cluster image sequences to form motor primitives. In a computational sense, primitives can be viewed as a basis set of motor programs that are sufficient, through combination operators, for generating the entire movement repertoire [1]. After the clustering, we propose a substructure discovery algorithm based on the minimum description length (MDL) principle.

In the following sections, the structure and learning algorithm of the self-organizing map are first introduced, followed by its application to video processing. Section 3 presents the basic idea of the recovery of primitives from the video sequence by searching. Section 4 describes the experiments and the research results. The final section gives some concluding remarks.

2 Clustering of the Self-Organizing Map

A key difficulty of a primitive-based approach is how to find and define those primitives. We propose an approach based on self-organizing maps. First, edge images are symbolized by clustering, where the video sequence is converted into a long symbolic series. Then, primitive actions are discovered by using a substructure searching algorithm.

The SOM usually consists of a 2D grid of nodes, each of which represents a model of some observation. Basically, the SOM can be regarded as a similarity graph, or a clustering diagram. After a nonparametric and unsupervised learning process, the models are organized into a meaningful order in which similar models are closer to each other than the more dissimilar ones.

The basic criterion for training a self-organizing map is the so-called *winner take all* principle, i.e., a winner node is selected and only this winner node will have a chance to learn its weights [7, 8, 9]. Further, in order to organize a map with cooperation between nodes, the learning area is expanded to a kernel around the winner node, with the learning rate linearly decreasing from the winner node to nodes on the boundary of the kernel. Then, the learning is performed in such a way that the reference vector represented by these weights is moved closer to the input pattern. Denote $\mathbf{m}_i$ as the weight vector for the ith node, and $\mathbf{x}$ as an input, the learning process is [7]

$$\mathbf{m}_i(t+1) = \mathbf{m}_i(t) + h_{c,i}(t)(\mathbf{x} - \mathbf{m}_i(t)), \tag{1}$$

where $h_{c,i}(t)$ is a decreasing function defined as follow

$$h_{c,i}(t) = \alpha(t) \exp\left(-\frac{||\mathbf{r}_i - \mathbf{r}_c||}{2\delta^2(t)}\right), \tag{2}$$

where $1 > \alpha(t) > 0$ is the learning rate that is a monotonically decreasing function, $\mathbf{r}_i$ and $\mathbf{r}_c$ are the vector locations of the ith node and cth node, respectively, $\delta(t)$ is the width of the kernel function that defines the size of the learning neighbourhood that decreases monotonically with time, and $||.||$ represents the Euclidean distance.

In this paper, we use a SOM to cluster images based on shape features. The objective is to find a representation of a video sequence to illustrate the property of an action as a time series. After training, the SOM is capable of generating a label for each input image, converting a video sequence to a label series. Then, a searching process for motor primitives is applied to construct a primitive vocabulary.

3 Searching for Primitives

After symbolizing the video sequences, computation cost is the key point for the searching algorithm of primitives. An exhaustive searching will result in an exponentially increasing complexity. Fortunately, exhaustive searching is not necessary when we consider the nature of the actions. Basically we can describe an action as a transfer from one pose to another. A pose accords to a serial of images that don't significantly change. Therefore, the whole searching space can be divided into multiple spaces by detecting the poses. Further, by using the minimum description length principle, the repetitive substructures, primitives, are identified.

For a given video sequence, the trained SOM maps all individual images onto a 2-dimensional (2D) network of neurons. Consider the time order of all images in the video. The video sequence forms some tracks/paths on the SOM map. These tracks represent some substructures in the video sequence, which appear repeatedly. We propose the following algorithm to discover these substructures.

1. Scan the 2D $N \times M$ SOM and form a 1D series of symbols, $\{S_1, S_2, \ldots, S_P\}$. The series length, P, equals to the number of neurons in the SOM map.
2. Create a matrix $C_{P \times P}$. Compute $C(i,j)$ as the number of times when a track from S_i to S_j is observed.
3. Find the maximal element of C. Denote it as $C_{i',j'}$. It represents a track from $S_{i'}$ to $S_{j'}$.
4. Fetch the j'th row of C. Find the maximal element of this row. Then, the corresponding symbol is the next symbol after $S_{j'}$.
5. Set the elements whose symbols have been tracked to zero. Then repeat Steps 4-5 until the current maximal element is less than half of the first maximal element.
6. After finding the global maximal element, the next process is to find the previous symbol by fetching the i'th column of C and searching the maximal element. This process is also repeated until the current maximal element is less than half of the first maximal element.
7. Repeat Steps 3-6 until there is no element larger than half of the first maximum.

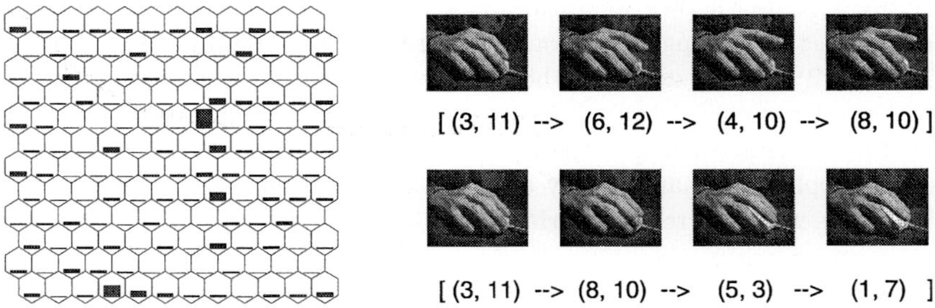

Fig. 1. (Left) Illustration of the sample distribution on the trained SOM. Totally there are 555 samples. The map is a 12×12 grid. The bar height demonstrates the number of samples that take the current node as the best-matching unit. (Right) Sample shots in the video sequence. The upper sequence shows a movement of the forefinger, while the lower sequence shows a movement of the middle finger. Each motion serial is symbolized to a neuron serials in the 2D map

The obtained sub-series of symbols represent the so-called primitives of motion. A new symbol can be defined for each primitive. Then, the whole video sequence can be represented by using these symbols, resulting in a concise representation of the video sequence.

4 Simulations

A web camera is used to capture a video sequence of a hand clicking on a mouse. With the resolution being 320×240 and the frequency being 15 frames/second, a 37 seconds sequence with 555 frames is used to test the proposed approach.

After we convert the video sequence into individual image files, the Matlab Image toolbox is used to compute shape-based Fourier feature vectors to which SOM can be applied to do the clustering. We first normalize the image size. The Prewitt method is used to compute the edge image. Then, an 8-point FFT is calculated. The resulted Fourier spectrum is low-pass filtered and decimated by the factor of 32, resulting in a 128D vector for each image [10].

The feature vectors obtained in the above process are fed into a 12×12 SOM for clustering. As there is no prior knowledge for the selection of the number of neurons, we apply a simple rule to help the selection, i.e., an even distribution of samples/features over the whole map. Basically , a too large map will fail to discover any similarity among samples while an extra small map might mess everything together. By monitoring the sample distribution, as shown in Figure 1(Left), we choose a heuristic structure with 12×12 neurons. The learning rate function $\alpha(t)$ is chosen as $\alpha(t) = a/(t+b)$ where a and b are chosen so that $\alpha(t = T) = 0.01 * \alpha(t = 0)$, with T is the last time interval and $\alpha(t = 0) = 0.05$. The kernel width $\delta(t)$ is set to be a linear function that changes from $\delta_{ini} = 12$ to $\delta_{final} = 1$. In particular, $\delta(t) = (\delta_{final} - \delta_{ini})/T * t + \delta_{ini}$.

Figure 1(Right) shows some sample shots of action in the video sequence. For example, the forefinger's action is well recognized by searching the serial of $\{(3, 11), (6, 12), ...\}$. By applying the substructure searching algorithm presented above, primitives are extracted as series of neurons, which are represented by a pair of numbers according to their positions on the map. Then, the whole video sequence is split automatically by dividing and representing the corresponding symbol series with the resulted primitives.

5 Conclusion

The video sequence processing approach proposed in this paper features two factors. First, due to the unsupervised learning mechanism of the self-organizing map, it saves us some tedious manual computation that is necessary for conventional approaches such as that based on hidden Markov models. Secondly, it gains support from cognitive studies of the motion primitives, as well as provides a better understanding of the biological sensory motor systems.

References

[1] E. Bizzi, S. Giszter, and F. A. Mussa-Ivaldi, "Computations Underlying the Execution of Movement: a Novel Biological Perspective", Science, 253: 287-291, 1991.

[2] A. Guo and S. X. Yang, "Neural Network Approaches to Visual Motion Perception", Science in China, Series B. Vol. 37, No. 2, pp. 177-189, 1994.

[3] A. Guo, H. Sun, and S. X. Yang, "A Multilayer Neural Network Model for Perception of Rotational Motion", Science in China, Series C. Vol. 40, No. 1, Feb. 1997, pp. 90-100, 1997.

[4] A. F. Bobick and J. W. Davis, "An Appearancebased Representation of Action", International Conference on Pattern Recognition, 1996.

[5] D. Ormoneit, H. Sidenbladh, M. J. Black, T. Hastie, and D. J. Fleet, "Learning and Tracking Human Motion Using Functional Analysis", Proc. IEEE Workshop on Human Modeling, Analysis and Synthesis, Hilton Head, SC, June 2000.

[6] C. Bregler, "Learning and Recognizing Human Dynamics in Video Sequences", Proc. IEEE Conf. Computer Vision and Pattern Recognition, San Juan, Puerto Rico, June 1997.

[7] T. Kohonen, "Self-Organizing Maps". Series in Information Sciences, Vol. 30, Springer, Heidelberg. Second ed. 1997.

[8] J. Vesanto and E. Alhoniemi, "Clustering of the Self-Organizing Map", IEEE Transactions on Neural Networks, Vol. 11, No. 3, May 2000.

[9] J. Laaksonen, M. Koskela, S. Laakso, and E. Oja, "Self-Organizing Maps as a Relevance Feedback Technique in Content-Based Image Retrieval". Pattern Analysis and Applications, 4(2+3): 140-152, June 2001.

[10] S. Brandt, J. Laaksonen, and E. Oja, "Statistical Shape Features in Content-Based Image Retrieval", In Proceedings of 15th International Conference on Pattern Recognition (ICPR 2000). Barcelona, Spain. September 2000.

Noun Sense Disambiguation with WordNet for Software Design Retrieval

Paulo Gomes, Francisco C. Pereira, Paulo Paiva, Nuno Seco, Paulo Carreiro, José Luís Ferreira, and Carlos Bento

CISUC - Centro de Informática e Sistemas da Universidade de Coimbra
Departamento de Engenharia Informática, Polo II, Universidade de Coimbra
3030 Coimbra
pgomes@dei.uc.pt
http://rebuilder.dei.uc.pt

Abstract. Natural language understanding can be used to improve the usability of intelligent Computer Aided Software Engineering (CASE) tools. For a software designer it can be helpful in two ways: a broad range of natural language terms in the naming of software objects, attributes and methods can be used; and the system is able to understand the meaning of these terms so that it could use them in reasoning mechanisms like information retrieval. But, the problem of word sense disambiguation is an obstacle to the development of computational systems that can fully understand natural language. In order to deal with this problem, this paper presents a word sense disambiguation method and how it is integrated with a CASE tool.

1 Motivation and Goals

Software design is one phase in software development [1], in which development teams use Computer Aided Software Engineering (CASE) tools to build design models of software systems. Most of these tools work as editors of design specification languages, revealing a lack of intelligent support to the designer's work. There are several ways to improve these tools, one possible way is to integrate reasoning mechanisms that can aid the software designer, like retrieval of relevant information, or generation of new software designs. But to accomplish a fruitful integration of these mechanisms in a CASE tool, they must be intuitive and easy to use by the software designers.

One way to provide a good communication environment between designer and tool is to integrate natural language understanding. The use of natural language queries for retrieval mechanisms, or the automatic classification of design elements using word sense disambiguation, are just two possible ways of achieving a good system-user communication interface. Nevertheless, natural language has some characteristics that are hard to mimic from the computational point of view. One of these aspects is the ambiguity of words. The same word can have different meanings, depending on the context in which it is used. This poses a big problem for a computational system that has to use natural language to

Y. Xiang and B. Chaib-draa (Eds.): AI 2003, LNAI 2671, pp. 537–543, 2003.

interact with humans. In the research field of natural language this problem has been named Word Sense Disambiguation (WSD), see [2]. In order for a system to use natural language it must deal with this important problem.

We are developing a CASE tool (REBUILDER) capable of helping a software designer in her/his work in a more intelligent way. This tool is capable of retrieving designs from a knowledge base, or generating new designs, thus providing the designer with alternative solutions. From the designer's point of view, REBUILDER is an Unified Modelling Language (UML [5]) editor with some special functionalities. The basic modelling units in UML (and in REBUILDER) are software objects. These objects must be classified so that they can be retrieved by REBUILDER. In order to do this classification, we use WordNet [4] as an index structure, and also as a general ontology. REBUILDER automates object classification, using the object's name to determine which classification the object must have. To do this, we have to tackle the WSD problem with just the object's name and the surrounding context, which in our case comprises object's attributes (in case of a class) and other objects in the same design model. This paper presents a WSD method for the domain of software design using UML models.

In the remaining of this paper we will start by describing the WordNet ontology. Section 3 presents our approach starting by an overview of REBUILDER, and then going into the definition of the WSD method used. We also describe how classification and retrieval are done in our system. Section 4 presents two experimental studies: one on the influence of the context in the accuracy of the WSD method, and the other on the influence of the semantic distance metric in the accuracy of the WSD method. Finally section 5 presents some of the advantages and limitations of our system.

2 WordNet

WordNet is a lexical resource that uses a differential theory where concept meanings are represented by symbols that enable a theorist to distinguish among them. Symbols are words, and concept meanings are called synsets. A synset is a concept represented by one or more words. If more than one word can be used to represent a synset, then they are called synonyms. There is also another word phenomenon important in WordNet: the same word can have more than one different meaning (polysemy). For instance, the word mouse has two meanings, it can denote a small rat, or it can express a computer mouse. WordNet is built around the concept of synset. Basically it comprises a list of word synsets, and different semantic relations between synsets. The first part is a list of words, each one with a list of synsets that the word represents. The second part, is a set of semantic relations between synsets, like *is-a* relations (rat *is-a* mouse), *part-of* relations (door *part-of* house), and other relations. Synsets are classified in four categories: nouns, verbs, adjectives, and adverbs. In REBUILDER we use the word synset list and four semantic relations: *is-a*, *part-of*, *substance-of*, and *member-of*.

3 REBUILDER

The main goals of REBUILDER are: to create a corporation's memory of design knowledge; to provide tools for reusing design knowledge; and to provide the software designer with a design environment capable of promoting software design reuse. It comprises four different modules: Knowledge Base (KB), UML Editor, KB Manager and Case-Based Reasoning (CBR [3]) Engine. It runs in a client-server environment, where the KB is on the server side and the CBR Engine, UML Editor and KB Manager are on the client side. There are two types of clients: the design user client, which comprises the CBR Engine and the UML Editor; and the KB administrator client, which comprises the CBR Engine and the KB Manager. Only one KB administrator client can be running, but there can be several design user clients.

The UML editor is the front-end of REBUILDER and the environment dedicated to the software designer. The KB Manager module is used by the administrator to manage the KB, keeping it consistent and updated. The KB comprises four different parts: the case library which stores the cases of previous software designs; an index memory that is used for efficient case retrieval; the data type taxonomy, which is an ontology of the data types used by the system; and WordNet, which is a general purpose ontology.

The CBR Engine is the reasoning part of REBUILDER. This module comprises six different parts: Retrieval, Design Composition, Design Patterns, Analogy, Verification, and Learning. The Retrieval sub-module retrieves cases from the case library based on the similarity with the target problem. The Design Composition sub-module modifies old cases to create new solutions. It can take pieces of one or more cases to build a new solution by composition of these pieces. The Design Patterns sub-module, uses software design patterns and CBR for generation of new designs. Analogy establishes a mapping between problem and selected cases, which is then used to build a new design by knowledge transfer between the selected case and the target problem. Case Verification checks the coherence and consistency of the cases created or modified by the system. The last reasoning sub-module is the retain phase, where the system learns new cases.

3.1 Object Classification

In REBUILDER cases are represented as UML class diagrams, which represent the software design structure. Class diagrams can comprise three types of objects (packages, classes, and interfaces) and four kinds of relations between them (associations, generalizations, realizations and dependencies). Class diagrams are very intuitive, and are a visual way of communication between software development members. Each object has a specific meaning corresponding to a specific synset, which we call context synset. This synset is then used for object classification, indexing the object in the corresponding WordNet synset. This association between software object-synset, enables the retrieval algorithm and the similarity metric to use the WordNet relational structure for retrieval efficiency and for similarity estimation, as it is shown in section 3.4.

3.2 Word Sense Disambiguation in REBUILDER

The object's class diagram is the context in which the object is referenced, so we use it to determine the meaning of the object. To obtain the correct synset for an object, REBUILDER uses the object's name, the other objects in the same class diagram, and the object's attributes in case it is a class. The disambiguation starts by extracting from WordNet the synsets corresponding to the object's name. This requires the system to parse the object's name, which most of the times is a composition of words. REBUILDER uses specific heuristics to choose the word to use. For instance, only words corresponding to nouns are selected, because commonly objects correspond to entities or things. A morphological analysis must also be done, extracting the regular noun from the word. After this, a word or a composition of words has been identified and will be searched in WordNet. The result from this search is a set of synsets. From this set of synsets, REBUILDER uses the disambiguation algorithm to select one synset, the supposed right one.

Suppose that the object to be disambiguated has the name *ObjName* (after the parsing phase), and the lookup in WordNet has yielded n synsets: s_1, ..., s_n. This object has the context *ObjContext*, which comprises several names: $Name_1, \ldots, Name_m$, which can be object names, and/or attribute names. Each of these context names has a list of corresponding synsets, for instance, $Name_j$ has p synsets: ns_{j1}, ..., ns_{jp}. The chosen synset for *ObjName* is given by:

$$ContextSynset(ObjName) = Min\{SynsetScore(s_i, ObjContext)\} \quad (1)$$

Where i is the ith synset of *ObjName* (i goes from 1 to n). The chosen synset is the one with the lower value of *SynsetScore*, which is given by:

$$SynsetScore(s, ObjContext) = \sum_{j=1}^{m} ShortestDist(s, Name_j) \quad (2)$$

Where m is the number of names in *ObjContext*. The *SynsetScore* is the sum of the shortest distance between synset s and the synsets of $Name_j$, which is defined as:

$$ShortestDist(s, Name_j) = Min\{SemanticDist(s, ns_{jk})\} \quad (3)$$

Where k is the kth synset of $Name_j$ (k goes from 1 to p). The shortest path is computed based on the semantic distance between synset s and ns_{jk}. Three semantic distances have been developed, the next section describes them.

The *ObjContext* mentioned before comprises a set of names. These names can be: object names and/or attribute names, depending on the type of object that is being disambiguated. For instance, a class can have as context a combination of three aspects: it's attributes, the objects in the class diagram which are adjacent to it, or all the objects in the diagram. Packages and interfaces do not have attributes, so only the last two aspects can be used. This yields the following combinations of disambiguation contexts:

- attributes (just for classes);
- neighbor objects;
- attributes and neighbor objects (just for classes);
- all the objects in the class diagram;
- attributes and all the objects in the class diagram (just for classes).

The experiments section presents a study of the influence of each of these context combinations on the disambiguation accuracy.

3.3 Semantic Distance

As said before three semantic distances were developed. The first semantic distance used is given by:

$$S_1(s_1, s_2) = 1 - \frac{1}{\ln\left(Min\{\forall Path(s_1, s_2)\} + 1\right) + 1} \quad (4)$$

Where Min is the function returning the smallest element of a list. $Path(s_1, s_2)$ is the WordNet path between synset s_1 and s_2, which returns the number of *is-a* relations between the synsets. ln is the natural logarithm.

The second semantic distance is similar to the one above, with the difference that the path can comprise other types of WordNet relations, and not just *is-a* relations. In REBUILDER we also use *part-of*, *member-of*, and *substance-of* relations. We name this distance as S_2.

The third semantic distance is more complex and tries to use other aspects additional to the distance between synsets. This metric is based on three factors. One is the distance between s_1 and s_2 in the WordNet ontology (D_1), using all the types of relations. Another one uses the Most Specific Common Abstraction ($MSCA$) between A and B synsets. The $MSCA$ is basically the most specific synset, which is an abstraction of both synsets. Considering the distance between s_1 and $MSCA$ ($D(s_1, MSCA)$), and the distance between s_2 and $MSCA$ ($D(s_2, MSCA)$), then the second factor is the relation between these two distances (D_2). This factor tries to account the level of abstraction in concepts. The last factor is the relative depth of $MSCA$ in the WordNet ontology (D_3), which tries to reflect the objects' level of abstraction. Formally we have: similarity metric between s_1 and s_2:

$$\begin{aligned} S_3(s_1, s_2) &= +\infty \Leftarrow does\_not\_exist\_MSCA \\ S_3(s_1, s_2) &= 1 - \omega_1 \cdot D_1 + \omega_2 \cdot D_2 + \omega_3 \cdot D_3 \Leftarrow exists\_MSCA \end{aligned} \quad (5)$$

Where w_1, w_2 and w_3 are weights associated with each factor. Weights are selected based on empirical work and are: 0.55, 0.3, and 0.15.

$$D_1 = 1 - \frac{D(s_1\ MSCA) + D(s_2, MSCA)}{2 \cdot DepthMax} \quad (6)$$

Where $DepthMax$ is the maximum depth of the *is-a* tree of WordNet. Current value is 17 for WordNet version 1.7.1.

$$\begin{aligned} D_2 &= 1 \Leftarrow s_1 = s_2 \\ D_2 &= 1 - \frac{|D(s_1, MSCA) - D(s_2, MSCA)|}{\sqrt{D(s_1, MSCA)^2 + D(s_2, MSCA)^2}} \Leftarrow s_1 \neq s_2 \end{aligned} \quad (7)$$

$$D_3 = \frac{Depth(MSCA)}{DepthMax} \tag{8}$$

Where $Depth(MSCA)$ is the depth of $MSCA$ in the *is-a* tree of WordNet.

3.4 Object Retrieval and Similarity

A case has a main package named root package (since a package can contain sub packages). REBUILDER can retrieve cases or pieces of cases, depending on the user query. In the first situation the retrieval module returns packages only, while in the second one, it can retrieve classes or interfaces. The retrieval module treats both situations the same way, since it goes to the case library searching for software objects that satisfy the query. The retrieval algorithm has two distinct phases: first it uses the context synsets of the query objects to get N objects from the case library. Where N is the number of objects to be retrieved. This search is done using the WordNet semantic relations that work like a conceptual graph, and with the case indexes that relate the case objects with WordNet synsets. The second phase ranks the set of retrieved objects using object similarity metrics.

In the first phase the algorithm uses the context synset of the query object as entry points in WordNet graph. Then it gets the objects that are indexed by this synset using the case indexes. Only objects of the same type as the query are retrieved. If the objects found do not reach N, then the search is expanded to the neighbor synsets using only the *is-a* relations. Then, the algorithm gets the new set of objects indexed by these synsets. If there are not yet enough objects, the system keeps expanding until it reaches the desired number of objects, or until there are nothing more to expand. The result of the previous phase is a set of N objects.

4 Experimental Results

The KB we use for tests comprises a case library with 60 cases. Each case comprises a package, with 5 to 20 objects (the total number of objects in the knowledge base is 586). Each object has up to 20 attributes, and up to 20 methods. The goal is to disambiguate each case object in the KB. After running the WSD method for each object we have collected the selected synsets, which are then compared with the synsets attributed by a human designer. The percentage of matching synsets determines the method accuracy. To study the influence of the context definition in the disambiguation accuracy, we considered five different combinations: C1 - only object attributes, C2 - only the neighbor objects, C3 - object attributes and neighbor objects, C4 - all objects, C5 - object attributes and all objects.

The accuracy results we obtained are: C1 - 60.19%, C2 - 68.47%, C3 - 68.79%, C4 - 71.18%, and C5 - 71.02% . These results show that the best result is reached by configuration C4, and that configuration C5 presents slightly worst results than C4. This is due to the abstract aspect of some of the attributes, which introduce ambiguity in the disambiguation method. For instance, if one of the attributes is *name*, it will not help in the disambiguation task, since this attribute is used in many objects and is a very ambiguous one.

REBUILDER uses three different semantic distances, as described in section 3.2. These distances are: using only the *is-a* links of WordNet (S_1), using the *is-a*, *part-of*, *member-of* and *substance-of links* (S_2), and S_3 described in section 3.2. The previous results are obtained with S_2. A combination of these three distances and the best context configurations (C4 and C5) were used to study the influence of the semantic distance in the accuracy of the WSD method. Results are: *S1*+C4 - 69.27%, *S2*+C4 - 71.18%, *S3*+C4 - 64.97%, *S1*+C5 - 69.11%, *S2*+C5 - 71.02%, *S3*+C5 - 65.13%. Experimental results show that semantic distance S_2 obtains the best accuracy values, followed by S_1, and finally S_3.

5 Conclusions

This paper presents an approach to the WSD problem applied to classification and retrieval of software designs. Some of the potential benefits of WSD in CASE tools are: providing software object classification, which enables a semantic retrieval and similarity judgment; and improving the system usability. Other advantage is to open the range of terms that can be used by the software designers in the objects names, attributes and methods, in opposition to a CASE tool that constraints the terms to be used. One of the limitations of our method is the lack of more specific semantic relations in WordNet. We think that with more semantic relations between synsets, it would improve the accuracy of our WSD method.

Acknowledgments

This work was supported by POSI - Programa Operacional Sociedade de Informação of Fundação Portuguesa para a Ciência e Tecnologia and European Union FEDER, under contract POSI/33399/SRI/2000, and by program PRAXIS XXI.

References

[1] Barry Boehm, *A spiral model of software development and enhancement*, IEEE Press, 1988.

[2] Nancy Ide and Jean Veronis, *Introduction to the special issue on word sense disambiguation: The state of the art*, Computational Linguistics **24** (1998), no. 1, 1–40.

[3] Janet Kolodner, *Case-based reasoning*, Morgan Kaufman, 1993.

[4] George Miller, Richard Beckwith, Christiane Fellbaum, Derek Gross, and Katherine J. Miller, *Introduction to wordnet: an on-line lexical database.*, International Journal of Lexicography **3** (1990), no. 4, 235 – 244.

[5] J. Rumbaugh, I. Jacobson, and G. Booch, *The unified modeling language reference manual*, Addison-Wesley, Reading, MA, 1998.

Not as Easy as It Seems: Automating the Construction of Lexical Chains Using *Roget's Thesaurus*

Mario Jarmasz and Stan Szpakowicz

School of Information Technology and Engineering
University of Ottawa
Ottawa, Canada, K1N 6N5
{mjarmasz,szpak}@site.uottawa.ca

Abstract. Morris and Hirst [10] present a method of linking significant words that are about the same topic. The resulting *lexical chains* are a means of identifying cohesive regions in a text, with applications in many natural language processing tasks, including text summarization. The first lexical chains were constructed manually using *Roget's International Thesaurus*. Morris and Hirst wrote that automation would be straightforward given an electronic thesaurus. All applications so far have used *WordNet* to produce lexical chains, perhaps because adequate electronic versions of *Roget's* were not available until recently. We discuss the building of lexical chains using an electronic version of *Roget's Thesaurus*. We implement a variant of the original algorithm, and explain the necessary design decisions. We include a comparison with other implementations.

1 Introduction

Lexical chains [10] are sequences of words in a text that represent the same topic. The concept has been inspired by the notion of cohesion in discourse [7]. A sufficiently rich and subtle lexical resource is required to decide on semantic proximity of words.

Computational linguists have used lexical chains in a variety of tasks, from text segmentation [10, 11], to summarization [1, 2, 12], detection of malapropisms [7], the building of hypertext links within and between texts [5], analysis of the structure of texts to compute their similarity [3], and even a form of word sense disambiguation [1, 11]. Most of the systems have used *WordNet* [4] to build lexical chains, perhaps in part because it is readily available. An adequate machine-tractable version of *Roget's Thesaurus* has not been ready for use until recently [8]. The lexical chain construction process is computationally expensive but the price seems worth paying if we then can incorporate lexical semantics in natural language systems.

We build lexical chains using a computerized version of the 1987 edition of Penguin's *Roget's Thesaurus of English Words and Phrases* [8, 9]. The original lexical chain algorithm [10] exploits certain organizational properties of *Roget's*. *WordNet*-based implementations cannot take advantage of *Roget's* relations. They

Y. Xiang and B. Chaib-draa (Eds.): AI 2003, LNAI 2671, pp. 544-549, 2003.

also usually only link nouns, as relations between parts-of-speech are limited in *WordNet*. Morris and Hirst wrote: "Given a copy [of a machine readable thesaurus], implementation [of lexical chains] would clearly be straightforward". We have set out to test this statement in practice. We present a step-by-step example and compare existing methods of evaluating lexical chains.

2 Lexical Chain Building Algorithms

Algorithms that build lexical chains consider one by one the words for inclusion in the chains constructed so far. Important parameters to consider are the lexical resource used, which determines the lexicon and the possible thesaural relations, the thesaural relations themselves, the transitivity of word relations and the distance — measured in sentences — allowed between words in a chain [10].

Barzilay and Elhadad [2] present the following three steps:

1. Select a set of candidate words;
2. For each candidate word, find an appropriate chain relying on a relatedness criterion among members of the chain;
3. If it is found, insert the word in the chain and update it accordingly.

Step1: Select a set of candidate words. Repeated occurrences of closed-class words and high frequency words are not considered [10]. We remove words that should not appear in lexical chains, using a 980-element stop list, union of five publicly-available lists: Oracle 8 ConText, SMART, Hyperwave, and lists from the University of Kansas and Ohio State University. After eliminating these high frequency words it would be beneficial to identify nominal compounds and proper nouns but our current system does yet not do so. *Roget's* allows us to build lexical chains using nouns, adjectives, verb, adverbs and interjections; we have therefore not found it necessary to identify the part-of-speech. Nominal compounds can be crucial in building correct lexical chains, as argued by [1]; considering the words *crystal* and *ball* independently is not at all the same thing as considering the phrase *crystal ball. Roget's* has a very large number of phrases, but we do not take advantage of this, as we do not have a way of tagging phrases in a text. There are few proper nouns in the *Thesaurus*, so their participation in chains is limited.

Step 2: For each candidate word, find an appropriate chain. Morris and Hirst identify five types of thesaural relations that suggest the inclusion of a candidate word in a chain [10]. We have decided to adopt only the first one, as it is the most frequent relation, can be computed rapidly and consists of a large set of closely related words. We also have simple term repetition. The two relations we use, in terms of the 1987 *Roget's* structure [8], are:

1. Repetition of the same word, for example: *Rome*, *Rome*.
2. Inclusion in the same *Head*. *Roget's Thesaurus* is organized in 990 Heads that represent concepts [8], for example: **343** *Ocean*, **747** *Restraint* and **986** *Clergy*. Two words that belong in the same head are about the same concept, for example: *bank* and *slope* in the Head **209** *Height*.

A Head is divided into paragraphs grouped by part-of-speech: nouns, adjectives, verbs and adverbs. A paragraph is divided into semicolon groups of closely related words, similar to a *WordNet* synset, for example *{mother, grandmother 169 maternity}* [8]. There are four levels of semantic similarity within a Head: two words or phrases located in the same semicolon group, paragraph, part-of-speech and Head.

Morphological processing must be automated to assess the relation between words. This is done both by *WordNet* and the electronic version of *Roget's*. Relations between words of different parts-of-speech seem to create very non-intuitive chains, for example: *{constant, train, train, rigid, train, takes, line, takes, train, train}*. The adjective *constant* is related to *train* under the Head **71** *Continuity: uninterrupted sequence* and *rigid* to *train* under the Head **83** *Conformity*, but these words do not seem to make sense in the context of this chain. This relation may be too broad when applied to all parts-of-speech. We have therefore decided to restrict it to nouns. *Roget's* contains around 100 000 words [8], but very few of them are technical. Any word or phrase that is not in the *Thesaurus* cannot be linked to any other except via simple repetition.

Step 3: Insert the word in the chain. Inclusion requires a relation between the candidate word and the lexical chain. This is the essential step, most open to interpretation. An example of a chain is *{cow, sheep, wool, scarf, boots, hat, snow}* [10]. Should all of the words in the chain be close to one another? This would mean that *cow* and *snow* should not appear in the same chain. Should only specific senses of a word be included in a chain? Should a chain be built on an entire text, or only segments of it? Barzilay [1] performs word sense disambiguation as well as segmentation before building lexical chains. In theory, chains should disambiguate individual senses of words and segment the text in which they are found; in practice this is difficult to achieve. What should be the distance between two words in a chain? These issues are discussed by [10] but not definitively answered by any implementation. These are serious considerations, as it is easy to generate spurious chains. We have decided that all words in a chain should be related via a thesaural relation. This allows building cohesive chains. The text is not segmented and we stop building a chain if no words have been added after seeing five sentences.

Step 4: Merge lexical chains and keep the strongest ones. This step is not explicitly mentioned by Barzilay [1] but all implementations perform it at some point. The merging algorithm depends on the intermediary chains built by a system. Section 4 discusses the evaluation of the strength of a chain.

3 Step-by-Step Example of Lexical Chain Construction

Ellman [3] has analyzed the following quotation, attributed to Einstein, for the purpose of building lexical chains. The words in bold are the candidate words retained by our system after applying the stop list.

We ***suppose*** *a very long* ***train travelling*** *along the* ***rails*** *with a* ***constant velocity*** *v and in the* ***direction*** *indicated in* ***Figure*** *1.* ***People travelling*** *in this* ***train*** *will with* ***advantage*** *use the* ***train*** *as a* ***rigid reference-body****; they* ***regard*** *all* ***events*** *in* ***reference*** *to the **train**. Then every **event** which **takes** place along the **line** also **takes** place at a particular point of the **train**. Also, the **definition** of **simultaneity** can be given **relative** to the **train** in exactly the same way as with **respect** to the **embankment**.*

All possible lexical chains (consisting of at least two words) are built for each candidate word, proceeding forward through the text. Some words have multiple chains, for example *{direction, travelling, train, train, train, line, train, train}*, *{direction, advantage, line}* and *{direction, embankment}*. The strongest chains are selected for each candidate word. A candidate generates its own set of chains, for example *{events, train, line, train, train}* and *{takes, takes, train, train}*. These two chains can be merged if we allow one degree of transitivity: *events* is related to *takes* since both are related to *train*. Once we have eliminated and merged chains, we get:

1. {train, travelling, rails, velocity, direction, travelling, train, train, events, train, takes, line, takes, train, train, embankment}
2. {advantage, events, event}
3. {regard, reference, line, relative, respect}

As a reference, the chains can be compared to the eight obtained by Ellman [4]: 1. {train, rails, train, line, train, train, embankment}, 2. {direction, people, direction}, 3. {reference, regard, relative-to, respect}, 4. {travelling, velocity, travelling, rigid}, 5. {suppose, reference-to, place, place}, 6. {advantage, events, event}, 7. {long, constant}, 8. {figure, body}. There also are nine chains obtained by St-Onge [4]: 1. {train, velocity, direction, train, train, train, advantage, reference, reference-to, train, train, respect-to, simultaneity}, 2. {travelling, travelling}, 3. {rails, line}, 4. {constant, given}, 5. {figure, people, body}, 6. {regard, particular, point}, 7. {events, event, place, place}, 8. {definition}, 9. {embankment}. We do not generate as many chains as Ellman or St-Onge, but we feel that our chains adequately represent the paragraph. Now we need an objective way of evaluating lexical chains.

4 Evaluating Lexical Chains

Two criteria govern the evaluation of a lexical chain: its strength and its quality. Morris and Hirst [10] identified three factors for evaluating strength: reiteration, density and length. The more repetitious, denser and longer the chain, the stronger it is. This notion has been generally accepted, with the addition of taking into account the type of relations used in the chain when scoring its strength [2, 3, 8, 12].

There should be an objective evaluation of the quality of lexical chains, but none has been developed so far. Existing techniques include assessing whether a chain is intuitively correct [4, 10]. Another technique involves measuring the success of lexical chains in performing a specific task, for example the detection of malapropisms [8], text summarization [2, 3, 12], or word sense disambiguation [1, 11]. Detection of malapropisms can be measured using precision and recall, but a large annotated corpus is not available. The success at correctly disambiguating word senses can also be measured, but requires a way of judging if this has been done correctly. [1] relied on a corpus tagged with *WordNet* senses, [11] used human judgment. There are no definite ways of evaluating text summarization.

5 Discussion and Future Work

We have shown that it is possible to create lexical chains using an electronic version of *Roget's Thesaurus*, but that it is not as straightforward as it originally seemed. *Roget's* has a much richer structure for lexical chain construction than exploited by [10]. Their thesaural relations are too broad to build well-focused chains or too computationally expensive to be of interest. *WordNet* implementations have different sets of relations and scoring techniques to build and select chains. Although there is a consensus on the high-level algorithm, there are significant differences in implementations. The major criticism of lexical chains is that there is no adequate evaluation of their quality. Until it is established, it will be hard to compare implementations of lexical chain construction algorithms. We plan to build a harness for testing the various parameters of lexical chain construction listed in this paper. We expect to propose a new evaluation procedure. For the time being, we intend to evaluate lexical chains as an intermediate step for text summarization.

Acknowledgments

We thank Terry Copeck for having prepared the stop list used in building the lexical chains. This research would not have been possible without the help of Pearson Education, the owners of the 1987 Penguin's *Roget's Thesaurus of English Words and Phrases*. Partial funding for this work comes from NSERC.

References

[1] Barzilay, R.: *Lexical Chains for Summarization*. Master's thesis, Ben-Gurion University (1997)

[2] Barzilay, R., Elhadad, M.: Using lexical chains for text summarization. In: *ACL/EACL-97 summarization workshop* (1987) 10–18

[3] Ellman, J.: *Using Roget's Thesaurus to Determine the Similarity of Texts*. Ph.D. Thesis, School of Computing, Engineering and Technology, University of Sunderland, England (2000)

[4] Fellbaum, C. (ed.) (1998a). *WordNet: An Electronic Lexical Database*. Cambridge: MIT Press

[5] Green, S.: Lexical Semantics and Automatic Hypertext Construction. In: *ACM Computing Surveys 31(4)*, December (1999)

[6] Halliday, M.A.K., Hasan, R.: *Cohesion in English*. Longman, London (1976)

[7] Hirst, G., St-Onge, D.: Lexical chains as representation of context for the detection and correction of malapropisms. In: Christiane Fellbaum, (ed.), *WordNet: An electronic lexical database*, Cambridge, MA: The MIT Press, (1998) 305–332

[8] Jarmasz, M., Szpakowicz, S.: The Design and Implementation of an Electronic Lexical Knowledge Base. *Proceedings of the 14th Biennial Conference of the Canadian Society for Computational Studies of Intelligence (AI 2001)*, Ottawa, Canada, June, (2001) 325–334

[9] Kirkpatrick, B.: *Roget's Thesaurus of English Words and Phrases*. Harmondsworth, Middlesex, England: Penguin, (1998)

[10] Morris, J., Hirst, G.: Lexical cohesion computed by thesaural relations as an indicator of the structure of text. *Computational Linguistics*, 17(1), (1991) 21–45

[11] Okumura, M., Honda, T.: Word sense disambiguation and text segmentation based on lexical cohesion. In *Proceedings of the Fifteen Conference on Computational Linguistics (COLING-94)*, volume 2, (1994) 755–761

[12] Silber, H., McCoy, K.: Efficient text summarization using lexical chains. Intelligent User Interfaces, (2000) 252–255

The Importance of Fine-Grained Cue Phrases in Scientific Citations

Robert E. Mercer[1] and Chrysanne Di Marco[2]

[1] University of Western Ontario, London, Ontario, N6A 5B7
mercer@csd.uwo.ca
[2] University of Waterloo, Waterloo, Ontario, N2L 3G1
cdimarco@uwaterloo.ca

Abstract. Scientific citations play a crucial role in maintaining the network of relationships among mutually relevant articles within a research field. Customarily, authors include citations in their papers to indicate works that are foundational in their field, background for their own work, or representative of complementary or contradictory research. But, determining the nature of the exact relationship between a citing and cited paper is often difficult to ascertain. To address this problem, the aim of formal citation analysis has been to categorize and, ultimately, automatically classify scientific citations. In previous work, Garzone and Mercer (2000) presented a system for citation classification that relied on characteristic syntactic structure to determine citation category. In this present work, we extend this idea to propose that fine-grained cue phrases within citation sentences may provide a stylistic basis for just such a categorization.

1 The Citation Problem: Automating Classification

1.1 The Purpose of Citations

Scientific citations play a crucial role in maintaining the network of relationships among articles within a research field by linking together works whose methods and results are in some way mutally relevant. Customarily, authors include citations in their papers to indicate works that are foundational in their field, background for their own work, or representative of complementary or contradictory research. A researcher may then use the presence of citations to locate articles she needs to know about when entering a new field or to read in order to keep track of progress in a field where she is already well-established. But, determining the nature of the exact relationship between a citing and cited paper, whether a particular article is relevant and, if so, in what way, is often difficult to ascertain. To address this problem, the aim of citation analysis studies has been to categorize and, ultimately, automatically classify scientific citations. An automated citation classifier could be used, for example, in scientific indexing systems to provide additional information to help users navigating a digital library of scientific articles.

Y. Xiang and B. Chaib-draa (Eds.): AI 2003, LNAI 2671, pp. 550–556, 2003.

1.2 Why Classify Citations? (And Why this Is Difficult)

A *citation* may be formally defined as a portion of a sentence in a citing document which references another document or a set of other documents collectively. For example, in sentence 1 below, there are two citations: the first citation is *Although the 3-D structure... progress*, with the set of references (Eger et al., 1994; Kelly, 1994); the second citation is *it was shown... submasses* with the single reference (Coughlan et al., 1986).

Example 1. Although the 3-D structure analysis by x-ray crystallography is still in progress (Eger et al., 1994; Kelly, 1994), it was shown by electron microscopy that XO consists of three submasses (Coughlan et al., 1986).

A *citation index* is used to enable efficient retrieval of documents from a large collection—a citation index consists of source items and their corresponding lists of bibliographic descriptions of citing works. A citation connecting the source document and a citing document serves one of many functions. For example, one function is that the citing work gives some form of credit to the work reported in the source article. Another function is to criticize previous work. When using a citation index, a user normally has a more precise query in mind than "Find all articles citing a source article". Rather, the user may wish to know whether other experiments have used similar techniques to those used in the source article, or whether other works have reported conflicting experimental results. In order to use a citation index in this more sophisticated manner, the citation index must contain not only the citation-link information, but also must indicate the function of the citation in the citing article.

In all cases, the primary purpose of scientific citation indexing is to provide researchers with a means of tracing the historical evolution of their field and staying current with on-going results. Citations link researchers and related articles together, and allow navigation through a space of mutually relevant documents which define a coherent academic discipline.

However, with the huge amount of scientific literature available, and the growing number of digital libraries, standard citation indexes are no longer adequate for providing precise and accurate information. Too many documents may be retrieved in a citation search to be of any practical use. And, filtering the documents retrieved may require great effort and reliance on subjective judgement for the average researcher. What is needed is a means of better judging the relevancy of related papers to a researcher's specific needs so that only those articles most related to the task at hand will be retrieved. For this reason, the goal of *categorizing* citations evolved out of citation analysis studies. If, for example, a researcher is new to a field, then he may need only the foundational work in the area. Or, if someone is developing a new scientific procedure, he will wish to find prior research dealing with similar types of procedures.

1.3 Background to the Research

As Garzone and Mercer ([2, 3]) demonstrated, the problem of classifying citation contexts can be based on the recognition of certain *cue words* or specific word usages in citing sentences. For example, in sentence 1, the phrase *still in progress* may be taken to indicate that the citation is referring to work of a concurrent nature.

In order to recognize these kinds of cue-word structures, Garzone and Mercer based their classifier system on what they called the *pragmatic parser.* The knowledge used by the parser to determine whether a certain pattern of cue words has been found was represented in a *pragmatic grammar.*

The purpose of the grammar was to represent the characteristic structural patterns that corresponded to the various citation functions (i.e., categories) in their classification scheme. The rules in the grammar were of two types: lexical rules based on cue words which were associated with functional properties and grammar-like rules which allowed more sophisticated patterns to be associated with functional properties.

The success obtained by Garzone and Mercer from using this cue-word–based approach for their classifier suggested that there may be value in looking for a more systematic and general definition of cues based on a document's rhetorical structure. An additional outcome of Garzone's experiment that seems noteworthy to pursue was the recognition of the important role that the preceding and following sentences could play in determining the category of a citation. Clearly, it seems useful to investigate whether incorporating some form of discourse analysis may enhance the current state of automated citation classifiers.

As a basis from which to develop our own approach to the citation problem, both the supporting work (i.e., Garzone and Mercer) and the opposing camp (e.g., Teufel) are useful references from which to start. In direct contrast to Garzone and Mercer, Teufel [9] questions whether fine-grained discourse cues do exist in citation contexts, and states that "many instances of citation context are linguistically unmarked." (p. 93). She goes on to add that while "overt cues" may be recognized if they are present, the problems of detecting these cues by automated means are formidable (p. 125). Teufel thus articulates the dual challenges facing us: to demonstrate that fine-grained discourse cues can play a role in citation analysis, and that such cues may be detected by automated means.

While Teufel does represent a counterposition to Garzone and Mercer, which we take as our starting-point, nevertheless her work lays important foundations for ours in a number of ways. Most importantly, Teufel acknowledges the importance of a recognizable rhetorical structure in scientific articles, the so-called 'IMRaD' structure, for *Introduction, Method, Results,* and *Discussion.* In addition, Teufel builds from this very global discourse structure a very detailed model of scientific argumentation that she proposes using as a basis for analyzing and summarizing the content of an article, including citation content.

At this point, Teufel diverges from us in her development of a method for analyzing the structure of articles based on a detailed discourse model and fine-grained linguistic cues. She does nonetheless give many instances of argumentative moves that may be signalled in citation contexts by specific cues.

Teufel acknowledges her concern with the "potentially high level of subjectivity" (p. 92) inherent in judging the nature of citations, a task made more difficult by the fine granularity of her model of argumentation and the absence, she claims, of reliable means of mapping from citations to the author's reason for including the citation: "[articles] often contain large segments, particularly in the central parts, which describe research in a fairly neutral [i.e., unmarked] way." (p. 93) As a consequence, Teufel reduces her model to a computationally tractable, but very broad-based set of seven categories, and confines the citation categories to only two types: the cited work either provides a basis for the citing work or contrasts with it.

2 The Role of Discourse Structure in Citation Analysis

The role of fine-grained discourse cues in the rhetorical analysis of general text (Knott [6] and Marcu [7]), together with models of scientific argumentation ([1, 4], [8]) may provide a means of constructing a systematic analysis of the role citations play in maintaining a network of rhetorical relationships among scientific documents. As the most basic discourse cue, a *cue phrase* can be thought of as a conjunction or connective that assists in building the coherence and cohesion of a text. Knott constructed a corpus of cue phrases, an enlarged version of which ([7]), is used in our study.

In addition to providing a formal means of defining cue phrases and compiling a large catalogue of phrases (over 350), Knott's other main result is of particular significance to us: he combines the two methods hitherto used in associating cue phrases with rhetorical relations to argue that "cue phrases can be taken as evidence for relations precisely if they are thought of as modelling psychological constructs" (p. 22). For our purposes then, Knott's supporting demonstration for this argument allows us to rely on his result that there is indeed a sound foundation for linking cue phrases with rhetorical relations.

3 The Frequency of Cue Phrases in Citations

The underlying premise of studies on the role of cue phrases in discourse structure (e.g., [5, 6, 7]) is that cue phrases are purposely used by the writer to make text coherent and cohesive. With this in mind, we are analyzing a dataset of scholarly science[1] articles. Our current task is to test our hypothesis that fine-grained discourse cues do exist in citation contexts in sufficient enough numbers to play a significant role in extra-textual cohesion. Our analysis, presented in the next section, confirms that cue phrases do occur in citation contexts with about the same frequency as their occurrence in the complete text.

We are using a dataset of 24 scholarly science articles. All of these articles are written in the IMRaD style. (Four articles have merged the Results and Discussion sections into a single section.) We are using the list of cue phrases from [7] in our analysis. Our belief that this list is adequate for this initial

[1] We are currently working with one scientific genre, biochemistry.

analysis results from the fact that it is an extension of the one from [6], which was derived from academic text.

We analyze the use of cue phrases in three components of the article: (1) five text sections: the *full text body* (which is the four IMRaD sections considered as a unit), and each IMRaD section considered independently, (in four papers the Results and Discussion sections are merged), (2) the *citation sentence* which is any sentence that contains at least one citation, and (3) the *citation window*, corresponding to a citation sentence together with the preceding and following sentences.

Some of of our analysis is given in the following discussion. In addition to the summaries, we provide some details, since it is instructive at this point to see how the papers vary in the various statistics.

Between one-tenth and one-fifth of the sentences in the 24 biochemistry articles that we investigated are citation sentences, with an average of 0.14. That citation sentences comprise between one-tenth and one-fifth of the sentences in a scientific article helps to demonstrate our earlier statement about the importance of making connections to extra-textual information. We contend that writers of scientific text use the same linguistic techniques to maintain cohesion between the textual and extra-textual material as they do to make their paper cohesive. The importance of these techniques, which we mentioned earlier, and the simple fact that their linguistic signals occur as frequently in citation sentences as in the rest of the text, which we discuss below, lends positive weight to our hypothesis, contra Teufel, that fine-grained discourse cues do exist in citation contexts and that they are relatively simple to find automatically.

Citations are well-represented in each of the IMRaD sections, suggesting that a purpose exists for relating each aspect of a scientific article to extra-textual material. Further analysis is required to catalogue these relationships and how they are signalled.

Table 1[2] corroborates our hypothesis that cue phrases do exist in citation contexts. In addition, the frequency of their occurrence suggests that cue phrases do play a significant role in citations: we note that the usage of cue phrases in citation sentences and citation windows is about the same as the usage in the full text body.

Another interesting feature that may be seen in this table is that cue-phrase usage in the Methods section is lower (one insignificant higher value), and sometimes significantly lower, than cue-phrase usage in the full text body. One of our hypotheses is that the rhetoric of science will be part of our understanding of text cohesion in this type of writing. The Methods section is highly stylized, often being a sequence of steps. Further analysis may reveal that this rhetorical style obviates the use of cue phrases in certain situations.

In addition to our global frequency analysis that we have given above, it is important to analyze the frequency of individual cue phrases. In Table 2 we show

[2] The cue phrase *and* is often used as a coordinate conjunction. We removed this word from the list of cue phrases to see if the analysis with and without this cue phrase differed. If anything, the result was stronger.

Table 1. Frequencies of cue phrases in various contexts ("and" not in cue phrase list)

Article	Full Body	Introduction	Methods	Results	Discussion	Citation	Cit Win
r1182	0.093	0.094	0.062	0.095	0.087	0.094	0.079
r1200	0.063	0.059	0.044	0.069		0.061	0.063
r1265	0.069	0.060	0.054	0.069	0.084	0.065	0.068
r1802	0.068	0.049	0.044	0.096	0.098	0.082	0.064
r1950	0.072	0.084	0.055	0.069	0.086	0.080	0.070
r1974	0.080	0.067	0.038	0.078	0.106	0.088	0.076
r1997	0.066	0.080	0.062	0.058	0.073	0.081	0.066
r2079	0.077	0.050	0.067	0.077	0.085	0.088	0.072
r2603	0.071	0.079	0.043	0.065	0.081	0.080	0.065
r263	0.094	0.107	0.057	0.081	0.107	0.091	0.101
r315	0.078	0.080	0.049	0.069	0.108	0.084	0.066
r3343	0.080	0.079	0.061	0.071	0.090	0.075	0.073
r3557	0.072	0.081	0.043	0.076		0.094	0.075
r3712	0.066	0.051	0.062	0.060	0.077	0.061	0.063
r3819	0.089	0.085	0.068	0.084	0.098	0.086	0.082
r432	0.070	0.056	0.049	0.074		0.066	0.076
r4446	0.079	0.062	0.078	0.075		0.065	0.067
r5007	0.076	0.073	0.066	0.070	0.090	0.072	0.080
r513	0.074	0.069	0.061	0.065	0.081	0.069	0.073
r5948	0.098	0.101	0.069	0.087	0.115	0.099	0.099
r5969	0.072	0.070	0.034	0.070	0.081	0.065	0.071
r6200	0.071	0.075	0.042	0.077	0.080	0.063	0.063
r7228	0.076	0.042	0.059	0.071	0.092	0.078	0.075
r7903	0.072	0.063	0.066	0.055	0.086	0.063	0.068

just a few instances from the 60 most frequently occurring cue phrases to point out some interesting patterns.

The cue phrase *previously* is three times more frequent in citation sentences than in the full text body and twice as frequent as in citation windows. This may indicate a strong tendency to indicate temporal coherence. The cue phrase *not* is used 50% more frequently in text/citation windows than in citations. Does this show that citation windows set up negative contexts? Similarly, *however* appears almost 50% more frequently in text/citation windows than in citations. Similar 'opposites' for *although*, *following*, and *in order to* seem to be present in the data.

4 Conclusions and Future Work

Our primary concern was to find evidence that fine-grained discourse cues exist in significant number in citation contexts. Our analysis of 24 scholarly science articles indicates that these cues do exist in citation contexts, and that their frequency is comparable to that in the full text. Secondarily, we are very interested

Table 2. Frequencies of example cue phrases

Citation sentences	Citation windows	Full text body
100 0.0316 previously	110 0.0170 previously	124 0.0102 previously
78 0.0246 not	199 0.0308 not	404 0.0333 not
28 0.0088 although	49 0.0076 although	70 0.0058 although
22 0.0069 however	63 0.0097 however	116 0.0096 however
11 0.0035 following	30 0.0046 following	78 0.0064 following
6 0.0019 in order to	16 0.0025 in order to	36 0.0030 in order to

in whether these cues are automatically detectable. Many of these discourse cues appear as cue phrases that have been previously catalogued in both academic and general texts. The detection of these cue phrases has been shown to be straightforward. What may be of equal importance are discourse cues that are not members of the current list of cue phrases: we envisage an extremely rich set of discourse cues in scientific writing and citation passages.

Of course, the main goal of this study of discourse relations is to use the linguistic cues as a means of determining the function of citations. Based on Knott, Marcu, and others, we can expect to be able to associate cue phrases with rhetorical relations as determiners of citation function. The interesting question then becomes: can we extend textual coherence/rhetorical relations signalled by cue phrases to extra-textual coherence relations linking citing and cited papers?

References

[1] Fahnestock, J.: *Rhetorical figures in science.* Oxford University Press (1999)

[2] Garzone, M.: *Automated classification of citations using linguistic semantic grammars.* M.Sc. Thesis, The University of Western Ontario (1996)

[3] Garzone, M., and Mercer, R. E.: Towards an automated citation classifier. In *AI'2000, Proceedings of the 13th Biennial Conference of the CSCSI/SCEIO*, Lecture Notes in Artificial Intelligence, v. 1822, H. J. Hamilton (ed.), Springer-Verlag, (2000) 337–346

[4] Gross, A. G.: *The rhetoric of science.* Harvard University Press (1996)

[5] Halliday, M. A. K., and Hasan, Ruqaiya.: *Cohesion in English.* Longman Group Limited (1976)

[6] Knott, A.: *A data-driven methodology for motivating a set of coherence relations.* Ph.D. thesis, University of Edinburgh (1996)

[7] Marcu, D.: *The rhetorical parsing, summarization, and generation of natural language texts.* Ph.D. thesis, University of Toronto (1997)

[8] Myers, G.: *Writing biology.* University of Wisconsin Press (1991)

[9] Teufel, S.: *Argumentative zoning: Information extraction from scientific articles.* Ph.D. thesis, University of Edinburgh (1999)

Fuzzy C-Means Clustering of Web Users for Educational Sites

Pawan Lingras, Rui Yan, and Chad West

Department of Mathematics and Computing Science
Saint Mary's University, Halifax, Nova Scotia, Canada, B3H 3C3

Abstract. Characterization of users is an important issue in the design and maintenance of websites. Analysis of the data from the World Wide Web faces certain challenges that are not commonly observed in conventional data analysis. The likelihood of bad or incomplete web usage data is higher than in conventional applications. The clusters and associations in web mining do not necessarily have crisp boundaries. Researchers have studied the possibility of using fuzzy sets for clustering of web resources. This paper presents clustering using a fuzzy c-means algorithm, on secondary data consisting of access logs from the World Wide Web. This type of analysis is called web usage mining, which involves applying data mining techniques to discover usage patterns from web data. The fuzzy c-means clustering was applied to the web visitors to three educational websites. The analysis shows the ability of the fuzzy c-means clustering to distinguish different user characteristics of these sites.

Keywords: Fuzzy C-means, Clustering, Web Usage mining, Unsupervised Learning.

1 Introduction

Clustering analysis is an important function in web usage mining, which groups together users or data items with similar characteristics. Clusters tend to have fuzzy or rough boundaries. Joshi and Krishnapuram [1] argued that the clustering operation in web mining involves modeling an unknown number of overlapping sets. They used fuzzy clustering to cluster web documents. Lingras [4] applied the unsupervised rough set clustering based on GAs for grouping web users of a first year university course. He hypothesized that there are three types of visitors: studious, crammers, and workers. Studious visitors download notes from the site regularly. Crammers download most of the notes before an exam. Workers come to the site to finish assigned work such as lab and class assignments. Generally, the boundaries of these clusters will not be precise. The present study applies the concept of fuzzy c-means [2,3] to the three educational websites analyzed earlier by Lingras *et al.* [6]. The resulting fuzzy clusters also provide a reasonable representation of user behaviours for the three websites.

Y. Xiang and B. Chaib-draa (Eds.): AI 2003, LNAI 2671, pp. 557-562, 2003.

2 Fuzzy C-Means

Cannon *et al.* [2] described an efficient implementation of an unsupervised clustering mechanism that generates the fuzzy membership of objects to various clusters. The objective of the algorithm is to cluster n objects into c clusters. Given a set of unlabeled patterns : $X = \{x_1, x_{2,}, ... x_n\}, x_i \in R^s$, where n is the number of patterns, and s is the dimension of pattern vectors (attributes). Each cluster is representated by the cluster center vector V. The FCM algorithm minimizes the weighted within group sum of the squared error objective function $J(U, V)$:

$$J(U,V) = \sum_{k=1}^{n} \sum_{i=1}^{c} u_{ik}^{m} d_{ik}^{2}. \qquad \sum_{k=1}^{c} u_{ik} = 1. \quad 0 < \sum_{i=1}^{n} u_{ik} < n. \tag{1}$$

where U represents the membership function matrix; u_{ik} is the elements of U ($u_{ik} \in [0,1]$, $i = 1, ... n$, $k = 1, ... c.$); V is the cluster center vector, $V = \{v_1, v_2, ... v_c\}$; n is the number of pattern; c is the number of clusters; d_{ik} represents the distance between x_i and v_k; m is the exponent of u_{ik} that controls fuzziness or amount of cluster overlap. Gao *et al.* [7] suggested the use of $m = 2$ in the experiments. The FCM algorithm is as follows :

Step 1: Given the cluster number c, randomly choose the initial cluster center V^0. Set $m = 2$, s, the index of the calculations, as 0, and the threshold ε, as a small positive constant.

Step 2: Based on V, the membership of each object U^s is calculated as:

$$u_{ik} = 1 \Big/ \sum_{j=1}^{c} \left(\frac{d_{ik}}{d_{jk}}\right)^{\frac{2}{(m-1)}}, \; i = 1, ... n, \; k = 1, ... c. \; d_{ik} = \|x_k - v_i\| > 0, \forall i, k. \tag{2}$$

for $d_{ik} = 0$, $u_{ik} = 1$ and $u_{jk} = 0$ for $j \neq i$.

Step 3: Increment s by one. Calculate the new cluster center vector V^s as :

$$v_i = \sum_{k=1}^{n} (u_{ik})^m x_k \Big/ \sum_{k=1}^{n} (u_{ik})^m, \; \forall i, \; i = 1, ... n. \tag{3}$$

Step 4: Compute the new membership U^s using the equation (2) in step 2.

Step 5: If $\left\| U^s - U^{(s-1)} \right\| < \varepsilon$, then stop, otherwise repeat step 3, 4, and 5.

3 Study Data and Design of the Experiment

The study data was obtained from web access logs of three courses. These courses represent a sequence of required courses for the computing science programme at Saint Mary's University. The first and second courses were for first year students. The third course was for second year students. Lingras [4] and Lingras and West [5] showed that visits from students attending the first course could fall into one of the following three categories:

1. Studious: These visitors download the current set of notes. Since they download a limited/current set of notes, they probably study class-notes on a regular basis.
2. Crammers: These visitors download a large set of notes. This indicates that they have stayed away from the class-notes for a long period of time. They are planning for pretest cramming.
3. Workers: These visitors are mostly working on class or lab assignments or accessing the discussion board.

The fuzzy c-means algorithm was expected to provide the membership of each visitor to the three clusters mentioned above. Data cleaning involved removing hits from various search engines and other robots. Some of the outliers with large number of hits and document downloads were also eliminated. This reduced the first data set by 5%. The second and third data sets were reduced by 3.5% and 10%, respectively. The details about the data can be found in Table 1. Five attributes are used for representing each visitor [4]:

1. On campus/Off campus access. (Binary value)
2. Day time/Night time access: 8 a.m. to 8 p.m. were considered to be the daytime. (Binary value)
3. Access during lab/class days or non-lab/class days: All the labs and classes were held on Tuesdays and Thursdays. The visitors on these days are more likely to be workers. (Binary value)
4. Number of hits. (Normalized in the range [0,10])
5. Number of class-notes downloads. (Normalized in the range [0,20])

4 Results and Discussion

Table 2 shows the fuzzy center vectors for the three data sets. It was possible to classify the three clusters as studious, workers, and crammers, from the results obtained using the fuzzy c-means clustering. The crammers had the highest number of hits and class-notes in every data set. The average numbers of notes downloaded by crammers varied from one set to another. The studious visitors downloaded the second highest number of notes. The distinction between workers and studious visitors for the second course was based on other attributes. It is also interesting to note that the crammers had a higher ratio of document requests to hits. The workers, on the other hand, had the lowest ratio of document requests to hits.

Table 1. Description of the Data Sets

Data Set	Hits	Hits after cleaning	Visits	Visits after cleaning
First	361609	343000	23754	7619
Second	265365	256012	16255	6048
Third	40152	36005	4248	1274

Table 2. Fuzzy Center Vectors

Course	Cluster Name	Campus Access	Day/Night Time	Lab Day	Hits	Document Requests
First	Studious	0.68	0.76	0.44	2.30	2.21
	Crammers	0.64	0.72	0.34	3.76	7.24
	Workers	0.69	0.77	0.51	0.91	0.75
Second	Studious	0.59	0.74	0.15	0.68	0.57
	Crammers	0.63	0.73	0.33	2.34	3.07
	Workers	0.82	0.86	0.71	0.64	0.49
Third	Studious	0.69	0.75	0.50	3.36	2.42
	Crammers	0.59	0.72	0.43	5.14	9.36
	Workers	0.62	0.77	0.52	1.28	1.06

Table 3. Visitors with Fuzzy Memberships Greater than 0.6

Course	Cluster Name	Number of Visitors with Memberships > 0.6
First	Studious	1382
	Crammers	414
	Workers	4354
Second	Studious	1419
	Crammers	317
	Workers	1360
Third	Studious	265
	Crammers	84
	Workers	717

Table 3 shows the cardinalities of sets with fuzzy memberships greater than 0.6. The choice of 0.6 is somewhat arbitrary. However, a membership of 0.6 (or above) for a cluster indicates a stronger tendency towards the cluster. The actual numbers in each cluster vary based on the characteristics of each course. For example, the first term course had significantly more workers than studious visitors, while the second term course had more studious visitors than workers. The increase in the percentage of studious visitors in the second term seems to be a natural progression. Similarly, the third course had significantly more studious visitors than workers. Crammers constituted less than 10% of the visitors.

The characteristics of the first two sites were similar. The third website was somewhat different in terms of the site contents, course size, and types of students.

The results discussed in this section show many similarities between the fuzzy c-means clustering for the three sites. The differences between the results can be easily explained based on further analysis of the websites. It is interesting to see that the fuzzy c-means clustering captured the subtle differences between the websites in the resulting clustering schemes. The clustering process can be individually fine-tuned for each website to obtain even more meaningful clustering schemes.

5 Summary and Conclusions

This paper described an experiment for clustering web users, including data collection, data cleaning, data preparation, and the fuzzy c-means clustering process. Web visitors for three courses were used in the experiments. It was expected that the visitors would be classified as studious, crammers, or workers. Since some of the visitors may not precisely belong to one of the classes, the clusters were represented using fuzzy membership functions. The experiments produced meaningful clustering of web visitors. The study of variables used for clustering made it possible to clearly identify the three clusters as studious, workers, and crammers. There were many similarities and a few differences between the characteristics of clusters for the three websites. These similarities and differences indicate the ability of the fuzzy c-means clustering to incorporate subtle differences between the usages of different websites.

Acknowledgment

The authors would like to thank Natural Sciences and Engineering Research Council of Canada for their financial support.

References

[1] A. Joshi and R. Krishnapuram: Robust Fuzzy Clustering Methods to Support Web Mining. In the Proceedings of the workshop on Data Mining and Knowledge Discovery, SIGMOD '98 (1998) 15/1-15/8.

[2] R. Cannon, J. Dave, and J. Bezdek: Efficient Implementation of the Fuzzy C-Means Clustering Algorithms. IEEE Trans. PAMI, Vol. 8 (1986) 248-255.

[3] T. Cheng, D.B. Goldgof, and L.O. Hall: Fast Clustering with Application to Fuzzy Rule Generation. In the proceedings of 1995 IEEE International Conference on Fuzzy Systems, Vol. 4 (1995) 2289-2295.

[4] P. Lingras: Rough Set Clustering for Web Mining. In the Proceedings of 2002 IEEE International Conference on Fuzzy Systems (2002).

[5] Lingras, and C. West: Interval Set Clustering of Web Users with Rough K-means. Submitted to Journal of Intelligent Information Systems (2002).

[6] P. Lingras, M. Hogo and M. Snorek: Interval Set Clustering of Web Users using Modified Kohonen Self-Organization Maps based on the Properties of Rough Sets. Submitted to Web Intelligence and Agent Systems: an International Journal (2002).
[7] X. Gao, J. Li, and W. Xie: Parameter Optimization in FCM Clustering Algorithms. In the Proceedings of 2000 IEEE 5th International Conference on Signal Processing, Vol. 3 (2000) 1457-1461.

Re-using Web Information for Building Flexible Domain Knowledge

Mohammed Abdel Razek, Claude Frasson, and Marc Kaltenbach

Computer Science Department and Operational Research University of Montreal
C.P. 6128, Succ. Centre-ville Montreal
Québec H3C 3J7 Canada
{abdelram,frasson,kaltenba}@iro.umontreal.ca

Abstract. Building a knowledge base for a given domain usually involves a subject matter expert (tutor) and a knowledge engineer. Our approach is to create mechanisms and tools that allow learners to build knowledge bases through a learning session on-line. The Dominant Meaning Classification System (DMCS) was designed to automatically extract, and classify segments of information (chunks). These chunks could well automate knowledge construction, instead of depending on the analysis of tutors. We use a dominant meaning space method to classify extracted chunks. Our experiment shows that this greatly improves domain knowledge

1 Introduction

Our Confidence Intelligent Tutoring System (CITS) [2] was designed to provide a Cooperative Intelligent Distance Learning Environment to a community of learners and thus improve on-line discussions about specific concepts. In the context of a learning session, the CITS can originate a search task, find updated information from the Web, filter it, and present it to learners in their current activity [3]. We claim that better eliciting, and classifying some chunks of this information can significantly improve domain knowledge. Accordingly, learners need services to elicit and classify knowledge in a simple and successful way.

Re-using Web information to improve domain knowledge constitutes a considerable algorithmic challenge. We need to extract chunks that optimize the Web information, and find adequate ways to classify the extracted chunks in a knowledge base. This paper describes the Dominant Meaning Classification System (DMCS). It enables learners to recognize information easily and extract chunks of it without worrying about technical details. The DMCS analyzes these chunks and classifies them with related concepts. For sound classification, we must specify a concept that is closely related to the chunk context. We use domain knowledge in CITS to indicate the latter. The idea is to represent domain knowledge as a hierarchy of concepts [1]. Each concept consists of some dominant meanings, and each of those is linked with some chunks to define it. The more dominant meanings; the better a concept relates to its chunk context. Using our dominant meaning space method [4], the proposed system analyzes these chunks.

Y. Xiang and B. Chaib-draa (Eds.): AI 2003, LNAI 2671, pp. 563–567, 2003.

This method measures semantic space between chunk and concepts. Accordingly, it can place this chunk under a suitable concept. For example, suppose that two learners browse a document about "Array-Based" concept in a course on Data Structure. Based on the dominant meaning space of the extracted chunk, the proposed classification algorithm has to return one of three concepts: a stack-related concept, a queue-related concept, or a list-related concept.

This paper is organized as follows. Section 2 discusses the role of the DMCS and describes our probabilistic dominant meanings method for classification algorithm. The results of experiments conducted to test our methods are presented in section 3. And section 4 concludes the paper.

2 Dominant Meaning Classification System

The feature of Web-based tutoring system is the ability to provide a learner adapted presentation of the subject matter which be taught [5]. CITS is a Web-based tutoring system for computer supported intelligent distance learning environment. To illustrate all this, let us say that two learners open a learning session using CITS. They are interested in a specific concept, say queue, from their course in data structure. The CBIA (for more details, see [3]) observes their discussions and captures some words. Using these words, along with their dominant meanings, the CBIA constructs a query about the context of the main concept. It searches the Web for related documents. When the CBIA receives the search results, it parses them and posts new recommended results to its user interface.

As shown in Fig.1, the CITS supplies these learners with two types of knowledge. The first type is a tree structure which represents the logical view of built in domain knowledge. In the case of data structure, we have a root node, under which there are different sections, "Structure", "Searching", "Queue", and so on. There might be subsections under each section. And each subsection might have a list of documents. The attributes and contents of these documents are represented as child nodes of subsections. Once the learner clicks on a section or a subsection of the tree, the corresponding document is shown in the middle window of the user interface.

The second type is a search-results list which shows the most highly recommended documents coming from the Web. This system allows learners to retrieve the full contents of these documents merely by clicking. If they are interested in a phrase or some other parts of a document, referred as a "chunk", they mark it for extraction to the DMCS. After they click on "Acquire" button, the DMCS automatically captures the chunk, and sends it to its classification processor.

The DMCS has two main components:

- Chunk extraction.
- Classification of the extracted chunk to a knowledge base of the domain knowledge.

A diagrammatic summary of CBIA and DMCS is shown in Fig.2, and the following section explains the two main components of DMCS.

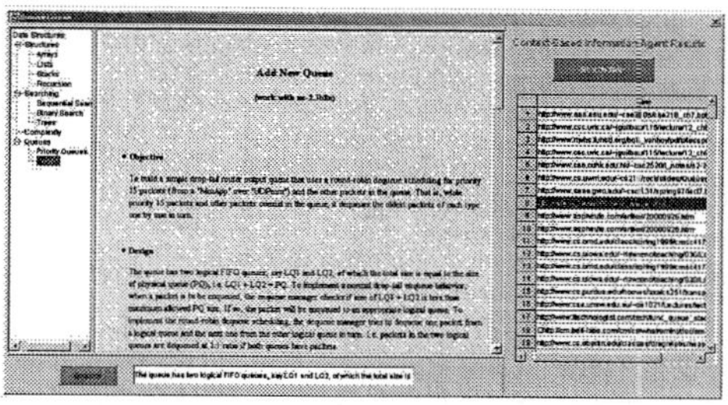

Fig. 1. User interface of CBIA

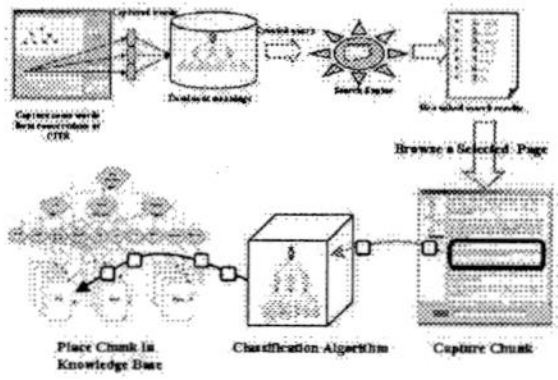

Fig.2. CBIA and DMCS Overview

3 Chunks Extraction and Classification Algorithm

The core of DMCS technology is a dominant meaning space, which provides a metric for measure distance between pairs of words. To guarantee a sound classification, we must specify the main concept of chunks. To extract the main concept of each chunk, three challenges must be met: how to construct the knowledge base in a way that helps the system classify chunks; how to construct dominant meanings for each chunk; and how the system identify intended meaning (concept) of a word needed for classification. The following subsections explain in more details our procedure.

3.1 Chunks Classification

We claim that the more dominant meanings in a chunk, the more closely these would be related to a chunk concept. Suppose that a general concept is C_h, and the extracted chunk is Γ. The set of dominant meanings of the concept C_h constructed by the DMG graph [3] is $\{w_1^h, ..., w_t^h\}$. The problem now is to find a suitable meaning to link Γ with it. Based on the dominant meaning probability [4], we compute the distance space between the chunk Γ and the meaning w_l, as follow:

$$P(\Gamma|w_l^h) = \frac{1}{t}\left[\sum_{j=1}^{j=t} \frac{F(\Gamma|w_j^h)}{F(\Gamma|w_l^h)}\right], \qquad (1)$$

where, the function $F(\Gamma|w_l^h)$ signifies the frequency of word w_l^h appearing in the chunk Γ. It is obvious that the less distance between the chunk Γ and the meaning w_l^h, the more closeness between them. To classify chunks, we follow a classification algorithm:

Classification Algorithm $(\{w_1^h, ..., w_t^h\}, \Gamma)$

- Put $Min = \infty$, and $r = 0$
- For each $w_l^h \in \{w_1^h, ..., w_t^h\}$;
  - Compute $P_l = P(\Gamma|w_l^h)$
  - If $P_l \leq Min$ then $Min = P_l$, and $r = l$
- **Traverse**$[w_r^h]$

Table 1. Collections used for experiment

Collection	Description
Number of learners in each experiment	10
Number of learners in each experiment	Data Structure Course
Tutoring sessions of the second experiment	Constructed Course by DMCS
Time period of the first experiment	4 week
Time period of the second experiment	1 week

The classification algorithm is designed to return a suitable dominant meaning place under C_h to link the chunk Γ with it. In the next section, we discuss our experiment and their.

4 Experiments and Results

In this section we describe our experiment to find out if learners discover a sound knowledge by using DMCS. We conducted two experiments on a group of 10 learners. Table 1 shows the main features of this group, the number of learners and their backgrounds, the type of the sessions, and the duration of experiment.

The first experiment was done with the original Domain knowledge, and the second with extraction knowledge. In the first experiment, learners were invited to discuss five concepts in a course on data structure. If they are interested in some chunks of documents coming from the Web, they marked these for extraction to the DMCS. We provided roughly four week of training. In the second experiment, learners were invited again to discuses the same concepts but without extracting chunks.

At the end, learner was also asked to fill out questionnaires. The goal was to see whether the system provides good tools to extract chunks, whether the extracted in-formation assists in improving domain knowledge, and whether these extracted chunks were classified in suitable places.

On average, learners found that the proposed system provides good tools (7 on a scale of 1-to-10) to easily extract chunks; that it was a good way (slightly over 8 on a scale of 1-to-10) to improve domain knowledge; and that it easily classified extracted chunks (8 on a scale of 1-to-10).

In short, our experiment shows that this method can greatly improve domain knowledge and provide tools by which the learners can easily extract chucks.

5 Conclusions

In this paper, we have presented the development of a Dominant Meaning Classification System (DMCS), a system that helps learners extract chunks (from a data-structure course) collected from the Web and automatically classify them into suitable knowledge-base classes. It is based on a new approach, called a dominant-meaning space, creates a new way of representing the knowledge base of domain knowledge, and classifies chunks. The experiments carried out on the two test collections showed that using our approach yields substantial improvements in retrieval effectiveness.

References

[1] De Bra,P.: Adaptive Educational Hypermedia on the Web. Communications of the ACM, Vol. 45, No. 5. (May 2002) 60-61

[2] Abdel Razek M., Frasson, C., and Kaltenbach M.: A Confidence Agent: Toward More Effective Intelligent Distance Learning Environments. Proceedings of the international Conferencew on Machine Learning and Applications (ICMLA'02), Las Vegas, USA (2002) 187-193

[3] Abdel Razek M., Frasson, C., Kaltenbach M.: Context-Based Information Agent for Supporting Intelligent Distance Learning Environment. The Twelfth International World Wide Web Conference , WWW03, 20-24 May, Budapest, Hungary, 2003

[4] Abdel Razek M., Frasson, C., Kaltenbach M.: UContext-Based Information Agent for Supporting Educationon the Web. The 2003 International Conference on Computational Science and Its Applications (ICCSA 2003) Springer-Verlag Lecture Notes in Computer Science volume. (2003)

[5] Vassileva, J.: DCG + WWW: Dynamic Courseware Generation on the WWW. Proceedings of AIED'97, Kobe, Japan, IOS Press, 18-22.08 (1997) 498-505

A New Inference Axiom for Probabilistic Conditional Independence

Cory J. Butz, S. K. Michael Wong, and Dan Wu

Department of Computer Science, University of Regina
Regina, SK, S4S 0A2, Canada

Abstract. In this paper, we present a hypergraph-based inference method for conditional independence. Our method allows us to obtain several interesting results on graph combination. In particular, our hypergraph approach allows us to strengthen one result obtained in a conventional graph-based approach. We also introduce a new inference axiom, called *combination*, of which the contraction axiom is a special case.

1 Introduction

In the design and implementation of a probabilistic reasoning system [5, 6], a crucial issue to consider is the *implication problem* [4]. The implication problem is to test whether a given set of independencies logically implies another independency. Given the set of independencies defining a Bayesian network, the *semi-graphoid inference axioms* [2] can derive every independency holding in the Bayesian network without resorting to their numerical definitions. Shachter [3] has pointed out that this logical system is equivalent to a graphical one involving multiple undirected graphs and some simple graphical transformations. More specifically, every independency used to define the Bayesian network is represented by an undirected graph. The axiomatic derivation of a new independency can then be seen as applying operations on the multiple undirected graphs such as combining two undirected graphs.

In this paper, we present a hypergraph-based inference method for conditional independence. Our method allows us to obtain several interesting results on graph combination, i.e., combining two individual hypergraphs into one single hypergraph. We establish a one-to-one correspondence between the separating sets in the combined hypergraph and certain separating sets in one of the individual hypergraphs. In particular, our hypergraph approach allows us to strengthen one result obtained by Shachter in the graph-based approach. Moreover, our analysis leads us to introduce a new inference axiom, called *combination*, of which the contraction axiom is a special case.

This paper is organized as follows. In Section 2, we review two pertinent notions. In Section 3, we introduce the notion of hypergraph combination. The combination inference axiom is introduced in Section 4. In Section 5, we present our main result. The conclusion is presented in Section 6.

Y. Xiang and B. Chaib-draa (Eds.): AI 2003, LNAI 2671, pp. 568–574, 2003.

2 Background Knowledge

In this section, we review the pertinent notions of probabilistic conditional independence and hypergraphs used in this study.

Let $R = \{A_1, A_2, \ldots, A_m\}$ denote a finite set of discrete variables. Each variable A_i is associated with a finite domain D_i. Let D be the Cartesian product of the domains $D_1, \ldots, D_m$. A *joint probability distribution* on D is function p on D, $p : D \rightarrow [0, 1]$, such that p is normalized. That is, this function p assigns to each tuple $t \in D$ a real number $0 \leq p(t) \leq 1$ and $\sum_{t \in D} p(t) = 1$. We write a joint probability distribution p as $p(A_1, A_2, \ldots, A_m)$ over the set R of variables.

Let X, Y, and Z be disjoint subsets of R. Let x, y and z be arbitrary values of X, Y and Z, respectively. We say Y and Z are *conditionally independent* given X under the joint probability distribution p, denoted $I(Y, X, Z)$, if $p(y|x, z) = p(y|x)$, whenever $p(x, z) > 0$. We call an independency $I(Y, X, Z)$ *full*, in the special case when $XYZ = R$. In the probabilistic reasoning theory, probabilistic conditional independencies are often graphically represented using hypergraphs.

A *hypergraph* [1] $\mathcal{H}$ on a finite set R of vertices is a set of subsets of R, that is, $\mathcal{H} = \{R_1, R_2, \ldots, R_n\}$, where $R_i \subseteq R$ for $i = 1, 2, \ldots, n$. (Henceforth, we will simply refer to the hypergraph $\mathcal{H}$ and assume $R = R_1 \cup R_2 \cup \ldots \cup R_n$). For example, two hypergraphs $\mathcal{H}_1 = \{h_1 = \{A, B, C, D, E\},\ h_2 = \{D, E, F\}\}$ and $\mathcal{H}_2 = \{\{A, B\}, \{A, C\}, \{B, D\}, \{C, E\}\}$ are shown in Figure 1 (i).

A hypergraph $\mathcal{H} = \{R_1, R_2, \ldots, R_n\}$ is *acyclic* [1], if there exists a permutation $S_1, S_2, \ldots, S_n$ of $R_1, R_2, \ldots, R_n$ such that for $j = 2, ..., n$, $S_j \cap (S_1 \cup S_2 \cup \ldots \cup S_{j-1}) \subseteq S_i$, where $i < j$. It can be verified that the two hypergraphs in Figure 1 (i) are each acyclic, whereas the one in Figure 1 (ii) is not.

If $\mathcal{H}$ is a hypergraph, then the set of conditional independencies *generated by* $\mathcal{H}$ is the set $CI(\mathcal{H})$ of full conditional independencies $I(Y, X, Z)$, where Y is the union of some disconnected components of the hypergraph $\mathcal{H} - X$ obtained from $\mathcal{H}$ by deleting the set X of nodes, and $Z = R - XY$. That is, $\mathcal{H} - X = \{h - X \mid h$ is a hyperedge of $\mathcal{H}\} - \{\emptyset\}$. We then say that X *separates off* Y from the rest of

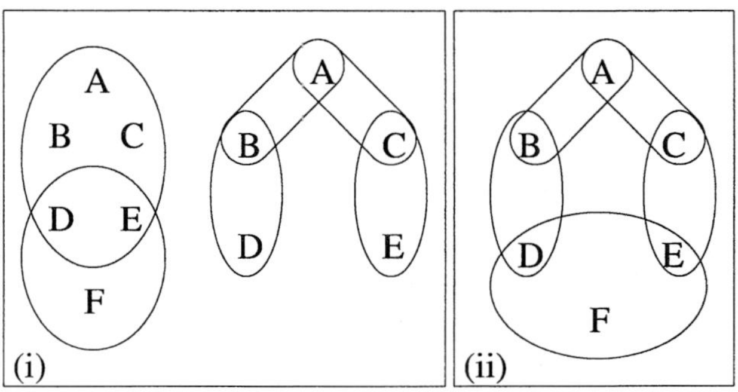

Fig. 1. Given $\mathcal{H}_1 = \{h_1 = \{A, B, C, D, E\}, h_2 = \{D, E, F\}\}$ and $\mathcal{H}_2 = \{\{A, B\}, \{A, C\}, \{B, D\}, \{C, E\}\}$ in (i), the *combination* of $\mathcal{H}_1$ and $\mathcal{H}_2$ is $\mathcal{H}_1^{h_1 \leftarrow \mathcal{H}_2}$ in (ii)

the nodes, and call X a *separating set* [1]. For example, consider the acyclic hypergraph $\mathcal{H}_2$ in Figure 1 (i). If $X = \{B, C\}$, then $\mathcal{H} - X = \{\{A\}, \{D\}, \{E\}\}$. By definition, $I(A, BC, DE)$ and $I(D, BC, AE)$ are two conditional independencies appearing in $CI(\mathcal{H})$.

The conditional independencies generated by a hypergraph $\mathcal{H}$, i.e., $CI(\mathcal{H})$, can be equivalently expressed using conventional undirected graphs and the separation method [1]. If H is a hypergraph, then the *graph of* H, denoted $G(H)$, is defined as: $G(H) = \{\ (A, B) \mid A \in h \text{ and } B \in h \text{ for some } h \in H\ \}$. For instance, the graph of the hypergraph $\mathcal{H}$ in Figure 1 (ii) is the undirected graph $G(\mathcal{H}) = \{(A, B), (A, C), (B, D), (C, E), (D, E), (D, F), (E, F)\}$. It can be verified that $CI(\mathcal{H}) = CI(G(\mathcal{H}))$.

3 Hypergraph Combination

This section focuses on the graphical combination of two individual hypergraphs into a single hypergraph.

Let $X_1Y_1Z_1 = R$ such that X_1, Y_1 and Z_1 are pairwise disjoint and each nonempty. Let $\mathcal{H}_1 = \{h_1 = Y_1X_1, h_2 = X_1Z_1\}$ be a binary acyclic hypergraph and $\mathcal{H}_2$ be any hypergraph defined on the set h_1 of variables. The *combination* of $\mathcal{H}_1$ and $\mathcal{H}_2$, written $\mathcal{H}_1^{h_1 \leftarrow \mathcal{H}_2}$, is defined as:

$$\mathcal{H}_1^{h_1 \leftarrow \mathcal{H}_2} = (\mathcal{H}_1 - \{h_1\}) \cup \mathcal{H}_2, \tag{1}$$

or equivalently,

$$\mathcal{H}_1^{h_1 \leftarrow \mathcal{H}_2} = \mathcal{H}_2 \cup \{h_2\}. \tag{2}$$

Example 1. Consider the two acyclic hypergraphs $\mathcal{H}_1 = \{h_1 = \{A, B, C, D, E\}, h_2 = \{D, E, F\}\}$ and $\mathcal{H}_2 = \{\{A, B\}, \{A, C\}, \{B, D\}, \{C, E\}\}$ in Figure 1 (i). The combination of $\mathcal{H}_1$ and $\mathcal{H}_2$ is the hypergraph $\mathcal{H}_1^{h_1 \leftarrow \mathcal{H}_2} = \{\{A, B\}, \{A, C\}, \{B, D\}, \{C, E\}, \{D, E, F\}\}$, as depicted in Figure 1 (ii).

As Shachter pointed out in [3], a set X may be a separating set in the combined hypergraph $\mathcal{H}_1^{h_1 \leftarrow \mathcal{H}_2}$ but not in $\mathcal{H}_1$. The set BE separates AC and DF in the combined hypergraph $\mathcal{H}_1^{h_1 \leftarrow \mathcal{H}_2}$ of Figure 1 (ii), but not in hypergraph $\mathcal{H}_1$ of Figure 1 (i). The next result precisely characterize the new separating sets.

Lemma 1. Let $\mathcal{H}_1 = \{Y_1X_1, X_1Z_1\}$ and $\mathcal{H}_2 = \{Y_2X_2, X_2Z_2\}$, where $X_1Y_1 = X_2Y_2Z_2$. If $Y_2 \cap X_1 = \emptyset$, then X_2 separates Y_2 and Z_1Z_2 in $\mathcal{H}_1^{h_1 \leftarrow \mathcal{H}_2}$.

Proof: Suppose $Y_2 \cap X_1 = \emptyset$. Since $X_1Y_1 = X_2Y_2Z_2$, we have $X_1 \subseteq X_2Z_2$. Thus, X_1 can be augmented by some subset $W \subseteq Y_1$ to be equal to X_2Z_2, namely, $X_1W = X_2Z_2$. Thus, X_1 separating Y_1 and Z_1 in $\mathcal{H}_1$ can be restated as X_1 separates Y_2W and Z_1 in $\mathcal{H}_1$. It immediately follows that X_1W separates Y_2 and Z_1 in $\mathcal{H}_1$. Since $X_1W = X_2Z_2$, we have X_2Z_2 separates Y_2 and Z_1 in $\mathcal{H}_1$. By *graphical contraction* [3], X_2 separating Y_2 and Z_2 in $\mathcal{H}_2$ and X_2Z_2 separating Y_2 and Z_1 in $\mathcal{H}_1$, implies that X_2 separates Y_2 and Z_1Z_2 in $\mathcal{H}_1^{h_1 \leftarrow \mathcal{H}_2}$. □

Lemma 1 can be understood using the database notion of *splits* [1]. Given a hypergraph $\mathcal{H}$, a set X *splits* two variables A and B, if X blocks every path between A and B. More generally, a set X splits a set W, if X splits at least two attributes of W. Lemma 1 then means that if the separating set X_2 does *not* split X_1, then X_2 will remain a separating set in the combined hypergraph.

Example 2. Consider again Figure 1. Here DE is the only separating set of $\mathcal{H}_1$. The separating set B of $\mathcal{H}_2$ in (i) *splits* DE, since D is separated from E by B. By Lemma 1, B will not be a separating set in $\mathcal{H}_1^{h_1 \leftarrow \mathcal{H}_2}$. On the other hand, the separating set BE of $\mathcal{H}_2$ in (ii) will indeed be a separating set in the combined hypergraph $\mathcal{H}_1^{h_1 \leftarrow \mathcal{H}_2}$ since BE does *not* split DE.

Lemma 2. There is a one-to-one correspondence between the separating sets of $\mathcal{H}_2$ that do *not* split X_1 and the *new* separating sets in $\mathcal{H}_1^{h_1 \leftarrow \mathcal{H}_2}$.

Proof: Suppose X_2 separates Y_2 and $Z_1 Z_2$ in $\mathcal{H}_1^{h_1 \leftarrow \mathcal{H}_2}$. It follows that X_2 separates Y_2 and Z_2 in the hypergraph obtained by projecting down to the context $X_2 Y_2 Z_2$, namely, $\mathcal{H}_1^{h_1 \leftarrow \mathcal{H}_2} - Z_1 = \{h - Z_1 \mid h \in \mathcal{H}_1^{h_1 \leftarrow \mathcal{H}_2}\} = \mathcal{H}_2 \cup \{X_1\}$. It is well-known [1, 2] that removing a hyperedge from a hypergraph can only add new separating sets, i.e., removing a hyperedge from a hypergraph cannot destroy an existing separating set. Thus, since X_2 separates Y_2 and Z_2 in $\mathcal{H}_2 \cup \{X_1\}$, X_2 separates Y_2 and Z_2 in the smaller hypergraph $\mathcal{H}_2$. □

Example 3. All of the separating sets of $\mathcal{H}_2$ are listed in the first column of Table 1. The horizontal line partitions those separating sets that do not split DE from those that do. Those separating sets that do *not* split DE are listed above the horizontal line, while those that split DE are listed below. The *new* separating sets in the combined hypergraph are given in the 3rd column. (The fact that DE separates F and ABC is already known from $\mathcal{H}_1$.) As indicated, there is a one-to-one correspondence between the separating sets in the smaller hypergraph $\mathcal{H}_2$ that do *not* split DE and the previously unknown separating sets in the combined hypergraph $\mathcal{H}_1^{h_1 \leftarrow \mathcal{H}_2}$.

4 The Combination Inference Axiom

Pearl's *semi-graphoid axiomatization* [2] is:

$$
\begin{array}{ll}
(SG1)\ Symmetry: & I(Y,X,Z) \Longrightarrow I(Z,X,Y),\\
(SG2)\ Decomposition: & I(Y,X,ZW) \Longrightarrow I(Y,X,Z)\ \&\ I(Y,X,W),\\
(SG3)\ Weak\ union: & I(Y,X,ZW) \Longrightarrow I(Y,XZ,W),\\
(SG4)\ Contraction: & I(W,XY,Z)\ \&\ I(Y,X,Z) \Longrightarrow I(WY,X,Z).
\end{array}
$$

We introduce *combination* (SG5) as a new inference axiom for CI:

$$(SG5)\ Combination: \quad I(Y_2,X_2,Z_2)\ \&\ I(Y_1,X_1,Z_1) \Longrightarrow I(Y_2,X_2,Z_1Z_2),$$

where $X_1Y_1 = X_2Y_2Z_2$ and $I(Y_2,X_2,Z_2)$ does not split X_1.

Table 1. There is a one-to-one correspondence between the separating sets in $\mathcal{H}_2$ that do *not* split DE and the *new* separating sets in the combined hypergraph

	separating sets of $\mathcal{H}_2$		separating sets in $\mathcal{H}_1^{h_1 \leftarrow \mathcal{H}_2}$
DE is *not* split	$I(B, AD, CE)$	$\longleftrightarrow$	$I(B, AD, CEF)$
	$I(C, AE, BD)$	$\longleftrightarrow$	$I(C, AE, BDF)$
	$I(A, BC, DE)$	$\longleftrightarrow$	$I(A, BC, DEF)$
	$I(AC, BE, D)$	$\longleftrightarrow$	$I(AC, BE, DF)$
	$I(AB, CD, E)$	$\longleftrightarrow$	$I(AB, CD, EF)$
	$I(A, BCD, E)$	$\longleftrightarrow$	$I(A, BCD, EF)$
	$I(A, BCE, D)$	$\longleftrightarrow$	$I(A, BCE, DF)$
DE is split	$I(BD, A, CE)$		-
	$I(D, B, ACE)$		-
	$I(E, C, ABD)$		-
	$I(D, AB, CE)$		-
	$I(BD, AC, E)$		-
	$I(D, BC, AE)$		-

Lemma 3. The *combination* inference axiom (SG5) is *sound* for probabilistic conditional independence.

Proof: Since $I(Y_2, X_2, Z_2)$ does not split X_1, at least one of Y_2 or Z_2 does not intersect with X_1. Without loss of generality, let $Y_2 \cap X_1 = \emptyset$.

By the proof of Lemma 1, $I(Y_1, X_1, Z_1)$ can be rewritten as $I(Y_2W, X_1, Z_1)$. By (SG3), we obtain $I(Y_2, X_1W, Z_1)$. Since $X_1W{=}X_2Z_2$, we have $I(Y_2, X_2Z_2, Z_1)$. By (SG4), $I(Y_2, X_2, Z_2)$ and $I(Y_2, X_2Z_2, Z_1)$ give $I(Y_2, X_2, Z_1Z_2)$. □

Lemma 3 indicates that $\{(SG1), (SG2), (SG3), (SG4)\} \Longrightarrow (SG5)$. The next result shows that (SG4) and (SG5) can be interchanged.

Theorem 1. $\{(SG1), (SG2), (SG3), (SG5)\} \Longrightarrow (SG4)$.

Proof: We need to show that any CI obtained by (SG4) can be obtained using $\{(SG1), (SG2), (SG3), (SG5)\}$. Suppose we are given $I(W, XY, Z)$ and $I(Y, X, Z)$. By (SG5), we obtain the desired CI $I(WY, X, Z)$. □

Corollary 1. The contraction inference axiom is a *special case* of the combination inference axiom.

By Theorem 1 and Lemma 3, we have:

$$\{(SG1), (SG2), (SG3), (SG4)\} \;\equiv\; \{(SG1), (SG2), (SG3), (SG5)\}.$$

The combination axiom can be used for *convenience*. For instance, consider deriving $I(AC, BE, DF)$ from $I(F, DE, ABC)$ and $I(D, BE, AC)$. Using the semi-graphoid axiomatization $\{(SG1), (SG2), (SG3), (SG4)\}$ requires four steps, whereas using $\{(SG1), (SG2), (SG3), (SG5)\}$ requires three steps.

5 Reasoning with Multiple Hypergraphs

In this section, we focus on those sets $\sum$ of CIs, where the semi-graphoid axioms are complete. That is, $\sum$ logically implies another independency σ if and only if σ can be derived from $\sum$ by applying the four inference axioms $\{(SG1), (SG2), (SG3), (SG4)\}$.

The main result is that the combination $\mathcal{H}_1^{h_1 \leftarrow \mathcal{H}_2}$ is a *perfect-map* of the full conditional independencies logically implied by the independencies in $\mathcal{H}_1$ together with those in $\mathcal{H}_2$.

A hypergraph $\mathcal{H}$ is an *independency-map* (I-map) [2] for a joint distribution $p(R)$, if every independency $I(Y, X, Z)$ in $CI(\mathcal{H})$ is satisfied by $p(R)$. A hypergraph $\mathcal{H}$ is a *perfect-map* (P-map) [2] for a joint distribution $p(R)$, if an independency $I(Y, X, Z)$ is in $CI(\mathcal{H})$ if and only if it is satisfied by $p(R)$.

In [3], Shachter established the following:

$$I(Y, X, Z) \in CI(\mathcal{H}_1^{h_1 \leftarrow \mathcal{H}_2}) \implies CI(\mathcal{H}_1) \cup CI(\mathcal{H}_2) \models I(Y, X, Z),$$

that is, if X separates Y and Z in the combined hypergraph $\mathcal{H}_1^{h_1 \leftarrow \mathcal{H}_2}$, then $I(Y, X, Z)$ is logically implied by $CI(\mathcal{H}_1) \cup CI(\mathcal{H}_2)$. Theorem 2 below shows that a CI $I(Y, X, Z)$ can be inferred by separation in the combined hypergraph $\mathcal{H}_1^{h_1 \leftarrow \mathcal{H}_2}$ iff $I(Y, X, Z)$ is logically implied by $CI(\mathcal{H}_1) \cup CI(\mathcal{H}_2)$, namely,

$$I(Y, X, Z) \in CI(\mathcal{H}_1^{h_1 \leftarrow \mathcal{H}_2}) \iff CI(\mathcal{H}_1) \cup CI(\mathcal{H}_2) \models I(Y, X, Z).$$

Theorem 2. The combined hypergraph $\mathcal{H}_1^{h_1 \leftarrow \mathcal{H}_2}$ is a *perfect-map* of the full conditional independencies logically implied by $CI(\mathcal{H}_1) \cup CI(\mathcal{H}_2)$.

Proof: ($\Rightarrow$) Let $I(Y, X, Z) \in CI(\mathcal{H}_1^{h_1 \leftarrow \mathcal{H}_2})$. Suppose $I(Y, X, Z) \in CI(\mathcal{H}_1)$. Then $CI(\mathcal{H}_1) \cup CI(\mathcal{H}_2) \models I(Y, X, Z)$. Suppose then that $I(Y, X, Z) \notin CI(\mathcal{H}_1)$. Since X does not separate Y and Z in $\mathcal{H}_1$, X must necessarily separate two nonempty sets Y_2 and Z_2 in $\mathcal{H}_2$. That is, $I(Y_2, X, Z_2) \in CI(\mathcal{H}_2)$. There are two cases to consider. Suppose $I(Y_2, X, Z_2)$ does *not* split X_1. Without loss of generality, let $Y_2 \cap X_1 = \emptyset$. By Lemma 3, $I(Y_2, X, Z_2)$ and $I(Y_1, X_1, Z_1)$ logically imply $I(Y_2, X, Z_1Z_2)$. Thus, $CI(\mathcal{H}_1) \cup CI(\mathcal{H}_2) \models I(Y_2, X, Z_1Z_2)$. We now show that $I(Y_2, X, Z_1Z_2) = I(Y, X, Z)$. Since $I(Y, X, Z) \in CI(\mathcal{H}_1^{h_1 \leftarrow \mathcal{H}_2})$, deleting X in $\mathcal{H}_1^{h_1 \leftarrow \mathcal{H}_2}$ gives two disconnected components Y and Z. Similarly, $I(Y_2, X, Z_1Z_2) \in CI(\mathcal{H}_1^{h_1 \leftarrow \mathcal{H}_2})$ means that deleting X in $\mathcal{H}_1^{h_1 \leftarrow \mathcal{H}_2}$ gives two disconnected components Y_2 and Z_1Z_2. By definition, however, the disconnected components in $\mathcal{H} - W$ are *unique* for any hypergraph on R and $W \subseteq R$. Thus, either $Y = Y_2$ and $Z = Z_1Z_2$ or $Y = Z_1Z_2$ and $Z = Y_2$. In either case, $CI(\mathcal{H}_1) \cup CI(\mathcal{H}_2) \models I(Y_2, X, Z_1Z_2)$. Now suppose $I(Y_2, X, Z_2)$ *splits* X_1. By the definition of splits, $X_1 \cap Y_2 \neq \emptyset$ and $X_1 \cap Z_2 \neq \emptyset$. But then contraction can never be applied:

$$I(Y_2, X, Z_2) \ \&\ I(Y_1 - W, X_1W, Z_1) \not\models I(Y_2, X, Z_1Z_2),$$

since $X_1W \neq XZ_2$ for every subset $W \subseteq Y_1$.

($\Leftarrow$) Suppose $CI(\mathcal{H}_1) \cup CI(\mathcal{H}_2) \models I(Y, X, Z)$. If $I(Y, X, Z) \in CI(\mathcal{H}_1)$, then X separates Y and Z in $\mathcal{H}_1$ and subsequently in $\mathcal{H}_1^{h_1 \leftarrow \mathcal{H}_2}$. Suppose then that

$I(Y, X, Z) \notin CI(\mathcal{H}_1)$. Since $\{(SG1), (SG2), (SG3), (SG4)\}$ can derive every logically implied independency and $\{(SG1), (SG2), (SG3)\}$ are all defined with respect to the same fixed set of variables, the contraction axiom $(SG4)$ must have been applied to derive $I(Y, X, Z)$, i.e,

$$I(Y_1, X_1, Z_1) \ \& \ I(Y_2, X_2, Z_2) \models I(Y, X, Z).$$

By definition of $(SG4)$, $I(Y_2, X_2, Z_2)$ does not split X_1, $X_2Y_2Z_2 = X_1Z_1$, $X = X_2$, $Y = Y_1Y_2$, and $Z = Z_1 = Z_2$. Interpreting the conditional independence statement $I(Y_1Y_2, X_2, Z_1)$ as a separation statement means that $X = X_2$ is a separator in the combined graph. That is, X separates Y and Z in $\mathcal{H}_1^{h_1 \leftarrow \mathcal{H}_2}$. Therefore, $I(Y, X, Z) \in CI(\mathcal{H}_1^{h_1 \leftarrow \mathcal{H}_2})$. □

6 Conclusion

This study emphasizes the usefulness of viewing graph combination from a hypergraph perspective rather than from a conventional undirected graph approach. Whereas it was previously shown by Shachter [3] that the combined hypergraph $\mathcal{H}_1^{h_1 \leftarrow \mathcal{H}_2}$ is an I-map of the full conditional independencies logically implied by $CI(\mathcal{H}_1) \cup CI(\mathcal{H}_2)$, Theorem 2 shows that $\mathcal{H}_1^{h_1 \leftarrow \mathcal{H}_2}$ is in fact a P-map of the full conditional independencies logically implied by $CI(\mathcal{H}_1) \cup CI(\mathcal{H}_2)$. Moreover, in Lemma 2, we were able to draw a one-to-one correspondence between the new separating sets in the combined hypergraph with the separating sets in the smaller hypergraph. Finally, our study of graphical combination lead to the introduction of a new inference axiom for conditional independence, called *combination*, which is a generalization of contraction as Corollary 1 establishes.

References

[1] Beeri, C., Fagin, R., Maier, D., Yannakakis, M.: On the desirability of acyclic database schemes. Journal of the ACM. **30**(3) (1983) 479–513

[2] Pearl, J.: Probabilistic Reasoning in Intelligent Systems: Networks of Plausible Inference. Morgan Kaufmann Publishers, San Francisco (1988)

[3] Shachter, R. D.: A graph-based inference method for conditional independence. *Proceedings of the Seventh Conference on Uncertainty in Artificial Intelligence*, 353–360, 1991.

[4] Wong, S. K. M., Butz, C. J., Wu, D.: On the implication problem for probabilistic conditional independency. IEEE Trans. Syst. Man Cybern. SMC-A **30**(6) (2000) 785–805

[5] Wong, S. K. M., Butz, C. J.: Constructing the dependency structure of a multiagent probabilistic network. IEEE Trans. Knowl. Data Eng. **13**(3) (2001) 395–415

[6] Xiang, X.: Probabilistic Reasoning in Multiagent Systems: A Graphical Models Approach. Cambridge University Press, New York (2002)

Probabilistic Reasoning for Meal Planning in Intelligent Fridges

Michael Janzen and Yang Xiang

University of Guelph, Canada
mjanzen@uoguelph.ca
yxiang@cis.uoguelph.ca

Abstract. In this paper, we investigate issues in building an intelligent fridge which can help a family to plan meals based on each member's preference and to generate a list for grocery shopping. The brute-force solution for this problem is intractable. We present the use of a BNF grammar to reduce the search space. We select the meal plan from alternatives following a decision-theoretic approach. The utility of a meal plan is evaluated by aggregating the utilities of meals and foods contained in meals. We propose an explicit representation of the uncertainty of each family member's food preference using extended Bayesian networks.

1 Introduction

As technology becomes more advanced, and the workload of people's schedules increases, there is an expectation for machines to complete tasks on behalf of the human owner. In the area of grocery shopping, human beings have had to determine what grocery items are needed based on their family's preferences, and the cost of the items. For some people, such as actors or other extremely busy professionals, a personal human shopping assistant may complete this task. The role of an intelligent fridge is to replace such a shopping assistant in the sense that the fridge will be able to determine what grocery items are needed for purchase.

To decide which grocery items to purchase, the fridge software needs to plan meals to be consumed and to determine the necessary grocery items for those meals. The desirability of a meal to a person can be represented as utility. However, the utility according to the person may not be known precisely by the fridge software. In this work, we propose to explicitly represent the uncertainty of the person's meal utility and to take this uncertainty into account in evaluation of alternative meal plans. This differs from the common approach where the events are represented as uncertain while the decision makers' utility for the events are assumed to be given.

The preferences for foods are not constant but rather depend on the context in which the food is consumed. This notion leads to the concept of a utility network which graphically shows the dependency between the consumption context of a food and its utility. This paper will present the implementation of such

Y. Xiang and B. Chaib-draa (Eds.): AI 2003, LNAI 2671, pp. 575–582, 2003.

a utility network using an equivalent Bayesian Network [2]. This is advantageous as inference methods for Bayesian Networks have been well studied [1].

The fridge has an intractable number of meal plans to examine. We observe that meals with a high utility typically have a structure associated with them. We propose to use a grammar to constrain the search space of potential meals. The use of a grammar also greatly aids the planning of meals for multiple people.

2 Problem Domain

The following terminologies will be used in this paper to describe the relevant objects and entities.

Group The set of users, typically a family, whose meals are to be planned.
Food A item that can be consumed by one or more users.
Meal A non-empty set of foods.
Meal of Day Meal of day can be breakfast, lunch, dinner, or snack. The meal of day indicates the time of the day at which the meal is consumed. For planning purposes, meals are considered to be consumed instantaneously.
Individual Meal A meal consumed by a single user.
Group Meal A meal that multiple users eat together. In such a meal the users will all eat the same foods, save foods that are specified as being individual.
Meal Plan A number of sequential meals planned for consumption by a group in future days.
Meal subplan A meal plan serves a group. A meal subplan for a given user in the group is the portion of a meal plan relevant to the user.

An output of the intelligent fridge would be a grocery shopping list that yields the maximum expected utility in terms of cost and food preference of the users. For the purposes of this paper it is assumed that the contents of the fridge are completely known in terms of identification and quantity. This may be accomplished by installing weigh scales and UPC scanners in the fridge. When a portion of an item is consumed, the fridge will consider the difference in weight in order to determine an accurate remaining quantity.

3 Technical Issues

As the meal planning involves choosing a sequence of meals over a time period, the problem may be conceived as a Markov decision process [3]. However, the Markov property holds if the transition probabilities from any given state depend only on the state and not on previous history [4]. In the case of meal planning the next meal depends strongly on the user's recent meal history. Hence, the Markov property is violated. Ignoring the recent history leads to an oscillating meal plan in which only a few foods are chosen repeatedly. One might incorporate the recent meal history into the current state in order to restore the Markov property. This would yield an exponential number of possible histories to consider in a policy which leads to a tractability problem.

$< start >$	$\longrightarrow < breakfast > \mid < dinner >$
$< breakfast >$	$\longrightarrow$ breakfast cereal
$< dinner >$	$\longrightarrow < steak\ dinner > \mid < stir\ fry\ dinner >$
$< steak\ dinner >$	$\longrightarrow$ steak $< side > < side > < drink >$ $< salad > < desert >$
$< stir\ fry\ dinner >$	$\longrightarrow$ stir fry $< drink > < desert >$
$< side >$	$\longrightarrow$ steamed broccoli | baked potato | french fries
$< drink >$	$\longrightarrow$ wine | Coca Cola | water
$< salad >$	$\longrightarrow$ garden salad | Caesar salad | Greek salad
$< desert >$	$\longrightarrow$ chocolate cake | ice cream | fresh fruit

Fig. 1. An example meal grammar

An alternative meal planning strategy is to generate all possible meals and then examine all possible meal plans consisting of those meals. The computation following this approach is intractable because the number of meals is exponential on the number of foods.

4 Reduce Search Space Using Meal Grammar

In general, a meal with a high utility is well structured. We expect dessert to end a supper but not a breakfast. A meal made of a set of foods that does not follow the normal structure usually has a low utility, such as a meal that has many, very spicy foods, but no drinks. Explicit representation of such a structure allows reduction of the number of meals to be considered and helps to alleviate the intractability problem outlined in the previous section.

We propose to represent the meal structure using the Backus Naur Form (BNF) grammar. Grammars are normally used for specifying syntax of natural or programming languages. Other applications include simulation of vehicle trajectories [5]. An example meal grammar is shown in figure 1 for 15 specific foods. A meal consistent with this grammar is $\{stir\ fry, water, chocolate\ cake\}$.

Using such a grammar reduces the number of meals to consider from 32767 to 92 under the assumption that duplication of foods is not allowed, and order is not important. It should be noted that, while recursion is allowed by BNF grammar, recursion should be avoided for meal grammars to reduce the potential number of meals.

The meal grammar can be alternatively represented as an and-or graph, which we refer to as a *food hierarchy.* Each non-leaf node in a food hierarchy is either an AND node (links going to its children are all AND branches) or an OR node (links going to its children are all OR branches). The root node corresponds to the *start* symbol of the meal grammar and is an OR node. Each leaf node represents a food and each internal node is an *abstract food* which corresponds to a term in the left-hand side of a rule in the meal grammar.

In addition to reducing the number of meals to examine for planning individual meals, the meal grammar also facilitates effective planning of group meals.

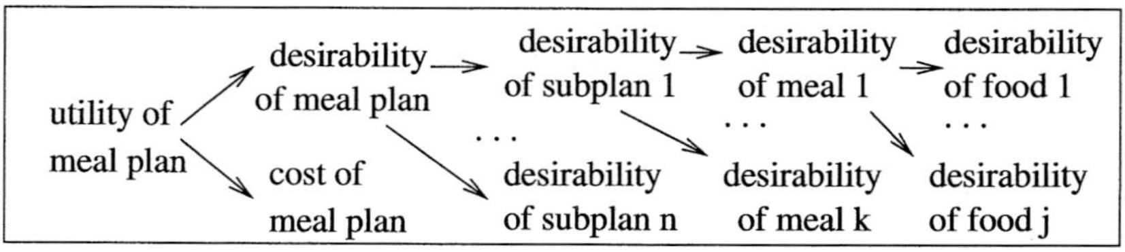

Fig. 2. Utility hierarchy

One way to perform the planning is to generate both the *common* foods as well as the *individual* foods. The meal plan is then evaluated relative to each individual's preference. Finally, the individual evaluations are aggregated to arrive at an overall evaluation. If the individual foods have k alternatives for each of n individuals, then for each set of common foods, k^n alternative combinations of individual foods need to be evaluated.

Alternatively, the individual foods can be independently planned by selecting the foods with high utility for each individual and then aggregating the meal plan. Suppose each individual chooses one set of individual foods from the k alternatives. Then only $k * n$ sets of individual foods need to be evaluated. For example, if $k = 10$ and $n = 4$, then $k^n = 10000$ but $k * n = 40$: a significant computational saving.

Using the meal grammar, the group meal planning can be performed as follows: Each abstract food to be planned individually will be tagged as individual and treated by the group planner as terminal. When all abstract foods in a meal have either been substituted for terminal foods or are tagged as individual, the group planning terminates and the individual planners continue to substitute individual foods and complete the meal plan.

5 Evaluating Meal Plans

The aim of the intelligent fridge is to select the meal plan with the highest utility. The utility of a meal plan can be decomposed according to a hierarchy as shown in figure 2.

The overall utility of a meal plan is aggregated from its utility based on desirability and its utility based on cost. The desirability-based utility of a food is determined by how much it is desired by a user and is user-dependent. A possible aggregation technique is weighted average.

The meal planning software is supported by a database that contains the mapping from each food to the required ingredients and the current price of each ingredient. This information can be used to determine the cost, in dollars, of a meal plan. The cost of a meal plan in general ranges from zero to infinity. The zero cost occurs when all the ingredients of a meal plan are free from the grocery supplier (which rarely happens) or are already in the fridge (which is more common). The infinite cost in general reflects the fact that no practical upper bound of cost can be found.

As the utility of cost must range from zero to one, we use the following function to map the cost to the utility, $Cost\ Utility = a^{-cost}$, where $a > 1.0$ is a constant which represents the relative altitude of the group towards cost. A large value of a corresponds to a group that is financially conservative. On the other hand, a smaller value of a corresponds to a group that is relatively wealthy.

The number of possible meal plans is still exponential on the number of meals included in the meal plan. We propose the use of a greedy search heuristic to make the computation manageable. The meal planning starts from the first meal of the day and proceeds to the subsequent meals in temporal order. At each step, the best meal for this meal of the day is selected from all possible alternatives. This heuristic reduces the computational complexity of meal plan selection from exponential to linear on the number of meals.

6 Handling Uncertain Utility of Food Desirability

The desirability of a given food to a given user depends on several factors, such as: how much the user likes the food in general, what other foods are present in the same meal, recent meal history (how recently the user consumed the same food), or other related foods and how much the user consumed, the preparation time of the food and whether the person has enough time on the corresponding date, and the season when the food is to be consumed.

We represent each user's utility about a food as a function from the above factors to $[0, 1]$. Let u_i be the utility of a given user for the food f_i. Let π_i be the set of variables that u_i depends on. The user's utility is denoted as $u_i(f_i|\pi_i)$.

For example, suppose $\pi_i = \{a_i, b_i\}$ and both a_i and b_i are binary. One possible utility function is $u_i(f_i|a_i = y, b_i = y) = 1.0, \quad u_i(f_i|a_i = y, b_i = n) = 0.6, ...$ Hence, given the values of a_i and b_i, we can approximate the utility of f_i.

Usually, the user's food preference is not precisely known. That is, we do not know the function $u_i(f_i|\pi_i)$ with certainty. In that case, we can represent our uncertain knowledge about each user's utility as a probability distribution over the possible utility functions: $P(u_i(f_i|\pi_i))$. For example, the uncertain knowledge about the above utility can be represented as

$$P(u_i(f_i|a_i = y, b_i = y) \in [0.75, 1.0]) = 0.6,$$
$$P(u_i(f_i|a_i = y, b_i = y) \in [0.5, 0.75)) = 0.3, ...$$

To simplify the notation, we denote $P(u_i(f_i|\pi_i))$ as $P(u_i|\pi_i)$, i.e.,

$$P(u_i \in [0.75, 1.0]|a_i = y, b_i = y) = P(u_i = u_{i3}|a_i = y, b_i = y) = 0.6,$$
$$P(u_i \in [0.5, 0.75)|a_i = y, b_i = y) = P(u_i = u_{i2}|a_i = y, b_i = y) = 0.3, ...$$

where u_{i0} denotes $u_i \in [0, 0.25)$, etc. If we know the values of a_i and b_i, we can determine the utility of f_i by weighted summation, e.g.,

$$E(u_i|a_i = y, b_i = y) =$$
$$0.125 * P(u_i = u_{i0}|a_i = y, b_i = y) + 0.375 * P(u_i = u_{i1}|a_i = y, b_i = y) +$$
$$0.625 * P(u_i = u_{i2}|a_i = y, b_i = y) + 0.875 * P(u_i = u_{i3}|a_i = y, b_i = y),$$

where the midpoint of each utility interval has been used.

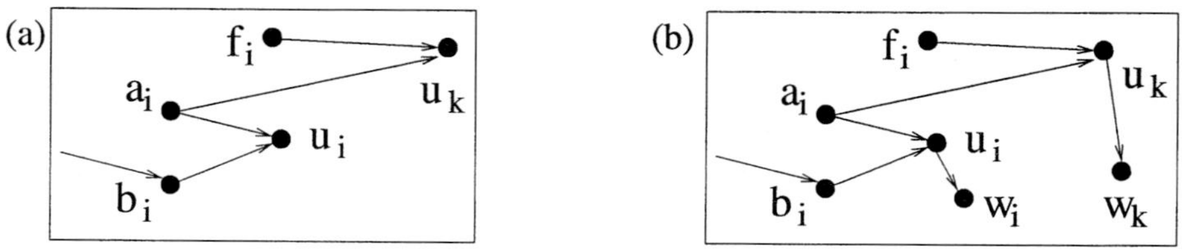

Fig. 3. Utility networks fragment to encode uncertain knowledge about a user's utility on food f_i

Given a meal subplan, some variables that u_i depends on will be instantiated. For instance, if a_i represents whether another food is present in the current meal, then $a_i = y$ if that food is present in the meal subplan. On the other hand, the values of other variables that u_i depends on may still be uncertain. For instance, if a_i represents the time needed to prepare the food and b_i represents the time that the user has on the date, then the value of b_i is unknown given the meal subplan. In general, b_i could depend on some other variables which are also unknown at the time of meal planning. Therefore, the above utility computation requires the calculation of $P(u_i|obs)$ where *obs* represents all variables whose values are observed at the time of meal planning. In other word, the above utility computation requires probabilistic inference.

To perform such inference, we use utility networks that extend Bayesian networks [2] with utility variables to represent the uncertain knowledge about the user's preference. The above knowledge $P(u_i|a_i, b_i)$ can be associated with the node u_i in the network fragment of figure 3(a). In the figure, the incoming arrow to b_i represents a variable that b_i depends on. The child node u_k of a_i and f_i represents the utility of another food f_k that depends on both of them.

For each meal subplan, a utility network (UN) can be constructed which encodes the uncertain knowledge on the desirability of each food according to a given user. The network thus contains a utility node for each food appearing in the meal subplan and the relevant nodes (variables) which the utility node depends on. Once such a network is constructed, variables whose values are known from the meal subplan can be instantiated accordingly (they are collectively represented as *obs*) and the probability distribution $P(u_i|obs)$ can be computed for each u_i using standard inference algorithms for Bayesian networks [1].

In the above example, when the utility $u_i \in [0, 0.25)$ (or $u_i = u_{i0}$), we have used the midpoint value 0.125 to approximate $E(u_i|a_i = y, b_i = y)$. We assume that for each utility variable u_i and each interval u_{ij}, a representative value w_{ij} for approximation is assigned (not necessarily the midpoint). We have: $E(u_i|obs) = \sum_j w_{ij}\ P(u_i = u_{ij}|obs)$. The utility of the meal subplan for the given user is then

$$\sum_i E(u_i|obs)/(\sum_i 1) = [\sum_i \sum_j w_{ij}\ P(u_i = u_{ij}|obs)]/(\sum_i 1),$$

where simple averaging is used to aggregate the utilities of multiple foods.

Note that the above consists of two stages of computation: the computation of $P(u_i|obs)$ by probabilistic inference using a UN and the computation of $\sum_i E(u_i|obs)$ given $P(u_i|obs)$. We can extend the UN representation to encode the representative utility values (w_{ij}) so that the computation of $E(u_i|obs)$ can be accomplished directly by probabilistic inference, as shown below.

For each utility node u_i, add a binary child node w_i with the space $\{y, n\}$. This is illustrated in figure 3(b). We associate with w_i the probability distribution $P(w_i|u_i)$ defined as follows:

$$P(w_i = y|u_i = u_{ij}) = w_{ij},$$
$$P(w_i = n|u_i = u_{ij}) = 1 - w_{ij}, \quad (j = 0, 1, ...).$$

The marginal probability of $P(w_i = y)$ is then

$$P(w_i = y|obs) = \sum_j P(w_i = y|u_i = u_{ij}, obs)P(u_i = u_{ij}|obs).$$

Due to the semantics of the network (graphical separation signifies probabilistic conditional independence), we have $P(w_i|u_i, obs) = P(w_i|u_i)$. Therefore, we derive

$$\begin{aligned} P(w_i = y|obs) &= \sum_j P(w_i = y|u_i = u_{ij})P(u_i = u_{ij}|obs) \\ &= \sum_j w_{ij}\ P(u_i = u_{ij}|obs) = E(u_i|obs). \end{aligned}$$

Using the utility network representation, after probabilistic inference, each $E(u_i|obs)$ can be retrieved directly from the node w_i and their aggregation will produce the utility of the meal subplan.

7 Experiment

An experiment was conducted using the concepts presented above. Sixty-four foods were used requiring 62 ingredients. Meals were planned for two users and the Bayesian network contained 515 nodes.

The history of the foods were grouped into time horizons of short, medium and long, refering to a couple of days, a week and a month respectively. The planner correctly determined that the desirability of the food was lower given that the user had consumed the given food recently. Group meals correctly contained the same foods for all users, save the foods that the user could choose on an individual basis.

Changing the groups attitude towards the cost of the meal changed the selected meal plan's composition and overall price. When the group was cost adverse, the foods chosen were more economical but less desirable. When the group was less cost adverse, the planner selected foods that were more desirable but also more expensive. In addition, the variety of foods increased.

Acknowledgements

Support in the form of NSERC PGS-A to the first author and NSERC Reserach Grant to the second author are acknowledged.

References

[1] B. D'Ambrosio. Inference in Bayesian networks. *AI Magazine*, 20(2):21–36, 1999.

[2] J. Pearl. *Probabilistic Reasoning in Intelligent Systems: Networks of Plausible Inference.* Morgan Kaufmann, 1988.

[3] M. L. Puterman. *Markov Decision Processes.* John Wiley, 1994.

[4] S. Russell and P. Norvig. *Artificial Intelligence: A Modern Approach.* Prentice Hall, 1995.

[5] R. Whitehair. *A framework for the analysis of sophisticated control.* PhD thesis, University of Massachusetts, 1996.

[6] Y. Xiang. *Probabilistic Reasoning in Multi-Agent Systems: A Graphical Models Approach.* Cambridge University Press, 2002.

Probabilistic Reasoning in Bayesian Networks: A Relational Database Approach

S. K. Michael Wong, Dan Wu, and Cory J. Butz

Department of Computer Science, University of Regina
Regina Saskatchewan, Canada S4S 0A2

Abstract. Probabilistic reasoning in Bayesian networks is normally conducted on a junction tree by repeatedly applying the local propagation whenever new evidence is observed. In this paper, we suggest to treat probabilistic reasoning as database queries. We adapt a method for answering queries in database theory to the setting of probabilistic reasoning in Bayesian networks. We show an effective method for probabilistic reasoning *without* repeated application of local propagation whenever evidence is observed.

1 Introduction

Bayesian networks [3] have been well established as a model for representing and reasoning with uncertain information using probability. Probabilistic reasoning simply means computing the marginal distribution for a set of variables, or the conditional probability distribution for a set of variables given evidence. A Bayesian network is normally transformed through moralization and triangulation into a junction tree on which the probabilistic reasoning is conducted.

One of the most popular methods for performing probabilistic reasoning is the so-called local propagation method [2]. The local propagation method is applied to the junction tree so that the junction tree reaches a consistent state, i.e., a marginal distribution is associated with each node in the junction tree. Probabilistic reasoning can then be subsequently carried out on this consistent junction tree [2].

In this paper, by exploring the intriguing relationship between Bayesian networks and relational databases [5], we propose a new approach for probabilistic reasoning by treating it as a database query. This new approach has several salient features. (1) It advocates using hypertree instead of junction tree for probabilistic reasoning. By selectively pruning the hypertree, probabilistic reasoning can be performed by employing the local propagation method *once* and can then answer any queries without another application of local propagation. (2) The structure of a fixed junction tree may be favourable to some queries but not to others. By using the hypertree as the secondary structure, we can dynamically prune the hypertree to obtain the best choice for answering each query. (3) Finally, this database perspective of probabilistic reasoning provides ample opportunities for well developed techniques in database theory, especially

Y. Xiang and B. Chaib-draa (Eds.): AI 2003, LNAI 2671, pp. 583–590, 2003.

techniques in query optimization, to be adopted for achieving more efficient probabilistic reasoning in practice.

The paper is organized as follows. We briefly review Bayesian networks and local propagation in Sect. 2. In Sect. 3, we first discuss the relationship between hypertrees and junction trees and the notion of Markov network. We then present our proposed method. We discuss the advantages of the proposed method in Sect. 4. We conclude our paper in Sect. 5.

2 Bayesian Networks and the Local Propagation

We use $U = \{x_1, \ldots, x_n\}$ to represent a set of discrete variables. Each x_i takes values from a finite domain denoted V_{x_i}. We use capital letters such as X to represent a subset of U and its domain is denoted by V_X. By XY we mean $X \cup Y$. We write $x_i = \alpha$, where $\alpha \in V_{x_i}$, to indicate that the variable x_i is instantiated to the value α. Similarly, we write $X = \beta$, where $\beta \in V_X$, to indicate that X is instantiated to the value β. For convenience, we write $p(x_i)$ to represent $p(x_i = \alpha)$ for all $\alpha \in V_{x_i}$. Similarly, we write $p(X)$ to represent $p(X = \beta)$ for all $\beta \in V_X$.

A *Bayesian network* (BN) defined over a set $U = \{x_1, \ldots, x_n\}$ of variables is a tuple $(\mathcal{D}, C)$. The $\mathcal{D}$ is a *directed acyclic graph* (DAG) and the $C = \{p(x_i|pa(x_i)) \mid x_i \in U\}$ is a set of *conditional probability distributions* (CPDs), where $pa(x_i)$ denotes the parents of node x_i in $\mathcal{D}$, such that $p(U) = \prod_{i=1}^{n} p(x_i|pa(x_i))$. This factorization of $p(U)$ is referred to as *BN factorization*. Probabilistic reasoning in a BN means computing $p(X)$ or $p(X|E = e)$, where $X \cap E = \emptyset$, $X \subseteq U$, and $E \subseteq U$. The fact that E is instantiated to e, i.e., $E = e$, is called the *evidence*.

The DAG of a BN is normally transformed through moralization and triangulation into a junction on which the local propagation method is applied [1]. After the local propagation finishes its execution, a marginal distribution is associated with each node in the junction tree. $p(X)$ can be easily computed by identifying a node in the junction tree which contains X and then do a marginalization; the probability of $p(X|E = e)$ can be similarly obtained by first incorporating the evidence $E = e$ into the junction tree and then propagating the evidence so that the junction tree reaches an updated consistent state from which the probability $p(X|E = e)$ can be computed in the same fashion as we compute $p(X)$. It is worth emphasizing that this method for computing $p(X|E = e)$ needs to apply the local propagation procedure every time when new evidence is observed. That is, it involves a lot of computation to keep the knowledge base consistent. It is also worth mentioning that it is not evident how to compute $p(X)$ and $p(X|E = e)$ when X is not a subset of any node in the junction tree [6]. A more formal technical treatment on the local propagation method can be found in [1].

The problem of probabilistic reasoning, i.e., computing $p(X|E = e)$, can then be equivalently stated as computing $p(X, E)$ for the set $X \cup E$ of variables [6]. Henceforth, probabilistic reasoning means computing the marginal distribution $p(W)$ for any subset W of U.

3 Probabilistic Reasoning as Database Queries

In this section, we show that the task of computing $p(X)$ for any arbitrary subset X can be conveniently expressed and solved as database query.

3.1 Hypertrees, Junction Trees, and Markov Networks

A hypergraph is a pair $(\mathbf{N}, \mathcal{H})$, where $\mathbf{N}$ is a finite set of nodes (attributes) and $\mathcal{H}$ is a set of edges (hyperedges) which are arbitrary subsets of $\mathbf{N}$ [4]. If the nodes are understood, we will use $\mathcal{H}$ to denote the hypergraph $(\mathbf{N}, \mathcal{H})$. We say an element h_i in a hypergraph $\mathcal{H}$ is a *twig* if there exists another element h_j in $\mathcal{H}$, distinct from h_i, such that $(\cup(\mathcal{H} - \{h_i\})) \cap h_i = h_i \cap h_j$. We call any such h_j a *branch* for the twig h_i. A hypergraph $\mathcal{H}$ is a *hypertree* [4] if its elements can be ordered, say $h_1, h_2, ..., h_n$, so that h_i is a twig in $\{h_1, h_2, ..., h_i\}$, for $i = 2, ..., n-1$. We call any such ordering a *hypertree (tree) construction ordering* for $\mathcal{H}$. It is noted for a given hypertree, there may exist multiple tree construction orderings. Given a tree construction ordering $h_1, h_2, ..., h_n$, we can choose, for each i from 2 to N, an integer $j(i)$ such that $1 \leq j(i) \leq i-1$ and $h_{j(i)}$ is a branch for h_i in $\{h_1, h_2, ..., h_i\}$. We call a function $j(i)$ that satisfies this condition a *branching* for the hypertree $\mathcal{H}$ with $h_1, h_2, ..., h_n$ being the tree construction ordering. For a given tree construction ordering, there might exist multiple choices of branching functions. Given a tree construction ordering $h_1, h_2, ..., h_n$ for a hypertree $\mathcal{H}$ and a branching function $j(i)$ for this ordering, we can construct the following multiset: $\mathcal{L}(\mathcal{H}) = \{h_{j(2)} \cap h_2, h_{j(3)} \cap h_3, ..., h_{j(n)} \cap h_n\}$. The multiset $\mathcal{L}(\mathcal{H})$ is the same for any tree construction ordering and branching function of $\mathcal{H}$ [4]. We call $\mathcal{L}(\mathcal{H})$ the *separator set* of the hypertree $\mathcal{H}$.

Let $(\mathbf{N}, \mathcal{H})$ be a hypergraph. Its *reduction* $(\mathbf{N}, \mathcal{H}')$ is obtained by removing from $\mathcal{H}$ each hyperedge that is a proper subset of another hyperedge. A hypergraph is *reduced* if it equals its reduction. Let $M \subseteq \mathbf{N}$ be a set of nodes of the hypergraph $(\mathbf{N}, \mathcal{H})$. The *set of partial edges* generated by M is defined to be the reduction of the hypergraph $\{h \cap M \mid h \in \mathcal{H}\}$.

Let $\mathcal{H}$ be a hypertree and X be a set of nodes of $\mathcal{H}$. The set of partial edges generated by X is also a hypertree [7]. A hypergraph $\mathcal{H}$ is a hypertree if and only if its reduction is a hypertree [4]. Henceforth, we will treat each hypergraph as if it is reduced unless otherwise noted.

It has been shown in [4] that given a hypertree, there exists a set of junction trees each of which corresponds to a particular tree construction ordering and a branching function for this ordering. On the other hand, given a junction tree, there always exists a unique corresponding hypertree representation whose hyperedges are the nodes in the junction tree.

Example 1. Consider the hypertree $\mathcal{H}$ shown in Fig 1 (i), it has three corresponding junction trees shown in Fig 1 (ii), (iii) and (iv), respectively. On the other hand, each of the junction trees in Fig 1 (ii), (iii) and (iv) corresponds to the hypertree in Fig 1 (i). The hypertree in Fig 1 (v) will be explained later.

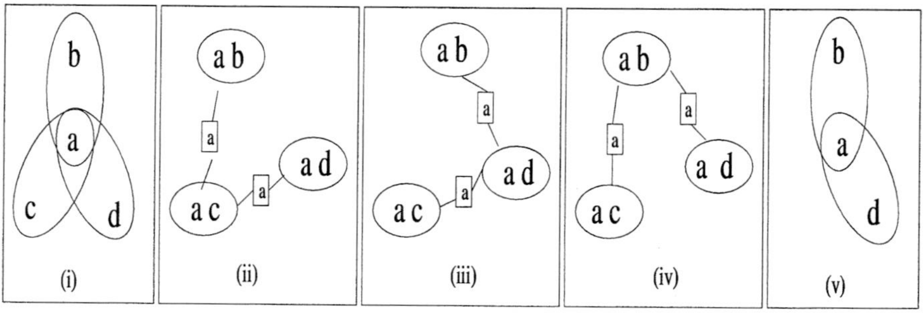

Fig. 1. (i) A hypertree $\mathcal{H}$, and its three possible junction tree representations in (ii), (iii), and (iv). The pruned hypertree with respect to b, d is in (v)

We now introduce the notion of Markov network. A (decomposable) *Markov network* (MN) [3] is a pair $(\mathcal{H},\ P)$, where (a) $\mathcal{H} = \{h_i | i = 1, \ldots, n\}$ is a hypertree defined over variable set U where $U = \bigcup_{h_i \in \mathcal{H}} h_i$ with $h_1, \ \ldots, \ h_n$ as a tree construction ordering and $j(i)$ as the branching function; together with (b) a set $P = \{p(h) \mid h \in \mathcal{H}\}$ of *marginals* of $p(U)$. The conditional independencies encoded in $\mathcal{H}$ mean that the jpd $p(U)$ can be expressed as *Markov factorization*:

$$p(U) = \frac{p(h_1) \cdot p(h_2) \cdot \ldots \cdot p(h_n)}{p(h_2 \cap h_{j(2)}) \cdot \ldots \cdot p(h_n \cap h_{j(n)})}. \tag{1}$$

Recall the local propagation method for BNs in Sect. 2. After finishing the local propagation without any evidence, we have obtained marginals for each node in the junction tree. Since a junction tree corresponds to a unique hypertree, the hypertree and the set of marginals (for each hyperedge) obtained by local propagation together define a Markov network [1].

3.2 An Illustrative Example for Computing $p(X)$

As mentioned before, the probabilistic reasoning can be stated as the problem of computing $p(X)$ where X is an arbitrary set of variables.

Consider a Markov network obtained from a BN by local propagation and let $\mathcal{H}$ be its associated hypertree. It is trivial to compute $p(X)$ if $X \subseteq h$ for some $h \in \mathcal{H}$, as $p(X) = \sum_{h-X} p(h)$. However, it is not evident how to compute $p(X)$ in the case that $X \not\subseteq h$. Using the Markov network obtained by local propagation, we use an example to demonstrate how to compute $p(X)$ for any arbitrary subset $X \subset U$ by selectively pruning the hypertree $\mathcal{H}$.

Example 2. Consider the Markov network whose associated hypertree $\mathcal{H}$ is shown in Fig 1 (i) and its Markov factorization as follows:

$$p(abcd) = \frac{p(ab) \cdot p(ac) \cdot p(ad)}{p(a) \cdot p(a)}. \tag{2}$$

Suppose we want to compute $p(bd)$ where the nodes b and d are not contained by any hyperedge of $\mathcal{H}$. We can compute $p(bd)$ by marginalizing out all the irrelevant variables in the Markov factorization of the jpd $p(abcd)$ in equation (2).

Notice that the numerator $p(ac)$ in equation (2) is the only factor that involves variable c. (Graphically speaking, the node c occurs only in the hyperedge ac). Therefore, we can sum it out as shown below.

$$p(bd) = \sum_{a,\,c} \frac{p(ab)\cdot p(ac)\cdot p(ad)}{p(a)\cdot p(a)} = \sum_{a} \frac{p(ab)\cdot p(ad)}{p(a)\cdot p(a)} \sum_{c} p(ac)$$

$$= \sum_{a} \frac{p(ab)\cdot p(ad)}{p(a)} \cdot \frac{p(a)}{p(a)} = \sum_{a} \frac{p(ab)\cdot p(ad)}{p(a)}. \qquad (3)$$

Note that $\frac{p(ab)\cdot p(ad)}{p(a)} = p(abd)$ and this is a Markov factorization. The above summation process graphically corresponds to deleting the node c from the hypertree $\mathcal{H}$ in Fig 1 (i), which results in the hypertree in Fig 1 (iv). Note that after the variable c has been summed out, there exists $p(a)$ both as a term in the numerator and a term in the denominator. The existence of the denominator term $p(a)$ is due to the fact that a is in $\mathcal{L}(\mathcal{H})$. Obviously, this pair of $p(a)$ can be canceled. Therefore, our original objective of computing $p(bd)$ can now be achieved by working with this "pruned" Markov factorization $p(abd) = \frac{p(ab)\cdot p(ad)}{p(a)}$ whose hypertree is shown in Fig 1 (iv).

3.3 Selectively Pruning the Hypertree of the Markov Network

The method demonstrated in Example 2 can actually be generalized to compute $p(X)$ for any $X \subset U$. In the following, we introduce a method for selectively pruning the hypertree $\mathcal{H}$ associated with a Markov network to the exact portion needed for computing $p(X)$. This method was originally developed in the database theory for answering database queries [7].

Consider a Markov network with its associated hypertree $\mathcal{H}$ and suppose we want to compute $p(X)$. In order to reduce the hypertree $\mathcal{H}$ to the exact portion that facilitates the computation of $p(X)$, we first mark those nodes in X and repeat the following two operations to prune the hypertree $\mathcal{H}$ until neither is applicable: (op1): delete an unmarked node that occurs in only one hyperedge; (op2): delete a hyperedge that is contained in another hyperedge. We use $\mathcal{H}'$ to denote the resulting hypergraph.

Note that the above procedure possesses the Church-Rosser property, that is, the final result $\mathcal{H}'$ is unique, regardless of the order in which (op1) and (op2) are applied [4]. It is also noted that the operators (op1) and (op2) can be implemented in linear time [7]. It is perhaps worth mentioning that (op1) and (op2) are *graphical* operators applying to $\mathcal{H}$. On the other hand, the method in [8] works with BN factorization and it sums out irrelevant variables *numerically*.

Let $\mathcal{H}_0, \mathcal{H}_1, \ldots, \mathcal{H}_j, \ldots, \mathcal{H}_m$ represent the sequence of hypergraphs (not necessarily reduced) in the pruning process, where $\mathcal{H}_0 = \mathcal{H}$, $\mathcal{H}_m = \mathcal{H}'$, $1 \le j \le m$, each $\mathcal{H}_j$ is obtained by applying either (op1) or (op2) to $\mathcal{H}_{j-1}$.

Lemma 1. Each hypergraph $\mathcal{H}_i$, $1 \leq i \leq m$, is a hypertree.

Lemma 2. $\mathcal{L}(\mathcal{H}^{'}) \subseteq \mathcal{L}(\mathcal{H})$.

Due to lack of space, the detailed proofs of the above lemmas and the following theorem will be reported in a separate paper.

For each $h_i^{'} \in \mathcal{H}^{'}$, there exists a $h_j \in \mathcal{H}$ such that $h_i^{'} \subseteq h_j$. We can compute $p(h_i^{'})$ as $p(h_i^{'}) = \sum_{h_j - h_i^{'}} p(h_j)$. In other words, the marginal $p(h_i^{'})$ can be computed from the original marginal $p(h)$ supplied with the Markov network $\mathcal{H}$. Therefore, after selectively pruning $\mathcal{H}$, we have obtained the hypertree $\mathcal{H}^{'}$ and marginals $p(h_i^{'})$ for each $h_i^{'} \in \mathcal{H}^{'}$.

Theorem 1. Let $(\mathcal{H}, P)$ be a Markov network. Let $\mathcal{H}^{'}$ be the resulting pruned hypertree with respect to a set X of variables. The hypertree $\mathcal{H}^{'} = \{h_1^{'}, h_2^{'}, \ldots, h_k^{'}\}$ and the set $P^{'} = \{p(h_i^{'}) \mid 1 \leq i \leq k\}$ of marginals define a Markov network.

Theorem 1 indicates that the original problem of computing $p(X)$ can now be answered by the new Markov network defined by the pruned hypertree $\mathcal{H}^{'}$. It has been proposed [5] that each marginal $p(h)$ where $h \in \mathcal{H}$ can be stored as a relation in the database fashion. Moreover, computing $p(X)$ from $\mathcal{H}^{'}$ can be implemented by database SQL statements [5]. It is noted that the result of applying (op1) and (op2) to $\mathcal{H}$ always yields a Markov network which is different than the method in [8].

4 Advantages

One salient feature of the proposed method is that it does not require any repeated application of local propagation. Since the problem of computing $p(X|E = e)$ can be equivalently reduced to the problem of computing $p(X, E)$, we can uniformly treat probabilistic reasoning as merely computing marginal distributions. Moreover, computing a marginal distribution, say, $p(W)$, from the jpd $p(U)$ defined by a BN, can be accomplished by working with the Markov factorization of $p(U)$, whose establishment only needs applying the local propagation method once on the junction tree constructed from the BN. It is worth mentioning that Xu in [6] reached the same conclusion and proved a theorem similar to Theorem 1 based on the local propagation technique on the junction tree.

Computing $p(W)$ in our proposed approach needs to prune the hypertree $\mathcal{H}$ to the exact portion needed for computing $p(W)$ as Example 2 demonstrates if $W \not\subseteq h$ for any $h \in \mathcal{H}$. A similar method was suggested in [6] by pruning the junction tree instead. Using hypertrees as the secondary structure instead of junction trees has valuable advantages as the following example shows.

Example 3. Consider the hypertree $\mathcal{H}$ shown in Fig 1 (i), it has three corresponding junction trees shown in Fig 1 (ii), (iii) and (iv), respectively. The method in [6] first fixes a junction tree, for example, say the one in Fig 1 (ii). Suppose we need to compute $p(bd)$, the method in [6] will prune the junction tree so that any irrelevant nodes will be removed as we do for pruning hypertree. However, in this junction tree, nothing can be pruned out according to [6]. In other words, $p(bd)$ *has* to be obtained by the following calculation: $p(bd) = \sum_a \frac{p(ab)}{p(a)} \cdot \sum_c \frac{p(ac) \cdot p(ad)}{p(a)}$. However, if we prune the hypertree in Fig 1 (i), the resulting pruned hypertree is shown in Fig 1 (v), from which $p(bd)$ can be obtained by equation (3). Obviously, the computation involved is much less. Observing this, one might decide to adopt the junction tree in Fig 1 (iii) as the secondary structure. This change facilitates the computation of $p(bd)$. However, in a similar fashion, one can easily be convinced that computing $p(bc)$ using the junction tree in (iii), computing $p(cd)$ using the junction tree in (iv) suffer exactly the same problem as computing $p(bd)$ using junction tree in (ii). In other words, regardless of the junction tree fixed in advance, there always exists some queries that are not favored by the pre-determined junction tree structure. On the other hand, the hypertree structure always provides the optimal pruning result for computing marginal [7].

5 Conclusion

In this paper, we have suggested a new approach for conducting probabilistic reasoning from the relational database perspective. We demonstrated how to selectively reduce the hypertree structure so that we can avoid repeated application of local propagation. This suggests a possible dual purposes database management systems for both database storage, retrieval and probabilistic reasoning.

Acknowledgement

The authors would like to thank one of the reviewers for his/her helpful suggestions and comments.

References

[1] C. Huang and A. Darwiche. Inference in belief networks: A procedural guide. *International Journal of Approximate Reasoning*, 15(3):225–263, October 1996.

[2] S. L. Lauritzen and D. J. Spiegelhalter. Local computation with probabilities on graphical structures and their application to expert systems. *Journal of the Royal Statistical Society*, 50:157–244, 1988.

[3] J. Pearl. *Probabilistic Reasoning in Intelligent Systems: Networks of Plausible Inference.* Morgan Kaufmann Publishers, San Francisco, California, 1988.

[4] G. Shafer. An axiomatic study of computation in hypertrees. School of Business Working Papers 232, University of Kansas, 1991.

[5] S. K. M. Wong, C. J. Butz, and Y. Xiang. A method for implementing a probabilistic model as a relational database. In *Eleventh Conference on Uncertainty in Artificial Intelligence*, pages 556–564. Morgan Kaufmann Publishers, 1995.

[6] H. Xu. Computing marginals for arbitrary subsets from marginal representation in markov trees. *Artificial Intelligence*, 74:177–189, 1995.
[7] Mihalis Yannakakis. Algorithms for acyclic database schemes. In *Very Large Data Bases, 7th International Conference, September 9-11, 1981, Cannes, France, Proceedings*, pages 82–94, 1981.
[8] N. Zhang and Poole.D. Exploiting causal independence in bayesian network inference. *Journal of Artificial Intelligence Research*, 5:301–328, 1996.

A Fundamental Issue of Naive Bayes

Harry Zhang[1] and Charles X. Ling[2]

[1] Faculty of Computer Science
University of New Brunswick
Fredericton, New Brunswick, Canada E3B 5A3
hzhang@unb.ca
[2] Department of Computer Science
The University of Western Ontario
London, Ontario, Canada N6A 5B7
ling@csd.uwo.ca

Abstract. Naive Bayes is one of the most efficient and effective inductive learning algorithms for machine learning and data mining. But the conditional independence assumption on which it is based, is rarely true in real-world applications. Researchers extended naive Bayes to represent dependence explicitly, and proposed related learning algorithms based on dependence. In this paper, we argue that, from the classification point of view, dependence distribution plays a crucial role, rather than dependence. We propose a novel explanation on the superb classification performance of naive Bayes. To verify our idea, we design and conduct experiments by extending the *ChowLiu* algorithm to use the dependence distribution to construct TAN, instead of using mutual information that only reflects the dependencies among attributes. The empirical results provide evidences to support our new explanation.

1 Introduction

Classification is a fundamental issue in machine learning and data mining. In classification, the goal of a learning algorithm is to construct a classifier given a set of training examples with class labels. Typically, an example E is represented by a tuple of attribute values $(a_1, a_2, , \cdots, a_n)$, where a_i is the value of attribute A_i. Let C represent the classification variable which takes value $+$ or $-$.

A classifier is a function that assigns a class label to an example. From the probability perspective, according to Bayes Rule, the probability of an example $E = (a_1, a_2, \cdots, a_n)$ being class C is

$$p(C|E) = \frac{p(E|C)p(C)}{p(E)}.$$

Assume that all attributes are independent given the value of the class variable (conditional independence), we obtain a classifier $g(E)$, called a naive Bayesian classifier, or simply naive Bayes (NB).

$$g(E) = \frac{p(C=+)}{p(C=-)} \prod_{i=1}^{n} \frac{p(a_i|C=+)}{p(a_i|C=-)}. \tag{1}$$

Y. Xiang and B. Chaib-draa (Eds.): AI 2003, LNAI 2671, pp. 591–595, 2003.

It is obvious that the conditional independence assumption is rarely true in most real-world applications. A straightforward approach to overcome the limitation of naive Bayes is to extend its structure to represent explicitly the dependencies among attributes. Tree augmented naive Bayes (TAN) is an extended tree-like naive Bayes [3], in which an attribute node can have only one parent from another attribute node. Algorithms for learning TAN have been proposed, in which detecting dependences among attributes is a major approach. The *Chowliu* algorithm is a popular one based on dependence [1, 3], illustrated below.

1. Compute $I(A_i, A_j|C)$ between each pair of attributes, $i \neq j$.
2. Build a complete undirected graph in which the nodes are the attributes A_1, $\cdots$, A_n. Annotate the weight of an edge connecting A_i to A_j by $I(A_i, A_j|C)$.
3. Build a maximum weighted spanning tree.
4. Transform the resulting undirected tree to a directed one by choosing a root attribute and setting the direction of all edges to be outward from it.
5. Construct a TAN model by adding a node labeled by C and adding an arc from C to each A_i.

Essentially, the *ChowLiu* algorithm for learning TAN is based-on the conditional mutual information $I(A_i, A_j|C)$.

$$I(A_i, A_j|C) = \sum_{A_i, A_j, C} P(A_i, A_j, C) ln \frac{P(A_i, A_j|C)}{P(A_i|C)P(A_j|C)} \tag{2}$$

2 A New Explanation on the Classification Performance of Naive Bayes

2.1 Learning TAN Based on Dependence Distribution

When we look at the essence of the *ChowLiu* algorithm, we find that Equation 2 reflects the dependences between two attributes. We can transform the form of $I(A_i, A_j|C)$ to an equivalent equation below.

$$I(A_i, A_j|C) = \sum_{A_i, A_j} (P(A_i, A_j, +) ln \frac{P(A_i|A_j, +)}{P(A_i|+)} + P(A_i, A_j, -) ln \frac{P(A_i|A_j, -)}{P(A_i|-)}) \tag{3}$$

A question arises when you think of the meaning of $I(A_i, A_j|C)$. When

$$\frac{P(A_i|A_j, +)}{P(A_i|+)} > 1$$

and

$$\frac{P(A_i|A_j, -)}{P(A_i|-)} < 1,$$

intuitively, the dependencies between A_i and A_j in both class + and − support classifying E into class +. Thus, both evidences support classifying E into class +. Therefore, from the viewpoint of classification, the information association between A_i and A_j should be the sum of them, but they actually cancel each other in Equation 3. Similarly, when

$$\frac{P(A_i|A_j,+)}{P(A_i|+)} > 1$$

and

$$\frac{P(A_i|A_j,-)}{P(A_i|-)} > 1,$$

the two evidences support different classifications. Thus, in terms of classification, they should cancel each other out, but Equation 3 reflects the opposite fact. That reminds us that we should pay more attention to dependence distribution; i.e., how the dependencies among attributes distribute in two classes.

We modify $I(A_i, A_j|C)$ and obtain a conditional mutual information as below.

$$I_D(A_i, A_j|C) = \sum_{A_i,A_j} P(A_i, A_j)(ln\frac{P(A_i|A_j,+)}{P(A_i|+)} - ln\frac{P(A_i|A_j,-)}{P(A_i|-)})^2 \tag{4}$$

Actually, $I_D(A_i, A_j|C)$ represents the dependence distribution of A_i or A_j in two classes, which reflects the influence of the dependence between A_i and A_j on classification. From the above discussion, it is more reasonable to use dependence distribution to construct a classifier, rather than dependence.

We propose an extended *ChowLiu* algorithm for learning TAN, in which $I(A_i, A_j|C)$ is replaced by $I_D(A_i, A_j|C)$. We call this algorithm *ddr-ChowLiu*.

We have conducted empirical experiments to compare our *ddr-ChowLiu* algorithm to the *ChowLiu* algorithm. We use twelve datasets from the UCI repository [4] to conduct our experiments. Table 1 lists the properties of the datasets we use in our experiments.

Our experiments follow the procedure below:

1. The continuous attributes in the dataset are discretized by the entropy-based method.
2. For each dataset, run *ChowLiu* and *ddr-ChowLiu* with the 5-fold cross-validation, and obtain the classification accuracy on the testing set unused in the training.
3. Repeat 2 above 20 times and calculate the average classification accuracy on the testing data.

Table 2 shows the experimental results of average classification accuracies of *ChowLiu* and *ddr-ChowLiu*. We conduct an unpaired two-tailed t-test by using 95% as the confidence level and the better one for a given dataset is reported in bold. Table 2 shows that *ddr-ChowLiu* outperforms *ChowLiu* in five datasets, losses in three datasets, and ties in four datasets. Overall, the experimental results show that *ddr-ChowLiu* outperforms slightly *ChowLiu*. Therefore, if we use

Table 1. Description of the datasets used in the experiments of comparing the *ddr-ChowLiu* algorithm to the *Chowliu* algorithm

Dataset	Attributes	Class	Instances
Australia	14	2	690
breast	10	10	683
cars	7	2	700
dermatology	34	6	366
ecoli	7	8	336
hepatitis	4	2	320
import	24	2	204
iris	5	3	150
pima	8	2	392
segment	19	7	2310
vehicle	18	4	846
vote	16	2	232

Table 2. Experimental results of the accuracies of *ChowLiu* and *ddr-ChowLiu*

Dataset	***ChowLiu***	***ddr-ChowLiu***
Australia	**76.7±0.32**	76.1±0.33
breast	73.3±0.37	73.3±0.33
cars	85.4±0.37	**87.1±0.28**
dermatology	97.7±0.17	97.7±0.17
ecoli	**96.1±0.23**	95.8±0.20
hepatitis	70.5±0.42	70.5±0.51
import	93.6±0.37	**95.6±0.34**
iris	91.2±0.48	91.3±0.50
pima	70.5±0.46	**71.8±0.51**
segment	82.3±0.17	**82.4±0.16**
vehicle	**89.3±0.23**	85.7±0.30
vote	78.6±0.61	**79.1±0.53**

directly dependence distribution, instead of using dependence, it will result in a better classifier. Further, this experiment provides evidence that it is dependence distribution that determines classification, not dependence itself.

2.2 A Novel Explanation for Naive Bayes

From Section 2.1, we observed that how dependence distributes in two classes determines classification, and the empirical experimental results provided evidence to support our claim. In fact, we can generalize this observation. In a given dataset, two attributes may depend on each other, but the dependence may distribute evenly in each class. Clearly, in this case, the conditional independence assumption is violated, but naive Bayes is still the optimal classifier. Further, what eventually affects classification is the combination of dependencies among

all attributes. If we just look at two attributes, there may exist strong dependence between them that affects classification. When the dependencies among all attributes work together, however, they may cancel each other out and no longer affect classification. Therefore, we argue that it is distribution of dependencies among all attributes over classes that affects classification of naive Bayes, not merely dependencies themselves. This explains why naive Bayes still works well on the datasets in which strong dependencies among attributes do exist [2].

3 Conclusions

In this paper, we investigated the *Chowliu* algorithm and proposed an extended algorithm for learning TAN that is based on dependence distribution, rather than dependence. The experimental results showed that the new algorithm outperforms the *Chowliu* algorithm. We generalized that observation, and proposed a new explanation on the classification performance of naive Bayes. We argue that, essentially, the dependence distribution; i.e., how the local dependence of an attribute distributes in two classes, evenly or unevenly, and how the local dependencies of all attributes work together, consistently (support a certain classification) or inconsistently (cancel each other out), plays a crucial role in classification. We explain why even with strong dependencies, naive Bayes still works well; i.e., when those dependencies cancel each other out, there is no influence on classification. In this case, naive Bayes is still the optimal classifier.

References

[1] Chow, C. K., Liu, C. N.: Approximating Discrete Probability Distributions with Dependence Trees. IEEE Trans. on Information Theory, Vol. 14 (1968), 462–467.

[2] Domingos P., Pazzani M.: Beyond Independence: Conditions for the Optimality of the Simple Bayesian Classifier. Machine Learning **29** (1997) 103-130

[3] Friedman, N., Geiger, D., Goldszmidt, M.: Bayesian Network Classifiers. Machine Learning, Vol: 29 (1997), 131–163.

[4] Merz, C., Murphy, P., Aha, D.: UCI Repository of Machine Learning Databases. In: Dept of ICS, University of California, Irvine (1997). http://www.www.ics.uci.edu/mlearn/MLRepository.html.

The Virtual Driving Instructor Creating Awareness in a Multiagent System

Ivo Weevers[1], Jorrit Kuipers[2], Arnd O. Brugman[2],
Job Zwiers[1], Elisabeth M. A. G. van Dijk[1], and Anton Nijholt[1]

[1] University of Twente, Enschede, the Netherlands
i.weevers@tm.tue.nl
{zwiers,bvdijk,anijholt}@cs.utwente.nl
[2] Green Dino Virtual Realities, Wageningen, the Netherlands
{jorrit,arnd}@greendino.nl

Abstract. Driving simulators need an Intelligent Tutoring System (ITS). Simulators provide ways to conduct objective measurements on students' driving behavior and opportunities for creating the best possible learning environment. The generated traffic situations can be influenced directly according to the needs of the student. We created an ITS - the Virtual Driving Instructor (VDI) - for guiding the learning process of driving. The VDI is a multiagent system that provides low cost and integrated controlling functionality to tutor students and create the best training situations.

1 Introduction

Driving simulators, such as the Dutch Driving Simulator developed by Green Dino Virtual Realities, offer great opportunities to create an environment in which novice drivers learn to control and drive a car in traffic situations. Although simulators still show some problems, such as simulator sickness [1], their main advantages are the objective measurements that can be carried out on the user's driving behavior and the creation of situations that suits the current student's skill level.

Driving instructors guide the students individually in acquiring the complex skills to become a proficient driver. In driving simulators, a student needs also this guidance. Since a simulator is capable of measuring the driving behavior objectively, the integration of an intelligent tutoring system with the driving simulator becomes a cheap and innovative educational technique. Accordingly, the system will evaluate the driving behavior in real-time and adapt the simulated environment to the student's needs, and a human driving instructor does not need to assist the student most of the time. In this paper, we present the Virtual Driving Instructor (VDI) - an intelligent tutoring multiagent system that recognizes and evaluates driving behavior within a given context using a hybrid combination of technologies. We will discuss driving education, awareness as the design principle for the system, and the architecture of the system.

Y. Xiang and B. Chaib-draa (Eds.): AI 2003, LNAI 2671, pp. 596-602, 2003.

2 Driving Education and Instruction

Driving involves carrying out driving tasks that suit the current situation. Driving education focuses on learning these tasks. Michon [2] discerned three driving task levels: strategic (route planning, higher goal selection), tactical (short-term objectives, such as overtaking and crossing an intersection) and operational (basic tasks, such as steering and using the clutch). McKnight and Adams [3] conducted an extensive task analysis on driving. Since this listing also includes tasks at all three levels, we used this listing for embedding driving knowledge into the VDI. Driving education not only implies knowing how to execute driving tasks, but also involves the evaluation and feedback processes. We carried out a two days empirical research on the practical experience of professional driving instructors at the Dutch national police school. This research provided insights into instruction aspects, such as feedback timing and the formulation of utterances. The most important results were that (1) the feedback usually is positively expressed; (2) that the student is being prepared for approaching complex situations by feedback; and (3) that the instructor mainly focuses on the aspects the exercise is meant for.

2.1 Awareness in Education

One of our design questions concerned the knowledge of the instructor. For several reasons it is important that the instructor has different types of common and specific knowledge. There has to be a mutual understanding between teacher and student, the instructor should know how to drive, how to apply a driving curriculum, and so on.

A driving instructor needs to possess situational awareness for a good understanding of and application of expert knowledge in traffic situations. In addition, driving instruction involves more than only situational awareness and therefore we defined more awareness types. According to Smiley and Michon [5], awareness is the domain-specific understanding to achieve goals for this domain. This definition shows that an instructor should not only have knowledge for different driving education aspects, but also has to be aware of achieving goals within those knowledge domains. Probably the most important is situational awareness; the VDI needs to recognize and evaluate the student's driving behavior in relation to the current situation. Subsequently, the VDI determines the best piece of advice for this behavior and presents it to the student. We decided to divide this knowledge into two awareness types: First, the adviser awareness concerns the feedback directly related to the situation element or driving task on which the feedback is generated. Second, the presentation awareness relates to the context in which the feedback may be provided. This context depends on former feedback, the current situation and the student. Third, we identified curriculum awareness for dealing with the structure and management of the driving program. We used the different awareness types for the design. The situational, adviser and presentation awareness types include the VDI's core functionality. We chose to add curriculum awareness, since the recent introduction of the new standard for the new Dutch driving program the RIS (Driving Education in Steps) makes the integration of this aspect attractive to the market.

3 Developing the Multiagent System

A recent approach to the design of intelligent tutoring systems is the multiagent system. We developed an agent for each awareness type: The Situation Agent implements situational awareness, the Presentation Agent implements presentation awareness and the Curriculum Agent implements curriculum awareness. The VDI's application domain is complex, unpredictable and uncertain. By using agents, we modularize the functionality of the design. In this way, the design becomes more flexible, easily changeable and extendible. The agents need to communicate for realizing intelligent tutoring behavior. We divided the agent's design into two layers. The communication layer deals with the communication with other agents. The agent layer implements the specific agent functionality and therefore differs for each agent.

3.1 Understanding and Evaluating the Situation and Driving Behavior

Situational awareness, as defined by Sukthankar [6], is one of the most fundamental awareness types for realizing the VDI. It involves recognition and evaluation of the driving behavior and the corresponding situation. Since both processes are closely related, we decided to combine them into one awareness type and thus into one agent: the Situation Agent. The VDI needs to perform a driving task and situation analysis. The VDI is only capable of accomplishing this when it knows the feasible driving tasks and situation elements. Sukthankar [6] decomposed these elements into three groups, which are (1) the road state, (2) traffic, speeds, relative positions and hypothesized intentions, and (3) the driver's self state. Since the groups concern only the situation and not driving tasks, we extended the knowledge of the driver's self state with these driving tasks. We used the task analysis conducted by McKnight and Adams [3], which is probably the most extensive driving task listing, for this purpose. Although the descriptions in the listing are sometimes too vague to express computationally, we used some empirically based parameters to apply to the description. By integrating the listing's tasks with the situational elements, we created relations amongst the elements and tasks. These are needed to understand the contextual coherence in the situation. We decided to integrate a continuous, dynamic and static driving task within the first analysis functionality to show that our design principle works for different situation types. We selected for speed control, car following and intersections.

Tree-like structures, as shown in figure 1, suit the integration of driving tasks with the situation elements. We adopted this idea from Decision Support Systems, which use the knowledge-based approach to declare the task structure. By defining the several tasks as different nodes in the structure, these tasks can be addressed separately. The nodes also represent the situation elements. When a situation element is present in the current situation or the student carries out a driving task, the corresponding node becomes active. Vice versa, when the element or task does not apply for the situation anymore, the node will be deactivated. The VDI recognizes the current situation and driving tasks by the activity status of the tree nodes. The VDI then is capable of generating rational feedback, since the structure allows evaluating whether the student performed or should have performed certain driving tasks in relation to the situation.

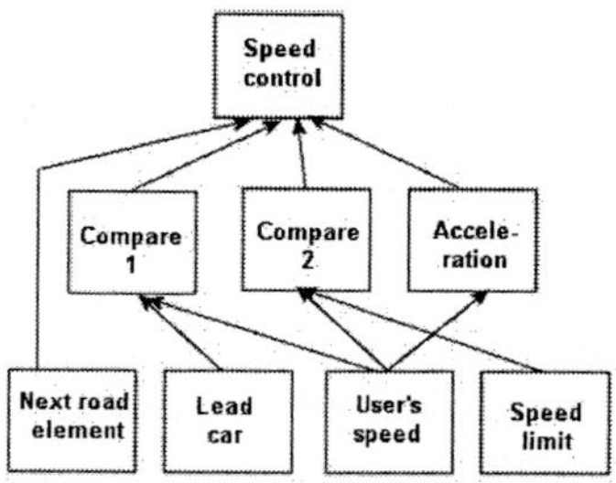

Fig. 1. Tree structure for speed control and car following

No matter what situation, a driver should always maintain an acceptable speed. The speed depends on current situational elements. We integrated some influencing situational elements that often occur in the simulator situations. These are the speed limit, acceleration or deceleration, turning intentions and the lead car's presence. Figure 1 shows the tree-like structure that combines the situation elements and driving tasks.

We discuss the structure by the components:

1. Next road element: Checks the next road element type.
2. Lead car: Checks whether there is a car in front of the driver.
3. User's speed: Determines the driver's speed. Speed limit: Determines the allowed speed for the current road.
4. Compare-1: Compares the user's speed to the distance to the lead car.
5. Compare-2: Compares the user's speed to the speed limit.
6. Acceleration: Checks whether the student is accelerating or slowing down.
7. Speed control: Determines which situational elements to consider as most important for the current situation.

We used arrows to indicate that one component (the speaker) might tell the other component (the listener) that its activity has changed. This speaker-listener principle - an event mechanism -has two advantages: (1) the speaker does not know what components are its listeners. In this way, the tree can be extended or changed easily, mostly without changing functionality of other parts of the tree. (2) The speaker only notifies its listeners when its activity state has changed. Therefore, the statuses of the components need not to be conveyed every update cycle, which will benefit the overall performance.

In all situations, the speed control component uses the compare-2 component for evaluating the user's speed in relation to the speed limit. However, in case there is a lead car (which is shown by the activity of the relating component) the relation of the user's speed to the lead car's distance is usually more important. Therefore, the VDI also considers the acceleration or deceleration by the student before evaluating the relation to the speed limit. By changing the speed, the student may be trying to achieve a higher or slower speed.

After the VDI conducted the recognition process for a given situation, the uppermost active component in the tree initiates the evaluation process. It coordinates the process by telling its speakers when to start their evaluation process. Subsequently, those speakers start their own evaluation process. In this case, the speed control component tells the compare-2 component (Figure 1) to evaluate, because the compare-2 component is active. If the compare-1 component is also active - because of an active lead car component - the speed control also tells that component to start evaluating.

Adviser Awareness Adviser awareness is embedded into the tree components. Each component evaluates a driving task or situation element and decides if it is important to provide feedback on that task or element. It measures the performance for that task by the current level and the progress, which both are classified in a local 'level x progress' matrix. The component calculates the level by using the deviation between the range of best values and the student's value. It determines the progress by comparing a range of previous levels and the current level. The matrix holds records for each field that maintain how much feedback is actually provided to the student on the specific component's status (level and progress). In this way, comments on a component can be chosen carefully with respect to a former status.

Each component may provide and time advice that is related to the driving task or situation element. After a component determines which piece of advice is currently needed, it passes it to its listeners. Some components receive pieces of advice from different speakers at the same moment. Since only one piece of advice can be provided at the same time, that component uses several methods to decide amongst those pieces of advice. First, predefined parameters assign the components a priority, which it uses to classify the pieces of advice. Second, the component knows the activities of the speakers' components and uses a simple rule-based choice algorithm to identify the most important piece of advice in case of a given component activity structure. A piece of advice is passed up through the tree. The highest coordinating component finally has the last judgment for the pieces of advice and puts forward the best overall piece of advice.

Evaluation Phases A major difference between different trees is the duration. Speed control applies all the time, while an intersection is a periodic event. We decompose the latter events into three phases: the motivating, mentoring and the correcting phase. The VDI uses the motivating phase to prepare the student for approaching the situation. This may be an introduction or a reminder of former task performances. The mentoring phase deals with evaluating the task behavior while the student is conducting that task. The correcting phase evaluates the task performances afterwards. This evaluation may be in the short term - how did the student perform the task this time - as well as in the long term - how does the last performance compare to previous performances.

A Hybrid Tree Structure Most tree components that recognize the presence of situational elements are straightforward, such as a lead car. However, the VDI also has to be capable of recognizing elements or driving tasks that are more vague, unpredictable and uncertain. For example, the other road user's intentions influence the situation intensively. These events are not easily captured by some parameters and depend on a variety of fuzzy data. Neural networks probably will help to guess such intentions. We can easily integrate another technique - such as a neural network - into the tree by creating a component that implements the technique internally, but externally works according to the speakers-listeners principle. This will result in a hybrid tree with the most suitable techniques for the related situational elements and driving tasks.

3.2 Contextual Adaptive Presentation of Feedback

Presentation awareness concerns the provision of natural feedback. This involves formulating natural utterances and timing the utterances both naturally and educationally. We implemented this awareness by creating the Presentation Agent. This agent receives advice information about what to present from the Situation Agent. The Presentation Agent schedules, formulates and presents the feedback. Scheduling involves ordering different pieces of advice according to their priority and possibly ignoring them if they are outdated. Furthermore, it decides on the timing of the next piece of advice. For example, pieces of advice should not follow each other too quickly, since this will cause an information overload to the student. However, when the piece of advice is about dangerous behavior, the VDI has to tell that right away. Scheduling also depends on the phase - motivation, mentor or correction - of the situation elements or driving task. Since the mentor phase concerns the current context, which may change immediately, feedback in this phase should not be delayed. However, feedback in the motivation and correction phase may be provided within a short time range.

4 A Flexible Architecture

One of the main design principles was to design a system that uses a flexible architecture, such that future changes and extensions can be carried out without changing the VDI's basis. The multiagent approach in combination with our common communication channel realizes this flexibility. Existing functionality may be changed or extended, which only causes internal agent adjustment. New functionality can be added by adding new agents. Another opportunity within the current architecture is to develop an instructor for another application domain. Apart from adaptations to the simulator, we can create a motorcycle instructor by adjusting and replacing some agents. The driving tasks almost equal those of car driving, except for operational tasks. This also counts for the driving curriculum. These aspects require some adjustments. Student awareness creates a student profile and can probably be reused. Another application domain of the VDI may be another country. Apart from adapting the language, traffic rules and driving program, nothing needs to be changed.

5 Conclusions

We have presented the Virtual Driving Instructor, a multiagent system that realizes different awareness types in order to create an intelligent learning environment. It achieves different learning objectives and provides ways for an adaptive teacher-student relationship. We used a flexible and easily extendible architecture for integrating the awareness types by agents.

We created situational awareness. The VDI conducts driving behavior analyses with respect to the current situation. It recognizes and evaluates speed control, car following and intersection. Within the three evaluation phases, motivation, mentor and correction, it provides feedback on the level and progress of the student's performances. We created a tree structure that follows a speaker-listener principle. Dependency is reduced in this way, which benefits the process of changing or extending the tree structure.

With adviser awareness, we added advice knowledge that depends on a situation element or driving task. It deals with relating the piece of advice to the current level and progress of the student's performance. We developed presentation awareness to make feedback provision context aware, well-timed and with adaptive expression.

Finally, we added curriculum awareness to the system. It implements elements of the new Dutch standard for driving curricula, relating to the driving tasks, which the Situation agent evaluates. It saves the current student's performance.

The first results are promising. The provided feedback has a high contextual dependency and we achieved the integration of important driving educational aspects. These include different phases of feedback provision, priority classification for tree components in a given situation and the use of a driving program.

Acknowledgements

We thank Rob van Egmond and Ronald Docter of the Dutch national police driving school, LSOP, for their support with the research. We would also like to thank the colleagues of Green Dino Virtual Realities.

References

[1] Casali, J.G. Vehicular simulation-induced sickness, Volume 1: An overview. IEOR, Technical report No. 8501, Orlando, USA (1986)

[2] Michon, J. A critical view of driver behavior models: What do we know, what should we do?. In Evans, L., and Schwing, R. (eds.), Human Behavior and Traffic Safety, Plemum (1985)

[3] McKnight, J., Adams, B. Driver education and task analysis volume 1: Task descriptions. Technical report, Department of Transportation, National Highway Safety Bureau (1970)

[4] Pentland, A., Liu, A. Towards augmented control systems. In Proceedings of IEEE Intelligent Vehicles (1995)

[5] Smiley, A. and Michon J.A. Conceptual framework for generic intelligent driving support. Deliverable GIDS/I, Haren, The Netherlands, Traffic Safety Centre (1989)

[6] Sukthankar, R. Situational awareness for tactical driving. Robotics Institute, Carnegie Mellon University, Pittsburgh, PA (1997)

Multi-attribute Exchange Market: Theory and Experiments

Eugene Fink, Josh Johnson, and John Hershberger

Computer Science, University of South Florida
Tampa, Florida 33620, USA
{eugene,jhershbe}@csee.usf.edu
joshjohnson@cfl.rr.com

Abstract. The Internet has opened opportunities for efficient on-line trading, and researchers have developed algorithms for various auctions, as well as exchanges for standardized commodities; however, they have done little work on exchanges for complex nonstandard goods. We propose a formal model for trading complex goods, present an exchange system that allows traders to describe purchases and sales by multiple attributes, and give the results of applying it to a used-car market and corporate-bond market.

1 Introduction

The growth of the Internet has led to the development of on-line markets, which include bulletin boards, auctions, and exchanges. Bulletin boards help buyers and sellers find each other, but they often require customers to invest significant time into reading multiple ads, and many buyers prefer on-line auctions, such as eBay (www.ebay.com). Auctions have their own problems, including high computational costs, lack of liquidity, and asymmetry between buyers and sellers. Exchange markets support fast-paced trading and ensure symmetry between buyers and sellers, but they require rigid standardization of tradable items. For example, the New York Stock Exchange allows trading of about 3,000 stocks, and a buyer or seller has to indicate a specific stock. For most goods, the description of a desirable trade is more complex. An exchange for nonstandard goods should allow the use of multiple attributes in specifications of buy and sell orders.

Economists and computer scientists have long realized the importance of auctions and exchanges, and studied a variety of trading models. The related computer science research has led to successful Internet auctions, such as eBay (www.ebay.com) and Yahoo Auctions (auctions.yahoo.com), as well as on-line exchanges, such as Island (www.island.com) and NexTrade (www.nextrade.org). Recently, researchers have developed efficient systems for combinatorial auctions, which allow buying and selling sets of commodities rather than individual items [1, 2, 7, 8, 9, 10]. Computer scientists have also studied exchange markets; in particular, Wurman, Walsh, and Wellman built a general-purpose system for auctions and exchanges [11], Sandholm and Suri developed an exchange

Y. Xiang and B. Chaib-draa (Eds.): AI 2003, LNAI 2671, pp. 603–610, 2003.

for combinatorial orders [9], and Kalagnanam, Davenport, and Lee investigated techniques for placing orders with complex constraints [6].

A recent project at the University of South Florida has been aimed at building an automated exchange for complex goods [3, 4, 5]. We have developed a system that supports large-scale exchanges for commodities described by multiple attributes. We give a formal model of a multi-attribute exchange (Sections 2 and 3), describe the developed system (Section 4), and show how its performance depends on the market size (Section 5).

2 General Exchange Model

We begin with an example of a multi-attribute market, and then define orders and matches between them.

Example. We consider an exchange for trading new and used cars. To simplify this example, we assume that a trader can describe a car by four attributes: model, color, year, and mileage. A prospective buyer can place a *buy order,* which includes a description of a desired car and a maximal acceptable price; for instance, she may indicate that she wants a red Mustang, made after 2000, with less than 20,000 miles, and she is willing to pay $19,000. Similarly, a seller can place a *sell order;* for example, a dealer may offer a brand-new Mustang of any color for $18,000. An exchange system must generate trades that satisfy both buyers and sellers; in the previous example, it must determine that a brand-new red Mustang for $18,500 satisfies the buyer and dealer.

Orders. When a trader makes a purchase or sale, she has to specify a set of acceptable items, denoted I, which stands for *item set.* In addition, a trader should specify a limit on the acceptable price, which is a real-valued function on the set I; for each item $i \in I$, it gives a certain limit $Price(i)$. For a buyer, $Price(i)$ is the maximal acceptable price; for a seller, it is the minimal acceptable price. If a trader wants to buy or sell several identical items, she can include their number in the order specification, which is called an *order size.* She can specify not only an overall order size, but also a minimal acceptable size. For instance, suppose that a Ford wholesale agent is selling one hundred cars, and she works only with dealerships that are buying at least ten cars. Then, she may specify that the overall size of her order is one hundred, and the minimal size is ten.

Fills. An order specification includes an item set I, price function $Price$, overall order size Max, and minimal acceptable size Min. When a buy order matches a sell order, the corresponding parties can complete a trade; we use the term *fill* to refer to the traded items and their price. We define a fill by a specific item i, its price p, and the number of purchased items, denoted *size.* If $(I_b, Price_b, Max_b, Min_b)$ is a buy order, and $(I_s, Price_s, Max_s, Min_s)$ is a matching sell order, then a fill must satisfy the following conditions:

1. $i \in I_b \cap I_s$.
2. $Price_s(i) \leq p \leq Price_b(i)$.
3. $\max(Min_b, Min_s) \leq size \leq \min(Max_b, Max_s)$.

3 Order Representation

We next describe the representation of orders in the developed exchange system.

Market Attributes. A specific market includes a certain set of items that can be bought and sold, defined by a list of attributes. As a simplified example, we describe a car by four attributes: model, color, year, and mileage. An attribute may be a set of explicitly listed values, such as the car model; an interval of integers, such as the year; or an interval of real values, such as the mileage.

Cartesian Products. When a trader places an order, she has to specify some set I_1 of acceptable values for the first attribute, some set I_2 for the second attribute, and so on. The resulting set I of acceptable items is the Cartesian product $I_1 \times I_2 \times \ldots$. For example, suppose that a car buyer is looking for a Mustang or Camaro, the acceptable colors are red and white, the car should be made after 2000, and it should have at most 20,000 miles; then, the item set is $I = \{\texttt{Mustang}, \texttt{Camaro}\} \times \{\texttt{red}, \texttt{white}\} \times [2001..2003] \times [0..20{,}000]$. A trader can use specific values or ranges for each attribute; for instance, she can specify a desired year as 2003 or as a range from 2001 to 2003. She can also specify a list of several values or ranges; for example, she can specify a set of colors as $\{\texttt{red}, \texttt{white}\}$, and a set of years as $\{[1900..1950], [2001..2003]\}$.

Unions and Filters. A trader can define an item set I as the union of several Cartesian products. For example, if she wants to buy either a used red Mustang or a new red Camaro, she can specify the set $I = (\{\texttt{Mustang}\} \times \{\texttt{red}\} \times [2001..2003] \times [0..20{,}000]) \cup (\{\texttt{Camaro}\} \times \{\texttt{red}\} \times \{2003\} \times [0..200])$. Furthermore, the trader can indicate that she wants to avoid certain items; for instance, a superstitious buyer may want to avoid black cars with 13 miles on the odometer. In this case, the trader must use a *filter function* that prunes undesirable items. This filter is a Boolean function on the set I, encoded by a C++ procedure, which gives FALSE for unwanted items.

Orders. An order includes an item set, defined by a union of Cartesian products and optional filter function, along with a price function and size. If the price function is a constant, it is specified by a numeric value; else, it is a C++ procedure that inputs an item and outputs the corresponding price limit. The size specification includes two positive values: overall size and minimal acceptable size.

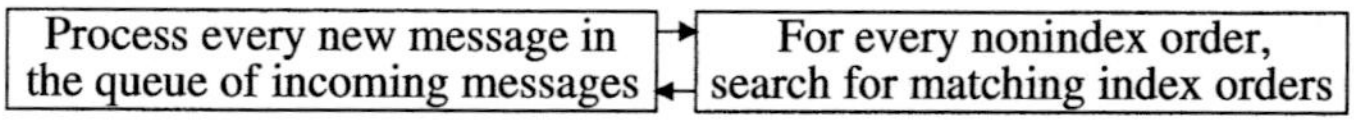

Fig. 1. Main loop of the matcher

4 Exchange System

The system consists of a central matcher and multiple user interfaces that run on separate machines. The traders enter orders through interface machines, which send the orders to the matcher. The system supports three types of messages to the matcher: placing, modifying, and cancelling an order.

The matcher includes a central structure for indexing of orders with fully specified items. If we can put an order into this structure, we call it an *index order*. If an order includes a set of items, rather than a fully specified item, the matcher adds it to an unordered list of *nonindex orders*. The indexing structure allows fast retrieval of index orders that match a given order; however, the system does not identify matches between two nonindex orders.

In Fig. 1, we show the main loop of the matcher, which alternates between processing new messages and identifying matches for old orders. When it receives a message with a new order, it immediately identifies matching index orders. If there are no matches, and the new order is an index order, then the system adds it to the indexing structure. Similarly, if the system fills only part of a new index order, it stores the remaining part in the indexing structure. If it gets a nonindex order and does not find a complete fill, it adds the unfilled part to the list of nonindex orders.

When the system gets a cancellation message, it removes the specified order from the market. When it receives a modification message, it makes changes to the specified order. If the changes can potentially lead to new matches, it immediately searches for index orders that match the modified order. For example, if a seller reduces the price of her order, the system immediately identifies new matches. On the other hand, if the seller increases her price, the system does not search for matches.

After processing all messages, the system tries to fill old nonindex orders; for each nonindex order, it identifies matching index orders. For example, suppose that the market includes an order to buy any red Mustang, and that a dealer places a new order to sell a red Mustang, made in 2003, with zero miles. If the market has no matching index orders, the system adds this new order to the indexing structure. After processing all messages, it tries to fill the nonindex orders, and determines that the dealer's order is a match for the old order to buy any red Mustang.

The indexing structure consists of two identical trees: one is for buy orders, and the other is for sell orders. The height of an indexing tree equals the number of attributes, and each level corresponds to one of the attributes (Fig. 2). The root node encodes the first attribute, and its children represent different values of this attribute. The nodes at the second level divide the orders by the second

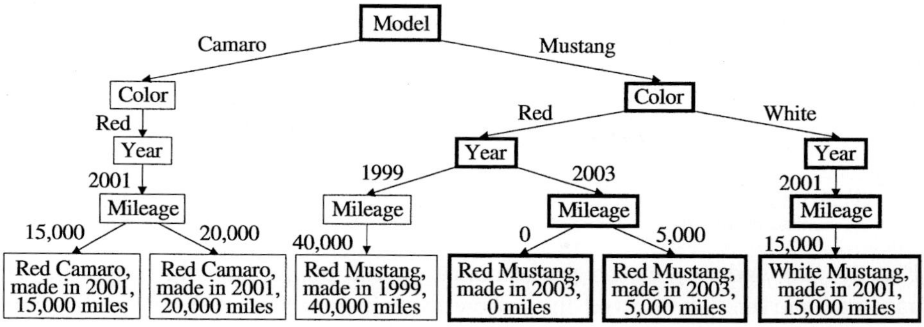

Fig. 2. Indexing tree for a used-car market. Thick boxes show the retrieval of matches for an order to buy a Mustang made after 2000, with any color and mileage

attribute, and each node at the third level corresponds to specific values of the first two attributes. In general, a node at level i divides orders by the values of the ith attribute, and each node at level $(i + 1)$ corresponds to all orders with specific values of the first i attributes. Every leaf node includes orders with identical items, sorted by price.

To find matches for a given order, the system identifies all children of the root that match the first attribute of the order's item set, and then recursively processes the respective subtrees. For example, suppose that a buyer is looking for a Mustang made after 2000, with any color and mileage, and the tree of sell orders is as shown in Fig. 2. The system identifies one matching node for the first attribute, two nodes for the second attribute, two nodes for the third attribute, and finally three matching leaves; we show these nodes by thick boxes. If the order includes the union of several Cartesian products, the system finds matches separately for each product. If the order includes a filter function, the system uses the filter to prune inappropriate leaves. After identifying the matching leaves, the system selects the best-price orders in these leaves.

5 Performance

We describe experiments with an extended used-car market and corporate-bond market. We have run the system on a 2-GHz Pentium computer with one-gigabyte memory. A more detailed report of the experimental results is available in Johnson's masters thesis [5].

The used-car market includes all car models available through AutoNation (www.autonation.com), described by eight attributes: transmission (2 values), number of doors (3 values), interior color (7 values), exterior color (52 values), year (103 values), model (257 values), option package (1,024 values), and mileage (500,000 values). The corporate-bond market is described by two attributes: issuing company (5,000 values) and maturity date (2,550 values).

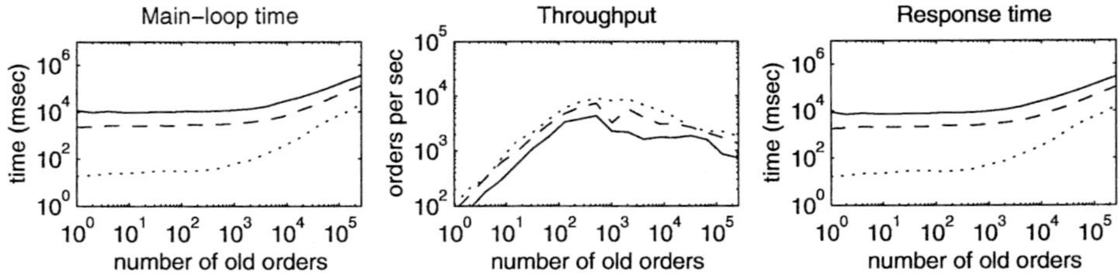

Fig. 3. Dependency of the performance on the number of old orders in the used-car market. The dotted lines show experiments with 300 new orders and matching density of 0.0001. The dashed lines are for 10,000 new orders and matching density of 0.001. The solid lines are for 10,000 new orders and matching density of 0.01

We have varied the number of old orders in the market from one to 300,000, which is the maximal possible number for one-gigabyte memory. We have also controlled the number of incoming new orders in the beginning of the system's main loop (Fig. 1); we have experimented with 300 and 10,000 new orders. In addition, we have controlled the *matching density,* defined as the mean percentage of sell orders that match a given buy order; in other words, it is the probability that a randomly selected buy order matches a randomly chosen sell order. We have considered five matching-density values: 0.0001, 0.001, 0.01, 0.1, and 1.

For each setting of the control variables, we have measured the main-loop time, throughput, and response time. The *main-loop time* is the time of one pass through the system's main loop (Fig. 1). The *throughput* is the maximal acceptable rate of placing new orders; if the system gets more orders per second, it has to reject some of them. Finally, the *response time* is the average time between placing an order and getting a fill.

In Figs. 3 and 4, we show how the performance changes with the number of old orders in the market; note that the scales of all graphs are *logarithmic.* The main-loop and response times are linear in the number of orders. The throughput in small markets grows with the number of orders; it reaches a maximum at about three hundred orders, and slightly decreases with further increase in the market size. The system processes 500 to 5,000 orders per second in the used-car market, and 2,000 to 20,000 orders per second in the corporate-bond market. In Figs. 5 and 6, we show that the main-loop and response times grow linearly with the matching density. On the other hand, we have not found any monotonic dependency between the matching density and the throughput.

6 Concluding Remarks

We have proposed a formal model for trading complex multi-attribute goods, and built an exchange system that supports markets with up to 300,000 orders on a 2-GHz computer with one-gigabyte memory. The system keeps all orders in

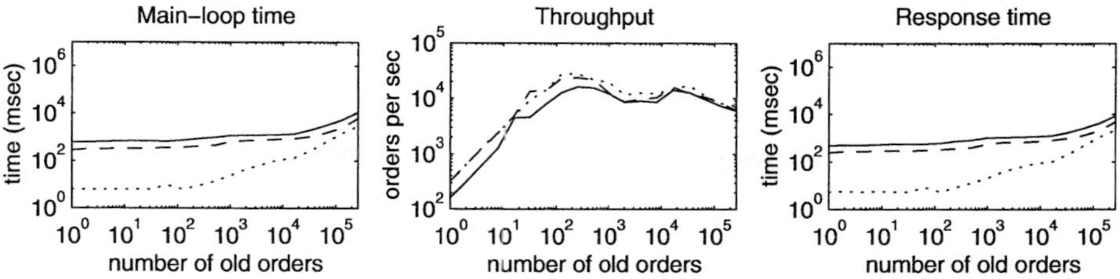

Fig. 4. Dependency of the performance on the number of old orders in the corporate-bond market. The dotted lines show experiments with 300 new orders and matching density of 0.0001. The dashed lines are for 10,000 new orders and matching density of 0.001. The solid lines are for 10,000 new orders and matching density of 0.01

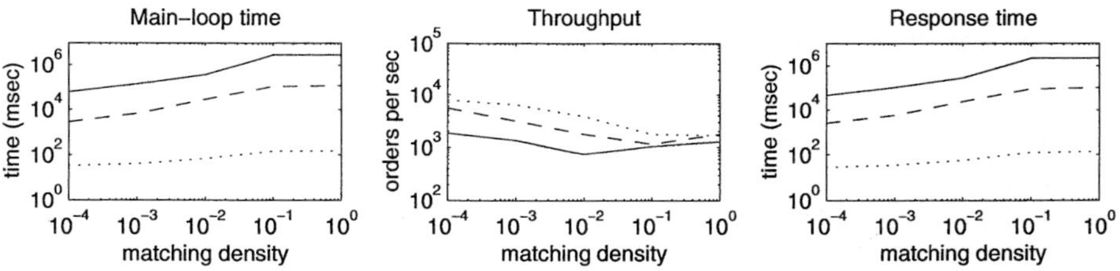

Fig. 5. Dependency of the performance on the matching density in the used-car market. The dotted lines show experiments with 300 old orders and 300 new orders. The dashed lines are for 10,000 old orders and 10,000 new orders. The solid lines are for 300,000 old orders and 10,000 new orders

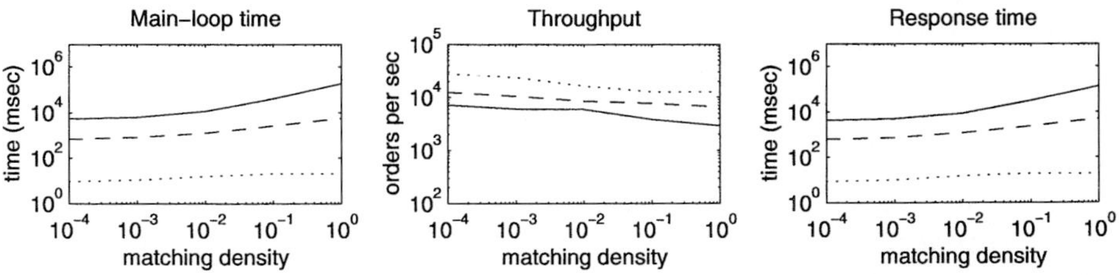

Fig. 6. Dependency of the performance on the matching density in the corporate-bond market. The dotted lines show experiments with 300 old orders and 300 new orders. The dashed lines are for 10,000 old orders and 10,000 new orders. The solid lines are for 300,000 old orders and 10,000 new orders

the main memory, and its scalability is limited by the available memory. We are presently working on a distributed system that includes a central matcher and multiple preprocessing modules, whose role is similar to that of stock brokers.

Acknowledgments

We are grateful to Hong Tang for her help in preparing this article, and to Savvas Nikiforou for his help with software and hardware installations. We thank Ganesh Mani, Dwight Dietrich, Steve Fischetti, Michael Foster, and Alex Gurevich for their feedback and help in understanding real-world exchanges. This work has been partially sponsored by the DYNAMiX Technologies Corporation and by the National Science Foundation grant No. EIA-0130768.

References

[1] Rica Gonen and Daniel Lehmann. Optimal solutions for multi-unit combinatorial auctions: Branch and bound heuristics. In *Proceedings of the Second* ACM *Conference on Electronic Commerce*, pages 13–20, 2000.

[2] Rica Gonen and Daniel Lehmann. Linear programming helps solving large multi-unit combinatorial auctions. In *Proceedings of the Electronic Market Design Workshop*, 2001.

[3] Jianli Gong. Exchanges for complex commodities: Search for optimal matches. Master's thesis, Department of Computer Science and Engineering, University of South Florida, 2002.

[4] Jenny Ying Hu. Exchanges for complex commodities: Representation and indexing of orders. Master's thesis, Department of Computer Science and Engineering, University of South Florida, 2002.

[5] Joshua Marc Johnson. Exchanges for complex commodities: Theory and experiments. Master's thesis, Department of Computer Science and Engineering, University of South Florida, 2001.

[6] Jayant R. Kalagnanam, Andrew J. Davenport, and Ho S. Lee. Computational aspects of clearing continuous call double auctions with assignment constraints and indivisible demand. Technical Report RC21660(97613), IBM, 2000.

[7] Noam Nisan. Bidding and allocation in combinatorial auctions. In *Proceedings of the Second* ACM *Conference on Electronic Commerce*, pages 1–12, 2000.

[8] Tuomas W. Sandholm. Approach to winner determination in combinatorial auctions. *Decision Support Systems*, 28(1–2):165–176, 2000.

[9] Tuomas W. Sandholm and Subhash Suri. Improved algorithms for optimal winner determination in combinatorial auctions and generalizations. In *Proceedings of the Seventeenth National Conference on Artificial Intelligence*, pages 90–97, 2000.

[10] Tuomas W. Sandholm and Subhash Suri. Market clearability. In *Proceedings of the Seventeenth International Joint Conference on Artificial Intelligence*, pages 1145–1151, 2001.

[11] Peter R. Wurman, William E. Walsh, and Michael P. Wellman. Flexible double auctions for electronic commerce: Theory and implementation. *Decision Support Systems*, 24(1):17–27, 1998.

Agent-Based Online Trading System

S. Abu-Draz and E. Shakshuki

Computer Science Department Acadia University
Nova Scotia, Canada 134P 2R6
{023666a;elhadi.shakshuki}@acadiau.ca

Abstract. This paper reports on an ongoing research on developing multi-agent system architecture for distributed, peer-to-peer, integrative online trading system. The system handles some limitations possessed by existing online trading systems such as single attribute based negotiation, the existence of a marketplace and lacking of a user profile. The system architecture is a three-tier architecture, consisting of software agents that cooperate, interact, and negotiate to find best tradeoff based upon the user preferences.

1 Introduction

The development of online shopping agents is a rapidly growing area accompanied by the growth of the Internet. Many online trading agent systems have been developed such as BargainFinder, Jango, Kasbah, AuctionBot, eBay's and FairMarket [1].

Such systems made some assumptions, and possessed some limitations that are not realistic in real world trading situations. For example, their negotiation strategy is based on single attribute, e.g. price. Essentially, in such negotiation strategy the merchant is pitted against the consumer in price-tug-of-wars [1]. In addition, they require a virtual marketplace in order for the negotiation to take place, instead of peer-to-peer interaction. One main problem with this approach is centralization. The agents must communicate within a time frame specified by the user else they will assume communication failure, halt execution and report to the user. Another limitation is that they do not cater for user profiling and keep track of user history and user profile.

This paper proposes multi-agent system architecture for online trading (AOTS). It focuses on the architecture of the system and addresses some of the limitations that exist in current online trading systems. The agents interact cooperatively with each other in a distributed, open, dynamic, and peer-to-peer environment. The agents use integrative negotiation [2] strategies, based on multiattributes, within a limited time frame suggested by the agents involved in negotiation. To reduce network congestion and bottleneck mobile agents are used for retrieving information from remote resources. The user interacts with the system through a user interface and allowed to submit requests and impose some constraints, such as time and preference over attributes. During each interaction session, the system builds a user profiles and adapt to them for future interactions and decision-makings.

Y. Xiang and B. Chaib-draa (Eds.): AI 2003, LNAI 2671, pp. 611–613, 2003.

2 Online Trading System Environment

All the components and the entities of the trading system environment are shown in Fig. 1. The system offers a three-tier architecture. It consists of three types of agents namely: Interface Agents (IA), Resource Agents (RA) and Retrieval Agents (RTA).

The interface agent is a stationery agent. It keeps track of user profiles, interacts with the user and other agents, creates retrieval agents and provides them with parameters, handles incoming retrieval agents, and interacts with the user using graphical user interface. The agents in this system can act both as a seller and a buyer. The retrieval agent is a mobile agent that is instantiated by the interface agent. It communicates with the interface agent at the remote host. Then it commences a negotiation session when necessary. The resource agent is a stationery agent and responsible for accessing, retrieving and monitoring the local databases.

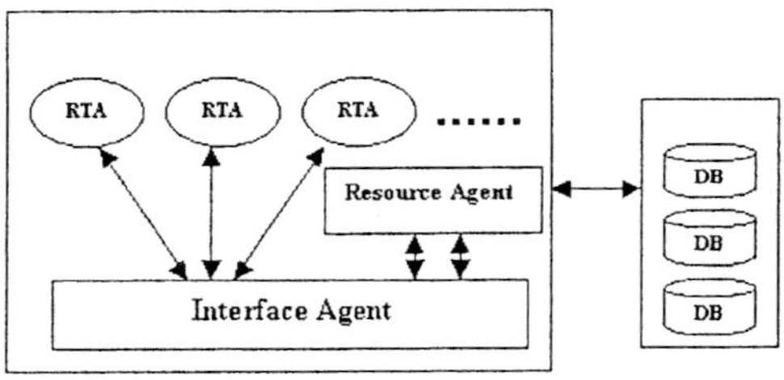

Fig. 1. AOTS Architecture

The interface agent consists of the following four components: user module, factory module, negotiation module, and user interface, as shown in Fig. 2a. Negotiation module is one of the main components of the interface agent and consists of two parts the bidder and the evaluator, as shown in Fig. 2b. The main function of the bidder is to generate bids. It consists of bid planner and bid generator. The function of the evaluator is to evaluate bids. It consists of the attributes evaluator and the utility evaluator. When agents engage in negotiation, they use integrative negotiation strategies based on multi-attributes utility theory [3].

3 Implementation

To demonstrate our approach, a simple prototype for a car trading systems is implemented using IBM Aglet SDK [4]. The user interface consists of user preferences, a display window, and user profiles list. The user model of the system is developed and the profile of the user is added to the local database. The communication between agents is implemented using Aglet messages in

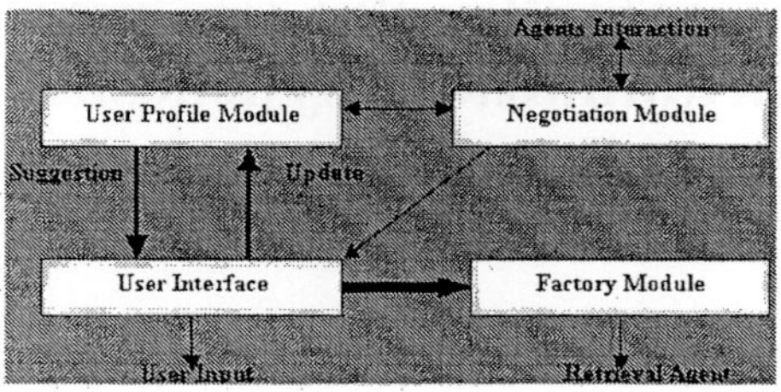

(a)

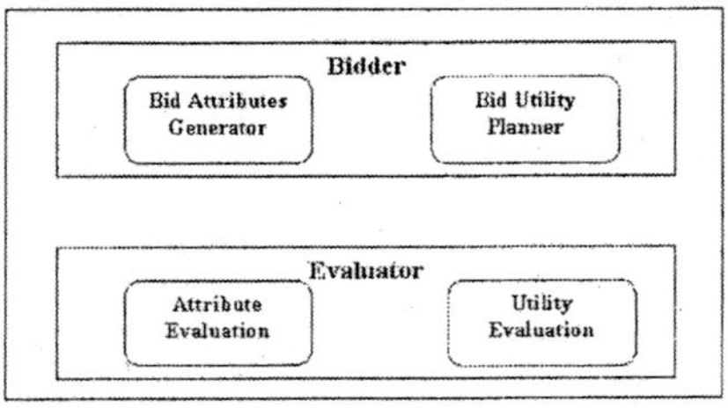

(b)

Fig. 2. (a) Interface Agent Architecture and (b) Negotiation Module

KQML [5] like format. Retrieval agents are mobile agents. They are developed and tested on remote hosts. All interactions are constrained by a time frame set by the user.

References

[1] Robert Guttman, and Pattie Maes. (1998). Agent-mediated Integrative Negotiation for Retail Electronic Commerce. MIT Media Lab.
[2] R. Lewicki, D. Saunders, and J. Minton. (1997). Essentials of Negotiation. Irwin.
[3] Winterfeld, D. von and Edwards, W. (1986). Decision Analysis and Behavioral Research. Cambridge, England: Cambridge University Press.
[4] IBM Aglet SDK `http://aglets.sourceforge.net/`.
[5] Tim Finin, Richard Fritzson, Don McKay and Robin McEntire. (1994). KQML as an Agent Communication Language.

On the Applicability of L-systems and Iterated Function Systems for Grammatical Synthesis of 3D Models

Luis E. Da Costa and Jacques-André Landry

Laboratoire d'Imagerie, Vision et Intelligence Artificielle-LIVIA-
Ecole de Technologie Supérieure - Montréal, Canada

Abstract. The elegance, beauty, and relative simplicity of the geometric models that characterize plant structure have allowed researchers and computer graphics practitioners to generate virtual scenes where natural development procedures can be simulated and observed. However, the synthesis of these models resembles more an artistic process than a scientific structured approach. The objective of this project is to explore the feasibility of constructing a computer vision system able to synthesize the 3D model of a plant from a 2D representation. In this paper we present the results of different authors' attempts to solve this problem, and we identify possible new directions to complement their development. We are also presenting the extent of applicability of L-systems and iterated function systems for solving our problem, and present some ideas in pursuit of a solution in this novel manner.

1 Description and Motivation

Modelling of complex objects is clearly a very important issue from a scientific, educational and economic viewpoint. As a result, we are able to simulate and observe features of natural organisms that can't be directly studied. Plants are a special case of "complex objects" that develop in a time-dependant manner. Computer-aided representation of these structures and the processes that create them combines science with art.

From a practical point of view, the detailed study of a plant (or of a set of plants from a field) is a precious source of information about their health, the treatments that the field has undergone and, consequently, about the schedule of treatments required. However, there is a physical impossibility in bringing all the specialized equipment needed to perform such a study. A novel approach to solve this constraint is to build a detailed model of the plant in order to make a detailed study with computer methods. So, the question of how to model a plant in a detailed manner (in a geometric, structural, or mathematical way) is an important point. The most commonly used models are called L-Systems, which are grammatical rewriting rules introduced in 1968 by Lindenmayer [2] to build a formal description of the development of a simple multicelular organism. This grammatical system is so expresively powerful that there exist languages

Y. Xiang and B. Chaib-draa (Eds.): AI 2003, LNAI 2671, pp. 614–615, 2003.

that can be described by context-free L-Systems, but can't be described by Chomsky's context-free class of grammars.

Because plant development and growth are highly auto-similar, L-Systems are used as a tool for modelling their immense complexity. Particularly, L-Systems have been devoted to study superior plants. With these ideas and a simple representation model (based on the LOGO *turtle*) researchers have been able to represent a large set of natural phenomena.

2 General and Specific Goals

L-systems allows complex objects to be described with a very reduced number of rules; however, the construction of a grammar that represents a specific structure is not a trivial task. We feel, just as Prusinkiewicz and Hanan in [5], that "*(...)it is advantageous to have a more systematic approach to the modelling of plants*". This defines the limits of a very specific problem, the *inverse problem*: can we define an automatic method to synthesize a grammar to represent a specific form?

The main goal of this project is to systematically explore different methods to do the reconstruction of 3D objects from partial 2D information. Jurgensen, Lindenmayer and Prusinciewicz (in [1], [3] and [4]) have proposed answers to this question. But no method is general enough, nor good enough. In this work we present the comparison of the 3 solutions, and we identify possible new directions to continue their development. We are also presenting the extent of applicability of L-systems and iterated function systems for solving our problem, and present some ideas in pursuit of a solution in this novel manner.

References

[1] H Jurgensen and A Lindenmayer. Modelling development by 0l-systems: inference algorithms for developmental systems with cell lineages. *Bulletin of Mathematical Biology*, 49(1):93–123, 1987.

[2] A Lindenmayer. Mathematical models for cellular interaction in development. parts i and ii. *Journal of Theoretical Biology*, 18:280–299 and 300–315, 1968.

[3] A Lindenmayer. Models for multicellular development: characterization, inference and complexity of l-systems. *Lecture Notes in Computer Science 281: Trends, techniques and problems in theoretical computer science*, 281:138–168, 1987.

[4] A Lindenmayer and P Prusinkiewicz. Developmental models of multicellular organisms: a computer graphics perspective. In C. Langton, editor, *Artificial Life: proceedings of an interdisciplinary workshop on the synthesis and simulation of living systems.* Addison-Wesley, Los Alamos, 1989.

[5] P Prusinkiewicz and Jim Hanan. Visualization of botanical structures and processes using parametric l-systems. In D. Thalmann, editor, *Scientific Visualization and Graphics Simulation*, pages 183–201. J. Wiley and sons, 1990.

An Unsupervised Clustering Algorithm for Intrusion Detection

Yu Guan[1], Ali A. Ghorbani[1], and Nabil Belacel[2]

[1] Faculty of Computer Science, University of New Brunswick
Fredericton, NB, E3B 5A3
{guan.yu,ghorbani}@unb.ca

[2] E-health, Institute for Information Technology, National Research Council
Saint John, NB, E2L 2Z6
nabil.belacel@nrc.ca

1 Introduction

As the Internet spreads to each corner of the world, computers are exposed to miscellaneous intrusions from the World Wide Web. Thus, we need effective intrusion detection systems to protect our computers from the intrusions. Traditional instance-based learning methods can only be used to detect known intrusions since these methods classify instances based on what they have learned. They rarely detect new intrusions since these intrusion classes has not been learned before. We expect an unsupervised algorithm to be able to detect new intrusions as well as known intrusions.

In this paper, we propose a clustering algorithm for intrusion detection, called Y-means. This algorithm is developed based on the H-means+ algorithm [2] (an improved version of the K-means algorithm [1]) and other related clustering algorithms of K-means. Y-means is able to automatically partition a data set into a reasonable number of clusters so as to classify the instances into 'normal' clusters and 'abnormal' clusters. It overcomes two shortcomings of K-means: *degeneracy* and *dependency on the number of clusters* .

The results of simulations that run on KDD-99 data set [3] show that Y-means is an effective method for partitioning large data set. An 89.89% detection rate and a 1.00% false alarm rate were achieved with the Y-means algorithm.

2 Y-means Algorithm

The amount of normal log data is usually overwhelmingly larger than that of intrusion data. Normal data are usually distinguished from the intrusions based on the Euclidean distance. Therefore, the normal instances form clusters with large populations, while the intrusion instances form remote clusters with a relatively small populations. Therefore, we can label these clusters as normal or intrusive according to their populations.

Y-means is our proposed clustering algorithm for intrusion detection. By splitting clusters and merging overlapped clusters, it is possible to automatically

Y. Xiang and B. Chaib-draa (Eds.): AI 2003, LNAI 2671, pp. 616–617, 2003.

partition a data set into a reasonable number of clusters so as to classify the instances into 'normal' clusters and 'abnormal' clusters. It also overcomes the shortcomings of the K-means algorithm.

We partitioned 2,456 instances of KDD-99 data using the H-means+ algorithm with different initial values of k. The decline of SSE is fast when the value of k is very small. When the value of k reaches 20, the decline of Sum of Square Error (SSE) becomes slow. In this experiment, the optimal value for k is found to be around 20. At this point, we obtained a 78.72% detection rate and a 1.11% false alarm rate. This result is probably the best that we can get with H-means+.

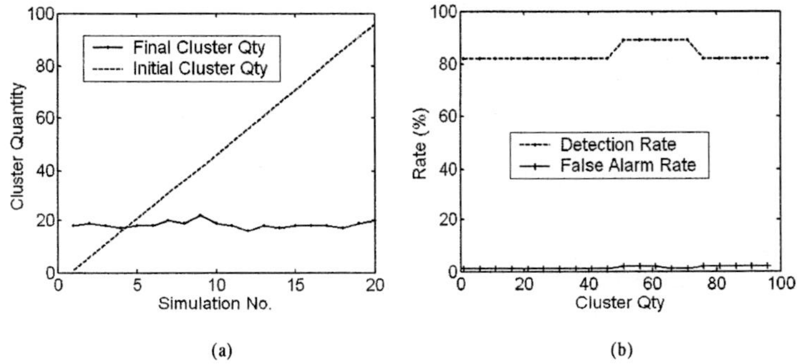

Fig. 1. a. Initial number vs. final number of clusters; b. Y-means with different initial number of clusters

Y-means partitioned the same data set into 16 to 22 clusters as shown by the approximately horizontal line in Figure 1 (a), when the initial number of clusters varied from 1 to 96. On average, the final number of clusters is about 20. This is exactly the value of the 'optimal' k in H-means+. On average, the Y-means algorithm detected 86.63% of intrusions with a 1.53% false alarm rate as shown in Figure 1 (b). The best performance was obtained when detection rate is 89.89% and false alarm rate is 1.00%.

In conclusion, the Y-means is a promising algorithm for intrusion detection, since it can automatically partition an arbitrarily sized set of arbitrarily distributed data into an appropriate number of clusters without supervision.

References

[1] MacQueen, J. B. "Some methods for classification and analysis of multivariate observations." Proceedings of Fifth Berkeley Symposium on Mathematical Statistics and Probability, Vol.2, pp.28-297, 1967.
[2] Hansen, P. and N. Mladenovic "J-Means: a new local search heuristic for minimum sum-of-squares clustering." Pattern Recognition 34 pp.405-413, 2002
[3] KDD Cup 1999 Data. University of California, Irvine. http://kdd.ics.uci.edu /databases/kddcup99/kddcup99.html, 1999.

Dueling CSP Representations: Local Search in the Primal versus Dual Constraint Graph

Mingyan Huang, Zhiyong Liu, and Scott D. Goodwin

School of Computer Science, University of Windsor
Windsor, Ontario, Canada N9B 3P4

Abstract. Constraint satisfaction problems (**CSPs**) have a rich history in Artificial Intelligence and have become one of the most versatile mechanisms for representing complex relationships in real life problems. A CSP's variables and constraints determine its primal constraint network. For every primal representation, there is an equivalent dual representation where the primal constraints are the dual variables, and the dual constraints are compatibility constraints on the primal variables shared between the primal constraints [1]. In this paper, we compare the performance of local search in solving Constraint Satisfaction Problems using the primal constraint graph versus the dual constraint graph.

1 Background

An excellent source for the necessary background for CSPs is [2].

A **graph** G is a structure <V, E>, where V = $\{v_1, v_2, \ldots, v_n\}$ is a finite set of elements called vertices (also referred to as nodes), and E = $\{e_1, e_2, \ldots, e_n\}$, is a finite set of elements of called edges, such that every element of E is a pair of distinct elements from V. V is called the vertex set of G, while E is called in the edge set.

The edges of a graph may be assigned specific values or labels, in which case the graph is called a **labelled graph.**

A **binary CSP** can be associated with a constraint graph G. N(G), which is the set of nodes(vertices) in G, corresponds to the set of variables and E(G), the set of edges in G, corresponds to the set of binary constraints.

The **primal constraint graph** associated with CSP is a labelled graph, where N=V, (Vi,Vj) $\in$ E iff exists Cx $\in$ C | Vx = {Vi,Vj}. Also the label on edge (Vi,Vj) is Cx.

The **dual constraint graph** associated with a CSP is a labelled graph, where N=C. For every pair of constraints Ci, Cj$\in$C, such that Vi $\cap$ Vj $\neq$ Ø, there is an edge in the dual graph, connecting nodes Ci and Cj.

Y. Xiang and B. Chaib-draa (Eds.): AI 2003, LNAI 2671, pp. 618-620, 2003.

2 Approach

In order to make the comparison objective and do the tests efficiently, we designed the experiments as follows: 1) represent constraints and variable domains extensionally; 2) test both binary and non-binary CSPs; 3) vary the number of variables, number of constraints, sizes of domains; 4) test different kinds of constraints; 5) consider several performance indicators (nodes visited, constraints checked, run time, etc.); 6) use the same programming language (Java); 7) use the same environment (hardware, operating system, Java virtual machine, etc.); 8) guarantee only one application is running in the same PC. We wrote two programs. Both implement local search based on steepest ascent hill climbing. One uses the primal constraint graph and the other uses the dual constraint graph. We designed a test suite for binary and non-binary CSPs as follows:

Binary CSP Test Suite:					Non-Binary CSP Test Suite:			
Vars/Cons	C<N	C=N	C>N		Vars/Cons	C<N	C=N	C>N
3	2 (NB1)	3 (NB2)	4 (NB3)		3	2 (B1)	3 (B2)	4 (B3)
10	4 (NB4)	10 (NB5)	20 (NB6)		10	4 (B4)	10 (B5)	20 (B6)

3 Results

Test Case No	Primal Graph					Dual Graph					
	Random Times	Node Visited	Constraints Checked	Search Time (ms)	Max memory usage (byte)	Random Times	Node Visited	Constraints Checked	Convert Time (ms)	Search Time (ms)	Max memory usage (bytes)
B1	1.2	6.9	13.8	61.1	3906.4	1.1	1.8	1.8	94.2	92	3104
B2	1.2	7.2	21.6	41	4544.8	1	4.9	14.7	120.3	146.2	5150.2
B3	1	8.6	34.4	40	4490.4	2.8	25.3	177.1	260.3	84.1	14608
B4	1.1	63.1	232.4	195.2	19168	1	2.4	2.4	224.4	71.1	5398.6
B5	14	1913.9	20129	428.5	278729.6	8.6	224	2930	440.5	321.6	121818.4
B6	2.4	383.5	7670	345.7	181924.8	37.9	14011.9	2387621.6	978.7	9742.8	936317.6
NB1	1.7	10.9	21.8	46	3824	1.6	6.9	20.7	116.1	118.1	5052
NB2	2.2	13.5	40.5	49	4596	2	32.2	289.8	245.2	84.1	15070.4
NB3	4.2	31	124	52	8294	5.7	274.5	4941	307.4	232.4	112364.8
NB4	1	9.1	36.4	138.1	17124	1	17.9	107.4	250.3	144.1	13712
NB5	1	28.6	286	181.2	22307.2	2.1	524.5	17833	596.1	675.7	164931.2
NB6	3.5	381.6	7385.4	444.6	195858.4	179.7	393585	62580015	731.2	255385.4	7532518.4

4 Conclusion

The analysis of the result table indicates when number of constraints is smaller than number of variables, the dual graph can out-perform the primal graph. For the other cases, local search in primal graph always out-performs the dual graph. Of course, these results are not conclusive but merely suggest further investigation is warranted. In particular, we need to consider some other factors that could influence the results such as: 1) tightness of constraints; 2) relative density or sparsity of solutions in the search space; 3) whether problem reduction techniques are more effective in one representation or the other.

References

[1] [1] S. Nagarajan, On Dual Encodings for Constraint Satisfaction, Ph.D. thesis, University of Regina, 2001.

[2] [2] E. Tsang, Foundation of Constraint Satisfaction, Academic Press, 1993.

A Quick Look at Methods for Mining Long Subsequences

Linhui Jiang

Department of Computer Science, University of Regina
Regina, SK, Canada S4S 0A2
linhui@cs.uregina.ca

1 Introduction

Pattern discovery, or the search for frequently occurring subsequences (called ***sequential patterns***) in sequences, is a well-known data-mining task. Sequences of events occur naturally in many domains. We address an abstract version of the problem of finding frequent sequences of page accesses in a log file by considering the problem of finding frequent subsequences in a sequence dataset. In the abstract problem, we use the 26 uppercase letters to represent the possible web pages, and examine the problem of finding frequently occurring subsequences of items in a very long sequence. The particular problem studied is to find all frequently occurring substrings of length K or less in a very long string. The advantage of Heuristic Depth-first (HDF) algorithm based on the Depth-First (DF) algorithm is explained by comparing with Breadth-First (BF) algorithm.

2 Approach

A specific problem is examined where the events in the sequence are restricted to the 26 uppercase letters and the maximum length of the subsequences is restricted to K. A threshold is used to determine the frequency.

For Breadth-First (BF) algorithm, the data file is read through K times and time complexity $O(K^2n)$. On the kth pass through the data file, all frequent subsequences s with length k are added to the trie. Any subsequence in the data with length k longer than 1 are inserted into the trie only when its prefixes count satisfied the threshold.

The Heuristic Depth-First (HDF) algorithm is based on Depth-First (DF) algorithm [Jia2003]. The data file is read only once, and time complexity is $O(Kn)$. Because of the shortcoming of Depth-First algorithm that it uses significantly more space because the threshold cannot be used before all the subsequences in a data are inserted into the trie. To apply pruning before the trie has been completely constructed as BF, we propose that the number of occurrences of a subsequence's prefixes be compared to the threshold before inserting the subsequence. If the prefix of a subsequence has not yet been shown to be frequent, then we choose not to start counting the occurrences of the subsequence itself. In this way, the accuracy is somehow scarifying for better memory utilization and elapsed time. This algorithm is appropriate when the $Kt<<n$, i.e., when the product of the maximum trie level and threshold is very small compared to the dataset length.

Y. Xiang and B. Chaib-draa (Eds.): AI 2003, LNAI 2671, pp. 621-623, 2003.

3 Results

An experiment was conducted by finding a long subsequence with length 100 in the dataset and set the threshold 10. When generating the dataset, we first defined a string with length equal to 100 and set the string's occupation in the dataset with 60%. We compare BF and HDF with dataset length $5 \cdot 10^5, 10^6, 5 \cdot 10^6, 10^7$. For DF, since it used up the memory when the dataset length reaches 10^5 before the complete construct the trie, we ignored it in this experiment.

As shown in the Table 3.1, for elapsed time, BF spent around more than 50 times than HDF. With the dataset length increase, the memory utilization for BF increases faster than DF until they reach the limit of memory. While the string we are searching always keep the same missing results, which less than the maximum missing result 990 with function $(K\text{-}1)t$, because for a subsequence with length k, beginning from the first length of patterns, there are t number of patterns lost at each length of its prefix. This explanation has been verified by detailed experiments (not shown).

Table 1. Comparison of BF and HDF

	Elapsed Time			**Memory Utilization**			**Missing Result**
Data Length	**BF**	**HDF**	**BF/HDF**	**HBF**	**DF**	**BF/HDF**	**BF-HDF**
$5 \cdot 10^5$	582.6	10.7	54.4	12733.6	5574.0	2.3	873
10^6	1199.5	22.0	54.5	38015.2	8951.8	4.2	873
$5 \cdot 10^6$	6551.8	140.1	46.8	203116.0	23258.6	8.7	873
10^7	13273.8	252.8	52.5	221127.1	49479.1	4.5	872

4 Conclusion

Two algorithms, BF and HDF, are compared in this paper to solve the problem of finding frequent sequential patterns in a large dataset. Two general approaches, breadth first insertion (BF) and depth first insertion (DF and HDF), are considered. HDF may miss some patterns, but it more efficient than BF to find long patterns, especially in a very large dataset. It sacrifices completeness for efficiency. We suggest that other variation on HDF be considered.

References

[AS1995] Agrawal, R., and Srikant, R., "Mining Sequential Patterns." *Proceedings IEEE International Conference on Data Engineering*, Taipei, Taiwan, 1995.

[Jia2003] Jiang, L., and Hamilton, H.J., "Methods for Mining Frequent Sequential Patterns." *Proceedings AI'2003,* this volume.

[PCY1995] Park, J.S., Chen, M.S., and Yu, P.S., "An Effective Hash-Based Algorithm for mining Association Rules." *Proceedings of the 1995 ACM SIGMOD International Conference on Management of Data*, San Jose, California, May 1995.

[Vil1998] Vilo, J., *Discovery Frequent Patterns from Strings*, Technical Report C-1998-9, Department of Computer Science, University of Helsinki, FIN-00014, University of Helsinki, May 1998.

Back to the Future: Changing the Direction of Time to Discover Causality

Kamran Karimi

Department of Computer Science, University of Regina
Regina, Saskatchewan, Canada S4S 0A2
karimi@cs.uregina.ca

Abstract. In this paper we present the idea of using the direction of time to discover causality in temporal data. The Temporal Investigation Method for Enregistered Record Sequences (TIMERS), creates temporal classification rules from the input, and then measures the accuracy of the rules. It does so two times, each time assuming a different direction for time. The direction that results in rules with higher accuracy determines the nature of the relation. For causality, TIMERS assumes the natural direction of time, which assumes that events in the past can cause a target event in the present time. For the acausality test, TIMERS considers a backward flow of time, which assumes that events in the future can cause a target event in the present. There is a third alternative that TIMERS considers, and that is an instantaneous relation, where events in the present occur at the same time as a target event.

Forward and Backward Directions of Time

We consider a set of rules to define a relationship among the condition attributes and the decision attribute. A temporal rule is one that involves variables from times different than the decision attribute's time of observation. An example temporal rule is:

If {(At time T_{-3}: $x = 2$) **and** (At time T_{-1}: $y > 1, x = 2$)}
then (At time T: $x = 5$). (Rule 1).

This rule indicates that the current value of x (at time T) depends on the value of x, 3 time steps ago, and also on the value of x and y, 1 time step ago. We use a preprocessing technique called flattening to change the input data into a suitable form for extracting temporal rules with tools that are not based on an explicit representation of time. With flattening, data from consecutive time steps are put into the same record, so if in two consecutive time steps we have observed the values of x and y as: Time n: <$x = 1, y = 2$>, Time $n + 1$: <$x = 3, y = 2$>, then we can flatten these two records to obtain <Time T - 1: $x_1 = 1$, $y_1 = 2$, Time T: $x_2 = 3$, $y_2 = 2$>. The "Time <number>" keywords are implied, and do not appear in the records. The initial

Y. Xiang and B. Chaib-draa (Eds.): AI 2003, LNAI 2671, pp. 624-626, 2003.

temporal order of the records is lost in the flattened records, and time always starts from (T - w - 1) inside each flattened record, and goes on until T. Time T signifies the "current time" which is relative to the start of each record. Such a record can be used to predict the value of either x_2 or y_2 using the other attributes. Since we refrain from using any condition attribute from the current time, we modify the previous record by omitting either x_2 or y_2.

In the previous example we used *forward flattening*, because the data is flattened in the same direction as the forward flow of time. We used the previous observations to predict the value of the decision attribute. The other way to flatten the data is *backward flattening*, which goes against the natural flow of time. Given the two previous example records, the result of a backward flattening would be < Time T: $y_1 = 2$, Time $T + 1$: $x_2 = 3$, $y_2 = 2$>. Inside the record, time starts at T, and ends at ($T + w$ - 1). This record could be used to predict the value of y_1 based on the other attributes. x_1 is omitted because it appears at the same time as the decision attribute y_1. In the backward direction, *future* observations are used to predict the value of the decision attribute.

There is no consensus on the definitions of terms like causality or acausality. For this reason we provide our own definitions here.

Instantaneous. An *instantaneous* set of rules is one in which the current value of the decision attribute in each rule is determined solely by the current values of the condition attributes in each rule. In other words, for any rule r in rule set R, if the decision attribute d appears at time T, then all condition attributes should also appear at time T. An instantaneous set of rules is an *atemporal* one. Another name for an instantaneous set of rules is a (atemporal) *co-occurrence*, where the values of the decision attribute are associated with the values of the condition attributes.

Causal. In a *causal* set of rules, the current value of the decision attribute relies only on the previous values of the condition attributes in each rule. In other words, for any rule r in the rule set R, if the decision attribute d appears at time T, then all condition attributes should appear at time $t < T$.

Acausal. In an *acausal* set of rules, the current value of the decision attribute relies only on the future values of the condition attributes in each rule. In other words, for any rule r in the rule set R, if the decision attribute d appears at time T, then all condition attributes should appear at time $t > T$.

All rules in a causal rule set have the same direction of time, and there are no attributes from the same time as the decision attribute. This property is guaranteed simply by not using condition attributes from the same time step as the decision attribute, and also by sorting the condition attributes in an increasing temporal order, until we get to the decision attribute. The same property holds for acausal rule sets, where time flows backward in all rules till we get to the decision attribute. Complementarily, in an instantaneous rule set, no condition attribute from other times can ever appear. The TIMERS methodology guarantees that all the rules in the rule set inherit the property of the rule set in being causal, acausal, or instantaneous.

More information about the TIMERS method can be found in the following papers, both by Kamran Karimi and Howard J. Hamilton. "Using TimeSleuth for Discovering Temporal/Causal Rules: A Comparison," In Proceedings of the Sixteenth Canadian

Artificial Intelligence Conference (AI'2003), Halifax, NS, Canada, June 2003. And ``Distinguishing Causal and Acausal Temporal Relations," In Proceedings of the Seventh Pacific-Asia Conference on Knowledge Discovery and Data Mining (PAKDD'2003), Seoul, South Korea, April/May 2003.

Learning Coordination in RoboCupRescue

Sébastien Paquet

DAMAS laboratory, Laval University, Canada
spaquet@damas.ift.ulaval.ca

Abstract. In this abstract, we present a complex multiagent environment, the RoboCupRescue simulation, and show some of the learning opportunities for the coordination of agents in this environment.

1 Introduction

A fundamental difficulty in cooperative multiagent systems is to find how to efficiently coordinate agents' actions in order to enable them to interact and achieve their tasks proficiently. One solution for this problem is to give the agents the ability to learn how to coordinate their actions. This type of solution is well suited for complex environments as RoboCupRescue, because the designer does not have to come up with all the rules for all possible situations.

2 RoboCupRescue

The goal of the RoboCupRescue simulation project is to build a simulator of rescue teams acting in large urban disasters [3]. More precisely, this project takes the form of an annual competition in which participants are designing rescue agents that are trying to minimize damages, caused by a big earthquake, such as civilians buried, buildings on fire and blocked roads. The RoboCupRescue simulation is a complex multiagent environment that has some major issues like: agents' heterogeneity, long-term planning, emergent collaboration and information access [2].

In the simulation, participants have approximately 30 agents of six different kinds to manage and each of them has different capabilities, for instance, *AmbulanceTeam* agents can rescue civilians, *FireBrigade* agents can extinguish fires and *PoliceForce* agents can clear roads. As we can see, this multiagent system is composed of heterogenous agents, having complementary capabilities, that will have to cooperate and coordinate their actions to accomplish their goals.

3 Coordination Approaches and Learning Opportunities

Solutions to coordination problems can be divided in three general classes [1]: those based on communication, those based on convention and those based on

Y. Xiang and B. Chaib-draa (Eds.): AI 2003, LNAI 2671, pp. 627–628, 2003.

learning. In the RoboCupRescue environment, approaches based on communication are not appropriate, because the constraints on communication are too restrictive. We could use an approach based on convention and presently it is the most used approach, because it is the simplest. However, since the RoboCupRescue simulation is a complex environment in which many different situations could occur, it becomes very difficult to find all the right conventions for all the possible situations. In such an environment, learning becomes interesting because it removes from the designer the hard job of defining all coordination procedures required for all possible situations.

We think that the RoboCupRescue environment is a good testbed for the study of coordination learning techniques in a complex real-time environment and we will show some of those learning opportunities in the next paragraphs.

The first learning approach consist of learning how to use the communication channel efficiently by enabling agents to learn, over some simulations, which messages are really useful and which ones are not. With this information, agents will take more enlightened decisions concerning the messages they send and the ones they listen to. By doing so, their coordination can be improved because the communication is more efficient; thus, the most important messages for the coordination have less chance to be lost.

The second approach consist of learning the best way to manage a disaster depending on which sectors of the city are in trouble. This improves the coordination because agents have a plan telling each one of them the more important things to do if there is a problem in a specific sector of the city.

The last approach presented in this short paper consist of enabling agents to anticipate their actions and other agents' actions. For this purpose, agents have to learn how the disaster evolves in time and how the agents' actions interact with the environment. With a better anticipation of the other agents' actions, each individual agent will be able to construct more accurate long-term plans, which plans will help to improve the coordination of their actions because each agent will have an idea about what the other agents are doing.

4 Conclusion

In conclusion, the RoboCupRescue simulation is a good testbed for the study of learning approaches used to improve agents' coordination in a complex real-time environment. It's an ongoing research project at our laboratory to design and test some learning algorithms that will be well suited and useful for this type of complex real-time systems.

References

[1] Boutilier Craig. (1996). Planning, Learning and Coordination in Multiagent Decision Processes. In *Proceedings of TARK-96*, De Zeeuwse Stromen, Hollande.

[2] Kitano Hiroaki. (2000). RoboCup Rescue: A Grand Challenge for Multi-Agent Systems. In *Proceedings of ICMAS 2000*, Boston, MA.

[3] RoboCupRescue Official Web Page. http://www.r.cs.kobe-u.ac.jp/robocup-rescue/

Accent Classification Using Support Vector Machine and Hidden Markov Model

Hong Tang and Ali A. Ghorbani

Faculty of Computer Science, University of New Brunswick
Fredericton, NB, E3B 5A3, Canada
{p518x, ghorbani}@unb.ca

Abstract. Accent classification technologies directly influence the performance of speech recognition. Currently, two models are used for accent detection namely: Hidden Markov Model (HMM) and Artificial Neural Networks (ANN). However, both models have some drawbacks of their own. In this paper, we use Support Vector Machine (SVM) to detect different speakers' accents. To examine the performance of SVM, Hidden Markov Model is used to classify the same problem set. Simulation results show that SVM can effectively classify different accents. Its performance is found to be very similar to that of HMM.

1 Introduction

Accent is one of the most important characteristics of speakers. Recently, accent detection became more focused and a number of researchers have published works not only on the features of foreign accent but also on accent identification. Levent and Hansen used Hidden Markov Model (HMM) codebooks based on the acoustic features to identify three accents (American, Turkish, Chinese) affecting English[1]. Currently, extensive researches are being carried out to find a suitable method that can effectively detect speakers' accents. There are two main factors – acoustic features and the classification models. This paper proposes another classification model-Support Vector Machine (SVM) to detect the accents.

2 Support Vector Machine

Besides HMM, ANN is the most popular model used to detect accents. Unfortunately, ANN suffers from number of limitations such as overfitting, fixed topology and slow convergence. Statistical learning techniques based on risk minimization such as Support Vector Machine (SVM) are found to be very powerful classification schemes. Compared with ANN, SVM has several merits: (1) Structural Risk Minimization techniques minimize a risk upper bound on the VC-dimension, (2) among all hyperplanes separating the data, SVM can find a unique hyperplane that maximizes the margin of separation between the classes and (3) the power of SVM lies in using kernel function to transform data from the low dimension space to the high dimension space and construct a linear binary classifier.

Y. Xiang and B. Chaib-draa (Eds.): AI 2003, LNAI 2671, pp. 629–631, 2003.

In general, SVM is a binary classifier. Recently, researchers have expanded the basic SVM to the multi-class SVM. Such multi-class SVM has been successfully applied to different kinds of classification problems. In our experiments, we use Pairwise SVM and DAGSVM to classify three accents – Canadian, Chinese and Indian accents. Pairwise Multi-class SVM is also called 1-to-rest algorithm. DAG multi-class method is 1 to 1 algorithm, which uses a Directed Acyclic Graph (DAG) to construct a binary tree.

3 Implementation

3.1 Speech Signal Database

The speech database consists of 60 male speakers speech signals (20 Chinese speakers, 20 Canadian speakers and 20 Indian speakers).The choice of collecting speech data of one gender type (i.e. male speakers) reduces the influence of the different pitch frequency that exists between males and females.

3.2 Feature Extraction

Foreign accent is a pronunciation feature of non-native speakers.Particular speech background groups generally exhibit some common acoustic features. We can identify different accent groups according to such features. There are four features we used in our experiments. (1) *Word-final Stop Closure Duration:* the duration of the silence between the lax stop and the full stop; (2) *Word Duration:* the time between the start and end of the speech signal; (3) *Intonation:* the intonation depends on the syntax, semantics, and phonemic structure of particular language; (4) *F2-F3 contour:* presents different tongue movements. The latter is the most powerful feature to distinguish different accents.

3.3 Experiment Results and Conclusions

To examine the performance of the SVM, we used HMM to detect the same accents. The test results are shown in Table 1. From the results obtained, we found that: Pairwise SVM is not as good as DAGSVM; DAGSVM has almost the same performance as HMM in three accents database; the simulation results show that SVM and HMM have almost the same convergence speed.

Table 1. Detection Rates for SVM and HMM

Pairwise SVM	DAGSVM	HMM
81.2%	93.8%	93.8%

References

[1] Levent Arslan, John H. L. Hansen Language Accent Classification in American English *Univeristy of Colorado Boulder, Speech Communication*, Vol. 18(4), pp.353-367, July 1996.
[2] Levent M. Arslan, John H. L. Hansen A study of Temporal Features and Frequency Characteristic in American English Foreign Accent, *Duck University, Robust Speech Processing Laboratory. http://www.ee.duke.edu/Resarch/speech*
[3] John C. Platt, Nello Cristianini, John Shawe-Taylor Large Margin DAGs for Multiclass Classification

A Neural Network Based Approach to the Artificial Aging of Facial Images

Jeff Taylor*

Department of Computer Science, The University of Western Ontario
jtaylo38@csd.uwo.ca

1 Introduction

After a child has been missing for a number of years, a photograph of the child is of limited use to law enforcement officials and the general public. In order for a picture to be of any use, it should be artificially aged to provide at least an estimate of what the child currently looks like. This age progression can be done by a forensic artist using specialized computer software; however, this is a subjective process that depends greatly on the skill and knowledge of the artist involved. Therefore, this research aims at developing a system that performs automated age progression on images of human faces, with special attention to the case of children in the range of five to fifteen years of age.

Aging is a complex process involving many factors that differ from individual to individual. Rowland and Perrett [1] describe a process that can transform facial images along different "dimensions" such as age, ethnicity, gender, and so on. Of all these transformations, aging is the only one that occurs naturally. This research intends to determine if the aging process can be learned by developing a neural network based system to perform artificial aging of images of human faces. Neural networks have been chosen to implement this system because of their ability to model complex, nonlinear relationships, and because of their applicability to problems involving pattern recognition.

This research will be done in three main phases: data collection, design and training of the neural network, and testing of the neural network.

2 Data Collection

In order to train the neural network, a large number of images will need to be collected, with the following restrictions: at least two images of each individual must be collected, and the age of the individual in each image must be known. These restrictions will require a certain amount of selectivity in data collection. Images cannot be taken from magazines or the Internet, for example, unless they meet the aforementioned restrictions. Therefore, it will be necessary to collect pictures from people who are willing to submit pairs of photographs of themselves.

* MSc student

Y. Xiang and B. Chaib-draa (Eds.): AI 2003, LNAI 2671, pp. 632–634, 2003.

3 Design and Training

The design of the neural network will need to be done with great care. Neural network design is largely a subjective, trial-and-error process. The complexity and unpredictability of the aging process mean that a suitable architecture may be difficult to obtain. In order to cut down on the complexity and training time of the neural network, the data will have to be preprocessed before it can be used in the system. Using individual pixels as inputs would lead to prohibitive training times; therefore, a number of feature points will be defined to describe each face. Hwang et al. [2] describe a method for face reconstruction using a small number of feature points; the feature points defined here can also be used for this research. After these feature points have been located, each face will have to be normalized to a standard position and size. A method for face normalization using the location of the eye strip is described by Gutta et al. [3]

While designing the neural network, the number and type of inputs will also need to be defined. The inputs to the system will consist of the coordinates of each feature point in the source image, the age, gender, and ethnicity of the source image, and the age of the target image.

We propose to use a modified version of the Backprop algorithm, such as Quickprop or Cascade-Correlation, to train the neural network. Once the neural network has been trained, its purpose will be to age input images artificially. A user need only enter values for the inputs defined above. Based on the values of these inputs, the system will determine the new locations of the feature points, map the new feature points onto the input image, and warp the input image so that it matches the new feature points.

4 Testing

The third and final phase of research will be the testing of the system. As the system is being trained, a number of pairs of images will be withheld and not used in the training of the system. This set of images will be used strictly to test the system. From each pair of images in the test set, the younger image will be input into the system. The output of the system can then be tested in two ways: objectively and subjectively. An objective test will measure how closely the feature points in the output image match those of the true older image. A subjective test can be performed by visually inspecting the output images and seeing how closely they resemble the subjects.

References

[1] Rowland, D., Perrett, D.: Manipulating Facial Appearance through Shape and Color. *IEEE Computer Graphics and Applications* **15** (1995), 70–76.

[2] Hwang, B., Volker, B., Vetter, T., Lee, S.: Face Reconstruction from a Small Number of Feature Points. *International Conference on Pattern Recognition* (2000), 842–845.

[3] Gutta, S., Huang, J., Takacs, B., Wechsler, H.: Face Recognition Using Ensembles of Networks. *International Conference on Pattern Recognition* (1996), 50–54.

Adaptive Negotiation for Agent Based Distributed Manufacturing Scheduling

Chun Wang[1], Weiming Shen[2], and Hamada Ghenniwa[1]

[1] Dept. of Electrical & Computer Engineering, The University of Western Ontario
London, Ontario, Canada, N6G 1H1
cwang28@uwo.ca
hghenniwa@eng.uwo.ca
[2] Integrated Manufacturing Technologies Institute,
National Research Council Canada
London, Ontario, Canada, N6G 4X8
weiming.shen@nrc.ca

1 Extended Abstract

Manufacturing scheduling problem is typically NP-hard. While traditional heuristic search based approaches have been considered not suitable for dynamic environments because of their inherent centralized nature, agent based approaches are promising for their decentralized, autonomous, coordinated, and rational natures. However, many challenging issues still need to be addressed when applying agent based approaches to complex distributed manufacturing scheduling environments. One of them, namely adaptive negotiation [2], is to integrate intelligence and rationality into negotiation mechanisms and make the system more adaptive in dynamic environments. This is very important to the manufacturing scheduling problem because the agent based scheduling process is essentially a coordination process among agents. Adaptive negotiation is a way to achieve the coordination in a dynamic scheduling environment. By adaptive negotiation we mean that more intelligence and rationality are integrated into the negotiation mechanism, thus make it adaptive to the changes of the dynamic scheduling environment. To achieve this, issues at three levels have to be addressed: system architecture, agent architecture, and heuristics. At the system architecture level, the system must have the architecture with corresponding characteristics to support adaptive negotiation among agents. At the agent architecture level, an agent must have rational abilities (decision making mechanisms) embedded in the architecture to transfer the knowledge (in our case, negotiation heuristics) and environment conditions into specific negotiation behaviors. The third level is the heuristics level. By this we mean the knowledge that needs to be integrated into the agent negotiation mechanism and can be used by agents in terms of rational decision making.

At the system architecture level, we propose a hybrid architecture that is suitable for both inter-enterprise and intra-enterprise manufacturing scheduling environments. The intra-enterprise environment consists of part agents, resource agents, a directory facilitator and a coordination agent. These agents work in a cooperative distributed environment, thus have the same goal. They communicate through an intranet behind a

Y. Xiang and B. Chaib-draa (Eds.): AI 2003, LNAI 2671, pp. 635-637, 2003.

firewall. The inter-enterprise environment consists of coordination agents from different enterprises. They negotiate in a self-interested multi-agent environment, and communicate through the Internet. The reasons that this architecture supports adaptive negotiation include: (i) this is a highly distributed architecture, no any agent in the system has the power over other agents; and each agent deals with dynamic environment autonomously, which increases the system responsiveness; (ii) the architecture integrates two kinds of manufacturing environments using coordination agents, which provides an infrastructure for enterprises to transfer the negotiation topics across the enterprise boundary, therefore, enhances the adaptive negotiation to the inter-enterprise level; (iii) the use of directory facilitator agents provides an easy way to update agents in the environment with up to date knowledge, which facilitates the adaptive nature of negotiation as well.

At the agent architecture level, we use the CIR (Coordinated Intelligent Rational) agent model [1] as our agent architecture. In the CIR model, an agent is viewed as a composition of knowledge and capability; the capability, in turn, consists of problem solver, interaction and communication. The CIR agent architecture accommodates adaptive negotiation in three aspects: (i) it focuses on the coordination which the adaptive negotiation has to achieve; (ii) interaction devices [1] are well classified and easy to be implemented with software components, which facilitates the selection of negotiation mechanisms in the context of adaptive negotiation; (iii) the decision making mechanism provided in the CIR agent architecture makes it easy for systems developers to design adaptive negotiation mechanisms.

Negotiation heuristics are the knowledge that an agent uses to make negotiation decisions under various situations. Our approach regarding this aspect focuses on negotiation heuristics from economics. We investigate the natures of different negotiation models used in economics; distinguish the important characteristics of different negotiation situations; and use a case based reasoning mechanism to match the different negotiation models to various situations.

A prototype environment for intra-enterprise manufacturing scheduling has been implemented at the National Research Council Canada's Integrated Manufacturing Technologies Institute. We are developing a new prototype that extends the current prototype into the inter-enterprise level by incorporating economically inspired negotiation mechanisms in the coordination agent of each enterprise, and integrating more adaptive negotiation mechanisms into the negotiation framework. Currently, the requirement specifications, system analysis and part of the detailed system design have been done for the new prototype. The detailed design and implementation of a software prototype are to be completed in Spring 2003.

In summary, we address adaptive negotiation issues at three levels: system architecture, agent architecture, and heuristics. Although the proposed approach seems to be complex, it has a very good potential to solving complex real world manufacturing scheduling problems as well as other complex resource management problems in dynamic environments.

References

[1] Ghenniwa, H and Kamel, M, Interaction Devices for Coordinating Cooperative Distributed Systems, *Automation and Soft Computing*, 6(2), 173-184, 2000.

[2] Shen, W., Li, Y., Ghenniwa, H. and Wang, C. Adaptive Negotiation for Agent-Based Grid Computing, Proceedings of AAMAS2002 Workshop on Agentcities: Challenges in Open Agent Environments, Bologna, Italy, July 2002, pp. 32-36.

Multi-agent System Architecture for Tracking Moving Objects

Yingge Wang and Elhadi Shakshuki

Computer Science Department
Acadia University
Nova Scotia, Canada B4P 2R6
050244w; elhadi.shakshuki@acadiau.ca

Abstract. There is an increasing demand for both tools and techniques that track the location of people or objects. This paper presents a multi-agent tracking system architecture that consists of several tracking software agents and uses GPS receivers as a signal-sending platform. The system acts as a mediator between the user and the tracking object environment. Objects carry Global Positioning System (GPS) receivers to locate their positions. These objects can move around within a predefined area, which is divided into several sub-areas. Each sub-area is monitored by one of the tracking agents. All agents of the system have similar architecture and functions and are able to communicate and coordinate their activities with each other to trade information about the position of the object. A prototype of this environment is being implemented to demonstrate its feasibility, using the ZEUS toolkit.

1 Introduction

Many distributed resource-tracking problems exhibit a high degree of uncertainty due to the object's movement, which makes it not easy to solve. Binding a signal-sending hardware onto a targeted object is the most common solution for detecting the target. However, the dynamism of the object's movement makes it a difficult task to detect the moving object's position in real time.

Agent-based technology is makes it possible to build a multi-agent system that can act as a mediator between the user and the moving object for tracking problems [1]. Our proposed system uses GPS receiver to determine the precise longitude, latitude and altitude of an object [2]. This location information changes as the object moves, so that the moving path can be traced. Agents gather real-time position data from GPS receivers on each object. At anytime, one tracking agent monitors the object. When the object moves to a common area that is shared by more than one tracking agent, the agents need to communicate and coordinate which one will track the object.

2 System Architecture and Implementation

In the object-tracking environment, the area in question is covered by identical circles, each with inner and outer rings that have the same centre points. The inner-circles are tangential with each other, and the outer-circles are large enough to envelope the common area surrounded by the inner-circles. A tracking agent resides in the centre of each circle at a predefined position. The agents continuously gather location information from GPS receivers and update their knowledge by sending/receiving information with other agents. The agents engage in negotiation with each other when the object moves to the area between the inner-circle and outer-circle.

The architecture of the agent consists of a set of modules, as shown in Fig. 1-a. In this application, the agent's knowledge includes the other agents' model and the object model. The other agents' model comprises information about the user (in terms of his/her requests), and other tracking agents (in terms of their names, addresses and the area under their control). An agent builds its knowledge from the information received from GPS receivers as well as from the information received from other agents. The agents utilize the information received from the GPS receivers, along with their own known position and predefined cover area, to determine whether the object is within their area and build their knowledge accordingly. The agents also generate

Y. Xiang and B. Chaib-draa (Eds.): AI 2003, LNAI 2671, pp. 638-639, 2003.

tracking history information, which is stored in a local database. Agents communicate with each other using Knowledge Query Manipulation Language (KQML) [3]. The user interacts with the system through a graphical user interface, as shown in Fig. 1-b. This interface also provides complete viewable information regarding the moving objects.

The Task Manager is a key component within a tracking agent. It controls a tracking agent's task in its sub-area and decides when to ask other agents for help. In addition, it checks an object's information by querying the Tracking Records Database. This module makes the agent capable of extrapolating and reasoning its knowledge, and then come up with the solution for the desired tracking task. The Communication Module allows the agent to exchange messages with other elements in the environment, including humans and other tracking agents. When a tracking agent needs help, it sends out a request to all other agents in the system. As soon as the other agents receive the request, they reply with answers to the sender agent within a pre-defined time frame. Through this process, they can decide who will track the object. The Database Manager is designed to record each object's information in the Tracking Records Database for review. During this process, the tracking agent keeps track of the object and also calculates the distance between the object and the location of the agent itself.

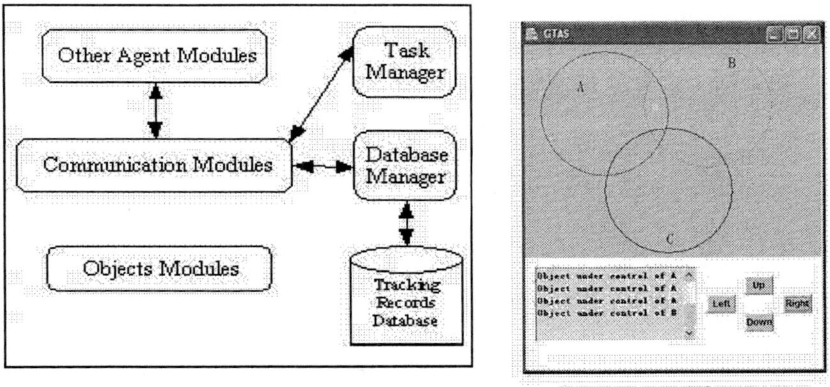

(a) (b)

Fig. 1. (a) Tracking Agent Architecture and (b) An example of a user interface.

A prototype of the proposed system has been implemented using Java and the ZEUS toolkit [4]. Each tracking agent acts as a publisher and when it is sending information and as a subscriber when it is receiving information. The tracking agent action, which furthers the negotiation, is the sending of a FIPA-ACL message. The only instance of waiting in a tracking agent's negotiation is that of waiting for the reply message. Three agents are created, namely: A, B and C. All agents use a common ontology as defined by ZEUS toolkit. The responsibilities of each agent that act as a publisher includes sending information to subscribers, responding to information received from subscribers, and performing its application-specific activities. All messages and rules are represented in the format of the FIPA Communicative Act Library Specification. To simplify the implementation, all tracking agents and objects are put at the same horizontal level.

References

[1] H.S. Nwana: "Software agents: an overview", The Knowledge Engineering Review, 11(3), 1996.

[2] GARMIN Corporation, "GPS Guide", 2000.

[3] Finin, T., Labrou, Y. and Mayfield, J., ''KQML as an Agent Communication Language'', In Bradshaw J.M. (Ed.) Software Agents, Cambridge, MA: AAA/MIT Press, pp. 291-316, 1997.

[4] J. C. Collis, D T Ndumu, H S Nwana and L C Lee, "The ZEUS agent building tool-kit" BT Technology J, 16(3), 1998.

Author Index

Lecture Notes in Artificial Intelligence (LNAI)

Vol. 2445: C. Anagnostopoulou, M. Ferrand, A. Smaill (Eds.), Music and Artificial Intelligence. Proceedings, 2002. VIII, 207 pages. 2002.

Vol. 2446: M. Klusch, S. Ossowski, O. Shehory (Eds.), Cooperative Information Agents VI. Proceedings, 2002. XI, 321 pages. 2002.

Vol. 2447: D.J. Hand, N.M. Adams, R.J. Bolton (Eds.), Pattern Detection and Discovery. Proceedings, 2002. XII, 227 pages. 2002.

Vol. 2448: P. Sojka, I. Kopecÿek, K. Pala (Eds.), Text, Speech and Dialogue. Proceedings, 2002. XII, 481 pages. 2002.

Vol. 2464: M. O'Neill, R.F.E. Sutcliffe, C. Ryan, M. Eaton, N. Griffith (Eds.), Artificial Intelligence and Cognitive Science. Proceedings, 2002. XI, 247 pages. 2002.

Vol. 2466: M. Beetz, J. Hertzberg, M. Ghallab, M.E. Pollack (Eds.), Advances in Plan-Based Control of Robotic Agents. Proceedings, 2001. VIII, 291 pages. 2002.

Vol. 2473: A. Gómez-Pérez, V.R. Benjamins, Knowledge Engineering and Knowledge Management. Proceedings, 2002. XI, 402 pages. 2002.

Vol. 2475: J.J. Alpigini, J.F. Peters, A. Skowron, N. Zhong (Eds.), Rough Sets and Current Trends in Computing. Proceedings, 2002. XV, 640 pages. 2002.

Vol. 2479: M. Jarke, J. Koehler, G. Lakemeyer (Eds.), KI 2002: Advances in Artificial Intelligence. Proceedings, 2002. XIII, 327 pages. 2002.

Vol. 2484: P. Adriaans, H. Fernau, M. van Zaanen (Eds.), Grammatical Inference: Algorithms and Applications. Proceedings, 2002. IX, 315 pages. 2002.

Vol. 2499: S.D. Richardson (Ed.), Machine Translation: From Research to Real Users. Proceedings, 2002. XXI, 254 pages. 2002.

Vol. 2504: M.T. Escrig, F. Toledo, E. Golobardes (Eds.), Topics in Artificial Intelligence. Proceedings 2002. XI, 432 pages. 2002.

Vol. 2507: G. Bittencourt, G.L. Ramalho (Eds.), Advances in Artificial Intelligence. Proceedings, 2002. XIII, 418 pages. 2002.

Vol. 2514: M. Baaz, A. Voronkov (Eds.), Logic for Programming, Artificial Intelligence, and Reasoning. Proceedings 2002. XIII, 465 pages. 2002.

Vol. 2522: T. Andreasen, A. Motro, H. Christiansen, H. Legind Larsen (Eds.), Flexible Query Answering. Proceedings 2002. XI, 386 pages. 2002.

Vol. 2527: F.J. Garijo, J.C. Riquelme, M. Toro (Eds.), Advances in Artificial Intelligence – IBERAMIA 2002. Proceedings 2002. XVIII, 955 pages. 2002.

Vol. 2531: J. Padget, O. Shehory, D. Parkes, N. Sadeh, W.E. Walsh (Eds.), Agent-Mediated Electronic Commerce IV. Proceedings, 2002. XVII, 341 pages. 2002.

Vol. 2533: N. Cesa-Bianchi, M. Numao, R. Reischuk (Eds.), Algorithmic Learning Theory. Proceedings 2002. XI, 415 pages. 2002.

Vol. 2541: T. Barkowsky, Mental Representation and Processing of Geographic Knowledge. X, 174 pages. 2002.

Vol. 2543: O. Bartenstein, U. Geske, M. Hannebauer, O. Yoshie (Eds.), Web Knowledge Management and Decision Support. Proceedings, 2001. X, 307 pages. 2003.

Vol. 2554: M. Beetz, Plan-Based Control of Robotic Agents. XI, 191 pages. 2002.

Vol. 2557: B. McKay, J. Slaney (Eds.), AI 2002: Advances in Artificial Intelligence. Proceedings 2002. XV, 730 pages. 2002.

Vol. 2560: S. Goronzy, Robust Adaptation to Non-Native Accents in Automatic Speech Recognition. Proceedings, 2002. XI, 144 pages. 2002.

Vol. 2569: D. Gollmann, G. Karjoth, M. Waidner (Eds.), Computer Security – ESORICS 2002. Proceedings, 2002. XIII, 648 pages. 2002.

Vol. 2577: P. Petta, R. Tolksdorf, F. Zambonelli (Eds.), Engineering Societies in the Agents World III. Proceedings, 2002. X, 285 pages. 2003.

Vol. 2581: J.S. Sichman, F. Bousquet, P. Davidsson (Eds.), Multi-Agent-Based Simulation II. Proceedings, 2002. X, 195 pages. 2003.

Vol. 2583: S. Matwin, C. Sammut (Eds.), Inductive Logic Programming. Proceedings, 2002. X, 351 pages. 2003.

Vol. 2586: M. Klusch, S. Bergamaschi, P. Edwards, P. Petta (Eds.), Intelligent Information Agents. VI, 275 pages. 2003.

Vol. 2592: R. Kowalczyk, J.P. Müller, H. Tianfield, R. Unland (Eds.), Agent Technologies, Infrastructures, Tools, and Applications for E-Services. Proceedings, 2002. XVII, 371 pages. 2003.

Vol. 2600: S. Mendelson, A.J. Smola, Advanced Lectures on Machine Learning. Proceedings, 2002. IX, 259 pages. 2003.

Vol. 2627: B. O'Sullivan (Ed.), Recent Advances in Constraints. Proceedings, 2002. X, 201 pages. 2003.

Vol. 2631: R. Falcone, S. Barber, L. Korba, M. Singh (Eds.), Trust, Reputation, and Security: Theories and Practice. Proceedings, 2002. X, 235 pages. 2003.

Vol. 2636: E. Alonso, D, Kudenko, D. Kazakov (Eds.), Adaptive Agents and Multi-Agent Systems. XIV, 323 pages. 2003.

Vol. 2637: K.-Y. Whang, J. Jeon, K. Shim, J. Srivastava (Eds.), Advances in Knowledge Discovery and Data Mining. Proceedings, 2003. XVIII, 610 pages. 2003.

Vol. 2639: G. Wang, Q. Liu, Y. Yao, A. Skowron (Eds.), Rough Sets, Fuzzy Sets, Data Mining, and Granular Computing. Proceedings, 2003. XVII, 741 pages. 2003.

Vol. 2645: M.A. Wimmer (Ed.), Knowledge Management in Electronic Government. Proceedings, 2003. XI, 320 pages. 2003.

Vol. 2663: E. Menasalvas, J. Segovia, P.S. Szczepaniak (Eds.), Advances in Web Intelligence. Proceedings, 2003. XII, 350 pages. 2003.

Vol. 2671: Y. Xiang, B. Chaib-draa (Eds.), Advances in Artificial Intelligence. Proceedings, 2003. XIV, 642 pages. 2003.

Lecture Notes in Computer Science

Vol. 2642: X. Zhou, Y. Zhang, M.E. Orlowska (Eds.), Web Technologies and Applications. Proceedings, 2003. XIII, 608 pages. 2003.

Vol. 2643: M. Fossorier, T. Høholdt, A. Poli (Eds.), Applied Algebra, Algebraic Algorithms and Error-Correcting Codes. Proceedings, 2003. X, 256 pages. 2003.

Vol. 2644: D. Hogrefe, A. Wiles (Eds.), Testing of Communicating Systems. Proceedings, 2003. XII, 311 pages. 2003.

Vol. 2645: M.A. Wimmer (Ed.), Knowledge Management in Electronic Government. Proceedings, 2003. XI, 320 pages. 2003. (Subseries LNAI).

Vol. 2646: H. Geuvers, F, Wiedijk (Eds.), Types for Proofs and Programs. Proceedings, 2002. VIII, 331 pages. 2003.

Vol. 2647: K.Jansen, M. Margraf, M. Mastrolli, J.D.P. Rolim (Eds.), Experimental and Efficient Algorithms. Proceedings, 2003. VIII, 267 pages. 2003.

Vol. 2648: T. Ball, S.K. Rajamani (Eds.), Model Checking Software. Proceedings, 2003. VIII, 241 pages. 2003.

Vol. 2649: B. Westfechtel, A. van der Hoek (Eds.), Software Configuration Management. Proceedings, 2003. VIII, 241 pages. 2003.

Vol. 2651: D. Bert, J.P. Bowen, S. King, M, Waldén (Eds.), ZB 2003: Formal Specification and Development in Z and B. Proceedings, 2003. XIII, 547 pages. 2003.

Vol. 2652: F.J. Perales, A.J.C. Campilho, N. Pérez de la Blanca, A. Sanfeliu (Eds.), Pattern Recognition and Image Analysis. Proceedings, 2003. XIX, 1142 pages. 2003.

Vol. 2653: R. Petreschi, Giuseppe Persiano, R. Silvestri (Eds.), Algorithms and Complexity. Proceedings, 2003. XI, 289 pages. 2003.

Vol. 2656: E. Biham (Ed.), Advances in Cryptology – EUROCRPYT 2003. Proceedings, 2003. XIV, 649 pages. 2003.

Vol. 2657: P.M.A. Sloot, D. Abramson, A.V. Bogdanov, J.J. Dongarra, A.Y. Zomaya, Y.E. Gorbachev (Eds.), Computational Science – ICCS 2003. Proceedings, Part I. 2003. LV, 1095 pages. 2003.

Vol. 2658: P.M.A. Sloot, D. Abramson, A.V. Bogdanov, J.J. Dongarra, A.Y. Zomaya, Y.E. Gorbachev (Eds.), Computational Science – ICCS 2003. Proceedings, Part II. 2003. LV, 1129 pages. 2003.

Vol. 2659: P.M.A. Sloot, D. Abramson, A.V. Bogdanov, J.J. Dongarra, A.Y. Zomaya, Y.E. Gorbachev (Eds.), Computational Science – ICCS 2003. Proceedings, Part III. 2003. LV, 1165 pages. 2003.

Vol. 2660: P.M.A. Sloot, D. Abramson, A.V. Bogdanov, J.J. Dongarra, A.Y. Zomaya, Y.E. Gorbachev (Eds.), Computational Science – ICCS 2003. Proceedings, Part IV. 2003. LVI, 1161 pages. 2003.

Vol. 2663: E. Menasalvas, J. Segovia, P.S. Szczepaniak (Eds.), Advances in Web Intelligence. Proceedings, 2003. XII, 350 pages. 2003. (Subseries LNAI).

Vol. 2665: H. Chen, R. Miranda, D.D. Zeng, C. Demchak, J. Schroeder, T. Madhusudan (Eds.), Intelligence and Security Informatics. Proceedings, 2003. XIV, 392 pages. 2003.

Vol. 2667: V. Kumar, M.L. Gavrilova, C.J.K. Tan, P. L'Ecuyer (Eds.), Computational Science and Its Applications – ICCSA 2003. Proceedings, Part I. 2003. XXXIV, 1060 pages. 2003.

Vol. 2668: V. Kumar, M.L. Gavrilova, C.J.K. Tan, P. L'Ecuyer (Eds.), Computational Science and Its Applications – ICCSA 2003. Proceedings, Part II. 2003. XXXIV, 942 pages. 2003.

Vol. 2669: V. Kumar, M.L. Gavrilova, C.J.K. Tan, P. L'Ecuyer (Eds.), Computational Science and Its Applications – ICCSA 2003. Proceedings, Part III. 2003. XXXIV, 948 pages. 2003.

Vol. 2670: R. Peña, T. Arts (Eds.), Implementation of Functional Languages. Proceedings, 2002. X, 249 pages. 2003.

Vol. 2671: Y. Xiang, B. Chaib-draa (Eds.), Advances in Artificial Intelligence. Proceedings, 2003. XIV, 642 pages. 2003. (Subseries LNAI).

Vol. 2674: I.E. Magnin, J. Montagnat, P. Clarysse, J. Nenonen, T. Katila (Eds.), Functional Imaging and Modeling of the Heart. Proceedings, 2003. XI, 308 pages. 2003.

Vol. 2675: M. Marchesi, G. Succi (Eds.), Extreme Programming and Agile Processes in Software Engineering. Proceedings, 2003. XV, 464 pages. 2003.

Vol. 2676: R. Baeza-Yates, E. Chávez, M. Crochemore (Eds.), Combinatorial Pattern Matching. Proceedings, 2003. XI, 403 pages. 2003.

Vol. 2678: W. van der Aalst, A. ter Hofstede, M. Weske (Eds.), Business Process Management. Proceedings, 2003. XI, 391 pages. 2003.

Vol. 2679: W. van der Aalst, E. Best (Eds.), Applications and Theory of Petri Nets 2003. Proceedings, 2003. XI, 508 pages. 2003.

Vol. 2686: J. Mira, J.R. Álvarez (Eds.), Computational Methods in Neural Modeling. Proceedings, Part I. 2003. XXVII, 764 pages. 2003.

Vol. 2687: J. Mira, J.R. Álvarez (Eds.), Artificial Neural Nets Problem Solving Methods. Proceedings, Part II. 2003. XXVII, 820 pages. 2003.

Vol. 2688: J. Kittler, M.S. Nixon (Eds.), Audio- and Video-Based Biometric Person Authentication. Proceedings, 2003. XVII, 978 pages. 2003.

Vol. 2692: P. Nixon, S. Terzis (Eds.), Trust Management. Proceedings, 2003. X, 349 pages. 2003.

Vol. 2694: R. Cousot (Ed.), Static Analysis. Proceedings, 2003. XIV, 505 pages. 2003.

Vol. 2695: L.D. Griffin, M. Lillholm (Eds.), Scale Space Methods in Computer Vision. Proceedings, 2003. XII, 816 pages. 2003.

Vol. 2701: M. Hofmann (Ed.), Typed Lambda Calculi and Applications. Proceedings, 2003. VIII, 317 pages. 2003.

Vol. 2706: R. Nieuwenhuis (Ed.), Rewriting Techniques and Applications. Proceedings, 2003. XI, 515 pages. 2003.

Vol. 2707: K. Jeffay, I. Stoica, K. Wehrle (Eds.), Quality of Service – IWQoS 2003. Proceedings, 2003. XI, 517 pages. 2003.